A READER'S REPERTOIRE

A READER'S REPERTOIRE

Aims and Perspectives

Gwendolyn Gong
The Chinese University of Hong Kong

Sam Dragga
Texas Tech University

HarperCollins*CollegePublishers*

Senior Editor: Patricia Rossi
Developmental Editor: Tom Maeglin
Project Editor: Lois Lombardo
Design Manager: Mary Archondes
Text Designer: Mary Archondes
Cover Designer: Kay Petronio
Art Studio: Vantage Art
Electronic Production Manager: Valerie A. Sawyer
Desktop Administrator: Hilda Koparanian
Manufacturing Manager: Helene G. Landers
Electronic Page Makeup: Molly Pike-Ricardi
Printer and Binder: RR Donnelley & Sons Company
Cover Printer: Phoenix Color Corp.

For permission to use copyrighted material, grateful acknowledgment is made to the copyright holders on pp. 509–513, which are hereby made part of this copyright page.

A Reader's Repertoire: Aims and Perspectives

Copyright © 1996 by HarperCollins College Publishers

HarperCollins® and ® are registered trademarks of HarperCollins Publishers Inc.

All rights reserved. Printed in the United States of America. No part of this book may be used or reproduced in any manner whatsoever without written permission, except in the case of brief quotations embodied in critical articles and reviews. For information address HarperCollins College Publishers, 10 East 53rd Street, New York, NY 10022. *For information about any HarperCollins title, product, or resource, please visit our World Wide Site at* **http: //www.harpercollins.com/college**.

Library of Congress Cataloging-in-Publication Data

Gong, Gwendolyn.
    A reader's repertoire: aims and perspectives/Gwendolyn Gong,
  Sam Dragga.
       p.   cm.
    Includes index.
    ISBN 0-673-99188-1 (Student Edition); 0-673-99189-X (Instructor's Edition)
    1. College readers. 2. English language—Rhetoric. I. Dragga,
Sam. II. Title.
PE1417.G584   1995
808'.0427—dc20   95-34156
                                                  CIP

95 96 97 98 9 8 7 6 5 4 3 2 1

CONTENTS

Alternate Thematic Contents   xi
Prologue   xvii

INTRODUCTION   1

    CRITICAL READING   2
       Planning   2
       Translating   3
       Reviewing   3
    READING PERSPECTIVES AND INFLUENCES   4
       Reading Perspectives   4
       Internal and External Influences   4
    UNDERSTANDING THE RHETORICAL SITUATION   6
       Determining Aims   6
       Analyzing Ways of Knowing   9
       Analyzing Audience   11
    DEVELOPING YOUR READING REPERTOIRE   11
       The Pie   15
         GARY SOTO

       Guide to Critical Reading   25

PART ONE
READING EXPRESSIVE AIM WRITING 27

    NARRATIVE 28
    POINT OF VIEW 29
    DESCRIPTIVE DETAIL 29
    CHARACTERS 29
    DIALOGUE 30
    SETTING 30
    SIGNIFICANCE OF THE EXPERIENCE 30

KNOWLEDGE BY PARTICIPATION

Little Deaths 31
T. H. WATKINS

Meditations on a Stolen Purse 36
MARION WINIK

And Then I Went to School 39
JOSEPH SUINA

How It Feels to Be Colored Me 44
ZORA NEALE HURSTON

Sylvia Plath: A Memoir 47
AL ALVAREZ

Hating Fred 59
HARRIET LERNER

Lessons from a Friend 61
FRANK DEFORD

Only Daughter 64
SANDRA CISNEROS

20/20 Hindsight 67
JAY FORD

KNOWLEDGE BY OBSERVATION

*Of Accidental Judgments and Casual
   Slaughters* 74
KAI ERIKSON

Columbus and His Four Fateful Voyages 83
DAVID GELMAN

Thoreau 90
VIRGINIA WOOLF

The Case of Harry Houdini 96
DANIEL MARK EPSTEIN

KNOWLEDGE BY PARTICIPATION AND OBSERVATION

Fat Like Me   107
LESLIE LAMPERT

My Grandmother's Pennies   113
CYNTHIA OZICK

Ghosts   118
BRUCE EDWARD HALL

Living In—and On—the Margins   126
DONALD McQUADE

On Being a Cripple   137
NANCY MAIRS

More Than Just a Shrine: Paying Homage to the Ghosts of Ellis Island   146
MARY GORDON

The House Where Martin Wept: Marks, Mississippi   150
WALT HARRINGTON

Grandmother's Country   153
N. SCOTT MOMADAY

A New Monument to Remembering—With a Mission   158
MICHAEL KERNAN

PART TWO
READING REFERENTIAL AIM WRITING   169

CREDIBILITY OF THE WRITER   170
THESIS AND SUPPORTING EVIDENCE   170
TECHNIQUES TO MOTIVATE READERS   171

KNOWLEDGE BY PARTICIPATION

Cultural Etiquette: A Guide for the Well-Intentioned   173
AMOJA THREE RIVERS

Falling for Apples   177
NOEL PERRIN

Shopping with Children   180
PHYLLIS THEROUX

How to Write a Letter   183
GARRISON KEILLOR

KNOWLEDGE BY OBSERVATION

A Practitioner's Guide to Research Methods 186
PATRICIA GOUBIL-GAMBRELL

Type A Behavior, Competitive Achievement-Striving, and Cheating Among College Students 201
ANTHONY R. PERRY, KEVIN M. KANE, KEVIN J. BERNESSER, AND PAUL T. SPICKER

Athenian Democracy 208
JOSIAH OBER AND CATHERINE VANDERPOOL

The Big New Mix 219
RENEE LOTH

The Underdog Concept in Sport 225
JIMMY A. FRAZIER AND ELDON E. SNYDER

Communication Stereotypes: Is Interracial Communication Possible? 234
REBECCA LEONARD AND DON C. LOCKE

Using Color Effectively: Designing to Human Specifications 242
GERALD M. MURCH

KNOWLEDGE BY PARTICIPATION AND OBSERVATION

Friends, Good Friends—and Such Good Friends 256
JUDITH VIORST

An Architect Who Takes Stairways One Step at a Time 260
RICHARD WOLKOMIR

The Mind of the Puzzler 267
ROBERT J. STERNBERG AND JANET E. DAVIDSON

Luis Jimenez's Outdoor Sculptures Slow Traffic Down 275
CHIORI SANTIAGO

The Bambi Syndrome 282
MATT CARTMILL

Peach Preserves and "A New Texas": A Rhetorical Analysis of the Inaugural Addresses of "Ma" Ferguson and Ann Richards 290
LINDA HATCHEL

*Alma's Bedside Ghost: Or the Importance of
    Cultural Similarity*   295
MARINA OPPENHEIMER

The Man Who Cries Wolf   300
FRED H. HARRINGTON

The Indian Image   306
JANE AND MICHAEL STERN

*Gender Bias and the 1992 Summer Olympic Games:
    An Analysis of Television Coverage*   314
CATRIONA T. HIGGS AND KAREN H. WEILLER

*Amphibian Alarm: Just Where Have All the Frogs
    Gone?*   325
BETH LIVERMORE

PART THREE
READING PERSUASIVE AIM WRITING   333

USING ADVERSARIAL AND CONCILIATORY PERSUASION   334
ESTABLISHING CREDIBILITY   334
OFFERING CLAIMS AND EVIDENCE   334
MOTIVATING READERS   335
USING PERSUASIVE INFORMATION AND TECHNIQUES
    ETHICALLY   336

KNOWLEDGE BY PARTICIPATION

The Outlaw Princesses   337
TERENCE RAFFERTY

It Is Time to Stop Playing Indians   340
ARLENE B. HIRSCHFELDER

Farewell to Fitness   343
MIKE ROYKO

Inside the Home   345
JILL FRAWLEY

I, Too, Am a Good Parent   348
DORSETT BENNETT

KNOWLEDGE BY OBSERVATION

*The "Bleaching Syndrome": Implications of Light
    Skin for Hispanic American Assimilation*   352
RONALD E. HALL

The Data Game   359
CYNTHIA CROSSEN

The Motherhood Myth   366
BETTY ROLLIN

Murder, Inc.   375
ROBERT SHERRILL

KNOWLEDGE BY PARTICIPATION AND OBSERVATION

Fenimore Cooper's Literary Offenses   386
MARK TWAIN (SAMUEL LANGHORNE CLEMENS)

Letter from Birmingham Jail   395
MARTIN LUTHER KING, JR.

Warning: Sports Stars May Be Hazardous to Your Health   409
JASON DEPARLE

Sexism in English: A 1990s Update   426
ALLEEN PACE NILSEN

The Language of Discretion   436
AMY TAN

From a Native Daughter   443
HAUNANI-KAY TRASK

Give Children the Vote   450
VITA WALLACE

Why Mow: The Case Against Lawns   454
MICHAEL POLLAN

Sensationalism Versus News of the Moral Life: Making the Distinction   463
KAREN L. SLATTERY

The Killing Game   473
JOY WILLIAMS

Amy Fisher and the Ethics of "Headline" Docudramas   484
ROD CARVETH

Hollywood: The Dark Side   496
SYLVESTER MONROE

History Is Not a Museum   502
ROBERT R. ARCHIBALD

Epilogue   508
Credits   509
Index   515

ALTERNATE THEMATIC CONTENTS

ART AND ENTERTAINMENT

The Case of Harry Houdini (expressive)   96
Luis Jimenez's Outdoor Sculptures Slow Traffic Down (referential)   275
The Outlaw Princesses (persuasive)   337
Amy Fisher and the Ethics of "Headline" Docudramas (persuasive)   484
Hollywood: The Dark Side (persuasive)   496

AFRICAN AMERICAN CULTURE

How It Feels to Be Colored Me (expressive)   44
Lessons From a Friend (expressive)   61
20/20 Hindsight (expressive)   67
The House Where Martin Wept: Marks, Mississippi (expressive)   150
Cultural Etiquette: A Guide for the Well-Intentioned (referential)   173
Letter from Birmingham Jail (persuasive)   395
Hollywood: The Dark Side (persuasive)   496

ASIAN AMERICAN CULTURE

Ghosts (expressive)   118
The Language of Discretion (persuasive)   436

xi

ETHICS

Meditations on a Stolen Purse (expressive) 36
Type A Behavior, Competitive Achievement-Striving, and Cheating Among College Students (referential) 201
Inside the Home (persuasive) 345
Murder, Inc. (persuasive) 375
Letter from Birmingham Jail (persuasive) 395
Warning: Sports Stars May Be Hazardous to Your Health (persuasive) 409
Sensationalism Versus News of the Moral Life: Making the Distinction (persuasive) 463
The Killing Game (persuasive) 473
Amy Fisher and the Ethics of "Headline" Docudramas (persuasive) 484

ENVIRONMENT

The Man Who Cries Wolf (referential) 300
Amphibian Alarm: Just Where Have All the Frogs Gone? (referential) 325
Why Mow: The Case Against Lawns (persuasive) 454

FAMILY

And Then I Went to School (expressive) 39
Only Daughter (expressive) 64
My Grandmother's Pennies (expressive) 113
Ghosts (expressive) 118
Living In—and On—the Margins (expressive) 126
Grandmother's Country (expressive) 153
Falling for Apples (referential) 177
Shopping with Children (referential) 180
Inside the Home (persuasive) 345

FRIENDSHIP

Sylvia Plath: A Memoir (expressive) 47
Lessons From a Friend (expressive) 61
Friends, Good Friends—and Such Good Friends (referential) 256

HISPANIC AMERICAN CULTURE

Only Daughter (expressive) 64
Luis Jimenez's Outdoor Sculptures Slow Traffic Down (referential) 275
Alma's Bedside Ghost: Or the Importance of Cultural Similarity (referential) 295
The "Bleaching Syndrome": Implications of Light Skin for Hispanic American Assimilation (persuasive) 352

HISTORY

Columbus and His Four Fateful Voyages (expressive) 83
Of Accidental Judgments and Casual Slaughters (expressive) 74
A New Monument to Remembering—With a Mission (expressive) 158
Athenian Democracy (referential) 208
From a Native Daughter (persuasive) 443
History Is Not a Museum (persuasive) 502

HUNTING

Little Deaths (expressive) 31
The Bambi Syndrome (referential) 282
The Killing Game (persuasive) 473

IMMIGRANTS AND IMMIGRATION

Ghosts (expressive) 118
Living In—and On—the Margin (expressive) 126
More Than Just a Shrine: Paying Homage to the Ghosts of Ellis Island (expressive) 146
The Big New Mix (referential) 219

JEWISH HISTORY AND TRADITIONS

My Grandmother's Pennies (expressive) 113
A New Monument to Remembering—With a Mission (expressive) 158

LANGUAGE AND COMMUNICATION

How to Write a Letter (referential)   183
Communication Stereotypes: Is Interracial Communication Possible? (referential)   234
Using Color Effectively: Designing to Human Specifications (referential)   242
Sexism in English: A 1990s Update (persuasive)   426
The Language of Discretion (persuasive)   436

MUSEUMS AND MONUMENTS

More Than Just a Shrine: Paying Homage to the Ghosts of Ellis Island (expressive)   146
The House Where Martin Wept: Marks, Mississippi (expressive)   150
A New Monument to Remembering—With a Mission (expressive)   158
History Is Not a Museum (persuasive)   502

NATIVE AMERICAN CULTURE

And Then I Went to School (expressive)   39
Grandmother's Country (expressive)   153
The Indian Image (referential)   306
It Is Time to Stop Playing Indians (persuasive)   340

NATURE

The Man Who Cries Wolf (referential)   300
Amphibian Alarm: Just Where Have All the Frogs Gone? (referential)   325

PARENTING

I, Too, Am a Good Parent (persuasive)   348
The Motherhood Myth (persuasive)   366

POLITICS

Athenian Democracy (referential)   208
Peach Preserves and "A New Texas": A Rhetorical Analysis of the Inaugural Addresses of "Ma" Ferguson and Ann Richards (referential)   290
Give Children the Vote (persuasive)   450

PREJUDICE

How It Feels to Be Colored Me (expressive)   44
Hating Fred (expressive)   59
Fat Like Me (expressive)   107
On Being a Cripple (expressive)   137
A New Monument to Remembering—With a Mission (expressive)   158
Communication Stereotypes: Is Interracial Communication Possible? (referential)   234
The Indian Image (referential)   306
The "Bleaching Syndrome": Implications of Light Skin for Hispanic American Assimilation (persuasive)   352
Letter from Birmingham Jail (persuasive)   395
The Language of Discretion (persuasive)   436

RESEARCH METHODS

Fat Like Me (expressive)   107
A Practitioner's Guide to Research Methods (referential)   186
Type A Behavior, Competitive Achievement-Striving, and Cheating Among College Students (referential)   201
An Architect Who Takes Stairways One Step at a Time (referential)   260
Communication Stereotypes: Is Interracial Communication Possible? (referential)   234
The Man Who Cries Wolf (referential)   300
Gender Bias and the 1992 Summer Olympic Games: An Analysis of Television Coverage (referential)   314
The Data Game (persuasive)   359

SPORTS

Lessons from a Friend (expressive)   61
The Underdog Concept in Sports (referential)   225
Gender Bias and the 1992 Summer Olympic Games: An Analysis of Television Coverage (referential)   314
Farewell to Fitness (persuasive)   343
Warning: Sports Stars May Be Hazardous to Your Health (persuasive)   409

TELEVISION

Gender Bias and the 1992 Summer Olympic Games: An Analysis of Television Coverage (referential) *314*
Sensationalism Versus News of the Moral Life: Making the Distinction (persuasive) *463*
Amy Fisher and the Ethics of "Headline" Docudramas (persuasive) *484*
Hollywood: The Dark Side (persuasive) *496*

WOMEN'S EXPERIENCES

Only Daughter (expressive) *64*
Fat Like Me (expressive) *107*
Friends, Good Friends—and Such Good Friends (referential) *256*
Peach Preserves and "A New Texas": A Rhetorical Analysis of the Inaugural Addresses of "Ma" Ferguson and Ann Richards (referential) *290*
Gender Bias and the 1992 Summer Olympic Games: An Analysis of Television Coverage (referential) *314*
The Outlaw Princesses (persuasive) *337*
The Motherhood Myth (persuasive) *366*
Sexism in English: A 1990s Update (persuasive) *426*

WRITERS AND WRITING

Sylvia Plath: A Memoir (expressive) *47*
Thoreau (expressive) *90*
Living In—and On—the Margins (expressive) *126*
How to Write a Letter (referential) *183*
Fenimore Cooper's Literary Offenses (persuasive) *386*

PROLOGUE

A Reader's Repertoire focuses on critical reading. *Critical reading* refers to the process of constructing meaning—meaning that you create when you decipher, interpret, analyze, and evaluate a text. It requires you to be a responsive participant, interacting with the verbal and visual images on a page. This book will offer you lots of opportunities to understand more fully the importance and power of being a critical reader.

In this book, the term *reading repertoire* has two specific meanings. First, reading repertoire suggests the range of written texts commonly encountered in academic and professional settings as well as in daily life. Memoirs, field notes, personal essays, biographies, physical descriptions, travelogues, news stories, reports, research articles, analyses, case histories, editorials, evaluations, reviews, proposals, letters, and feasibility studies are examples of these kinds of texts. *A Reader's Repertoire* includes expressive, referential, and persuasive aim selections in which writers draw from various ways of knowing to gain understanding about their subjects. Specifically, writers use personal experience (knowledge by participation), external oral and written sources (knowledge by observation), or a combination of the two (knowledge by participation and observation).

Second, the term reading repertoire refers to the storehouse of strategies you can employ when reading different kinds of texts. Because of the research of reading experts, we now know more about how people read than we ever thought possible. According to the research findings, people use a variety of approaches, depending upon the kind of text they are reading as well as their motives for reading. For example, if you were reading *A Reader's Repertoire* to remember facts for a test, you might read in a deliberate fashion, highlighting ideas in the text and taking notes as you read. However, if you were compiling a tentative list of essays on a particular theme, you might simply check the alternate table of contents or scan the essay titles and headnotes to determine quickly which sources might be pertinent. Knowing more about how you read can enable you to be a more careful and a more thoughtful reader—a critical reader.

In *A Reader's Repertoire,* you will find information about how to read, followed by a wide array of essays, written for diverse readerships, and published in a broad range of magazines and journals. As the thematic table of contents indicates, you can find clusters of essays that pertain to a variety of subjects, such as ethics, the environment, family, friendship, hunting, language and communication, politics, prejudice, research methods, sports, television, and writers and writing. *A Reader's Repertoire* consists of an introduction and 66 essays divided into three major parts. The essays all appear in their entirety rather than in excerpted form.

The Introduction provides a general overview of critical reading. We define and explain the processes involved in the act of reading, exploring how motives and various constraints such as attitude, fatigue, environment, and technology can affect readers. In addition, we explain the key concepts of the rhetorical situation—the tension among writer, reader, and subject—as well as the aims and purposes of writing. We conclude this section by presenting a Guide to Critical Reading and two student analyses of an essay.

The three major parts in *A Readers's Repertoire* are Part One: **Reading Expressive Aim Writing;** Part Two: **Reading Referential Aim Writing;** and Part Three: **Reading Persuasive Aim Writing.** Each of these parts begins with introductory information on a particular aim of writing, followed by 22 essays, organized according to the authors' ways of knowing about their subjects. The selections have been chosen with care. The essays include both individually and collaboratively authored works, written for general and professional readerships, published in a wide range of popular magazines and scholarly journals, and conforming to various documentation style guides, including MLA and APA.

Every essay concludes with two kinds of activities. **Questions for Discussion** focus on critical reading: the questions reinforce and augment the "conversation" initiated by a Guide to Critical Reading, thus helping you to read critically—to decipher, interpret, analyze, and evaluate. **Opportunities for Writing** emphasize composing: the activities suggest possible subjects and rhetorical situations.

A Reader's Repertoire is the result of the collaborative efforts of a great many people. We wish to thank the undergraduate and graduate students in our writing and reading classes for their honesty and understanding. As we've taken our ideas and applied them in the classroom, our students voiced what they found helpful. Even more valuable was their willingness to work with us to modify and strengthen our teaching. We appreciate their allowing us to learn from them.

We also acknowledge the teachers who have inspired us to love learning, and who have challenged us to pass that passion on to our students. They taught us the power of language, knowing, and communication.

In the process of writing and editing this book, our reviewers have also been our teachers and deserve our thanks: Chris Baker, Armstrong State College; Ralph G. Dillie, University of Southern Colorado; Maurice Hunt, Baylor University; Rodney Keller, Ricks College; Lisa McClure, Southern Illinois University; John Miller, Normandale Community College; Charlotte Rotkin, Pace University; Charlotte Smith, Virginia Polytechnic Institute and State University; Isabel Stanley, East Tennessee State University; Dean Stover, Arizona State University; Sally Young, University of Tennessee at Chattanooga.

Thanks also go to our collaborators and close friends at HarperCollins: Tisha Rossi, Tom Maeglin, Lois Lombardo, and Lee Paradise, our editors. Special recognition also goes to Jane Kinney and Laurie Likoff for their continued support and encouragement.

We are especially privileged to acknowledge our families for their unwavering love and support: our parents, Kung Woo and Lee Chiles Sit Gong and Sam and Theresa Dragga; our spouses, John Powers and Linda Dragga; and our children, Devereux Gong Powers and Timothy and Nicholas Dragga. We are grateful for their hugs and smiles, patience and understanding. Collaborating on this book while living on two different continents has often required us to steal time from our families, traveling long distances across the Pacific, writing at our offices late into the night, and settling for the sound of their voices on the telephone or "reading" their voices on e-mail. No words can capture our deep gratitude for their love and encouragement.

Gwendolyn Gong
Sam Dragga

A READER'S REPERTOIRE

INTRODUCTION

Can you remember the first time you read? What did you read? How old were you? You may never have thought about it before, but you haven't ever stopped reading since the day you learned to read. In fact, you couldn't stop reading, even if you tried. As an experiment, try *not* to read for a day; it's not as easy as you may think.

Once we know how to read, we cannot help but engage in the act of reading. We read the words that we see involuntarily, and we often "see" mental pictures of words as we hear or think of them. In effect, reading has become for us an integral part of what it means to be human and to communicate.

The subject and practice of reading are the focuses of this book. In the following pages, you will find information about ways to become actively involved in what you read, accompanied by a wide range of essays to broaden your reading experiences. All of the essays in *A Reader's Repertoire* appear in their entirety rather than in excerpted form.

What does *reading repertoire* mean? In this book, we emphasize two definitions of the term. First, *reading repertoire* refers to the range of written texts commonly encountered in academic and professional settings as well as in daily life. Examples of these kinds of texts include memoirs, field notes, personal essays, biographies, physical descriptions, and travelogues; news stories, reports, research articles, analyses, and case histories; as well as editorials, evaluations, reviews, proposals, letters, and feasibility studies.

Second, *reading repertoire* refers to the storehouse of strategies you can employ when reading different kinds of texts. What do you do when you read? Reading experts report that we use a variety of approaches, depending upon the kind of text we are reading as well as our reasons or motives for reading. For example, when reading a textbook to remember facts for a test, you may read more deliberately, highlighting ideas in the text and taking notes as you read. However, when compiling a working list of sources, you may simply scan a series of abstracts to determine quickly which sources to actually look up. By knowing more about how you read, you will be a more careful and a more thoughtful reader: that is, you'll learn to be a critical reader.

CRITICAL READING

Critical reading amounts to more than a single, simple process. It actually involves three overlapping and ongoing processes that you use to construct meaning: *planning, translating,* and *reviewing* (Flower; Spivey; Baker and Brown; Haas and Flower; Brandt; Courage). That is, meaning isn't something that resides *passively* in a text for you to uncover or to receive; it isn't like liquid that can be "poured" into you as if you were a water glass. Instead, meaning is something that you must *actively* create by interacting with words to decipher, interpret, analyze, and evaluate a text.

Why make this effort? Consider this example. Suppose your physician prescribes some high-blood-pressure medicine for you; on the label, the only directive is "Take one tablet after dinner." When is dinnertime? For most people, *dinner* refers to their evening meal. But for many in the American South, *dinner* suggests lunch, and *supper* refers to the evening meal. In order to take your medicine appropriately, you can't simply read the directive (i.e., passively "receive" information); you must analyze it and, in this case, perhaps call your doctor or pharmacist for clarification (i.e., actively "make" meaning or sense of information). Critical reading is an important ability that you need to use daily, regardless of the setting or circumstance—at college, on the job, or at home.

Planning

Planning is a reading process during which you survey the text and inventory your knowledge and attitude about the subject. When surveying a text, you identify its major characteristics. For example, you note the text's title, author, publication date, research approach, headings, and illustrations. Because the meaning of the text is shaped by what a reader already knows about the subject, you take stock of your impressions, biases, experiences, and attitudes. And if you are reading a text (e.g., an essay, a recipe, a chapter in a book) that is followed by questions or instructions (as is the case in this book), you might quickly read through them before reading that text. This planning process provides you with a quick overview of the text.

For example, if you were going to see a movie, your perception of the movie would be influenced by the movie's title, its rating, the reputation of the director and the actors, movie reviews, conversations with friends, advertisements, and previews. All of this occurs before you see the movie. All of this is part of planning. Your perception of books and articles is subject to similar influences.

Although planning begins before you read the text, it continues as you read. While you are reading, for example, you might recall additional details about the subject or notice a heading you'd overlooked earlier.

Translating

Translating refers to the process of deciphering and interpreting a text. (This is the kind of activity you might have engaged in when searching for the intended meaning of the word *dinner* that appeared on the high-blood-pressure medicine.) Translating means more than simply decoding the words on the page. It is also more than paraphrasing and summarizing. Translating involves continual experimentation with "making meaning"—developing and questioning different possible interpretations, taking into account the understanding that you can bring to the text.

Consider again the example of seeing a movie. While you watch the film, the images flashing across the screen contribute to your understanding and appreciation, but so does your continual monitoring of actions, motives, and consequences. As the movie progresses, without realizing that you're doing so, you probably ask yourself a series of questions that help you to investigate and make meaning: Are the characters believable? Is the plot feasible? Is the ending satisfactory? The knowledge you bring to the film—all of the movies you have seen as well as all of your life experiences—will influence your answers to such questions. Your ongoing involvement in making such judgments about the movie is similar to decisions you might make while reading a text.

Reviewing

Reviewing is a process during which you analyze and evaluate your reading plans and translations. Often your reviewing will begin as soon as you start planning, and it may result in your writing notes in the margins or highlighting key words or ideas. While you identify the characteristics in a text, consider your knowledge and attitudes about the subject, and experiment with meaning by deciphering and interpreting, you might change your view of one or more portions of the text, from a brief passage to a major section. This "re-viewing" or rethinking is a pivotal process because it triggers the back-and-forth movement between planning and translating.

Imagine again that you're watching a movie. Are the attitudes that you derived from seeing advertisements or previews justified? Are the expectations that arose after conversations with friends fulfilled? Do you initially perceive certain characters as foolish, but later consider them wise? Do you originally think some event or object is insignificant, but later decide that it is important? Whenever you make such adjustments and refinements to your plans and translations, you are engaged in the dynamic process of reviewing.

Critical reading thus consists of the interactive and recursive processes of planning, translating, and reviewing. That is, these processes can occur again and again as you read, and more than one process can happen at the same time.

Reading Perspectives and Influences

Now that you've gotten a sense of the processes involved in the act of reading a text, let's consider two factors that are associated with how you read:

- perspectives for reading
- internal and external influences

Reading Perspectives

According to reading researchers, you adopt these different perspectives when you approach a text: the *content perspective,* the *function/feature perspective,* and the *rhetorical perspective* (Haas and Flower 174–176).

When you are reading from the content perspective, you strive to retrieve information from a text (e.g., who, what, when, where, why, how). You focus on "what a text is about." As a student, you may find that you are a content reader, especially when fulfilling "read-to-take-a-test assignments" (Haas and Flower 170). Or as a manager reading sales reports, you might be a content reader in order to access information accurately and efficiently.

Unlike the content perspective, the function/feature perspective focuses on what a text is doing (Haas and Flower 175). That is, you locate major parts of a text such as the introduction, conclusion, thesis, title, and headings in a piece of writing. The function/feature perspective helps you to understand the relationship among the parts of a text. For example, you might preview the table of contents in a book as a way to orient yourself and guide your reading.

If you read from the rhetorical perspective, you consider the writer, audience, and subject of the text. You examine who the author is and what he or she hopes to accomplish by addressing a particular audience. While the *content reader* seeks key information and the *function/feature reader* focuses on organization, the *rhetorical reader* stresses *what, how,* and *why* something is said within a particular context.

Readers shift perspectives to accommodate different reading situations. If, for example, you're reading a history assignment while rushing to class, you may only have time to scan the topic headings to get a sense of what and how material is presented. Your perspective in this case emphasizes functions/features. If you're reading to prepare for the written portion of a driving test, however, you'd want to take the time to study both the topic headings and the sentences that accompany them. Here you approach reading from a content perspective. And if you're reading a letter from a friend requesting a cash loan, you might consider his or her predicament and motives carefully before withdrawing money from the bank, thus assuming a rhetorical perspective for reading.

From which perspective do you most frequently read? Depending upon your reading situations, you use all three, sometimes in isolation and sometimes in combination. In *A Reader's Repertoire,* we encourage you to be mindful of these three perspectives. That is, rather than reading exclusively from a content, function/feature, or rhetorical perspective, try to incorporate all three into your reading repertoire. In doing so, you'll understand what you're reading more effectively: you will be reading critically.

Internal and External Influences

Reading doesn't happen in a vacuum. Granted, you might find a quiet corner of your college library to read your notes or assignments. Or you could curl up on your sofa with a favorite novel and a cup of cocoa. In these two instances, the conditions seem conducive for effective reading.

These conditions, however, can't always be maintained. We've all experienced times when circumstances beyond our control have altered our reading situation and, as a result, our ability to read well. For example, we've all been distracted by loud noise, music, or talking in the next room. Often, we are tempted to pay more attention to the sounds coming from our neighbor's apartment than our reading assignment.

The different types of conditions just described are examples of internal and external influences—influences that can promote, hinder, or altogether prohibit you in your efforts to be an effective reader.

Internal influences are physical, emotional, and intellectual constraints that exist within you at the time you are reading (McLeod). Here are some questions that might help you to assess possible internal influences on your reading processes: Do you have a cold, allergies, or headache, or some other chronic illness? Are you well-rested or fatigued? Do you think the text you're reading is easy, challenging, or frustrating? Does what you're reading correspond or conflict with what you believe about the subject? Do you have enough information to understand what you're reading? Is your understanding of the subject gained from personal experience (participation), outside sources (observation), or both?

External influences are factors that impinge upon you as you read. Some outside factors are task, time, environment, technology, and collaborators. Whenever these factors change, they alter your reading perspective or reason for reading. Consider these questions when evaluating external influences on your reading processes: Is your purpose for reading clear? How manageable is your reading assignment? Is this text similar to others you've read before? If so, how did you approach those texts and how effective was your reading? How will that previous experience (or any others) influence you this time? How long do you have to read the text? Does having time limits help or hinder you? Are you reading in a familiar or comfortable setting? Do you have enough light? Are you reading a paper copy or words on a computer screen? Are you making suggestions or editing the text as you read? Do you like to read a text and talk about it with others?

Your ability to identify the different constraints on your reading process will allow you to anticipate and compensate for their impact. Your reading experiences, however, will differ each time you read because no two reading situations—neither the texts you are reading nor your internal and external influences—will be identical.

Understanding the Rhetorical Situation

Reading processes are shaped and affected by not only different reading perspectives and constraints but also a text's rhetorical situation. The rhetorical situation is the dynamic relationship among a writer, a reader, and a subject. For example, a writer communicates information about a subject to you, the reader. In doing so, the writer must consider what he or she knows about the subject and about you. Likewise, to read effectively, you need to consider what you know about the subject and writer. Successful communication and meaning-making require interaction among the *writer, subject,* and *reader*. The communication triangle illustrates this important relationship (see Figure 1).

In other words, understanding the relationships among the writer, subject, and reader within a specific context can help you assess

- the writer's objective and motives for writing
- the accuracy or credibility of the writer's information, and
- the appropriateness of the writing for the intended or likely readers.

Determining Aims

According to theorist James L. Kinneavy in *A Theory of Discourse,* there are *four aims of writing:* expressive, referential, persuasive, and literary (18–19, 37–40). As shown in Figure 2, these aims derive from the communication triangle—*writer, reader,* and *subject*—that is expanded to include *language* (Kinneavy; Jakobson). The writings that you read in college, on the job, and at your leisure all involve different degrees of emphasis among the four aims of the communication triangle. For this reason, let's quickly review each aim.

When the *writer* corner is emphasized, the writing aim is called *expressive*. How can you tell if a text is expressive? If an individual or group of writers use language to express personal perceptions and accounts about how people, ideas, places, and things have affected them and their values, the text can be said to be expressive, emphasizing the *writer* corner (Kinneavy 38–39). Why compose expressive aim writing? Writers produce expressive aim texts to achieve certain purposes, such as to recount events, portray characters, and

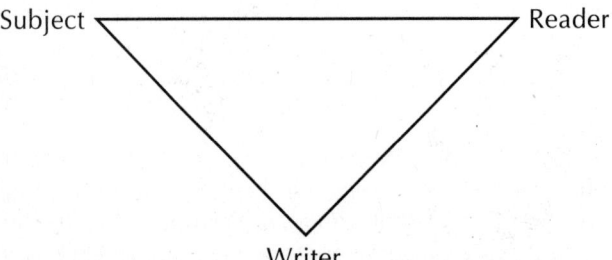

Figure 1. The Communication Triangle and the Rhetorical Situation

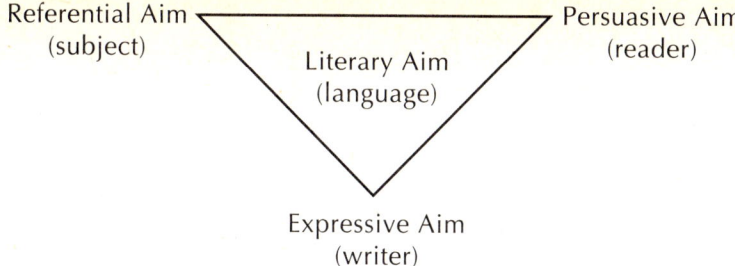

Figure 2. Aims and the Communication Triangle

depict places. These types of texts are commonly considered to be examples of expressive aim writing:

autobiographies	personal journals
personal letters	diaries
confessions	travelogues
personal essays	memoirs

When the *subject* corner is stressed, writers produce *referential* aim texts. Referential aim writing informs or teaches readers and is sometimes referred to as expository writing. When reading referential writing, you'll typically find that the purpose of the text may be either to explain or to analyze a subject, or both. Here are some examples of referential aim texts:

biographies	case histories
news reports	minutes of a meeting
accident reports	court testimonies
research articles	historical analyses
medical diagnoses	laboratory or field experiments
investigative reports	Supreme Court decisions
textbooks	summaries
questionnaires	definitions
hypothesis-support essays	problem-solving alternatives
user's manuals	guidebooks

When a writer emphasizes the *reader* corner, *persuasive* aim writing results. Almost all writing is at least partially persuasive; however, a text is primarily persuasive if it focuses chiefly on its audience or readership. The common purposes of persuasive writing are to declare a position on an issue, propose a solution to a problem, or evaluate a subject. The following are examples of persuasive aim writing:

advertisements	political messages
religious sermons	editorials
proposals	fund-raising appeals
sales letters	legislative debates
position letters	reviews of products and services
job evaluations	letters of recommendation

Which have you read before? Did you consider them to be persuasive at the time? Why?

Persuasive texts strive to convince readers to see an issue from a particular perspective or to move readers to take action. For a hostile audience, persuasion may actually lead readers to adopt a different opinion on a subject; for a neutral audience, it may offer readers a fresh viewpoint on a subject; and for a friendly audience, persuasion may reinforce readers' views about an issue.

Literary aim writing focuses on *language* instead of the writer, subject, or audience corners of the triangle. Authors of literary works are concerned about the effect of language on the reader; as a consequence, they may experiment with and, as much as possible or appropriate, try to reform or perfect the form that language takes. Unlike expressive, referential, and persuasive aim writing that is nonfiction, literary writing is fiction. For instance, the people, places, and events in literary works may either spring from the author's imagination or be a combination of both history and imagination—the real and the unreal. Short stories, poetry, drama, jokes, limericks, and novels are illustrations of this type of writing. (If you want to learn how to compose literary aim writing, for instance, you might enroll in fiction, poetry, or drama writing classes.)

The words *literature* and *literary* are both sometimes used to refer to the same kind of texts; in a more precise sense, however, each term has a distinct meaning. The noun *literature* is a general term that refers to *all* writing, be it in the humanities, fine arts, business, sciences, or engineering. Literature includes expressive, referential, persuasive, and literary aim texts. The adjective *literary*, on the other hand, is a term that refers only to texts such as short stories, poems, plays, novels, and so on. Writing that analyzes (referential aim) and evaluates (persuasive aim) literary aim texts is called *literary criticism.*

In *A Reader's Repertoire,* we focus on developing your reading repertoire in terms of these three aims: expressive, referential, and persuasive aim texts, including literary criticism. These are the types of texts that you will most often read and write in school and on the job.

While the basic aims of writing are expressive, referential, persuasive (and literary), these aims may coexist and overlap. For instance, a referential description of Ellis Island may contain personal insights and experiences in addition to the impressions of a random sampling of visitors. Or it may have persuasive overtones: readers who have never traveled to the island before may be drawn to its exhibits as a result of reading the personal anecdotes in the description and may add this site to their list of places to visit next summer. It is important to know, however, that even when aims do overlap, one aim will emerge as dominant.

Why is this important to know? Writers compose with certain purposes in mind. When you read, you must determine how well the author's intended purpose matches the actual achieved purpose in the text. Analysis of purpose leads us to another key consideration: the analysis of ways of knowing.

Figure 3. The Knowledge Continuum

Analyzing Ways of Knowing

Everyone gains knowledge along a continuum in three ways: knowledge by participation, knowledge by observation, and knowledge by participation and observation (see Figure 3).

The knowledge continuum illustrates the spectrum of knowledge structures from the writer's and reader's *knowledge by participation* (the left line) to *knowledge by observation* (the right line). By identifying the kind of knowing a writer uses in an essay, for example, you can better analyze both the quality of information in a text and the credibility of the writer. How can you use knowing as a means to analyze these two aspects of a text? To answer this question, you need to understand the definitions of the three ways of knowing and consider some brief examples.

Knowledge by participation refers to information gained from firsthand experience—direct, personal interaction. When you see first-person "I" used often or hear the author's voice used prominently, you assume that he or she gained knowledge through personal experience. You expect that he or she writes about a topic with authority and credibility because the author has firsthand experience or knowledge of the subject.

Suppose an eyewitness to a traffic accident makes a statement in a police report about what he saw; that evidence would be considered knowledge gained by participation. Now suppose you read the police report. You would scrutinize the statement in light of the reliability and accuracy of the witness's evidence—what he could reasonably see and remember. Imagine the witness says he saw a bus driver remove her eyeglasses just before her bus crashed into a parked car. Consider these questions: Could the witness really see the bus driver take off her eyeglasses from where he was standing? Could he do so given the time of day (i.e., the morning light too bright, the afternoon sky too overcast and rainy, or the evening sky too cloudy for anyone to have seen the driver in such detail)? Suppose the eyewitness admits in the report that although he was at the scene of the accident, his statement is really a compilation of remarks he heard from those around him (e.g., most of his sentences begin with "he," "she," "they," rather than "I")? In reading this eyewitness's statement, you might challenge his "I was there" account and credibility, for the evidence he provides has instead been gained from others. While his statement would still be valuable, in a legal context this account would probably be considered as "hearsay" evidence. And the statement—evidence—should be presented as such to be ethical and accurate.

Knowledge by observation refers to information learned from other people's experiences—external sources—which can range from data collected in interviews, polls, and surveys to journal articles, research and annual reports, legislative records, and books. When a writer uses the ideas of others, you expect that the text is written from the perspective of knowledge by observation. As a consequence, other people's findings and voices (i.e., especially when direct quotations are used) may emerge more prominently than the writer's own personal voice. In effect, the writer inspires reader trust and establishes credibility by citing appropriate sources and incorporating their views and findings into the text.

In this case, for example, suppose a reporter writes an article about the bus accident. Although the reporter wasn't present when the mishap occurred, she investigates and reconstructs the accident, relying on the observations of bystanders, police officers, as well as transportation and safety experts. The experts comment on such matters as the speed of the bus, the visibility on that date and time of day, and road conditions. As you read the article, you would want to check the sources, making certain that the experts were respected and experienced in this kind of case. You would check to see if the reporter documented or credited sources by including their names, job titles, credentials, familiarity with the case, and so on. Depending upon the type of article and the place of publication, a writer might use either a formal system of documentation (e.g., bibliographical notes or parenthetical references) or informal tagging of sources (e.g., "according to Dr. Smith"). If sources aren't cited appropriately, both the writer and the information in the article might be suspect.

Knowledge by participation and observation is a combination of knowledge gained through personal experience and knowledge gained from the reported experiences of others. How can you tell if you're reading a text written from this way of knowing? Here are two specific kinds of information to look for:

- evidence gained from others to be formally or informally documented (i.e., establishes the ethics and credibility of the sources as well as those of the writer; provides authoritative, reliable information) and
- insights and data gained from personal experience (i.e., "I was there" evidence strengthens credibility and quality of information).

For example, a detective might know some details about a traffic accident because she witnessed it, but she might also investigate it further by reading newspaper accounts and speaking to other witnesses. As in the earlier examples, you would read to double-check the accuracy and credibility of the information and references.

Analyzing texts according to ways of knowing allows you to examine both the quality of information included and the credibility of both the writer and sources cited.

Analyzing Audience

When deciding whether a text seems effective, you need to consider the intended audience. Ask yourself: "Was this text written for someone like me?" If not, how similar am I to the intended readers? Just because a text doesn't appeal to you or doesn't seem to achieve its objective doesn't necessarily mean that it is an ineffective piece of prose. It may instead be a text that is written for readers very different from you. For example, an article about how to set animal traps in the wild might be quite informative and interesting for you to read; however, others in this class might find it gory and violent, perhaps clashing with their personal views on this practice. In trying to analyze a text fairly, then, your responsibility doesn't stop with just analyzing information: you must also try to determine the target audience.

To analyze the intended audience, you may develop a profile of the readers (e.g., their age, education, experience, and cultural background). The more you understand the characteristics of these readers, the more likely you are to understand and appreciate the text. For example, you might consider cues in the text such as word choice, phrasing, allusion, voice, format of information in the text, level and kind of information, references in the text, documentation system, and place of publication. We examine these cues in greater detail in the discussion of analyzing the intended readers in the next section.

DEVELOPING YOUR READING REPERTOIRE

The following questions are designed to guide your planning, translating, and reviewing processes as you read and analyze the selections in this book. By responding to this series of questions, you will improve your ability to approach a text from all three reading perspectives: content, function/feature, and rhetorical. You will also clarify your relationship to the subject, author, and intended audience.

- **What do you know about the subject of the text? How do you know this information?**
    Preview the text. That is, before actually reading the text, scan it to determine what the essay is about.
    Then list key words or ideas about the subject.
    Circle the key words and ideas that you learned about from personal experience (knowledge by participation).
    Place a check mark beside the key words and ideas that you learned about from others (knowledge by observation).

As you read a text, you interpret and evaluate the information an author presents in light of the information that you already know about the subject. For example, suppose you're reading an essay about the health benefits of hiking. Imagine, however, that you once were an avid hiker who was forced to give up the practice because hiking triggered chronic asthma attacks and aggravated bone spurs in your feet. This information gained from personal experience (participation) may certainly influence your attitude about hiking and thus may color your sense of how effective the text may be. For this reason, you need to consider your own knowledge of the subject of a text so that you can see how it might affect your interpretation and assessment of what the text says and how effectively it says it.

- **What does the author know about the subject? How does the author know this information?**
  Read the text, and list key words or ideas about the subject.
  Circle the key words and ideas that the author learned about from personal experience (knowledge by participation).
  Place a check mark beside the key words and ideas that the author learned about from others (knowledge by observation).

Reading critically requires you to scrutinize the evidence presented in a text. And this is why you'll want to list the key words or ideas that the author includes in his or her text. What specific information is included? Did the author gain that information by participation, observation, or both participation and observation?

Look at the information that was gained from personal experience. Is the author's experience representative or novel? Is the information believable, specific, and accurate? Do you think the author's experience could provide him or her with these kinds of details? Why or why not? Is the information organized in a logical and meaningful way?

Examine the evidence gained from other sources. Is it formally or informally documented (notes, parenthetical references, or tagging)? Compare the publication dates of the sources to the publication date of the author's text. In most cases, the majority of sources should be recent ones, containing the most current data about the subject at the time the author was researching and writing. However, this is not always the case; the appropriateness and usefulness of older or newer sources often depends on the subject and discipline.

For example, suppose you're reading an essay on the subject of AIDS. Because of the rapid development of medical, social, political, and legal information associated with this virus, new findings are constantly replacing or modifying previous ones. As a consequence, you'd expect the sources in the essay to be recent research, published around the same time as the essay itself.

On the other hand, suppose you're reading an essay recounting how Alexander Graham Bell invented the telephone. In this case, you'd expect the author to rely heavily on historical documents, such as the letters, diaries, notes, reports, and personal accounts of Bell as well as his family, friends, and colleagues. You might find some contemporary research in the essay, but it probably would not be used as extensively as the historical documents. If the author only used recent sources, would his or her credibility be affected? How and why?

- **What is the author's aim?**
  Is the author's aim expressive, referential, or persuasive?
  What does the author hope to accomplish in the text?
  Are there subordinate aims?

By identifying the dominant aim of a text, you determine what you think the author is trying to achieve, enabling you to judge whether or not the author has achieved that objective.

In expressive aim writing, the author emphasizes the personal value and significance of ideas, people, places, objects, and so on. Referential aim writing reports information about ideas, people, places, and objects. In contrast, in persuasive aim writing, the author strives to convince readers to think or act in the way he or she advocates.

After you identify the dominant aim of the text, consider whether or not there is a subordinate aim. For example, suppose you read an essay in which the author describes how her job as a 911 operator has increased her self-esteem and her ability to calm and instruct people in trouble. In her description, suppose that she explains the procedure for keeping her caller on the line as she alerts police and medical emergency personnel of the problem. Although her explanation of her job is representative of referential aim writing, her main objective is expressive: to stress how doing her job has affected her.

Imagine that the same author wrote another essay about the life of a 911 operator. In her text, suppose that she describes the personal rewards of the job (expressive aim), explains the application process (referential aim), and urges readers to consider this exciting career (persuasive aim). How do you know which aim is dominant? Try to locate the author's objective in the text. Often, an author will state his or her reason for writing in the introduction or conclusion of a text. Look at the body of the essay, where ideas are refined and developed. What does the bulk of the evidence attempt to accomplish?

- **Who are the intended readers?**
  For whom do you think this text was intended?
  Try to list the groups of readers who might learn from or enjoy this text.
  In making your list, consider cues in the text such as language, direct address or naming of readers, and context; these cues can reveal a great deal about intended readers' ages, levels of education, academic majors, and cultural heritages.
  Circle readers you think share the author's attitudes and interests about this subject.

As you read an essay, remember that every message is written to be read by someone. In fact, you might examine the text to find cues that suggest targeted readers. For example, locate specialized jargon or technical information in the text; you can use these cues to identify the possible readers (e.g., professionals, hobbyists, general readers) who would understand and appreciate these terms and data. Notice if and how the author refers to the audience—background, age, academic major—in the essay. What do these references or cues reveal about the intended readers?

- "Classical music lovers will rush out and buy this new compact disk."
- "If you've ever needed a guide for buying a used car, read this article."
- "Before administering any medication to patients, double-check their medical charts for prescription changes to see if doctors have revised medication and dosages."
- "Graduating from high school is an important accomplishment."
- "When you file your tax form, remember to include your social security number in the appropriate blanks."

Where was the article published? If an article on heart disease appeared in a medical journal, you might expect health professionals to be the key readership. Few patients would probably subscribe to or routinely read medical publications. On the other hand, an article about heart disease published in *Readers' Digest* would have a broad readership, from general readers to highly specialized health professionals.

Given textual cues and context, for whom might this message or text be written? Try to imagine those readers as best as you can. How would you characterize them? Why do you think they would be appropriate or likely readers for this text? Do you consider the information in the text to be informative and interesting for this audience? Why or why not?

- **What is your relationship to the intended readers?**
    Are you like any of the intended readers you've listed? If so, how?
    Go back and add your name to the list, placing it near the group you might be most similar to.
    If you're not like the intended audience, how are you different?
    How do you think this difference influences your reading of the text?

Sometimes you may think that a text is ineffective because it doesn't spark your interest or move you. Before making this conclusion, consider who the author envisioned as the audience. If you list the intended readers and decide that you fit their profile, then you may be right: the text may be ineffective. The author may have failed to communicate to his or her audience.

But if you find that you aren't similar to the intended readers, you need to do more analysis before judging the text. Reread the text as if you were a member of the intended readers. Does the meaning in the text seem more engaging and important when you read from another person's viewpoint? If so, you may find that the text is effective but just does not appeal to you.

For example, have you ever read a research article published in a professional journal? As a student reader, you may have found that text pretentious, jargon-ridden, full of indecipherable data in figures and tables, and thus incomprehensible. Given that this article has been written for other researchers in a specific field of expertise, your assessment of the text is understandable; nevertheless, try to judge the text from the viewpoint of the author's peers in that profession. Would they find the text too difficult, the specialized terminology unnecessary, and the data confusing or superfluous? Being a critical reader requires that you attempt to understand the text in its rhetorical context.

Next we show how two students have used the questions in the preceding discussion to guide them as they read "The Pie" by Gary Soto. Before examining their responses, read Soto's essay.

The Pie

GARY SOTO

I knew enough about hell to stop me from stealing. I was holy in almost every bone. Some days I recognized the shadows of angels flopping on the backyard grass, and other days I heard faraway messages in the plumbing that howled underneath the house when I crawled there looking for something to do.

But boredom made me sin. Once, at the German market, I stood before a rack of pies, my sweet tooth gleaming and the juice of guilt wetting my underarms. I gazed at the nine kinds of pie, pecan and apple being my favorites, although cherry looked good, and my dear, fat-faced chocolate was always a good bet. I nearly wept trying to decide which to steal and, forgetting the flowery dust priests give off, the shadow of angels and the proximity of God howling in the plumbing underneath the house, sneaked a pie behind my coffee-lid frisbee and walked to the door, grinning to the bald grocer whose forehead shone with a window of light.

"No one saw," I muttered to myself, the pie like a discus in my hand, and hurried across the street, where I sat on someone's lawn. The sun wavered between the branches of a yellowish sycamore. A squirrel nailed itself high on the trunk, where it forked into two large bark-scabbed limbs. Just as I was going to work my cleanest finger into the pie, a neighbor came out to the porch for his mail. He looked at me, and I got up and headed for home. I raced on skinny legs to my block, but slowed to a quick walk when I couldn't wait any longer. I held the pie to my nose and breathed in its sweetness. I licked some of the crust and closed my eyes as I took a small bite.

In my front yard, I leaned against a car fender and panicked about stealing the apple pie. I knew an apple got Eve in deep trouble with snakes because Sister Marie had shown us a film about Adam and Eve being cast into the desert, and what scared me more than falling from grace was being thirsty for the rest of my life. But even that didn't stop me from clawing a chunk from the pie tin and pushing it into the cavern of my mouth. The slop was sweet and gold-colored in the afternoon sun. I laid more pieces on my tongue, wet finger-dripping pieces, until I was finished and felt like crying because it was about the best thing I had ever tasted. I realized right there and then, in my sixth year, in my tiny body of two hundred bones and three or four sins, that the best things in life came stolen. I wiped my sticky fingers on the grass and rolled my tongue over the corners of my mouth. A burp perfumed the air.

I felt bad not sharing with Cross-Eyed Johnny, a neighbor kid. He stood over my shoulder and asked, "Can I have some?" Crust fell from my mouth, and my teeth were bathed with the jam-like filling. Tears blurred my eyes as I remembered the grocer's forehead. I remembered the other pies on the rack, the warm air of the fan above the door and the car that honked as I crossed the street without looking.

"Get away," I had answered Cross-Eyed Johnny. He watched my fingers greedily push big chunks of pie down my throat. He swallowed and said in a whisper, "Your hands are dirty," then returned home to climb his roof and sit watching me eat the pie by myself. After a while, he jumped off and hobbled away because the fall had hurt him.

I sat on the curb. The pie tin glared at me and rolled away when the wind picked up. My face was sticky with guilt. A car honked, and the driver knew. My mom, peeling a mountain of potatoes at the Redi-Spud factory, knew. I got to my feet, stomach taut, mouth tired of chewing, and flung my frisbee across the street, its shadow like the shadow of an angel fleeing bad deeds. I retrieved it, jogging slowly. I flung it again until I was bored and thirsty.

I returned home to drink water and help my sister glue bottle caps onto cardboard, a project for summer school. But the bottle caps bored me, and the water soon filled me up more than the pie. With the kitchen stifling with heat and lunatic flies, I decided to crawl underneath our house and lie in the cool shadows listening to the howling sound of plumbing. Was it God? Was it Father, speaking from death, or Uncle with his last shiny dime? I listened, ear pressed to a cold pipe, and heard a howl like the sea. I lay until I was cold and then crawled back to the light, rising from one knee, then another, to dust off my pants and squint in the harsh light. I looked and saw the glare of a pie tin on a hot day. I knew sin was what you take and didn't give back.

Now, let's see how David, an 18-year-old college student, analyzed the rhetorical situation for "The Pie." Notice how his experience of stealing a candy bar at age 9 influences

- what he considers to be the key information in "The Pie."
- who he thinks the readers might be.
- how he imagines himself to be similar to the intended readers as well as the writer in experience and attitude.

David responds to the reading questions, recording his thoughts in his reading journal. Here is his journal entry containing his analysis.

- **What do you know about the subject of the text? How do you know this information?**
  Preview the text. That is, before actually reading the text, scan it to determine what the essay is about.
  Then list key words or ideas about the subject.
  Circle the key words and ideas that you learned about from personal experience (knowledge by participation).
  Place a check mark beside the key words and ideas that you learned about from others (knowledge by observation).

  At first, I didn't know what the essay was really about. The meaning of the title wasn't clear to me until I began to read it. For this reason, I didn't write anything in response to this step.

While reading the first half of the essay, I realized I had done this kind of thing when I was a little boy. I stole a candy bar from a corner store. Guess I should jot down those "key words and ideas" now. Everything I remember is from my experience, so I guess I'll circle it all. I wonder if it's okay to do this after I've started reading?

- (9 years old)
- (stole candy bar)
- (had money, though)
- (why did I steal it?)
- (stolen candy tasted good)
- (Mrs. Jones saw?)
- (never confessed, never got caught)
- (guilt pangs)
- (can't eat a Baby Ruth now)
- (too late to say I sinned)
- (I'm still a good guy)
- (Everyone makes mistakes)
- (I was only 9)

- **What does the author know about the subject? How does the author know this information?**
  Read the text, and list key words or ideas about the subject.
  Circle the key words and ideas that the author learned about from personal experience (knowledge by participation).
  Place a check mark beside the key words and ideas that the author learned about from others (knowledge by observation).

I've read the essay and I really can identify with this writer. Soto wrote the story from personal experience (knowledge by participation). I'm supposed to write down words and ideas that strike me as important. Here goes.

- boredom
- sin
- German Market
- 9 kinds of pie
- steal
- Adam and Eve
- Sister Marie
- 6 years old
- best things in life came stolen
- Cross-Eyed Johnny
- Mrs. Hancock
- my mom at the Redi Spud Factory
- my sister and bottle factory
- heat and flies, under house
- howling plumbing, God
- dead father, uncle
- harsh light
- hot day
- sin
- you take it, don't give it back

I think words about the action-stealing-are very important. Also, I think words that show Soto is sorry and scared and all are a big part of this essay. Even if he wishes he hadn't stolen that pie, he can't undo what's already been done. Just like me. I can't give Mrs. Jones her Baby Ruth back (or could I?).

- **What is the author's aim?**
  Is the author's aim expressive, referential, or persuasive?
  What does the writer hope to accomplish in the text?
  Are there subordinate aims?

Expressive. I think it's expressive. Soto is writing about something that he did when he was a kid. Stealing that pie affected him, and he'll never forget what he did and how it made him feel.

Is there a subordinate aim? I keep reading the essay and going back to read what this subordinate aim is supposed to be, but I don't think there is any. Soto's not trying to convince me stealing is good or bad, is he? He has to explain what he did here. Does that mean he's being referential? Could that be it?

- **Who are the intended readers?**
  For whom do you think this text was intended?
  Try to list the groups of readers who might learn from or enjoy this text.
  In making your list, consider cues in the text such as language, direct address or naming of readers, and context; these cues can reveal a great deal about intended readers' ages, levels of education, academic majors, and cultural heritages.
  Circle readers you think share the author's attitudes and interests about this subject.

people who never stole anything   (people/kids who've stolen once and knew it was wrong   DAVID)

people who think they've never made mistakes   people/kids who steal all the time and think it's cool

I think the readers fall into two basic groups: people or kids who have or haven't stolen. I think most people are like Soto. They've taken something when they knew they shouldn't have, and they're sorry. Trouble is, they never were caught and I guess that's good because they never got into trouble. But then they live with the guilt. I think that's like Soto. Can't cry over spilt milk, even if you want to. These readers like this story. They see themselves in it.

Some people steal all of the time and feel no guilt. They are a world away from Gary Soto (and me). They probably would think this story is sappy because the guy feels scared and bad about stealing the pie. Guys who steal and get away with it are supposed to be street smart. Not scared their dead fathers, mothers, uncles, and neighbors might know or care or anything.

About the other readers. I see one group being the "straight as an arrow" guys who never stole anything. They'd like this story, though. The guy in the story has a conscience. That's how he and these readers are alike.

There's another group of readers I see. They're the people who are self-righteous because they think they've never even made a mistake in their lives, much less ever stolen anything. They are kind of neutral about the story because they can't identify with the writer, and they think they're very different from him, but in reality, I don't think they are that different.

- **What is your relationship to the intended readers?**
  Are you like any of the intended readers you've listed? If so, how?
  Go back and add your name to the list, placing it near the group you might be most similar to.
  If you're not like the intended audience, how are you different?
  How do you think this difference influences your reading of the text?

I put myself with the people/kids who've stolen once and knew it was wrong—the "Soto group." His story made me remember a time that I'm not proud of. Reading his story was like reliving my own sin.

For my first time to use these questions and read by myself, I think I've done okay. If I have time later, I want to add a few more feelings about my own experience to my list. Maybe I can use the ideas to write an essay one day. Wonder if this will make me feel better about such a silly mistake? Everyone makes them, don't they? Even if they won't admit it.

Teresa's response to "The Pie" is very different from David's. Teresa is a thirty-something single parent; she works part-time at a local convenience store and doesn't share David's empathy with Soto. Customers come in and steal during her shift, and she's angry about it. As you read Teresa's analysis of the knowledge she brings to the text, Soto's key ideas and aim, and audience, try to recall David's comments. These two readers' interpretations and appreciation of the essay will undoubtedly differ. How do these readers' backgrounds and experiences influence their perceptions of Soto's audience and objective?

Like David, Teresa relies on the reading questions to analyze the rhetorical situation. She also uses her reading journal to record her analysis of her own knowledge of the subject, the author's main ideas and writing aim, and the audience.

- **What do you know about the subject of the text? How do you know this information?**
  Preview the text. That is, before actually reading the text, scan it to determine what the essay is about.
  Then list key words or ideas about the subject.
  Circle the key words and ideas that you learned about from personal experience (knowledge by participation).
  Place a check mark beside the key words and ideas that you learned about from others (knowledge by observation).

What is this essay about? I'm curious. If it's about loving pies, making them, giving them to others, well, great. I can't imagine this writer's a pie expert. But maybe he's a food critic or something.

I sneaked a peak and I'm really disappointed. I came to college to learn something, not to read about the glorification of shoplifters. I can't believe this guy gets paid to tell about being a thief. Am I paying for childcare to study this stuff?

I'm supposed to write about my knowledge of shoplifting. Well, there's always something in the news about crime, but I also know about it directly, especially shoplifting. I am a clerk at the store on 8th and Pearl. The school kids come in around 3:45 and try to steal me blind. They come into the store in groups of five or six, so it's hard to watch them all. One picks up ice cream, another a can drink, somebody else a Twinkie, another a package of cold cuts. They all want to test you. Some will pick up something, look you in the eye, smile, and walk right out of the door. That's when they run. Time to make my list.

(Typical story) ✓
See it in the newspaper everyday – neighborhood crimes are reported all the time ✓
CNN story on kids doing crimes for kicks ✓

Convenience store
Kids steal all the time
Look you in the eye, smile, run
Don't care about themselves or me
I could lose job ✓

Store manager says: Kids steal, clerks pay ✓
Store manager told me stories about kids stealing. Sad thing is, even if you catch them, he says the police won't do anything to them. They'll be out within the hour. ✓

People feel sorry for kids
People should be in my shoes
Crime pays – I pay for crimes ✓
Bleeding hearts love this kind of story ✓

22 INTRODUCTION

My boss has a policy. Clerks pay for whatever is stolen (if he finds out). If kids steal a lot during your shift, you can be fired. The manager says if I can figure out a better solution, let him know. What else can he do? He thinks the police are soft on minors who shoplift—it's a "petty" crime. So, clerks pay since kids don't. It makes sense. Your paycheck is hardly anything after he deducts everything he takes out. I can't stand to pay for those shoplifters. They're not worth it.

- **What does the author know about the subject? How does the author know about this information?**
  Read the text, and list key words or ideas about the subject.
  Circle the key words and ideas that the author learned about from personal experience (knowledge by participation).
  Place a check mark beside the key words and ideas that the author learned about from others (knowledge by observation).

> German Market
> rack of pies
> sneaked a pie under coffee lid
> steal
> No one saw, neighbors looked
> 6 years old
> best things in life come stolen
> Cross-Eyed Johnny, Mrs. Hancock
> my Mom, my sister
> heat and flies, under house
> howling plumbing, God
> dead father, uncle
> harsh light
> hot day
> sin – means take

Soto knows about shoplifting because he is a shoplifter. I can circle everything on the list, no problem. Picking out key words and ideas is pretty easy. Soto is a 6-year-old thief who thinks the best things in life are stolen. Doesn't care about what the neighbors think, his mom or sister. They might know, but he never owns up to his sin; what's more, they never make him own up. That's the trouble with the system. I put down a lot of key words, but the most important one is SIN.

- **What is the author's aim?**
  Is the author's aim expressive, referential, or persuasive?
  What does the writer hope to accomplish in the text?
  Are there subordinate aims?

  > Soto has two reasons for writing this. First, I think he's got to tell his story-expressive. Second, I think he wants readers to like what he has to say about how he sinned and knew it was stealing and all. Funny thing, he never owned up to anything. But he wants me to let him off the hook for doing this wrong thing-persuasive. I just don't buy it.

- **Who are the intended readers?**
  For whom do you think this text was intended?
  Try to list the groups of readers who might learn from or enjoy this text.
  In making your list, consider cues in the text such as language, direct address or naming of readers, and context; these cues can reveal a great deal about intended readers' ages, levels of education, academic majors, and cultural heritages.
  Circle readers you think share the author's attitudes and interests about this subject.

  > (one time shoplifters)   (habitual shoplifters)
  >
  > (people who aren't familiar with situations where customers shoplift)   people who work at places where patrons shoplift
  >
  > TERESA
  >
  > I read this essay three times and got madder every time. Who are the readers? There are readers like me who have to put up with people like Soto. I don't see myself as like this writer or as liking what he writes. Then there are readers who don't have any idea that shoplifters are such a problem. These people are probably like bleeding hearts, blaming society for kids "having" to steal. They'd really like this story and feel pretty close to Soto.
  > After thinking about this more, I added some others to my list:
  >   1. One-time shoplifters-just like Soto and love this story
  >   2. Habitual shoplifters-more criminal than Soto; they love this story

- **What is your relationship to the intended readers?**
  Are you like any of the intended readers you've listed? If so, how?

Go back and add your name to the list, placing it near the group you might be most similar to.
If you're not like the intended audience, how are you different?
How do you think this difference influences your reading of the text?

> *I am on the other side of the counter from Soto. I'm the clerk he's stealing that apple pie from. I don't like him or this essay.*

Notice how David and Teresa read the same essay, yet construct different interpretations of it. Their interpretations are influenced by the knowledge and experience they bring to Soto's childhood experience. David identifies with Soto and is a very motivated and enthusiastic reader; his analysis of the rhetorical situation illustrates how his knowledge is complementary to Soto's. Teresa, on the other hand, assumes an adversarial attitude toward the writer and subject. She reads this essay but isn't especially happy about it.

David and Teresa both identify the key ideas in "The Pie." They summarize the event similarly. But that's where the similarity ends. When they construct meaning by combining their knowledge with the author's, new meaning emerges. While both readers agree that the dominant aim—the major objective—is expressive, Teresa perceives a persuasive subordinate aim or objective. Do you agree with her? Why? Given these readers' backgrounds and experiences, one interpretation may not necessarily be "better" or more "correct" than the other. In fairness to the text and the author, however, it is important that interpretations and evaluations of a text be reasonable and justifiable in light of the intended audience.

David's and Teresa's responses to the reading questions try to take into account Soto's intended readers. At the same time, their comments also illustrate how and why their reactions to "The Pie" differ from each other. David and Teresa clearly demonstrate the dynamic process of critical reading: the relationship that a reader shares with the writer and subject of a text.

Now it's your turn to try. Using the Guide to Critical Reading, analyze "The Pie." Do your responses to the questions resemble either those of David or Teresa? In what specific ways do they differ? Just because your responses differ from other people's doesn't necessarily mean your analysis is less appropriate; it means that you bring different background, experiences, and so on to the text when you're reading. And this difference is what makes critical reading an exciting, dynamic process. Critical reading enriches us, enabling us to achieve new insights and to make new connections between ourselves and other people, places, experiences, cultures, times, and ideas.

In *A Reader's Repertoire*, we invite you to discover your relationship to a wide variety of writers and subjects—to journey across the territory of rhetoric, stopping to investigate expressive, referential, and persuasive aim writing. We offer you opportunities for planning, translating, and reviewing; for exploring your reading perspectives; for assessing the influences on your reading processes; and for expanding your repertoire of critical reading abilities.

Guide to Critical Reading

- **What do you know about the subject of the text? How do you know this information?**

    Preview the text. That is, before actually reading the text, scan it to determine what the essay is about.

    Then list key words or ideas about the subject.

    Circle the key words and ideas that you learned about from personal experience (knowledge by participation).

    Place a check mark beside the key words and ideas that you learned about from others (knowledge by observation).

- **What does the author know about the subject? How does the author know this information?**

    Read the text, and list key words or ideas about the subject.

    Circle the key words and ideas that the author learned about from personal experience (knowledge by participation).

    Place a check mark beside the key words and ideas that the author learned about from others (knowledge by observation).

- **What is the author's aim?**

    Is the author's aim expressive, referential, or persuasive?

    What does the author hope to accomplish in the text?

    Are there subordinate aims?

- **Who are the intended readers?**

    For whom do you think this text was intended?

    Try to list the groups of readers who might learn from or enjoy this text.

    In making your list, consider cues in the text such as language, direct address or naming of readers, and context; these cues can reveal a great deal about intended readers' ages, levels of education, academic majors, and cultural heritages.

    Circle readers you think share the author's attitudes and interests about this subject.

- **What is your relationship to the intended readers?**

    Are you like any of the intended readers you've listed? If so, how?

    Go back and add your name to the list, placing it near the group you might be most similar to.

    If you're not like the intended audience, how are you different?

    How do you think this difference influences your reading of the text?

Works Cited

Baker, Linda, and Ann L. Brown. "Metacognitive Skills and Reading." *Handbook of Reading Research.* Ed. R. Barr, Michael L. Kamil, and Peter Mosenthal. New York: Longman, 1984. 353–394.

Brandt, Deborah. *Literacy as Involvement: The Acts of Writers, Readers, and Texts.* Carbondale: Southern Illinois UP, 1990.

Courage, Richard. "The Interaction of Public and Private Literacies." *College Composition and Communication* 44 (1993): 484–496.

Flower, Linda. "Interpretive Acts: Cognition and the Construction of Discourse." *Poetics* 16 (April 1987): 109–130.

Haas, Christina, and Linda Flower. "Rhetorical Reading Strategies and the Construction of Meaning." *College Composition and Communication* 39 (May 1988): 167–183.

Jakobson, Roman. "Linguistics and Poetics." *Essays on the Language of Literature.* Ed. Seymour Chatman and Samuel L. Levin. Boston: Houghton Mifflin, 1967. 296–322.

Kinneavy, James L. *A Theory of Discourse.* New York: Norton, 1971.

McLeod, Susan. "Some Thoughts About Feelings: The Affective Domain and the Writing Process." *College Composition and Communication* 38 (1987): 426–435.

Spivey, Nancy N. "Construing Constructivism: Reading Research in the United States." *Poetics* 16 (April 1987): 169–193.

PART ONE

READING EXPRESSIVE AIM WRITING

Every day, you write and read numerous expressive aim texts. For example, whenever you dash off a note or letter to a relative, read postcards and electronic mail from a friend who's far away, as well as write and read your journal or diary, you're in some way involved with expressive aim writing. Simply put, expressive aim texts focus on personal experiences, people, ideas, places, and things and may be produced by one or more authors.

As is true of the other aims of writing, expressive aim writing combines aims. That is, texts that have a dominant expressive aim can also have subordinate aims. For example, imagine you're reading an article that provides a profile of an author's favorite teacher. You might expect to read a description of how this educator inspired the author or influenced his or her choice of majors. Because the author emphasizes the significance of this teacher, the resulting essay is chiefly expressive. By including the details of the teacher's personal and professional life, the essay is also referential. If the essay declares that students today deserve more such inspiring teachers, it is also persuasive. As you can see, whether you're the writer or reader of an expressive aim text, you can benefit from being able to recognize the dominant and subordinate aims of writing: as a writer, understanding your aims for writing can guide you as you plan, translate, and review your developing expressive text; as a reader, considering aims can help you to interpret, analyze, and evaluate it.

You can also benefit from understanding the different ways of knowing. For example, as a writer, you can focus your efforts, researching knowledge by participation, by observation, or both. For instance, you could describe your gymnastics coach, a quiet spot you like to visit, or your earliest athletic or academic triumph—direct, personal experiences that you consider important or meaningful. Or you might choose to discuss a historical person you've only read about in books but who particularly impressed or influenced you; similarly, you might describe a place you've never been but have heard a lot about

27

and that is therefore special to you, such as the church or temple where your parents were married. Or you could discuss the personal significance of an event that you know about both by participating in it and reading about it in newspapers and magazines, such as the political campaign of your favorite candidate. When incorporating information gained by observation, you would consider the most appropriate way to cite your sources (i.e., formal or informal documentation system).

As a reader, you might examine the information in a text and ask: What ways of knowing has the author used? Is the evidence accurate and sufficient? Has the author appropriately cited sources? How credible and ethical does the author seem to be, based on the specific evidence used in the text? Notice that by analyzing and evaluating a text in terms of ways of knowing, you can consider the quality as well as the quantity of the evidence and specific details included in the text.

You can also come to write and read expressive aim texts more effectively by being aware of the following characteristics.

NARRATIVE

When you hear the term *narrative,* you may automatically associate it with the kind of writing found in literary aim texts (e.g., short stories and novels). Narratives, however, are commonly found in all kinds of writing, and expressive aim texts are no exception. In most expressive aim writing, the narrative usually involves one or more characters grappling with internal or external conflicts. The typical narrative comprises five stages of plot. The *introduction* presents the characters and setting. The *rising action* describes events that lead to conflict within a character or among characters. The *climax* is the point in the narrative when the most important action happens. The *falling action* describes events that lead to the easing of the conflict. The *resolution* details the outcome of the story.

It is important to note that not all narratives follow the pattern described. For example, historical narratives (i.e., nonfiction accounts that are chronologically arranged) may not develop in the way a traditional plot does. Some essays may, in fact, seem more effective and realistic when the authors break away from a traditional pattern.

In reading expressive aim essays, consider the following questions:

- Does every action in the story line seem appropriate and necessary? If not, which actions might the author delete?
- Which sequences of action are the most important to the logical building of tension and foreshadowing of meaning in the essay?
- Which sequences of action are less important and might be consolidated and summarized?

Point of View

The perspective from which an author writes is called point of view. If the author is a participant in the narrative action, he or she will usually write from a first-person point of view, using the pronoun *I* (if individually authored) or *we* (if collaboratively authored or if the writer is narrating on behalf of a group of people). If the author strictly observes the narrative action, he or she will usually write from a third-person point-of-view, often using the pronouns *he, she, it,* and *they*. If the author adopts a participant-observer's voice, he or she will integrate first-person and third-person perspectives, sometimes relating personal experiences and sometimes citing the experiences of others.

Given the author's way of knowing about the subject, what is the most appropriate voice for the writer to adopt: participant, observer, or participant-observer?

Descriptive Detail

Expressive aim writing *shows* rather than *tells* readers about experience, offering a sense of realism and authenticity by incorporating vivid and accurate descriptive details. Authors refer to people, places, and things by name; identify the color, make, model, and year of a car; specify the look, smell, and taste of food, the high-pitched laugh of a delighted child, the quiet cries of a grieving widow. Such specifics instill readers with a feeling that they are there experiencing the same conflict and resolution that the author is.

Does the author remember that you have five senses, not just one or two? Does the essay make familiar experiences more immediate for you? Does the author introduce you to new sensory impressions or insights?

Characters

The people who appear in expressive writing can be thought of as characters. *Minor characters* are usually simple and static. *Major characters,* on the other hand, are typically complex and dynamic. Expressive writing usually involves some kind of change in the way major characters act or think. As a result, readers need to see how and why major characters think and act as they do.

Does the author breathe life into the characters by revealing their names and occupations, by detailing their physical appearance, actions, thoughts, and emotions? Do the descriptive details create coherent dominant impressions of the characters? Can you draw a vivid mental picture of each major character?

Dialogue

Dialogue captures the speech of characters as they actually have expressed their ideas. The more real that characters are, the more involved readers become in the story. Dialogue can also help to advance narrative action. By talking to one another, characters can reveal the conflict, develop the climax, or explain the resolution of a story.

Do the characters speak so that you can hear their voices? Does the dialogue sound authentic and realistic? Is the dialogue purposeful? Do the characters convey important information in distinctive ways?

Setting

Setting indicates where and when something happens. The setting can affect how characters and their actions are interpreted. For example, if a man brings flowers to his wife's grave during the middle of the night, he is likely to be judged bizarre and his activity considered weird and suspicious. If he visits the grave during the middle of the day, however, he will probably be viewed sympathetically and his activity considered tragically romantic.

Are the details of setting vivid enough to make you imagine that you are there? What impressions does the setting create? How does or should the setting change as the narrative progresses? Why?

Significance of the Experience

The fundamental fascination of expressive writing resides in its ability to tap human experience, either directly or indirectly: the author's experience provokes intellectual and emotional responses among readers to similar situations in their own lives. If expressive writing is successful, readers will see something of themselves in the author's text; they will identify with the author's experience and learn from it too. Without the inclusion of some thoughtful interpretation of human experience, expressive writing may seem empty or pointless to readers. That is, readers rightfully expect an answer to the question, "So what?"

What significance does the author ascribe to his or her subject? Does the significance realized from this incident, person, place, or thing seem logical? Are there other more important lessons or insights that the author might have derived? Has the text made its point without being heavy-handed and didactic?

The following essays display various ways of integrating the characteristics of expressive aim writing. Organized by ways of knowing, these essays recount events, portray characters, and depict places while incorporating subordinate referential and persuasive aims.

Use the Guide to Critical Reading to direct your reading processes and develop your reading perspectives—content, function/feature, and rhetorical. Consider also the internal and external influences on your planning, translating, and reviewing abilities. Your critical examination of expressive aim writing will be a challenging addition to your reading repertoire.

KNOWLEDGE BY PARTICIPATION

Little Deaths

T. H. WATKINS

T. H. Watkins was born in Loma Linda, California. Among his numerous book-length works are California: An Illustrated History *(1973), which was nominated for a Pulitzer Prize;* American Landscape *(1987);* On the Shore of the Sundown Sea *(1990); and* Righteous Pilgrim: The Life and Time of Harold Ickes *(1990). Watkins has also contributed over 200 articles to such publications as* American Heritage, American West, *and the* Sierra Club Bulletin. *In "Little Deaths," which first appeared in a 1974 issue of the* Sierra Club Bulletin, *Watkins recounts his personal experience of accompanying his cousin, a field trapper, and interprets the significance of that experience from the perspective of an environmentalist and historian. Watkins draws from knowledge by participation in order to write this narrative.*

It has been more than ten years since the day my cousin let me walk his traplines with him. We never see each other now. Our worlds, never very close, have grown even farther apart. He left California several years ago to become a trapping supervisor somewhere in Nevada, while I have joined the ranks of those who would cheerfully eliminate his way of life. He would, rightly enough, consider me one of his natural enemies, and it is not likely that we would have much to say if we did meet. Still, I am grateful to him for giving me a glimpse into the reality of a world normally hidden from us, a dark little world where death is the only commonplace.

At the time, my cousin was a lowly field trapper at the beck and call of any rancher or farmer who made an official complaint to the trapping service about varmint troubles—coyotes or wildcats getting after newborn lambs, foxes sneaking into chicken coops, that sort of thing. His current assignment was to trap out the varmint population of some ranchland high in the Diablo Hills southeast of Oakland, a country of rolling grassland, scrub oak, and chaparral dominated by the 3,000-foot upthrust of Mount Diablo. His base was a house trailer planted on the edge of one of the ranches he was servicing near Livermore, although he got into Oakland quite a lot for weekend visits to a lady

31

of his acquaintance. I lived in Oakland at the time, and he usually made a point of stopping by to see my children, of whom he was particularly fond.

I was then a practicing student of western history and thoroughly intrigued by the glittering adventure that pervaded my reading—especially in the stories of the mountain men, those grizzled, anarchic beings with a lust for far places and far things, stubborn individualists who had lived freer than any Indian and had followed their quest for beaver pelts into nearly all the mysterious blanks of the American West, from Taos, New Mexico, to Puget Sound, from the Marys River of the northern Rockies to the Colorado River of the Southwest; hopelessly romantic creatures with a predilection for Indian women, a talent for profanity, and a thirst for liquor profound enough to melt rivets. And here was my cousin, the literary—if not lineal—descendant of the mountain man. True, he was neither grizzled nor given much to profanity, nor had he, so far as I knew, ever offered his blanket to an Indian woman. Still, he was a *trapper*, by God, and when on one of his visits he invited me to accompany him on his rounds, I was entranced with the notion.

Late one spring afternoon I bundled wife and children into the car and drove down to Livermore and out to the ranch where he was staying. After a dinner cooked in the trailer's tiny kitchen, my wife and the children bedded down in the trailer's two little bunks. "When we get back tomorrow afternoon," my cousin told the children, "I'll take you out and show you some spring lambs. You'd like that, right?" he added, giving them a pinch and tickle that set them to giggling in delight. He and I bundled up in sleeping bags on the ground outside.

5   It was pitch black when he woke me that next morning at five o'clock. After shocking ourselves out of sleep by bathing our faces in water from the outside faucet, we got into his pickup and drove off for breakfast at an all-night diner on the road. Dawn was insinuating itself over the dark hills by the time we finished breakfast, and had laid a neon streak across the sky when we finally turned off the highway and began climbing a rutted dirt road that led to the first trapline (we would be walking two traplines, my cousin explained, one on the western side of the hills, one on the eastern; these were two of the six he had scattered over the whole range, each of them containing between 15 and 20 traps and each checked out and reset or moved to a new location every ten days or so). As we bumped and rattled up the road, daylight slowly illuminated the hills. For two or three months in the spring, before the summer sun turns them warm and brown, these hills look as if they had been transplanted whole from Ireland or Wales. They are a celebration of green, all shades of green, from the black-green of manzanita leaves to the bright, pool-table green of the grasses. Isolated bunches of cows and sheep stood almost motionless, like ornaments added for the effect of contrast, and morning mist crept around the base of trees and shrouded dark hollows with the ghost of its presence. Through all this, the exposed earth of the road cut like a red scar, and the sounds of the pickup's engine and the country-western music yammering out of its radio intruded themselves on the earth's silence gracelessly.

We talked of my cousin's father, whom he worshipped and emulated. My cousin was, in fact, almost literally following in his father's footsteps, for "the old man" had been a state trapper himself and was now a trapping supervisor. Before that, back in the deep of the Depression, he had been a lion hunter for the state, when a mountain lion's ears were good as money, and before that he had "cowboyed some," as he put it; at one time, according to family tradition, his grandfather's ranch had encompassed much of what became the town of San Bernardino in Southern California. At one point in his life, he had led jaguar-hunting trips to the jungles of northwestern Mexico, and he was still a noteworthy hunter, though now he confined himself principally to an occasional deer, antelope, or bear. My cousin had grown up in a house where skins of various types served as rugs and couchthrows, where stuffed heads glared unblinkingly from the walls, where sleek hounds were always in-and-out, where hunting magazines dominated the tables, hunting talk dominated the conversations, and everywhere was the peculiarly masculine smell of newly oiled guns, all kinds of guns—pistols (including an old Colt once used by my cousin's great-grandfather, legend had it, to kill a man), rifles, shotguns. It was a family that had been killing things for a long time, sometimes for meat, sometimes for a living, sometimes for what was called the sport of it, and one of my cousin's consuming ambitions was to bag a bighorn sheep, something his father had never managed to do.

I had never killed anything in my life except fish, and since fish neither scream, grunt, squeal, nor moan when done in, it had never seemed like killing at all. In any case, I was by no means prepared for the first sight of what my cousin did to earn his bread. I don't know what I had expected with my romantic notions of the trapper's life, but surely it was something other than what I learned when we crawled up the road through increasingly heavy underbrush and stopped to check out the first of my cousin's traps.

We got out of the truck and beat our way through the brush to a spot perhaps 30 feet from the road. I did not see the animal until we were nearly on top of it. It was a raccoon, the first raccoon I had ever seen in person, and at that moment I wished that I never had seen one. It was dead, had been dead for several days, my cousin informed me. "Hunger, thirst, and shock is what kills them, mostly," he said in response to my question. "That, and exhaustion, I reckon." The animal seemed ridiculously tiny in death. It lay on its side, its small mouth, crawling with ants, open in a bared-tooth grin, and its right rear leg in the clutch of the steel trap. It was easy to see how the animal had exhausted itself; it had been at its leg. A strip of flesh perhaps three inches in width had been gnawed away, leaving the white bone and a length of tendon exposed. Tiny flies sang about the ragged wound and over the pool of dried blood beneath the leg. There was a stink in the air, and it suddenly seemed very, very warm to me there in the morning shadows of the brush.

"Once in a while," my cousin said, prying open the curved jaws of the trap, "one of them will chew his way loose, and if he doesn't lose too much blood he can live. I caught a three-legged coyote once. Too stupid to learn, I guess."

"Do you ever find one of them still alive?" I asked.

"Sometimes."

"What do you do with them?"

He looked up at me. "Do with them? I shoot them," he said, patting the holstered pistol at his waist. He lifted the freed raccoon by the hind legs and swung it off into the brush. "Buzzard meat," he said. He then grabbed the steel stake to which the trap was attached by a chain and worked it out of the ground. "I've had this line going for over a month, now. The area's just about trapped out." He carried the trap back to the road, threw it in the back of the pickup, and we drove up the increasingly rough road to the next trap. It was empty, as was the one after it. I was beginning to hope they would all be empty, but the fourth one contained a small skunk, a black-and-white pussycat of a creature that had managed to get three of its feet in the trap at once and lay huddled in death like a child's stuffed toy. It, too, was disengaged and tossed into the brush. A little further up the ridge, and we found a fox, to my cousin's visible relief. "Great," he said. "That has to be the mate to the one I got a couple of weeks ago. Pregnant, too. There won't be any little foxes running around this year." Into the brush the animal went.

By the time we reached the top of the long ridge on which my cousin had set his traps, the morning had slipped toward noon and our count had risen to seven animals: three raccoons, three skunks, and the pregnant fox. There was only one trap left now, but it was occupied by the prize of the morning, a bobcat. "I'll be damned," my cousin said, "I've been after that bugger all month. Just about give up hope." The bobcat had not died well, but in anger. The marks of its rage and anguish were laid out in a torn circle of earth described by the length of the chain that had linked the animal to its death. Even the brush had been ripped and clawed at, leaves and twigs stripped from branches, leaving sweeping scars Yellow tufts of the animal's fur lay scattered on the ground, as if the bobcat had torn at its own body for betraying it, and its death-mask was a silent howl of outrage. My cousin took it out of the trap and heaved it down the side of the hill. Buzzard meat.

15   We had to go back down the hills and around the range in order to come up the eastern slopes and check out the second trapline, and on the way we stopped at a small roadhouse in Clayton for a hamburger and a beer. I found I could eat, which surprised me a little, and I certainly had a thirst for the beer. We sat side-by-side at the bar, not saying much. Something Wallace Stegner had once written kept flashing through my mind. "Like most of my contemporaries," he had said, "I grew up careless. I grew up killing things." I wondered if my cousin would know what Stegner had been talking about, and decided it would be best not to bring it up. I could have cancelled out right there, I suppose, asking him to take me back to his camp, explaining that I had seen enough, too much, of the trapper's life. I could always plead exhaustion. After all, the day's hiking had been more real exercise than I had had in months, and I was, in fact, tired. A stubborn kernel of pride would not let me do it. I would see the day through to the end.

So the ritual continued. We climbed back up into the hills on the east side of the range in the oven-heat of a strong spring sun. The day's count rose even more as the pickup bounced its way up the ragged weedgrown road: two more skunks, another fox, two more raccoons. The work went more slowly than the morning's run, for this was a new line, and each trap had to be reset. My cousin performed this task with an efficient swiftness and the kind of quiet pride any craftsman takes in his skill, snapping and locking the jaws of the traps, covering them with a thin scattering of earth and twigs, sprinkling the ground about with dog urine from a plastic squeeze bottle to cover up the man-smell. By the time we were ready to approach the last three traps of the line, it was well after three o'clock. We were very high by then, well up on the slopes of Mount Diablo itself, and we had to abandon the pickup to hike the rest of the way on foot. We broke out of the brush and walked along a spur of the hills. About 1,500 feet below us and some miles to the east, we could see the towns of Pittsburgh and Martinez sending an urban haze into the air. Ahead of me, my cousin suddenly stopped.

"Wait a minute. Listen," he said.

A distant thrashing and rattling sound came from the slope below us. "That's where the trap is," he said. "Might be a bobcat, but I didn't expect to get him so soon. Come on."

The slope was very steep, and we slid much of the way down to the trap on our bottoms, slapped at and tangled by brush. The animal was not a bobcat. It was a dog, a large, dirty-white mongrel whose foreleg was gripped in the trap. The dog snarled at us as we approached it. Saliva had gathered at its lips and there was a wildness in its eyes.

"*Dammit,*" my cousin said. He had owned dogs all his life. "A wild dog. Probably abandoned by somebody. They do it all the time. Dogs turn wild and start running in packs. Some people ought to be shot."

I didn't know what he wanted to do. He hadn't pulled out his gun. "Can we turn him loose? Maybe he isn't wild. Maybe he just wandered up here on his own."

My cousin looked at me. "Maybe. There's a noose-pole in the back of the truck—a kind of a long stick with a loop of rope at the end. Why don't you get it?"

I scrambled back up the slope and made my way back to the pickup, where I found the noose-pole. As thick as a broomhandle and about five feet in length, it looked like a primitive fishing pole. When I got back down to the trap, the dog was still snarling viciously. My cousin took the pole from me, opened the loop at the end, and extended it toward the dog. "If I can hook him," he said, "I'll hold his head down while you open the trap. You've seen how I do it."

It was useless. The dog fought at the loop frantically in a madness of pain and fear. After perhaps 15 minutes, my cousin laid the pole down. "He just isn't going to take it."

"What'll we do?" I asked, though I'm sure I knew.

He shrugged. "Can't just leave him here to die." He unsnapped his holster and pulled out the gun. He duck-walked to within a couple of feet of the animal, which watched him suspiciously. "I'll try to do it with one shot," he said. The gun's discharge slammed into the silence of the mountain. The dog howled once, a long, penetrating song of despair that ran in echoes down the hill. My cousin nudged the animal with his boot. It was dead. He opened the trap, freed the leg, and heaved the body down the slope. The crashing of its fall seemed to go on for a long time. My cousin reset the trap. "Come on," he said. "It's getting late."

The last trap of the day held a dead raccoon.

My cousin was pleased with the day's work. "If it keeps up like this," he said as we rattled down the highway toward his trailer, "I could be out of here in a month."

"What's the hurry?"

He indicated a small housing development by the side of the road. "Too much civilization around here for me. Too many people. I need to get back up into the mountains."

There was plenty of light left when we got back, and true to his promise, my cousin took the children out into the fields to see a newborn lamb. While its mother bleated in protest, he ran one down and brought it to my children so they could pet it. I watched his face as he held the little creature. There was no hint in it of all the death we had harvested that day, no hint of the half-eaten legs we had seen, no hint of the fearful thrashing agony the animals had endured before dying. No hint, even, of the death-howl of the dirty white dog that may or may not have been wild. There was neither irony nor cynicism in him. He held the lamb with open, honest delight at the wonder my children found in touching this small, warm, live thing.

My cousin is not an evil man. We are none of us evil men.

Questions for Discussion

1. Identify the stages of plot. Which passages compose the introduction? rising action? climax? falling action? resolution?
2. Notice that none of the characters are named. Instead the author refers to "my wife," "the children," and "my cousin." Why do you think the narrator avoids proper names?
3. In describing the dead raccoon, the author includes a number of grisly details. Is this necessary? Why do you think it is or isn't?
4. What significance does the author derive from this experience? How does the author communicate this significance?
5. This essay was written for readers who are especially committed to protecting the environment and preserving the natural habitat of plants and animals. If the author were writing for an audience of farmers or ranchers, what suggestions for revision could you offer? Could he still write using only knowledge by participation?

Opportunities for Writing

1. Recount the first time you realized that shoes and belts were made from the skins of animals or that some of your favorite foods were made from animals. Address your essay to the membership of a local animal rights organization.
2. Describe your earliest memories of hunting, fishing, hiking, or camping. Compose your essay for the sports section of your school newspaper.
3. Portray a friend or member of your family with whom you once were close. What did you two have in common? How have you grown apart?
4. Depict a forest, desert, river, mountain, or canyon that you consider inspiring, a place you've only read about or heard about but are eager to visit. Write your essay for a friend you would like to accompany you.

Meditations on a Stolen Purse

MARION WINIK

Marion Winik is featured regularly as an essayist on National Public Radio's All Things Considered. *She was awarded a fellowship in creative nonfiction by the National Endowment for the Arts in 1993. Her commentaries also appear in such publications as* Texas Monthly, Glamour, The Austin Chronicle, *American Airlines'* American Way, The Houston Chronicle, Parenting, *and* Utne Reader. *"Meditations on a Stolen Purse" is an essay from* Telling: Confessions, Concessions, and Other Flashes of Light *(1994). This essay chronicles Winik's experience of learning that her handbag has been taken and the realization that occurs afterward. From this ordinary story about loss, Winik is led to consider extraordinary instances of tragic losses: an old friend's suicide or a brother-in-law's AIDS complications.*

As part of an endless series of handbag-related disasters in my life, the most beautiful purse in the world was stolen from my car while it was parked outside my condo on my friendly street in my quiet neighborhood in Yuppieville, U.S.A. Someone strolled into the parking lot, saw a purse under my dash, opened the door, took it, and left. This happened on a sunny Thursday afternoon with me sitting in my living room not ten yards away.

When I first saw it wasn't in the car, I thought, Hmmm, must have left it in the house. When a quick search of the house yielded nothing, I thought, Hmmm, better take another look in the car. I went on like this, not the least bit worried, until the next day. When it was time to go to work, and I went to find my purse, and frantic rummagings through closets, under couches, in the freezer, through the laundry basket, and back out in the car proved fruitless, I began to realize the awful truth: I would never see the most beautiful purse in the world again.

I hesitate to describe it, for I know I can't do it justice. If I had to guess, I'd say it was a souvenir from the gift shop at Yellowstone Park circa 1953. It was hand-tooled, hand-stitched leather decorated with bison and deer and elk, sky and grass and mountains, blue and green and brown and white. It had two short wooden handles, also covered in leather, and was lined with soft brown moiré. Okay, now, whatever you're picturing, it was twenty times more beautiful. Plus the lady at the store gave it to me for eight dollars off the marked price. Life could not have been more sweet. I transferred everything out of my boring old purse into my beautiful new purse before I even left the store.

Five short days later, it was gone. No ransom note, no footprints, no trail of bobby pins, no response to the signs I tacked up around the neighborhood. HANDSOME REWARD FOR BEAUTIFUL PURSE, they proclaimed.

5   Okay, I admit it. My car wasn't locked. But I was only going upstairs for a minute. Okay, an hour. Okay, two hours and forty-five minutes. Okay, I was asking for it. That doesn't help.

The problem is, you want to feel safe. You don't want to think that you live in a world where crazy, bad people do stupid, cruel things. That every once in a while your number comes up, you're the victim of this random badness, and just like that, something you love is gone. If you're lucky, it's only a purse. At first, you can't stop seeing the lost things in your mind's eye. The little gold clasp. The dog-eared business card stuck in the inside pocket. The alligator checkbook case. The Scarlet Moon lipstick (a shade since discontinued). A favorite pen, with a brand-new ink cartridge. Small plastic cards with your name on them that can be used to purchase everything from gasoline to silk shirts to airplane tickets to Paris. Library cards, video club cards, photos of your niece and nephew, phone numbers, paint formulas, I can't go on. But you can see it all so clearly, you can almost touch it. As long as it's that clear, it's hard to believe it won't just come back at any moment. Then gradually, over days and weeks, it starts to fade. That's time, healing all wounds. That's letting go.

Sometimes something much more terrible than having your purse stolen happens—you hear an old friend from high school committed suicide, or they tell you your brother-in-law has AIDS—and you protect yourself psychically. You say it's terrible, it's terrible. You even cry a little. But somehow you don't let yourself really feel the full feeling. You don't let it get all the way in. It's too scary. Then something that is by contrast very minor will happen. Like the theft of the most beautiful purse in the world. And you just go for it. You wallow in it, you roll around in it, you poke it like a black-and-blue mark to see how bad it hurts. You walk around for days with a dark cloud over your head and yell at yourself and feel sorry for yourself and mourn. And think what a jerk you are, going completely nuts over a stupid purse, when your old high school friend is dead, your brother-in-law has AIDS, half the world is starving, and God knows what else.

So what I want to know is: who did it, and where is it now? I drive around my neighborhood, eyeing the little boys on their bikes and the sorority girls in their BMWs. I peek into other people's trash cans. I squint at their handbags. I peer into lighted windows at night. Was it you? I ask. No? Then who? Sometimes I think I'll get a phone call. Excuse me, the voice will say, are you Marion Winik? I think I've found something of yours. It gives me goose bumps just to imagine it.

Questions for Discussion

1. Examine the author's use of descriptive detail. Which senses does she appeal to in describing "the most beautiful purse in the world"? Which details do you consider important? Which are unnecessary?
2. Occasionally, the author addresses the reader directly: "Okay, now, whatever you're picturing, it was twenty times more beautiful." What is your impression of this technique? Do you like it or dislike it? What purpose does it serve?
3. Do you consider the title effective? Why or why not?
4. What significance does the author derive from the experience? Is this appropriate?
5. How would this essay differ if the author were also using knowledge by observation (e.g., police records, newspaper stories)?

Opportunities for Writing

1. Discuss your experience of losing something you considered important. What did you do when you noticed it was gone? How did you look for it? Did you ever find it? What is the significance of this experience? Compose this essay for a friend who has just lost something important.
2. Describe your most prized possession. What is it? What does it look like? How did you acquire it? Why is it important to you? What does it reveal about you, your friends, your society?
3. Your school newspaper is soliciting articles for a special issue on families. In your article, characterize a family member who frequently loses things or has things stolen. Why do such terrible things seem to always happen to this individual?

4. Recall the last time something happened to you that troubled you more than perhaps it should have—something that left you feeling sorry for yourself. What did you learn from this experience? Write this essay for a younger brother or sister.

And Then I Went to School

Joseph Suina

Joseph Suina lives on the Cochiti Pueblo Reservation in New Mexico, where he was born and raised. Suina is a member of the Department of Curriculum and Instruction in Multicultural Teacher Education at the University of New Mexico and has coauthored An Instructional Strategy *(1982). "And Then I Went to School" is an essay that appeared in* Linguistic and Cultural Influences on Learning Mathematics *(1988). Suina recalls his childhood memories of Pueblo life: his friends and family—especially his grandmother, prayers and celebrations, Pueblo language and songs, food, and homes, contrasting them with the values introduced by whites at the Bureau of Indian Affairs boarding school. Drawing from knowledge by participation, he remembers the transition from reservation life to boarding school life, thus resulting in a bittersweet insight for Suina: "There was no choice left but to compete with the white man on his terms for survival. For that I knew I had to give up a part of my life."*

I lived with my grandmother from the ages of 5 through 9. It was the early 1950s when electricity had not yet invaded the homes of the Cochiti Indians. The village day school and health clinic were first to have it and to the unsuspecting Cochitis this was the approach of a new era in their uncomplicated lives.

Transportation was simple then. Two good horses and a sturdy wagon met most needs of a villager. Only five or six individuals possessed an automobile in the Pueblo of 300. A flatbed truck fixed with wooden rails and a canvas top made a regular Saturday trip to Santa Fe. It was always loaded beyond capacity with Cochitis taking their wares to town for a few staples. With an escort of a dozen barking dogs, the straining truck made a noisy exit, northbound from the village.

During those years, Grandmother and I lived beside the plaza in a one-room house. It consisted of a traditional fireplace, a makeshift cabinet for our few tin cups and dishes, and a wooden crate that held our two buckets of all-purpose water. At the far end of the room were two rolls of bedding we used as comfortable sitting "couches." Consisting of thick quilts, sheepskin, and assorted blankets, these bed rolls were undone each night. A wooden pole the length of one side of the room was suspended about 10 inches from the ceiling beams. A modest collection of colorful shawls, blankets, and sashes draped over the pole making this part of the room most interesting. In one corner was a bulky metal trunk for our ceremonial wear and few valuables. A dresser, which was traded for some of my grandmother's well-known pottery, held the few articles of clothing we owned and the "goody bag." Grandmother always had a flour sack filled with candy, store bought cookies, and Fig Newtons. These were saturated with a sharp odor of moth balls. Nevertheless, they made a fine snack with coffee before we turned in for the night. Tucked securely in my blankets, I listened to one of her stories or accounts of how it was when she was a little girl.

These accounts seemed so old fashioned compared to the way we lived. Sometimes she softly sang a song from a ceremony. In this way I fell asleep each night.

Earlier in the evening we would make our way to a relative's house if someone had not already come to visit us. I would play with the children while the adults caught up on all the latest. Ten-cent comic books were finding their way into the Pueblo homes. For us children, these were the first link to the world beyond the Pueblo. We enjoyed looking at them and role playing as one of the heroes rounding up the villains. Everyone preferred being a cowboy rather than an Indian because cowboys were always victorious. Sometimes, stories were related to both children and adults. These get-togethers were highlighted by refreshments of coffee and sweet bread or fruit pies baked in the outdoor oven. Winter months would most likely include roasted piñon nuts or dried deer meat for all to share. These evening gatherings and sense of closeness diminished as the radios and televisions increased over the following years. It was never to be the same again.

5   The winter months are among my fondest recollections. A warm fire crackled and danced brightly in the fireplace and the aroma of delicious stew filled our one-room house. To me the house was just right. The thick adobe walls wrapped around the two of us protectingly during the long freezing nights. Grandmother's affection completed the warmth and security I will always remember.

Being the only child at Grandmother's, I had lots of attention and plenty of reasons to feel good about myself. As a pre-schooler, I already had the chores of chopping firewood and hauling in fresh water each day. After "heavy work," I would run to her and flex what I was certain were my gigantic biceps. Grandmother would state that at the rate I was going I would soon attain the status of a man like the adult males in the village. Her shower of praises made me feel like the Indian Superman of all times. At age 5, I suppose I was as close to that concept of myself as anyone.

In spite of her many years, grandmother was still active in the village ceremonial setting. She was a member of an important women's society and attended all the functions taking me along to many of them. I would wear one of my colorful shirts she handmade for just such occasions. Grandmother taught me the appropriate behavior at these events. Through modeling she taught me to pray properly. Barefooted, I would greet the sun each morning with a handful of cornmeal. At night I would look to the stars in wonderment and let a prayer slip through my lips. I learned to appreciate cooperation in nature and my fellowmen early in life. About food and material things, grandmother would say, "There is enough for everyone to share and it all comes from above, my child." I felt very much a part of the world and our way of life. I knew I had a place in it and I felt good about me.

At age 6, like the rest of the Cochiti 6-year-olds that year, I had to begin my schooling. It was a new and bewildering experience. One I will not forget. The strange surroundings, new concepts about time and expectations, and a foreign tongue were overwhelming to us beginners. It took some effort to return the second day and many times thereafter.

To begin with, unlike my grandmother, the teacher did not have pretty brown skin and a colorful dress. She was not plump and friendly. Her clothes were one color and drab. Her pale and skinny form made me worry that she was very ill. I thought that explained why she did not have time just for me and the disappointed looks and orders she seemed to always direct my way. I didn't think she was so smart because she couldn't understand my language. "Surely that was why we had to leave our 'Indian' at home." But then I did not feel so bright either. All I could say in her language was "yes teacher," "my name is Joseph Henry," and "when is lunch time." The teacher's odor took some getting used to also. In fact, many times it made me sick right before lunch. Later, I learned from the girls that this odor was something she wore called perfume.

The classroom too had its odd characteristics. It was terribly huge and smelled of medicine like the village clinic I feared so much. The walls and ceiling were artificial and uncaring. They were too far from me and I felt naked. The fluorescent light tubes were eerie and blinked suspiciously above me. This was quite a contrast to the fire and sunlight that my eyes were accustomed to. I thought maybe the lighting did not seem right because it was man-made, and it was not natural. Our confinement to rows of desks was another unnatural demand from our active little bodies. We had to sit at these hard things for what seemed like forever before relief (recess) came midway through the morning and afternoon. Running carefree in the village and fields was but a sweet memory of days gone by. We all went home for lunch because we lived within walking distance of the school. It took coaxing and sometimes bribing to get me to return and complete the remainder of the school day.

School was a painful experience during those early years. The English language and the new set of values caused me much anxiety and embarrassment. I could not comprehend everything that was happening but yet I could understand very well when I messed up or was not doing so well. The negative aspect was communicated too effectively and I became unsure of myself more and more. How I wished I could understand other things just as well in school.

The value conflict was not only in school performance but in other areas of my life as well. For example, many of us students had a problem with head lice due to "the lack of sanitary conditions in our homes." Consequently, we received a severe shampooing that was rough on both the scalp and the ego. Cleanliness was crucial and a washing of this type indicated to the class how filthy a home setting we came from. I recall that after one such treatment I was humiliated before my peers with a statement that I had "She'na" (lice) so tough that I must have been born with them. Needless to say, my Super Indian self-image was no longer intact.

My language, too, was questionable from the beginning of my school career. "Leave your Indian (language) at home" was like a trademark of school. Speaking it accidentally or otherwise was a sure reprimand in the form of a dirty look or a whack with a ruler. This punishment was for speaking the language of my people which meant so much to me. It was the language of my grandmother and I spoke it well. With it, I sang beautiful songs and prayed from my heart. At that young and tender age, comprehending why I had to part with it was most difficult for me. And yet at home I was encouraged to attend school so that I might have a better life in the future. I knew I had a good village life already but this was communicated less and less each day I was in school.

As the weeks turned to months, I learned English more and more. It would appear comprehension would be easier. It got easier to understand all right. I understood that everything I had and was a part of was not nearly as good as the white man's. School was determined to undo me in everything from my sheepskin bedding to the dances and ceremonies that I learned to believe in and cherish. One day I fell asleep in class after a sacred all-night ceremony. I was startled to awakening by a sharp jerk on my ear and informed coldly, "That ought to teach you not to attend 'those things' again." Later, all alone I cried. I could not understand why or what I was caught up in. I was receiving two very different messages, both intending to be for my welfare.

15   Life-style values were dictated in various ways. The Dick and Jane reading series in the primary grades presented me with pictures of a home with a pitched roof, straight walls, and sidewalks. I could not identify with these from my Pueblo world. However, it was clear I did not have these things and what I did have did not measure up. At night, long after grandmother went to sleep, I would lay awake staring at our crooked adobe walls casting uneven shadows from the light of the fireplace. The walls were no longer just right for me. My life was no longer just right. I was ashamed of being who I was and I wanted to change right then and there. Somehow it became so important to have straight walls, clean hair and teeth, and a spotted dog to chase after. I even became critical and hateful toward my bony fleabag of a dog. I loved the familiar and cozy surroundings of grandmother's house but now I imagined it could be a heck of a lot better if only I had a white man's house with a bed, a nice couch, and a clock. In school books, all the child characters ever did was run around chasing their dog or a kite. They were always happy. As for me, all I seemed to do at home was go back and forth with buckets of water and cut up sticks for a lousy fire. "Didn't the teacher say that drinking coffee would stunt my growth?" "Why couldn't I have nice tall glasses of milk so I could have strong bones and white teeth like those kids in the books?" "Did my grandmother really care about my well-being?"

I had to leave my beloved village of Cochiti for my education beyond Grade 6. I left to attend a Bureau of Indian Affairs boarding school 30 miles from home. Shined shoes and pressed shirt and pants were the order of the day. I managed to adjust to this just as I had to most of the things the school shoved at me or took away from me. Adjusting to leaving home and the village was tough indeed. It seemed the older I got, the further away I became from the ways I was so much a part of. Because my parents did not own an automobile, I saw them only once a month when they came up in the community truck. They never failed to come supplied with "eats" for me. I enjoyed the outdoor oven bread, dried meat, and tamales they usually brought. It took a while to get accustomed to the diet of the school. I longed for my grandmother and my younger brothers and sisters. I longed for my house. I longed to take part in a Buffalo Dance. I longed to be free.

I came home for the 4-day Thanksgiving break. At first, home did not feel right anymore. It was much too small and stuffy. The lack of running water and bathroom facilities were too inconvenient. Everything got dusty so quickly and hardly anyone spoke English. I did not realize I was beginning to take on the white man's ways, the ways that belittled my own. However, it did not take long to "get back with it." Once I established my relationships with family, relatives, and friends I knew I was where I came from and where I belonged.

Leaving for the boarding school the following Sunday evening was one of the saddest events in my entire life. Although I enjoyed myself immensely the last few days, I realized then that life would never be the same again. I could not turn back the time just as I could not do away with school and the ways of the white man. They were here to stay and would creep more and more into my life. The effort to make sense of both worlds together was painful and I had no choice but to do so. The schools, television, automobiles, and other white man's ways and values had chipped away at the simple cooperative life I grew up in. The people of Cochiti were changing. The winter evening gatherings, exchanging of stories, and even the performing of certain ceremonies were already only a memory that someone commented about now and then. Still the demands of both worlds were there. The white man's was flashy, less personal, but comfortable. The Indian was both attracted and pushed toward these new ways that he had little to say about. There was no choice left but to compete with the white man on his terms for survival. For that I knew I had to give up a part of my life.

Determined not to cry, I left for school that dreadfully lonely night. My right hand clutched tightly the mound of cornmeal grandmother placed there and my left hand brushed away a tear as I made my way back to school.

Questions for Discussion

1. What is the essay's subordinate aim? Cite specific passages to support your answer.
2. Does the essay give you a vivid picture of the setting? If so, how? If not, why not? Which descriptive details do you consider essential?
3. Are the major characters static or dynamic? Explain your answer.
4. Do you see something of yourself and your situation in the author's experience? Do you think you have learned something from the author's experience? Why or why not?
5. Is the emotional ending appropriate or excessive? Explain your answer.

Opportunities for Writing

1. To accompany a museum display on Native Americans, describe a specific incident in the history of the Cochiti people. What was the incident? When and where did it occur? Why do you consider it especially important or meaningful?
2. Depict a typical village of Cochiti Indians. How big is the village? Where is it located? What is life like for its residents? What is your impression of this village?
3. Portray a schoolteacher you especially liked or disliked. What grade were you in? What subject did he or she teach? Why did you like or dislike this teacher?
4. Describe a favorite ritual or tradition of your ethnic or religious group. What do you do? Why? What is the significance of this ritual or tradition? Why is it your favorite? Address this essay to a friend who is curious.

How It Feels to Be Colored Me

ZORA NEALE HURSTON

Zora Neale Hurston (1901–1960) was educated at Howard University, Barnard College, and Columbia University. An author and anthropologist, Hurston wrote Jonah's Gourd Vine *(1934),* Mules and Men *(1935),* Their Eyes Were Watching God *(1937),* Tell My Horse *(1938),* Voodoo Gods *(1939),* Moses, Man of the Mountain *(1939), and* Dust Tracks on a Road *(1942). "How It Feels to Be Colored Me" is an essay in which Hurston tells of four different times in her life—times when her understanding of the word* colored *and of herself—took on changed meanings. This essay is autobiographical, and the information is gained exclusively from personal experience and reflection—from knowledge by participation.*

I am colored but I offer nothing in the way of extenuating circumstances except the fact that I am the only Negro in the United States whose grandfather on the mother's side was *not* an Indian chief.

I remember the very day that I became colored. Up to my thirteenth year I lived in the little Negro town of Eatonville, Florida. It is exclusively a colored town. The only white people I knew passed through the town going to or coming from Orlando. The native whites rode dusty horses, the Northern tourists chugged down the sandy village road in automobiles. The town knew the Southerners and never stopped cane chewing when they passed. But the Northerners were something else again. They were peered at cautiously from behind curtains by the timid. The more venturesome would come out on the porch to watch them go past and got just as much pleasure out of the tourists as the tourists got out of the village.

The front porch might seem a daring place for the rest of the town, but it was a gallery seat to me. My favorite place was atop the gate-post. Proscenium box for a born first-nighter. Not only did I enjoy the show, but I didn't mind the actors knowing that I liked it. I usually spoke to them in passing. I'd wave at them and when they returned my salute, I would say something like this: "Howdy-do-well-I-thank-you-where-you-goin'?" Usually the automobile or the horse paused at this, and after a queer exchange of compliments, I would probably "go a piece of the way" with them, as we say in farthest Florida. If one of my family happened to come to the front in time to see me, of course negotiations would be rudely broken off. But even so, it is clear that I was the first "welcome-to-our-state" Floridian, and I hope the Miami Chamber of Commerce will please take notice.

During this period, white people differed from colored to me only in that they rode through town and never lived there. They liked to hear me "speak pieces" and sing and wanted to see me dance the parse-me-la, and gave me generously of their small silver for doing these things, which seemed strange to me for I wanted to do them so much that I needed bribing to stop. Only they didn't know it. The colored people gave no dimes. They deplored any joyful tendencies in me, but I was their Zora nevertheless. I belonged to them, to the nearby hotels, to the county—everybody's Zora.

5   But changes came in the family when I was thirteen, and I was sent to school in Jacksonville. I left Eatonville, the town of the oleanders, as Zora. When I disembarked from the river-boat at Jacksonville, she was no more. It

seemed that I had suffered a sea change. I was not Zora of Orange County any more, I was now a little colored girl. I found it out in certain ways. In my heart as well as in the mirror, I became a fast brown—warranted not to rub nor run.

But I am not tragically colored. There is no great sorrow dammed up in my soul, nor lurking behind my eyes. I do not mind at all. I do not belong to the sobbing school of Negrohood who hold that nature somehow has given them a lowdown dirty deal and whose feelings are all hurt about it. Even in the helter-skelter skirmish that is my life, I have seen that the world is to the strong regardless of a little pigmentation more or less. No, I do not weep at the world—I am too busy sharpening my oyster knife.

Someone is always at my elbow reminding me that I am the granddaughter of slaves. It fails to register depression with me. Slavery is sixty years in the past. The operation was successful and the patient is doing well, thank you. The terrible struggle that made me an American out of a potential slave said "On the line!" The Reconstruction said "Get set!"; and the generation before said "Go!" I am off to a flying start and I must not halt in the stretch to look behind and weep. Slavery is the price I paid for civilization, and the choice was not with me. It is a bully adventure and worth all that I have paid through my ancestors for it. No one on earth ever had a greater chance for glory. The world to be won and nothing to be lost. It is thrilling to think—to know that for any act of mine, I shall get twice as much praise or twice as much blame. It is quite exciting to hold the center of the national stage, with the spectators not knowing whether to laugh or to weep.

The position of my white neighbor is much more difficult. No brown specter pulls up a chair beside me when I sit down to eat. No dark ghost thrusts its leg against mine in bed. The game of keeping what one has is never so exciting as the game of getting.

I do not always feel colored. Even now I often achieve the unconscious Zora of Eatonville before the Hegira. I feel most colored when I am thrown against a sharp white background.

For instance at Barnard. "Beside the waters of the Hudson" I feel my race. Among the thousand white persons, I am a dark rock surged upon, overswept by a creamy sea. I am surged upon and overswept, but through it all, I remain myself. When covered by the waters, I am; and the ebb but reveals me again.

Sometimes it is the other way around. A white person is set down in our midst, but the contrast is just as sharp for me. For instance, when I sit in the drafty basement that is The New World Cabaret with a white person, my color comes. We enter chatting about any little nothing that we have in common and are seated by the jazz waiters. In the abrupt way that jazz orchestras have, this one plunges into a number. It loses no time in circumlocutions, but gets right down to business. It constricts the thorax and splits the heart with its tempo and narcotic harmonies. This orchestra grows rambunctious, rears on its hind legs and attacks the tonal veil with primitive fury, rending it, clawing it until it breaks through to the jungle beyond. I follow those heathen—follow them exultingly. I dance wildly inside myself; I yell within, I whoop; I shake my assegai above my head, I hurl it true to the mark *yeeeeooww!* I am in the jungle and living in the jungle way. My face is painted red and yellow and my body is painted blue. My pulse is throbbing like a war drum. I want to slaughter something—give pain, give death to what, I do not know. But the piece ends. The men of the orchestra wipe their lips and rest their fingers. I creep back slowly to the veneer we call civilization with the last tone and find the white friend sitting motionless in his seat, smoking calmly.

"Good music they have here," he remarks, drumming the table with his fingertips.

Music! The great blobs of purple and red emotion have not touched him. He has only heard what I felt. He is far away and I see him but dimly across the ocean and the continent that have fallen between us. He is so pale with his whiteness then and I am *so* colored.

At certain times I have no race, I am *me*. When I set my hat at a certain angle and saunter down Seventh Avenue, Harlem City, feeling as snooty as the lions in front of the Forty-Second Street Library, for instance. So far as my feelings are concerned, Peggy Hopkins Joyce on the Boule Mich with her gorgeous raiment, stately carriage, knees knocking together in a most aristocratic manner, has nothing on me. The cosmic Zora emerges. I belong to no race nor time. I am the eternal feminine with its string of beads.

15   I have no separate feeling about being an American citizen and colored. I am merely a fragment of the Great Soul that surges within the boundaries. My country, right or wrong.

Sometimes, I feel discriminated against, but it does not make me angry. It merely astonishes me. How *can* any deny themselves the pleasure of my company! It's beyond me.

But in the main, I feel like a brown bag of miscellany propped against a wall. Against a wall in company with other bags, white, red and yellow. Pour out the contents, and there is discovered a jumble of small things priceless and worthless. A first-water diamond, an empty spool, bits of broken glass, lengths of string, a key to a door long since crumbled away, a rusty knife-blade, old shoes saved for a road that never was and never will be, a nail bent under the weight of things too heavy for any nail, a dried flower or two, still a little fragrant. In your hand is the brown bag. On the ground before you is the jumble it held—so much like the jumble in the bags, could they be emptied, that all might be dumped in a single heap and the bags refilled without altering the content of any greatly. A bit of colored glass more or less would not matter. Perhaps that is how the Great Stuffer of Bags filled them in the first place—who knows?

Questions for Discussion

1. What do you think of the essay's title? Does it arouse your curiosity? What other titles would be appropriate for this essay?
2. Notice the variety of similes (explicit comparisons using *like* or *as*) and metaphors (implicit comparisons). What is the purpose of such comparisons? Is the technique effective?

3. Does the essay reveal a subordinate referential aim? A subordinate persuasive aim? Explain your answer.
4. Is the setting vivid? Why do you think it is or isn't? Cite specific passages.
5. Do you see something of yourself and your situation in the author's experience? Do you think you have learned something from the author's experience? Why or why not?

Opportunities for Writing

1. Discuss the time you first noticed that people are different colors. How old were you? How did you come to this realization? What did you do?
2. Write a letter to your family describing a new friend of yours who is of a different race or from a different geographical region. How did you come to be friends? How do you discuss your racial or regional differences?
3. Relate a particular episode in the struggle for racial equality that you consider especially important or meaningful. Compose your essay for a school magazine to be published in commemoration of the assassination of Malcolm X.
4. Address a local civil rights group regarding a racial incident that you observed. When and where did it happen? Who was the victim? How did it make you feel?

Sylvia Plath: A Memoir

AL ALVAREZ

Al Alvarez is a literary critic, editor, teacher, poet, and fiction writer. Among his numerous works are the novels, Hunt *(1979) and* Hers *(1974); poetry collections,* Autumn to Autumn and Selected Poems, 1953–1976 *(1978),* Apparition *(1971), and* Lost *(1968); and critical studies:* Samuel Beckett *(1973),* Beyond All This Fiddle *(1968),* The New Poetry *(1962),* The School of Donne *(1961), and* Stewards of Excellence *(1958). Alvarez is known also for his study of literary works and suicide,* The Savage God: A Study of Suicide *(1971), from which this essay is taken. "Sylvia Plath: A Memoir" gives readers a character sketch of the young poet, wife, mother, and friend from the vantage point of a critic, editor, personal friend, and neighbor. Alvarez describes Plath as a genius who tried to exorcise depression and suicide by writing about it and "challenging" it; in this essay, he tells of a certain Monday, February 11, however, when her attempt failed.*

They were living in a tiny flat not far from the Regent's Park Zoo. Their windows faced onto a run-down square: peeling houses around a scrappy wilderness of garden. Closer to the Hill, gentility was advancing fast: smart Sunday newspaper house-agents had their boards up, the front doors were all fashionable colors—"Cantaloupe," "Tangerine," "Blueberry," "Thames Green"—and everywhere was a sense of gleaming white interiors, the old houses writ large and rich with new conversions.

Their square, however, had not yet been taken over. It was dirty, cracked, and racketty with children. The rows of houses that led off it were still occupied by the same kind of working-class families they had been built for eighty years before. No one, as yet, had made them chic and quadrupled their price—though that was to come soon enough. The Hughes' flat was one floor up a bedraggled staircase, past a pram in the hall and a bicycle. It was so small that everything seemed sideways on. You inserted yourself into a hallway so narrow and jammed that you could scarcely take off your coat. The kitchen seemed to fit one person at a time, who could span it with arms outstretched. In the living room you sat side by side, longways on, between a wall of books and a wall of pictures. The bedroom off it, with its flowered wallpaper, seemed to have room for nothing except a double bed. But the colors were cheerful, the bits and pieces pretty, and the whole place had a sense of liveliness about it, of things being done. A typewriter stood on a little table by the window, and they took turns at it, each working shifts while the other minded the baby. At night they cleared it away to make room for the child's cot. Later, they borrowed a room from another American poet, W. S. Merwin, where Sylvia, worked the morning shift, Ted the afternoon.

This was Ted's time. He was on the edge of a considerable reputation. His first book had been well received and won all sorts of prizes in the States, which usually means that the second book will be an anticlimax. Instead, *Lupercal* effortlessly fulfilled and surpassed all the promises of *The Hawk in the Rain*. A figure had emerged on the drab scene of British poetry, powerful and undeniable. Whatever his natural hesitations and distrust of his own work, he must have had some sense of his own strength and achievement. God alone knew how far he was eventually going, but in one essential way he had already arrived. He was a tall, strong-looking man in a black corduroy jacket, black trousers, black shoes; his dark hair hung untidily forward; he had a long, witty mouth. He was in command.

In those days Sylvia seemed effaced; the poet taking a back seat to the young mother and housewife. She had a long, rather flat body, a longish face, not pretty but alert and full of feeling, with a lively mouth and fine brown eyes. Her brownish hair was scraped severely into a bun. She wore jeans and a neat shirt, briskly American: bright, clean, competent, like a young woman in a cookery advertisement, friendly and yet rather distant.

5   Her background, of which I knew nothing then, belied her housewifely air: she had been a child prodigy—her first poem was published when she was eight—and then a brilliant student, winning every prize to be had, first at Wellesley High School, then at Smith College: scholarships all the way, straight A's, Phi Beta Kappa, president of this and that college society, and prizes for everything. A New York glossy magazine, *Mademoiselle,* had picked her as an outstanding possibility and wined her, dined her, and photographed her all over Manhattan. Then, almost inevitably, she had won a Fulbright to Cambridge, where she met Ted Hughes. They were married in 1956, on Bloomsday. Behind Sylvia was a self-sacrificing, widowed mother, a schoolteacher who had worked herself into the ground so that her two children might flourish. Sylvia's father—ornithologist, entomologist, ichthyologist, international authority on bumblebees, and professor of biology at Boston University—had died when she was nine. Both parents were of German stock and were German-speaking, academic, and intellectual. When she and Ted went to the States after Cambridge, a glittering university career seemed both natural and assured.

On the surface it was a typical success story: the brilliant examination-passer driving forward so fast and relentlessly that nothing could ever catch up with her. And it can last a lifetime, provided nothing checks the momentum, and the vehicle of all those triumphs doesn't disintegrate into sharp fragments from sheer speed and pressure. But already her progress had twice lurched to a halt. Between her month on *Mademoiselle* and her last year in college she had had the nervous breakdown and suicide attempt which became the theme of her novel, *The Bell Jar.* Then, once reestablished at Smith—"an outstanding teacher," said her colleagues—the academic prizes no longer seemed worth the effort. So in 1958 she had thrown over university life—Ted had never seriously contemplated it—and gone free-lance, trusting her luck and talent as a poet. All this I learned much later. Now Sylvia had simply slowed down; she was subdued, absorbed in her new baby daughter, and friendly only in that rather formal, shallow, transatlantic way that keeps you at your distance.

Ted went downstairs to get the pram ready while she dressed the baby. I stayed behind a minute, zipping up my son's coat. Sylvia turned to me, suddenly without gush:

"I'm so glad you picked *that* poem," she said. "It's one of my favorites but no one else seemed to like it."

For a moment I went completely blank; I didn't know what she was talking about. She noticed and helped me out.

"The one you put in *The Observer* a year ago. About the factory at night."

"For Christ's sake, Sylvia *Plath*." It was my turn to gush. "I'm sorry. It was a lovely poem."

"Lovely" wasn't the right word, but what else do you say to a bright young housewife? I had picked it from a sheaf of poems which had arrived from America, immaculately typed, with self-addressed envelope and international reply coupon efficiently supplied. All of them were stylish and talented but that in itself was not rare in those days. The late fifties was a period of particularly high style in American verse, when every campus worth its name had its own "brilliant" poetic technician in residence. But at least one of these poems had more going for it than rhetorical elegance. It had no title, though later, in *The Colossus,* she called it "Night Shift." It was one of those poems which starts by saying what it is *not* about so strongly that you don't believe the explanations that follow:

> It was not a heart, beating,
> That muted boom, that clangor
> Far off, not blood in the ears
> Drumming up any fever
>
> To impose on the evening.
> The noise came from outside:
> A metal detonating
> Native, evidently, to
>
> These stilled suburbs: nobody
> Startled at it, though the sound

Shook the ground with its pounding.
It took root at my coming . . .

It seemed to me more than a piece of good description, to be used and moralized upon as the fashion of that decade dictated. The note was aroused and all the details of the scene seemed continually to be turning inward. It is a poem, I suppose, about fear, and although in the course of it the fear is rationalized and explained (that pounding in the night is caused by machines turning), it ends by reasserting precisely the threatening masculine forces there were to be afraid of. It had its moments of awkwardness—for example, the prissy, pausing flourish in the manner of Wallace Stevens: "Native, evidently, to . . ." But compared with most of the stuff that thudded unsolicited through my letterbox every morning, it was that rare thing: the always unexpected, wholly genuine article.

I was embarrassed not to have known who she was. She seemed embarrassed to have reminded me, and also depressed.

After that I saw Ted occasionally, Sylvia more rarely. He and I would meet for a beer in one of the pubs near Primrose Hill or the Heath, and sometimes we would walk our children together. We almost never talked shop; without mentioning it, we wanted to keep things unprofessional. At some point during the summer Ted and I did a broadcast together. Afterward we collected Sylvia from the flat and went across to their local. The recording had been a success and we stood outside the pub, around the baby's pram, drinking our beers and pleased with ourselves. Sylvia, too, seemed easier, wittier, less constrained than I had seen her before. For the first time I understood something of the real charm and speed of the girl.

15 About that time my wife and I moved from our flat near Swiss Cottage to a house higher up in Hampstead, near the Heath. A couple of days before we were due to move I broke my leg in a climbing accident, and that put out everything and everyone, since the house had to be decorated, broken leg or not. I remember sticking black and white tiles to floor after endless floor, a filthy dark brown glue coating my fingers and clothes and gumming up my hair, the great, inert plaster cast dragging behind me like a coffin as I crawled. There wasn't much time for friends. Ted occasionally dropped in and I would hobble with him briefly to the pub. But I saw Sylvia not at all. In the autumn I went to teach for a term in the States.

While I was there *The Observer* sent me her first book of poems to review. It seemed to fit the image I had of her: serious, gifted, withheld, and still partly under the massive shadow of her husband. There were poems that had been influenced by him, others which echoed Theodore Roethke or Wallace Stevens; clearly, she was still casting about for her own style. Yet the technical ability was great, and beneath most of the poems was a sense of resources and disturbances not yet tapped. "Her poems," I wrote, "rest secure in a mass of experience that is never quite brought out into the daylight. . . . It is this sense of threat, as though she were continually menaced by something she could see only out of the corners of her eyes, that gives her work its distinction."

Throughout this time the evidence of the poems and the evidence of the person were utterly different. There was no trace of the poetry's despair and unforgiving destructiveness in her social manner. She remained remorselessly bright and energetic: busy with her children and her beekeeping in Devon, busy flat-hunting in London, busy seeing *The Bell Jar* through the press, busy typing and sending off her poems to largely unreceptive editors (just before she died she sent a sheaf of her best poems, most of them now classics, to one of the national British weeklies; none was accepted). She had also taken up horse-riding again, teaching herself to ride on a powerful stallion called Ariel, and was elated by this new excitement.

Cross-legged on the red floor, after reading her poems, she would talk about her riding in her twanging New England voice. And perhaps because I was also a member of the club, she talked, too, about suicide in much the same way; about her attempt ten years before which, I suppose, must have been very much on her mind as she corrected the proofs of her novel, and about her recent car crash. It had been no accident; she had gone off the road deliberately, seriously, wanting to die. But she hadn't, and all that was now in the past. For this reason I am convinced that at this time she was not contemplating suicide. On the contrary, she was able to write about the act so freely because it was already behind her. The car crash was a death she had survived, the death she sardonically felt herself fated to undergo once every decade:

> I have done it again.
> One year in every ten
> I manage it—
>
> A sort of walking miracle . . .
> I am only thirty.
> And like the cat I have nine times to die.
>
> This is Number Three . . .

In life, as in the poem, there was neither hysteria in her voice, nor any appeal for sympathy. She talked about suicide in much the same tone as she talked about any other risky, testing activity: urgently, even fiercely, but altogether without self-pity. She seemed to view death as a physical challenge she had, once again, overcome. It was an experience of much the same quality as riding Ariel or mastering a bolting horse—which she had done as a Cambridge undergraduate—or careening down a dangerous snow slope without properly knowing how to ski— an incident, also from life, which is one of the best things in *The Bell Jar.* Suicide, in short, was not a swoon into death, an attempt "to cease upon the midnight with no pain"; it was something to be felt in the nerve-ends and fought against, an initiation rite qualifying her for a *life* of her own.

God knows what wound the death of her father had inflicted on her in her childhood, but over the years this had been transformed into the conviction that to be an adult meant to be a survivor. So, for her, death was a debt to be met once every decade: in order to stay alive as a grown woman, a mother, and a poet, she had to pay—in some partial, magical way—with her life. But because this impossible payment involved also the fantasy of joining or regaining her beloved dead father, it was a passionate act, instilled as much with love as with hatred and despair. Thus in that strange, upsetting poem "The Bee Meeting," the detailed, doubtless accurate description of a gathering of local beekeepers in her Devon village gradually becomes an invocation of some deadly ritual in which she is sacrificial virgin whose coffin, finally, waits in the sacred grove. Why this should happen becomes, perhaps, slightly less mysterious when you remember that her father was an authority on bees; so her beekeeping becomes a way of symbolically allying herself to him, and reclaiming him from the dead.

The tone of all these late poems is hard, factual and, despite the intensity, understated. In some strange way, I suspect she thought of herself as a realist: the deaths and resurrections of "Lady Lazarus," the nightmares of "Daddy," and the rest had all been proved on her pulses. That she brought to them an extraordinary inner wealth of imagery and associations was almost beside the point, however essential it is for the poetry itself. Because she felt she was simply describing the facts as they had happened, she was able to tap in the coolest possible way all her large reserves of skill: those subtle rhymes and half-rhymes; the flexible, echoing rhythms and offhand colloquialism by which she preserved, even in her most anguished probing, complete artistic control. Her internal horrors were as factual and precisely sensed as the barely controllable stallion on which she was learning to ride or the car she had smashed up.

So she spoke of suicide with a wry detachment, and without any mention of the suffering or drama of the act. It was obviously a matter of self-respect that her first attempt had been serious and nearly successful, instead of a mere hysterical gesture. That seemed to entitle her to speak of suicide as a subject, not as an obsession. It was an act she felt she had a right to as a grown woman and a free agent, in the same way as she felt it to be necessary to her development, given her queer conception of the adult as a survivor, an imaginary Jew from the concentration camps of the mind. Because of this there was never any question of motives: you do it because you do it, just as an artist always knows what he knows.

Perhaps this is why she scarcely mentioned her father, however clearly and deeply her fantasies of death were involved with him. The autobiographical heroine of *The Bell Jar* goes to weep at her father's grave immediately before she holes up in a cellar and swallows fifty sleeping pills. In "Daddy," describing the same episode, she hammers home her reasons with repetitions:

> At twenty I tried to die
> And get back, back, back to you.
> I thought even the bones would do.

I suspect that finding herself alone again now, however temporarily and voluntarily, all the anguish she had experienced at her father's death was reactivated: despite herself, she felt abandoned, injured, enraged, and bereaved as purely and defenselessly as she had as a child twenty years before. As a result, the pain that had built up steadily inside her all that time came flooding out. There was no need to discuss motives because the poems did that for her.

These months were an amazingly creative period, comparable, I think, to the "marvellous year" in which Keats produced nearly all the poetry on which his reputation finally rests. Earlier she had written carefully, more or less painfully, with much rewriting and, according to her husband, with constant recourse to *Roget's Thesaurus*. Now, although she abandoned none of her hard-earned skills and discipline, and still rewrote and rewrote, the poems flowed effortlessly, until, at the end, she occasionally produced as many as three a day. She also told me that she was deep into a new novel. *The Bell Jar* was finished, proofread and with her publishers; she spoke of it with some embarrassment as an autobiographical apprentice-work which she had to write in order to free herself from the past. But this new book, she implied, was the genuine article.

Considering the conditions in which she worked, her productivity was phenomenal. She was a full-time mother with a two-year-old daughter, a baby of ten months, and a house to look after. By the time the children were in bed at night she was too tired for anything more strenuous than "music and brandy and water." So she got up very early each morning and worked until the children woke. "These new poems of mine have one thing in common," she wrote in a note for a reading she prepared, but never broadcast, for the BBC, "they were all written at about four in the morning—that still blue, almost eternal hour before the baby's cry, before the glassy music of the milkman, settling his bottles." In those dead hours between night and day, she was able to gather herself into herself in silence and isolation, almost as though she were reclaiming some past innocence and freedom before life got a grip on her. Then she could write. For the rest of the day she was shared among the children, the housework, the shopping, efficient, bustling, harassed, like every other housewife.

Yet lonely she was, touchingly and without much disguise, despite her buoyant manner. Despite, too, the energy of her poems, which are, by any standards, subtly ambiguous performances. In them she faced her private horrors steadily and without looking aside, but the effort and risk involved in doing so acted on her like a stimulant; the worse things got and the more directly she wrote about them, the more fertile her imagination became. Just as disaster, when it finally arrives, is never as bad as it seems in expectation, so she now wrote almost with relief, swiftly as though to forestall further horrors. In a way, this is what she had been waiting for all her life, and now it had come she knew she must use it. "The passion for destruction is also a creative passion," said Michael Bakunin, and for Sylvia also this was true. She turned anger, implacability, and her roused, needle-sharp sense of trouble into a kind of celebration.

I have suggested that her cool tone depends a great deal on her realism, her sense of fact. As the months went by and her poetry became progressively more extreme, this gift of transforming every detail grew steadily until, in the last weeks, each trivial event became the occasion for poetry: a cut finger, a fever, a bruise. Her drab domestic life fused with her imagination richly and without hesitation. Around this time, for example, her husband produced a strange radio play in which the hero, driving to town, runs over a hare, sells the dead animal for five shillings, and with the blood money buys two roses. Sylvia pounced on this, isolating its core, interpreting and adjusting it according to her own needs. The result was the poem "Kindness," which ends:

> The blood jet is poetry,
> There is no stopping it.
> You hand me two children, two roses.

There was, indeed, no stopping it. Her poetry acted as a strange, powerful lens through which her ordinary life was filtered and refigured with extraordinary intensity. Perhaps the elation that comes of writing well and often helped her to preserve that bright American façade she unfailingly presented to the world. In common with her other friends of that period, I chose to believe in this cheerfulness against all the evidence of the poems. Or rather, I believed in it, and I didn't believe. But what could one do? I felt sorry for her but she clearly didn't want that. Her jauntiness forestalled all sympathy, and, if only by her blank refusal to discuss them otherwise, she insisted that her poems were purely poems, autonomous. If attempted suicide is, as some psychiatrists believe, a cry for help, then Sylvia at this time was not suicidal. What she wanted was not help but confirmation: she needed someone to acknowledge that she was coping exceptionally well with her difficult routine life of children, nappies, shopping, and writing. She needed, even more, to know that the poems worked and were good, for although she had gone through a gate Lowell had opened, she was now far along a peculiarly solitary road on which not many would risk following her. So it was important for her to know that her messages were coming back clear and strong. Yet not even her determinedly bright self-reliance could disguise the loneliness that came from her almost palpably, like a heat haze. She asked for neither sympathy nor help but, like a bereaved widow at a wake, she simply wanted company in her mourning. I suppose it provided confirmation that, despite the odds and the internal evidence, she still existed.

It was an unspeakable winter, the worst, they said, in a hundred and fifty years. The snow began just after Christmas and would not let up. By New Year the whole country had ground to a halt. The trains froze on the tracks, the abandoned trucks froze on the roads. The power stations, overloaded by million upon pathetic million of hopeless electric fires, broke down continually; not that the fires mattered, since the electricians were mostly out on strike. Water pipes froze solid; for a bath you had to scheme and cajole those rare friends with centrally heated houses, who became rarer and less friendly as the weeks draped on. Doing the dishes became a major operation. The gastric rumble of water in outdated plumbing was sweeter than the sound of mandolins. Weight for weight, plumbers were as expensive as smoked salmon, and harder to find. The gas failed and Sunday joints went raw. The lights failed and candles, of course, were unobtainable. Nerves failed and marriages crumbled. Finally, the heart failed. It seemed the cold would never end. Nag, nag, nag.

In December *The Observer* had published a still uncollected poem by Sylvia called "Event"; in mid-January they published another, "Winter Trees." Sylvia wrote me a note about it, adding that maybe we should take our children to the zoo and she would show me "the nude verdigris of the condor." But she no longer dropped into my studio with poems. Later that month I met the literary editor of one of the big weeklies. He asked me if I had seen Sylvia recently.

"No. Why?"

"I was just wondering. She sent us some poems. Very strange."

"Did you like them?"

"No," he replied. "Too extreme for my taste. I sent them all back. But she sounds in a bad state. I think she needs help."

Her doctor, a sensitive, overworked man, thought the same. He prescribed sedatives and arranged for her to see a psychotherapist. Having been bitten once by American psychiatry, she hesitated for some time before writing for an appointment. But her depression did not lift, and finally the letter was sent. It did no good. Either her letter or that of the therapist arranging a consultation went astray; apparently the postman delivered it to the wrong address. The therapist's reply arrived a day or two after she died. This was one of several links in the chain of accidents, coincidences, and mistakes that ended in her death.

I am convinced by what I know of the facts that this time she did not intend to die. Her suicide attempt ten years before had been, in every sense, deadly serious. She had carefully disguised the theft of the sleeping pills, left a misleading note to cover her tracks, and hidden herself in the darkest, most unused corner of a cellar, rearranging behind her the old firelogs she had disturbed, burying herself away like a skeleton in the nethermost family closet. Then she had swallowed a bottle of fifty sleeping pills. She was found late and by accident, and survived only by a miracle. The flow of life in her was too strong even for the violence she had done it. This, anyway, is her description of the act in *The Bell Jar;* there is no reason to believe it false. So she had learned the hard way the odds against successful suicide; she had learned that despair must be counterpoised by an almost obsessional attention to detail and disguise.

By these lights she seemed, in her last attempt, to be taking care not to succeed. But this time everything conspired to destroy her. An employment agency had found her an *au pair* girl to help with the children and housework while Sylvia got on with her writing. The girl, an Australian, was due to arrive at nine o'clock on the morning of Monday, February 11th. Meanwhile, a recurrent trouble, Sylvia's sinuses were bad; the pipes in her newly converted flat froze solid; there was still no telephone, and no word from the psychotherapist; the weather continued monstrous. Illness, loneliness, depression, and cold, combined with the demands of two small children, were too much for her. So when the weekend came she went off with the babies to stay with friends in another part of London. The plan was, I think, that she would leave early enough on Monday morning to be back in time to welcome the Australian girl. Instead, she decided to go back on the Sunday. The friends were against it but she was insistent, made a great show of her old competence and seemed more cheerful than she had been for some time. So they let her go. About eleven o'clock that night she knocked on the door of the elderly painter who lived below her, asking to borrow some stamps. But she lingered in the doorway, drawing out the conversation until he told her that he got up well before nine in the morning. Then she said goodnight and went back upstairs.

Around six A.M. she went up to the children's room and left a plate of bread and butter and two mugs of milk, in case they should wake hungry before the *au pair* girl arrived. Then she went back down to the kitchen; sealed the door and window as best she could with towels, opened the oven, laid her head in it, and turned on the gas.

The Australian girl arrived punctually at nine A.M. She rang and knocked a long time but could get no answer. So she went off to search for a telephone kiosk in order to phone the agency and make sure she had the right address. Sylvia's name, incidentally, was not on either of the doorbells. Had everything been normal, the neighbor below would have been up by then; even if he had overslept, the girl's knocking should have aroused him. But as it happened, the neighbor was very deaf and slept without his hearing aid. More important, his bedroom was immediately below Sylvia's kitchen. The gas seeped down and knocked him out cold. So he slept on through all the noise. The girl returned and tried again, still without success. Again she went off to telephone the agency and ask what to do; they told her to go back. It was now about eleven o'clock. This time she was lucky: some builders had arrived to work in the frozen-up house, and they let her in. When she knocked on Sylvia's door there was no answer and the smell of gas was overpowering. The builders forced the lock and found Sylvia sprawled in the kitchen. She was still warm. She had left a note saying. "Please call Dr. —" and giving his telephone number. But it was too late.

Had everything worked out as it should—had the gas not drugged the man downstairs, preventing him from opening the front door to the *au pair* girl—there is no doubt she would have been saved. I think she wanted to be; why else leave her doctor's telephone number? This time, unlike the occasion ten years before, there was too much holding her to life. Above all, there were the children: she was too passionate a mother to want to lose them or them to lose her. There were also the extraordinary creative powers she now unequivocally knew she possessed: the poems came daily, unbidden and unstoppable, and she was again working on a novel about which, at last, she had no reservations.

40   Why, then, did she kill herself? In part, I suppose, it was "a cry for help" which fatally misfired. But it was also a last, desperate attempt to exorcise the death she had summoned up in her poems. I have already suggested that perhaps she had begun to write obsessively about death for two reasons. First, when she and her husband separated, however mutual the arrangement, she went through again the same piercing grief and bereavement she had felt as a child when her father, by his death, seemed to abandon her. Second, I believe she thought her car crash the previous summer had set her free; she had paid her dues, qualified as a survivor, and could now write about it. But, as I have written elsewhere, for the artist himself art is not necessarily therapeutic; he is not automatically relieved of his fantasies by expressing them. Instead, by some perverse logic of creation, the act of formal expression may simply make the dredged-up material more readily available to him. The result of handling it in his work may well be that he finds himself living it out. For the artist, in short, nature often imitates art. Or, to restate the cliché, when an artist holds a mirror up to nature he finds out who and what he is; but the knowledge may change him irredeemably so that he becomes that image.

I think Sylvia, in one way or another, sensed this. In an introductory note she wrote to "Daddy" for the BBC, she said of the poem's narrator, "she has to act out the awful little allegory once over before she is free of it." The allegory in question was, as she saw it, the struggle in her between a fantasy Nazi father and a Jewish mother. But perhaps it was also a fantasy of containing in herself her own dead father, like a woman possessed by a demon (in the poem she actually calls him a vampire). In order for her to be free of him, he has to be released like a genie from a bottle. And this is precisely what the poems did: they bodied forth the death within her. But they also did so in an intensely living and creative way. The more she wrote about death, the stronger and more fertile her imaginative world became. And this gave her everything to live for.

I suspect that in the end she wanted to have done with the theme once and for all. But the only way she could find was "to act out the awful little allegory once over." She had always been a bit of a gambler, used to taking risks. The authority of her poetry was in part due to her brave persistence in following the thread of her inspiration right down to the Minotaur's lair. And this psychic courage had its parallel in her physical arrogance and carelessness. Risks didn't frighten her; on the contrary, she found them stimulating. Freud has written, "Life loses in interest, when the highest stake in the game of living, life itself, may not be risked." Finally, Sylvia took that risk. She gambled for the last time, having worked out that the odds were in her favor, but perhaps, in her depression, not much caring whether she won or lost. Her calculations went wrong and she lost.

It was a mistake, then, and out of it a whole myth has grown. I don't think she would have found it much to her taste, since it is a myth of the poet as a sacrificial victim, offering herself up for the sake of her art, having been dragged by the Muses to that final altar through every kind of distress. In these terms, her suicide becomes the whole point of the story, the act which validates her poems, gives them their interest, and proves her seriousness. So people are drawn to her work in much the same spirit as *Time* featured her at length: not for the poetry but for the gossipy, extra-literary "human interest." Yet just as the suicide adds nothing at all to the poetry, so the myth of Sylvia as a passive victim is a total perversion of the woman she was. It misses altogether her liveliness, her intellectual appetite and harsh wit, her great imaginative resourcefulness and vehemence of feeling, her control. Above all, it misses the courage with which she was able to turn disaster into art. The pity is not that there is a myth of Sylvia Plath but that the myth is not simply that of an enormously gifted poet whose death came recklessly, by mistake, and too soon.

I used to think of her brightness as a façade, as though she were able, in a rather schizoid way, to turn her back on her suffering for the sake of appearances, and pretend it didn't exist. But maybe she was also able to keep her unhappiness in check because she could write about it, because she knew she was salvaging from all those horrors something rather marvelous. The end came when she felt she could stand the subject no longer. She had written it out and was ready for something new.

> The blood-jet is poetry,
> There is no stopping it.

The only method of stopping it she could see, her vision by then blinkered by depression and illness, was that last gamble. So having, as she thought, arranged to be saved, she lay down in front of the gas oven almost hopefully, almost with relief, as though she were saying, "Perhaps this will set me free."

45   On Friday, February 15th, there was an inquest in the drab, damp coroner's court behind Camden Town: muttered evidence, long silences, the Australian girl in tears. Earlier that morning I had gone with Ted to the undertakers in Mornington Crescent. The coffin was at the far end of a bare, draped room. She lay stiffly, a ludicrous ruff at her neck. Only her face showed. It was gray and slightly transparent, like wax. I had never before seen a dead person and I hardly recognized her; her features seemed too thin and sharp. The room smelled of apples, faint, sweet but somehow unclean, as though the apples were beginning to rot. I was glad to get out into the cold and noise of the dingy streets. It seemed impossible that she was dead.

Even now I find it hard to believe. There was too much life in her long, flat, strongly boned body, and her longish face with its fine brown eyes, shrewd and full of feeling. She was practical and candid, passionate and compassionate. I believe she was a genius. I sometimes catch myself childishly thinking I'll run into her walking on Primrose Hill or the Heath, and we'll pick up the conversation where we left off. But perhaps that is because her poems still speak so distinctly in her accents: quick, sardonic, unpredictable, effortlessly inventive, a bit angry, and always utterly her own.

Questions for Discussion

1. Did you already knew something about Sylvia Plath before reading this essay? If you did, does this essay change your impression? If you didn't, does this essay arouse your curiosity about her and her writings? Explain your answer.
2. What is the essay's subordinate aim? Cite specific passages to support your answer.
3. How would this essay differ if the author's knowledge of the subject were primarily through observation?
4. What do you think of the opening? Is a more effective or appropriate opening possible? How would you start this essay?
5. The author occasionally quotes lines of poetry by Sylvia Plath. What is the purpose of these quotations? Should the author have included more such quotations? Why or why not?

Opportunities for Writing

1. Your local library is soliciting essays for a display on favorite authors. In your essay, characterize a writer you especially admire. What is (or was) this individual like? How did this writer influence you?
2. Depict the home of a friend. What does it look like? How does it reveal the characteristics of your friend?
3. Recall a time that you tried to write poetry. What did you write about? What did you do for inspiration? Was the writing difficult?

4. Write a letter to a friend, discussing your reaction to the suicide of a famous person you and your friend liked. How did you hear about this suicide? How did you feel? What did you do?

Hating Fred

Harriet Lerner

Harriet Lerner, Ph.D., is a staff psychologist at the Menniger Clinic in Topeka, Kansas. She is the author of the best-selling trilogy The Dance of Anger, The Dance of Intimacy, *and* The Dance of Deception. *"Hating Fred" is a personal essay that appeared in the* Family Therapy Networker *(March/April 1994), a magazine for mental health professionals. Lerner has written articles for both professional journals as well as popular magazines such as* Cosmopolitan, Ms., Working Mother, *and* Nation's Business.

Several months ago, the reverend Fred Phelps was the subject of ABC's *20/20,* in a segment aptly dubbed, "A Gospel of Hate." For those who missed the show, Phelps is a Primitive Baptist minister and disbarred attorney who has made it his spiritual mission and full-time job to eradicate homosexuality from the planet. He has started in his hometown and mine, Topeka, Kansas.

Fred and his small following, most of them members of his family, hit our streets almost every day, rain or shine, carrying huge signs reading, "God Hates Gays," "Death to Gays," and "Gays=AIDS." He pickets parades, performance halls, parks, homes and even funerals if he suspects an AIDS-related death. And he sends thousands of faxes to lawyers, city officials and legislators attacking homosexuals and anyone else who publicly opposes him.

Not long ago, my friend Tom Averill, who teaches English at Washburn University in Topeka, performed a satirical piece about Fred on public radio. Two days later, Fred sent faxes to university departments and scores of people that said, "Washburn University has become Fag University and is a rat's nest of filthy fags like Mr. Averill." Tom is married to journalist Jeffrey Ann Goudie, and when she made oblique reference to Fred in her column in the morning newspaper, Fred sent her a fax that said, "Dear Jeff, are you a bull dike [sic] or what?" The bottom left-hand corner of the fax read, "Fag Goudie, Moralphobic Bible-Basher."

Fred has near-zero support for his particular brand of homophobia. He hates "fags" and "fag-lovers," and Topekans hate Fred. The citizens of Topeka organize counterdemonstrations and offer support to the victims of Fred's harassment; we meet with attorneys; we help pass ordinances restricting his picketing at funerals and private homes. No one asks why Topekans hate Fred. It's obvious.

5   But I've always felt uneasy with the simplicity of our hatred. In a society that considers heterosexuality the only form of living and loving that can be celebrated, validated or mentioned, why *does* everyone hate Fred? Not long ago, a young woman in my doctor's waiting room told me how much she despises

Fred. Her daughter had danced with a local ballet company, and Fred and his followers had picketed their performance.

"I could hardly keep from swerving my car into the whole group of them," the young mother told me. "Why should my daughter have to know about those people?"

Those people. I thought at first she was talking about Fred and his relatives, but it turned out she meant homosexuals. Her daughter had seen Fred's signs and asked a lot of questions about "sodomites and fags." "My daughter is only nine," said the irate mother. "She shouldn't be exposed to homosexuality and things like that."

Is this why some Topekans hate Fred? Long before he hit the streets and the fax machine, homophobia was as deeply entrenched in Topeka as it is almost everywhere. There wasn't much talk about hating homosexuals then, because no one acknowledged their existence, except in tasteless jokes. Gays and lesbians didn't feel free to come out of hiding in my town—and they still don't, but that's not Fred's doing, "We are not just asked to keep a secret," a gay friend told me. "We are asked to be a secret."

I found myself thinking about my being Jewish. What would be the lesser of two evils, I wondered, enforced invisibility or being hated outright? Outright hate frightens me. I would sleep less well if Fred's signs said, "God Hates Jews" and "Death to Jews." "But even that would acknowledge that we Jews do, indeed, exist.

10   What about enforced invisibility—a life in the closet? At first, it seemed like the less terrifying choice. But I knew how deeply, over time, it would erode my dignity and self-regard. I imagined myself in a community preaching "tolerance"—but not visibility and celebration—of my Jewishness. ("It's unfortunate, but after all, she was born that way.") I imagined the young mother in the waiting room, angry that her daughter was forced to know about "my kind." I pictured my neighbors reacting to my son's Bar Mitzvah ("Well, I think it's fine that the Lerners are Jewish, but must they *flaunt* it?"). I imagined having to lie, to conceal, to pretend each day to be what I am not.

To be erased by the dominant culture is a terrible thing. Once, flying home to Topeka from the West Coast, I spotted a famous runner on the plane and asked him for an autograph for my younger son. He wrote, "To Ben: Run for Jesus." I was stunned by his assumptions—and equally stunned that I didn't gather the courage to tell him we were Jewish and to ask him for a different autograph.

It's this assumption—that all the world is just like us—that may be the seeding ground from which more virulent and elaborate forms of bigotry grow.

A lesbian-feminist friend recently reminded me that she feels erased almost daily from the categories of humans and women. She attends panels and workshops on "Love in the Nineties," or "Adjusting to Mastectomy" or "Mothers and Daughters." The programs do not include lesbians, and the experts talk as if homosexuals don't exist. Heterosexuals, she says, are like the runner on the airplane: They assume everyone is just like them, or should be.

Bigotry has many faces. Fred may be dangerous, but he represents only one danger. It is also dangerous to pretend that the Freds of the world are the containers of all prejudice, while the rest of us are on the side of virtue. Perhaps the citizens of Topeka should thank Fred for reminding us daily that homosexuals exist—and that people *do* hate them.

Questions for Discussion

1. This essay was written for a specific readership of family therapists. If the author were addressing a general audience, would revisions be necessary? If so, how might she revise this essay? If not, why not?
2. Would this essay be more effective if it included knowledge by observation? Explain your answer?
3. The author cites several examples of Fred's hatred. Which do you consider the most telling example? Are more examples necessary? Why or why not?
4. In this essay, is Fred a major character or a minor character? Explain your answer.
5. Notice that the title is ambiguous: Is Fred the one who is hating or the one who is hated? What do you think of using ambiguous titles?

Opportunities for Writing

1. Portray a man or woman you know who is actively opposed to or supportive of homosexuals. What motivates this individual? What have you learned from this individual?
2. In a letter to the editor of your school newspaper, recall a specific time that you ridiculed a man or woman because of his or her sexual orientation. When and where did this incident occur? Why did you act the way you did? Would you do it again? How did you feel about this experience afterward? What is the significance of this experience?
3. Recall a political demonstration that you consider especially meaningful or important. It could be a demonstration that you participated in yourself or that you read about or heard about. Write your essay for a newspaper article to be published on the anniversary of this demonstration.

Lessons from a Friend

Frank DeFord

A Princeton graduate, Frank DeFord is a journalist and author. A featured commentator on National Public Radio, DeFord is also a senior writer for Sports Illustrated *and is the author of a number of books including* Alex: The Life of a Child *(1983),* Everybody's All-American *(1981),* The Owner *(1976), and* There She Is: The Life and Times of Miss America *(1971). He also served as Arthur Ashe's collaborator on a 1975 autobiography,* Arthur Ashe: Portrait in Motion. *"Lessons from a Friend" appeared in* Newsweek *(February 22, 1993). The abstract of the article in the table of contents describes DeFord's personal and professional tribute this way: "The outpouring of grief for Arthur Ashe, who died of complications from AIDS at 49, was extraordinary, transcending his status as a sports great. Frank DeFord celebrates Ashe as a man who was honored more for his nobility than for his celebrity."*

A personal note to begin with: I remember my grandfather, who grew up in Richmond, telling me about the day when he was a little boy, and they let all the children out of school so they could help pull Robert E. Lee's new statue to its assigned place on Monument Avenue, there to rest amidst the other statues of all the beloved Virginia heroes. And my grandfather would then show me a little piece of frayed rope, which he'd saved all these decades, cut with his penknife from the tow rope after the general's statue was safely set. Virginians have ways taken their champions very seriously.

I thought back on that last Wednesday, in Richmond, a century later, when Arthur Ashe, the Virginian, was monumentalized. I tried to imagine how ever I could have explained that to my grandfather—how the hero that came next to Richmond after Robert E. Lee, general in chief, Confederate States of America—that next Virginian was merely a tennis player, who was also, of all things, black.

As much as that would have confounded my grandfather, it is also still difficult for me to understand quite how deeply Arthur Ashe's death touched so many people. Bill Rhoden, who is black, a sports columnist for *The New York Times,* even observed that the outpouring overshadowed that which had been bestowed upon Thurgood Marshall—not to mention surpassing the affection granted to those other distinguished world citizens who have left us, one after another, in these first sad weeks of 1993: Dizzy Gillespie, Rudolf Nureyev, Audrey Hepburn. Has any athlete—not to mention *former* athlete—ever been lionized so at his death? It wasn't as if Arthur was the best player ever; why, he wasn't even the best of his time. Rather, he was just a very good tennis player who had come to be recognized as an altogether exceptional human being. I think that, by the time he died, Arthur Ashe had become everybody's favorite athlete. Not just All-American, more just all ours.

Obviously, there was some rare chord that Arthur plucked on people's heart-strings. Probably, too, that twang reveals more about our society right now than it does about the man himself. Andrew Young, eulogizing Arthur at the service in Richmond, may have drawn closest, saying that Ashe had come to represent "the role of innocence in our time." And innocence, like love, sometimes is found in funny places—even in professional athletics.

5   It was the tennis player who came to triumph in society even as he was grotesquely defeated by fate, the tennis player who was the one who exhibited the dignity and decency that we simply no longer expect from people of consequence. Jesse Jackson characterized it in an intriguing way, saying that Arthur managed to "build a code of conduct for the gifted." Somehow, the public correctly divined that essential goodness of Ashe, so that he really was honored more for his nobility than for his celebrity—which is truly amazing in these Warholian times. That's what a lot of last week was about: us saying, we will pause now for just a moment to honor honor. It felt good, so we were even more profligate in our giving.

Nothing, of course, distinguished Ashe so much as the way he handled adversity. It was enough to suffer a heart attack when still in his 30s—while still, for that matter, ranked in the top 10 of tennis players. But then, to contract AIDS from a blood transfusion given after heart-bypass surgery . . . well, that was just impossibly unfair. The intensity of anger that the public feels about how he was subsequently violated by the media, when he was forced to reveal his condition or be "outed" by *USA Today,* remains palpable. Anybody in the press who dismisses the public's disgust at the encroachment upon a private man's privacy does so at their future peril.

But above all, race was forever crucial to understanding the way in which the world dealt with Arthur Ashe. He was, I came to think, in matters of race, *The Universal Soldier,* some kind of keystone figure we need if ever brothership is to triumph. He was black, but he perfectly infiltrated white American society as much as he needed to, and even beyond that he was just terribly interested in everybody everywhere in the world.

Those legions who paid tribute last week kept talking about how Ashe was a "transcendent figure" above tennis, mere sports, but, I'm sorry, the much greater, dearer point was quite the opposite: he was the sort of person who was always down in the ditches, connecting things, tying people together. Arthur would have been mortified to have been reduced to being labeled transcendent.

Anyway, even if we throw around high-falutin' words like "transcend," most everybody really sensed otherwise; by the end, all the world wanted to associate itself closely with Arthur. The International Olympic Committee made him the first athlete member of the Olympic Order never to have had anything to do with the Olympics. The bell was sounded 10 times for him at the Bowe-Dokes championship fight, the first time that any but a fallen fighter had ever been so honored. African-Americans exalted him as one of theirs, even though there were occasions in the past when Arthur was painted as effete for failing to scream out and an elitist for failing to go along with politically correct racial dogma. And whites, of course, loved to cozy up to Ashe and cite him as the black ideal—why can't they all be like him?—missing the point that there are precious few whites that live up to that standard, either.

As a matter of fact, nothing blindsided some whites as much as Ashe's recent comment that, as difficult as it was having AIDS, that wasn't nearly as trying as being black. "No question," he snapped.

Arthur Ashe said that? Certainly not Arthur. Not the man who was always so civil and understanding. But the thought wasn't anything new with him. I can remember him years ago instructing me that "equal" though things may seem, he could never achieve that estate because so much of his time—of any black person's time—must be spent simply thinking about race. "You can get up in the morning and just walk outside and start your day. I can't do that. I always have to think: well, here goes a black guy walking outside. So, you see, you'll always have an advantage over me."

But the fact that Arthur Ashe could say things about race, however passionately, without bitterness, is what made them so meaningful. Obviously, Arthur Ashe meant more to black people, but, notwithstanding, he was capable of engaging white people; he was capable of causing change in them and their world. In the end, the outpouring of emotion we gave to him spoke selfishly to our hope—that if we could not save his life, what he stood for might help save us.

Although this adulation Arthur received this past week would have embarrassed him terribly, he must have sensed the effluence of affection that would flow with his death. In a way, you see, the revelation of last April that was wrenched from him produced the first draft of his obituaries while he was still alive to read them. His pre-death also, he recognized, made him a more valuable advocate of the causes he cared about, so he could make us cosign for his borrowed time. He wanted to steal a few more months, too, and he thought he would, but he was accepting of what would come of him, whenever it did.

The last time I saw him was only a couple weeks before he died, but it preceded any sense of urgency. Still, he was in the hospital, so he wanted to put me at ease. "You know," he said, "everything in my life is just wonderful now—except for the hospital stuff."

15   When I looked a little skeptical—as if to say out loud: excuse me, you are reducing AIDS to "hospital stuff"?—he added: "Really, everything is almost perfect."

I left almost believing him. Arthur Ashe had a very good attitude, and it was catching. He was a more infectious person even than what incidentally killed him.

Questions for Discussion

1. What do you think of the two opening paragraphs? Why do you think the author starts the essay this way? How would you have started this essay?
2. Notice the organization of the essay: it starts with the funeral of Arthur Ashe, recalls his public life, and concludes with his dying in the hospital. Why is the essay organized this way? Do you consider this organization effective? Why or why not?
3. Consider the author's use of descriptive detail. Does the essay show us who Arthur Ashe was or tell us who he was? Explain your answer.
4. This essay was written for a general audience. How would you revise this essay for a specific audience of tennis players? Of African Americans? Of AIDS patients?
5. Why does the author mention the deaths of Thurgood Marshall, Dizzy Gillespie, Rudolf Nureyev, and Audrey Hepburn?

Opportunities for Writing

1. Portray a man or woman you admire who has AIDS. How has this individual influenced you? How is he or she living with the disease? Address your essay to the membership of a local AIDS association.
2. Write a special essay for the sports page of your local newspaper describing your favorite athlete. What are his or her achievements? Why do you admire this individual?
3. In a letter to your family, discuss your reaction to the death of a friend. How did this individual die? How did you feel? What did you do? What will you try to remember about him or her?

Only Daughter

SANDRA CISNEROS

Sandra Cisneros is one of seven children; her father is Mexican and her mother Chicana. Her family and her cultural background serve as important sources for her prose and poetry. She has published a collection of narratives, Woman Hollering Creek

(1992), a novel—The House on Mango Street *(1983)—and a collection of poetry,* My Wicked Wicked Ways *(1987). In "Only Daughter," Cisneros provides readers with a firsthand account of what it is like being an only daughter in her Mexican American family; in addition, she recounts how going home for Christmas led to her receiving a great "gift" from her father.*

Once, several years ago, when I was just starting out my writing career, I was asked to write my own contributor's note for an anthology I was part of. I wrote: "I am the only daughter in a family of six sons. *That* explains everything."

Well, I've thought about that ever since, and yes, it explains a lot to me, but for the reader's sake I should have written: "I am the only daughter in a *Mexican* family of six sons." Or even: "I am the only daughter of a Mexican father and a Mexican-American mother." Or: "I am the only daughter of a working-class family of nine." All of these had everything to do with who I am today.

I was/am the only daughter and *only* a daughter. Being an only daughter in a family of six sons forced me by circumstance to spend a lot of time by myself because my brothers felt it beneath them to play with a *girl* in public. But that aloneness, that loneliness, was good for a would-be writer—it allowed me time to think and think, to imagine, to read and prepare myself.

Being only a daughter for my father meant my destiny would lead me to become someone's wife. That's what he believed. But when I was in the fifth grade and shared my plans for college with him, I was sure he understood. I remember my father saying, "*Qué bueno, mi'ja,* that's good." That meant a lot to me, especially since my brothers thought the idea hilarious. What I didn't realize was that my father thought college was good for girls—good for finding a husband. After four years in college and two more in graduate school, and still no husband, my father shakes his head even now and says I wasted all that education.

5   In retrospect, I'm lucky my father believed daughters were meant for husbands. It meant it didn't matter if I majored in something silly like English. After all, I'd find a nice professional eventually, right? This allowed me the liberty to putter about embroidering my little poems and stories without my father interrupting with so much as a "What's that you're writing?"

But the truth is, I wanted him to interrupt. I wanted my father to understand what it was I was scribbling, to introduce me as "My only daughter, the writer." Not as "This is only my daughter. She teaches." *Es maestra*—teacher. Not even *profesora.*

In a sense, everything I have ever written has been for him, to win his approval even though I know my father can't read English words, even though my father's only reading includes the brown-ink *Esto* sports magazines from Mexico City and the bloody *¡Alarma!* magazines that feature yet another sighting of *La Virgen de Guadalupe* on a tortilla or a wife's revenge on her philandering husband by bashing his skull in with a *molcajete* (a kitchen mortar made of volcanic rock). Or the *fotonovelas,* the little picture paperbacks with tragedy and trauma erupting from the characters' mouths in bubbles.

My father represents, then, the public majority. A public who is uninterested in reading, and yet one whom I am writing about and for, and privately trying to woo.

When we were growing up in Chicago, we moved a lot because of my father. He suffered bouts of nostalgia. Then we'd have to let go our flat, store the furniture with mother's relatives, load the station wagon with baggage and bologna sandwiches and head south. To Mexico City.

We came back, of course. To yet another Chicago flat, another Chicago neighborhood, another Catholic school. Each time, my father would seek out the parish priest in order to get a tuition break, and complain or boast: "I have seven sons."

He meant *siete hijos,* seven children, but he translated it as "sons." "I have seven sons." To anyone who would listen. The Sears Roebuck employee who sold us the washing machine. The short-order cook where my father ate his ham-and-eggs breakfasts. "I have seven sons." As if he deserved a medal from the state.

My papa. He didn't mean anything by that mistranslation, I'm sure. But somehow I could feel myself being erased. I'd tug my father's sleeve and whisper: "Not seven sons. Six! and *one daughter."*

When my oldest brother graduated from medical school, he fulfilled my father's dream that we study hard and use this—our heads, instead of this—our hands. Even now my father's hands are thick and yellow, stubbed by a history of hammer and nails and twine and coils and springs. "Use this," my father said, tapping his head, "and not this," showing us those hands. He always looked tired when he said it.

Wasn't college an investment? And hadn't I spent all those years in college? And if I didn't marry, what was it all for? Why would anyone go to college and then choose to be poor? Especially someone who had always been poor.

Last year, after ten years of writing professionally, the financial rewards started to trickle in. My second National Endowment for the Arts Fellowship. A guest professorship at the University of California, Berkeley. My book, which sold to a major New York publishing house.

At Christmas, I flew home to Chicago. The house was throbbing, same as always; hot *tamales* and sweet *tamales* hissing in my mother's pressure cooker, and everybody—my mother, six brothers, wives, babies, aunts, cousins—talking too loud and at the same time, like in a Fellini film, because that's just how we are.

I went upstairs to my father's room. One of my stories had just been translated into Spanish and published in an anthology of Chicano writing, and I wanted to show it to him. Ever since he recovered from a stroke two years ago, my father likes to spend his leisure hours horizontally. And that's how I found him, watching a Pedro Infante movie on Galavisión and eating rice pudding.

There was a glass filmed with milk on the bedside table. There were several vials of pills and balled Kleenex. And on the floor, one black sock and a plastic urinal that I didn't want to look at but looked at anyway. Pedro Infante was about to burst into song, and my father was laughing.

I'm not sure if it was because my story was translated into Spanish, or because it was published in Mexico, or perhaps because the story dealt with Tepeyac, the *colonia* my father was raised in and the house he grew up in, but at any rate, my father punched the mute button on his remote control and read my story.

I sat on the bed next to my father and waited. He read it very slowly. As if he were reading each line over and over. He laughed at all the right places and read lines he liked out loud. He pointed and asked questions: "Is this So-and-so?" "Yes," I said. He kept reading.

When he was finally finished, after what seemed like hours, my father looked up and asked: "Where can we get more copies of this for the relatives?"

Of all the wonderful things that happened to me last year, that was the most wonderful.

Questions for Discussion

1. Do you think the title is appropriate? Why do you think it is or isn't? What other titles could you give this essay?
2. Notice that the author introduces several Spanish words. What is her purpose in doing so? Do you like this technique? Is it effective? Why or why not?
3. Does the author give you a vivid picture of her father? Which descriptive details are essential to his characterization? Are all the details necessary?
4. This essay was originally published in a woman's magazine. How might the author revise this essay for a Mexican American audience? What changes would you advise?
5. How would this essay differ if it were written using knowledge by observation?

Opportunities for Writing

1. Portray a friend of yours who enjoys writing. What types of things does he or she write? Essays? Poems? Short stories? Why is this man or woman your friend?
2. Depict your home during a holiday celebration. How is it decorated? What sounds and smells do you notice? Is it filled with people? What are your impressions of your home at this time? Write this essay as a holiday gift for your family.
3. Your local newspaper is soliciting essays for a special Father's Day issue. In your essay, describe a time you accomplished something that made your father particularly proud of you. What did you do? What was his reaction? How did he make you feel? What did you learn from this experience?

20/20 Hindsight

Jay Ford

A native New Yorker, Jay Ford was educated at Wesleyan University, where he majored in African American history. In "20/20 Hindsight," Ford recalls his four-month trip to East Africa, as a student participating in an academic program in Kenya called "An Experiment in International Living." Living, visiting, and traveling with Africans in rural and urban parts of the country taught Ford—an African American—an invaluable lesson about Kenyan culture, people, and himself.

Born into a middle class African-American family on the upper west side of Manhattan, I have spent most of my life chasing the (white) American dream.

Absorbing the rhetoric brewed by the media, school curricula, and, more important, my teachers, I was graduated from high school with the goal of travelling to Europe, achieving a college degree, becoming a corporate lawyer and, eventually, marrying a spouse who would be most likely white or a light-skinned black. We would have two homes and probably three children. This was my rough sketch of my future, one with which I was satisfied. I would be a success and this was very important because I clearly represent what W. E. B. DuBois coined as the "talented tenth." Therefore, I had a responsibility to my people to succeed, to vanquish the disabilities associated with my color and earn my place in white America, my America.

In starting off on my journey to success, I met my first obstacle as I neared the end of my sophomore year in college. The student body had taken over the administration building in hopes of persuading the University to divest monies invested in corporations in South Africa. A meeting between the students and the administration had been arranged during which the administration had thoroughly explained its position on divestment. Now it was the students' turn to respond. As student after student approached the microphone, explaining what he/she believed to be the most important reasons for disinvesting, an unsettling feeling began to overwhelm me. Although all of the explanations were more than legitimate reasons to disinvest, none of them had touched my personal reasons for protesting the University's position on divestment.

When it was my turn, I did not actually know what I wanted to say, but I was determined to say something. "My name is Julius J. Ford. I am an Afro-American. Inherent in my title is the word African, meaning "of Africa." My ancestry is from Africa. Africans are therefore my people, my history. So as long as you continue to oppress my people through violence or investment or silence, you oppress me. And as long as you oppress me, I will fight you! I will fight you!" As I returned to my seat, my friend leaned over, patted me on the back and said, "That was great, I never really knew you felt that way." I turned to him and said, "Neither did I."

It was this event that made me question myself. How could I be satisfied with my sketch of success when it had no background or depth? Why had I not felt this strongly about Africa or Africans before? Why was I more attracted to women who possessed European features (straight hair, light skin, thin nose) than those who possessed African features? Why did I feel that Europe was so great and Africa so primitive? Why did I choose to call myself an African-American when I knew virtually nothing about Africa? These questions would trouble my soul for the remainder of the year. In fact, they would push me to apply to a student exchange program in East Africa, Kenya.

Called "An Experiment in International Living," the program would offer me travel throughout the country, during which time I would live in both rural and urban areas, in both huts and hotels, for approximately four months from February through mid-May, 1989. I would be equipped with two academic directors with numerous university and government contacts and ensured a variety of learning opportunities, as I would stay with native families and be allowed to venture off on my own.

Even though this program seemingly presented an optimum opportunity to find answers to all my pending questions, I was still apprehensive about my decision to go. But, perhaps if there was one specific incident that canceled any wavering on my part, it was that Friday afternoon at drama class. On Fridays, I taught drama to about twenty 9–14-year-old kids from predominantly black families with low incomes at a community center about twenty minutes from my college. On this particular day I had decided to ask the class what they thought about my taking a trip to Africa. They shot off these responses: "Why would you want to go to Africa to get even blacker than you are now?", "Why don't you take a trip somewhere nice like Paris, London, Rome?", "But they say in Africa every one is backwards, they can't teach you anything," "People are so black and ugly there." And, although some of the comments from the children were said specifically to make the other children laugh, many of them were exemplifications of how our educational system and other forms of external social propaganda affect a black child's mind.

When I first arrived in Kenya, we stayed in its capital city, Nairobi. Surprisingly enough, my first impression of Nairobi was that it was just like any American city: skyscrapers, movie theatres, discos, and crime. In fact, I was a bit disappointed, feeling that I had travelled fifteen hours in a Pan Am jet just to come back to New York City. But upon more detailed observation, I realized that this city was quite different from any other I had visited before. This city was black and, when I say black, I'm not talking your coffee-colored Atlanta, Oakland, Harlem black people. I mean black! I mean when you were small and used to play games and chose to embarrass the darkest kid on the block by calling him "midnight," "shadow," and "teeth black."

But the lesson to be learned in Nairobi was that all shades of black were equally attractive and the small children did not penalize attractiveness according to shade of skin, or length of hair, or size of nose. Furthermore, being in a black city, knowing I was in a mostly black country that sits on a predominantly black continent, enhanced my confidence and hence my actions. For the first time in my life I felt as though I could do anything, fit in anywhere, be welcomed by everyone because of my color. This was the feeling I had often assumed blacks felt during the Twenties, the period of the Harlem Renaissance. It was wonderful! I would go for days without being aware of my color. It did not seem to matter.

It was only a few weeks into the program, however, when I began to notice racial insecurities developing within my peer group (of twenty-four I was the only black). As many as half a dozen of the other students declared that they had begun to view black children as more beautiful than white, that black women and black features were more pleasing to the eye than white ones. Others simply segregated themselves from the black society as much as possible, refusing to stay with families without another white person present. Perhaps, then, inherent in the role of minority come feelings of inferiority, a certain lack of confidence, insecurity.

Because there is much tribalism in Kenya, the first title I had to drop was African-American. When people around me refer to themselves as Masai or Kikuyu as opposed to Kenyan or East African, then how could I refer to myself as an African? Furthermore, the language I spoke, my values, morals and education were not African. So this put me in an awkward position. No one could question my ancestry as African because of my color, so I enjoyed most benefits of majority status. Yet, to many Kenyans, I was much more similar to a white American than an African so there was a wide gap between us.

It was here I realized that to be an accepted descendant of Africa I had a lot of work to do. I needed to learn a new language and a new culture. I needed to assimilate, and I figured that that shouldn't be too hard as I had twenty years of experience in that in the United States. But, the difference between my American and Kenyan assimilations is that in Kenya it seemed to be welcomed if not encouraged by the majority. The more knowledge I attained of Kenya and the more I left my English at home and spoke Swahili or another tribal language, the more cultural doors opened to me. For example, as I became increasingly familiar with Gidiam tribal customs and my use of Kiswahili improved, I was able to travel along the coast for days never worrying about food or lodging. I was often given the opportunity to sit and discuss with elders, and take part in tribal ceremonies and had responsibilities bestowed on me by elder men, *Mzees,* or my temporary *Mama.* In fact, toward the end of my trip, when travelling alone, it was often difficult for me to convince people that I was African-American. They would tell me, *"Una toka Africa qwa sababo una weza kusema Kiswahili na una famhamu Africa life"* (You are from Africa because you are able to speak Kiswahili and you understand African life). The more I learned, the more comfortable I was with the title African-American.

I also took more pride in myself. Here it was important to learn that the black empowerment was not from sheer numbers, it was from the fact that the blacks in Africa possess a communal sense of self, a shared past that is to never be forgotten, that has passed through generations, and is used as a reference for modern-day experiences. An exemplification of this concept is the way in which Kenyans and Africans in general treat their elderly. In Kenya you are told that you never grow to equal your parents' authority or knowledge. Your elders will forever be your elders and respected as such. In Kenya, elderly people are cherished not forgotten.

As we visited small villages in the areas of Kisumu, Nakru, and on the coast, villages which by American standards were far below the poverty line, we were welcomed with feasts of foods, drinks, people and music. To them we were guests paying them the honor of visitation. Even on a more individual level, most Kenyan families were extraordinarily hospitable. To be welcomed into a stranger's home and be offered food, wine, and a bed for an unlimited number of days is shocking to Americans and even more so to a New Yorker.

This humanistic view was very difficult to adapt to because it affected every level of Kenyan society. For example, Kenyans have a very limited concept of personal space (but in a country with a population growth rate of 4.3 percent that is quite understandable). So it was often difficult for me to discover that my four newly acquired brothers were also my newly acquired bedmates, to change money at the bank while the people behind me were looking over my shoulder examining my passport and money exchange papers, and to learn not to tell your family that you would like to be left alone because crazy people stay by themselves.

15   Also, Americans are lost outside of a linear society. We are taught from kindergarten to stay in line. Order for us is symbolically represented by the line, and we therefore choose to see all other forms of non-linear collective activity as chaotic. Kenyans, however, do not have this same view of order. They choose to mass together, aggressively seeking out their desires and bringing new mean-

ing to the words "organized chaos." Mobs catch buses, herds are seen at ticket counters, and, unfortunately, until your adjustment period is complete, you stand apart from the chaos, "jaw dropped," staring at the stampede of people. As a result, you do not obtain a ticket or get on the bus.

This conception of order plus the Kenyan view of personal space make for exciting moments in the public sphere. For example, there is a type of Kenyan public transportation called *matatus*. Matatus are small privately owned minivans that serve as buses for local citizens. To ride a matatu is like taking the most crowded New York City subway car during rush hour, placing that car on Broadway, and allowing a taxicab driver to control the wheel. Matatus do not actually stop at designated bus stops; in fact, they do not actually stop at all. Instead, they simply slow down and those who need to get off push and shove their way to the front of the van and jump out. And as for those who wish to board, they simply chase the matatu down and shove and push their way onto the van. As with circus clown cars, there is always room for one more.

Another linear concept I was introduced to was time. In rural areas there would sometimes be days when we would have no activities planned. It was at these moments when I would curse my directors for poor planning. But I was soon to learn that doing nothing was not necessarily wasted time. This time to think, relax, conversationalize was most important for a peaceful state of mind. I finally understood that it is not imperative even in America to eat breakfast, read the paper in the street while you are running to the subway, or to work two jobs just to pay off your life insurance bill. Here there was not "so much to do and so little time"; here there was a great deal to do but also the belief that that which is supposed to get done will get done in time.

For example, during the last month of my stay in Kenya I visited a small farm in Kisumu Kaubu, Uganda, with a woman and her three sons. I was only to stay for a day and one night. I had come to visit just prior to the time the rains were expected, so I had assumed that the family was going to spend very little time relaxing with me because it was imperative that the soil and seeds for the year be prepared for the rains which could come at any moment.

However, once I arrived, we did very little field work. We talked instead—about the history of her people, about America, and about American perceptions of Kenya. Of course this was hard work since their English was very limited and my Swahili is fair at best. And as the day crept on to the night, I asked her how she could afford to give her attentions to me when the threat of the rains could come at any day now. *"Pole Pole, bu'ana,"* she replied (We have not neglected our work to the fields. We have only delayed our work so to welcome our new son, who by joining us will ease our workload). I then asked her, "But, Mama, it is already 11:00 and I leave tomorrow at 9:00." She replied, "Don't worry, bwana, we start to work the cattle (plow) at 2:00 A.M. Good night."

It seemed as though Kenyan culture chose to be humanistic rather than materialistic. The value placed on human life and interaction is much greater than in the States. To shake hands, to share a meal or even your home with a foreigner is an honor, not a burden. And, for you as a guest to turn down that hand, meal, or bed is an insult. How wonderfully strange to travel to a foreign land where people who can hardly understand what language you speak are ready to take you home and make you part of the family. They wouldn't last too long in New York, I thought.

In most places in Kenya, it was common knowledge for one to know his/her environment. People could name the types of trees along the roads, tell you animals indigenous to the area, and explain which types of soil were best for growing specific crops. They could tell you the staple foods of different parts of Kenya *or* even the U.S. In fact, their world geography was superior to that of most American college students. Access to information, whether at home or in schools, was a privilege to be appreciated by those involved and then passed down to younger generations orally. I wonder why I did not feel this way. My country offers more educational opportunities than any other in the world and yet seldom are these opportunities fully exploited. American students go to school, but they do not go to learn. They go to get A's and move up economically. They go to play the game, the educational game of success that I like to refer to as DT (Diploma Training), a process that verifies one's intelligence by certificate as opposed to action or common sense.

Furthermore, along with this overwhelming appreciation for knowledge, Kenyans show reverence for everyday simplicities which we in America take for granted: the appreciation for candlelight, running water, a toilet with a seat cover, a long hot shower every day. Learning to live is to stay in Kenya and survive with twenty-three other people living mostly off rain water, sleeping in huts, and eating many fruits and vegetables with only the occasional beef meal. I felt as though Kenya taught me a new dimension of life, a rebirth of sorts. It put objectives, time, goals, values into a new perspective. It did not tell me, "Please be aware of how much water you use because a drought warning is in effect." It gave me a gallon of water and told me to drink and bathe for an undetermined period. It did not tell me of the beauties of nature, rather it revealed them to me by greeting me in the morning with the sights of Mt. Kenya, Kilimanjaro, and Lake Victoria. I saw no need for *National Geographic* or wildlife television, for when it wanted to introduce me to animals, a monkey, leopard, or family of raccoons would become my fellow pedestrians. There was no urge to tell me of the paradox of zoos when it could show me national parks with hundreds of acres of land.

In Kenya I felt more free than I have ever felt before. The only thing holding me captive was the earth which would grow the food, the sky which would quench the earth of its thirst, and the sun which would warm and help all things to grow. But these masters were sure to give back all that you have put in. When you worked hard, your rewards were great and if you chose to relax so would your crop and cattle. And with a give-and-take relationship like this, one learns that it is okay to take time, time for others, for oneself, time to enjoy and appreciate all that life and earth offer. Some choose to call this type of relationship religion, a covenant with the Lord and her divinity (sky, earth, and animals and I will not deny that there was a strong sense of God or Allah or Sa or Buddha).

A forest burning to the ground germinates the soil, allowing new life to grow. The omnipotence of nature—floods, lightning, hurricanes, earthquakes, the beauty of a cheetah or giraffe running, an open field, the sky, the mountains, the sea—is overwhelming and foreign to me living so long in a concrete jungle. When all of this engulfed me and I took the time to embrace it, I became convinced that there exists a master craftsperson of this creation, that there exists a God.

Kenya has more than (just) given me a new perception of the world; Kenya has widened my world view. I now realize that there are other significant cultures in the world besides a western one. I no longer think of the world in First, Second, and Third World terms. There are aspects of Kenyan values which should be regarded as more First World than American: humanistic sentiments, importance of family, pride of ancestry, appreciation and respect for other peoples' differences.

Also, whereas I ventured off to Kenya to learn about a new culture and its new people, I found that most of the more important discoveries and evaluations were about myself. Upon leaving Kenya I feel that I have grown more confident about my African-Americanness, my perceptions of the world around me, and my expectation of 21/21 vision and beyond. I do not believe I could have gone anywhere else on earth and been as personally challenged.

Questions for Discussion

1. Do you consider the title effective? Why do you think it is or isn't?
2. How important is the essay's referential aim? Is it as important as the expressive aim? Could this essay be considered referential aim writing? Explain your answer.
3. Identify the stages of plot in the author's narrative. Which passages constitute the introduction? the rising action? the climax? the falling action? the resolution?
4. Consider the author's use of dialogue. When and where does he use dialogue? Why does he include the dialogue he does? What is its purpose? Should he use dialogue more often? Why or why not?
5. What significance does the author derive from this experience? How does he communicate this significance? Cite specific passages.

Opportunities for Writing

1. In a letter to a friend, recall your visit to a different country. Where did you go? What did you see and do? How did the visit impress you?
2. Describe your experience of learning to speak a second language. What prompted you to learn a second language? Was it easy or difficult? Why?
3. Portray a friend or acquaintance who is a visitor to this country. What is he or she like? What brought this individual to your city? How is he or she adjusting to life here?
4. Your school is revising its recruiting materials. Compose a series of brief essays depicting the local community. What are its major attractions? What would a visitor to this city find especially interesting or unusual?

KNOWLEDGE BY OBSERVATION

Of Accidental Judgments and Casual Slaughters

KAI ERIKSON

Born in Austria, Kai Erikson is a sociologist, teacher, and writer. He has been on the faculty at Pittsburgh, Emory, and Yale. His publications include A New Species of Trouble: Explorations in Disaster, Trauma, and Community *(1994),* Everything in Its Path: Destruction of Community in the Buffalo Creek *(1976) and* Wayward Puritans: A Study of the Sociology of Deviance *(1966). In addition to his own books, Erikson has also edited* In Search of Common Ground *(1973), a work by psychoanalyst Erik Erikson, his famous father. "Of Accidental Judgments and Casual Slaughters" first appeared in* The Nation; *in this essay, Erikson reconstructs the events leading up to the nuclear bombings of Hiroshima and Nagasaki, focusing on the possible alternatives that political, military, and scientific leaders might have considered. To explore this time and this historical event, Erikson uses information gained by observation. This author doesn't use formal documentation (i.e., parenthetic references or formal notes); he instead uses a technique called tagging, so that he can integrate information from external sources within his own sentences.*

The bombings of Hiroshima and Nagasaki, which took place forty years ago this month, are among the most thoroughly studied moments on human record. Together they constitute the only occasion in history when atomic weapons were dropped on living populations, and together they constitute the only occasion in history when a decision was made to employ them in that way.

I want to reflect here on the second of those points. The "decision to drop"—I will explain in a minute why quotation marks are useful here—is a fascinating historical episode. But it is also an exhibit of the most profound importance as we consider our prospects for the future. It is a case history well worth attending to. A compelling parable.

If one were to tell the story of that decision as historians normally do, the details arranged in an ordered narrative, one might begin in 1938 with the discovery of nuclear fission, or perhaps a year later with the delivery of Einstein's famous letter to President Roosevelt. No matter what its opening scene, though, the tale would then proceed along a string of events—a sequence of appointees named, committees formed, reports issued, orders signed, arguments won and lost, minds made up and changed—all of it coming to an end with a pair of tremendous blasts in the soft morning air over Japan.

The difficulty with that way of relating the story, as historians of the period all testify, is that the more closely one examines the record, the harder it is to make out where in the flow of events something that could reasonably be called a decision was reached at all. To be sure, a kind of consensus emerged from the sprawl of ideas and happenings that made up the climate of wartime Washington, but looking back, it is hard to distinguish those pivotal moments in the story when the crucial issues were identified, debated, reasoned through, resolved. The decision, to the extent that one can even speak of such a thing, was shaped and seasoned by a force very like inertia.

Let's say, then, that a wind began to blow, ever so gently at first, down the corridors along which power flows. And as it gradually gathered momentum during the course of the war, the people caught up in it began to assume, without ever checking up on it, that it had a logic and a motive, that it had been set in motion by sure hands acting on the basis of wise counsel.

Harry Truman, in particular, remembered it as a time of tough and lonely choices, and titled his memoir of that period *Year of Decisions*. But the bulk of those choices can in all fairness be said to have involved confirmation of projects already under way or implementation of decisions made at other levels of command. Brig. Gen. Leslie R. Groves, military head of the Manhattan Project, was close to the mark when he described Truman's decision as "one of noninterference—basically, a decision not to upset the existing plans." And J. Robert Oppenheimer spoke equally to the point when he observed some twenty years later: "The decision was implicit in the project. I don't know whether it could have been stopped."

In September of 1944, when it became more and more evident that a bomb would be produced in time for combat use, Franklin Roosevelt and Winston Churchill met at Hyde Park and initialed a brief *aide-mémoire,* noting, among other things, that the new weapon "might, perhaps, after mature consideration, be used against the Japanese." This document does not appear to have had any effect on the conduct of the war, and Truman knew nothing at all about it. But it would not have made a real difference in any case, for neither chief of state did much to initiate the "mature consideration" they spoke of so glancingly, and Truman, in turn, could only suppose that such matters had been considered already. "Truman did not inherit the question," writes Martin J. Sherwin, "he inherited the answer."

What would "mature consideration" have meant in such a setting as that anyway?

First of all, presumably, it would have meant seriously asking whether the weapon should be employed at all. But we have it on the authority of virtually all the principal players that no one in a position to do anything about it ever really considered alternatives to combat use. Henry L. Stimson, Secretary of War:

At no time, from 1941 to 1945, did I ever hear it suggested by the President, or by any other responsible member of the government, that atomic energy should not be used in the war.

Harry Truman:

I regarded the bomb as a military weapon and never had any doubt that it should be used.

General Groves:

Certainly, there was no question in my mind, or, as far as I was ever aware, in the mind of either President Roosevelt or President Truman or any other responsible person, but that we were developing a weapon to be employed against the enemies of the United States.

Winston Churchill:

There never was a moment's discussion as to whether the atomic bomb should be used or not.

And why should anyone be surprised? We were at war, after all, and with the most resolute of enemies, so the unanimity of that feeling is wholly understandable. But it was not, by any stretch of the imagination, a product of mature consideration.

"Combat use" meant a number of different things, however, and a second question began to be raised with some frequency in the final months of the war, all the more insistently after the defeat of Germany. Might a way be devised to demonstrate the awesome power of the bomb in a convincing enough fashion to induce the surrender of the Japanese without having to destroy huge numbers of civilians? Roosevelt may have been pondering something of the sort. In September of 1944, for example, three days after initialing the Hyde Park *aide-mémoire,* he asked Vannevar Bush, a trusted science adviser, whether the bomb "should actually be used against the Japanese or whether it should be used only as a threat." While that may have been little more than idle musing, a number of different schemes were explored within both the government and the scientific community in the months following.

One option involved a kind of *benign strike:* the dropping of a bomb on some built-up area, but only after advance notice had been issued so that residents could evacuate the area and leave an empty slate on which the bomb could write its terrifying signature. This plan was full of difficulties. A dud under those dramatic circumstances might do enormous damage to American credibility, and, moreover, to broadcast any warning was to risk the endeavor in other ways. Weak as the Japanese were by this time in the war, it was easy to imagine their finding a way to intercept an incoming airplane if they knew where and when it was expected, and officials in Washington were afraid that it would occur to the Japanese, as it had to them, that the venture would come to an abrupt end if American prisoners of war were brought into the target area.

The second option was a *tactical strike* against a purely military target—an arsenal, railroad yard, depot, factory, harbor—without advance notice. Early in the game, for example, someone had nominated the Japanese fleet concentration at Truk. The problem with this notion, however—and there is more than a passing irony here—was that no known military target had a wide enough compass to contain the whole of the destructive capacity of the weapon and so display its full range and power. The committee inquiring into likely targets wanted one "more than three miles in diameter," because anything smaller would be too inadequate a canvas for the picture it was supposed to hold.

The third option was to stage a kind of *dress rehearsal* by detonating a bomb in some remote corner of the world—a desert or empty island, say—to exhibit to international observers brought in for the purpose what the device could do. The idea had been proposed by a group of scientists in what has since been called the Franck Report, but it commanded no more than a moment's attention. It had the same problems as the benign strike: the risk of being embarrassed by a dud was more than most officials in a position to decide were willing to take, and there was a widespread feeling that any demonstration involving advance notice would give the enemy too much useful information.

The fourth option involved a kind of *warning shot.* The thought here was to drop a bomb without notice over a relatively uninhabited stretch of enemy land so the Japanese high command might see at first hand what was in store for them if they failed to surrender soon. Edward Teller thought that an explosion at night high over Tokyo Bay would serve as a brilliant visual argument, and Adm. Lewis Strauss, soon to become a member (and later chair) of the Atomic Energy Commission, recommended a strike on a local forest, reasoning that the blast would "lay the trees out in windrows from the center of the explosion in all directions as though they were matchsticks," meanwhile igniting a fearsome firestorm at the epicenter. "It seemed to me," he added, "that a demonstration of this sort would prove to the Japanese that we could destroy any of their cities at will." The physicist Ernest O. Lawrence may have been speaking half in jest when he suggested that a bomb might be use to "blow the top off" Mount Fujiyama, but he was quite serious when he assured a friend early in the war: "The bomb will never be dropped on people. As soon as we get it, we'll use it only to dictate peace."

15 Now, hindsight is too easy a talent. But it seems evident on the face of it that the fourth of those options, the warning shot, was much to be preferred over the other three, and even more to be preferred over use on living targets. I do not want to argue the case here. I do want to ask, however, why that possibility was so easily dismissed.

The fact of the matter seems to have been that the notion of a demonstration was discussed on only a few occasions once the Manhattan Project neared completion, and most of those discussions were off the record. So a historian trying to reconstruct the drift of those conversations can only flatten an ear against the wall, as it were, and see if any sense can be made of the muffled voices next door. It seems very clear, for example, that the options involving advance notice were brought up so often and so early in official conversations that they came to *mean* demonstration in the minds of several important players. If a James Byrnes, say, soon to be named Secretary of State, were asked why one could not detonate a device in unoccupied territory, he might raise the problem posed by prisoners of war, and if the same question were asked of a James

Bryant Conant, another science adviser, he might speak of the embarrassment that would follow a dud—thus, in both cases, joining ideas that had no logical relation to each other. Neither prisoners of war nor fear of failure, of course, posed any argument against a surprise demonstration.

There were two occasions, however, on which persons in a position to affect policy discussed the idea of a nonlethal demonstration. Those two conversations together consumed no more than a matter of minutes, so far as one can tell at this remove, and they, too, were off the record. But they seem to represent virtually the entire investment of the government of the United States in "mature consideration" of the subject.

The first discussion took place at a meeting of what was then called the Interim Committee, a striking gathering of military, scientific and government brass under the chairmanship of Secretary Stimson. This group, which included James Byrnes and Chief of Staff Gen. George C. Marshall, met on a number of occasions in May of 1945 to discuss policy issues raised by the new bomb, and Stimson recalled later that at one of their final meetings the members "carefully considered such alternatives as a detailed advance warning or a demonstration in some uninhabited area." But the minutes of the meeting, as well as the accounts of those present, suggest otherwise. The only exchange on the subject, in fact, took place during a luncheon break, and while we have no way of knowing what was actually said in that conversation, we do know what conclusion emerged from it. One participant, Arthur H. Compton, recalled later:

> Though the possibility of a demonstration that would not destroy human lives was attractive, no one could suggest a way in which it could be made so convincing that it would be likely to stop the war.

And the recording secretary of the meeting later recalled:

> Dr. Oppenheimer ... said he doubted whether there could be devised any sufficiently startling demonstration that would convince the Japanese they ought to throw in the sponge.

Two weeks later, four physicists who served as advisors to the Interim Committee met in Los Alamos to consider once again the question of demonstration. They were Arthur Compton, Enrico Fermi, Ernest Lawrence and Robert Oppenheimer—as distinguished an assembly of scientific talent as could be imagined—and they concluded, after a discussion of which we have no record: "We can propose no technical demonstration likely to bring an end to the war; we see no acceptable alternative to direct military use." That, so far as anyone can tell, was the end of it.

We cannot be sure that a milder report would have made a difference, for the Manhattan Project was gathering momentum as it moved toward the more steeply pitched inclines of May and June, but we can be sure that the idea of a demonstration was at that point spent. The Los Alamos report ended with something of a disclaimer ("We have, however, no claim to special competence ... "), but its message was clear enough. When asked about that report nine years later in his security hearings, Oppenheimer said, with what might have been a somewhat defensive edge in his voice, "We did not think exploding one of those things as a firecracker over the desert was likely to be very impressive."

Perhaps not. But those fragments are telling for another reason. If you listen to them carefully for a moment or two, you realize that these are the voices of nuclear physicists trying to imagine how a strange and distant people will react to an atomic blast. These are the voices of nuclear physicists dealing with psychological and anthropological questions about Japanese culture, Japanese temperament, Japanese will to resist—topics, we must assume, about which they knew almost nothing. They did not know yet what the bomb could actually do, since its first test was not to take place for another month. But in principle, at least, Oppenheimer and Fermi reflecting on matters relating to the Japanese national character should have had about the same force as Ruth Benedict and Margaret Mead reflecting on matters relating to high-energy physics, the first difference being that Benedict and Mead would not have presumed to do so, and the second being that no one in authority would have listened to them if they had.

The first of the two morals I want to draw from the foregoing—this being a parable, after all—is that in moments of critical contemplation, it is often hard to know where the competencies of soldiers and scientists and all the rest of us begin and end. Many an accidental judgment can emerge from such confusions.

But what if the conclusions of the scientists had been correct? What if some kind of demonstration had been staged in a lightly occupied part of Japan and it *had* been greeted as a firecracker in the desert? What then?

Let me shift gears for a moment and discuss the subject in another way. It is standard wisdom for everyone in the United States old enough to remember the war, and for most of those to whom it is ancient history, that the bombings of Hiroshima and Nagasaki were the only alternative to an all-out invasion of the Japanese mainland involving hundreds of thousands and perhaps millions of casualties on both sides. Unless the Japanese came to understand the need to surrender quickly, we would have been drawn by an almost magnetic force toward those dreaded beaches. This has become an almost automatic pairing of ideas, an article of common lore. If you lament that so many civilians were incinerated or blown to bits in Hiroshima and Nagasaki, then somebody will remind you of the American lives thus saved. Truman was the person most frequently asked to account for the bombings, and his views were emphatic on the subject:

> It was a question of saving hundreds of thousands of American lives. I don't mind telling you that you don't feel normal when you have to plan hundreds of thousands of complete, final deaths of American boys who are alive and joking and having fun while you are doing your planning. You break your heart and your head trying to figure out a way to save one life. The name given to our invasion plan was "Olympic," but I saw nothing godly about the killing of all the people that would be necessary to make that invasion. I could not worry about what history would say about my personal morality. I made the only decision I ever knew how to make. I did what I thought was right.*

Veterans of the war, and particularly those who had reason to suppose that they would have been involved in an invasion, have drawn that same connection

---

*Merle Miller notes, in *Plain Speaking: An Oral Biography of Harry S. Truman,* that Truman may have had moments of misgiving: "My only insight into Mr. Truman's feeling about the Bomb and its dropping, and it isn't much, came one day in his private library at the Truman Memorial Library. In one corner was every book ever published on the bomb, and at the end of one was Horatio's speech in the last scene of *Hamlet.*" Truman had underlined these words:

(continued on p. 80)

repeatedly, most recently Paul Fussell in the pages of *The New Republic*. Thank God for the bomb, the argument goes, it saved the lives of countless numbers of us. And so, in a sense, it may have.

But the destruction of Hiroshima and Nagasaki had nothing to do with it. It only makes sense to assume, even if few people were well enough positioned in early August to see the situation whole, that there simply was not going to be an invasion. Not ever.

For what sane power, with the atomic weapon securely in its arsenal, would hurl a million or more of its sturdiest young men on a heavily fortified mainland? To imagine anyone ordering an invasion when the means were at hand to blast Japan into a sea of gravel at virtually no cost in American lives is to imagine a madness beyond anything even the worst of war can induce. The invasion had not yet been called off, granted. But it surely would have been, and long before the November 1 deadline set for it.

The United States did not become a nuclear power on August 6, with the destruction of Hiroshima. It became a nuclear power on July 16, when the first test device was exploded in Alamogordo, New Mexico. Uncertainties remained, of course, many of them. But from that moment on, the United States knew how to produce a bomb, knew how to deliver it and knew it would work. Stimpson said shortly after the war that the bombings of Hiroshima and Nagasaki "ended the ghastly specter of a clash of great land armies," but he could have said, with greater justice, that the ghastly specter ended at Alamogordo. Churchill came close to making exactly that point when he first learned of the New Mexico test:

> To quell the Japanese resistance man by man and conquer the country yard by yard might well require the loss of a million American lives and half that number of British . . . Now all that nightmare picture had vanished.

It *had* vanished. The age of inch-by-inch crawling over enemy territory, the age of Guadalcanal and Iwo Jima and Okinawa, was just plain over.

The point is that once we had the bomb and were committed to its use, the terrible weight of invasion no longer hung over our heads. The Japanese were incapable of mounting any kind of offensive, as every observer has agreed, and it was our option when to close with the enemy and thus risk casualties. So we could have easily afforded to hold for a moment, to think it over, to introduce what Dwight Eisenhower called "that awful thing" to the world on the basis of something closer to mature consideration. We could have afforded to detonate a bomb over some less lethal target and then pause to see what happened. And do it a second time, maybe a third. And if none of those demonstrations had made a difference, presumably we would have had to strike harder: Hiroshima

---

And let me speak to the yet unknowing world
How these things came about. So shall you hear
Of carnal, bloody, and unnatural acts,
Of accidental judgments, casual slaughters
Of deaths put on by cunning and forced cause,
And, in this upshot, purposes mistook
Fall'n on the inventors' heads.

and Nagasaki would still have been there a few weeks later for that purpose, silent and untouched—"unspoiled" was the term Gen. H. H. Arnold used—for whatever came next. Common lore also has it that there were not bombs enough for such niceties, but that seems not to have been the case. The United States was ready to deliver a third bomb toward the end of August, and Groves had already informed Marshall and Stimson that three or four more bombs would be available in September, a like number in October, at least five in November, and seven in December, with substantial increases to follow in early 1946. Even if we assume that Groves was being too hopeful about the productive machinery he had set in motion, as one expert close to the matter has suggested, a formidable number of bombs would have been available by the date originally set for invasion.

Which brings us back to the matter of momentum. The best way to tell the story of those days is to say that the "decision to drop" had become a force like gravity. It had taken life. The fact that it existed supplied its meaning, its reason for being. Elting E. Morison, Stimson's biographer, put it well:

> Any process started by men toward a special end tends, for reasons logical, biological, aesthetic or whatever they may carry forward, if other things remain equal, to its climax. [This is] the inertia developed in a human system . . . In a process where such a general tendency has been set to work it is difficult to separate the moment when men were still free to choose from the moment, if such there was, when they were no longer free to choose.

I have said very little about Nagasaki so far because it was not the subject of any thought at all. The orders of the bomber command were to attack Japan as soon as the bombs were ready. One was ready on August 9. Boom. When Groves was later asked why the attack on Nagasaki had come so soon after the attack on Hiroshima, leaving so little time for the Japanese to consider what had happened to them, he simply said: "Once you get your opponent reeling, you keep him reeling and never let him recover." And that is the point, really. There is no law of nature that compels a winning side to press its superiority, but it is hard to slow down, hard to relinquish an advantage, hard to rein the fury. The impulse to charge ahead, to strike at the throat, is so strong a habit of war that it almost ranks as a reflex, and if that thought does not frighten us when we consider our present nuclear predicament, nothing will. Many a casual slaughter can emerge from such moods.

If it is true, as I have suggested, that there were few military or logistic reasons for striking as sharply as we did and that the decision to drop moved in on the crest of an almost irreversible current, then it might be sensible to ask, on the fortieth anniversary of the event, what some of the drifts were that became a part of that larger current. An adequate accounting would have to consider a number of military, political and other matters far beyond the reach of this brief essay, the most important of them by far being the degree to which the huge shadow of the Soviet Union loomed over both official meetings and private thoughts. It is nearly impossible to read the remaining record without assuming that the wish to make a loud announcement to the Russians was a persuasive factor in the minds of many of the principal participants. There were other drifts as well, of course, and I would like to note a few of the sort that sometimes occur to social scientists.

For one thing, an extraordinary amount of money and material had been invested in the Manhattan Project—both of them in short supply in a wartime economy—and many observers thought that so large a public expense would be all the more willingly borne if it were followed by a striking display of what the money had been spent for.

And, too, extraordinary investments had been made in men and talent, both of them in short supply in a wartime economy. The oldest of the people involved in the Manhattan Project—soldiers, engineers and scientists—made sacrifices in the form of separated families, interrupted careers and a variety of other discomforts, and it makes a certain psychological sense that a decisive strike would serve as a kind of vindication for all the trouble. The youngest of them, though, had been held out of combat, thus avoiding the fate of so many men of their generation, by accidents of professional training, personal skill and sheer timing. The project was their theater of war, and it makes even more psychological sense that some of them would want the only shot they fired to be a truly resonant one.

The dropping of such a bomb, moreover, could serve as an ending, something sharp and distinct in a world that had become ever more blurred. The Grand Alliance was breaking up, and with it all hope for a secure postwar world. Roosevelt was dead. The future was full of ambiguity. And, most important, everybody was profoundly tired. In circumstances like that, a resounding strike would serve to clarify things, to give them form, to tidy them up a bit.

There are other matters one might point to, some of them minor, some of them major, all of them strands in the larger weave. There was a feeling, expressed by scientists and government officials alike, that the world needed a rude and decisive shock to awaken it to the realities of the atomic age. There was a feeling, hard to convey in words but easy to sense once one has become immersed in some of the available material, that the bomb had so much power and majesty, was so compelling a force, that one was almost required to give it birth and a chance to mature. There was a feeling, born of war, that for all its ferocity the atomic bomb was nevertheless no more than a minor increment on a scale of horror that already included the firebombings of Tokyo and other Japanese cities. And there was a feeling, also born of war, that living creatures on the other side, even the children, had somehow lost title to the mercies that normally accompany the fact of being human.

The kinds of points I have been making need to be stated either very precisely or in some detail. I have not yet learned to do the former; I do not have space enough here for the latter. So let me just end with the observation that human decisions do not always emerge from reflective counsels where facts are arrayed in order and logic is the prevailing currency of thought. They emerge from complex fields of force, in which the vanities of leaders and the moods of constituencies and the inertias of bureaucracies play a critical part. That is as important a lesson as one can learn from the events of 1945—and as unnerving a one.

The bombings of Hiroshima and Nagasaki supply a rich case study for people who must live in times like ours. It is not important for us to apportion shares of responsibility to persons who played their parts so long ago, and I have not meant to do so here: these were unusually decent and compassionate people for the most part, operating with reflexes that had been tempered by war. We need to attend to such histories as this, however, because they provide the clearest illustrations we have of what human beings can do—this being the final moral to be drawn from our parable—when they find themselves in moments of crisis and literally have more destructive power at their disposal than they know what to do with. That is as good an argument for disarming as any that can be imagined.

Questions for Discussion

1. Do you like the title of this essay? If you do, explain why. If you don't, offer a title you think is more effective or appropriate.
2. How important is the essay's subordinate persuasive aim? Could this essay be classified as persuasive aim writing? Explain your answer.
3. This essay was written for a politically liberal readership. How would this essay differ if the author were writing for political conservatives? What changes would you recommend?
4. Why does the author call his story a "parable"? What is the desired impact of this word choice?
5. Explain the organization of this essay. Why is it organized the way it is?

Opportunities for Writing

1. Describe the city of Hiroshima or Nagasaki before or after the dropping of the atomic bomb. Write your essay for a special issue of your school newspaper on the anniversary of the Hiroshima and Nagasaki bombings.
2. Interview a man or woman who served as a soldier during World War II. How did this individual serve during the war? How did this experience influence his or her life? Is this individual's experience pertinent to your life? Explain why it is or isn't.
3. Recall your memories of a war that you participated in directly or observed indirectly through newspapers and television. What did you learn from this war? Address your essay to a friend or family member who is joining the military.

Columbus and His Four Fateful Voyages

DAVID GELMAN

David Gelman was born in New York and attended Brooklyn College (now part of the City University of New York). A journalist, Gelman has been a reporter for the New York Post *and* Newsday. *In addition, he has been an evaluation officer and special projects director for the U.S. Peace Corps. For most of his career, Gelman has written for* Newsweek; *he won the National Magazine Award for his story "Negro in America" (1968), a citation for excellence from the Overseas Press Club for a Vietnam story (1973), and a Page One Award from the Newspaper Guild (1978). "Columbus and His Four Fateful Voyages" was published in a special issue of* Newsweek *(Fall/Winter 1991) that focused on the quincentennial of Columbus's first voyage. This issue was produced in conjunction with the "Seeds of Change," a Smithsonian exhibit that featured the "'intermingling of peoples, animals, plants, and diseases that resulted when the old and new worlds collided." Using frequent tagging of his sources within the text, Gelman writes this essay from the perspective of knowledge by observation.*

Marooned on Jamaica, ailing and out of favor, with perhaps two embittered years of life remaining to him, Christopher Columbus dispatched to his monarchs a rambling, semi-coherent letter invoking at one point a tribute to himself, written as if it were meant to be sung by angels:

> "When He saw thee of an age with which He was content, He caused thy name to sound marvellously in the land. The Indies, which are so rich a part of the world, He gave thee for thine own ... Of the barriers of the Ocean Sea, which were closed with such mighty chains, He gave thee the keys ... "

It was an encomium he could no longer expect from the world. Returning from his epic first voyage, Columbus had been welcomed with honors, a triumphal march, a summons to dine with the king and queen. By the time he died 13 years later, many of his rights and titles had been stripped away, and the crown barely acknowledged his existence. He had become an embarrassment, blamed for instigating a ruthless slave trade in the New World and making a botch of the settlements he established there. To a large extent, this extraordinary reversal of fortune was brought on by his own blundering greed. Yet the fault was not entirely his. Above all, perhaps, he was guilty of having been too faithful to his mission, an endeavor launched "in the name of Jesus," but more palpably driven by the quest for gold. Columbus was first and foremost a man of his time, the product of an ethos shaped as much by commerce as by Christianity, in which it seemed equally the work of the Lord to find the gold and propagate the faith.

It's easy enough to be cynical about him nowadays. Over the centuries, his reputation has tended to expand and deflate like some unruly Thanksgiving Day parade balloon. Yet in the broad sweep of history, most scholars agree, Columbus is a figure of unique importance. If his landing on American soil was not the first by a European (that distinction probably belongs to the Norseman, Leif Eriksson, who is believed to have touched somewhere on the Newfoundland coast around 1000), it was the most decisive. It marked the beginning of sustained contact between the Old World and the New—the beginning, really, of the world we know. "The likelihood of transatlantic voyages before Columbus was so great, you can probably say it did happen, but there was no impact, no consequence," says historian William McNeill. "What makes Columbus's voyage important was the response of Europe to the news of the discovery. Europe was poised to follow up."

5   Europe had been seeking some such expansion of its horizons for centuries. By the Middle Ages, Europeans were already beguiled by the opulent East, which remained, however, veiled in mystery. The elite could purchase precious silks, carpets and spices from Genoese, Venetian or Pisan merchants, who got them from Turkish traders at Alexandria, Aleppo or Damascus. But, for the most part, they were blocked from venturing any farther eastward. "This was the Iron Curtain of the late Middle Ages," writes Daniel Boorstin, author of "The Discoverers." Then, observes Boorstin, "for a single century, from about 1250

to about 1350, that curtain was lifted, and there was direct human contact between Europe and China."

The brief opening arose courtesy of Genghis Khan, who led his Mongol armies down to Beijing in 1214 and spent the next 50 years expanding his empire across much of Eastern Asia and Eastern Europe. The khan may have been looked on as a barbarian, but he and his heirs encouraged free commercial trade by offering the Europeans well-policed roads with low customs fees. One taker was the adventurous 17-year-old Venetian named Marco Polo, who made the overland trek to China with his father and uncle and returned 24 years later with tales of unbounded wealth and luxury. Observes Boorstin: "Without Marco Polo, who stirred the European imagination with impatience to reach Cathay [the khans' capital city], would there have been a Columbus?"

The Chinese conquest of the Mongols in 1368 rang down the curtain on land travel to the East again, shifting momentum to the search for a sea route. No one pushed this quest more zealously than the Portuguese. Historians believe the Portuguese launched several forays westward on the Atlantic in the decades before 1492, but their main thrust was toward the southern tip of Africa. Portuguese ships kept inching down the west coast of the continent until a skipper named Bartolomeu Dias rounded the Cape of Good Hope and confirmed the existence of a water connection to the Indian Ocean. Forced to turn back by his men in the face of threatening seas, Dias returned to Lisbon with the news just in time to squelch the patiently nurtured ambitions of a Genoese named Columbus.

Picture the Discoverer at this moment in his life: an obscure navigator nearing 40, deeply in debt, sustained only by a daring notion of sailing west to reach the East and a cockeyed idea of how much ocean he must cross to get there. When Dias's storm-battered caravels limped into the harbor of Lisbon in December 1488, Columbus is thought to have been in Portugal trying for the second time to wangle King João II's backing for a westward expedition. With the eastward passage around Africa now feasible, Columbus's project was judged superfluous.

But the navigator was used to rejection. Since 1484, Columbus had devoted himself to promoting his "Enterprise of the Indies," first in Portugal and then in Spain. Now, like some wild-eyed adventurer in a Robert Louis Stevenson novel, Columbus petitioned Ferdinand and Isabella, flourishing a map that he had modified with the dubious geographic calculations of Ptolemy and Marco Polo. In 1491, a special commission, headed by Isabella's confessor, rendered an unfavorable opinion of the plan; in the spring of 1492, a second commission dismissed it anew. But after 10 years of war, Spain succeeded that spring in liberating Granada from the Moors, freeing the monarchs to turn to other matters. A last-ditch effort by Columbus's supporter Luis de Santángel, the king's financial adviser, convinced them that they might gain huge influence from Columbus's venture at relatively small cost. After eight desperate years, the plan was at last approved.

On the whole, Columbus is probably given less credit than he deserves for his almost fanatical persistence. Given that he was an impecunious foreigner with an uncertain grasp of geography, he "had to have been a very convincing public-relations man," says McNeill. "That a foreigner would be able to sell that bill of goods to the Spanish crown is really quite amazing."

After all the struggle and rejection, Columbus at last had a contract in his pocket, signed by the Spanish monarchs. In the Capitulations of Santa Fe, as the document was called, the crown agreed to grant him noble status, together with the offices of admiral, viceroy and governor in all the islands and mainlands that he might claim for Castile in the Atlantic. As for profits from the venture, one tenth, plus some investment options, would go to Columbus and the rest to the crown. "Here he was, an outsider from Genoa who was promised one tenth of all the riches and who managed to get himself classified as a noble in Spanish society," notes McNeill. "Columbus did extremely well for himself."

Finally, the great voyage of discovery got underway. The day before Columbus set sail was also the deadline for all Jews to leave the country. The same tide that bore him seaward carried the last of Spain's estimated 100,000 Jews into centuries-long exile. Samuel Eliot Morison, the patrician yachtsman-historian who wrote what has become the standard reference work on Columbus, imagined the embarkation scene as it might have been painted by El Greco: "One of those gray, calm days" under motionless cloud masses, "when the sea is like a mirror of burnished rigged steel." The three square-rigged sailing vessels—the largest, the *Santa María,* was no bigger than a tennis court—begin moving down the Saltés River at about 5:15 A.M. It is Friday, Aug. 3, 1492. Not a leaf stirs as the men pull the oars. Morison even hears the friars chanting their morning prayer in the monastery of La Rábida on a cliff overlooking the harbor: "The Captain General, who often had joined in that hymn during his stay at La Rábida removes his hat; seamen who are not working follow his example . . ." It's a scene of hushed, poetic piety, one we almost want to believe—because history, in fact, is about to take one of its great leaps.

But between the embarkation and the sighting of land in the Americas, there was almost no drama. There were no storms or prolonged calms; the winds were brisk and steady. Compared with what later befell explorers Vasco da Gama and Ferdinand Magellan, or some of Columbus's own subsequent crossings, it was practically a luxury cruise. The days were balmy, the men went swimming at times in the glassy sea; at night they slept on deck.

Not all was serene, even so. Columbus kept a detailed journal of the voyage, which comes down to us in the form of an abstract by a Dominican monk, Bartolomé de Las Casas, sometimes in Columbus's words, more often in his own. From the journal and other sources it emerges that, experienced though they were, the crew were scarcely eager to sail off into a limitless sea. It was a measure of their uneasiness that little more than a week after they left the Canary Islands the voyagers began seeing signs of land on every side: "Friday, September 14th: The crew of the *Niña* stated that they had seen a tern and a tropic bird; and these birds never go more than twenty-five leagues from land."

"Monday, September 17th: They saw much vegetation and it was very delicate and was weed from rocks . . . They concluded that they were near land."

By Oct. 8, they did seem to be nearing something. "Thanks be to God," wrote Columbus, "the breezes were softer than in April at Seville . . . they are so laden with scent." And still there was no land. "Here the men could now bear no more; they complained of the long voyage." By some accounts, the crew wanted to turn back, but Columbus pleaded, if they didn't reach land in two or three days, "cut off my head and you shall return."

It was not until two hours past midnight on Oct. 12 that a lookout on the *Pinta* actually saw what looked like a line of white cliffs to the west. Ten weeks after he embarked from Palos de la Frontera, Columbus landed on an island he christened San Salvador. Scholars still debate whether this was Samana Cay, San Salvador (Watlings Island) or any of a number of small islands in the Bahamas. What we do know is that after Columbus landed, his explorations took him to several other islands, including Cuba and Hispaniola (today, the Dominican Republic and Haiti). On Christmas Eve, 1492, the *Santa María* ran aground on shoals off Haiti's coast and had to be abandoned. Columbus had to leave 39 men behind in a colony he named La Navidad (for Christmas). Not to waste an opportunity, he ordered them to trade goods with the natives in exchange for gold.

The hope of finding some putative mother lode of gold drove Columbus relentlessly through the islands. Gold danced before his eyes, in the necklaces, bracelets and nose rings the natives wore: "October 13th:. . . So I resolved to go to the south-west to seek the gold and precious stones." "October 23rd: I did not delay longer here [on Cabo del Isleo] since I see that here there is no gold mine." In "The Conquest of Paradise," author Kirkpatrick Sale, a dedicated Columbus revisionist, counts no fewer than 140 uses of the word *oro* (gold) in Columbus's journal of the first voyage. He apparently could not admire the lush beauty of the islands without also estimating their potential value. "Here was a true son of Renaissance materialism," Sale snorts. Historian Carla Phillips demurs. Columbus, she argues, was desperate to justify the costs of the enterprise. "It's important for him to find vast harbors and rich mines in order to confirm his theories about what is out there."

Toward the natives, Columbus behaved with a kind of schizoid duplicity. From the moment he beheld them he saw an attractive, peaceable and friendly people who would make good Christians and "good servants." He rewarded their generosity with hawk bells, glass beads and other "trifles of small value," and periodically took them captive. And sometimes he dropped all pretense of good will: ". . . these people are very unskilled in arms . . . when Your Highnesses so command, they can all be carried off to Castile or held captive in the island itself, since with fifty men they would be all kept in subjection and forced to do whatever may be wished." Given the attitude of their visitors, it's not surprising the natives grew hostile—so that before he left for home, Columbus felt obliged to fortify La Navidad settlement, which was nevertheless wiped out to the last man by the islanders.

Meanwhile, Columbus grew increasingly anxious about finding the mainland. He still seemed to believe Cipango (Japan) or Cathay (China) was just around the next cove. But there were only more islands. (On his second voyage, still thwarted in the search, he would take depositions from his crew declaring Cuba to be part of the Asia mainland.) He sailed home, finally, aboard the Niña, picking up the westerlies he needed by heading north from Hispaniola, and arriving on March 15, 1493, 32 weeks after he left, without having lost a man at sea. "He was a very competent seaman," says McNeill.

When Leif Eriksson reached the North American continent the news fell like a tree in the forest; almost no one heard it. When Columbus announced his discovery, in a letter to Luis de Santángel written during his return voyage, the word spread quickly, thanks to an already vigorous printing industry. Though some challenged Columbus's assertion that he had reached the Indies, the impact on the European imagination was profound, providing a forward thrust to the whole enterprise of New World exploration.

In response to his famous missive, Columbus received a letter from Ferdinand and Isabella, commanding him to court and addressing him as "Don Cristóbal Colón, their Admiral of the Ocean Sea, Viceroy and Governor of the Islands that he hath discovered in the Indies." He would never again experience anything like the grand reception he was accorded, first at Córdoba, then at Barcelona, where he created a sensation by presenting to the monarchs seven natives of "the Indies," along with gold artifacts and samples of allegedly rare spices. "It would have been well for him had he then taken his profits and retired with honor, leaving to others the responsibility of colonization," observes Morison. Instead, he embarked westward again, this time in the panoply of 17 ships, with 1,500 crewmen, soldiers and colonists and the requisite plants, domestic animals and tools for a permanent settlement. But the cresting hopes that rode with him were doomed to failure. From the moment of his return, the arc of the admiral's career sweeps downward. His relations with the natives rapidly descended into a kind of Kurtzian darkness.

With La Navidad destroyed, Columbus founded a new colony at La Isabela, closer to the rumored source of gold. But it was plagued by illness and rebellion. The admiral had no gift for administration; he could not control hundreds of Spaniards avid for conquest. There were repeated episodes of rape, pillage and murder by marauding bands of Spaniards. Returning from a trip to find a mutiny brewing, Columbus placed all munitions on board his flagship under command of his younger brother Diego. But when Columbus was away, the violence erupted again. Later, several of the troublemakers seized some caravels that Columbus's other brother Bartolomé had brought from Spain and sailed home, where they circulated slanders against the Columbus brothers.

Historians say Columbus may have made a fatal mistake at this point when he ignored a summons from Ferdinand and Isabella to come home. Instead of appeasing the monarchs and silencing the slanders, he decided to deal with the turbulent situation at La Isabela and try to begin regular exports to Spain. As a first step, he rounded up about 1,600 Tainos who had been resisting the Spaniards and crammed 550 of them aboard four ships, to be transported home as slaves. Then he and his brothers set about subjugating all of Hispaniola to reap its gold, with the use of slave labor.

25 They did, finally, find a rich vein of gold in the southern part of the island; eventually, the gold strike made Columbus rich and repaid the crown some of its initial investment. He nevertheless returned home under a cloud, still having failed to establish a stable colony. What's more, he had angered the monarchs by enslaving people now regarded as Spanish subjects. It was more than a year before the crown would outfit another voyage. On this third crossing, he managed at last to reach mainland America—Venezuela, as it happened. Ill at the time and slipping into what some historians think was a half-mad mysticism, he speculated that he had found the Garden of Eden itself. Phillips insists he was sane. "He had a very firm belief that he was chosen by God," she argues. "His whole mental map was Biblical."

Meanwhile, conditions on Hispaniola had grown worse under Diego, who had been left in charge. Because of the negative reports filtering back,

Ferdinand and Isabella ordered an investigation, which ended with all three Columbus brothers shipped home in chains. The monarchs appointed a new governor of the islands, Nicolás de Ovando, who set sail with a fleet twice the size of Columbus's largest. When Columbus embarked on his fourth and final voyage in 1502, still hoping to find a direct passage from Cuba to Asia, he was reduced to four small ships and a kind of renegade status, barred from the colony at Santo Domingo. His worm-eaten boats, barely afloat, had to be grounded on a Jamaican reef. A caravel rescued the expedition a year later, but after his return to Spain in November 1504, the admiral never sailed again.

Columbus spent the rest of his life lobbying to have his grants and titles restored. On May 20, 1506, he died at 55, feeling betrayed by the monarchs he thought he had served with the steadfastness of a Job. The glory passed to those who came after him. After Amerigo Vespucci reached the mainland of the New World, the German cartographer Martin Waldseemüller named it America on his famous map of 1507, in Vespucci's honor. Europe, at any rate, remained less interested in settling the Americas than finding ways around them. Just before the end of the 15th century, a Portuguese named Vasco da Gama completed the trip that Bartolomeu Dias had begun, sailing around the tip of Africa to Calicut, on the southwest coast of India. By 1515, the treasures of India, China and Japan were coming to Europe around the Cape of Good Hope on Portuguese ships.

In 1513, another explorer searching for gold in the Americas, Vasco Núuñez de Balboa, climbed a peak on the Panamanian isthmus and beheld the mighty Pacific, the first European to do so. And in 1519, Ferdinand Megellan, a Portuguese of aristocratic birth, sailing for the Spanish crown, undertook the most extraordinary voyage of all. Setting out with five barely seaworthy ships, racked by violent storms, near starvation and a mutiny, he managed to find a passage from the east coast of South America to the Pacific through the straits that now bear his name. His ships, or what was left of them, then completed a three-year circumnavigation of the globe that Magellan himself did not survive.

Yet it is the comparatively idyllic first voyage of Columbus that has come down to us, in almost folkloric colors, as the great voyage of discovery. We know little of what the Vikings felt as they sailed to Vinland in the icy dawn of modern history. But it is Columbus, pressing confidently into uncharted seas, leaning forward to catch the first spice-laden scent of a continent he never doubted he would find, who speaks to the voyager in all of us.

Questions for Discussion

1. This essay displays a complex chronology: it starts during the fourth voyage of Columbus, then flashes back to the time before his first voyage. Why does the author organize the narrative this way? What impact does this organization have on your initial impression of Columbus?
2. Notice that the author uses a literary allusion to a major character from Conrad's *Heart of Darkness*—Mr. Kurtz: "His relations with the natives rapidly descended into a kind of Kurtzian darkness." What is the purpose of this literary allusion? Do you consider it effective? What do you think of this technique of using literary allusions?

3. This essay was written for a general readership. How would the author revise this essay for an audience of historians? sailors? Native Americans? What specific changes would you recommend?
4. Do you like this title? If so, why? If not, how would you title this essay?
5. What is the author's attitude toward Columbus? Cite specific passages to support your answer.

Opportunities for Writing

1. Depict the island of Hispaniola as it was before and after the voyages of Columbus. What did it look like? Who lived there? What was it like to live there? Write your essay for a museum display on the voyages of Columbus.
2. For the October 9 (Leif Eriksson Day) issue of your local newspaper, chronicle the voyage of Leif Eriksson to America. What was his voyage like? What lessons do you learn from his experience?
3. Discuss the reaction of the people of Europe to the "discovery" of a new world. What did people think? How did it influence their lives? What do you consider interesting or important about their reaction?
4. Recall your experience of "discovering" something. How old were you? What did you "discover"? How did you feel?

Thoreau

VIRGINIA WOOLF

A British novelist, essayist, and critic, Virginia Woolf (1882–1941) is considered to be one of the foremost novelists of the twentieth century. She was a member of a famous group of intellectuals called the Bloomsburys and cofounded the Hogarth Press, which published the writing of such authors as E. M. Forster, Gertrude Stein, T. S. Eliot, and Katherine Mansfield; Hogarth Press also published some of Woolf's writing. Woolf's works include these titles: Between the Acts *(1941),* The Years *(1937),* Flush *(1933),* The Waves *(1931),* A Room of One's Own *(1929),* To the Lighthouse *(1927),* Jacob's Room *(1927),* The Common Reader *(1925),* Mrs. Dalloway *(1925),* Night and Day *(1919), and* The Voyage Out *(1919). In the following essay, Woolf presents a character sketch of Henry David Thoreau and writes this biographical account, marking Thoreau's 100th birthday. The details in "Thoreau" are drawn from knowledge by observation—from her research of this "egoist" who calls for "simplicity," his friends, his world view, and his writings.*

A hundred years ago, on July 12, 1817, was born Henry David Thoreau, the son of a pencil maker in Concord, Massachusetts. He has been lucky in his biographers, who have been attracted to him not by his fame so much as by their sympathy with his views, but they have not been able to tell us a great deal about him that we shall not find in the books themselves. His life was not eventful; he had, as he says, "a real genius for staying at home." His mother was quick and voluble, and so fond of solitary rambling that one of her children narrowly escaped coming into the world in an open field. The father, on the other hand, was a "small, quiet, plodding man," with a faculty for making the best lead pencils in America, thanks to a secret of his own for mixing levigated plumbago with fuller's earth and water, rolling it into sheets, cutting it into strips, and burning it. He could at any rate afford, with much economy and a little help, to send his son to Harvard, although Thoreau himself did not attach much importance to this expensive opportunity. It is at Harvard, however, that he first becomes visible to us. A class mate saw much in him as a boy that we recognize later in the grown man, so that instead of a portrait we will quote what was visible about the year 1837 to the penetrating eye of the Rev. John Weiss:

> He was cold and unimpressible. The touch of his hand was moist and indifferent, as if he had taken up something when he saw your hand coming, and caught your grasp on it. How the prominent grey-blue eyes seemed to rove down the path, just in advance of his feet, as his grave Indian stride carried him down to University Hall. He did not care for people; his class-mates seemed very remote. This reverie hung always about him, and not so loosely as the odd garments which the pious household care furnished. Thought had not yet awakened his countenance; it was serene, but rather dull, rather plodding. The lips were not yet firm; there was almost a look of smug satisfaction lurking round their corners. It is plain now that he was preparing to hold his future views with great setness and personal appreciation of their importance. The nose was prominent, but its curve fell forward without firmness over the upper lip, and we remember him as looking very much like some Egyptian sculpture of faces, large-featured, but brooding, immobile, fixed in a mystic egoism. Yet his eyes were sometimes searching, as if he had dropped, or expected to find, something. In fact his eyes seldom left the ground, even in his more earnest conversations with you. . . .

He goes on to speak of the "reserve and inaptness" of Thoreau's life at college.

Clearly the young man thus depicted, whose physical pleasures took the form of walking and camping out, who smoked nothing but "dried lily stems," who venerated Indian relics as much as Greek classics, who in early youth had formed the habit of "settling accounts" with his own mind in a diary, where his thoughts, feelings, studies, and experiences had daily to be passed under review by that Egyptian face and searching eye—clearly this young man was destined to disappoint both parents and teachers and all who wished him to cut a figure in the world and become a person of importance. His first attempt to earn his living in the ordinary way by becoming a schoolmaster was brought to an end by the necessity of flogging his pupils. He proposed to talk morals to them instead. When the committee pointed out that the school would suffer from this "undue leniency" Thoreau solemnly beat six pupils and then resigned, saying that school-keeping "interfered with his arrangements." The arrangements that the penniless young man wished to carry out were probably assignations with certain pine trees, pools, wild animals, and Indian arrowheads in the neighbourhood, which had already laid their commands upon him.

But for a time he was to live in the world of men, at least in that very remarkable section of the world of which Emerson was the centre and which professed the Transcendentalist doctrines. Thoreau took up his lodgings in Emerson's house and very soon became, so his friends said, almost indistinguishable from the prophet himself. If you listened to them both talking with your eyes shut you could not be certain where Emerson left off and Thoreau began ". . . in his manners, in the tones of his voice, in his modes of expression, even in the hesitations and pauses of his speech, he had become the counterpart of Mr Emerson." This may well have been so. The strongest natures, when they are influenced, submit the most unreservedly: it is perhaps a sign of their strength. But that Thoreau lost any of his own force in the process, or took on permanently any colours not natural to himself the readers of his books will certainly deny.

The Transcendentalist movement, like most movements of vigour, represented the effort of one or two remarkable people to shake off the old clothes which had become uncomfortable to them and fit themselves more closely to what now appeared to them to be the realities. The desire for readjustment had, as Lowell has recorded and the Memoirs of Margaret Fuller bear witness, its ridiculous symptoms and its grotesque disciples. But of all the men and women who lived in an age when thought was remoulded in common, we feel that Thoreau was the one who had least to adapt himself, who was by nature most in harmony with the new spirit. He was by birth among those people, as Emerson expresses it, who have "silently given in their several adherence to a new hope, and in all companies do signify a greater trust in the nature and resources of man than the laws of the popular opinion will well allow." There were two ways of life which seemed to the leaders of the movement to give scope for the attainment of these new hopes; one in some cooperative community, such as Brook Farm; the other in solitude with nature. When the time came to make his choice Thoreau decided emphatically in favour of the second. "As for the communities," he wrote in his journal, "I think I had rather keep bachelor's quarters in hell than go to board in heaven." Whatever the theory might be, there was deep in his nature "a singular yearning to all wildness" which would have led him to some such experiment as that recorded in "Walden," whether it seemed good to others or not. In truth he was to put in practice the doctrines of the Transcendentalists more thoroughly than any one of them, and to prove what the resources of man are by putting his entire trust in them. Thus, having reached the age of 27, he chose a piece of land in a wood on the brink of the clear deep green waters of Walden Pond, built a hut with his own hands, reluctantly borrowing an axe for some part of the work, and settled down, as he puts it, "to front only the essential facts of life, and see if I could not learn what it had to teach, and not, when I came to die, discover that I had not lived."

5 And now we have a chance of getting to know Thoreau as few people are known, even by their friends. Few people, it is safe to say, take such an interest in themselves as Thoreau took in himself; for if we are gifted with an intense egoism we do our best to suffocate it in order to live on decent terms with our neighbours. We are not sufficiently sure of ourselves to break completely with the established order. This was Thoreau's adventure; his books are the record of that experiment and its results. He did everything he could to intensify his own understanding of himself, to foster whatever was peculiar, to isolate himself from contact with any force that might interfere with his immensely valuable gift of personality. It was his sacred duty, not to himself alone but to the world; and a man is scarcely an egoist who is an egoist on so grand a scale. When we read "Walden," the record of his two years in the woods, we have a sense of beholding life through a very powerful magnifying glass. To walk, to eat, to cut up

logs, to read a little, to watch the bird on the bough, to cook one's dinner—all these occupations when scraped clean and felt afresh prove wonderfully large and bright. The common things are so strange, the usual sensations so astonishing that to confuse or waste them by living with the herd and adopting habits that suit the greater number is a sin—an act of sacrilege. What has civilization to give, how can luxury improve upon these simple facts? "Simplicity, simplicity, simplicity!" is his cry. "Instead of three meals a day, if it be necessary eat but one; instead of a hundred dishes, five; and reduce other things in proportion."

But the reader may ask, what is the value of simplicity? Is Thoreau's simplicity simplicity for its own sake, and not rather a method of intensification, a way of setting free the delicate and complicated machinery of the soul, so that its results are the reverse of simple? The most remarkable men tend to discard luxury because they find that it hampers the play of what is much more valuable to them. Thoreau himself was an extremely complex human being, and he certainly did not achieve simplicity by living for two years in a hut and cooking his own dinner. His achievement was rather to lay bare what was within him—to let life take its own way unfettered by artificial constraints. "I did not wish to live what was not life, living is so dear; nor did I wish to practice resignation, unless it was quite necessary. I wanted to live deep and suck out all the marrow of life...." "Walden"—all his books, indeed—are packed with subtle, conflicting, and very fruitful discoveries. They are not written to prove something in the end. They are written as the Indians turn down twigs to mark their path through the forest. He cuts his way through life as if no one had ever taken that road before, leaving these signs for those who come after, should they care to see which way he went. But he did not wish to leave ruts behind him, and to follow is not an easy process. We can never lull our attention asleep in reading Thoreau by the certainty that we have now grasped his theme and can trust our guide to be consistent. We must always be ready to try something fresh; we must always be prepared for the shock of facing one of those thoughts in the original which we have known all our lives in reproductions. "All health and success does me good, however far off and withdrawn it may appear; all disease and failure helps to make me sad and do me evil, however much sympathy it may have with me or I with it." "Distrust all enterprises that require new clothes." "You must have a genius for charity as well as for anything else." That is a handful, plucked almost at random, and of course there are plenty of wholesome platitudes.

As he walked his woods, or sat for hours almost motionless like the sphinx of college days upon a rock watching the birds, Thoreau defined his own position to the world not only with unflinching honesty, but with a glow of rapture at his heart. He seems to hug his own happiness. Those years were full of revelations—so independent of other men did he find himself, so perfectly equipped by nature not only to keep himself housed, fed, and clothed, but also superbly entertained without any help from society. Society suffered a good many blows from his hand. He sets down his complaints so squarely that we cannot help suspecting that society might one of these days have come to terms with so noble a rebel. He did not want churches or armies, post-offices or newspapers, and very consistently he refused to pay his tithes and went into prison rather than pay his poll tax. All getting together in crowds for doing good or procuring pleasure was an intolerable infliction to him. Philanthropy was one of the sacrifices, he said, that he had made to a sense of duty. Politics seemed to him "unreal, incredible, insignificant," and most revolutions not so important as the drying up of a river or the death of a pine. He wanted only to be left alone tramping the woods in his suit of Vermont grey, unhampered even by those two pieces of limestone which lay upon his desk until they proved guilty of collecting the dust, and were at once thrown out of the window.

And yet this egoist was the man who sheltered runaway slaves in his hut; this hermit was the first man to speak out in public in defence of John Brown; this self-centred solitary could neither sleep nor think when Brown lay in prison. The truth is that anyone who reflects as much and as deeply as Thoreau reflected about life and conduct is possessed of an abnormal sense of responsibility to his kind, whether he chooses to live in a wood or to become President of the Republic. Thirty volumes of diaries which he would condense from time to time with infinite care into little books prove, moreover, that the independent man who professed to care so little for his fellows was possessed with an intense desire to communicate with them. "I would fain," he writes, "communicate the wealth of my life to men, would really give them what is most precious in my gift. . . . I have no private good unless it be my peculiar ability to serve the public. . . . I wish to communicate those parts of my life which I would gladly live again." No one can read him and remain unaware of this wish. And yet it is a question whether he ever succeeded in imparting his wealth, in sharing his life. When we have read his strong and noble books, in which every word is sincere, every sentence wrought as well as the writer knows how, we are left with a strange feeling of distance; here is a man who is trying to communicate but who cannot do it. His eyes are on the ground or perhaps on the horizon. He is never speaking directly to us; he is speaking partly to himself and partly to something mystic beyond our sight. "Says I to myself," he writes, "should be the motto to my journal," and all his books are journals. Other men and women were wonderful and very beautiful, but they were distant; they were different; he found it very hard to understand their ways. They were as "curious to him as if they had been prairie dogs." All human intercourse was infinitely difficult; the distance between one friend and another was unfathomable; human relationships were very precarious and terribly apt to end in disappointment. But, although concerned and willing to do what he could short of lowering his ideals, Thoreau was aware that the difficulty was one that could not be overcome by taking pains. He was made differently from other people. "If a man does not keep pace with his companions, perhaps it is because he hears a different drummer. Let him step to the music which he hears, however measured or far away." He was a wild man, and he would never submit to be a tame one. And for us here lies his peculiar charm. He hears a different drummer. He is a man into whom nature has breathed other instincts than ours, to whom she has whispered, one may guess, some of her secrets.

"It appears to be a law," he says, "that you cannot have a deep sympathy with both man and nature. Those qualities which bring you near to the one estrange you from the other." Perhaps that is true. The greatest passion of his life was his passion for nature. It was more than a passion, indeed; it was an affinity; and in this he differs from men like White and Jefferies. He was gifted, we are told, with an extraordinary keenness of the senses; he could see and hear what other men could not; his touch was so delicate that he could pick up a dozen pencils accurately from a box holding a bushel; he could find his way alone through thick woods at night. He could lift a fish out of the stream with his hands; he could charm a wild squirrel to nestle in his coat; he could sit so still that the animals went on with their play round him. He knew the look of the country so intimately that if he had waked in a meadow he could have told the time of year within a day or two from the flowers at his feet. Nature had made it easy for him to pick up a living without effort. He was so skilled with his hands that by labouring forty days he could live at leisure for the rest of the year. We scarcely know whether to call him the last of an older race of men, or the first of one that is to come. He had the toughness, the stoicism, the unspoilt senses of an Indian, combined with the self-consciousness, the exacting discontent, the susceptibility of the most modern. At times he seems to reach beyond our human powers in what he perceives upon the horizon of humanity. No philanthropist ever hoped more of mankind, or set higher and nobler tasks before him, and those whose ideal of passion and of service is the loftiest are those who have the greatest capacities for giving, although life may not ask of them all that they can give, and forces them to hold in reserve rather than to lavish. However much Thoreau had been able to do he would still have seen possibilities beyond; he would always have remained, in one sense, unsatisfied. That is one of the reasons why he is able to be the companion of a younger generation.

He died when he was in the full tide of life, and had to endure long illness within doors. But from nature he had learnt both silence and stoicism. He had never spoken of the things that had moved him most in his private fortunes. But from nature, too, he had learnt to be content, not thoughtlessly or selfishly content, and certainly not with resignation, but with a healthy trust in the wisdom of nature, and in nature, as he says, there is no sadness. "I am enjoying existence as much as ever," he wrote from his deathbed, "and regret nothing." He was talking to himself of moose and Indian when, without a struggle, he died.

Questions for Discussion

1. The author includes a long quotation describing Thoreau. What is the purpose of this quotation? Is it necessary? Why do you think it is or isn't?
2. Are you satisfied with the way the author has identified sources of information? Do you know which information comes from which source?
3. Consider the essay's characterization of Thoreau. Does the essay paint a vivid picture of this individual? If so, which of the descriptive and narrative details do you consider essential to the portrait? If not, which details do you think are missing?
4. Why do you think the author concludes this essay with the death of Thoreau? What is her purpose in doing so? Do you like this ending? Would this essay be more or less effective without the final paragraph?
5. What significance does the author derive from this portrait of Thoreau? Does this seem logical and appropriate to you? Why or why not?

Opportunities for Writing

1. Depict Walden Pond as it looks today. What sights and sounds characterize it? Do you think Thoreau would still enjoy it? Explain why you believe he would or wouldn't. In studying this subject, interview visitors to the site and review pertinent newspaper and magazine articles, especially for available photographs. Address your essay to the membership of a local conservation society.
2. Compose a portrait of Thoreau's friend and teacher, Ralph Waldo Emerson. Several biographies are available that could serve as your sources of information. Who was he? Why is he important? What is your impression of him?
3. Discuss your favorite experience of walking through a woods. How old were you? Where did you go? What did you think? How did you feel? Do you still go walking through this woods?
4. Describe a friend of yours who enjoys solitude. What is he or she like? How did you come to be friends? Write your essay as a gift to this friend.

The Case of Harry Houdini

Daniel Mark Epstein

*A writer and teacher, Daniel Mark Epstein was born in Washington, D.C., and graduated from Kenyon College. Among his publications are three collections of poetry—*Young Men's Gold *(1978),* The Follies *(1977), and* No Vacancies in Hell *(1973), as well as two stage plays—*The Gayety Burlesque *(1978) and* Jenny and the Phoenix *(1977). "The Case of Harry Houdini" first appeared in* The New Criterion *in October 1986 and can also be found in Epstein's* The Star of Wonder *(1986). To research Houdini and his "magic," Epstein relies on knowledge by observation—for example, Epstein's father's memories of Houdini's act; various newspaper accounts; comments of Bess Houdini, his wife; and observations of Houdini's personal friend Sir Arthur Conan Doyle.*

When my grandfather was a boy he saw the wild-haired magician escape from a riveted boiler. He would remember that image as long as he lived, and how Harry Houdini, the rabbi's son, defeated the German Imperial Police at the beginning of the twentieth century. Hearing those tales and others even more incredible, sixty years after the magician's death we cannot help but wonder: What did the historical Houdini *really* do? And how on earth did he do it?

The newspaper accounts are voluminous, and consistent. The mere cataloguing of Houdini's escapes soon grows tedious, which they were not, to be sure, in the flesh. But quickly: the police stripped him naked and searched him thoroughly before binding his wrists and ankles with five pairs of irons. Then they would slam him into a cell and turn the key of a three-bond burglar-proof lock. He escaped, hundreds of times, from the most secure prisons in the world. He hung upside down in a straitjacket from the tallest buildings in America, and escaped in full view of the populace. He was chained hand and foot and nailed into a packing case weighted with lead; the packing case was dropped from a tugboat into New York's

East River and ninety seconds later Houdini surfaced. The packing case was hauled up intact, with the manacles inside, still fastened. He was sealed into a paper bag and got out without disturbing the seal. He was sewn into a huge football, into the belly of a whale, and escaped. In California he was buried six feet underground, and clawed his way out. He did this, he did that. These are facts that cannot be exaggerated, for they were conceived as exaggerations. We know he did these things because his actions were more public than the proceedings of Congress, and most of them he performed over and over, so no one would miss the point.

How did he do such things? For all rational people who are curious, sixty years after the magician's death, there is good news and bad news. The good news is that we know how the vast majority of Houdini's tricks were done, and the explanations are as fascinating as the mystery was. Much of our knowledge comes from the magician's writings, for Houdini kept ahead of his imitators by exposing his cast-off tricks. We have additional information from technicians and theater historians. No magician will reveal Houdini's secrets—their code forbids it. But so much controversy has arisen concerning his powers—so much conjecture they may have been supernatural—that extraordinary measures have been taken to assure us Houdini was a *mortal* genius. Many secrets have leaked out, and others have been discovered from examining the props. So at last we know more about Houdini's technique than any other magician's.

The disturbing news is that, sixty years after his last performance, some of his more spectacular escapes remain unexplained. And while magicians such as Doug Henning are bound not to expose their colleagues, they are free to admit what mystifies them. They know how Houdini walked through the brick wall at Hammerstein's Roof Garden, in 1914, but they do not know how he made the elephant disappear in 1918. This trick he performed only for a few months in New York. And when people asked him why he did not continue he told them that Teddy Roosevelt, a great hunter, had begged him to stop before he exhausted the world's supply of pachyderms.

5   But before we grapple with the mysteries, let us begin with what we can understand. Let us begin with my grandfather's favorite story, the case of Harry Houdini versus the German Police. Houdini's first tour of Europe depended upon the good will and cooperation of the law. When he arrived in London in 1900 the twenty-six-year-old magician did not have a single booking. His news clippings eventually inspired an English agent, who had Houdini manacled to a pillar in Scotland Yard. Seeing that Houdini was securely fastened, Superintendent Melville of the Criminal Investigation Department said he would return in a couple of hours, when the escapist had worn himself out. By the time Melville got to the door the magician was free to open it for him.

The publicity surrounding his escape from the most prestigious police force in the world opened up many another door for the young magician. Booked at the Alhambra Theater in London, he performed his "Challenge" handcuff act, which had made him famous on the vaudeville circuit. After some card tricks and standard illusions, Houdini would stand before the proscenium and challenge the world to restrain him with ropes, straitjackets, handcuffs, whatever they could bring on, from lockshops, prisons, and museums. A single failure might have ruined him. There is no evidence that he ever failed, though in several cases he nearly died from the effort required to escape from sadistic shackles. The "Challenge" act filled the Alhambra Theater for two months. Houdini might have stayed there if Germany had not already booked him; the Germans could hardly wait to get a look at Houdini.

As he had done in America and England, Houdini began his tour of Germany with a visit to police headquarters. The Dresden officers were not enthusiastic, yet they could hardly refuse the magician's invitation to lock him up. That might suggest a crisis of confidence. And like their colleagues the world over, the Dresden police viewed Houdini's news clippings as so much paper in the balance with their locks and chains. Of course the Dresden police had no more success than those of Kansas City, or San Francisco, or Scotland Yard. Their manacles were paper to him. The police chief reluctantly signed the certificate Houdini demanded, but the newspapers gave him little coverage.

So on his opening night at Dresden's Central Theatre, Houdini arranged to be fettered in the leg irons and manacles of the Mathildegasse Prison. Some of the locks weighed forty pounds. The audience, packed to the walls, went wild over his escape, and the fact that he spoke their language further endeared him. If anything could have held him captive it would have been the adoring burghers of Dresden, who mobbed the theater for weeks. The manager wanted to buy out Houdini's contract with the Wintergarten of Berlin, so as to hold him over in Dresden, but the people of Berlin could not wait to see the magician.

Houdini arrived in Berlin in October of 1900. The first thing he did was march into the police station, strip stark naked, and challenge the jailors. They could not hold him. This time Count von Windheim, the highest ranking policeman in Germany, signed the certificate of Houdini's escape. The Wintergarten was overrun. The management appealed to the theater of Houdini's next engagement, in Vienna, so they might hold him over an extra month in Berlin. The Viennese finally yielded, demanding an indemnity equal to Houdini's salary for one month. When the magician, at long last, opened at the Olympic Theater in Paris, in December of 1901, he was the highest paid foreign entertainer in French history.

10   But meanwhile there was big trouble brewing in Germany. It seems the police there had little sense of humor about Houdini's peculiar gifts, and the Jew had quickly exhausted what little there was. In Dortmund he escaped from the irons that had bound Clowisky, a notorious murderer, beheaded three days before. At Hanover the police chief, Count von Schwerin, plotted to disgrace Houdini, challenging him to escape from a special straitjacket reinforced with thick leather. Houdini agonized for one and a half hours while von Schwerin looked on, his jubilant smile melting in wonder, then rage, as the magician worked himself free.

The cumulative anger of the German police went public in July of 1901. Inspector Werner Graff witnessed Houdini's escape from all the manacles at the Cologne police station and vowed to end the humiliation. It was not a simple matter of pride. Graff, along with von Schwerin and other officials, feared Houdini was weakening their authority and inviting jailbreaks, if not other kinds of antisocial behavior. So Graff wrote a letter to Cologne's newspaper, the

Rheinische Zeitung. The letter stated that Houdini had escaped from simple restraints at the police headquarters, by trickery; but his publicity boasted he could escape from restraints of *any kind*. Such a claim, Graff wrote, was a lie, and Houdini ought to be prosecuted for fraud.

Though he knew the letter was nonsense the magician could not ignore it, for it was dangerous nonsense. If the police began calling him a fraud in every town he visited, Houdini would lose his audience. So he demanded that Graff apologize and the newspaper publish a retraction. Graff refused, and other German dailies reprinted his letter. Should Harry Houdini sue the German policeman for libel? Consider the circumstances. Germany, even in 1901, was one of the most authoritarian states in the world. Houdini was an American, a Jew who embarrassed the police. A libel case against Graff would turn upon the magician's claim that he could escape from *any* restraint, and the courtroom would become an international theater. There a German judge and jury try his skill, and, should they find it wanting, Houdini would be washed up, exiled to play beer halls and dime museums. Only an artist with colossal pride and total confidence in his methods would act as Houdini did. He hired the most prominent trial lawyer in Cologne, and ordered him to sue Werner Graff and the Imperial Police of Germany for criminal libel.

There was standing room only in the Cologne *Schöffengericht*. The judge allowed Werner Graff to seek out the most stubborn locks and chains he could find, and tangle Houdini in them, in full view of everyone. Here was a hitch, for Houdini did not wish to show the crowd his technique. He asked the judge to clear the courtroom, and in the ensuing turmoil the magician released himself so quickly no one knew how he had done it. The *Schöffengericht* fined the astonished policeman and ordered a public apology. So Graff's lawyer appealed the case.

Two months later Graff was better prepared. In the *Strafkammer*, or court of appeals, he presented thirty letters from legal authorities declaring that the escape artist could not justify his advertisements. And Graff had a shiny new pair of handcuffs. The premier locksmith of Germany had engineered the cuffs especially for the occasion. Werner Graff explained to the judge that the lock, once closed, could never be opened, even with its own key. Let Houdini try to get out of these.

This time the court permitted Houdini to work in privacy, and a guard led the magician to an adjacent chamber. Everyone else settled down for a long wait, in a chatter of anticipation. They were interrupted four minutes later by the entrance of Houdini, who tossed the manacles on the judge's bench. So the *Strafkammer* upheld the lower court's decision, as did the *Oberlandesgericht* in a "paper" appeal. The court fined Werner Graff thirty marks and ordered him to pay for the trials as well as a published apology. Houdini's next poster showed him in evening dress, his hands manacled, standing before the judge, jurors, and a battery of mustachioed policemen. Looking down on the scene is a bust of the Kaiser against a crimson background, and a scroll that reads: "The Imperial Police of Cologne slandered Harry Houdini . . . were compelled to advertise 'An Honorary Apology' and pay costs of the trials. By command of Kaiser Wilhelm II, Emperor of Germany."

Now this is surely a wondrous tale, like something out of the Arabian Nights, and it will seem no less wonderful when we understand the technique that made it come true. In 1901, when Houdini took on the Imperial Police, he was not whistling in the dark. By the time he left America at the end of the nineteenth century he had dissected every kind of lock he could find in the New World, and whatever he could import from the old one. Arriving in London Houdini could write that there were only a few kinds of British handcuffs, "seven or eight at the utmost," and these were some of the simplest he had ever seen. He searched the markets, antique shops, and locksmiths, buying up all the European locks he could find so he could dismantle and study them.

Then during his Berlin engagement he worked up to ten hours a day at Mueller's locksmith on the Mittelstrasse, studying restraints. He was the Bobby Fischer of locks. With a chessmaster's foresight Houdini devised a set of picks to release every lock in existence, as well as *any he could imagine*. Such tireless ingenuity produced the incandescent light bulb and the atom bomb. Houdini's creation of a theatrical metaphor made a comparable impact on the human spirit. He had a message which he delivered so forcefully it goes without mentioning in theater courses: humankind cannot be held in chains. The European middle class had reached an impressionable age, and the meaning of Houdini's theater was not lost upon them. Nor was he mistaken by the aristocracy, who stayed away in droves. The spectacle of this American Jew bursting from chains by dint of ingenuity did not amuse the rich. They wanted desperately to demythologize him.

It was not about to happen in the German courtroom. When Werner Graff snapped the "new" handcuffs on Houdini, they were not strange to the magician. He had already invented them, so to speak, as well as the pick to open them, and the pick was in his pocket. Only a locksmith whose knowledge surpassed Houdini's could stop him; diligent study assured him that, as of 1901, there could be no such locksmith on the face of the earth.

What else can we understand about the methods of Harry Houdini, born Ehrich Weiss? We know he was a superbly conditioned athlete who did not smoke or take a drop of alcohol. His straitjacket escapes he performed in full view of the world so they could see it was by main force and flexibility that he freed himself. He may or may not have been able to dislocate his shoulders at will—he said he could, and it seems no more marvelous than certain other skills he demonstrated. Friends reported that his toes could untie knots most of us could not manage with our fingers. And routinely the magician would hold his breath for as long as four minutes to work underwater escapes. To cheapen the supernatural claims of the fakir Rahman Bey, Houdini remained underwater in an iron box for ninety minutes, as against the Egyptian's sixty. Examining Houdini, a physician testified that the fifty-year-old wizard had halved his blood pressure while doubling his pulse. Of course, more wonderful than any of these skills was the courage allowing him to employ them, in predicaments where any normal person would panic.

These things are known about Houdini. The same tireless ingenuity, when applied to locks and jails, packing cases and riveted boilers; the same athletic prowess, when applied at the bottom of the East River, or while dangling from a rope attached to the cornice of the Sun Building in Baltimore—these talents account for the vast majority of Houdini's exploits. As we have mentioned, theater historians, notably Raymund Fitzsimons in his *Death and the Magician,* have carefully exposed Houdini's ingenuity, knowing that nothing can tarnish the miracle of the man's existence. Their accounts are technical and we need not dwell on them, except to say they *mostly* support Houdini's oath that his effects were achieved by natural, or mechanical means. The Houdini problem arises from certain outrageous effects no one has ever been able to explain, though capable technicians have been trying for more than sixty years.

Let us briefly recall those effects. We have mentioned the Disappearing Elephant. On January 7, 1918, Houdini had a ten-thousand-pound elephant led onto the bright stage of the Hippodrome in New York City. A trainer marched the elephant around a cabinet large enough for an elephant, proving there was space behind. There was no trapdoor in the floor of the Hippodrome, and the elephant could not fly. Houdini ushered the pachyderm into the cabinet and closed the curtains. Then he opened them, and where the elephant had stood there was nothing but empty space. Houdini went on with his program, which might have been making the Hippodrome disappear, for all the audience knew. A reporter for the *Brooklyn Eagle* noted "The program says that the elephant vanished into thin air. The trick is performed fifteen feet from the backdrop and the cabinet is slightly elevated. That explanation is as good as any." After Houdini stopped making elephants disappear, nineteen weeks later, the trick would never be precisely duplicated.

That is the single "conventional" illusion of Houdini's repertoire that remains unexplained. He was not the greatest illusionist of his time, though he was among them. His expertise was the "escape" act, that specialty of magic furthest removed from theater, for its challenges are quite real and sometimes beyond the magician's control. It was the escapes, as his wife later wrote, that were truly dangerous, and Houdini privately admitted some anxieties about them. Give a wizard twenty years to build a cabinet which snuffs an elephant, and you will applaud his cleverness if he succeeds, in the controlled environment of his theater. But surrender the same man, stark naked, to the Russian police, who stake their honor upon detaining him in a convict van, and you may well suspect the intercession of angels should he get out.

And that is exactly what Houdini did, in one of the strangest and most celebrated escapes of his career. Strange, because it was Houdini's habit to escape only from barred jail cells where the locks were within easy reach, and then only after inspection, so he might hide picks in crannies, or excuse himself if he foresaw failure. But the Siberian Transport Cell made his blood boil. On May 11, 1903, the chief of the Russian secret police searched the naked Houdini inside and out. The revolt of 1905 was in its planning stages and the Imperial Police were understandably touchy. The magician's wrists were padlocked and his ankles fettered before the police locked him into the *carette*. Mounted on a wagon, the zinc-lined steel cell stood in the prison courtyard in view of chief Lebedoeff, his staff, and a number of civilians. Twenty-eight minutes later Houdini was walking around the courtyard, stretching. Nobody saw him get out, but he was out. The police ran to the door of the *carette*. The door was still locked and the shackles lay on the floor of the undamaged van. The police were so furious they would not sign the certificate of escape, but so many people had witnessed the event that the news was soon being shouted all over Moscow. Doug Henning has written: "It remains one of his escapes about which the real method is pure conjecture."

In the Houdini Museum at Niagara Falls, Canada, you may view the famous Mirror Handcuffs. If you are a scholar you can inspect them. In March of 1904 the London *Daily Mirror* discovered a blacksmith who had been working for five years to build a set of handcuffs no mortal man could pick. Examining the cuffs, the best locksmiths in London agreed they had never seen such an ingenious mechanism. The newspaper challenged Houdini to escape from them. On March 17, before a house of four thousand in the London Hippodrome, a journalist fastened the cuffs on Houdini's wrists and turned the key six times. The magician retired to his cabinet onstage, and the band struck up a march. He did not emerge for twenty minutes. When he did, it was to hold the lock up to the light. Remember that most "Challenge" handcuffs were regulation, and familiar to Houdini. He studied the lock in the light, and then went back into the cabinet, as the band played a waltz.

Ten minutes later Houdini stuck his head out, asking if he could have a cushion to kneel on. He was denied. After almost an hour Houdini came out of the cabinet again, obviously worn out, and his audience groaned. He wanted the handcuffs to be unlocked for a moment so he could take off his coat, as he was sweating profusely. The journalist denied the request, since Houdini had never before seen the handcuffs unlocked, and that might give him an advantage. Whereupon Houdini, in full view of the four thousand, extracted a penknife from his pocket and opened it with his teeth. Turning the coat inside out over his head, he shredded it loose with the penknife, and returned to the cabinet. Someone called out that Houdini had been handcuffed for more than an hour. As the band played on, the journalists of the London *Daily Mirror* could taste the greatest scoop of the twentieth century. But ten minutes later there was a cry from the cabinet and Houdini leapt out of it, free, waving the handcuffs high in the air. While the crowd roared, several men from the audience carried Houdini on their shoulders around the theater. He was crying as if his heart would break.

For all his other talents Houdini was a notoriously wooden actor, and we may assume the rare tears were altogether real, the product of an uncounterfeitable emotion. It is as if the man himself had been overwhelmed by his escape. Eighty years of technological progress have shed no light upon it. We know how Houdini got out of other handcuffs, but not these. As far as anyone can tell, the Mirror Handcuffs remain as the blacksmith described them—a set of handcuffs no mortal man could pick. One is tempted to dismiss the whole affair as mass hypnosis.

In the same Canadian museum you may view the Chinese Water Torture Cell, in which the magician was hung upside down, in water, his ankles padlocked to the riveted roof. His escape from this cell was the crowning achievement of his stage career, and though he performed it on tour during the last ten years of his life, no one has the slightest notion how he did it. The gifted Doug Henning revived the act in 1975, on television. But he would be the first to tell you his was *not* Houdini's version, but his own, and he would not do it onstage before a live audience seven nights a week, with matinees on Wednesday and Saturday, because the trick would be unspeakably dangerous even if he could perform it there. When Houdini died he willed the contraption to his brother Hardeen, a fine magician in his own right. But Hardeen would not get in it either, and the instructions were to be burned upon his death. Again, as with the Vanishing Elephant, we are reviewing a stage illusion under controlled conditions, and may bow to a master's technical superiority, without fretting that he has used supernatural powers.

But the Mirror Handcuffs and the Siberian Van Escape are troublesome, as are certain of Houdini's escapes from reinforced straitjackets, and packing cases underwater. So is the fact that he was buried six feet underground, and clawed his way out. He only tried it once, and nearly died in the struggle, but the feat was attested, and you do not need a degree in physics to know it is as preposterous as rising from the dead. The weight of the earth is so crushing you could not lift it in the open air. Try doing this with no oxygen. The maestro himself misjudged the weight, and, realizing his folly, tried to signal his crew when the grave was not yet full. They could not hear him and kept right on shoveling as fast as they could, so as not to keep him waiting. Then they stood back, to watch. A while later they saw his bleeding hands appear above the ground.

If we find Houdini's record unsettling, imagine what our grandparents must have thought of him. They knew almost nothing of his technique. Where we remain troubled by a few of his illusions and escapes, our ancestors were horrified by most of them. The European journalists thought he was some kind of hobgoblin, a shapeshifter who could crawl through keyholes, or dematerialize and reappear at will. One can hardly blame them. Despite his constant reassurances that his effects were technical, and natural, the practical-minded layman could not believe it, and even fellow magicians were disturbed by his behavior.

30   So we come to the central issue in the case of Harry Houdini. It is an issue he carefully avoided in public, while studying it diligently in private. To wit: Can a magician, by the ultimate perfection of a technique, generate a force which, at critical moments, will achieve a supernatural result? Houdini's writings show this was the abiding concern of his intellectual life. It is, of course, the essential mystery of classical magic since before the Babylonians. Yet it remained a private and professional concern until Houdini's career forced it upon the public.

With the same determination that opened the world's locks, Houdini searched for an answer. His own technique was so highly evolved that its practice might have satisfied him, but his curiosity was unquenchable. He amassed the world's largest collection of books pertaining to magic and the occult, and no less a scholar than Edmund Wilson honored Houdini's authority. The son of a rabbi, Houdini pursued his studies with rabbinic thoroughness. And, from the beginning of his career, he sought out the living legends of magic and badgered them in retirement, sometimes with tragicomic results.

As far back as 1895 it seemed to Houdini something peculiar was going on when he performed the Metamorphosis with his wife Bess. You have probably seen this classic illusion. Two friends of mine once acted it in my living room, as a birthday present. When the Houdinis performed the Metamorphosis, Bess would handcuff Harry, tie him in a sack, and lock him in a trunk. She would draw a curtain hiding the trunk and then it would open, showing Houdini free upon the stage. Where was Bess? Inside the trunk, inside the sack, handcuffed—there was Bess. The method of this trick is only mysterious if you cannot pay for it. But the Houdinis' *timing* of the Metamorphosis got very mysterious indeed. They polished the act until it happened in less than three seconds—three rather blurred seconds in their own minds, to be sure. Believe me, you cannot get *in* to the trunk in less than three seconds. So when the Houdinis had done the trick they were often as stunned as their audience. It seemed a sure case of technique unleashing a supernatural force. Perplexed, Houdini planned to interview Hermann the Great, the pre-eminent conjuror in America in 1895, and ask Hermann what was up. But Hermann died as Houdini was about to ask him the question.

And Houdini shadowed the marvelous Harry Kellar, cross-examining him, and Alexander Heimburger, and the decrepit Ira Davenport, who had been a medium as well as a magician. But the great magicians flatly denied the psychic possibility, and Davenport would not answer to Houdini's satisfaction. In 1903 he discovered that Wiljalba Frikell, a seemingly mythic wizard of the nineteenth century, was still alive, in retirement near Dresden. When the ancient mage would not acknowledge his letters, Houdini grew convinced Wiljalba Frikell was the man to answer his question. He took the train to Dresden and knocked on Frikell's door. His wife sent Houdini away. On the road in Germany and Russia, Houdini continued to send letters and gifts to Frikell. And at last, six months after he had been turned away from Frikell's door, the reclusive magician agreed to see him.

Houdini rang the doorbell at 2:00 P.M. on October 8, 1903, the exact hour of his appointment. The door swung open. An hour earlier Wiljalba Frikell had dressed in his best suit, and laid out his scrapbooks, programs, and medals for Houdini to view. Houdini excitedly followed Frikell's wife into the room where the master sat surrounded by the mementos of his glorious career. But he would not be answering any of the questions that buzzed in Houdini's brain. The old man was stone dead.

35   Throughout his life Houdini categorically denied that any of his effects were achieved by supernatural means. He crusaded against mediums, clairvoyants, and all who claimed psychic power, advertising that he would reproduce any of their manifestations by mechanical means. In the face of spiritualists who accused *him* of being a physical medium, he protested that all his escapes and illusions were tricks. He was probably telling the truth, as he understood it. But Rabbi Drachman, who spoke at Houdini's funeral, and had been in a position to receive confidences, said: "Houdini possessed a wondrous power that he never understood, and which he never revealed to anyone in life."

Houdini was not Solomon; he was a vaudeville specialist. If he ever experienced a psychic power it surely humbled his understanding. And to admit such a power, in his position, would have been a monumental stupidity. Why? If for no other reason, Talmudic law forbids the performance of miracles, and Houdini was the obedient son of Rabbi Weiss. Also, in case he should forget the Jewish law, it is strictly against the magician's code to claim a supernatural power, for reasons impossible to ignore. Mediums made such claims, at their own risk. Two of the more famous mediums of the nineteenth century, Ira and William Davenport, achieved manifestations similar to Houdini's. Audiences in Liverpool, Leeds, and Paris rioted, stormed the stage, and ran the mediums out of town, crying their performances were an outrage against God and a danger to man. Whether or not the acts were supernatural is beside the point—billing them as such was bad business, and hazardous to life and limb. Yet the Davenports were no more than a sideshow, compared to Houdini. The man was blinding. There had not been such a public display of apparent miracles in nearly two thousand years. Had the Jew so much as hinted his powers were spiritual he might have expected no better treatment than the renegade Hebrew of Nazareth.

Houdini was the self-proclaimed avatar of nothing but good old American know-how, and that is how he wished to be remembered. His wife of thirty years, Beatrice Houdini (known as "Bess"), was loyal to him in this, as in all other things. Pestered for revelations about Houdini's magic long after his death, the widow swore by her husband's account. But against her best intentions, Bess clouded the issue by saying just a little more than was necessary. It was in a letter to Sir Arthur Conan Doyle, who had been a close friend of hers and Houdini's.

The friendship was an odd one. The author of Sherlock Holmes believed in Spiritualism, and championed the séance with all the fervor with which Houdini opposed it. There were two great mysteries in Doyle's life: the powers of Sherlock Holmes and Harry Houdini. Doyle knew the Houdinis intimately, and nothing the magician said could shake Sir Arthur's conviction that certain of Houdini's escapes were supernatural. Doyle never stopped trying to get Houdini to confess. In 1922 it was more than a personal issue. The séance had become big business in America, with millions of bereaved relatives paying to communicate with their dear departed. Spiritualism was a home-grown, persuasive religious movement, a bizarre reaction to American science and pragmatism. The great critic Edmund Wilson, who admired Houdini and understood his gifts, recognized that the magician had appeared at a critical moment in the history of Spiritualism. Houdini was the only man living who had the authority, and the competence, to expose the predatory mediums, and his success was decisive.

Yet Houdini's lecture-demonstrations, and exposures of false mediums, only fueled Doyle's suspicions that his friend was the real thing, a physical medium. In all fairness, Sir Arthur Conan Doyle was a credulous old gentleman, who knew nothing of Houdini's techniques. But his instinct was sound. Two months after Houdini died, Sir Arthur wrote to Bess in despair of ever learning the truth from the magician's lips, and she wrote Doyle a long letter. What concerns us here are a few sentences which, coming from the woman who shared his life and work, and maintained her loyalty to Houdini alive and dead, we must regard as altogether startling.

> I will never be offended by anything you say for him or about him, but that he possessed psychic powers—he never knew it. As I told Lady Doyle often he would get a difficult lock, I stood by the cabinet and I would hear him say, "This is beyond me," and after many minutes when the audience became restless I nervously would say "Harry, if there is anything in this belief in Spiritism,—why don't you call on them to assist you," and before many minutes had passed Houdini had mastered the lock.
>
> We never attributed this to psychic help. We just knew that that particular instrument was the one to open that lock, and so did all his tricks.

The tone of this letter penned so soon after her husband's death is somber throughout, painfully sincere. This was not a subject for levity, this being the central issue in the life of Harry Houdini. So what on earth is Bess trying to tell Sir Arthur when she testifies to the invocation of spirits in one sentence, and repudiates psychic help in the next? What kind of double-talk is this, when the widow refers to the summoning of spiritual aid as "that particular instrument," as if a spirit were no different from any other skeleton key? It sounds like sheer euphemism; it sounds like the Houdinis' lifetime of work had uncovered a power so terrifying they would not admit it to each other, let alone the world. Would that Albert Einstein had been so discreet in 1905.

So what if Harry Houdini, once in a while, "spirited" himself out of a Siberian Van, or a pair of Mirror Handcuffs, or a packing case at the bottom of the East River? It is perhaps no more remarkable than that an American Jew won a verdict against the German Police for criminal libel in 1901, or reversed a religious movement in America in 1922. Houdini died in Detroit on Halloween in 1926, of acute appendicitis. He was born in Budapest on March 24, 1874, but told the world he was born in Appleton, Wisconsin on April 6. Not until after World War II did Americans discover that their greatest magician was an alien. Houdini's work was no more miraculous than his life. His life was no more miraculous than the opening and closing of a flower.

Questions for Discussion

1. What significance does the author derive from his exploration of this subject? How does he communicate that significance?
2. What is the essay's subordinate aim? Cite specific passages to support your answer.
3. The author describes a number of Houdini's magic tricks. Which of these do you consider essential to the essay? Which do you think might be unnecessary?
4. Notice the way the author identifies his sources of information. Do you consider his tagging of sources satisfactory? Explain your answer.
5. In the opening paragraph, the author asks two questions: "What did the historical Houdini *really* do? And how on earth did he do it?" Do you think the essay satisfactorily answers these two questions? What do you think of this technique of starting with questions that the essay will try to answer?

Opportunities for Writing

1. Portray a famous magician such as Doug Henning or David Copperfield. What is this individual like? How did he or she train to be a magician? Which illusion is this magician's favorite? Why?
2. Depict the Houdini Museum in Niagara Falls, Canada. What does it look like outside and inside? How big is it? How many items are on display? Why is it located in Niagara Falls? What do you think of a museum being dedicated to Harry Houdini? Interview visitors to the museum for their observations. Also review fliers and brochures from the museum itself.
3. Recount the death of Harry Houdini on October 31, 1926. What happened? What was the public reaction? Why do you think this event is important or interesting? Write your essay for the October 31 edition of your local newspaper.
4. Characterize a friend or acquaintance who claims to possess special psychic or spiritual power. How did he or she discover this power? How is it displayed? What is your impression of his or her power?

Knowledge by Participation and Observation

Fat Like Me

Leslie Lampert

"Fat Like Me" reveals the prejudice that overweight individuals experience. Leslie Lampert took the challenging investigative assignment for the Ladies' Home Journal: *she wears a custom-made "fat suit" that transforms her into a 250-pound woman. This essay, published in the May 1993 issue of* Ladies' Home Journal, *contains both Lampert's personal feelings and account of this experience as well as the attitudes and reactions of other people toward her. Lampert is a regular reporter for the* Ladies' Home Journal *and the author of many articles for this popular magazine, including "Can a Woman be Fat and Happy?" (March 1995).*

One morning I gained one hundred fifty pounds, and my whole life changed. My husband looked at me differently, my kids were embarrassed, friends felt sorry for me, and strangers were shamelessly disgusted by my presence. The pleasures of shopping, family outings and going to parties turned into wrenchingly painful experiences. In truth, I became depressed by just the thought of running even the most basic errands; a trip to the grocery store or the video shop was enough to put me in a bad mood. But mostly, I became angry. Angry because what I experienced in the week that I wore a "fat suit"—designed to make me look like a two-hundred-fifty-plus-pound woman—was that our society not only hates fat people, it feels entitled to participate in a prejudice that at many levels parallels racism and religious bigotry. And in a country that prides itself on being sensitive to the handicapped and the homeless, the obese continue to be the target of cultural abuse.

To many, obesity symbolizes an inability to control oneself or to maintain personal health. Fat people are often perceived as smelly, dirty, lazy failures (whose extra girth must also be expected to shield them from cruel insults and blatant disdain). The issue of personal space also plays a prominent role in this prejudice—many feel that fat people take up more than their justifiable territory on the bus, in movie theaters, in store aisles, in general. Judging from my recent experience as a counterfeit obese person, it seems we are more tolerant of ill-mannered, indecent individuals who are slim than we are of honorable, oversize citizens.

We are a society that worships slimness and fears the full figure. I am no different. After having given birth to three children, waved good-bye to thirty long ago and succumbed to the natural laws of gravity, I found myself holding on to twenty or so pounds that I've never looked upon in a friendly way. And anyone who knows me could reveal my own on-off-on-off dieting battles. But nothing could have prepared me for the shame and disrespect imposed upon the clinically obese (that is, those more than 20 percent over ideal weight for a given height).

When Goldie Hawn was weighted down with two hundred extra pounds in last year's movie *Death Becomes Her*, I thought, I wonder what it would really be like to look so big? Then I asked myself, What would it be like to live like that? And so this experiment was born.

5   Each morning during the first week, I slipped into a custom-made "fat suit" designed by special-effects artist Richard Tautkus of New York City (he's responsible for costumes worn in The Ringling Bros. Circus, the upcoming *Star Wars* road show and a number of hit movies and Broadway shows), and made my way into a world where I was alternately treated as invisible or regarded as a spectacle. Following is my diary:

FRIDAY

10 A.M. I take a taxi from the *Ladies' Home Journal* offices in Manhattan to Richard Tautkus Studio, in Long Island City, for Richard and his assistants, Jim and Steven, to finish sculpting me into my new persona. I am nervous about this assignment, especially when I recall a recent newspaper series reporting a study of former fat people (all of whom had lost significant amounts of weight after intestinal bypass surgery) who said they'd rather be blind, deaf or have a leg amputated than be fat again. Can it really be that bad?

The costumers can hardly believe the swelled-up me before them. The costume—made from air-conditioner filters—is surprisingly lightweight, but its bulk is already making me sweat. I'm led to a three-way, full-length mirror. I'm stunned. I look authentic. Too authentic!

I am uncomfortable seeing myself like this. "You're still pretty," comforts one of the guys jokingly, "—for a fat girl." I do not laugh.

12 P.M. I take my first taxi ride in the fat suit. Did the driver sneer at me? I must be imagining it. It took me a little longer than usual to maneuver myself into the cab. Was the driver impatient? I arrive at the photo studio and, with difficulty, get out of the car. Did I say something funny? The driver is openly laughing.

10 **8 P.M.** I show my husband and kids the before-and-after pictures from the photo session. My husband reconsiders his willingness to go out to dinner with me in my disguise. "It makes me sad to think of you this fat," he says. "I'll be uncomfortable knowing that people will be staring at you and making fun of you." My kids chorus, "Don't pick me up at school looking like that."

We talk about fat discrimination. "I don't dislike fat people," says Elizabeth, my ten-year-old. "It's just that I wouldn't want anyone to say mean things about you." Nine-year-old Amanda says flatly, "You scare me." Alex, my seven-year-old son, laughs nervously and wants to try on the costume.

11 P.M. I am trying to fall asleep in my own body. My husband is quietly snoring. I am hurt by his reaction to the fat me. While he's never made a disparaging comment about my body in the twelve years we've been married, I feel awful at having seen the look of repulsion on his face when he saw the photos.

MONDAY

7 A.M. I suit up and take the commuter train to work. No one sits next to me. I feel incredibly self-conscious. People look long enough to let me know that they disapprove, then go back to reading their morning newspapers. Two women go as far as to whisper blatantly, glaring at me with a how-could-you-let-yourself-get-like-that attitude. I take up one and a half seats, and, yes, I feel embarrassed. Yet shame takes a backseat to the resentment I'm feeling. How dare these people judge me on the basis of my dress size?

8 A.M. At the office, everyone is eager to hear about my experiences and to see if my disguise has had an impact on the real me. One editor remarks that in my fat suit, my body movements seem more aggressive. A staff member asks me how I'll feel if while on assignment I bump into an old boyfriend. Another one says I seem depressed. Yes, I am depressed—and, suddenly, very hungry.

1 P.M. I am lunching with two colleagues at a swank restaurant uptown. I am cranky, conscious of all the smirks and stares. In an effort to seem helpful, the waiter pulls my chair way out so that I can fit at the table. My embarrassment at having to shimmy into the chair with too-tight armrests is certainly noticed by the other patrons, who are sneaking looks whenever they can.

Okay, I'm fat, I'm thinking. But I'll bet some of you are pill-poppers, embezzlers, adulterers and lousy parents. I wish you had to display symbols of those character flaws as openly as I have to reveal my above-average body size (which some medical experts are beginning to define as a genetically linked trait—not a personality weakness). We skip dessert and leave.

5:30 P.M. Driving home from the train station, I stop at a red light next to a car with two teenage boys in it. I look over. The boy on the passenger side puffs out his cheeks at me and bursts out laughing.

6:30 P.M. Pick up the kids at school and go to a take-out chicken shop to get dinner. My kids make me walk in first.

I order two roast chickens, potatoes, gravy, veggies, corn and a half-dozen brownies. Some kids in the restaurant refer to me as That Fat Lady; the adults with them muffle their amusement.

While the man at the cash register is ringing up my order, he asks me how many people I'm feeding. I reply indignantly, "Six people. Why?" He says that had he known, he could have suggested a less expensive family-pack meal. I am upset for assuming he was trying to ridicule me.

Tuesday

10 A.M. On my way to Bloomingdale's to go shopping, I stop for ice cream at Häagen-Dazs. I order a double scoop of chocolate-chocolate chip, and as I watch the youngster behind the counter evaluate my size, I fight the urge to say something defensive. Walking down the street eating the cone, I see one well-dressed man shake his head in disparagement and another laugh out loud as he passes me.

Walking into Bloomingdale's is difficult. First, I can barely fit in the revolving door, and when I get inside, I feel all eyes are on me. Interestingly, I am not ignored the way I thought I would be. Two perfumers practically attack me with their latest fragrance. One man behind the counter asks me if I want a makeover.

I proceed to the elevator. Have to squeeze in. A couple of women giggle. I ask the saleswoman for help in the sportswear section. She refers me nicely to the "big gals" department.

On the way home, I buy a dozen bagels at a bakery in Grand Central Terminal. I eat one on the train. Why do people find it so repulsive to watch a large person eat? I do not give in to the frowning looks. I am hungry.

Wednesday

10 A.M. I'm having a consultation at a beauty salon near my home. I tell the hairstylist, who's thin as a rail, that I want a different look. She gently explains that I need a fuller hairstyle to compensate for my ample figure. I am not offended. She has been honest, but not insulting. We talk about the difficulties of dieting. I have made a friend.

1 P.M. I am meeting some friends for lunch at a restaurant in the suburbs. They can't wait to see my transformation and hear about my project. I am feeling depressed and do not want to go. I am getting tired of constantly being on the defensive. My friends jokingly argue over who gets to sit next to me, so that they can feel skinny. I am delighted when I see another large woman seated at the table next to us. I notice that she is eating a salad. I order one, too.

2:30 P.M. I go grocery shopping. Everyone peers into my cart to see what the fat lady is buying. A couple of women are exasperated at not being able to get by me in the canned goods aisle. I apologize and turn sideways. I dread the candy aisle, but I promised my kids Skittles. I grab the bag of candy and look to see if anyone is watching. I discreetly put it in my cart. I feel like a criminal.

4 P.M. I worry that I'm getting paranoid about others' reaction to me. I decide to talk to an overweight woman to see if she has the same feelings. Unfortunately, she does. "I am sick of being judged by what I put in my mouth," Denise Rubin says. Rubin, thirty-two, an attorney, is five feet two and weighs over two hundred pounds. "I'm tired of being regarded as less-than because of my more-than size. When are we going to understand that fat is an adjective, not an epithet?"

I listen sympathetically, but do not have an answer for her.

Thursday

9:30 A.M. Elizabeth has told her fifth grade class about my assignment, and the teacher has asked me to come, in my fat suit, to share my experience with the students. Elizabeth is no longer embarrassed to let her friends see me. During this week, we have all been transformed. We are anxious to tell my story to others; to make people understand the prejudice. The kids in this classroom—most of whom know me—laugh at first, and then fire questions faster than I can answer them: How did I feel? Were people mean to me? What's it like to be fat?

2 P.M. I drive to the city to finish up some work at the office. I must admit, being behind the wheel at this weight has not been easy. I have had to adjust my seat to the farthest position so that I can fit comfortably, but, as a result, I can barely reach the pedals.

7:30 P.M. I'm having dinner at a see-and-be-seen kind of place in the city with my costumer, Richard. We have made plans to meet in the lobby of a nearby hotel, so that I wouldn't have to walk into the chic restaurant all by myself. Richard is late, so I window-shop in the lobby. I am met with the looks of disdain that I have come to expect. Richard finally arrives at seven forty-five, and he kisses me hello. We walk arm-in-arm to dinner. I feel safe.

The nightmare begins. A sea of beautiful people are sitting at the bar. It is so crowded I can barely manage to take off my coat. Richard, a good-looking man, whispers from behind. He can't believe how blatantly I am being made fun of by the crowd at the bar. I wait in line to tell the hostess we have arrived, but she pretends not to see me. Richard steps in, gives her our name, and she shows us to our table.

We had asked for a table in front. We get seated in the back by the hostess. The two thirtysomething women next to me can barely contain their horror as I clumsily try to pass through the space between our tables to slide onto the banquette seat. The water glasses shake as I unwittingly rock both tables. Richard and I order a drink, and I take a roll from the bread basket. The two women are glaring at me. I order a goat-cheese salad and pasta with cream sauce. They giggle. The rest of the meal proceeds in much the same manner. Richard and I look at the dessert menu, ignoring the two women.

I excuse myself to go to the ladies' room. Once there, I change out of my fat suit and into my own clothes. I know that sounds crazy, but I'm so upset that I have to do it. I come back and slink into my place. The two women are stupefied. Richard is ready to take revenge. He tells me that as soon as I left, one of them asked him, "What are you doing with that fat pig?" He replied, "She's my girlfriend." "That's not possible," said one woman. "You must be a hustler." My blood is boiling. Richard tells them about my project. They are angry at me. *Angry* at me! They quickly pay the check and leave.

Richard and I leave after our coffee. I am put off by flirtatious looks from the same men at the bar who were previously so rude to me.

Friday

4 P.M. I take my kids to the mall to buy clothes for our upcoming trip down south. Today while we're shopping I get two "Wows," countless dirty looks and one snort from various strangers. But I care less about what people are thinking. Perhaps it's because I know the project is coming to an end; perhaps I am resigned to society's disfavoring of me, the fat person. I still feel the sting of the everyday prejudice I experienced, but I feel less rebellious. I feel worn out.

7:30 P.M. I'm out to dinner with my husband (sans fat suit). I am surprisingly sulky, not all rejoicing in my instant weight loss. Instead, I feel ashamed of my culture and how much pain we cause people who are less than our concept of ideal. I'm thinking about ways I can help obese people feel more powerful; what I can do to deliver the message about maintaining positive self-esteem. Yet I am still using all my willpower to refrain from ordering dessert.

Questions for Discussion

1. The title of this essay alludes to John Howard Griffin's *Black Like Me,* a book published in 1961 about a white man who disguises himself as a black man and discovers how blacks are treated by white society. What do you think of the author's adaptation of that earlier title? What is she trying to imply? Is the title of this essay effective? Why or why not?
2. This essay is unconventional: a brief discussion followed by nineteen entries in a diary, all of which together reveal the author's experience. What do you think of this way of organizing and displaying the information? Why does the author choose to do it this way? How would this essay differ if it were written as a conventional piece?
3. What significance does the author derive from this experience? How does she communicate that significance?
4. This essay was written for a women's magazine? How would this essay differ if it were written for a men's magazine? How might the author revise it? What specific changes would you advise?
5. How important is this essay's subordinate persuasive aim? Is it as important as the expressive aim? Could you classify this essay as persuasive aim writing? Explain your answer.

Opportunities for Writing

1. Portray a friend of yours who is obese. What is he or she like? Does his or her obesity disturb you? If so, why? If not, why not?
2. In a letter to a friend of yours who is obese, recount a specific time that you ridiculed a man or woman because of his or her weight. What did you do? Why? How did you feel about this incident at the time? How do you feel about it now?
3. Characterize a famous man or woman who is or was obese. How does (or did) this individual live with his or her obesity? Do you think this individual's experience is applicable to your life? If so, how? If not, how does your experience differ?
4. Describe your experience with dieting. Why were you dieting? Was it easy or difficult? How did this experience make you feel about yourself?

Write this essay for a magazine on dieting and nutrition published by your local hospital.

My Grandmother's Pennies
Cynthia Ozick

Cynthia Ozick was born in New York and was educated at New York University and Ohio State University. A novelist, essayist, critic, translator, and short fiction writer, Ozick has won numerous awards and fellowships for her works. Her fiction titles include The Messiah of Stockholm *(1987),* The Cannibal Galaxy *(1983),* Trust *(1983),* Levitation: Five Fictions *(1982),* Bloodshed and Three Novellas *(1976), and* The Pagan Rabbi *(1971). Critic Doris Grumbach has stated that Ozick is "an important voice in American fiction, a woman whose intellect . . . is so impressive that it pervades the words she chooses, the stories she elects to tell, and every careful phrase and clause in which they are conveyed" (as quoted in* Contemporary Authors, *New Revision Series 300). In "My Grandmother's Pennies," Ozick describes Hanukkah and derives its personal significance to her and her daughter. This essay first appeared in the December 1978 issue of* McCall's *and reflects knowledge by both participation and observation.*

I keep in my dresser drawer an unusual heirloom. When people speak of heirlooms, they mean, I suppose, grand old clocks with brass pendulums and carved oak cases, or perhaps a ribboned bundle of weighty Victorian silver. There are houses that are heirlooms, too, lived in by the same family for generations, and antique lockets with ancestral ringlets in them, and fine old bridal lace, and cracked-leather chairs like hereditary thrones.

Our heirloom is different. It is made of rags, and if you tried to price it, it would fetch no more than 18 cents. Every darkening December, as the evening before the 25th day of the Hebrew month of Kislev approaches, my daughter and I take out our heirloom and renew our familiarity with its shapes and parts.

The first shape we see is an elongated cheesecloth bag, more yellowed now than white, knotted at the top. The seams are machine-sewn and hardy; it is the kind of homely sack in which, long ago, a whole cheese used to be packed.

We lift out of it a drawstring bag. Now, without warning, we are in the presence of something royal: This second bag is of a resplendent crimson velvet, hand-sewn with large, precise stitches in a broad green double thread. The neck of it, housing the drawstring, is green and white; tiny blossoms winding over a meadow. The colors are as fresh and bright as the day my grandmother cut out the fabric, a month or so before my first Hanukkah. The velvet is as deep and thick as the day my grandmother embroidered on its face the Hebrew letters that my daughter and I now begin to read together.

The first letters spell out a surprise: my daughter's own name! There it is, embroidered in a brilliant blue on the blazing velvet: *Rachel*. Yet how can this be? Rachel is 13, and the bag was sewn almost half a century ago. Instantly, there is the crackle of a magical connection—my grandmother, my daughter's great-grandmother, was also named Rachel. She sewed the letters of her own name into the velvet. Did she know that one day this rich sack and its homely contents would come into the hands of another Rachel?

Ah, she knew. Among Jews of eastern European origin, it is a nearly universal practice to name children in memoriam, to bring alive one's nearest forebears on one's daily tongue. "I am never lonely," my grandmother Rachel used to say to me when I was still very young. "I have my mother and father with me always." She meant my brother and me; he is (in Hebrew) Judah, and I am (in Hebrew) Susannah; we are named for our great-grandparents, Judah and Susannah. So my grandmother knew, when she emblazoned her name, that in time there would surely be another Rachel to read it and claim it as her own inheritance. The first Rachel was born in 1861; the second, in 1965. The blue embroidery binds them.

And so does the Hebrew language. At Hanukkah last year the younger Rachel came to the traditional age of bat mitzvah, which means "daughter of the Commandments," and signifies a ripening into moral, religious and communal responsibility. All of this implies, of course, a scholarly obligation to the language of the Bible. The Hebrew name *Rachel,* glowing on this velvet sack, flows backward not only to the Rachel born into Czarist Russia, but back and back and back to, at last, the Rachel of the Bible who is the mother of the Jewish people. All the history of the Children of Israel flickers in the blue strands my grandmother sewed one winter night long ago.

And now the younger Rachel takes up the velvet heirloom sack and reads the simple Hebrew legend embroidered under her name:

> The gifts of Hanukkah
> An inheritance
> Let it not pass

Let it not pass! My mother sews Hanukkah *baytelakh* for Rachel, and I will sew them for Rachel's children, and Rachel for her grandchildren, and so on into history-to-come, and it will not pass, this dedicated old task. But what, after all, does the velvet sack hold? Rachel stretches open its drawstring neck and spills out the contents. Onto the kitchen table there falls a small hill of colorful smaller sacks, each with its drawstring. In Yiddish—the language my grandmother and I used to converse in—the little sacks are called *baytelakh.*

We count them, there are only ten, because my grandmother died in the summer after my 11th birthday, months before Hanukkah. She had not yet sewn the eleventh. The *baytelakh* are made mostly of motley scraps of silk and reminiscence—here is a bit of redolent old shawl, and a fragment of unforgotten dress (how I used to bury my head in its lap!), and still another vivid swatch of someone's skirt, and here is a little sack of red and purple, material bought on purpose for making *baytelakh.* Each Hanukkah my grandmother sewed 22 *baytelakh,* one for each grandchild.

And all the while my grandmother was stitching, stitching—I see her worn, creased hands and the lightning glint of the needle—Hitler was thumping his fists, and his soldiers were thumping their boots, and Jewish life in Europe was growing dimmer and dimmer, passing, passing into ash; and my grandmother's needle flashed its defiant light. Then it was 1939, and something called the British White Paper sent its terrible flashes into our kitchen, and my grandmother sat weeping over her Yiddish newspaper, beating her breast with a crumpled hand, because the British were turning back to Hitler's death-ridden Germany ships packed with Jewish orphans coming to seek refuge in the Holy Land.

In the kitchen now, it is time for the younger Rachel to open her great-grandmother's *baytelakh.* Inside are the gifts of Hanukkah—what will they be? Out of each miniature sack there tumbles, still shiny, 18 pennies!

It is a night in dark December. All of America is occupied with gifts—the stores are giddy with shoppers, mountains of boxes rise in closets and behind doors, cascades of brilliant wrapping paper wind themselves around tantalizing shapes, rivers of ribbons curl into bows. Gifts, gifts, gifts everywhere—toys and things to wear, bicycles and perfumes, cameras and television sets; in an American December the gifts ascend. But in our kitchen at Hanukkah, from Rachel to Rachel, there are only the bags of 18 pennies, some old enough to show their Indian heads, all as shiny as the day they were slipped into a little silken sack cut from a worn-out shawl.

There are 18 pennies because in Hebrew (as with Roman numerals) the letters of the alphabet also stand for numbers. The Hebrew letters that make up the number 18 are *khet* and *yud* (the latter is the *jot* of the Gospels: *Till heaven and earth pass, one jot or one tittle shall in no wise pass from the law,* says Jesus), and *khet* and *yud* together spell the Hebrew word *khai,* which means life. So there are 18 symbolic pennies for Hanukkah *gelt*—Hanukkah money—not because of the gift of "buying power," but because of the powerful gift of life. My grandmother Rachel, who died in 1939, the year Hitler swarmed over Europe like a death's-head, calls to her unknown-but-known great-granddaughter Rachel: Choose life, life!

We set up the menorah, a candelabrum with eight candle holders—nine, counting the kindling candle. We recite the blessings and sing the hymn. We fry potato pancakes (latkes, these are called in Yiddish) in oil—the reason for the oil will soon emerge—and eat them by the dozens, with sour cream or apple sauce. We play a game called dreydl, a four-sided wooden top spun for a prize of nuts. The sides of the dreydl are engraved with the Hebrew letters that stand for the words *A Great Miracle Happened There.* We light the candles, recite the blessings and sing the hymn for eight days—a matter of a few minutes each afternoon at dusk. And that, in all its simplicity and fun, is the whole of the Hanukkah celebration. In our family, because of grandmother Rachel's lightning needle and the foresight of her embroidery, the 18 pennies come in *baytelakh.* Other families give Hanukkah gelt in other ways—but always in units of 18, to remember life. And the candles blaze, like trees of life.

Choosing life is the theme of Hanukkah—as it is the cry of Jewish history—because again and again oppressors have tried to snuff out the lives of Jews, lives made witness to dedication ever since God spoke to Abraham, the first Jew. Only three and a half decades ago six million Jews were gassed and incinerated by Hitler. But Hanukkah began more than two thousand years ago, when there arose in Greek culture an ancient precursor of Hitler, a rapacious persecutor called Antiochus. His troops marched into Jerusalem and raised up idols everywhere. In the Temple on Mount Zion Antiochus's men tore apart the altar, poured pigs' blood over the scrolls of Scripture and then set fire to them;

and in the charred and desolated Temple they set up a vast idol, a towering statue of Zeus. Jewish practices and customs were outlawed, and the study of Scripture was decreed a crime punishable by death. All Jews, Antiochus declared, had to bow before Zeus and a host of other gods, or die. They had to look, eat and behave like Greeks, or die. Blood ran in all the villages of Israel; even when the fearful Jews obeyed, they were killed. The Greek soldiers went from town to town all over the land, killing Jews and burning books. Antiochus's army was in the thousands. The Jews, an occupied people, had no army, and were only a handful of anguished citizens. But the handful of Jews fought back, inspired by the cry, "Whoever is for the Lord, come!"—and won.

Hanukkah marks the first time in the history of the world that a people struggled for freedom of religion.

Stuffed with pancakes, we roll out of the kitchen, settle down on the hall floor and begin spinning the dreydl. It's my turn. The dreydl whirls, then falls on the letter *Hey,* for Half. I take six out of the 12 walnuts in the pot. It's Rachel's turn. She lands on *Gimel,* for Get-All—all my winnings!

It's such an easy game—even though suspenseful—that we can make up another game while we're busy with this one. The game we invent is based on the letter *Nun.* When the dreydl rolls *Nun,* for Nothing, nobody gets anything.

The *Nun* game asks this question: If Israel had lost to Antiochus over two thousand years ago, if Judaism had been extinguished—and how close it came to that!—160 years before the birth of Jesus, what would our civilization be like now?

Answer: *Nun.* Nothing.

The Ten Commandments would not have been inherited by the nations of the world.

There would be no Christianity or Islam.

There would now be no Christmas to light the dark of an American December.

The pagan way would have won out over the centuries.

A scary game!

The Hanukkah candles are still spilling their radiance on the windowsill. Across the street the neighbors' electric Christmas lights are winking on strings along all the porches.

The two kinds of lights appear to be paired, if only by the darkness.

But the two *events* are not paired, except by a coincidence of the calendar. Hanukkah is by no means what some negligently call it, "the Jewish Christmas" (any more than Christmas is the Christian Hanukkah!). The two celebrations—the great one of multitudinous lights and abundant gifts and the modest one of eight lights and 18 pennies—have not a jot or tittle in common, and certainly ought not to be observed in tandem. And yet Christmas is joined to Hanukkah by a single vital bond. If Judaism had not been preserved against the onslaught of Antiochus, there would have been no Jewish family to give birth to Jesus, and no Jewish Jesus to give birth to Christianity.

But look, a wonder among the walnuts! The last four throws of the dreydl have come out in order! Rachel throws *Nun.* I throw *Gimel.* She gets *Hey.* I land on *Shin.* The walnuts are scattered everywhere, the game's in disarray—the dreydl has, unbidden, spelled out its historic reminder: *Nes Gadol Hayah Sham.*

A Great Miracle Happened There.

But why, after all, "great"? It was, in fact, as miracles go, a very modest one.

This is how it happened:

When at last the Jewish citizen-soldiers of Jerusalem entered the defiled Temple their jubilation at their courageous victory was shadowed by signs of hatred and vandalism all around. They got rid of the idol and began to clean up. They swept up the debris, washed away the dried pigs' blood, put up new curtains, rebuilt broken walls and doors. And then they began to look around for some oil to light the candelabrum with, to show that the Temple was renewed and rededicated to the idea of the One Creator.

But Antiochus's soldiers had spilled out nearly all the stock of consecrated oil, and only one jar was left. All it held was a few drops, enough to burn for one day.

Now comes the miracle (and notice how modest it is!): The few drops of oil burned for eight full days, long enough for a fresh supply of oil to be secured for the candelabrum.

This is the miracle that Hanukkah records and celebrates, and that is why Hanukkah lasts for eight days, beginning with the lighting of a single candle, until, on the eighth night, by the addition of a new candle daily, the glory has grown and all eight candles are afire at once.

The rabbis who first began to mark Hanukkah—which means dedication—thought this small miracle more important than any victory, even a victory for freedom of religion, even a victory over a brutal oppressor. We can understand why the rabbis emphasized the miracle of the little bit of oil that lasted and lasted, and endured beyond all expectation. The oil reminds us of the burning bush that burned and burned and was not consumed, and out of which the Voice of the Lord was heard. The oil reminds us of the Children of Israel—the saving remnant of the Jewish people—who are often endangered, but who live and live and will always live, eternally choosing freedom.

On the Sabbath that occurs during the eight days of Hanukkah, a special cycle of Psalms is sung in the synagogue, and these words from the prophet Zechariah are recited:

Not by might, nor by power, but by my Spirit, saith the Lord . . .

I think this must be what my grandmother Rachel continues to tell her great-granddaughter Rachel each year at Hanukkah, when we read the words her precious old fingers embroidered into our unusual heirloom. A message written in a remnant, not from a far-off time but from the future: *Let it not pass.* Hanukkah and life. The inheritance they bring is freedom.

Questions for Discussion

1. Do you consider the title appropriate? What are other possible titles for this essay?
2. Is the essay organized effectively? Why do you think it is or isn't?
3. How would this essay differ if the author were writing to a Jewish audience?
4. The author includes information on the ancient origins of Hanukkah—knowledge by observation—without citing sources. Does this damage the author's credibility. Why do you think it does or doesn't?
5. Consider the author's use of descriptive detail. Which details do you consider important? Which do you consider unnecessary? Why?

Opportunities for Writing

1. In a letter to a young member of your family or a new member through marriage, describe a family heirloom. What is it? What does it look like? How long has it been in your family? Why is it something your family treasures?
2. Depict the ancient city of Jerusalem. What was this city like in the time of King David or King Solomon? What do you consider interesting or important about this ancient city?
3. Your local religious congregation publishes a weekly magazine of religious news and essays. Writing for this magazine, discuss a specific episode in the history of your religion that you believe is especially meaningful.

Ghosts

BRUCE EDWARD HALL

Bruce Edward Hall describes himself as a "preppy white guy from Connecticut. My mother is blonde and blue-eyed, the very image of a Donna Reed. . . . Except that, unlike Alex Stone, my father is Chinese." In "Ghosts," Hall draws on details derived from his memory and from outside sources to give readers a rich introduction to "old" New York Chinatown and Chinatown "ghosts"—his friends and family. This essay appeared in the October 4, 1993, issue of New York *magazine.*

There are ghosts in Chinatown. They're all there, lined up, waiting to see me whenever I venture down Mott Street, squeezing past the crowds inspecting the sidewalk vendors' fruit or firecrackers or windup birds that really fly. There are ghosts of men and women, some in exotic clothes, some gambling, bent over little ivory tiles, some eating. No, everyone's eating. Inside a certain shop, there is the ghost of a man in a broad-sleeved jacket and long braid, creating an awe-inspiring work of art. On a tiny street, a vintage black Cadillac, driven by a little man with a big cigar, careers away from the curb, full of flowers and that day's race receipts. On a narrow sidewalk is the image of a shy young woman in magnificent ceremonial clothes, venturing uncertainly into the sunlight. And then there is the ghost of a little boy with a blue blanket, being carted up a staircase to a mysterious place full of dragons and phoenixes and, once, even a bowl of Chinese Cheerios. These are my personal spirits, shadows of my existence reaching out to me from over 120 years. To me they are dollops or magic—magic that can still be found by those who know where to look.

    Basically, I'm a preppy white guy from Connecticut. My mother is blonde and blue-eyed, the very image of a Donna Reed—sitcom housewife. Except that, unlike Alex Stone, my father is Chinese.

    Actually, he's third-generation Chinese American, born in Chinatown, raised in Brooklyn, and sounding remarkably like Walter Cronkite. His was a classic poor-boy-makes-good story: The youngest of five children, he was blessed with exquisite good looks and opportunity, and graduated from Columbia at 19; then, as a wartime Army Air Corps cadet in Denver, he married the beautiful southern blonde he met at a church social—a scandalous move in 1944. Chinatown was far behind him when, as an up-and-coming corporate executive in the late forties, he Anglicized his name to Hall from Hor, a name many Chinese Americans modify for obvious reasons. Pronounced "Haw," the Chinese character seems to mean "What?" (although some say it more accurately translates to "Huh?").

Our house *was* the ethnic neighborhood in Madison, Connecticut. My mother's acquaintances from bridge at the country club supposed we four kids were Korean War orphans. But Mrs. Hall, ever the southern lady, would always smile sweetly and say, "Guess again!"

5   Perhaps the enchantment I feel in Chinatown stems from the fact that we would visit only a few times a year, months of atmosphere and mystery crammed into forays lasting only as long as it took to consume a twenty-course banquet. I am talking of old Chinatown, those few blocks of Mott from Canal south to Chatham Square, and then up the Bowery to Doyers and Pell Streets, then west back to Mott—three little streets to which a whole universe had been transplanted, in miniature.

The ghosts are loud at Quong Yuen Shing & Company, at 32 Mott. Once a grocery, now selling dishes, it is hard to believe any time has passed since the store opened in 1891. Delicate portraits of gentlemen and ladies from old China still hang near the ceiling. In a glass case by the window is a large blue-and-white vase, left as collateral for a loan taken out by some immigrant Chinese man generations ago, when this store functioned as a credit union, mail drop, and social center for the lonely Chinese bachelors who once made up most of Chinatown's population. Against the rear wall is a bank of cubbyholes, once fitted with square drawers containing herbs that, according to ancient tradition, would cure all manner of ailments. And framing the back counter is an arch of wood, fantastically carved into the shapes of peacocks and fish in the branches of a tree and, since my childhood, solemnly pointed out to me as the handiwork of my great-grandfather Hor Lup Chut, the patriarch who arrived in this country in California as a 16-year-old boy in 1866.

He must have taken up residence in New York right at the founding of Chinatown in the 1870s or 1880s. Apparently a young man of some education, he had been lured to America by the promise of wealth and adventure, following the thousands coming to work on the railroads. My older relatives have always insisted that he was a cook and did no manual labor, but that might be wishful thinking.

At any rate, anti-Chinese violence drove him east, where wood-carving and whatever else he did earned him enough money to enable him to return several times to his home village near Canton and build three connecting houses, each with curving dragon eaves, to hold his three wives, one of whom he eventually brought to Mott Street. Descendants of the other wives still live in the crumbling remains of the old compound. When my sister Amy rediscovered them on a visit near there in 1986, she became the first American family member to make contact since Hor Lup Chut had died, in 1919. Her letter of introduction was hastily answered by a two-word telegram, "Bring money."

Diagonally across the street from 32 Mott is a redbrick apartment building sitting right on the bend of the street. Built in the early twenties, it is still known as *"sun lau,"* or "new building," the last apartment house built on lower Mott and the first to have real bathrooms. It was here that my father was born in 1923, and the spirits fairly shout at me as I walk by. There were nine people crammed into three rooms on the fourth floor—five small children, two parents, Great-Grandmother, and my great-aunt Bik, born to Hor Lup Chut and his wife on a family trip to China in 1913. They all slept on wooden planks set up nightly on sawhorses; Great-Grandmother had a hard porcelain pillow, like a hollow brick, which the Chinese found softer than down.

Research in China revealed that Great-Grandmother's name was Kan, but she was referred to only as "the mother of Pun" or "my No. 3 Wife." Back then, it was not uncommon for children to grow to adulthood without ever knowing their mothers' names, and Great-Grandmother's children may have gone to their graves never having uttered hers. She had bound feet, like all daughters of anyone with social pretensions, and one of my father's earliest memories is a horrifying image of the feet unbound—two fists of flesh with a single toe each—propped up on a chair.

Chin Shih was my grandmother's name, a fact also unknown until recently. She had given birth to five living children and endured hardship and unhappiness before succumbing in 1925, at the age of 28, to—heart failure? Tuberculosis? No one is sure. She had been brought from China under duress by Hor Lup Chut's son, my grandfather George Pun Hor, in 1914, after the family had sent him there with orders to marry and have children with the girl they had selected. But 16-year-old George was in love with a girl back in New York. He wrote to Great-Grandmother, pleading to be allowed to marry her. Her curt reply announced that he would marry the girl they had chosen or he would not be allowed to return from China. George Pun Hor did not question his orders again.

We have only one picture of Chin Shih—the formal family portrait perhaps taken in 1919 to celebrate the arrival of the First Son, my uncle Everett, who sits, fat and happy, decked out in the ceremonial First Son's crown. My aunts, Constance and Thelma, are there, and Chin Shih is off to the side, serenely beautiful but looking a little sad. She is remembered only vaguely by my father's generation, primarily as a source of warmth and quiet kindness. However, Everett recalls standing with her and Great-Grandmother in front of the New Building, both ladies dressed to the nines in elaborate, embroidered Chinese robes with flowers adorning their hair. A taxi pulled up to the curb, the entire party climbed in the back door, and they were driven about ten yards to a building across the street, where they climbed out the other door. Apparently, the ladies didn't want to risk soiling their precious clothes on the pavement.

It was to a neighbor's First Son celebration that they were being driven, and nearly 70 years later, Uncle Everett can still remember what they had to eat. But then, everything revolves around food in a society where the common greeting is not "Hello" but "Have you eaten yet?"

A glossy restaurant on the corner of Mott and Bayard Streets has replaced the wonderful, smelly, chaotic grocery we'd visit on our trips in from the suburbs when I was a child. It was always fun to see the reactions of both proprietors and tourists as my Waspish mother asked for various cooked meats or strange vegetables in her very tortured Chinese. There aren't any places like that anymore, but in the more modern supermarkets on Mott or Mulberry you can still buy dried skate, or 1,000-year eggs, or black-skin chickens to cook down into a medicinal broth. (Somehow, though, a bucket of raw chicken feet is a lot more interesting to a 12-year-old when it's lying out in the open with flies all over it than when it's packaged in plastic and found on a refrigerator shelf.)

15   Of course, restaurants assumed an almost ritualistic importance—like Lee's, where waiters rushed take-out meals through the narrow streets with food, dishes, and chopsticks arrayed on a big board balanced on their heads, or Joy Luck, where the owner would offer my grandfather "tea that burns" (a teapot full of scotch).

Those restaurants are gone, but walking down Pell and turning onto Doyers Street, one can still find the Nom Wah Tea Parlor, at No. 13–15, tucked into the elbow of the tiny, crooked lane. It has remained very much the same since the twenties, when it was the place to which my family would repair for Sunday-afternoon lunches of yum cha (tea food), now more popularly known as dim sum. Nom Wah's interior is worn and comfortable—probably never redecorated since my father's childhood. Against one wall is a collection of ancient tea and hot-water urns standing on curvy little legs. Open shelves, reaching to the ceiling, are full of colorful tea canisters. Hanging on another wall are panoramic pictures of the Shanghai waterfront, made when the restaurant was new, and probably not dusted since then. Sitting in your aged red booth, you can get steamed white dumplings stuffed with the sweet roasted pork known as cha shao; shao mai, little balls of steamed ground pork and fish; the square fried turnip cakes called lou bo gao; little shrimp, xia jiao; and all sorts of other things that I've never quite figured out. You don't have to know what anything is called: At Nom Wah, there are no menus, and patrons still make their selections from the big trays the waitress brings to their table. Tea food is all they serve, and when the meal is over, Mr. Tang will come over and figure your bill by counting the empty dishes, each size and shape commanding a different price.

For dessert, Mr. Tang provides some of the best pastries in Chinatown. And so does Fung Wong, my favorite childhood bakery, which still beckons from 30 Mott, with cases piled high with melon cakes or lotus-seed pastries, delicately sweet and delicious. In the window are little yellow egg custards and cookies shaped like fish. But during the days leading up to the Autumn Moon Festival (September 30), Fung Wong sells only dense moon cakes, made of lotus paste, elaborately shaped and decorated—and definitely an acquired taste.

No Chinese-food experience, even those accompanied by generous amounts of tea that burns, can compare with the banquet, that catchall celebratory event that Chinese families stage at the drop of a hat. And for my entire childhood, for my father's entire childhood—for my grandfather's entire childhood—a banquet meant a trip to Port Arthur, the Best Restaurant That Ever Was.

No. 7–9 Mott is a Chinese supermarket now; its second floor, where Port Arthur used to be, is devoted to the sale of dishes and cooking utensils. But once upon a time, the old staircase with the big brass rail delivered me into a murky world full of carved teak furniture and magnificent painted screens. Elaborate silk lanterns, festooned with dragons gripping long red tassels in their teeth, competed with ancient electric fans for ceiling space. Lifting the starched tablecloths, I discovered that the big round tables were merely huge pieces of plywood slapped over wonderful antiques, beautifully carved and inlaid with marble and mother-of-pearl. And down the corridor leading to the venerable bathrooms was the room set aside for brides to change into their wedding dresses—four elaborate costumes, each a different shade of red, worn during four different parts of the celebration.

I can see right through the housewares to the past. Over by the display of electrified household shrines was the table where my mother sneaked me a bowl of cereal because, as a 3-year-old, I wouldn't eat anything else. "These are really good Chinese Cheerios!" I announced in a loud voice, something that has been repeated to me at every banquet I've attended since 1961.

Over by the shelf with the electric rice cookers was where my great-aunt Bik held her sixtieth-birthday banquet. The sixtieth birthday is special, the cause for a really big celebration, and I was determined to be at my favorite aunt's party. So—my first solo motor trip to the big city. Knowing that Broadway would take me to the vicinity of Chinatown, I exited the expressway at the first "Broadway" sign I saw—in Yonkers. Two and a half hours later, I made a breathless entry into Port Arthur just as the last dish was being finished. "Bruce is here!" Aunt Bik cried. "Everyone sit down!" and she had the waiters bring me every one of the eighteen or twenty courses while the family grumbled and told me to eat faster. There was whole roasted duck, mysteriously boned from within, leaving the skin intact, so that when you sliced into it, you found only the shredded duck meat mixed with rice and vegetables. There were three-foot-long life noodles to be laboriously wound around chopsticks, because breaking them before they entered your mouth would be bad luck for the celebrant. And there was the dreaded almond juice, hot, thick, and cloyingly sweet, which had to be drunk to the hostess's health. It was a great party; the only thing missing was my grandfather, gravely ill in a hospital room and dreaming of his long-dead mother hobbling to him on bound feet, warning that he would be with her soon.

Everyone knew my grandfather. Today, twenty years after his death, I can still identify myself to almost anyone of a certain age on Mott Street by saying, "I'm Hock-Shop's grandson." People say, "Oh, Hock-Shop! I lost a lot of money in his store!" and they laugh at the memory, Hock-Shop. Hockie. It's a play on his name, Pun, pronounced "Pawn"—Pawn Shop, hence. . . . Okay, it's a stretch, but the name really suited him. He smoked huge cigars. He drove fancy cars at breakneck speed. During the late twenties, he toured with my great-uncles Sun and Fong in a vaudeville act called "The Chinese Whoopee Revue." And eventually, he became one of the most popular bookies in Chinatown.

We have a wonderful photograph of Hock-Shop with his foot up on the running board of his pride and joy, the big black 1938 LaSalle convertible that he talked about for years after its demise. You can still see what he saw as he wrestled that monster around the corner onto Park (now Mosco) Street, undoubtedly one of the smallest streets in New York. There's the wooden outdoor Chinese pastry booth, seemingly held together by countless coats of red paint. Next is the perennially open door of the kitchen to Hop Kee, always with an off-duty cook smoking a cigarette on the doorstep. And opposite was Hockie's flower shop, providing its indispensable service to the community.

He did sell flowers, mostly to the funeral home on the corner, but behind the tiny store was the real heart of the business. There, in the back room, Great-Uncle Fong would sit at a little table piled high with money and betting slips, ready to receive wagers on that day's horse races. The bookmaking didn't bring in huge amounts of cash, but it was enough to enable Hock-Shop to help out family members like his younger brother, who found that being named Fong Hor made it difficult to get a decent job in thirties New York.

If anyone wanted to gamble at *pai gow,* the pokerlike game played with dominoes, or the fast-paced fan-tan, where players bet on the number of beans shaken out of a cup, they had to go to one of the other secret little rooms or basements that could be found all over Chinatown. Gambling, after all, is in Chinese blood, and it was faithfully protected by the tong.

The Tong. A business association formed to protect Chinese interests and pastimes. The word conjures up images of mayhem and slaughter by sinister Asian gangsters, but much of that was a fabrication by the early-twentieth-century press. Well, it wasn't *entirely* fabricated, but compared with the recently arrived gangs of drug-smuggling thugs, tongs were decidedly benign operations.

Most businessmen had to belong to a tong, and Hock-Shop was no exception. His tong, the On Leong, controlled Mott Street. The Hip Sing tong controlled Pell and Doyers Streets, and never the twain would meet. One could not open a business without the tong's approval, and tongs carefully regulated the flow of stores and restaurants in an attempt to avoid unhealthy competition. It was strictly understood that a member of one tong would not try to open a shop in the other tong's territory; that might provoke an unwelcome visit from the opposition. Life in Chinatown was carefully taken care of. There were family associations that could find you a job, an apartment, or even food. Churches like the True Light Lutheran or the First Chinese Baptist looked after souls. Tongs regulated business. It was an all-encompassing cocoon in a time when welfare was unknown.

The tongs still exist, though in a vastly faded condition. Hip Sing shares a building with a newly established Buddhist temple at 16 Pell. On Leong's balconies, red columns, and pagoda roof preside over the corner of Mott and Canal. The old family associations like Lung Kong Tin Yee, at 23 Division, still provide low-cost meals and other help to needy members. Dominating their new meeting room (not open to the public) is the lovingly maintained ancestors' altar, brought from China in 1888. The Sun Wei Village Association building at 24 Pell, with its dragons and scrollwork painted in the traditional good-luck colors of green, red, and gold—peeling now—is obviously from another time and place. And flanking the door at the Yee Fon Toy Family Association, at 81 Bayard, is a poem identifying the very first Yee, who lived thousands of years ago, and proclaiming that the Yee family will continue for another 10,000 years.

It was at some of these places that my grandfather insisted on stopping during his final trip. Three days after Great-Aunt Bik's party, Hock-Shop died, as his mother's spirit had forewarned. However, later that day, while Aunt Bik was talking to my father on the phone about funeral arrangements for her brother, she had a heart attack and died, too, leaving my father stranded and helpless in Connecticut, frantically trying to figure out how to place a long-distance call to

New York's 911. Uncle Fong finally rushed over to find Aunt Bik lying on her bed. Her husband was in the living room, having assumed that his wife had fallen asleep while talking to her friends.

It seemed as if all Chinatown was at the Wah Wing Sang Funeral Corporation, at 26 Mulberry, for their funerals. Once again I came down from school, only this time I flew, to make sure I got there on time. On entering the room, mourners were compelled to take a piece of hard candy from a dish by the door, to wash away the bitterness of the occasion. A little towel was provided to "wipe away the tears." On one side of the coffin were mounds of flowers from the family; on the other, those from friends, all adorned with little scrolls in Chinese paying tribute to the deceased. Streams of mourners—mah-jongg partners, aged tong members, distant relatives—lined up in front of the casket to bow three times in a show of respect. For my grandfather, an awkward eulogy that went to great lengths to avoid mention of horses or the tong was delivered in English and Cantonese by a Mandarin Catholic priest for whom both were foreign languages. Pallbearers wrestled the coffins out the door, hoisting my aunt's at arm's length above their heads in a strange, dramatic gesture. The company filed out, each reaching into a bowl to grab a little twist of paper with a nickel inside, for buying a piece of candy at the first opportunity, to continue sweetening the bitterness.

I counted more than 30 cars in the funeral procession. Led by an Italian brass band (Aunt Bik's husband wanted to hire professional mourners, but the family drew the line), we wound through and around the streets of the congested neighborhood, stopping in front of any location that was important in the deceased's life. Tradition said that the closest family members were supposed to leave the limousines at each stop and bow three times before the open door of the hearse, but out of respect for the family, the funeral director did it for us, clapping loudly to alert the souls of the dead that we had stopped and they should take one last look around. It was a mournful tour of Chinatown's history, past Quong Yuen Shing, Port Arthur Restaurant, the On Leong Tong, the flower shop, and the New Building, with its real bathrooms and faded memories.

Today, at the National Archives, Kaimon Chin assists professor Betty Lee Sung as she patiently sorts through the 600 boxes of immigration records she recently discovered in a New Jersey warehouse. They document Chinese who, like Hor Lup Chut, suffered through years of a South Africa-like apartheid system before they were allowed to become full citizens of the country they called home. (In fact, my great-grandfather never *could* become a citizen, though he lived in America for 53 years; foreign-born Chinese were not allowed to be naturalized until 1943.)

At the tiny Chinatown History Museum, on the second floor of 70 Mulberry Street, young historians try to preserve memories of what was essentially a Cantonese village grafted onto the New York City streets. But Old Chinatown seemed to die with Bik and Hock-Shop in 1973, as greatly relaxed immigration laws opened up the old neighborhood to a flood of Asians from around the world. Where once you heard only Cantonese, now the streets are full of Thai, Vietnamese, and Malay—welcome, to be sure, but a little hard to keep up with. Chinatown even threatens to swallow up Little Italy as a new generation of entrepreneurs rips out the old wooden shops and replaces them with burnished-silver and brass finishes in an attempt to transform Mott Street into a Long Island-style shopping mall.

The family has long since left Chinatown for corporate jobs and homes in the suburbs. Our banquets barely fill one table now, and they are held in vast restaurants where uniformed hostesses brandishing walkie-talkies meet customers at the door and send them up escalators to a madhouse of noise and rush and confusion. Oh, the food is always delicious, and the service prompt. But my ghosts are slowly floating away, getting lost in a neighborhood where there is no longer time to clear the table for a post-dinner game of mah-jongg or for the owner to sit down with his favorite bookie over a pot of tea that burns.

Questions for Discussion

1. What do you think of the opening paragraph? Is this opening effective? Why do you think it is or isn't?
2. This essay was written for a general readership. How might the author revise this essay if he were addressing a specific audience of Chinese Americans? What changes would be appropriate?
3. Notice that the author occasionally gives the Chinese word for something he is describing. What is his purpose in doing this? Do you think he should do this more often? Explain your answer.
4. Do you see something of yourself and your situation in the author's experience? Do you think you have learned something from the author's experience?
5. What is this essay's subordinate aim? Cite specific passages to support your answer.

Opportunities for Writing

1. Your school newspaper is running a series of articles on families. In your submission for this series, describe your earliest memories of a special family gathering such as a wedding or a funeral. Where was it located? How many of your family's friends and relatives were there? How old were you at the time? Why do you remember this family gathering? How did you feel about it then? How do you feel about it now?
2. Recount your visit to the city or neighborhood where one or both of your parents or grandparents lived as a child. What did you see? What did you think?
3. Describe a Chinese neighborhood in your city. How big is the neighborhood? How old is it? What is your impression of it? What symbols and decorations do you notice? What shops and restaurants does it offer? Address your essay to a friend who might enjoy visiting this neighborhood.

Living In—and On—the Margins

Donald McQuade

Donald McQuade was born in New York and educated at Saint Francis College and Rutgers University. A writer and teacher, McQuade has edited and contributed to a number of books, including The Harper American Literature *(1986);* Student Writers at Work *(edited with Nancy Sommers, 1986);* Linguistics, Stylistics, and the Teaching of Composition *(1985);* Thinking in Writing: Structures for Composition *(with Robert Atwan, 1983); and* Selected Writings of Ralph Waldo Emerson *(1981). He has taught at Queens College, the University of Pennsylvania, and the University of California–San Diego. He is currently a professor of English and Dean of Undergraduate and Interdisciplinary Studies at the University of California–Berkeley. "Living In—and On—the Margins" is a version of McQuade's Chair's Address to the opening session of the 1991 College Composition and Communication Conference in Boston. This essay about his Italian mother, Adelina Pisano, draws on knowledge by participation and observation; it appeared in the February 1992 issue of* College Composition and Communication, *a professional journal for the study of reading and writing at the college level.*

I would like to invoke a brief—but I think memorable—assertion from Isak Dinesen. It reads: "All sorrows can be borne if you put them into a story or tell a story about them."[1] I come to this podium this morning fully conscious of the rather daunting responsibility attached to this occasion—a responsibility heightened by what my distinguished predecessors have said in their Chair's Addresses. Mindful of that tradition, I do not intend this morning to speak *for* our profession, nor to try to prepare a different focus for our individual or collective work. Nor do I intend to argue for the need to establish either greater coherence for or a different map of the shifting demarcations within the field of composition studies. Rather, I've come here prepared simply to tell a story about writing, about writing as a matter of life and death, a story about how I now know much better what I thought I had known before—about the dignity and the importance of what we try to do each day in our public and private conversations about the importance of the work of words in the lives of our students and in our own lives.

I pause nervously at the door to room 216, trying with one last deep breath to compose myself for what I have been told I'm about to see. It's late in the afternoon on January 16th, a day already shrouded by low-hung dark rain clouds and the specter of the first salvos in what will soon be a deadly and destructive war in the Gulf. I adjust my eyes to the darkness in the room, and I enter its silence. I follow the invitation of the only light that's on—a small and soft green light on the monitor next to the shapeless form on the bed. The light casts a pale glow over the motionless figure. I stand at the foot of the bed, and I suddenly recall the smell of a decomposing body from my summers working at the beach. I decide that this odor is slightly different—that it might be a leak in the catheter that hangs nearly filled on the far side of the bed. I taste the bitterness churning in the pit of my stomach and swallow uneasily. I stare at what is in front of me, trying to figure out if it's the person I traveled across the country to see and to talk with—perhaps for the last time.

I linger there for a moment or two, and then I decide to pick up her chart—to confirm her identity and to peer at the medical staff's judgment of her illness. Standing at the foot of the bed, her past and her future in my hands, I suddenly remember that she never had a birth certificate. I recall that she told us once that there was apparently no official record of her birth—anywhere. There was only a baptismal certificate. I saw it once; it said: Adelina Pisano, Blessed Sacrament Church, January 21, 1907. She had no reason not to trust her parents when they told her she was born on Christmas Day. She always seemed pleased that I had been born on December 26th. We celebrated our birthdays together late on Christmas night, and she always had a kind word to offset the disappointment I invariably felt when our relatives wished me a Merry Christmas *and* a Happy Birthday with a single present.

But there is no voice to hear this afternoon. Her lips are motionless; the rings around her eyes underscore the darkness of her sleep. Her body seems shorter, her head smaller than the image I carry around with me. Several wisps of thin grey hair evade the snarls of the net she no doubt struggled to put on—so that she wouldn't bother the nurses with having to comb her hair before her children's arrival each day during visiting hours. Smiling at the sight of the black hair net, I remember how self-effacing she is, how she never wants to bother anyone, how she doesn't expect anything from anyone, and how—when someone does try to help her—she responds with embarrassment and with the conviction that she hasn't done anything to deserve the attention, how someone else needs it more.

5   She never claims any authority for herself—for her perceptions, for her experiences, for her distinctive sense of self. She habitually disqualifies her point of view—before she speaks it. I recall from my childhood her most often repeated phrase: "Go ask your father. He'll know about that." I remember her telling us that she didn't get upset when the nuns in grammar school "officially" changed her name from Adelina to Edna—to make it easier to pronounce her name. "What was I going to do? Those nuns were tough then—not like today. They all wore stiff habits, even in the summer—not like today. Then, they didn't take any guff from anybody. . . ." I can hear her constantly interrupt herself to say "I know I shouldn't say this." The soft stillness of the body lying in that bed reminds me that she sees herself at the receiving end of experience rather than at its origins. She doesn't seem to determine the history of her own life. After she was robbed by the young man she had asked to help her cross an icy and busy street on her way to daily Mass, she told her children, "Look, you gotta take what comes your way . . . the bad with the good. But don't worry, I asked Josie the tailor to sew pockets on the inside of my overcoat. When that bum tries to steal my pocketbook again, he'll be surprised. There won't be nothing in it next time." It seemed almost as if she were eager to see him again and to stare at him with contempt. But she allows herself few instances of such sweet revenge.

As I look intently down at her, I remind myself that she never likes to call attention to herself. She talks a great deal, but always about others—and especially about her sons, about her daughters-in-law, and, whenever *anyone* would listen, about her grandchildren and how blessed—and lucky—she is. As hard as I try, I can recall no time when she allows herself to be at the center of anything public. She somehow manages to make herself inconspicuous, even the time when she was invited to City Hall to receive a certificate—suitable of course for framing—from then-Mayor Ed Koch for her volunteer work among the elderly. She was proud of her award, but modesty, if not embarrassment, seemed almost to compel her to cover at least partially her mouth whenever she spoke about the occasion. Her family seemed much more excited than she allowed herself to be, and none of us was surprised that we had a difficult time trying to find her in the official photograph; she had tucked herself into a tiny space between two beaming—and large—women at what, as fortune would have it, turned out to be the edge of the photograph. As I move my eyes slowly across her deeply-lined face, I see there reminders that in virtually every significant sense, she probably still views herself as unimportant, as someone who doesn't matter, as someone who finally sees herself as fundamentally expendable.

I notice that her chest moves slowly—to the rhythm of the monitor. Her skin takes on a slightly yellow hue in the soft green light, and it drapes loosely—and even elegantly—over the small, brittle bones that somehow still keep her body together. Her wrists are attached with thin rubber tubing to the metal bed rails—to protect her, they say, from hurting herself if she suffers another stroke. I sit down at the bedside and reach for the short, stubby fingers that are open to view, fingers that I imagine still bear traces from the years she devoted to raising her children, years when, as she hesitantly told us, she "helped make ends meet" by typing address labels at the kitchen table against a never-ending cycle of pressured deadlines from an insurance company that wanted its renewal notices out on time.

Her hands are ice cold, and I slide my nervous fingers up to her wrist—in search of what I expect will be her faint pulse. I'm no longer surprised by what I see and touch. She looks as if she's dying quietly, if not peacefully. Her arm moves slightly, and I am quickly drawn to her face, and then to her flickering eyes. She opens them and turns her head toward me—but slowly. I lean closer to her, but she doesn't speak. I sense her surprise and wait for her to say something. She looks at me with more focused attention, smiles, and tries to force words out of her body. I feel the attention in her quickening pulse and sense the emotion that pushes the words through her stiffened jaw and parched lips. Her voice finally relaxes, taking comfort in recognizing its own distinctive sound. She whispers: "Da Professor!"

She seems too weak for conversation, so I launch into a hurried—and scattered—report on her grandchildren in California. The news seems to course through her fragile veins, and I try to make her stronger with funny stories about the children, about life on the west coast, and about the trips she took with us after her husband died. I ask her if she remembers the trip on TWA to the old country—when one of my former students bumped all of us up into first class. "Somebody should fly first class," he said, "Why not you and your family?" When I remind her that I found that logic compelling, her smile broadens and deepens. She says softly: "I was a nervous wreck for the first half-hour. I had my rosary beads out. What if they found out that we didn't belong?!"

10   I lean back into the chair and ask: "Do you remember what happened when we landed in Rome?"

"Yeah. I wouldn't speak Italian. I didn't want to embarrass you and Susanne by speaking with such a terrible accent. They'd know I was from Brooklyn in a second. . . ." I remind myself that she won't speak for either herself or for others, and I conclude, mistakenly, that she remains not simply—but profoundly—inarticulate.

As we relax into each other's company and settle into a quiet conversation, a hospital orderly announces himself and reminds her that it's five o'clock. Positioning her dinner tray over her now raised-bed, he proudly announces "I've got something special for you tonight. I know you gonna like this." He releases the restraints on her wrists and sweeps the metal cover from over the plate, like a magician heightening the anticipation before revealing a surprise. He backs away from the bed with the metal lid still in his hand, and as he turns to leave, he takes special pleasure in trumpeting the word "Lasagne!"

Almost immediately, her head drops, as if it has been suddenly disconnected from the rest of her body. She moves it back and forth, trying to muster a sigh of despair at the same time. She tries to arch her head back up to see if the orderly has left. "They're very nice people here," she says in a hushed voice. "They bring you your tray right to your bed. I don't want them to be insulted, but I can't eat this stuff. Look at it. They serve carrots with lasagne! I tasted the sauce yesterday." Her eyes dart toward the doorway. She tries to lean forward, but she resorts to another whisper: "They don't know how to make sauce—not like we do."

I try to reassure her that I understand. "I know," I say softly, "but try to eat it anyway. If you wanna get outta here, you have to eat. You know you need to get strong."

"I know.... I know...." Her hand moves slowly, reluctantly toward the fork. She lifts a small lump of the lasagne from the right side of the plate, and as she moves it haltingly—and almost horizontally—across the plate toward her, the fork touches the carrots. She doesn't seem either willing or able to hold the fork any longer. Her eyes move away from the food, and she stares intently at me. Her tongue reaches the edge of her lips, but she doesn't speak.

I fill the silence with a nervous refrain: "You have to eat it if you want to get strong, if you want to get out of this place."

She forces herself to lift her right hand with her left and to move it once again toward the fork. She picks it up and tilts it slightly toward herself, perhaps hoping that some of the lasagne will slide off and onto her pale green nightgown, putting an end to the awkwardness we both feel.

But the sauce glues the pasta to the fork. "I'll try," she murmurs, "but I can't promise that I'll eat all of it. This sauce is so lousy."

"Try.... Do the best you can."

The second bite is even more reluctant than the first. "I can't eat it. It'll kill me."

"You gotta eat," I say, and somewhat impatiently. "All right. Leave the lasagne. Try the carrots...."

She responds more quickly, and with a slightly sharper edge in her voice. "The carrots?! I just tried the lasagne. I can't eat the carrots now, not with lasagne."

"You gotta get stronger if you wanna get out of here."

"I know. But I can't eat this stuff. The lasagne and the carrots are cold. Nobody can eat cold lasagne. It'll kill me."

Her eyes reach for the cup of lime Jello. "Let me try the Jello. It's got fruit cocktail in it. What the hell can they do to Jello?!" Her fork disturbs the sheen of the Jello. The surface wobbles like she knows it should. She forces a slight smile, and as she eats it she says "Everybody knows how to make Jello."

At 7:15 that night, I'm sitting at a linen-lined table in my younger brother's dining room, eating a steaming plate of ravioli. Our eyes are glued to the television set nervously propped atop the credenza so that we could eat and watch the news before returning to the hospital. At precisely the same moment that news reports from Baghdad announce that the war has begun, raining steel on that city, the phone rings. Annoyed by the distraction, I pick it up and before I can say anything the voice on the other end urges "Come to the hospital—fast."

As soon as my brother, sister-in-law, and I arrive at room 216, we're redirected to the intensive care unit, where my older brother paces the hallway. "She's had another episode," he reports anxiously. "I don't know if she's gonna make it this time." I spend what seems like the next hour or two sitting on a vinyl-covered couch, thinking—nervously—about the word "episode." Finally, the doctor emerges and asks us to step outside the waiting room to find a corner or a wall that will provide some semblance of privacy.

"She's had another stroke, but this one is far more serious. She's also suffered respiratory arrest, but because the nurses and the doctor were working on her in less than a minute, I'm confident that there's no brain damage. We can always do a CAT-scan later. She didn't seem able to keep her food down, and it came back up into her lungs. I'm afraid she's also suffering from double pneumonia—a combination of bacterial and gastric infections in her lungs. Look, I hate to bring this up, but the hospital staff needs to know whether you'd like us to try to resuscitate her should she experience another episode like the one tonight. She's stabilized now. There isn't anything you can do for her at this point. Don't let me push you into a decision. Why don't you go home and try to get some sleep."

Even in the face of her own death, she doesn't have the opportunity to speak for herself.

30   The next morning brings the startling news that she's made remarkable progress during the night. We take turns going in to see her. When my brother and I reach her bedside, we're stunned by the sight of the number of tubes running into, and through, her body. While technology rained death on Baghdad and Allied forces used "smart" bombs equipped with cameras to film their own success in living color, one tiny, frail Italian woman was kept alive by six humming consoles and by what apparently was an indomitable will to live.

She looks up at us from the center of the other side of that terrifying sight. The tubes prevent her from speaking, but her eyes plead for an explanation. We tell her, as best we can, what has happened to her. We don't tell her that the doctor has asked us to decide whether *we* want the hospital to resuscitate her should she have another stroke. Neither of us is ready to say that, at least not yet. We try to keep talking, to reach beyond the veil of silence that seems to have descended over her.

The more we try to offer her encouragement, the more her eyes seem to dart around the room. She fixes her attention on the table to the right of where I'm standing. She motions toward the table with her eyes. The only items on it are a stack of the bookmark-sized prayers she carries around with her, a half-filled cup of water, a pencil, and some sheets of paper with "Mercy Hospital" written across the top and "PROGRESS NOTES" printed in large boldface beneath it. Instinctively, I gather up the prayers and ask her if she'd like me to read them to her. Her eyes dart left and right. Once again, she uses her eyes to motion toward the table. After what seemed like the longest—and most awkward—moments in my life, I finally realize that she wants me to hand her the paper and pencil. I rush to the nurse's station and ask for a clipboard. Within seconds of my return, a torrent of prose rushes across that piece of paper.

It seemed as though nothing—nor her ninth grade education, her shaky handwriting, her weak grammar, not her spotty punctuations—could encumber what she wanted, almost desperately, to tell us about what had happened to her. Here's a sampling of what she wrote:

> Last night after you left they started working on me from 8:00 to through the night. The doctors and nurses never left me. No sleep until 5:00 o'clock a.m. in the morning. They were good to me. I will not ever forget them in my prayers. They all very very nice to me and I hope you all feel the same way about them. Sorry. Bad handwriting. Love and Prayers.

She wrote virtually continuously for twenty minutes that morning, pausing only to allow us to figure out what the appropriate next question was and to press her for greater detail. She wrote until she slid into exhaustion and a deep sleep. That afternoon, as soon as we arrived, she was back at it. And the next day, when her grown grandchildren arrived, she told them slightly different versions of the same story in writing. She was proud that she had survived, but she couldn't fully release herself into saying that directly.

It seems as if she is writing to keep herself alive, almost as if her self would be lost if she stopped—lost, or suffocated, in the maze of tubes and wires and contraptions that not only were keeping her alive but also allowing her to speak from the other side of her silence. Each time we visit she pours out one "Progress Note" after another. Each becomes more detailed, more compelling. She writes, for example, about the CAT-scan they put her through on the night she suffered her last stroke. She describes feeling trapped inside that silver machine, feeling as though she had died and had been placed inside a silver casket. She writes that she felt so alone and that she is glad she can tell us about that experience, and how she hopes she won't have to go through it again. "Next time," she writes, "just bury me."

Over the course of several visits, we ease her—or she eases us—into taking up different subjects, but she invariably returns to the events surrounding her last stroke and to their aftermath. She seems to shy away from describing the central event, the "episode," in any detail, but she doesn't hesitate in the least to take us inside the world of the machines she's still hooked up to. She explains, for example, that she sometimes feels as though she no longer has a body, that she is little more than an extension of the equipment. "I don't know how I'll ever get out of this place," she writes. Yet, slowly her tone grows slightly more confident. She seems able for the first time in her notes to distance herself from the trauma by characterizing it in a phrase we heard applied for years to anything she judges unpleasant. "You have no idea. I went through the tortures of hell." Everyone smiles, knowingly. It's also time to leave. She motions me to stay, and as soon as she is sure that everyone else has left the room, she starts to write again. After about a minute, she hands me the clipboard, and smiles wistfully and coyly: "It was the bad lasagne I had. . . ."

Driving home from that evening, I take pleasure in the fact that perhaps for the first time in her life, Adelina Pisano has chosen to reserve for herself the authority to make—as well as to articulate—a decision. Needing to tell her stories, but trapped in silence, she turns to the only medium available to her: writing. Writing for her took on a life of its own; it became not only a self-affirming but also a life-affirming activity.

Another day—her final day in intensive care. The doctor reports that she's "out of the woods now" and that they plan to move her in the morning to a bed in intermediate care. We thank him for his help, and he turns toward me: "When are you going home?"

"I guess I can go back tomorrow night."

The ride to JFK is unusual; that is, it is uneventful. There is no traffic, no accidents, and I remark to my brother that the road looks "really clean," that I haven't seen a single abandoned—or stripped—car along the side of the highway. He acknowledges my point with a quick "uh huh" but never takes his eyes off the car in front of him.

The flight to San Francisco proves more intriguing. With threats of global terrorism, it's not surprising that the plane is far less than half full. Yet I can't understand why I don't sleep on the long flight home.

My body is in neutral, if not reverse, but my mind jump starts the takeoff. Before we reach cruising altitude, I realize I need to make some sense of what we all have just gone through. I order some wine—to celebrate Adelina Pisano's will to live and to toast her for caring enough about her family and finally about herself to tell them each day through her "Progress Notes" that she is alive and that she hopes—with the help of God and some good luck—to stay alive. I take pleasure and pride in the dignity of her struggle and in her resourcefulness with language and the power she now exercises over it. But I quickly caution myself to resist sentimentalizing her and what she is accomplishing as a newly-practiced, although still self-effacing writer. I remind myself of my rekindled anger about the resources of language denied to her as well as about the skills she denied to herself. I know that her resourcefulness with language is culturally as well as personally determined, but I can't decide which prevails in Adelina Pisano's life—then and now. I can't figure out where she is in relation to her own experience—whether she is at the center or at the margins of her own articulateness.

I sit in a silver cylinder at 35,000 feet, alone with my thoughts and plenty of time, so I decide to pursue some better understanding of what it means to be "marginal" or "marginalized" and to live "in" and "on" the margins. It doesn't take long for the negative associations to surface. Those who are "marginal" or "marginalized" lead lives determined—in fundamental ways—by others. Characteristically, they are reported by others to regard themselves as closed out, if not shut down, from experience. Characteristically, they are reported to be viewed—and treated—by others as though they were inert, ignored, forgotten, left out too long—like a faded shirt hanging on a clothesline at the back of an abandoned tenement.

The prevailing view of living "on the margins" doesn't differ markedly. To be "on the margins" is to be in a condition which closely approximates the limit below or beyond which something ceases to be possible or desirable. Viewed from another angle—from on the other side of a boundary—to be on the margins is to be superfluous. After all, a margin (of profit, of space, of time, of material goods) is an amount that is available—or allowed—in addition to what is estimated to be strictly necessary for or essential to a predefined purpose.

I gaze out the window and reflect on the significance the term bears when viewed from the perspective of spatial relations. To be "on" the margin means to locate oneself—or to be located—at the edge of a boundary. This place—this state of mind, this socio-economic condition, this linguistic or political or sexual identity—is in some way marked off or distinguished from the rest of what is perceived. In this sense, to be "in" or "on" the margin is to be identified as different—but negatively so—to be seen as unlike the rest. But the demarcations between the center and the margins are always in flux. And complex identities result from these shifting grounds—what Gloria Anzaldua calls "Borderlands." In a compelling blend of poetry and prose, Anzaldua describes the shadowy spaces of her own childhood along the Texas/Mexico border, caught between two cultures, and an alien in both. Anzaldua charts the intersections of ethnic, linguistic, and sexual identity with both searing insight and a powerful and cohesive vision of a dignified future for those who live in what she calls "this place of contradiction," a place where the self struggles "amidst adversity and violation; with the confluence of primordial images; with the unique positionings consciousness takes at these confluent streams; and with [an] almost instinctive urge to communicate, to speak, to write about life on the borders, life in the shadows."[2]

45   I realize that the terms of Adelina Pisano's life—and especially its shifting grounds—offer another confirmation of the contradictions of living "on the borders" and "in the shadows." I begin to challenge the applicability of the traditional definitions of the word "margins," each of which focuses on some limitation of the place or the person described with this term. The inaccuracies and the inadequacies of these definitions become clearer—when applied to individual acts of self-identification, to individual acts of self-articulation, when applied to speaking, thinking, and writing.

For Gloria Anzaldua—and for Adelina Pisano—to live "in" and "on" the margins might well bear more positive implications. For these two women, in very different places and in very different ways, to live "in" and "on" the margins is, in many respects, to be free: to try to reach out, to speak out from behind the veil of silence, to take risks, to take chances, to open themselves to experience in what are possibly, although not assuredly, informative and enduring ways. To live productively "in" and "on" the margins is to be "on edge," to recognize and explore both the terms for experience as well as the relations between and among the terms, those seemingly silent gaps, those seemingly still spaces between one experience and another. The voice of William James resonates as I pause to take a deep breath. "Experience itself, taken at large, can grow by its edges," James reminds me. "Life is in the transitions as much as in the terms connected: often indeed, [life] seems to be there more emphatically, as if our spurts and sallies forward were the real firing line of flame advancing across the dry autumnal field which the farmer proceeds to burn. In this line, we live prospectively as well as retrospectively."[3] I ponder those lines in James, and

I *think* I understand the connection: the margin is not only a place, it is a locus for relations. It may even be an activity. It's *more*—not less—than a noun. It's a noun in process—like the word "education," or "knowledge," or "experience."

I spend the rest of the flight conjuring up images that might sharpen the distinctions between and among such terms as "margins," "borders," "edges," "boundaries," and "fringes." I think first of the students I teach. I realize that the margins are where most teachers—especially teachers of writing—live in relation to our students. It's a location (a place) as well as an opportunity for us to demonstrate (an activity) the generosity that distinguishes our work as teachers—the reciprocity we express in response to what they have written. I suddenly find it curious that teachers and students call such writing "marginal notes," and I remind myself that I need to think more often—and more seriously—about the nature and the implications of the writing I so routinely do in the classes I teach. Being "in" and "on" the margins of our students' lives is where they ordinarily expect us to be—and rightfully so. Versions of the dialectic surface in all corners of the academy. I begin to understand that the margins may well be where many students *and* faculty spend their time thinking and writing—even though every one of us is expected to do something quite different: to speak and think and write and perform at the center of the intellectual communities and the cultures in which each of us seeks to posit his or her voice.

My thoughts drift to the difficulties, to the strains, to the pain some—and perhaps many—students and teachers experience as they struggle with the pressures and expectations imposed on them: to toe the line rather than, as James says, to live *in* the line, that is to "live prospectively as well as retrospectively." Remembering my mother's eagerness—and struggle—to write prompts me to think of my student Emily Hampton, who loved to write sentences. Emily Hampton wrote many brilliant and elegant sentences. She worked relentlessly on them, shaping and reshaping them to satisfy her own extraordinary standards. But Emily Hampton had trouble seeing the relations between her sentences. Transitions—from one sentence to the next, from one paragraph to another—remained impossibly difficult for her. A perfectionist in every sense, Emily Hampton was stuck *on* the line. She had trouble living and writing either prospectively or retrospectively. Because Emily Hampton was convinced—by herself or by others—that she couldn't ever produce paragraphs and essays that would satisfy the expectations she imagined others set for her, she did violence to her sentences and finally to herself. She killed herself the day after she participated in the commencement ceremony at Berkeley. With my chin leaning on my hand, I sit staring at the seat in front of me—thinking only of my failures, for a long time.

The silence is broken by the sounds of the voices of Emily and Adelina, by the painful edges of these women's stories, and I recall another. Francine du Plessix Gray's account of a recurring—and harrowing—nightmare from her youth. "Facing a friend, I struggle for words and emit no sound," she says. "I have an urgent message to share but am struck dumb. My jaw is clamped shut as in a metal vise. I gasp for breath and cannot set my tongue free. And at the dream's end, my friend has fled, and I am locked into the solitude of silence." du Plessix Gray attributes the nightmare, at least in part, to her father's impatience with her youthful writing, to his swift and sardonic tongue, and to his having constantly interrupted her when she tried to speak. Later as a student in a workshop at Black Mountain, du Plessix Gray submitted revisions of several prize-winning stories. Her mentor, no less an imposing figure than the 6 foot 8 inch poet Charles Olson, told her "You're writing pure junk.... If you want to be a writer keep it to a journal.... And above all don't try to publish anything for ten years."

Francine du Plessix Gray's first piece of fiction was published in *The New Yorker* one year *past* the distant deadline Olson had set for her. In struggling to come to terms with why she persisted at writing, she says: "I write out of a desire for revenge against reality, to destroy forever the stuttering powerless child I once was, to gain the love and attention that silenced child never had, to allay the dissatisfaction I still have with myself, to be something other than what I am.... I remain sustained," she says, "by a definition of faith once offered me by Ivan Illich: 'faith is a readiness for the surprise.' I write because I have faith in the possibility that I can eventually surprise myself."[4]

That image of a jaw clamped shut, that sense of revenge against reality, that definition of faith, that readiness for the surprise propel me back to the place I left nearly eight hours before.

I am standing at Adelina Pisano's bedside. She finally frees herself from the machines that regulated her recovery. She can talk now, but I know that she won't—not unless she has her teeth in. We're both nervous. We hold each other's hand tightly, but stiffly. Neither of us dares to be the first to talk. I feel the quiet tension between us. I finally say: "I'm leaving tonight. I have to go. Susanne has been alone with the kids for a long time, and I start a new semester in two days."

"I understand."

I tell her how happy I am to have spent time with her, even in such difficult circumstances. I tell her how sorry I am to leave, and I try to deflect attention from my sadness by reminding her of the funny stories we traded on the first day I visited her. She looks at me and fixes my attention on her eyes for what seems like a very long minute. Finally, she speaks. "I understand. I've caused you boys too much trouble already. Don't worry about me. I'll be all right." Her voice rushes forward. "Listen, say hello to Susanne and the kids, and send me a new picture of Christine and Marc. The ones I have are getting old. I bet he's grown a lot."

She pauses, but only for a few seconds, perhaps to summon a word, to change the subject. "Oh, they say I can have a phone in my new room. Call me once in a while." She drops her hand slightly, but her eyes hold mine. "You take care of yourself, do you hear . . . and write when you get a chance."[5]

Notes

1. This quotation from Isak Dinesen appears as an epigraph to chapter five of Hannah Arendt's *The Human Condition* (175).
2. See the "Preface" to Gloria Anzaldua's *Borderlands/La Frontera: The New Mestiza*.
3. William James makes this point in an essay, "A World of Pure Experience," in *Essays in Radical Empiricism* (42).
4. Francine du Plessix Gray's statement appeared in a *New York Times Book Review* article, "I Write for Revenge Against Reality" (3).
5. Adelina Pisano died on August 6, 1991.

For their generous encouragement and assistance in preparing several drafts of this essay, I would like to thank Patrick W. Hoy III, June Jordan, Anne Middleton, Kathleen Moran, and Nancy Sommers. I would also like to express my gratitude to the students in English 180J at the University of California, Berkeley who read an earlier draft of this essay and offered invaluable suggestions for improving it.

Works Cited

Anzaldua, Gloria. *Borderlands/La Frontera: The New Mestiza.* San Francisco: Spinsters/Aunte Lute, 1987.

Arendt, Hannah. *The Human Condition.* Chicago: U of Chicago P, 1958.

Gray, Francine du Plessix. "I Write for Revenge Against Realty," *The New York Times Book Review.* September 12, 1982: 3.

James, William. "A World of Pure Experience," *Essays in Radical Empiricism.* Cambridge: Harvard UP, 1976.

Questions for Discussion

1. Identify the stages of plot in this essay. Which passages constitute the introduction? rising action? climax? falling action? resolution?
2. Examine the descriptive and narrative details with which the author characterizes Adelina Pisano. Which details do you consider essential to this characterization? Explain your answer.
3. What is your opinion of the narrator? How does he characterize himself? What is his attitude toward his subject?
4. Is the title appropriate? Why do you think it is or isn't?
5. This essay was written for a specific audience of college composition teachers. If the author were addressing a general audience, how might he revise this essay? What changes would you recommend?

Opportunities for Writing

1. Recall a time you visited a friend or relative in the hospital. Why was he or she in the hospital? What was his or her condition? What did you see and do? How did your visit make your friend or relative feel? How did it make you feel?
2. Depict a hospital you have visited. What does it look like? When was it built? How many patients does it serve daily? How many doctors and nurses work there? What sounds and smells did you notice on your visit? What was your impression of this hospital? What did you consider especially interesting or important about it?
3. Recount a time in your life when you relied heavily on writing—when your ability to write was especially important to you. Why were you writing? What sorts of things did you to write? To whom did you write? Address this essay to a teacher who influenced your writing.
4. Without mentioning his or her name, describe a man or woman you know who is "marginalized"—who lives on the margins of society. What is this individual like? How and why is he or she marginalized?

What have you learned from this individual? What is your relationship to him or her? Write this essay for the contributors to a charitable organization in your community.

On Being a Cripple
NANCY MAIRS

Nancy Mairs is a poet and essayist. She was born in Long Beach, California, and went to Wheaton College and the University of Arizona. As revealed in this essay, Mairs has been a technical editor as well as high school and college writing teacher. Her numerous publications include Voice Lessons: On Becoming a (Woman) Writer *(1994),* Carnal Acts: Essays *(1990), and* Remembering the Bone House: An Erotics of Place and Space *(1989). "On Being a Cripple" appeared in* Plaintext: Essays *(1986). In this text, Mairs traces the onset and development of the crippling disease, multiple sclerosis (MS), and shares what her physical condition has taught her. Notice the inclusion of information that Mairs has come to understand by having MS, by knowing others who also have the disease, by reading, and by speaking to doctors.*

> *To escape is nothing. Not to escape is nothing.*
>
> Louise Bogan

The other day I was thinking of writing an essay on being a cripple. I was thinking hard in one of the stalls of the women's room in my office building, as I was shoving my shirt into my jeans and tugging up my zipper. Preoccupied, I flushed, picked up my book bag, took my cane down from the hook, and unlatched the door. So many movements unbalanced me, and as I pulled the door open I fell over backward, landing fully clothed on the toilet seat with my legs splayed in front of me: the old beetle-on-its-back routine. Saturday afternoon, the building deserted, I was free to laugh aloud as I wriggled back to my feet, my voice bouncing off the yellowish tiles from all directions. Had anyone been there with me, I'd have been still and faint and hot with chagrin. I decided that it was high time to write the essay.

First, the matter of semantics. I am a cripple. I choose this word to name me. I choose from among several possibilities, the most common of which are "handicapped" and "disabled." I made the choice a number of years ago, without thinking, unaware of my motives for doing so. Even now, I'm not sure what those motives are, but I recognize that they are complex and not entirely flattering. People—crippled or not—wince at the word "cripple," as they do not at "handicapped" or "disabled." Perhaps I want them to wince. I want them to see me as a tough customer, one to whom the fates/gods/viruses have not been kind, but who can face the brutal truth of her existence squarely. As a cripple, I swagger.

But, to be fair to myself, a certain amount of honesty underlies my choice. "Cripple" seems to me a clean word, straightforward and precise. It has an honorable history, having made its first appearance in the Lindisfarne Gospel in the tenth century. As a lover of words, I like the accuracy with which it describes my condition: I have lost the full use of my limbs. "Disabled," by contrast, suggests an incapacity, physical or mental. And I certainly don't like "handicapped," which implies that I have deliberately been put at a disadvantage, by whom I can't imagine (my God is not a Handicapper General), in order to equalize chances in the great race of life. These words seem to me to be moving away from my condition, to be widening the gap between word and reality. Most remote is the recently coined euphemism "differently abled," which partakes of the same semantic hopefulness that transformed countries from "undeveloped" to "underdeveloped," then to "less developed," and finally to "developing" nations. People have continued to starve in those countries during the shift. Some realities do not obey the dictates of language.

Mine is one of them. Whatever you call me, I remain crippled. But I don't care what you call me, so long as it isn't "differently abled," which strikes me as pure verbal garbage designed, by its ability to describe anyone, to describe no one. I subscribe to George Orwell's thesis that "the slovenliness of our language makes it easier for us to have foolish thoughts." And I refuse to participate in the degeneration of the language to the extent that I deny that I have lost anything in the course of this calamitous disease; I refuse to pretend that the only differences between you and me are the various ordinary ones that distinguish any one person from another. But call me "disabled" or "handicapped" if you like. I have long since grown accustomed to them; and if they are vague, at least they hint at the truth. Moreover, I use them myself. Society is no readier to accept crippledness than to accept death, war, sex, sweat, or wrinkles. I would never refer to another person as a cripple. It is the word I use to name only myself.

5   I haven't always been crippled, a fact for which I am soundly grateful. To be whole of limb is, I know from experience, infinitely more pleasant and useful than to be crippled; and if that knowledge leaves me open to bitterness at my loss, the physical soundness I once enjoyed (though I did not enjoy it half enough) is well worth the occasional stab of regret. Though never any good at sports, I was a normally active child and young adult. I climbed trees, played hopscotch, jumped rope, skated, swam, rode my bicycle, sailed. I despised team sports, spending some of the wretchedest afternoons of my life sweaty and humiliated, behind a field-hockey stick and under a basketball hoop. I tramped alone for miles along the bridle paths that webbed the woods behind the house I grew up in. I swayed through countless dim hours in the arms of one man or another under the scattered shot of light from mirrored balls, and gyrated through countless more as Tab Hunter and Johnny Mathis gave way to the Rolling Stones, Creedence Clearwater Revival, Cream. I walked down the aisle. I pushed baby carriages, changed tires in the rain, marched for peace.

When I was twenty-eight I started to trip and drop things. What at first seemed my natural clumsiness soon became too pronounced to shrug off. I consulted a neurologist, who told me that I had a brain tumor. A battery of tests, increasingly disagreeable, revealed no tumor. About a year and a half later I developed a blurred spot in one eye. I had, at last, the episodes "disseminated in space and time" requisite for a diagnosis: multiple sclerosis. I have never been sorry for the doctor's initial misdiagnosis, however. For almost a week, until the negative results of the tests were in, I thought that I was going to die right away. Every day for the past nearly ten years, then, has been a kind of gift. I accept all gifts.

Multiple sclerosis is a chronic degenerative disease of the central nervous system, in which the myelin that sheathes the nerves is somehow eaten away and scar tissue forms in its place, interrupting the nerves' signals. During its course, which is unpredictable and uncontrollable, one may lose vision, hearing, speech, the ability to walk, control of bladder and/or bowels, strength in any or all extremities, sensitivity to touch, vibration, and/or pain, potency, coordination of movements—the list of possibilities is lengthy and yes, horrifying. One may also lose one's sense of humor. That's the easiest to lose and the hardest to survive without.

In the past ten years, I have sustained some of these losses. Characteristic of MS are sudden attacks, called exacerbations, followed by remissions, and these I have not had. Instead, my disease has been slowly progressive. My left leg is now so weak that I walk with the aid of a brace and a cane; and for distances I use an Amigo, a variation on the electric wheelchair that looks rather like an electrified kiddie car. I no longer have much use of my left hand. Now my right side is weakening as well. I still have the blurred spot in my right eye. Overall, though, I've been lucky so far. My world has, of necessity, been circumscribed by my losses, but the terrain left me has been ample enough for me to continue many of the activities that absorb me: writing, teaching, raising children and cats and plants and snakes, reading, speaking publicly about MS and depression, even playing bridge with people patient and honorable enough to let me scatter cards every which way without sneaking a peek.

Lest I begin to sound like Pollyanna, however, let me say that I don't like having MS. I hate it. My life holds realities—harsh ones, some of them—that no right-minded human being ought to accept without grumbling. One of them is fatigue. I know of no one with MS who does not complain of bone-weariness; in a disease that presents an astonishing variety of symptoms, fatigue seems to be a common factor. I wake up in the morning feeling the way most people do at the end of a bad day, and I take it from there. As a result, I spend a lot of time *in extremis* and, impatient with limitation, I tend to ignore my fatigue until my body breaks down in some way and forces rest. Then I miss picnics, dinner parties, poetry readings, the brief visits of old friends from out of town. The offspring of a puritanical tradition of exceptional venerability, I cannot view these lapses without shame. My life often seems a series of small failures to do as I ought.

I lead, on the whole, an ordinary life, probably rather like the one I would have led had I not had MS. I am lucky that my predilections were already solitary, sedentary, and bookish—unlike the world-famous French cellist I have read about, or the young woman I talked with one long afternoon who wanted only to be a jockey. I had just begun graduate school when I found out something was wrong with me, and I have remained, interminably, a graduate student. Perhaps I would not have if I'd thought I had the stamina to return to a full-time job as a technical editor; but I've enjoyed my studies.

In addition to studying, I teach writing courses. I also teach medical students how to give neurological examinations. I pick up freelance editing jobs here and there. I have raised a foster son and sent him into the world, where he has made me two grandbabies, and I am still escorting my daughter and son through adolescence. I go to Mass every Saturday. I am a superb, if messy, cook. I am also an enthusiastic laundress, capable of sorting a hamper full of clothes into five subtly differentiated piles, but a terrible housekeeper. I can do italic writing and, in an emergency, bathe an oil-soaked cat. I play a fiendish game of Scrabble. When I have the time and the money, I like to sit on my front steps with my husband, drinking Amaretto and smoking a cigar, as we imagine our counterparts in Leningrad and make sure that the sun gets down once more behind the sharp childish scrawl of the Tucson Mountains.

    This lively plenty has its bleak complement, of course, in all the things I can no longer do. I will never run again, except in dreams, and one day I may have to write that I will never walk again. I like to go camping, but I can't follow George and the children along the trails that wander out of a campsite through the desert or into the mountains. In fact, even on the level I've learned never to check the weather or try to hold a coherent conversation: I need all my attention for my wayward feet. Of late, I have begun to catch myself wondering how people can propel themselves without canes. With only one usable hand, I have to select my clothing with care not so much for style as for ease of ingress and egress, and even so, dressing can be laborious. I can no longer do fine stitchery, pick up babies, play the piano, braid my hair. I am immobilized by acute attacks of depression, which may or may not be physiologically related to MS but are certainly its logical concomitant.

    These two elements, the plenty and the privation, are never pure, nor are the delight and wretchedness that accompany them. Almost every pickle that I get into as a result of my weakness and clumsiness—and I get into plenty—is funny as well as maddening and sometimes painful. I recall one May afternoon when a friend and I were going out for a drink after finishing up at school. As we were climbing into opposite sides of my car, chatting, I tripped and fell, flat and hard, onto the asphalt parking lot, my abrupt departure interrupting him in mid-sentence. "Where'd you go?" he called as he came around the back of the car to find me hauling myself up by the door frame. "Are you all right?" Yes, I told him, I was fine, just a bit rattly, and we drove off to find a shady patio and some beer. When I got home an hour or so later, my daughter greeted me with "What have you done to yourself?" I looked down. One elbow of my white turtleneck with the green froggies, one knee of my white trousers, one white kneesock were blood-soaked. We peeled off the clothes and inspected the damage, which was nasty enough but not alarming. That part wasn't funny: The abrasions took a long time to heal, and one got a little infected. Even so, when I think of my friend talking earnestly, suddenly, to the hot thin air while I dropped from his view as though through a trap door, I find the image as silly as something from a Marx Brothers movie.

    I may find it easier than other cripples to amuse myself because I live propped by the acceptance and the assistance and, sometimes, the amusement of those around me. Grocery clerks tear my checks out of my checkbook for me, and sales clerks find chairs to put into dressing rooms when I want to try on clothes. The people I work with make sure I teach at times when I am least likely to be fatigued, in places I can get to, with the materials I need. My students, with one anonymous exception (in an end-of-the-semester evaluation) have been unperturbed by my disability. Some even like it. One was immensely cheered by the information that I paint my own fingernails; she decided, she told me, that if I could go to such trouble over fine details, she could keep on writing essays. I suppose I became some sort of bright-fingered muse. She wrote good essays, too.

15   The most important struts in the framework of my existence, of course, are my husband and children. Dismayingly few marriages survive the MS test, and why should they? Most twenty-two- and nineteen-year-olds, like George and me, can vow in clear conscience, after a childhood of chickenpox and summer colds, to keep one another in sickness and in health so long as they both shall live. Not many are equipped for catastrophe: the dismay, the depression, the extra work, the boredom that a degenerative disease can insinuate into a relationship. And our society, with its emphasis on fun and its association of fun with physical performance, offers little encouragement for a whole spouse to stay with a crippled partner. Children experience similar stresses when faced with a crippled parent, and they are more helpless, since parents and children can't usually get divorced. They hate, of course, to be different from their peers, and the child whose mother is tacking down the aisle of a school auditorium packed with proud parents like a Cape Cod dinghy in a stiff breeze jolly well stands out in a crowd. Deprived of legal divorce, the child can at least deny the mother's disability, even her existence, forgetting to tell her about recitals and PTA meetings, refusing to accompany her to stores or church or the movies, never inviting friends to the house. Many do.

But I've been limping along for ten years now, and so far George and the children are still at my left elbow, holding tight. Anne and Matthew vacuum floors and dust furniture and haul trash and rake up dog droppings and button my cuffs and bake lasagne and Toll House cookies with just enough grumbling so I know that they don't have brain fever. And far from hiding me, they're forever dragging me by racks of fancy clothes or through teeming school corridors, or welcoming gaggles of friends while I'm wandering through the house in Anne's filmy pink babydoll pajamas. George generally calls before he brings someone home, but he does just as many dumb thankless chores as the children. And they all yell at me, laugh at some of my jokes, write me funny letters when we're apart—in short, treat me as an ordinary human being for whom they have some use. I think they like me. Unless they're faking. . . .

Faking. There's the rub. Tugging at the fringes of my consciousness always is the terror that people are kind to me only because I'm a cripple. My mother almost shattered me once, with that instinct mothers have—blind, I think, in this case, but unerring nonetheless—for striking blows along the fault-lines of their children's hearts, by telling me, in an attack on my selfishness, "We all have to make allowances for you, of course, because of the way you are." From the distance of a couple of years, I have to admit that I haven't any idea just what she meant, and I'm not sure that she knew either. She was awfully angry. But at the time, as the words thudded home, I felt my worst fear, suddenly realized. I could bear being called selfish: I am. But I couldn't bear the corroboration that those around me were doing in fact what I'd always suspected them of doing, professing fondness while silently putting up with me because of the way I am. A cripple. I've been a little cracked ever since.

Along with this fear that people are secretly accepting shoddy goods comes a relentless pressure to please—to prove myself worth the burdens I impose, I guess, or to build a substantial account of goodwill against which I may write drafts in times of need. Part of the pressure arises from social expectations. In our society, anyone who deviates from the norm had better find some way to compensate. Like fat people, who are expected to be jolly, cripples must bear their lot meekly and cheerfully. A grumpy cripple isn't playing by the rules. And much of the pressure is self-generated. Early on I vowed that, if I had to have MS, by God I was going to do it well. This is a class act, ladies and gentlemen. No tears, no recriminations, no faint-heartedness.

One way and another, then, I wind up feeling like Tiny Tim, peering over the edge of the table at the Christmas goose, waving my crutch, piping down God's blessing on us all. Only sometimes I don't want to play Tiny Tim. I'd rather be Caliban, a most scurvy monster. Fortunately, at home no one much cares whether I'm a good cripple or a bad cripple as long as I make vichyssoise with fair regularity. One evening several years ago, Anne was reading at the dining-room table while I cooked dinner. As I opened a can of tomatoes, the can slipped in my left hand and juice spattered me and the counter with bloody spots. Fatigued and infuriated, I bellowed, "I'm so sick of being crippled!" Anne glanced at me over the top of her book. "There now," she said, "do you feel better?" "Yes," I said, "yes, I do." She went back to her reading. I felt better. That's about all the attention my scurviness ever gets.

20   Because I hate being crippled, I sometimes hate myself for being a cripple. Over the years I have come to expect—even accept—attacks of violent self-loathing. Luckily, in general our society no longer connects deformity and disease directly with evil (though a charismatic once told me that I have MS because a devil is in me) and so I'm allowed to move largely at will, even among small children. But I'm not sure that this revision of attitude has been particularly helpful. Physical imperfection, even freed of moral disapprobation, still defies and violates the ideal, especially for women, whose confinement in their bodies as objects of desire is far from over. Each age, of course, has its ideal, and I doubt that ours is any better or worse than any other. Today's ideal woman, who lives on the glossy pages of dozens of magazines, seems to be between the ages of eighteen and twenty-five; her hair has body, her teeth flash white, her breath smells minty, her underarms are dry; she has a career but is still a fabulous cook, especially of meals that take less than twenty minutes to prepare; she does not ordinarily appear to have a husband or children; she is trim and deeply tanned; she jogs, swims, plays tennis, rides a bicycle, sails, but does not bowl; she travels widely, even to out-of-the-way places like Finland and Samoa, always in the company of the ideal man, who possesses a nearly identical set of characteristics. There are a few exceptions. Though usually white and often blonde, she may be black, Hispanic, Asian, or Native American, so long as she is unusually sleek. She may be old, provided she is selling a laxative or is Lauren Bacall. If she is selling a detergent, she may be married and have a flock of strikingly messy children. But she is never a cripple.

Like many women I know, I have always had an uneasy relationship with my body. I was not a popular child, largely, I think now, because I was peculiar: intelligent, intense, moody, shy, given to unexpected actions and inexplicable notions and emotions. But as I entered adolescence, I believed myself unpopular because I was homely: my breasts too flat, my mouth too wide, my hips too narrow, my clothing never quite right in fit or style. I was not, in fact, particularly ugly, old photographs inform me, though I was well off the ideal; but I carried this sense of self-alienation with me into adulthood, where it regenerated in response to the depredations of MS. Even with my brace I walk with a limp so pronounced that, seeing myself on the videotape of a television program on the disabled, I couldn't believe that anything but an inchworm could make progress humping along like that. My shoulders droop and my pelvis thrusts forward as I try to balance myself upright, throwing my frame into a bony S. As a result of contractures, one shoulder is higher than the other and I carry one arm bent in front of me, the fingers curled into a claw. My left arm and leg have wasted into pipe-stems, and I try always to keep them covered. When I think about how my body must look to others, especially to men, to whom I have been trained to display myself, I feel ludicrous, even loathsome.

At my age, however, I don't spend much time thinking about my appearance. The burning egocentricity of adolescence, which assures one that all the world is looking all the time, has passed, thank God, and I'm generally too caught up in what I'm doing to step back, as I used to, and watch myself as though upon a stage. I'm also too old to believe in the accuracy of self-image. I know that I'm not a hideous crone, that in fact, when I'm rested, well dressed, and well made up, I look fine. The self-loathing I feel is neither physically nor intellectually substantial. What I hate is not me but a disease.

I am not a disease.

And a disease is not—at least not singlehandedly—going to determine who I am, though at first it seemed to be going to. Adjusting to a chronic incurable illness, I have moved through a process similar to that outlined by Elizabeth Kübler-Ross in *On Death and Dying*. The major difference—and it is far more significant than most people recognize—is that I can't be sure of the outcome, as the terminally ill cancer patient can. Research studies indicate that, with proper medical care, I may achieve a "normal" life span. And in our society, with its vision of death as the ultimate evil, worse even than decrepitude, the response to such news is, "Oh well, at least you're not going to *die*." Are there worse things than dying? I think that there may be.

I think of two women I know, both with MS, both enough older than I to have served as models. One took to her bed several years ago and has been there ever since. Although she can sit in a high-backed wheelchair, because she is incontinent she refuses to go out at all, even though incontinence pants, which are readily available at any pharmacy, could protect her from embarrassment. Instead, she stays at home and insists that her husband, a small quiet man, a retired civil servant, stay there with her except for a quick weekly foray to the supermarket. The other woman, whose illness was diagnosed when she was eighteen, a nursing student engaged to a young doctor, finished her training, married her doctor, accompanied him to Germany when he was in the service, bore three sons and a daughter, now grown and gone. When she can, she travels with her husband; she plays bridge, embroiders, swims regularly; she works, like me, as a symptomatic-patient instructor of medical students in neurology. Guess which woman I hope to be.

At the beginning, I thought about having MS almost incessantly. And because of the unpredictable course of the disease, my thoughts were always terrified. Each night I'd get into bed wondering whether I'd get out again the next morning, whether I'd be able to see, to speak, to hold a pen between my fingers. Knowing that the day might come when I'd be physically incapable of killing myself, I thought perhaps I ought to do so right away, while I still had the strength. Gradually I came to understand that the Nancy who might one day lie inert under a bedsheet, arms and legs paralyzed, unable to feed or bathe herself, unable to reach out for a gun, a bottle of pills, was not the Nancy I was at present, and that I could not presume to make decisions for that future Nancy, who might well not want in the least to die. Now the only provision I've made for the future Nancy is that when the time comes—and it is likely to come in the form of pneumonia, friend to the weak and the old—I am not to be treated with machines and medications. If she is unable to communicate by then, I hope she will be satisfied with these terms.

Thinking all the time about having MS grew tiresome and intrusive, especially in the large and tragic mode in which I was accustomed to considering my plight. Months and even years went by without catastrophe (at least without one related to MS), and really I was awfully busy, what with George and children and snakes and students and poems, and I hadn't the time, let alone the inclination, to devote myself to being a disease. Too, the richer my life became, the funnier it seemed, as though there were some connection between largesse and laughter, and so my tragic stance began to waver until, even with the aid of a brace and cane, I couldn't hold it for very long at a time.

After several years I was satisfied with my adjustment. I had suffered my grief and fury and terror, I thought, but now I was at ease with my lot. Then one summer day I set out with George and the children across the desert for a vacation in California. Part way to Yuma I became aware that my right leg felt funny. "I think I've had an exacerbation," I told George. "What shall we do?" he asked. "I think we'd better get the hell to California," I said, "because I don't know whether I'll ever make it again." So we went on to San Diego and then to Orange, and up the Pacific Coast Highway to Santa Cruz, across to Yosemite, down to Sequoia and Joshua Tree, and so back over the desert to home. It was a fine two-week trip, filled with friends and fair weather, and I wouldn't have missed it for the world, though I did in fact make it back to California two years later. Nor would there have been any point in missing it, since in MS, once the symptoms have appeared, the neurological damage has been done, and there's no way to predict or prevent that damage.

The incident spoiled my self-satisfaction, however. It renewed my grief and fury and terror, and I learned that one never finishes adjusting to MS. I don't know now why I thought one would. One does not, after all, finish adjusting to life, and MS is simply a fact of my life—not my favorite fact, of course—but as ordinary as my nose and my tropical fish and my yellow Mazda station wagon. It may at any time get worse, but no amount of worry or anticipation can prepare me for a new loss. My life is a lesson in losses. I learn one at a time.

30 And I had best be patient in the learning, since I'll have to do it like it or not. As any rock fan knows, you can't always get what you want. Particularly when you have MS. You can't, for example, get cured. In recent years researchers and the organizations that fund research have started to pay MS some attention even though it isn't fatal; perhaps they have begun to see that life is something other than a quantitative phenomenon, that one may be very much alive for a very long time in a life that isn't worth living. The researchers have made some progress toward understanding the mechanism of the disease: It

may well be an autoimmune reaction triggered by a slow-acting virus. But they are nowhere near its prevention, control, or cure. And most of us want to be cured. Some, unable to accept incurability, grasp at one treatment after another, no matter how bizarre: megavitamin therapy, gluten-free diet, injections of cobra venom, hypothermal suits, lymphocytopharesis, hyperbaric chambers. Many treatments are probably harmless enough, but none are curative.

The absence of a cure often makes MS patients bitter toward their doctors. Doctors are, after all, the priests of modern society, the new shamans, whose business is to heal, and many an MS patient roves from one to another, searching for the "good" doctor who will make him well. Doctors too think of themselves as healers, and for this reason many have trouble dealing with MS patients, whose disease in its intransigence defeats their aims and mocks their skills. Too few doctors, it is true, treat their patients as whole human beings, but the reverse is also true. I have always tried to be gentle with my doctors, who often have more at stake in terms of ego than I do. I may be frustrated, maddened, depressed by the incurability of my disease, but I am not diminished by it, and they are. When I push myself up from my seat in the waiting room and stumble toward them, I incarnate the limitation of their powers. The least I can do is refuse to press on their tenderest spots.

This gentleness is part of the reason that I'm not sorry to be a cripple. I didn't have it before. Perhaps I'd have developed it anyway—how could I know such a thing?—and I wish I had more of it, but I'm glad of what I have. It has opened and enriched my life enormously, this sense that my frailty and need must be mirrored in others, that in searching for and shaping a stable core in a life wrenched by change and loss, change and loss, I must recognize the same process, under individual conditions, in the lives around me. I do not deprecate such knowledge, however I've come by it.

All the same, if a cure were found, would I take it? In a minute. I may be a cripple, but I'm only occasionally a loony and never a saint. Anyway, in my brand of theology God doesn't give bonus points for a limp. I'd take a cure; I just don't need one. A friend who also has MS startled me once by asking, "Do you ever say to yourself, 'Why me, Lord?'" "No, Michael, I don't," I told him, "because whenever I try, the only response I can think of is 'Why not?'" If I could make a cosmic deal, who would I put in my place? What in my life would I give up in exchange for sound limbs and a thrilling rush of energy? No one. Nothing. I might as well do the job myself. Now that I'm getting the hang of it.

Questions for Discussion

1. Consider the opening paragraph. Why does the author start the essay with this episode? Is this opening effective? Why do you think it is or isn't?
2. Does this essay have a subordinate aim? If you think it does, cite specific passages to support your answer. If you think it doesn't, how might the author revise this essay to include a subordinate referential or persuasive aim?
3. In writing this essay, the author chiefly uses knowledge by participation. Identify the passages that display knowledge by observation. How important are these passages? Which, if any, could be omitted? Why does the author include this information?

4. Do you think you have learned something from the author's experience? Explain your answer.
5. Does the author paint a vivid picture of herself? If so, which descriptive and narrative details do you consider essential to her self-portrait? If not, which details do you think are missing?

Opportunities for Writing

1. Describe a friend or relative who is disabled. What is this individual like? How does this individual live with the disability? Does his or her disability disturb you? What have you learned from this individual?
2. Recall a time in your life when you were temporarily disabled (e.g., a broken arm, a broken leg). What happened to you? How did you live with your disability? How did you feel about yourself? How has this experience influenced you?
3. Your local newspaper is running a series of articles on the lives of the disabled. In your essay for this series, depict the home of a disabled friend or relative. What accommodations have been made for the disabled individual? What is your impression of his or her home?
4. Compose a portrait of a leading activist in the fight for the rights of people with disabilities. What is this man or woman like? What has been his or her experience? Has this individual inspired or influenced you? If possible, interview the activist and his or her friends and relatives. Also review newspaper and magazine articles that might have been written regarding his or her activities.

More Than Just a Shrine
Paying Homage to the Ghosts of Ellis Island

Mary Gordon

Novelist, short story writer, essayist, and writing teacher, Mary Gordon was born in Long Island, New York. She attended Barnard College and Syracuse University. Among her writings are The Company of Women *(1981) and* Final Payments *(1978); she is also a contributor to many popular and scholarly publications. "More Than Just a Shrine: Paying Homage to the Ghosts of Ellis Island" appeared in* The New York Times. *In this essay, Gordon recounts her trip to Ellis Island, the first "American" place her Irish ancestors passed through as new immigrants in New York. Gordon blends her own impressions of what she imagined happened and what sources have told her happened as immigrants were processed on Ellis Island. As you will see, this trip provides Gordon with insights about her "differentness": a sense of identification with and pride in the "ghosts" of Ellis Island.*

I once sat in a hotel in Bloomsbury trying to have breakfast alone. A Russian with a habit of compulsively licking his lips asked if he could join me. I was afraid to say no; I thought it might be bad for détente. He explained to me that he was a linguist, and that he always liked to talk to Americans to see if he could make any connection between their speech and their ethnic background. When I told him about my mixed ancestry—my mother is Irish and Italian, my father a Lithuanian Jew—he began jumping up and down in his seat, rubbing his hands together, and licking his lips even more frantically.

"Ah," he said, "so you are really somebody who comes from what is called the boiling pot of America." Yes, I told him, yes I was, but I quickly rose to leave. I thought it would be too hard to explain to him the relation of the boiling potters to the main course, and I wanted to get to the British Museum. I told him that the only thing I could think of that united people whose backgrounds, histories, and points of view were utterly diverse was that their people had landed at a place called Ellis Island.

I didn't tell him that Ellis Island was the only American landmark I'd ever visited. How could I describe to him the estrangement I'd always felt from the kind of traveler who visits shrines to America's past greatness, those rebuilt forts with muskets behind glass and sabers mounted on the walls and gift shops selling maple sugar candy in the shape of Indian headdresses, those reconstructed villages with tables set for fifty and the Paul Revere silver gleaming? All that Americana—Plymouth Rock, Gettysburg, Mount Vernon, Valley Forge—it all inhabits for me a zone of blurred abstraction with far less hold on my imagination than the Bastille or Hampton Court. I suppose I've always known that my uninterest in it contains a large component of the willed: I am American, and those places purport to be my history. But they are not mine.

Ellis Island is, though; it's the one place I can be sure my people are connected to. And so I made a journey there to find my history, like any Rotarian traveling in his Winnebago to Antietam to find his. I had become part of that humbling democracy of people looking in some site for a past that has grown unreal. The monument I traveled to was not, however, a tribute to some old glory. The minute I set foot upon the island I could feel all that it stood for: insecurity, obedience, anxiety, dehumanization, the terrified and careful deference of the displaced. I hadn't traveled to the Battery and boarded a ferry across from the Statue of Liberty to raise flags or breathe a richer, more triumphant air. I wanted to do homage to the ghosts.

5   I felt them everywhere, from the moment I disembarked and saw the building with its high-minded brick, its hopeful little lawn, its ornamental cornices. The place was derelict when I arrived; it had not functioned for more than thirty years—almost as long as the time it had operated at full capacity as a major immigration center. I was surprised to learn what a small part of history Ellis Island had occupied. The main building was constructed in 1892, then rebuilt between 1898 and 1900 after a fire. Most of the immigrants who arrived during the latter half of the nineteenth century, mainly northern and western Europeans, landed not at Ellis Island but on the western tip of the Battery at Castle Garden, which had opened as a receiving center for immigrants in 1855.

By the 1880s the facilities at Castle Garden had grown scandalously inadequate. Officials looked for an island on which to build a new immigration center because they thought that on an island immigrants could be more easily protected from swindlers and quickly transported to railroad terminals in New Jersey. Bedloe's Island was considered, but New Yorkers were aghast at the idea of a "Babel" ruining their beautiful new treasure, "Liberty Enlightening the World." The statue's sculptor, Frédéric Auguste Bartholdi, reacted to the prospect of immigrants landing near his masterpiece in horror; he called it a "monstrous plan." So much for Emma Lazarus.

Ellis Island was finally chosen because the citizens of New Jersey petitioned the federal government to remove from the island an old naval powder magazine that they thought dangerously close to the Jersey shore. The explosives were removed; no one wanted the island for anything. It was the perfect place to build an immigration center.

I thought about the island's history as I walked into the building and made my way to the room that was the center in my imagination of the Ellis Island experience: the Great Hall. It had been made real for me in the stark, accusing photographs of Louis Hine and others who took those pictures to make a point. It was in the Great Hall that everyone had waited—waiting, always, the great vocation of the dispossessed. The room was empty, except for me and a handful of other visitors and the park ranger who showed us around. I felt myself grow insignificant in that room, with its huge semicircular windows, its air, even in dereliction, of solid and official probity.

I walked in the deathlike expansiveness of the room's disuse and tried to think of what it might have been like, filled and swarming. More than sixteen million immigrants came through that room: approximately 250,000 were rejected. Not really a large proportion, but the implications for the rejected were dreadful. For some, there was nothing to go back to, or there was certain death; for others, who left as adventurers, to return would be to adopt in local memory the fool's role, and the failure's. No wonder that the island's history includes reports of three thousand suicides.

Sometimes immigrants could pass through Ellis Island in mere hours, though for some the process took days. The particulars of the experience in the Great Hall were often influenced by the political events and attitudes on the mainland. In the 1890s and the first years of the new century, when cheap labor was needed, the newly built receiving center took in its immigrants with comparatively little question. But as the century progressed, the economy worsened, eugenics became both scientifically respectable and popular, and World War I made American xenophobia seem rooted in fact.

Immigration acts were passed; newcomers had to prove, besides moral correctness and financial solvency, their ability to read. Quota laws came into effect, limiting the number of immigrants from southern and eastern Europe to less than 14 percent of the total quota. Intelligence tests were biased against all non-English-speaking persons and medical examinations became increasingly strict, until the machinery of immigration nearly collapsed under its own weight. The Second Quota Law of 1924 provided that all immigrants be inspected and issued visas at American consular offices in Europe, rendering the center almost obsolete.

On the day of my visit, my mind fastened upon the medical inspections, which had always seemed to me most emblematic of the ignominy and terror the immigrants endured. The medical inspectors, sometimes dressed in uniforms like soldiers, were particularly obsessed with a disease of the eyes called trachoma, which they checked for by flipping back the immigrants' top eyelids with a hook used for buttoning gloves—a method that sometimes resulted in the transmission of the disease to healthy people. Mothers feared that if their children cried too much, their red eyes would be mistaken for a symptom of the disease and the whole family would be sent home. Those immigrants suspected of some physical disability had initials chalked on their coats. I remembered the photographs I'd seen of people standing, dumbstruck and innocent as cattle, with their manifest numbers hung around their necks and initials marked in chalk upon their coats: "E" for eye trouble, "K" for hernia, "L" for lameness, "X" for mental defects, "H" for heart disease.

I thought of my grandparents as I stood in the room; my seventeen-year-old grandmother, coming alone from Ireland in 1896, vouched for by a stranger who had found her a place as a domestic servant to some Irish who had done well. I tried to imagine the assault it all must have been for her; I've been to her hometown, a collection of farms with a main street—smaller than the athletic field of my local public school. She must have watched the New York skyline as the first- and second-class passengers were whisked off the gangplank with the most cursory of inspections while she was made to board a ferry to the new immigration center.

What could she have made of it—this buff-painted wooden structure with its towers and its blue slate roof, a place *Harper's Weekly* described as "a latter-day watering place hotel"? It would have been the first time she'd have heard people speaking something other than English. She would have mingled with people carrying baskets on their heads and eating foods unlike any she had ever seen—dark-eyed people, like the Sicilian she would marry ten years later, who came over with his family, responsible even then for his mother and sister. I don't know what they thought, my grandparents, for they were not expansive people, nor romantic; they didn't like to think of what they called "the hard times," and their trip across the ocean was the single adventurous act of lives devoted after landing to security, respectability, and fitting in.

15 What is the potency of Ellis Island for someone like me—an American, obviously, but one who has always felt that the country really belonged to the early settlers, that, as J. F. Powers wrote in "Morte D'Urban," it had been "handed down to them by the Pilgrims, George Washington and others, and that they were taking a risk in letting you live in it." I have never been the victim of overt discrimination; nothing I have wanted has been denied me because of the accidents of blood. But I suppose it is part of being an American to be engaged in a somewhat tiresome but always self-absorbing process of national definition. And in this process, I have found in traveling to Ellis Island an important piece of evidence that could remind me I was right to feel my differentness. Something had happened to my people on that island, a result of the eternal wrongheadedness of American protectionism and the predictabilities of simple greed. I came to the island, too, so I could tell the ghosts that I was one of them, and that I honored them—their stoicism, and their innocence, the fear that turned them inward, and their pride. I wanted to tell them that I liked them better than the Americans who made them pass through the Great Hall and stole their names and chalked their weaknesses in public on their clothing. And to tell the ghosts what I have always thought: that

American history was a very classy party that was not much fun until they arrived, brought the good food, turned up the music, and taught everyone to dance.

Questions for Discussion

1. Are you satisfied with the way the author identifies sources of information? How does she know the history of Ellis Island? What is the source of this information?
2. Why does this essay start with the episode of the Russian man? Is it appropriate? Is it effective? How would you have started this essay?
3. Do you think the essay is logically organized? If so, why? If not, how would you revise the organization?
4. Does the author derive appropriate significance from this experience? Does she communicate this significance effectively? Explain your answer.
5. Consider the author's use of descriptive detail. Is she showing you or telling you? Does she offer you a vivid picture of Ellis Island? Cite specific passages to support your answer.

Opportunities for Writing

1. Portray a friend or family member who immigrated to America. What is your relationship to this man or woman? Why did he or she immigrate to America? When? What have you learned from this individual?
2. To publicize his or her visit to your community, write a portrait of a famous man or woman who immigrated to America. Why did this individual immigrate? How? When? Where? What has life in America been like for this individual? What has he or she contributed to American society? What do you consider interesting or important about this individual?
3. In a letter to a friend, describe your visit to a historic site. What happened at this site? When? Why did you decide to visit this site? What were your expectations? How did you feel being there?

The House Where Martin Wept
Marks, Mississippi

WALT HARRINGTON

Walt Harrington earned his Master's degrees in journalism and sociology from the University of Missouri. He is an award-winning staff writer for the Washington Post Magazine *and author of* Crossings *(1993), a collection of narratives that chronicle Harrington's trek across America—in particular rural and predominantly black communities. "The House Where Martin Wept" appears in this collection. On the dust jacket for* Crossings, *Harrington is described as a "white man married to a black woman and [father of] two children." In* Crossings, *he offers a complex and fresh understanding of African American people and places from the perspective of a white man with an African American family. As such, this essay combines Harrington's knowledge by both participation and observation.*

In the midst of field after field of flat farmland demarcated by distant tree lines that separate red-flowered cotton plants, stumpy soy beans, and stalks of rice that roll in the breeze like the waves of a bright green sea, Marks, Mississippi, is a brief footnote in history. Only weeks before his assassination in 1968, Martin Luther King, Jr., visited the town's poor black Cotton Street neighborhood and was so moved by the destitution he saw that he cried. Marks became "the town where Martin wept."

I'm headed to Clarksdale, the Mississippi Delta town where blues music was born, to visit Wade Walton, the barber and harmonica player recommended to me back in Williamsburg, Virginia. I'm hoping to have some fun. But Marks is on the way, so when I see the sign that says WELCOME TO MARKS, I stop at Holmans Amoco for directions. I make the few turns necessary to find Cotton Street, a beaten lane surrounded by some of the roughest-looking houses I've ever seen–shot-gun shacks with rusty tin roofs, shanties with barn-wood siding cracked to the weather, places built haphazardly with cast-off lumber. I turn onto the gravel path that is Sims Street and follow it a short distance until it disappears into a field of tall weeds. To my right, shrouded in undergrowth, is what's left of the house where local legend says Martin wept.

It's a tiny green-roofed shack, abandoned and twisting in different directions as if it can't decide which way to fall. The gray asbestos siding has risen with the distortion, the window mullions have popped their eyes, the front porch has collapsed at one end, and the brick chimney has tilted. When Martin Luther King came to the Cotton Street neighborhood, he visited many homes, and this one on Sims was no better or worse. But the neighborhood often flooded after heavy rains, and that day the end of Sims Street was a lake. King got to the house by small boat, and there he found a family living as if on an island in the floodwaters, an island of poverty amid an American sea of plenty. He cried.

The front door to the house is hanging off its hinges today, and, while wondering just what kind of snakes populate the Mississippi Delta, I push it aside and walk in. The three rooms of the house are revealed in shards of light that cast through the naked windows and the holes in the roof. Once my eyes have adjusted, I can see that no one has lived here, I hope, for a long time. A fragment of ratty green carpet covers a piece of the floor. Hunks of cheap paneling are falling off the walls and ceiling and their newspaper-insulation innards have settled around the room. Doors have fallen backwards, wasps fly everywhere, and red paint has been splattered on a remaining white wall. In the sweltering Mississippi heat, the whole place has the humid, claustrophobic smell of water-rotting wood. But if you swept up the trash, chased out the wasps, and painted the walls, this house wouldn't be much worse than some of the others in the neighborhood.

Across the street, at a sagging clapboard house, I talk to Bertha Lee Turner, a short and thick eighty-one-year-old black woman in a crisply clean white house dress and white go-ahead slippers. She lived here when King visited, although she wasn't home that day. "It's worser now than it's ever been," Ms. Turner says. She points to the floodwater line a couple feet above her foundation. "It gets higher and higher every year." Of the shack across the road, she says, "That house wasn't in that bad a shape. That house was a *good* house."

I ask, "Are things better since Martin came?"

"I think so. They get food stamps and lots of 'em on the welfare. I think it's better. They ain't workin' hard like they used ta. They used ta have ta chop cotton, pick cotton. I know'd I was poor. We poor yet ain't we? I'm poor now."

At one of the many other shanty houses in the neighborhood are seven black children laughing and running, playing in a dirt yard. A stagnant canal of cloudy green septic water reeks at their feet. They stop and stand stiffly when I introduce myself. I ask if they know that Martin Luther King once visited their neighborhood. They stare at the ground, kick the dirt for a long moment, until an older boy, a boy in high school, speaks up confidently. "He fell to his knees and cried at that house over there."

I ask, "You got any good white friends?"

"Skateboard friends," a different boy says.

"Do you go visit them?"

"Sometimes."

"You ever invite them to your house?"

A long silence. "They don't know how ta get here."

Then the confident boy speaks again. "Maybe they won't like our neighborhood. The way we live."

"What way is that?"

"Floodwater, tin houses, stuff like that."

"Is it that they wouldn't like the way you live or do you not want them to *see* the way you live?"

Another long pause, until the confident boy speaks. "We don't want them ta *see* the way we live."

"It's embarrassing to you?"

"Yeah."

"Do the white kids live this way?"

"No! Brick houses, big *fine houses,* sidewalks."

"What do you think when you visit them?"

He hesitates. "Why couldn't we live in houses like theirs?"

"And why can't you?"

"Our parents didn't have the right educations."

"How do you do in school?"

"Straight-A work."

"What do you want to be?"

"An architect."

"Where do you want to go to college?"

"Harvard. Or Yale."

His answer catches me off guard, and I feel simultaneously glad for his ambition and saddened at the long odds he faces. More than twenty years after Martin Luther King wept on this street, I can think of nothing to say except, "I wish you the best."

Questions for Discussion

1. Do you like the title? Does it arouse your curiosity? What other titles could you give this essay?

2. Consider the author's use of dialogue. Why does he record his conversation with the seven children? Why doesn't he summarize their conversation? What is the impact of their words on you?
3. Does the ending satisfactorily convey the significance of the author's experience? Why or why not?
4. Notice the author's use of descriptive detail. Does he offer you a vivid picture of the setting? Explain your answer.
5. How would this essay differ if it were written using only knowledge by participation? How would it differ if it were written using only knowledge by observation?

Opportunities for Writing

1. Depict a poor neighborhood in your city. What do the houses look like? Who lives there? How old is the neighborhood? How big is it? What is your impression of it? What do you think is noteworthy about this neighborhood?
2. Portray a child from a poor neighborhood. How old is this boy or girl? What is life like for this child in this neighborhood? What are his or her ambitions? What is your relationship with this child? What do you think of him or her? Address your essay to the principal of the child's school.
3. Recount a specific incident in the fight for racial equality. When and where did this incident occur? Why do you consider it especially important or meaningful? Write your essay for a special issue of your local newspaper to be published on the anniversary of this incident.

Grandmother's Country

N. SCOTT MOMADAY

N. Scott Momaday was born in Lawton, Oklahoma, and is a member of the Kiowa tribe. He earned degrees from the University of New Mexico and Stanford University and now teaches at the University of Arizona. Momaday is best known for his prose: he won the Pulitzer Prize for The Way to Rainy Mountain *(1969), a collection of his people's legends and folktales. He has also written* The Names *(1976) and* The House Made of Dawn *(1968). Through his poetry and paintings, Momaday also captures and preserves images of the Kiowa people and culture. Appearing on January 27, 1967, in* The Reporter, *"Grandmother's Country" is an essay about his people, their rituals, and the land. Momaday's grandmother, Aho, embodies his conception of all three. As this writer visits Aho's grave, he realizes the importance of knowing and maintaining Kiowa traditions. And by incorporating knowledge that he has learned on his own as well as from Aho and others, Momaday passes on the tribal traditions.*

A single knoll rises out of the plain in Oklahoma, north and west of the Wichita Range. For my people, the Kiowas, it is an old landmark, and they give it the name Rainy Mountain. The hardest weather in the world is there. Winter brings blizzards, hot tornadic winds arise in the spring, and in summer the prairie is an anvil's edge. The grass turns brittle and brown, and it cracks beneath your feet. There are green belts along the rivers and creeks, linear groves of hickory and pecan, willow and witch hazel. At a distance in July or August the steaming foliage seems almost to writhe in fire. Great green and yellow grasshoppers are everywhere in the tall grass, popping up like corn to sting the flesh, and tortoises crawl about on the red earth, going nowhere in the plenty of time. Loneliness is an aspect of the land. All things in the plain are isolate; there is no confusion of objects in the eye, but *one* hill or *one* tree or *one* man. To look upon that landscape in the early morning, with the sun at your back, is to lose the sense of proportion. Your imagination comes to life, and this, you think, is where Creation was begun.

I returned to Rainy Mountain in July. My grandmother had died in the spring, and I wanted to be at her grave. She had lived to be very old and at last infirm. Her only living daughter was with her when she died, and I was told that in death her face was that of a child.

I like to think of her as a child. When she was born, the Kiowas were living the last great moment of their history. For more than a hundred years they had controlled the open range from the Smoky Hill River to the Red, from the headwaters of the Canadian to the fork of the Arkansas and Cimarron. In alliance with the Comanches, they had ruled the whole of the southern Plains. War was their sacred business, and they were among the finest horsemen the world has ever known. But warfare for the Kiowas was preeminently a matter of disposition rather than of survival, and they never understood the grim, unrelenting advance of the U.S. Cavalry. When at last, divided and ill-provisioned, they were driven onto the Staked Plains in the cold rains of autumn, they fell into panic. In Palo Duro Canyon they abandoned their crucial stores to pillage and had nothing then but their lives. In order to save themselves, they surrendered to the soldiers at Fort Sill and were imprisoned in the old stone corral that now stands as a military museum. My grandmother was spared the humiliation of those high gray walls by eight or ten years, but she must have known from birth the affliction of defeat, the dark brooding of old warriors.

Her name was Aho, and she belonged to the last culture to evolve in North America. Her forebears came down from the high country in western Montana nearly three centuries ago. They were a mountain people, a mysterious tribe of hunters whose language has never been positively classified in any major group. In the late seventeenth century they began a long migration to the south and east. It was a journey toward the dawn, and it led to a golden age. Along the way the Kiowas were befriended by the Crows, who gave them the culture and religion of the Plains. They acquired horses, and their ancient nomadic spirit was suddenly free of the ground. They acquired Tai-me, the sacred Sun Dance doll, from that moment the object and symbol of their worship, and so shared in the divinity of the sun. Not least, they acquired the sense of destiny, therefore courage and pride. When they entered upon the southern Plains they had been transformed. No longer were they slaves to the simple necessity of survival; they were a lordly and dangerous society of fighters and thieves, hunters and priests of the sun. According to their origin myth, they entered the world through a hollow log. From one point of view, their migration was the fruit of an old prophecy, for indeed they emerged from a sunless world.

Although my grandmother lived out her long life in the shadow of Rainy Mountain, the immense landscape of the continental interior lay like memory in her blood. She could tell of the Crows, whom she had never seen, and of the Black Hills, where she had never been. I wanted to see in reality what she had seen more perfectly in the mind's eye, and traveled fifteen hundred miles to begin my pilgrimage.

Yellowstone, it seemed to me, was the top of the world, a region of deep lakes and dark timber, canyons and waterfalls. But, beautiful as it is, one might have the sense of confinement there. The skyline in all directions is close at hand, the high wall of the woods and deep cleavages of shade. There is a perfect freedom in the mountains, but it belongs to the eagle and the elk, the badger and the bear. The Kiowas reckoned their stature by the distance they could see, and they were bent and blind in the wilderness.

Descending eastward, the highland meadows are a stairway to the plain. In July the inland slope of the Rockies is luxuriant with flax and buckwheat, stonecrop and larkspur. The earth unfolds and the limit of the land recedes. Clusters of trees, and animals grazing far in the distance, cause the vision to reach away and wonder to build upon the mind. The sun follows a longer course in the day, and the sky is immense beyond all comparison. The great billowing clouds that sail upon it are shadows that move upon the grain like water, dividing light. Farther down, in the land of the Crows and Blackfeet, the plain is yellow. Sweet clover takes hold of the hills and bends upon itself to cover and seal the soil. There the Kiowas paused on their way; they had come to the place where they must change their lives. The sun is at home on the plains. Precisely there does it have the certain character of a god. When the Kiowas came to the land of the Crows, they could see the dark lees of the hills at dawn across the Bighorn River, the profusion of light on the grain shelves, the oldest deity ranging after the solstices. Not yet would they veer southward to the caldron of the land that lay below; they must wean their blood from the northern winter and hold the mountains a while longer in their view. They bore Tai-me in procession to the east.

A dark mist lay over the Black Hills, and the land was like iron. At the top of a ridge I caught sight of Devil's Tower upthrust against the gray sky as if in the birth of time the core of the earth had broken through its crust and the motion of the world was begun. There are things in nature that engender an awful quiet in the heart of man; Devil's Tower is one of them. Two centuries ago, because they could not do otherwise, the Kiowas made a legend at the base of the rock. My grandmother said:

> Eight children were there at play, seven sisters and their brother. Suddenly the boy was struck dumb; he trembled and began to run upon his hands and feet. His fingers became claws, and his body was covered with fur. Directly there was a bear where the boy had been. The sisters were terrified; they ran, and the bear after them. They came to the stump of a great tree, and the tree spoke to them. It bade them climb upon it, and as they did so it began to rise into the air. The bear came to kill them, but they were just beyond its reach. It reared against the tree and scored the bark all around with its claws. The seven sisters were borne into the sky, and they became the stars of the Big Dipper.

From that moment, and so long as the legend lives, the Kiowas have kinsmen in the night sky. Whatever they were in the mountains, they could be no more. However tenuous their well-being, however much they had suffered and would suffer again, they had found a way out of the wilderness.

My grandmother had a reverence for the sun, a holy regard that now is all but gone out of mankind. There was a wariness in her, and an ancient awe. She was a Christian in her later years, but she had come a long way about, and she never forgot her birthright. As a child she had been to the Sun Dances; she had taken part in those annual rites, and by them she had learned the restoration of her people in the presence of Tai-me. She was about seven when the last Kiowa Sun Dance was held in 1887 on the Washita River above Rainy Mountain Creek. The buffalo were gone. In order to consummate the ancient sacrifice—to impale the head of a buffalo bull upon the medicine tree—a delegation of old men journeyed into Texas, there to beg and barter for an animal from the Goodnight herd. She was ten when the Kiowas came together for the last time as a living Sun Dance culture. They could find no buffalo; they had to hang an old hide from the sacred tree. Before the dance could begin, a company of soldiers rode out from Fort Sill under orders to disperse the tribe. Forbidden without cause the essential act of their faith, having seen the wild herds slaughtered and left to rot upon the ground, the Kiowas backed away forever from the medicine tree. That was July 20, 1890, at the great bend of the Washita. My grandmother was there. Without bitterness, and for as long as she lived, she bore a vision of deicide.

10   Now that I can have her only in memory, I see my grandmother in the several postures that were peculiar to her: standing at the wood stove on a winter morning and turning meat in a great iron skillet; sitting at the south window, bent above her beadwork, and afterwards, when her vision failed, looking down for a long time into the fold of her hands; going out upon a cane, very slowly as she did when the weight of age came upon her; praying. I remember her most often at prayer. She made long, rambling prayers out of suffering and hope, having seen many things. I was never sure that I had the right to hear, so exclusive were they of all mere custom and company. The last time I saw her she prayed standing by the side of her bed at night, naked to the waist, the light of a kerosene lamp moving upon her dark skin. Her long, black hair, always drawn and braided in the day, lay upon her shoulders and against her breasts like a shawl. I do not speak Kiowa, and I never understood her prayers, but there was something inherently sad in the sound, some merest hesitation upon the syllables of sorrow. She began in a high and descending pitch, exhausting her breath to silence; then again and again—and always the same intensity of effort, of something that is, and is not, like urgency in the human voice. Transported so in the dancing light among the shadows of her room, she seemed beyond the reach of time. But that was illusion; I think I knew then that I should not see her again.

Houses are like sentinels in the plain, old keepers of the weather watch. There, in a very little while, wood takes on the appearance of great age. All colors wear soon away in the wind and rain, and then the wood is burned gray and the grain appears and the nails turn red with rust. The windowpanes are black and opaque; you imagine there is nothing within, and indeed there are many ghosts, bones given up to the land. They stand here and there against the sky, and you approach them for a longer time than you expect. They belong in the distance; it is their domain.

Once there was a lot of sound in my grandmother's house, a lot of coming and going, feasting and talk. The summers there were full of excitement and reunion. The Kiowas are a summer people; they abide the cold and keep to themselves, but when the season turns and the land becomes warm and vital they cannot hold still; an old love of going returns upon them. The aged visitors who came to my grandmother's house when I was a child were made of lean and leather, and they bore themselves upright. They wore great black hats and bright ample shirts that shook in the wind. They tubbed fat upon their hair and wound their braids with strips of colored cloth. Some of them painted their faces and carried the scars of old and cherished enmities. They were an old council of warlords, come to remind and be reminded of who they were. Their wives and daughters served them well. The women might indulge themselves; gossip was at once the mark and compensation of their servitude. They made loud and elaborate talk among themselves, full of jest and gesture, fright and false alarm. They went abroad in fringed and flowered shawls, bright beadwork and German silver. They were at home in the kitchen, and they prepared meals that were banquets.

There were frequent prayer meetings, and great nocturnal feasts. When I was a child I played with my cousins outside, where the lamplight fell upon the ground and the singing of the old people rose up around us and carried away into the darkness. There were a lot of good things to eat, a lot of laughter and surprise. And afterwards, when the quiet returned, I lay down with my grandmother and could hear the frogs away by the river and feel the motion of the air.

Now there is a funeral silence in the rooms, the endless wake of some final word. The walls have closed in upon my grandmother's house. When I returned to it in mourning, I saw for the first time in my life how small it was. It was late at night, and there was a white moon, nearly full. I sat for a long time on the stone steps by the kitchen door. From there I could see out across the land; I could see the long row of trees by the creek, the low light upon the rolling plains, and the stars of the Big Dipper. Once I looked at the moon and caught sight of a strange thing. A cricket had perched upon the handrail, only a few inches away from me. My line of vision was such that the creature filled the moon like a fossil. It had gone there, I thought, to live and die, for there, of all places, was its small definition made whole and eternal. A warm wind rose up and purled like the longing within me.

15   The next morning I awoke at dawn and went out on the dirt road to Rainy Mountain. It was already hot, and the grasshoppers began to fill the air. Still, it was early in the morning, and the birds sang out of the shadows. The long yellow grass on the mountain shone in the bright light, and a scissortail hied above the land. There, where it ought to be, at the end of a long and legendary way, was my grandmother's grave. Here and there on the dark stones were ancestral names. Looking back once, I saw the mountain and came away.

Questions for Discussion

1. What is the essay's subordinate aim? Cite specific passages to support your answer.
2. Does the essay offer you a vivid picture of the setting? Which descriptive details do you consider essential? Which are unnecessary?
3. Why does the author include information on the origins and traditions of the Kiowas?
4. Why doesn't the author cite the sources of historical information? Does this omission damage his credibility? Why do you think it does or doesn't?
5. What significance does the author derive from this experience? How does he communicate that significance?

Opportunities for Writing

1. Depict your grandmother's or grandfather's house. Where is it located? What does it look like? How big or small is it? How old is it? What is it like inside? How does it reveal the character of its owner? What do you think is curious or noteworthy about this house?
2. In a letter to your mother or father, describe a visit with your grandmother or grandfather. How did he or she look? What did you do? How long did you stay? What did you especially like or dislike about this visit?
3. Describe a place you often visited as a child. Where was this place? How long did it take to get there? How old were you? Why did you go there? How important was this place to you at the time? Why? How important is it to you today? Why?
4. Your school is soliciting essays for a special exhibit on the histories, traditions, and practices of the various Native American peoples. In your essay, discuss a specific historical episode that you consider especially important or meaningful. In studying this subject, interview Native Americans and locate historical records of the incident. In writing your essay, integrate appropriate illustrations.

A New Monument to Remembering—With a Mission

Michael Kernan

Michael Kernan was born in Utica, New York. He was educated at Harvard University and has been a writer and reporter, contributing regularly to numerous magazines and newspapers. He has published a book-length nonfiction work, The Violet Dots *(1978), in which Kernan integrates various sources—diary accounts, interviews, letters, songs, news articles—in order to portray a British soldier who fought in the battle of the Somme on July 1, 1916. In "A New Monument to Remembering—With a Mission," Kernan takes readers to the United States Holocaust Memorial Museum in Washington, D.C., dedicated on April 22, 1993. This writer was a teenager during World War II and went to Auschwitz in 1991 with someone who had escaped the camp in 1943. Using information about the Holocaust gained from his own visit and from outside sources, Kernan tells of this museum and its profound effect on and significance to visitors. This essay appeared in the April 1993 issue of* The Smithsonian.

How do you think about millions?

Stand in the morning fog at Auschwitz II, the killing camp known as Birkenau, and everywhere around you are chimneys, all that is left of the barracks where the inmates were kept, for the Nazis burned down many of the sheds as the Allies approached. The rough wooden barracks were designed as stables, but each was packed with more than half a thousand living skeletons. Once each building had a wood stove with a crude heating system, hence the chimneys, but little heat was provided for these prisoners.

The dark brick chimneys loom up in the mist, row after row after row, as far as you can see. Dozens, scores, hundreds of them, marking the last shelter of a thousand people and then of a thousand more when the first ones died of starvation or a bullet or the gas chambers, and then of a thousand more, and then of a thousand more. And perhaps as you begin to understand, to grasp the meaning of a million, of six million, you begin to comprehend the Holocaust, this thing that the human race did to itself.

On April 26 the United States Holocaust Memorial Museum will open in Washington, D.C. Mandated by a unanimous act of Congress in 1980, it stands on 1.9 acres of land given by the federal government between 14th and 15th Streets just off Independence Avenue and the Mall. The five-story building contains 265,000 square feet of space. Dedication ceremonies will be held April 22.

The money for the structure and its 36,000-square-foot permanent exhibition, a fund that will total some $168 million, comes from private donations obtained by the Presidentially appointed 55-member United States Holocaust Memorial Council.

It is a monument to remembering, with a mission "to tell the full, horrible truth about the Holocaust," according to Harvey M. Meyerhoff, the council chairman.

But any memorial dedicated to the Holocaust presents a unique problem. The dilemma is that this event must be spoken of—yet must remain unspeakable. It must never be allowed, as Nobel Peace Prize winner Elie Wiesel has said, to become ordinary, to be absorbed into the normal fabric of human history.

"There are those who believe the story of the Holocaust cannot be told, that only those who were there can understand," says Michael Berenbaum, the museum's project director. But, he adds, there are things that must be learned, for though the Jews were the central victims, the lessons of this tragedy are universal. "History has imposed upon us the responsibility of telling the story of the Holocaust."

Even before the building was designed, objections were heard from some who thought such a memorial did not belong in America, so remote from the death camps of Eastern Europe, or in Washington, whose politicians in 1939 had rejected the refugee ship *St. Louis*—sending its passengers back to almost certain death—or especially on the fringes of the Mall, with its cheerful folk festivals and upbeat museums of American accomplishment.

As for the concern that the museum might be too grim for that site, museum director Jeshajahu Weinberg has this to say: "It is not morbid. It is an historical museum devoted to a world-shattering event in which the United States was very deeply involved. And beyond the American aspect, this was an event in world history that has implications and moral lessons for all humankind."

The Holocaust, he notes, was basically a racist event—"racism taken to its climax. Everybody who goes there will ask the question: 'How would I have behaved?' It is a major moral question that we face almost daily in our lives. Jews happened to be the major victims of that event, but it is certainly relevant for everybody."

Originally the Holocaust Commission, appointed by President Jimmy Carter and headed by Wiesel, considered a monument similar to other emotion-laden Holocaust memorials all over the world, even at the camps themselves. But the final recommendation was for a historical museum to inform as well as to remind.

Wiesel, an Auschwitz survivor and author who perhaps more than any other living human has come to personify our struggle to cope with the Holocaust, resigned in 1986, after getting the project launched, to make way for someone more versed in fundraising, design and construction. He plans to attend the opening ceremonies.

As it was, the demands of designing the building almost defeated architect James Ingo Freed, a principal in the firm of Pei Cobb Freed & Partners and a Jewish refugee who fled Germany in 1939 at the age of 9.

"I gave myself three months to plan it," he said recently. "I didn't know that much about the Holocaust, so I immersed myself in reading and films. My wife got so depressed she moved out of the bedroom. Nothing came to me. Should the building try to tell the story? Should it be poetic?"

He asked himself: How would the structure relate to the other buildings on and near the Mall? Could it? Should it? He would be asking the casual tourists of summer in their shorts and funny shirts to shift abruptly 50 years into the past, to confront an ugly world they might know little about, nor care to have their children see.

The months passed. Freed was on the point of giving up, when he decided to visit the camps in person. He saw what was left of the ovens at Auschwitz, with their manufacturer's plaques proudly displayed. Tramping through the mud of the Polish camp, he found his shoes flecked with bits of human bone.

"Finally I began to respond. I wanted to convey the feeling of constantly being watched, of things closing in. I was thinking of the Warsaw ghetto. The bridges that the Jews had to cross over to get from one part of the ghetto to another, so they wouldn't contaminate others. I wanted the feeling of a procession. Of choices: either/or. Selections. The long lulls and sudden bumps forward, the steps to death."

His solution to the problem is brilliant. The massive facade on 14th Street has a grave beauty, a solemnity that imposes its mood on the passer-by. The succession of towers down the flank suggests the march of the years, leading back to the Hall of Remembrance, a six-sided memorial to silence, a place where visitors can meditate on what they have seen.

Subtly, in certain slightly off-kilter features, the building evokes a world of dislocation, a world askew. To those walking through it, the vistas seem disorienting. Perspectives are forced. Diagonals don't always appear quite right. The framework of the 304 large glass panels of the ceiling of the central Hall of

Witness is skewed, twisted, the way the wreckage at the camps was crazily wrenched by fire, the way the world had become twisted.

For those who have seen Auschwitz and the other places, specific visual references are everywhere. The tapered staircase leading up from the ground floor looks weirdly like the famous perspective shot of the railroad tracks at Birkenau with the arch looming above, a familiar picture to anyone who lived through the '40s. The brick walls contain decorative curved lintels, echoing the grim shape of the oven doors. Steel braces set into the walls recall the braces that the Nazis had to install to reinforce the brick of the ovens because of the extreme heat.

This is very much a public place, and for some, the building may just be too huge, too imposing, too grand to speak for the terribly private experience of death. For some, it may instruct but not move to tears as does, say, the memorial in Paris. But to most visitors, who haven't been to the camps, the Holocaust Memorial Museum can be a tremendous awakening experience.

The heart of the experience, of course, is the actual process of the visit itself.

As I enter the museum I pick up a computer-generated ID card of a Holocaust victim. Every visitor will get such a card. My new identity is Arthur Menke, born 1927—the same year I was born—in Hamburg, Germany. His father owned a small rubber-stamp factory.

Now I take an elevator to the fourth floor to begin a long, winding journey down through three floors of exhibitions. The experience actually begins as the steel doors of the elevator snap shut. The recorded voice of a liberator from the U.S. Army tells of coming upon the camps and of the horror he found there. A video monitor runs footage of the liberation. When I arrive on the fourth floor, the elevator doors open on a large photomural of G.I.'s entering a camp.

As I wend my way past murals and exhibits the story of Hitler's rise to power in 1933 is thrust at me. The gradual increase of legally sanctioned government pressure on the Jews is demonstrated. In his great documentary novel *The Wall,* about the Warsaw ghetto, in which a half-million Jews were literally walled in, John Hersey listed the sequence: "casual looting of Jewish property; kosher slaughter forbidden; *Kehilla* [the traditional Jewish community council] disbanded and *Judenrat* [Nazi-sponsored Jewish leadership] formed; public worship forbidden; census; registration for labor . . . armbands; bank accounts frozen; limitations on change of residence; registration of Jews' jewelry; schools closed; restrictions on travel; registration of property; Jews barred from trolleys and buses . . . wall sections built . . . "

There is an exhibit on the systematic racism practiced by the Nazis, the obsession with physiognomy, eye and hair color, caliper measurements of head proportions, nose length, cheek width, forehead height, to prove the superiority of "Aryans." Also on display is a Hollerith machine used by the Nazis for the national census. Benign in itself, the elaborate tabulating device, sort of a punch-card computer, was put to sinister use classifying citizens by race and religion, thus making it easy for the Nazis to identify and locate Jews and other "undesirables."

The Nuremberg Laws of 1935, legalizing the war against the Jews, are described, as is the 1938 Evian Conference, called by President Franklin Roosevelt to deal with the international refugee crisis brought on by Jews fleeing Germany and Austria. Basically, the 32 nations at the conference turned their backs on the refugees. A hotel register shows the names of diplomats who attended the conference.

Suddenly my progress is stopped by a horizontal bar, like those used at European borders. I can see beyond the bar but have to detour. My movement is controlled.

As I walk to the left, there are artifacts from Kristallnacht, November 9, 1938, when in a government-orchestrated national frenzy of hate, hundreds of Jewish-owned stores, schools and synagogues were smashed and burned, and scores of Jews beaten and killed. Here is a wooden Torah ark from a German synagogue, slashed with maniacal fury. The sheer energy of the hatred visible in these gouges is appalling. There are Nazi hate posters and books like *The Poison Mushroom,* which infected small children with hatred of Jews; and an actual Gypsy wagon from Czechoslovakia, to symbolize the attack on other minorities, from homosexuals to Jehovah's Witnesses.

Inexorably, I am moving forward. There seems to be no turning back. I am a witness as the fear builds among the Jews of Germany. A number manage to flee the country, a few find ways to fight back.

As I continue, I insert my ID card at a computer station and am given a first-person update on Arthur Menke. I find that the Nazis have seized his father's business and that the family has been moved to another part of town. "My sister and I make our own 'Nazi' flag and hang it out of the window," the boy says. "But my parents get angry with us and reel it back in. We don't understand why we can't support our own country."

Now I walk across a bridge—a glass floor, a change of footing and a view down onto the central skylit concourse through a glass wall etched with the names of 5,000 European towns and villages and shtetls that were attacked or simply obliterated by the Nazis—and through a tower hung with hundreds of photographs of men, women and children from one such town.

Stairs lead down to the third floor, which covers the most horrific phase of the Holocaust, 1940–44. Now the surface beneath my feet changes disconcertingly from granite to cobblestone to wood. This is another device meant to disorient—to upset the visitor's sense of order and rightness and logic. Here are the murals of ghettos and ghetto life, and a casting of a section of the wall that surrounded Warsaw's Jewish sector. The gate of the Jewish cemetery from Tarnow, Poland, is also here, as are photographs of Theresienstadt, the Potemkin Village camp set up by the Germans in western Czechoslovakia. The faces shown here bear little likeness to the smiling workers and happy children depicted in Hitler's propaganda film about the camp or to the staged scenes he arranged for a Red Cross inspection to quell rumors about the mistreatment of Jews. In reality, Theresienstadt was nothing more than a way station to the death camps.

The exhibits grow more and more terrible. Some may be so hard to take that special walls hide them from child visitors. One of the freight cars that was thought to have transported Jews and others to their deaths stands alongside a wooden platform. Found on a remote siding in Poland, the car was presented to the museum by the Polish government. Visitors can enter the car, walk right through it to the other side, or choose to detour around it. I walk through.

Near the train car are samples of the mountains of ordinary possessions confiscated at the Birkenau siding from the thousands who were marched straight from the railroad cars to the gas chambers—toothbrushes, combs, mirrors, kitchen utensils, suitcases—some of them with names carefully painted on: Josef Rederer, Ida Pollak, Julius Simon, Oskar Popper . . .

I move on, walking under a casting of the notorious iron *"Arbeit Macht Frei"* sign over the entrance to Auschwitz, a bit of heavyhanded Nazi humor, telling the prisoners that work would make them free. Part of an actual barracks from Birkenau is here, and a casting of a gas chamber door and canisters of Zyklon B, the toxic gas used for the killings. There is a pile of stone blocks from the Mauthausen quarry, where inmates were forced to work and sometimes pushed to their deaths by SS guards. And there is a mesmerizing sculpture by Polish artist Mieczyslaw Stobierski depicting, with hundreds of small white plaster figures, the whole process of selecting, gassing and burning at Auschwitz.

Among the vast trove of images is one of Janusz Korczak, the Warsaw orphanage director who marched with his charges onto the deportation trains, though he could have escaped. His story has been celebrated in books and movies, but it is necessary to remember that hundreds, perhaps thousands, of unsung mothers also rejected the offer of life in the camps and chose to die with their children.

Amazingly, the museum has one of two milk cans in which historian Emanuel Ringelblum buried his archive of the Warsaw ghetto. The second is in Warsaw. The museum has collected 23,000 such artifacts, filling two warehouses—remnants of the nightmare. Some are as ordinary and nondescript as ID cards and prayer shawls; some are as elaborate as the intricate model of the Lodz ghetto, complete with all the streets and bridges, built inside a sort of violin case by Leon Jacobson and later buried in the Polish ghetto. After the war, Jacobson's brothers found the model in the rubble of the ghetto and returned it to him. He in turn has given it to the museum.

From all over the world, people have donated items that once meant everything to them: a doll from the Krakow ghetto (the girl who owned it ended up in Buchenwald, was liberated and later reunited with the doll, which was left behind in Krakow and saved for her by non-Jews), a mica necklace, a frayed old cloth belt that Ruth Meyerowitz, now of West Orange, New Jersey, found in the dirt when she was a 13-year-old at Auschwitz and wore, though such decorations were forbidden, and cherished for years afterward until she thought to give it to the museum.

Though the museum has not specifically sought out Nazi paraphernalia, a few important items are in the collection, including stacks of propaganda, execution notices, medical instruments, and geneticists' measuring tools, one with a brass nameplate: Dr. Eugen Fischer.

I sit down at a rest point and listen to recorded voices of survivors telling what life was like in Auschwitz-Birkenau. I think of Bergen-Belsen and Buchenwald and the thousand other places from France to Russia. There are bowls from the camps here, 4,000 shoes, a picture of the hair of 40,000 human beings on exhibit at Auschwitz. Here, too, are castings of a door from an Auschwitz oven and a zinc dissecting table used to salvage valuables, such as gold fillings, from the dead.

Continuing my tour, I once again cross over a bridge, this time with a glass wall etched with the first names of victims, and then on to the other side and through the bottom level of the tower of snapshots.

And here surely is the most powerful single exhibit in the museum. A woman named Yaffa Sonenson Eliach was 4 years old when the Jewish population (some 4,000 souls) of her Polish town, Ejszyszki, was wiped out in 1941 by the guns of the mobile death squads, the German *Einsatzgruppen,* forerunners of the more efficient gas chambers. Only 29 survived the massacre, Eliach and her immediate family among them. Now living in Brooklyn, she has spent much of her life collecting some 6,000 photographs, a family album of her shtetl. Most of them are reproduced here, some discolored, some bent and cracked, all of them unspeakably moving in their portrait of a lost world.

45   Many are studio portraits, for Eliach's grandmother was one of the town's photographers, and Eliach and her brother managed to retrieve some of her photographs after the war. Most of the images, however, were painstakingly acquired by Eliach from friends and relatives of the victims. Four sisters pose together, all of them handsome, one a stunning beauty. They wear pleated skirts, slingback heels and '30s hairstyles. Here is an old bearded grandfather and a small girl in a white lace dress wearing a locket. (Where is that locket today?) Two men in Polish uniforms, the hats too big for them. A dashing youth with cigarette in mouth, riding a bicycle through the woods. A baby in a sled. The family Glombocki standing before a house of unpainted rough wood. Five boys in Zionist scout uniforms, dated June 10, 1930. The Portnoy sisters, clear-eyed, standing with a vase of roses. Eliach herself as a wide-smiling small girl feeding the chickens. Wedding parties, school groups, young couples smiling dreamily, schoolboys in knickers, with clipped hair. Snow scenes in unknown cities, summer scenes with leaf and shadow. A girl standing in a broad field holding three eggs. A boy with bangs in an embroidered shirt, chin in hand, the other hand resting possessively on a typescript as he looks intelligently at us, staring straight at us, into the future. His nails are dirty. You can multiply these pictures by a thousand, but you don't have to. By themselves, they say what has to be said.

Down now to the final floor of the tour. I learn that Arthur Menke has been deported to a giant ghetto in Russia to cut blocks of peat for fuel for the German Army. "The soldiers are regular army and don't abuse the prisoners as badly as do the SS here," he reports. "Walking to and from our labor site, I push the guard's bicycle for him. Food is so scarce that one day he locks me in the potato cellar so I can steal potatoes for him. He allows me to take some for myself."

After two years in Minsk, Arthur Menke was deported to Poland and in 1945 was liberated while on a forced march to Dachau. (Some ID cards record the holder's death; others testify to survival.) On this floor I learn about the Jews who fought back. Trees from the Rudniki forest in Lithuania that provided a haven for partisans tell of their resistance. One of the small fishing boats by which the Danes ferried many Jews to safety in Sweden is here. And a vendor's sign from Lidice, the Czech village wiped off the face of the Earth in retaliation for the assassination of Reinhard Heydrich, the executor of the Final Solution. At the end of the hall is a row of photographs, the killers, the mass murderers—the perpetrators of the Holocaust.

Finally there is a reprise of the role of the liberators. The conquering Allied armies were the first outsiders to enter the death camps, though escapees had been coming out of Europe for years to tell the terrible story, and aerial photographs clearly showed the prison barracks and the transports.

Now I move out of the exhibition area and into the 70-foot-high Hall of Remembrance, lit by a domed skylight and a few tall slivers of windows. The walls seem to stand unsupported, the glass gaps between them reminding one of the thin shafts of light in the barracks. The symmetry of the space stands in sharp contrast to much of the rest of the museum, restoring a sense of order and calm and comfort. Candles may be lit and left in niches. There are steps for people to sit on, in the quiet.

Earth gathered from the camps and ghettos of Europe has been buried in one area beneath the hall's floor. An eternal flame will sit above the spot.

The problem of how much to beautify this solemn memorial has been with the designers from the beginning. "Most museums deal in the beautiful," Michael Berenbaum has said. "We are dealing with the anti-beautiful." "The tragedy cuts through all the time—in nightmares and in speechless anger and incomprehension," adds Raye Farr, director of the permanent exhibition. "But we go on trying to make it visible, even if we can never explain why it happened."

Some of the artwork that embellishes the walls and open spaces comes straight from history, like Roman Vishniac's celebrated photographs of Jewish life in Eastern Europe before the war. Some has been specially commissioned. Notably, four artists—Ellsworth Kelly, Sol LeWitt, Richard Serra and Joel Shapiro—have been asked to create sculptures or wall drawings for the museum's public spaces.

Then there is the Children's Wall of Remembrance, which features 3,300 ceramic tiles painted by American schoolchildren in memory of the 1.5 million children lost in the Holocaust. The Tile Project, started by educational advocate Adeline Yates in 1986, is part of the museum's campaign to teach elementary school pupils about the event.

Children are a special concern at the museum, and an exhibit titled "Remember the Children" has been set up for those ages 8 and older. It follows a composite child named Daniel through the Holocaust to his eventual survival. His room, toys and furniture are there in replica to be touched and studied. A similar children's show, with photographs but no artifacts, has been traveling around the country as part of the museum's outreach program, which is considerable.

Along with the four classrooms of the educational center, there are two exhibition galleries for temporary shows and two auditoriums on the lower levels—in addition to the small auditoriums that are part of the permanent exhibition. These larger chambers, seating 414 and 178 respectively, will be available to the public for performing arts events, films, concerts and lectures.

In the computer-based Wexner Learning Center on the second floor, visitors can work some of the museum's 24 interactive computers to call up tapes of survivors telling their stories, or to study in detail specific aspects of the Holocaust, such as Swedish attaché Raoul Wallenberg's rescue of thousands of Hungarians—often literally ordering them off the deportation trains by simply reading out names in a loud voice while the Nazi guards gaped, so imposing was his presence—until his disappearance into the Soviet Union.

On the top floor are the library and archives, occupying 16,000 square feet of space. In addition to a 20,000-volume library, the facility contains a huge mass of Holocaust records, including reels of microfilmed documents stored in a special climate-controlled room. The collapse of Communism brought to the museum an immeasurably valuable collection of captured German and other material from the former Soviet Union and Eastern Europe. The library and archives, along with the museum's oral history, photography and film collections, constitutes the United States Holocaust Research Institute, which is expected to develop into an international center for Holocaust scholarship.

One important aspect of this scholarship is the continuing search for information about the dead, so many of whom simply disappeared without trace. People want to know, if possible, just what happened to their lost families. Once in a great while, survivors from the same family are reunited.

Nazi records of deportation trains, lists of names for work details, transport lists, camp death books (complete with fictitious causes of death: "pneumonia" or "shot trying to escape"), documents on euthanasia—the handicapped were the first to be eliminated—kept with insane meticulousness, are being catalogued by the museum in cooperation with the National Archives, which holds much of this material. As the museum sifts through these records, it coordinates with the American Red Cross to identify documents that may be helpful in tracing Holocaust victims.

The American Red Cross has been tracing lost people for years, since the Civil War in fact. A special unit set up in Baltimore two years ago has accepted more than 13,000 tracing requests connected to the Holocaust and has reunited survivors in some 100 cases.

"We work with the museum to increase people's awareness of this service," said Diane Paul, director of the Red Cross unit in Baltimore. "So many were totally forgotten. These records prove they existed."

The Red Cross also coordinates with the International Tracing Service in Arolsen, Germany, which holds 46 million such documents relating to more than 14 million people.

Some Nazi records give not only the victim's name, and place and date of birth—unreliable because many lied about their age to survive—but occupation and religion, and sometimes the name of the SS officer responsible for that person's death. Some of the people listed in the Mauthausen camp death book were U.S. citizens. A few were captured American fliers.

The staggering job of finding individual names in this sea of handwritten lists from all over Europe is just one of the projects of Holocaust researchers.

And unfortunately, tragically, such work today is not the quaint, musty, abstruse thing that scholarship can be. Taking note of the ominous resurgence of racial strife around the world and of neo-Nazi activity in Germany and elsewhere, the museum's deputy director, Elaine Heumann Gurian, says, "It is frightening to think about the relevance of our museum. I think we would have liked to be less relevant."

On the other hand, one remembers the words of a Polish tailor named Ignacy Kunin, who died just a few years ago. A Jew who made it to America after surviving five years in Auschwitz, Buchenwald and three other places because of his skill, a man who once, in order to stay alive, made a sky-blue uniform for the ineffable Reichsmarschall Hermann Göring, Kunin was a wire-tough, sardonic survivor who escaped death-by-selection a dozen times in the crazy lottery that was life in the Nazi camps: "I consider it was a victory. I consider that we won. Hitler is gone, and we're still here."

Questions for Discussion

1. Explain the organization of this essay. Why is it organized the way it is? Do you consider this organization effective? If so, why? If not, how would you revise the organization?
2. Could you classify this essay as referential aim writing? Explain your answer.
3. What do you think of the final paragraph? Is this a satisfactory way to conclude this essay? Why do you think it is or isn't?
4. This essay was written for a general audience. If the author were addressing a specific audience of Jews, how might he revise this essay? What changes would you recommend?
5. What significance does the author derive from his visit to this museum? Does this seem logical and appropriate to you? If so, why? If not, why not?

Opportunities for Writing

1. Depict the concentration camp at Auschwitz. How big was it? What did it look like? How many people lived and died there? When? Why? How? Why is this concentration camp important? Why is it important to you?
2. A local human rights organization is soliciting essays for a book about the Holocaust. Compose a portrait of a local man or woman who lived through the Holocaust. Interview this survivor, if possible, and his or her family and friends. What was life like for this survivor before, during, and after the Holocaust? What have you learned from this individual's experience?
3. Discuss a specific incident in the Nazi persecution of Jews and other minorities? What happened? When and where did it happen? Why do you consider this episode especially meaningful or noteworthy? Address your essay to the membership of a local Jewish congregation on the anniversary of this incident.

PART TWO

READING REFERENTIAL AIM WRITING

As a college student, you write and read referential texts all of the time. What is referential aim writing? It is writing that explains and analyzes. You go to school to learn about new subjects or to explore familiar subjects more fully; consequently, much of the school writing and reading you do involves referential texts, a very important kind of academic writing. Have you ever written or read texts that analyzed a character in a novel? Defined a concept in psychology? Explained a marketing strategy? Examined a current trend? Provided instructions for how to keep score in a sport such as tennis, baseball, bowling, basketball, or football? Summarized something you've read (e.g., an article or book) or seen (e.g., a movie, play, event)? Or have you reported the results of a chemistry experiment you've completed? Announced a meeting or presented the minutes of a meeting? If so, you have had firsthand experience writing and reading referential aim texts.

Texts that have a dominant referential aim often have subordinate expressive or persuasive aims. For example, a computer manual may be instructive, offering objective and clear directions about how to use a certain word processing program (referential aim). At the same time, the manual may include comparisons of this software with another popular program—comparisons that point out how one program is superior to the other (persuasive aim). If the writer also offers an autobiographical account of how this word processing software changed his or her life as a writer, the manual would also have an expressive subordinate aim. When you write or read texts, identify the dominant and subordinate aims. Doing so will help you to develop your understanding of referential texts.

In addition, consider the different ways of knowing: participation, observation, or both participation and observation. For example, as a writer you might compose a page of instructions for changing a bicycle tire, using your experience (participation) as a clerk in a local bicycle shop. Or you might choose to explain the operation of a saccharometer, relying exclusively on information you obtained from reading several chemistry books and from interviewing a chemist (observation). Or you might analyze a poem, integrating your personal insights (participation) as well as ideas you discovered in journal articles by literary critics (observation). What and how you write about your subject is directly influenced by what and how you know about that subject.

When you read referential texts, you can determine the way that an author researched the subject, too. How accurate and sufficient is the information? Are the sources appropriately cited? By reading in this way, you can consider both the quality and quantity of the information in the text. And given the specific details in the text, you can consider the author's credibility as well.

For our purposes, let's take a quick look at three concerns, among the many, of a writer or reader of referential aim texts.

CREDIBILITY OF THE WRITER

Credibility is a writer's reputation for fairly and thoroughly discussing a subject. A writer establishes credibility by identifying his or her qualifications to discuss a subject or by displaying knowledge of the subject.

THESIS AND SUPPORTING EVIDENCE

A *thesis* is a writer's major assertion regarding the subject. The thesis may be explicit (overt and direct) or implicit (implied or indirect); it may appear at the beginning, end, or beginning and end of a text. For example, if an author poses a question at the beginning of an essay, the writer's response might be the entire essay. The author's thesis would be implicitly rather than explicitly stated; the reader would have to infer the thesis. On the other hand, suppose an author asks a question and immediately answers it; the response would represent an explicit thesis.

A writer can develop and clarify his or her thesis by offering *supporting evidence* that is sufficient, plausible, and pertinent. A writer's information is *sufficient* if it anticipates and responds to the questions readers may have regarding the subject. The writer must consider the intended audience to determine how much readers need to know about the subject and how much readers already know. A writer can intimidate readers with too much information or confuse them with too little. If the writer is in doubt here, it is probably better to offer more information. If a writer omits information and it proves necessary to your understanding as a reader, the writer essentially paralyzes you and leaves you incapable of digesting or using the information given.

Information is *plausible* if it identifies reliable and likely sources of information. Reliable sources of information include accurate information from rigorous experiments, prestigious newspapers, professional journals, and interviews with subject specialists. If a source typically supplies correct information or has a reputation for accuracy and integrity, it will probably be considered, for the most part, to be trustworthy and to have integrity. Conversely, inconsistent or contradictory ideas ought to raise questions among readers.

A writer's information is *pertinent* if it directs the reader's attention to the thesis and avoids unnecessary details or digressions. Once again, the writer must be sensitive to his or her readers, deciding which information is essential (is needed to clarify the explanation or analysis) and which information is distracting (interferes with the reader's understanding).

TECHNIQUES TO MOTIVATE READERS

As a reader you probably don't automatically examine every piece of referential writing that is offered to you. The writer's job, therefore, is to motivate you to read an explanation or analysis and add it to your previous knowledge of a subject. Writers can motivate readers by emphasizing the significance of the information—by showing why the explanation or analysis is important to know. Here are some common techniques you may find in referential essays:

> *Examples* identify practical applications or specific occurrences of the subject, making information easier to remember.
> *Illustrations* display the vital characteristics of a subject, thereby helping readers to visualize it.
> *Narratives* dramatize and personalize a subject, making information easier to understand and remember.
> *Comparison and contrast* reveal the ways a new subject is similar to or different from a subject with which readers are already familiar, thus simplifying information and easing understanding.
> *Division* identifies the components of the subject, allowing readers to digest information more readily.

While these techniques, among others, all help to make writing more accessible to readers, writers also know that as a reader you will tolerate difficult texts if you believe there is a good reason for that difficulty. When approaching a text that might be difficult to read, therefore, ask yourself the following questions:

- Why do you need the information being offered? That is, how can you use or apply it?
- How will you benefit from reading this text?
- Has the writer integrated techniques (e.g., examples, illustrations) into his or her writing to aid you in your reading? If so, how?

The following referential aim essays explain and analyze subjects while incorporating expressive and persuasive subordinate aims. As you read these selections, you'll notice that they represent the various ways of knowing as well as a broad range of academic writing; these essays advance readers' understanding of a subject's meaning, characteristics, importance, composition, operation, causes, effects, or similarities to and differences from associated subjects. In your planning, translating, and reviewing of these essays, notice the variety of rhetorical strategies used to establish credibility, support the thesis, and motivate the reader.

Using the Guide to Critical Reading, explore the essays from a content, function/feature, and rhetorical perspective. Consider also the internal and external influences on your reading processes. By critically examining this referential aim writing, you will significantly expand your reading repertoire.

Knowledge by Participation

Cultural Etiquette
A Guide for the Well-Intentioned

Amoja Three Rivers

Amoja Three Rivers cofounded the Accessible African Heritage Project. In this essay published in Ms. *in 1991, she identifies language that promotes "cultural and racial bigotry," following each example with her own advice concerning the proper "etiquette" in the situation. This etiquette guide is based on Three Rivers's personal understanding of cultural and racial prejudice. As you read, consider Three Rivers's tone and use of definitions, negative definitions, and the imperative mood (e.g., "Do not . . . "). Does her way of knowing about the language of prejudice justify or clarify what she says and how she "talks" to her readers?*

Cultural Etiquette is intended for people of all "races," nationalities, and creeds, not necessarily just "white" people, because no one living in Western society is exempt from the influences of racism, racial stereotypes, race and cultural prejudices, and anti-Semitism. I include anti-Semitism in the discussion of racism because it is simply another manifestation of cultural and racial bigotry.

All people are people. It is ethnocentric to use a generic term such as "people" to refer only to white people and then racially label everyone else. This creates and reinforces the assumption that whites are the norm, the real people, and that all others are aberrations.

"Exotic," when applied to human beings, is ethnocentric and racist.

While it is true that most citizens of the U.S.A. are white, at least four fifths of the world's population consists of people of color. Therefore, it is statistically incorrect as well as ethnocentric to refer to us as minorities. The term "minority" is used to reinforce the idea of people of color as "other."

A cult is a particular system of religious worship. If the religious practices of the Yorubas constitute a cult, then so do those of the Methodists, Catholics, Episcopalians, and so forth.

A large radio/tape player is a boom-box, or a stereo or a box or a large metallic ham sandwich with speakers. It is not a "ghetto blaster."

Everybody can blush. Everybody can bruise. Everybody can tan and get sunburned. Everybody.

Judaism is no more patriarchal than any other patriarchal religion.

Koreans are not taking over. Neither are Jews. Neither are the Japanese. Neither are the West Indians. These are myths put out and maintained by the ones who really have.

All hair is "good" hair. Dreadlocks, locks, dreads, natty dreads, et cetera, is an ancient traditional way that African people sometimes wear their hair. It is not braided, it is "locked." Locking is the natural tendency of African hair to knit and bond to itself. It locks by itself, we don't have to do anything to it to make it lock. It is permanent; once locked, it cannot come undone. It gets washed just as regularly as anyone else's hair. No, you may not touch it, don't ask.

One of the most effective and insidious aspects of racism is cultural genocide. Not only have African Americans been cut off from our African tribal roots, but because of generations of whites pitting African against Indian, and Indian against African, we have been cut off from our Native American roots as well. Consequently, most African Native Americans no longer have tribal affiliations, or know for certain what people they are from.

Columbus didn't discover diddly-squat.

Slavery is not a condition unique to African people. In fact, the word "slave" comes from the Slav people of Eastern Europe. Because so many Slavs were enslaved by other people (including Africans), their very name came to be synonymous with the condition.

Native Americans were also enslaved by Europeans. Because it is almost impossible to successfully enslave large numbers of people in their own land, most enslaved Native Americans from the continental U.S. were shipped to Bermuda, and the West Indies, where many inter-married with the Africans.

People do not have a hard time because of their race or cultural background. No one is attacked, abused, oppressed, pogromed, or enslaved because of their race, creed, or cultural background. People are attacked, abused, oppressed, pogromed, or enslaved because of racism and anti-Semitism. There is a subtle but important difference in the focus here. The first implies some inherent fault or shortcoming within the oppressed person or group. The second redirects the responsibility back to the real source of the problem.

Asians are not "mysterious," "fatalistic," or "inscrutable."

Native Americans are not stoic, mystical, or vanishing.

Latin people are no more hot-tempered, hot-blooded, or emotional than anyone else. We do not have flashing eyes, teeth, or daggers. We are lovers pretty much like other people. Very few of us deal with any kind of drugs.

Middle Easterners are not fanatics, terrorists, or all oil-rich.

Jewish people are not particularly rich, clannish, or expert in money matters.

Not all African Americans are poor, athletic, or ghetto-dwellers.

Most Asians in the U.S. are not scientists, mathematicians, geniuses, or wealthy.

Southerners are no less intelligent than anybody else.

It is not a compliment to tell someone: "I don't think of you as Jewish/Black/Asian/Latina/Middle Eastern/Native American." Or "I think of you as white."

Do not use a Jewish person or person of color to hear your confession of past racist transgressions. If you have offended a particular person, then apologize directly to that person.

Also don't assume that Jews and people of color necessarily want to hear about how prejudiced your Uncle Fred is, no matter how terrible you think he is.

If you are white and/or gentile, do not assume that the next Jewish person or person of color you see will feel like discussing this guide with you. Sometimes we get tired of teaching this subject.

If you are white, don't brag to a person of color about your overseas trip to our homeland. Especially when we cannot afford such a trip. Similarly, don't assume that we are overjoyed to see the expensive artifacts you bought.

Words like "gestapo," "concentration camp" and "Hitler" are only appropriate when used in reference to the Holocaust.

"Full-blood," "half-breed," "quarter-blood." Any inference that a person's "race" depends on blood is racist. Natives are singled out for this form of bigotry and are denied rights on that basis.

"Scalping": a custom also practiced by the French, the Dutch, and the English.

Do you have friends or acquaintances who are terrific except they're really racist? If you quietly accept that part of them, you are giving their racism tacit approval.

As an exercise, pretend you are from another planet and you want an example of a typical human being for your photo album. Having never heard of racism, you'd probably pick someone who represents the majority of the people on the planet—an Asian person.

How many is too many? We have heard well-meaning liberals say things like "This event is too white. We need more people of color." Well, how many do you need? Fifty? A hundred? Just what is your standard for personal racial comfort?

People of color and Jewish people have been so all their lives. Further, if we have been raised in a place where white gentiles predominate, then we have been subjected to racism/anti-Semitism all our lives. We are therefore experts on our own lives and conditions. If you do not understand or believe or agree with what someone is saying about their own oppression, do not automatically assume that they are wrong or paranoid or oversensitive.

It is not "racism in reverse" or "segregation" for Jews or people of color to come together in affinity groups for mutual support. Sometimes we need some time and space apart from the dominant group just to relax and be ourselves. If people coming together for group support makes you feel excluded, perhaps there's something missing in your own life or cultural connections.

The various cultures of people of color often seem very attractive to white people. (Yes, we are wonderful, we can't deny it.) But white people should not make a playground out of other people's cultures. We are not quaint. We are not exotic. We are not cool.

Don't forget that every white person alive today is also descended from tribal peoples. If you are white, don't neglect your own ancient traditions. They are as valid as anybody else's, and the ways of your own ancestors need to be honored and remembered.

"Race" is an arbitrary and meaningless concept. Races among humans don't exist. If there ever was any such thing as race, there has been so much constant crisscrossing of genes for the last 500,000 years that it would have lost all meaning anyway. There are no real divisions between us, only a continuum of variations that constantly change, as we come together and separate according to the movement of human populations.

40 Anyone who functions in what is referred to as the "civilized" world is a carrier of the disease of racism.

Does reading this guide make you uncomfortable? Angry? Confused? Are you taking it personally? Well, not to fret. Racism has created a big horrible mess, and racial healing can sometimes be painful. Just remember that Jews and people of color do not want or need anybody's guilt. We just want people to accept responsibility when it is appropriate, and actively work for change.

Questions for Discussion

1. What are the subordinate aims of this essay? Cite specific passages to support your answer.
2. Notice the frequency of single-sentence paragraphs. Do you consider this technique effective? Why or why not?
3. What is the thesis of the essay? How does the author try to develop and clarify the thesis?
4. Do you consider the author a credible source of information on this subject? If so, why? If not, why not?
5. How would this essay differ if it were written using only knowledge by observation? Would the essay be more or less effective? Explain your answers.

Opportunities for Writing

1. Explain a tradition or practice of your religious or ethnic group. How do you participate in this tradition or practice? When? Where? What is its meaning? What are its origins?
2. Analyze a common misunderstanding about your religious or ethnic group. What is this misunderstanding? How did it get started? What is its impact on your religious or ethnic group? Compose your essay as a guest editorial for your local newspaper.
3. Write a letter to a friend, offering guidelines for polite behavior within your religious or ethnic group. How should "outsiders" conduct themselves during conversations, while dining, or at special celebrations?

Falling for Apples

Noel Perrin

Born in New York, Noel Perrin attended Williams College and Duke University. Perrin has taught at Dartmouth College since 1959 and has been named a Guggenheim Fellow twice and a Fulbright Fellow at the University of Warsaw. An environmental studies educator and columnist, Perrin has been a prolific writer; among his publications are A Reader's Delight *(1988),* Third Person Rural *(1983), and* Second Person Rural *(1980), from which "Falling for Apples" is taken. This essay explains "cidering," a process that Perrin thinks is best learned and appreciated directly (knowledge by participation). And it is from this perspective that Perrin instructs readers.*

The number of children who eagerly help around a farm is rather small. Willing helpers do exist, but many more of them are five years old than fifteen. In fact, there seems to be a general law that says as long as a kid is too little to help effectively, he or she is dying to. Then, just as they reach the age when they really could drive a fence post or empty a sap bucket without spilling half of it, they lose interest. Now it's cars they want to drive, or else they want to stay in the house and listen for four straight hours to The Who. That sort of thing.

There is one exception to this rule. Almost no kid that I have ever met outgrows an interest in cidering. In consequence, cider making remains a family time on our farm, even though it's been years since any daughter trudged along a fencerow with me, dragging a new post too heavy for her to carry, or begged for lessons in chainsawing.

It's not too hard to figure out why. In the first place, cidering gives the child instant gratification. There's no immediate reward for weeding a garden (unless the parents break down and offer cash), still less for loading a couple of hundred hay bales in the barn. But the minute you've ground and pressed the first bushel of apples, you can break out the glasses and start drinking. Good stuff, too. Cider has a wonderful fresh sweetness as it runs from the press.

In the second place, making cider on a small scale is simple enough so that even fairly young children—say, a pair of nine-year-olds—can do the whole operation by themselves. Yet it's also picturesque enough to tempt people of any age. When my old college roommate was up last fall—and we've been out of college a long time—he and his wife did four pressings in the course of the weekend. They only quit then because I ran out of apples.

5 Finally, cider making appeals to a deep human instinct. It's the same one that makes a housewife feel so good when she takes a bunch of leftovers and produces a memorable casserole. At no cost, and using what would otherwise be wasted, she has created something. In fact, she has just about reversed entropy.

Cidering is like that. You take apples that have been lying on the ground for a week, apples with blotches and cankers and bad spots, apples that would make a supermarket manager turn pale if you merely brought them in the store, and out of this unpromising material you produce not one but two delicious drinks. Sweet cider now. Hard cider later.

The first step is to have a press. At the turn of the century, almost every farm family did. They ordered them from the Sears or Montgomery Ward catalogue as routinely as one might now order a toaster. Then about 1930 little presses ceased to be made. Pasteurized apple juice had joined the list of American food-processing triumphs. It had no particular flavor (still hasn't), but it would keep almost indefinitely. Even more appealing, it was totally sterile. That was the era when the proudest boast that, let's say, a bakery could make was that its bread was untouched by human hands. Was touched only by stainless-steel beaters and stainless-steel wrapping machines.

Eras end, though, and the human hand came back into favor. One result: in the 1970s home cider presses returned to the market. They have not yet returned to the Sears catalogue, but they are readily available. I know of two companies in Vermont that make them, another in East Aurora, New York, and one out in Washington state. If there isn't someone making them in Michigan or Wisconsin, there soon will be. Prices range from about 175 to 250 dollars.

Then you get a couple of bushels of apples. There *may* be people in the country who buy cider apples, but I don't know any of them. Old apple trees are too common. I get mine by the simple process of picking up windfalls in a derelict orchard that came with our place. I am not choosy. Anything that doesn't actually squish goes in the basket.

10 With two kids to help, collecting takes maybe twenty minutes. Kids tend to be less interested in gathering the apples than in running the press, but a quiet threat of no-pickee, no-pressee works wonders. Kids also worry about worms sometimes, as they scoop apples from the ground—apples that may be wet with dew, spiked with stubble, surrounded by hungry wasps. Occasionally I have countered with a short lecture on how much safer our unsprayed apples are than the shiny, wormless, but heavily sprayed apples one finds in stores. But usually I just say that I have yet to see a worm in our cider press. That's true, too. Whether it's because there has never been one, or whether it's because in the excitement and bustle of grinding you just wouldn't notice one little worm, I don't dare to say.

As soon as you get back with the apples, it's time to make cider. Presses come in two sizes: one-bushel and a-third-of-a-bushel. We have tried both. If I lived in a suburb and had to buy apples, I would use the very efficient third-of-a-bushel press and make just under a gallon at a time. Living where I do, I use the bigger press and make two gallons per pressing, occasionally a little more.

The process has two parts. First you set your pressing tub under the grinder, line it with a pressing cloth, and start grinding. Or, better, your children do. One feeds apples into the hopper, the other turns the crank. If there are three children present, the third can hold the wooden hopper plate, and thus keep the apples from bouncing around. If there are four, the fourth can spell off on cranking. Five or more is too many, and any surplus over four is best made into a separate crew for the second pressing. I once had two three-child crews present, plus a seventh child whom my wife appointed the official timer. We did two pressings and had 4¼ gallons of cider in 43 minutes and 12 seconds. (Who won? The second crew, by more than a minute. Each crew had one of our practiced daughters on it, but the second also had the advantage of watching the first.)

As soon as the apples are ground, you put the big pressing plate on and start to turn the press down. If it's a child crew, and adult meddling is nevertheless tolerated, it's desirable to have the kids turn the press in order of their age, starting with the youngest: at the end it takes a fair amount of strength (though it's not beyond two nine-year-olds working together), and a little kid coming after a big one may fail to produce a single drop.

The pressing is where all the thrills come. As the plate begins to move down and compact the ground apples, you hear a kind of sighing, bubbling noise. Then a trickle of cider begins to run out. Within five or ten seconds the trickle turns into a stream, and the stream into a ciderfall. Even kids who've done it a dozen times look down in awe at what their labor has wrought.

15 A couple of minutes later the press is down as far as it will go, and the container you remembered to put below the spout is full of rich, brown cider. Someone has broken out the glasses, and everybody is having a drink.

This pleasure goes on and on. In an average year we start making cider the second week of September, and we continue until early November. We make all we can drink ourselves, and quite a lot to give away. We have supplied whole church suppers. One year the girls sold about ten gallons to the village store, which made them some pocket money they were prouder of than any they ever earned by baby-sitting. Best of all, there are two months each year when all of us are running the farm together, just like a pioneer family.

Questions for Discussion

1. What do you think of the essay's title? What other titles would be appropriate for this essay?
2. How is the essay organized? How would you organize this essay if you were writing it?
3. In this essay, the author addresses the readers directly using *you* (e.g., "You take apples that have been lying on the ground . . ."). What do you think of this technique? Is it appropriate? Why do you think it is or isn't?
4. This essay was written for families with children. How would it differ if it were written for readers without children?
5. How does the author try to motivate his audience? Is he effective? Why or why not?

Opportunities for Writing

1. Explain how to prepare your favorite food. What are the ingredients? What utensils are required? Write your essay for the food section of your local newspaper.
2. Compare and contrast a homemade food item with its sterilized supermarket version (e.g., bread). What similarities and differences do you notice regarding nutrition, enjoyment, cost, safety, and time?
3. Explain how to include children in the preparation of a food (e.g., ice cream). Does the process change according to the age of the children? If so, how? Address your essay to the membership of a parenting organization.
4. Analyze the impact of new technology on a specific food item (e.g., orange juice). How has the processing of this food item changed? Interview appropriate food technicians and visit their facilities.

Consider integrating photographs or diagrams of their machines as well as illustrations of their processes.

Shopping with Children

Phyllis Theroux

Phyllis Theroux often draws on her own experience as a parent to comment on parent-child relationships. A regular contributor to publications such as The New York Times, Reader's Digest, Washington Post, *and* McCall's, *Theroux has compiled three collections of her essays:* Night Lights *(1987);* Peripheral Visions *(1982); and* California and Other States of Grace: A Memoir *(1980). "Shopping with Children" appears in* Night Lights.

Once upon a time there were three little children. By and large, dressing them was a joyful thing. At a moment's notice, their mother could turn the boys into baby Rothschilds, the girl into a shipping heiress, or even a Kennedy. In those early days of motherhood, I used to take a lot of photographs for the scrapbook. Now I flip through the scrapbook sometimes to remind myself that "those were the days."

The eldest son was the first to establish his individuality: sleeveless Army jackets, kneecap bandannas and a pierced ear hidden under a lengthening hair style. Then the youngest son discovered dirt. He formed a club, still active, called "The All Dirt Association." To qualify, one had to roll in the mud.

Fortunately, the little girl grows increasingly more tasteful and immaculate. She will get up at 5:30 A.M. to make sure she has enough time to wash and curl her hair so that it bounces properly on her shoulders when she goes off to school, and she screams as if bitten by an adder if a drop of spaghetti sauce lands on her Izod. The entire house is thrown into an uproar while she races for the Clorox bottle. This is a family of extremists, and nobody dresses for the kind of success I had in mind.

Time will tell what happens to these children. Who can say whether my son the dirt bomb will wind up sewing buttons on a seersucker sports jacket, or my daughter the Southamptonian will discover the joys of thrift-shop browsing. They are still evolving toward personal statements that are, at this writing, incomplete.

5   In the meantime, however, they must be dressed, which means taking them to stores where clothing for their growing bodies can be purchased. Shopping with children is exactly as awful as shopping with parents. But if the experience is to be survived there are certain rules all adults must follow. (If you are a child, you may not read any further. This is for your parents, who will deal with you very harshly if you read one more word!)

Rule I: Never shop with more than one child at a time. This rule is closely related to another rule—never raise more than one child at a time. If you understand the second rule, there is no need to elaborate upon the first.

Rule II: Dress very nicely yourself. After the age of nine, children do not like to be seen with their mothers in public. You are a blot upon their reputation, a shadow they want to shake. I, myself, always insisted that my mother walk ten paces behind me, take separate elevators and escalators and speak only when spoken to—which brings me to the next rule.

Rule III: Do not make any sudden gestures, loud noises or heartfelt exclamations such as "How adorable you look in that!" or "Twenty-nine ninety-five! Are you kidding? For a shirt?" Children are terribly embarrassed by our eccentricities, and it goes without saying that you must never buy their articles of "intimate apparel" in their presence. Children, until enough sleazy adults teach them that it is old-fashioned, are very modest creatures. One time I ran out of the store and took the bus home by myself after my mother asked a salesclerk where the "underpants" counter was. Everyone in the store heard her. I had no choice.

Rule IV: Know your child's limits. If he can be coerced into a department store, coaxed into telling you that he wouldn't mind wearing this shirt or that pair of pants, don't insist that he go the whole distance—i.e., don't force him to try them on. Keep the sales slips; if something doesn't fit when he tries it on at home, return it. If he cannot be made to enter the store at all, say, "Fine. When you run out of clothes, wear your sister's." Children who won't go shopping at all save their parents a lot of time.

Rule V: Know your own limits. Do not be dragged to every sneaker store in the metropolitan area to find the exact shoes your child has in mind. Announce: "We're going to Sears—and Sears only—unless you want to wait for six more weeks, which is the next time I am free." Some children, with nothing but time and a passion to improve their image, will cheerfully go to three stores they know about and six more they don't, without blinking an eye.

Rule VI: Keep your hand on your checkbook. This is a very hard rule to follow if you are not strong-minded. Children can accuse you of ruining their lives because you do not genuflect before the entire line of Ocean Pacific sportswear, and girls have a way of filling you with guilt by telling you that every other girl in their confirmation class is going to be wearing Capezio sandals and if you want to make her look funny in front of the bishop she will never forgive you as long as she lives.

Rule VII: Keep on top of the laundry. Or, if you can't keep on top of the laundry, remember that the wardrobe your son or daughter wants is probably lying in the bottom of a hamper waiting to be retrieved. When packing a trunk for camp or school, insist that everything the child owns be washed (preferably by him or her), folded and ready to be inventoried before you go to the store to fill in the gaps. Your children will hate you for enforcing this rule, but remember that true love is strong.

Rule VIII: Avoid designer clothes. Shut your eyes to labels. Do not be intimidated by the "fact" that your daughter cannot go to the movies without swinging a Bermuda Bag, or that your son will not be able to concentrate in the library without Topsiders on his feet. Tell your children that the best thing about Gloria Vanderbilt is her bank account, fattened by socially insecure people which, thank God, they are not!

Having laid down the rules, it is important to refresh the adult's memory with "remembrances of things past." I have never met a child who did not remind me of how difficult it is to present a confident face to the world. Clothing is only the top blanket shielding them from the elements, and children need all the protective covering they can get.

15   As a child, I knew in an inarticulate way that I stood a better chance of surviving a windstorm in a circle of trees. My aim was to be the tree in the middle, identical and interchangeable with every other sapling in the grove. How I dressed had everything to do with feeling socially acceptable and when I inadvertently slipped into an individualism I could not back up with sustained confidence, I would try to think what I could do to regain my place in the grove.

It seemed to me that social success depended on having at least one of three commodities: a fabulous personality, fame, or a yellow Pandora sweater. These were the building blocks upon which one could stand.

A fabulous personality was beyond my power to sustain on a daily basis. Fame, like lightning, seemed to strike other people, none of whom I even knew. But a yellow Pandora sweater could be purchased at Macy's, if only my mother would understand its cosmic importance. Fortunately, she did.

For several days, or as long as it took for the sweater cuffs to lose their elasticity, I faced the world feeling buttoned up, yellow and self-confident—almost as confident as Susan Figel, who had a whole drawerful of Pandora sweaters in different shades to match her moods.

Unfortunately, I remember that yellow Pandora sweater a little too vividly. When I am shopping with my children, empathy continually blows me off course in the aisles. On the one hand, nobody wants her child to look funny in front of the bishop. On the other, it has yet to occur to my children that the bishop in full regalia looks pretty funny himself.

Questions for Discussion

1. Notice the opening sentence: "Once upon a time there were three little children." What attitudes and expectations does this opening sentence create? Do you consider this opening appropriate? Why or why not?
2. How important is this essay's expressive aim? Is it as important as the referential aim? Could this essay be appropriately classified as expressive aim writing? Why or why not?
3. If the author were revising this essay for a children's magazine, what changes would you recommend?
4. How could the author integrate knowledge by observation (e.g., advice from child psychologists)? What impact would such information have on this essay? Would it be more or less effective? Why?
5. Does the author do a satisfactory job of establishing credibility and motivating the audience? Cite specific passages to support your answer.

Opportunities for Writing

1. Write a letter to a brother or sister analyzing your relationship with your parents. How do they treat you? As an adult or as a child? How do you treat them? What do they do that you especially like or dislike? What do you do that elicits their praise or disapproval?
2. Analyze the impact of "designer" fashions on the clothing industry. What is the origin of designer fashions? Why do people choose designer fashions? Write your essay for the fashion page of your local newspaper.

3. Analyze how your attitudes toward clothing have changed over the years. Does your clothing contribute as much to your self-confidence today as it did while you were in high school? Why do you think it does or doesn't?

How to Write a Letter

Garrison Keillor

Known widely for his public radio program, A Prairie Home Companion, *featuring his "News from Lake Wobegon" characters and stories, Garrison Keillor has been called the "voice of mid-America." Born in Anoka, Minnesota, background for the mythical town described in* Lake Wobegon Days *(1985), Keillor writes humorous stories and commentaries about common folk and their daily lives. Keillor has written a novel,* WLT *(1991), and* We Are Still Married, Stories and Letters *(1986), dedicated to Corrine Guntzel, a friend and classmate. "How to Write a Letter" is taken from that collection and is written for Corrine. Notice how Keillor offers Corrine instructions on letter writing in the form of a friendly, personal letter. While he could include "textbook" advice about how to write a letter, he chooses to present only his own ideas on the subject.*

We shy persons need to write a letter now and then, or else we'll dry up and blow away. It's true. And I speak as one who loves to reach for the phone, dial the number, and talk. I say, "Big Bopper here—what's shakin', babes?" The telephone is to shyness what Hawaii is to February, it's a way out of the woods, *and yet:* a letter is better.

Such a sweet gift—a piece of handmade writing, in an envelope that is not a bill, sitting in our friend's path when she trudges home from a long day spent among wahoos and savages, a day our words will help repair. They don't need to be immortal, just sincere. She can read them twice and again tomorrow: *You're someone I care about, Corinne, and think of often and every time I do you make me smile.*

We need to write, otherwise nobody will know who we are. They will have only a vague impression of us as A Nice Person, because, frankly, we don't shine at conversation, we lack the confidence to thrust our faces forward and say, "Hi, I'm Heather Hooten; let me tell you about my week." Mostly we say "Uh-huh" and "Oh, really." People smile and look over our shoulder, looking for someone else to meet.

So a shy person sits down and writes a letter. To be known by another person—to meet and talk freely on the page—to be close despite distance. To escape from anonymity and be our own sweet selves and express the music of our souls.

5   Same thing that moves a giant rock star to sing his heart out in front of 123,000 people moves us to take ballpoint in hand and write a few lines to our dear Aunt Eleanor. *We want to be known.* We want her to know that we have fallen in love, that we quit our job, that we're moving to New York, and we want to say a few things that might not get said in casual conversation: *Thank you for what you've meant to me, I am very happy right now.*

The first step in writing letters is to get over the guilt of *not* writing. You don't "owe" anybody a letter. Letters are a gift. The burning shame you feel when you see unanswered mail makes it harder to pick up a pen and makes for a cheerless letter when you finally do. *I feel bad about not writing, but I've been so busy,* etc. Skip this. Few letters are obligatory, and they are *Thanks for the wonderful gift* and *I am terribly sorry to hear about George's death* and *Yes, you're welcome to stay with us next month,* and not many more than that. Write those promptly if you want to keep your friends. Don't worry about the others, except love letters, of course. When your true love writes, *Dear Light of My Life, Joy of My Heart, O Lovely Pulsating Core of My Sensate Life,* some response is called for.

Some of the best letters are tossed off in a burst of inspiration, so keep your writing stuff in one place where you can sit down for a few minutes and *(Dear Roy, I am in the middle of a book entitled* We Are Still Married *but thought I'd drop you a line. Hi to your sweetie, too)* dash off a note to a pal. Envelopes, stamps, address book, everything in a drawer so you can write fast when the pen is hot.

A blank white eight-by-eleven sheet can look as big as Montana if the pen's not so hot—try a smaller page and write boldly. Or use a note card with a piece of fine art on the front; if your letter ain't good, at least they get the Matisse. Get a pen that makes a sensuous line, get a comfortable typewriter, a friendly word processor—whichever feels easy to the hand.

Sit for a few minutes with the blank sheet in front of you, and meditate on the person you will write to, let your friend come to mind until you can almost see her or him in the room with you. Remember the last time you saw each other and how your friend looked and what you said and what perhaps was unsaid between you, and when your friend becomes real to you, start to write.

10   Write the salutation—*Dear* You—and take a deep breath and plunge in. A simple declarative sentence will do, followed by another and another and another. Tell us what you're doing and tell it like you were talking to us. Don't think about grammar, don't think about lit'ry style, don't try to write dramatically, just give us your news. Where did you go, who did you see, what did they say, what do you think?

If you don't know where to begin, start with the present moment: *I'm sitting at the kitchen table on a rainy Saturday morning. Everyone is gone and the house is quiet.* Let your simple description of the present moment lead to something else, let the letter drift gently along.

The toughest letter to crank out is one that is meant to impress, as we all know from writing job applications; if it's hard work to slip off a letter to a friend, maybe you're trying too hard to be terrific. A letter is only a report to someone who already likes you for reasons other than your brilliance. Take it easy.

Don't worry about form. It's not a term paper. When you come to the end of one episode, just start a new paragraph. You can go from a few lines about the sad state of pro football to the fight with your mother to your fond memories of Mexico to your cat's urinary-tract infection to a few thoughts on personal indebtedness and on to the kitchen sink and what's in it. The more you write, the easier it gets, and when you have a True True Friend to write to, a *compadre,* a soul sibling, then it's like driving a car down a country road, you just get behind the keyboard and press on the gas.

Don't tear up the page and start over when you write a bad line—try to write your way out of it. Make mistakes and plunge on. Let the letter cook along and let yourself be bold. Outrage, confusion, love—whatever is in your mind, let it find a way to the page. Writing is a means of discovery, always, and when you come to the end and write *Yours ever* or *Hugs and kisses,* you'll know something you didn't when you wrote *Dear Pal.*

15   Probably your friend will put your letter away, and it'll be read again a few years from now—and it will improve with age. And forty years from now, your friend's grandkids will dig it out of the attic and read it, a sweet and precious relic of the ancient eighties that gives them a sudden clear glimpse of you and her and the world we old-timers knew. You will then have created an object of art. Your simple lines about where you went, who you saw, what they said, will speak to those children and they will feel in their hearts the humanity of our times.

You can't pick up a phone and call the future and tell them about our times. You have to pick up a piece of paper.

Questions for Discussion

1. In this essay, the author uses incomplete sentences and comma splices. What do you think of the author's writing style? Is it appropriate?
2. What is the essay's subordinate aim? Cite specific passages to support your answer?
3. Notice the frequency of italics. What is the author's purpose in using italics? Is this technique effective? Why do you think it is or isn't?
4. What is the thesis of this essay? How does the author develop and clarify the thesis?
5. How would this essay differ if it were written using knowledge by observation? What impact would this new information have on the author's credibility? On the author's writing style? On the organization of the essay?

Opportunities for Writing

1. Offer your guidelines for writing a letter to a friend. Explain your techniques for getting started, for filling pages, and for closing.
2. Compare and contrast the process of writing with a pen, a typewriter, and a word processor. Cite your personal experience and interview friends, teachers, and business people. What similarities and differences do you notice? Why do people choose to write with a pen, a typewriter, or a word processor?
3. In a letter to a friend, analyze the impact of the telephone on the writing of letters. Are you more likely to call your friend or to write? Why?
4. Discuss the history of letter writing. When and where did this practice start? Why? How has this practice evolved? Write your essay for a special exhibit at your local museum on the history of writing.

KNOWLEDGE BY OBSERVATION

A Practitioner's Guide to Research Methods

PATRICIA GOUBIL-GAMBRELL

Patricia Goubil-Gambrell is an assistant professor in the Technical Communication Program at Texas Tech University, where she teaches graduate and undergraduate courses in research methods, document design, and the theory and practice of technical communication. She has given numerous presentations on technical communication at regional, national, and international conventions. Goubil-Gambrell is a member of the Association of Teachers of Technical Writing, the Society for Technical Communication, and the Institute of Electrical and Electronic Engineers Professional Communication Society. In this essay, the author provides readers with an overview of the different methods that generate knowledge in the field: quantitative research, qualitative research, scholarly inquiry, and practitioner inquiry. In addition, she explains how readers can effectively judge studies by analyzing and evaluating their methodology and results. "A Practitioner's Guide to Research Methods" appeared in Technical Communication. *The internal references and notes at the end of the article follow the style required by this periodical and illustrate a variation of the IEEE system of documentation.*

SUMMARY

Practitioners can help the professional growth of technical communication by becoming more knowledgeable about the research methods that generate knowledge in the field. Methods for research on writing are typically quantitative—experimental with randomized subject selection, treatment, and control groups—or qualitative—case or ethnographic study with representative subjects in a naturalistic setting. Both methods are important. The greatest strength of quantitative research is its ability to describe cause-and-effect relationships. The greatest strength of qualitative research is its in-depth depiction of subjects in an actual setting. Because of the complexity involved in any type of research on *writing, whatever method is used, the reader should analyze a study carefully before generalizing from it.*

If you are a Macintosh user and your boss or supervisor did not send you a copy of a certain article that appeared in *Academic Computing* in January 1990 *[1]*, you may be more rare than an endangered species. That article "proved" that writing produced on an IBM was better than writing produced on a Macintosh. The "findings" of this article appeared in a number of popular and academic publications, and they created quite a stir in the academic as well as the computer world *[2–4]*.

The article has the aura of scientific research: It has what sounds like scientific research terminology and it refers to what appear to be experimental methods. Thus, its conclusions were taken as scientific proof by many readers. Such readers focused on the article's conclusions, not on the method used to arrive at them. Whether readers skipped over the methodology or didn't know what to make of it—just that it sounded scientific—the result was the same. People thought that they now had proof that writers produced better writing with one brand of computer than with another brand. But the research methodology of the article is flawed, and as a result, the conclusions are virtually meaningless.

Unfortunately, research methodology in the field of rhetoric and professional communication is a subject that isn't widely understood. Technical writers in industry, even some who have a degree in technical communication, may not have been exposed to the concepts that let one know how much a given piece of research can be relied on. And these writers often are aware that a knowledge of research findings can be useful. They want to believe.

In fact, in the 1990 survey of the readers of *Technical Communication,* the second most common request by survey respondents was that the journal publish more research-based articles. Frank R. Smith, who analyzed the survey results, notes that "if we are to grow as a profession, we must begin to found our work in solid research instead of working on the basis of intuition, guess, habit, and prejudice" *[5]*.

Similarly, Mary Sue MacNealy comments that the development of a field proceeds in two stages: "In the first, a concern with training and with description of practices and projects predominates, indicating an interest in establishing common procedures and topics of importance. In the second stage, systematic research supplants or complements the earlier, more impressionistic work" *[6]*.

Based on her analysis of systematic research presented in the proceedings of the International Professional Communication Conference (IPCC) and the International Technical Communication Conference (ITCC), MacNealy sees technical communication moving beyond the first stage of a discipline under development. She concludes that "Those technical communicators and their coworkers who are interested in the development of technical communication as a discipline must begin to find ways to foster the systematic research needed to complement the earlier, impressionistic work" *[6]*.

Further emphasis on the need for technical communicators to be knowledgeable about research methods comes from Wenger and Spyridakis, writing about usability testing. They say, "It is going to be increasingly more difficult for practitioners to rationalize a lack of concern for appropriate methods" *[7]*.

Thus, while the importance of conducting and reporting research to the field is generally acknowledged, practitioners must also know how to evaluate this research. Interestingly, Earl McDowell found that practitioners rated courses in research methodology higher in importance to the field than did academicians; however, such courses did not rank in the top 10 of important courses [8]. The need to understand research methodology is a concern of practitioners.

What Practitioners Should Learn About Research Methods

This article has two objectives: first, to identify the main types of methodology in business and technical communication research, and second, to help technical communication practitioners understand the distinguishing characteristics of these methodologies.

The purpose here is not to turn practitioners into researchers but to give them an overview of research methodologies so that they can be more informed readers and users of research. The most common error made in reading research is overlooking the methodology and concentrating on the conclusions. Yet if the methodology isn't sound, the conclusions and subsequent recommendations won't be sound.

Sometimes the methodology is not available for the reader to examine. The reports on business and technical writing research printed in trade magazines and the popular press usually focus so narrowly on the results that much of the discussion of methodology in the original reports is eliminated. Thus, practitioners may have to seek out the original study before they can make an informed judgment about applying particular research conclusions. However, even then they cannot be assured of finding an adequate discussion of methodology.

MacNealy notes that authors who fail to include basic information on methodology "in order to have more space for discussing findings" do themselves a disservice "because such an omission raises questions about the soundness of their conclusions" [6]. Whatever the case, practitioners should not blindly accept the findings of any piece of research without first examining its methodology in order to make their own judgments about whether the research's conclusions can be generalized.

At this point the reader should understand that the following guide to research takes great liberty in simplifying a complex subject, stripping away many of its nuances. This is necessary to make the subject of research methodology accessible to the users of research, and the reader should not be misled by this reductionist approach to the subject.

Types of Research on Writing

Naming the types of research methodologies that exist in research on writing depends, to a degree, on whom you read and with whose classification that you agree. There are two empirical methodologies—**quantitative** and **qualitative**—that come to writing research primarily by way of the social sciences and through educational research. Two other methodologies or approaches come primarily by way of the English department: **scholarly inquiry** and **practitioner inquiry.**

Quantitative and qualitative research are the types of academic research that the practitioner will often find in academic journals and at academically sponsored conferences. The two other methodologies, scholarly inquiry and practitioner inquiry, are included here to provide a more complete review of the kinds of methodologies used in research on writing. The names of these other two categories derive from, and came into popular usage from, *The Making of Knowledge in Composition* by Stephen North [9].

Quantitative Research

Quantitative research attempts to quantify key aspects, or variables, of a situation and relate them to one another. The researcher performs an experiment that manipulates these variables in some way. The manipulation is usually called a treatment. The results of the treatment are measured and statistically analyzed. The purpose of quantitative research is to establish cause-and-effect relationships.

Qualitative Research

Qualitative research is descriptive in nature. The researcher observes a specific situation. The researcher doesn't tamper with this setting in any way. The purpose of qualitative research is identifying key variables in a given situation that may prove useful in framing questions to be explored further, by qualitative research or by other modes of inquiry.

An Example of Quantitative and Qualitative Research

What if you were interested in online manuals and wanted to design a study? What might you do?

If you were designing a quantitative study, you might want to see whether a relationship existed between how much experience users had with online documentation (one variable) and how quickly they were able to use your online manual to solve a particular problem (another variable). The results might prove that your online manual was so easy to use that a novice could work with it as quickly as an experienced user.

If you were designing a qualitative study, you might go into a setting where online manuals were in use and observe the people using them. You wouldn't try to prove that there was a relationship between how much experience with online documentation the users had had and how quickly they were able to use an online manual to solve a particular problem; rather you would be interested in how online manuals were used, who used them, how often they were used, whether or not people liked using them, and so on.

Scholarly Inquiry

Scholarly inquiry is in a sense a text-based approach to research. According to North, the purpose of scholarly inquiry is dialectic, "the seeking of knowledge via the deliberate confrontation of opposing points of view" *[9, 60]*. If one thinks of the traditional approaches to studying literature and then applies these approaches to other kinds of writing, one has the essence of the scholarly approach.

In research on writing, these "other kinds of writing" may include the freshman essay, the engineering lab report, the software manual, or copy for a print advertisement. In scholarly inquiry one may study the writing from a historical, a critical, or even a philosophical point of view. For the first two types of study, the researcher gathers and analyzes documents according to some scheme or theory. Philosophical inquiry, as the name implies, ponders fundamental assumptions and beliefs about writing and communication.

Practitioner Inquiry

Practitioner inquiry is basically a report, or story, of how an individual handled a particular writing problem or situation. That situation may be how to teach students to write a comparison/contrast essay, or how to produce a hypertext documentation for a software package. It is "experienced-based testimony" *[9, 36]*. As North says, "It is concerned with what has worked, is working or might work in teaching, doing, or learning writing" *[9, 23]*. Its purpose is to provide an account of what to do in a particular situation.

Evaluating the Types of Research on Writing

One type of research is not necessarily better than another. Each method does different things. However, in the past couple of years, the methodology of most of the articles in the proceedings of the IPCC and of the ITCC has ranged from "anecdotal evidence to quasi-empirical evidence," according to MacNealy *[6]*. Moreover, she notes that "few carefully regulated, empirically-based research articles" have appeared in the proceedings. Most articles are descriptive or are training presentations (what North would probably call practitioner inquiry).

According to Bereiter and Scardamalia, there are various levels of inquiry in research on composition. The types of methodologies used in writing research are not hierarchical but are part of a recursive cycle. Key variables of a situation identified in qualitative studies are often then tested in quantitative studies. The results of the latter usually suggest other questions, and so a new cycle begins "but with a heightened understanding acquired from the preceding cycle" *[10]*. Thus, both types of research are important and useful.

The Problem of Generalization of Research Results

A common problem, though, in interpreting the results of any type of research is overgeneralization. Every qualitative study and every quantitative study has limitations due to the circumstances in which the data were collected. These constraints put limits on how much one can generalize a study's results. The problem is that most people look at the results and don't note the constraints that should temper the generalizations.

Writing research is notoriously hard to generalize from because the qualitative studies are so situation-specific and because the quantitative studies, with their experimental apparatus, are so unnatural for the behavior they are studying. Hence, all results in writing research are surrounded by a gray area. Engineers, for example, can cope with this gray area by reporting results as falling in a range, "X ± 3." Researchers in rhetoric and professional communication usually attempt to do this by qualifying the generalizations. But the problem remains: readers of the research skip the qualifiers and gravitate to the generalizations.

CHARACTERISTICS OF QUANTITATIVE RESEARCH

Quantitative research in writing is of two types: experimental and quasi-experimental:

- Experimental research is characterized by (1) random sampling, or selection, of subjects; (2) introduction of a treatment; and (3) use of a control group for comparing subjects who don't receive the treatment with those who do.
- A quasi-experimental methodology is different because the subjects are not randomized; that is, a researcher using a quasi-experimental method will use intact groups of subjects, for example, students in one classroom, or workers in one department in an organization.

Random Selection of Subjects

One of the greatest strengths of quantitative research is that the subjects are randomized; that is, the subjects are drawn by chance from the general population of interest and have nothing in common with each other except what would be expected by chance. Random samples are representative of the populations from which they are drawn because every member of a population has an equal chance of being included.

This is an important characteristic because it means the results can be generalized. Randomization means that any differences a researcher finds between the group that received the "experimental" treatment and the control group that didn't are the result of the treatment and not the result of chance.

Random samples may also be stratified. That is, when the composition of a population is known and a population with specific characteristics is desired for study, the random sample can be selected from this subgroup of the population. For example, the population of a study might be engineers and an aspect of the study might involve gender differences. If the researcher knows the ratio of women to men in the population, the sample can be drawn so that proportionate numbers of women and men are selected.

Because the groups are not randomized in quasi-experiments, the researcher seeking to draw on the power of the experimental method must do something to establish that the groups are comparable. This something is called a pretest. It may be simply background information on subjects such as "years of computer use experience," or it may be more "test-like," as in a questionnaire to determine subjects' previous knowledge about a topic related to the study.

Hypotheses in Quantitative Research

Quantitative research, being experimental, is hypothesis-driven. That is, the researcher has a hypothesis about what should happen as a result of a treatment. A treatment is some condition applied to the experimental group, for example, receiving a certain type of instruction or using a particular type of online documentation. The researcher has an experimental group that receives a treatment and a control group that does not. The null hypothesis states that after the treatment there will be no difference between the control and experimental groups. If there is a difference between the groups after the treatment, it is assumed that it can be attributed to the treatment. The researcher can then make a cause-and-effect statement.

The quality of the hypotheses themselves should be evaluated:

- First, a hypothesis should be conceptually clear, with concepts defined operationally, if possible.
- Second, a hypothesis should have empirical referents; it should not include value judgments.
- Third, a hypothesis should be specific so that it can be determined whether it is testable.
- Fourth, a hypothesis should be related to available testing techniques.
- Fifth, a hypothesis should be related to a body of theory *[12, 33–35]*.

Statistics in Quantitative Research

The reason for all the statistical apparatus in quantitative research is to explain that relationships between variables are due not to chance but to cause-and-effect relationships. Statistical methods "enable us to study and to describe precisely averages, differences, and relationships" *[12, 243]*.

Some of the more common questions that researchers ask and use statistics to answer are

- Is there a significant difference between these two (or more) groups on this variable?
- What confidence can I have that observed differences did not occur by chance?
- Is there an association between these two (or more) variables? If so, how close is the association *[12, 243]*?

Spyridakis, Wenger, and Andrew have written a helpful guide to statistics commonly used in research about writing *[13]*. As they note, there are two kinds of statistics, descriptive and inferential:

- **Descriptive statistics** allow a researcher to describe data in an orderly fashion. The most common descriptive statistics are frequency distributions: Mean, median, and mode—the average score in a data set, the score in the exact middle of a data set, and the most frequent score in a data set.
- **Inferential statistics** allow a researcher to infer that relationships exist among variables. The most common descriptive statistics are chi-square, a t-test, and an F-test.

These statistics indicate whether a data set is distributed according to theoretical expectations and whether there are significant differences between groups on the variables being studied.

Because in current statistical thinking an effect is considered to be the result of a number of interacting causes, especially in explaining human behavior, multivariate analysis–considering two or more treatment variables and their interaction with the independent variable—is very important in statistics. Causes, according to Miller, manifest themselves in four ways:

1. Causes may occur in a sequence to produce an effect.
2. Several causes may converge or cluster to produce an effect.
3. The effects of a single cause may disperse outward into many different areas.
4. The preceding three manifestations of cause may all occur to create a complex network of causes for an effect *[12, 258–259]*.

In quantitative research, the researcher must identify independent and dependent variables carefully:

- An independent variable is the cause of something in a relationship; it is the treatment in an experiment, the activity that will make a difference in the outcome of an experiment if indeed there is a cause-and-effect relationship among variables.
- A dependent variable is the effect. The effect is the change or difference that occurs as a result of the manipulation of the independent variable.

So if you were studying whether there was a relationship between how much experience users had with online documentation and how quickly they were able to use your online manual to solve a particular problem, the independent variable would be the amount of experience users had with using online documentation, and the dependent variable would be how much time it took them to use the online manual to solve a problem.

You might also decide to administer a treatment—give the users a short tutorial on your online manual—then measure how much time it took them to solve the problem. In that case you would be manipulating the independent variable by changing the amount of experience that the subjects of your study had with online documentation.

Given the myriad ways that causes may manifest themselves, one begins to understand the difficulties that the researcher faces in creating an experimental design that might uncover a relationship between or among variables that is truly statistically significant. So while statistics would seem to make the results of a study more generalizable, the complexity involved in creating an experimental design should make one cautious in accepting the results of an experimental study. Moreover, while statistics are useful for showing trends and indicating probabilities, they don't necessarily tell us what is going to happen in a particular case.

Validity and Reliability in Quantitative Research

No discussion of quantitative methodology is complete without noting the concepts of validity and reliability.

- **Validity** refers to whether the experiment actually measures what it says it will measure. An experimental study must have internal and external validity. Internal validity means that the difference in the dependent variable is actually a result of the independent variable. External validity means that the results of the study are generalizable to other groups and environments outside the experimental setting.
- **Reliability** refers to whether the experiment precisely measures a single dimension of human ability *[11, 286]*.

In reporting the results of their research, researchers should discuss whether there were any threats to validity or reliability.

Problems with Quantitative Research

Quantitative research focuses on isolated variables in a structured situation. These characteristics enable the researcher to draw fairly explicit and definitive conclusions, but they also pose problems *[11]*. Many argue that the settings of experimental research do not mirror the conditions under which people actually write, consult a manual, or use online documentation.

Another problem is that the need to isolate and to control variables may eliminate other variables that would affect the research results. Thus, while the conclusions of quantitative research seem to be definitive, they are based on unnatural conditions. Moreover, it is not always possible to conduct a "true" experiment as opposed to a quasi-experiment in research on writing. In a sample drawn from a general population, important variables such as sex, socioeconomic status, ethnic background, or previous experiences cannot be randomly assigned *[11]*.

CHARACTERISTICS OF QUALITATIVE RESEARCH

Qualitative research in rhetoric and professional communication is of two types: case study and ethnographic study.

- **Case study,** as its name implies, is research about a particular individual or a small group of individuals.
- **Ethnographic study,** on the other hand, is research about the whole environment in which an individual or a group of individuals function as communicators.

In practice it is often difficult to identify a piece of research as a case study or as an ethnographic study. In research about writing, the line between the two can become fuzzy. Also, the line between case study and practitioner inquiry can sometimes seem fuzzy. However, the practitioner inquiry will not be as concerned with analysis of the "case," that is, the why and what it means. Instead, the practitioner inquiry will be more concerned with presenting the details of the case.

Subjects

In a qualitative study, subjects are not randomly selected from a population. A researcher may try to pick subjects who are representative of a group, but there is no statistical assurance that they are, and often a researcher will have to select subjects based on their availability rather than subjects who fit a certain profile. However, purposeful sampling can enhance the weight of the results of a qualitative study.

Purposeful sampling attempts to select "information-rich" cases for study *[14, 169]*. There are 15 strategies for selecting a purposeful sample. The importance of this technique is that it allows the researcher to create a reasonable rationale for studying a particular group of subjects. So, while qualitative researchers cannot make cause-and-effect statements, the researchers with a purposeful sample can make an argument for the validity of their in-depth qualitative findings.

Some representative strategies that are applicable to research on writing include extreme case sampling, intensity sampling, and maximum variation sampling:

- **Extreme case sampling** focuses on subjects who are unusual or special in some way. The logic is that "lessons may be learned about unusual conditions or extreme outcomes" that are relevant to typical cases *[14, 170]*. In research on writing, for example, this strategy could manifest itself in studies that compare novice writers and experienced writers.
- **Intensity sampling** looks for cases "that manifest the phenomenon of interest intensely (but not extremely)" because "extreme or deviant cases may be so unusual as to distort the manifestation of the phenomenon of interest" *[14, 171]*. If a researcher is concerned with "skillful" users of online documentation, for example, it would not make sense to study all or just any users of online documentation. Rather, the researcher should focus attention on users who have skill with online documentation but who are not the very "best" ones.
- **Maximum variation sampling** focuses on what common patterns emerge from a diverse group. The common patterns that emerge from great variation capture "core experiences" *[14, 172]*. Thus, in studying experienced and novice users of online documentation, the researcher would seek out their common experiences to help describe what happens when someone uses online documentation.

Data Collection and Analysis

No treatment is involved in qualitative research, since it is exploratory and attempts only to describe what goes on in a communication situation. The setting is naturalistic; the subjects are observed as they are and no change, or "treatment," is attempted. For example, the researcher would observe how technical writers actually collaborate in doing their jobs rather than putting a group of them through a training program on collaboration and then measuring the effect of such training on them as compared with a control group that had not had the training. The qualitative researcher does not attempt to isolate variables to determine how they interact, as in experimental research. The purpose of qualitative research is to identify salient features or variables in the situation. Administering a treatment would interfere with that goal.

Because there is no randomization of subjects, no identification of variables, and no treatment, it is important that the qualitative researcher provide readers with a full description of the setting where the data were collected and how they were collected. For example, not only should the researcher discuss subject selection as indicated above, but also site selection, the researcher's role, data-collection techniques (observation, interviews, surveys, videos, etc.), management and recording of data (field notes, transcripts of audio tapes, etc.), and data-analysis strategies *[15, 50]*.

In qualitative research, the relationship of the researcher to the data differs from that in quantitative research. The researcher is usually a participant-observer in the setting rather than someone who is measuring the relationship between predefined variables. Thus it is also important for researchers to indicate their role in the setting: How much and what kind of participation in the setting occurred? Did it influence the interpretation of the results of the observation?

Triangulation is an important concept in qualitative research. It helps to reduce systematic bias in the data *[14, 470]* and it contributes to the verification and validation of the qualitative analysis *[14, 464]*. Triangulation is basically comparison. There are four types of triangulation:

1. Data triangulation
2. Methods triangulation
3. Researcher triangulation
4. Theory triangulation.

Data triangulation involves comparing and cross-checking the consistency of information gathered at different times with the same method, for example, interviews at the beginning, middle, and end of a study.

Methods triangulation involves checking the consistency of information gathered by different means—field notes by the researcher, interviews with people in the setting, documents written and used by people in the setting, and so on.

Researcher triangulation is achieved by having more than one researcher interpret the data. Agreement among several researchers about what went on in a situation enhances the validity of the interpretations.

Theory triangulation involves looking at the same data from different perspectives.

Judging a Qualitative Study

Because of the numerous factors involved. Marshall and Rossman recommend that reports of qualitative studies be judged on the following ten criteria *[15, 148]*:

1. Data collection methods are explicit.
2. Data are used to document analytic constructs.
3. Negative instances of the findings are displayed and accounted for.
4. Biases are discussed, including personal and professional biases, and theoretical biases and assumptions.

5. Strategies for data collection and analysis are made public.
6. Field decisions altering strategies or substantive focus are documented.
7. Competing hypotheses are presented and discussed.
8. Data are preserved.
9. Participants' truthfulness is assessed.
10. Theoretical significance and generalizability are made explicit.

If a study discusses all of the above topics, the reader can have greater confidence in the researcher's thoroughness and in the credibility of the conclusions reached in the study.

An Advantage and Disadvantage of Qualitative Research

The strength of qualitative research is that it depicts business and technical writing situations as they truly are. Its weakness is that these findings cannot be generalized because the sample on which they are based has not been randomized.

As Lauer and Asher have noted, co-occurrences are often misinterpreted as cause-and-effect relationships in qualitative research *[11]*. Factors that appear to have a cause-and-effect relationship may be due only to chance, and we have no way of knowing whether they are or are not.

Although the conclusions of qualitative research are not so generalizable as conclusions from quantitative research, generalizations may be made if they are limited to the subjects and the settings studied.

OTHER RESEARCH METHODS

Very often researchers in writing research mix methodologies, creating a sort of hybrid for the readers to evaluate. Thus one might have a study that provides an ethnographic account of a writing setting (qualitative methodology) and also includes the results of a survey (quantitative methodology) of the writers in that setting. The survey would be analyzed in a statistical manner, and these results might play a role in interpretation of the setting.

In judging the study, the reader would have to realize that the quantitative results in this hybrid situation differ somewhat from the quantitative results in a purely quantitative study. The survey might help the researcher quantify some of the impressionistic and anecdotal data gathered in the qualitative part of the study.

DEVELOPING METHODOLOGICAL LITERACY

In discussing various research methodologies, one is tempted to identify the "best" one and to dismiss the others as having too many shortcomings. But research on writing is not really an either/or situation. Each method, when carefully implemented, can provide us with insights about how people produce and process texts. It is also important to remember the complexity of what we are studying—human behavior that occurs in a social context—and thereby also resist the temptation to overgeneralize the results of any one study, regardless of the methodology.

Both quantitative and qualitative research have "truth value"—quantitative research with its applicability, consistency, and neutrality, and qualitative research with its credibility, transferability, dependability, and confirmability *[15, 145]*. While quantitative methods may seem "better" because of their origins in science and thus their ability to predict and to describe cause-and-effect relationships, both methods generate information that helps us get at the truth.

The way that qualitative methods get at the truth, though, may not be as familiar to readers as the way of quantitative methods. Qualitative methods can be judged by four constructs to assess their truth value:

- First, **credibility** is created when the researcher demonstrates that the study was conducted in such a way as to ensure that the subject was accurately identified and described *[15, 145]*. The parameters of a study must also be adequately stated.
- Second, the **transferability** of the conclusions of the study may be demonstrated. Transferability, or generalizability, is the most problematic aspect of qualitative research, and it is more of a problem to a researcher who wants to use the findings of a qualitative study than to the original researcher. The original researcher's use of a theoretical framework that guided data collection and analysis as well as triangulation of data can enhance a study's transferability to other settings.
- Third, **dependability** is created when the researcher "attempts to account for changing conditions in the phenomenon chosen for study" *[15, 146]*. Quantitative research rests on positivist notions of an unchanging reality, a direct contrast to qualitative assumptions that the social world is always changing. So rather than replicability, the qualitative researcher seeks to be able to explain the changes that occur.
- Finally, **confirmability** demonstrates that the findings of the study could be confirmed by another, that is, the findings of the study are "objective." To obtain objectivity, the qualitative researcher must pay scrupulous attention to documenting methodology, use more than one researcher to record and interpret data, and maintain the collected data on a study in retrievable form so that another researcher can reanalyze the data to confirm the conclusions.

Among the various skills that professional technical communicators are trying to attain, a knowledge of research methodology should be a primary one. With such knowledge, practitioners will be able to assess the value and meaning of research confidently for their own work experiences and needs as professional communicators.

Some fundamental questions that such a reader of research should consider when examining a study are given in the guide for analyzing research methodology. This checklist of questions gives practitioners a simple and systematic way to ask some of the appropriate questions about a study. With their understanding of the basics of the methods that produce knowledge in their field, these practitioners will contribute to the increasing professionalization of technical communication.

Guide for Analyzing Research Methodology

1. The Problem
   What question is the researcher trying to answer?
2. The Data
   What kinds of data need to be collected to answer the question?
   What kind of data did the researcher collect? Was it the type that will be needed to answer the question?
   Was more than one kind of data collected so that results can be triangulated if need be?
3. The Subjects
   Who were the subjects for the research? How many subjects were there?
   What are their demographic characteristics?
   What background do they have that makes them appropriate subjects for this research?
   How were these subjects recruited to participate in this research? Were they volunteers? Were they paid?
4. The Methods
   What were the subjects asked to do that produced the data that will provide an answer for the research question?
   Did the task seem appropriately related to the research question being asked?
5. The Analysis
   How were the data analyzed?
   Were appropriate statistical techniques used?
   If data were to be interpreted by raters, how many raters were there? How were they trained? What criteria did they use in interpreting the data?
6. The Conclusions
   How much does the researcher generalize in the conclusions?
   Did the researcher generalize beyond the bounds that are appropriate for the research method used?
   - Quantitative research can establish cause-and-effect relationships.
   - Qualitative research can generalize only about the particular subjects that were studied and can make an argument that they are representative of others with similar characteristics.

Acknowledgments

I wish to thank the four reviewers of this article for their helpful comments on the manuscript.

References

1. Marcia Peoples Halio, "Student Writing: Can the Machine Maim the Message?" *Academic Computing* 4, no. 4 (January 1990): 16–19, 45.
2. *Computers and Composition* 7, no. 3 (1990): 73–107.
3. "Letters," *MacWorld* 8, no. 4 (February 1991): 37, 40.
4. "Letters," *Chronicle of Higher Education* 36, no. 32 (April 25, 1990): B4.
5. Frank R. Smith, "Response to Reader Survey," *Technical Communication* 38, no. 1 (First Quarter 1991): 13–16.
6. Mary Sue MacNealy, "Moving Toward Maturity: Research in Technical Communication," *IEEE Transactions on Professional Communication* 33, no. 4 (1990): 197–204.
7. Michael J. Wenger and Spyridakis, Jan H., "The Relevance of Reliability and Validity to Usability Testing," *IEEE Transactions on Professional Communication* 32, no. 4 (1989): 265–271.
8. Earl McDowell, "Surveys of Undergraduate and Graduate Technical Communication Programs and Courses in the United States," *Technical Writing Teacher* 18, no. 1 (1991): 29–36.
9. Stephen M. North, *The Making of Knowledge in Composition: Portrait of an Emerging Field* (Upper Monclair, NJ: Boynton Cook Publishers, Inc., 1987).
10. Carl Bereiter and Marlene Scardamalia, "Levels of Inquiry in Writing Research," in *Research on Writing: Principles and Methods,* eds. Mosenthal, Tamor, and Walmsley (New York: Longman, 1983), 3–25.
11. Janice M. Lauer and J. William Asher, *Composition Research: Empirical Designs* (New York: Oxford University Press, 1988).
12. Delbert C. Miller, *Handbook of Research Design and Social Measurement,* 5th ed. (Newbury Park, CA: Sage Publications, 1991).
13. Jan H. Spyridakis, Michael J. Wenger, and Sarah H. Andrew, "The Technical Communicator's Guide to Understanding Statistics and Research Design," *Journal of Technical Writing and Communication* 21, no. 3 (1991): 207–219.
14. Michael Quinn Patton, *Qualitative Evaluation and Research Methods,* 2nd ed. (Newbury Park, CA: Sage Publications, 1990).
15. Catherine Marshall and Gretchen B. Rossman, *Designing Qualitative Research* (Newbury Park, CA: Sage Publications, 1989).

Questions for Discussion

1. How do the headings contribute to your reading of the essay? Are the headings necessary? Why or why not?
2. Does the author establish herself as a credible source of information on this subject? Cite specific passages to support your answer.
3. Consider the author's explicit statement of purpose: "This article has two objectives: first to identify the main types of methodology in business and technical communication research, and second, to help technical communication practitioners understand the distinguishing characteristics of these methodologies." What do you think of using explicit statements of purpose? Do you think this technique is effective? Is it appropriate here?
4. What is the essay's thesis? How does the author develop and clarify the thesis?
5. How would this essay differ if it were written using knowledge by participation? Would it be more or less effective? Explain your answer.

Opportunities for Writing

1. Explain the meaning of *practitioner* as it applies to your academic major. In your field, who is a *practitioner?* What does he or she do? What are his or her qualifications? Address your explanation to a friend or relative who is curious about your academic major.
2. Compare and contrast the research methods characteristic of your academic major and academic minor. Interview instructors from the two disciplines and survey the appropriate research journals. Are the methods similar or different? Why do you think these similarities or differences occur?
3. Analyze the research of a scholar in your field. What was the subject of his or her research? What research methods did he or she use? What were his or her important findings? Compose your essay for a special exhibit at your school library on the achievements of this scholar.

Type A Behavior, Competitive Achievement-Striving, and Cheating Among College Students

ANTHONY R. PERRY, KEVIN M. KANE, KEVIN J. BERNESSER, AND PAUL T. SPICKER

This article reports the results of a study conducted by Anthony R. Perry, Kevin M. Kane, Kevin J. Bernesser, and Paul T. Spicker. At the time this study was published in Psychological Reports *in 1990, all four were researchers at the University of Cincinnati. As you read, observe the text conventions (i.e., summary, headings, and tables) and the APA documentation style (internal citations and references at the end of the article). This study is based on knowledge by observation. Consider how you might analyze and evaluate the quality and quantity of information as well as the credibility of the sources in this kind of research report.*

SUMMARY

The present study examined the cheating behavior in competitive and noncompetitive situations of 40 college students classified as Type A (16 women, 24 men) and 40 as Type B (19 women, 21 men). Type A-scoring students were more likely to cheat than Type B-scoring students irrespective of competition. The results suggest that in some situations, especially where expectations for success cannot be met, Type A-scoring students may cheat to achieve success.

In the late 1950s, two cardiologists (Friedman & Rosenman, 1959) reported that the majority of their coronary heart disease patients showed a set of behavioral characteristics that they labeled the Type A behavior pattern. This purported relationship has generated considerable interest in recent years among both medical and psychological researchers. Clinical and epidemiological studies have demonstrated both prospectively and retrospectively that the Type A pattern is associated with at least twice the incidence of coronary heart disease relative to the noncoronary-prone pattern called Type B (Brand, 1978; Cooper, Detre, & Weiss, 1981; Friedman & Rosenman, 1974; Jenkins, Rosenman, & Zyzanski, 1974; Manuck, Kaplan, & Matthews, 1986; Matthews & Haynes, 1986).

Since it was first described by Friedman and Rosenman (1959), the Type A pattern has been characterized by extremes of impatience, aggressiveness and hostility, competitive achievement striving, and time urgency that are evoked by a variety of environmental situations (Glass, 1977, 1983; Kirmeyer & Biggers, 1988; Matthews, 1982). These major characteristics were captured in the following description of the Type A pattern provided by Friedman and Rosenman (1974): it is "an action-emotion complex that can be observed in any person who is aggressively involved in a chronic, incessant struggle to achieve more and more in less and less time, and if required to do so, against the opposing efforts of other things or other persons" (p. 67).

As the description suggests, competitive achievement-striving is an important component of the Type A pattern and has been viewed by some researchers as underlying the other characteristics (Carver & Humphries, 1982). For example, the Type A-scoring person's chronic sense of time urgency may be seen as growing out of an attempt to accomplish more and more in less time. The evidence for this orientation and its manifestations has come from a variety of sources. For example, several studies suggest that there is a relationship between the Type A pattern and measures of achievement motivation. Significant relationships have been found between scores on the student version of the Jenkins Activity Survey and scores on the Edwards (1957) measure of achievement motivation (see Glass, 1977). Matthews and Saal (1978) found no significant relationship between the Type A pattern and TAT measures of need for achievement. However, it should be noted that subjects who were very high in achievement motivation but who had little fear of failure also had high Type A scores on the Jenkins Survey. In a more recent investigation (Davis, Grover, Sadowski, Tramill, & Kleinhammer-Tramill, 1986), Type A scorers were shown to have a higher level of impact achievement motivation than Type B scorers, that is, Type A scorers reported being concerned with the effects of achievements rather than with the process of achieving.

Certainly, one would expect that having a positive psychological orientation toward achievement striving might result in greater actual achievement. There is, in fact, much evidence that supports this relationship. In an interview study of college students' Type A behavior and achievement striving conducted by Glass (1977), Type A-scoring students reported participating in more extracurricular activities, holding positions of leadership in these activities, and reported more academic honors in college than Type B-scoring students. A similar pattern, though nonsignificant, was also obtained for academic honors in high school. In addition, a greater proportion of Type A scorers reported being interested in subsequent graduate or professional school training as opposed to seeking employment immediately. Studies have also found relationships between Type A pattern and educational attainment as well as occupational and socioeconomic status (Mettlin, 1976; Waldron, 1978; Waldron, Zyzanski, Shekelle, Jenkins, & Tannenbaum, 1977).

Similarly, the Type A pattern has been related significantly to placing high importance on grades and achieving higher grades than Type B scorers in college. Grimm and Yarnold (1984) reported that Type A-scoring students set higher performance standards on college examinations than Type B scorers. In an investigation of physical attractiveness and academic achievement, Sparacino and Hansell (1979) found that Type A-scoring women reported higher GPAs and that study time was significantly related to their GPAs. Other studies have confirmed that Type A-scoring college students achieve higher academic success and report devoting more time to classes, studying, and academic and extracurricular activities than Type B scorers (Ovcharchyn, Johnson, & Petzel, 1981; Suls, Becker, & Mullen, 1981; Tang, 1988; Waldron, Hickey, McPherson, Butensky, Gruss, Overall, Schmader, & Wohlmuth, 1980).

One question that arises from the research on the competitive achievement orientation of the Type A pattern is what strategies do they use in achieving their goals? In terms of academic success, the studies just described have shown Type A scorers to report they put forth greater effort than Type B scorers (e.g., devoting more time to studying). However, in some situations it may be that Type A scorers use other means to achieve their goals. Given their greater concern with success, it is possible that Type A scorers would be more likely to cheat to achieve success than Type B scorers. The present experiment examined this possibility among Type A- and Type B-scoring college students in both competitive and noncompetitive conditions. The method by which cheating was assessed was one in which subjects reporting higher than possible scores on a word-forming task were considered to have cheated. What was possible was judged by comparison with control groups treated identically except that the opportunity to cheat was eliminated, so cheating was not directly observed but was inferred probabilistically.

METHOD

Subjects   Subjects were 80 undergraduate students (40 women, 40 men) enrolled in introductory psychology courses at the University of Cincinnati who participated in exchange for course credit. Subjects' ages ranged from 18 to 27 yr., with a mean of 19.2 yr.

Materials   Form C of the Jenkins Activity Survey (Jenkins, Zyzanski, & Rosenman, 1979) was administered to all subjects to measure Type A behavior. The experimental task was a word-forming task similar to that used by Cooper and Peterson (1980). On each of five cards (3- × 5-in.) were seven uppercase black letters. The letters on the cards (in the order of appearance) were (1) SGADBEE, (2) ODIFICL, (3) ETKPLAD, (4) KLOITWN, and (5) NAIGEVC.

Procedure   Prior to the experimental session, subjects were identified as scoring either Type A or Type B estimated by a median split of the Jenkins Activity Survey scores (*Mdn* = 247.5, Type A scores ranged from 259 to 383, Type B scores ranged from 76 to 236). Subjects were then randomly assigned to one of the experimental conditions. During the experimental session the experimenter was unaware of the subjects' behavior pattern classification. Upon their arriving for the experimental session, the experimenter explained the word-forming task to the subjects. Subjects were told they would be given five cards, on each were seven randomly selected letters. Working with the letters on one card at a time, subjects were to use the letters to write down as many words as possible. Points were awarded for the number of letters used in each word; 2 points were given for a two-letter word, 3 points for a three-letter word, and so on. There was a time limit of 30 sec. per card.

In the no-competition groups, subjects participated individually. They were told, "A score of 26.5 points per card is average for college students. Try to score as many points as you can." In reality, pilot data* and previous research (Cooper & Peterson, 1980) showed that such a score was out of the range in which subjects could be expected to score. In the competition groups, subjects were tested in pairs. They were told, "A score of 26.5 points per card is average for college students. The other person is your opponent. Try to outscore him." For subjects in the groups without opportunity to cheat (control groups), the experimenter scored the words. For subjects in the groups with opportunity to cheat, the experimenter instructed the subjects to score the words themselves and turn in their scores at the end of the session. Subjects were told they could keep the words they produced or throw them away so subjects could cheat by employing inadmissible words and/or adding points to their scores.

RESULTS

Preliminary analysis indicated the absence of sex differences; accordingly, these data were pooled across sex of subjects for the subsequent analyses. Means and standard deviations on the word-forming task were determined for each subject in each experimental condition and are shown in Table 1.

A 2 × 2 × 2 between-groups analysis of variance with the factors of behavior pattern (Type A, Type B), competition (yes, no), and opportunity to cheat (yes, no) was computed on the word-forming scores. The analysis of these data indicated significant main effects for the behavior pattern ($F_{1,72} = 8.18$, $p < .006$, $\eta^2 = .07$) and for the opportunity to cheat ($F_{1,72} = 18.34$, $p < .0002$, $\eta^2 = .17$). The two-way interaction between behavior pattern and opportunity to cheat was also significant ($F_{1,72} = 5.81$, $p < .02$, $\eta^2 = .06$). The significant main effects are best interpreted by the significant two-way interaction, which showed that Type A-scoring students given the opportunity to cheat scored significantly higher than Type A-scoring students given no opportunity to cheat or Type B scorers with or without the opportunity to cheat ($p < .05$) by the Tukey HSD procedure (Hays, 1981).

---

*Pilot data were collected from 5 graduate students and 5 undergraduate students enrolled at the University of Cincinnati. The mean score on the word-forming task for this group was 14.6 (no competition, no opportunity to cheat).

TABLE 1 MEAN SCORES ON WORD-FORMING TASK

	NO COMPETITION		COMPETITION	
GROUP	M	SD	M	SD
Type A Behavior Pattern				
Opportunity to Cheat	18.44	2.33	20.12	2.36
No Opportunity	13.78	4.80	14.04	2.24
Type B Behavior Pattern				
Opportunity to Cheat	14.60	3.98	15.50	4.74
No Opportunity	13.26	4.41	13.84	2.40

Note: Higher scores are associated with greater cheating in the opportunity to cheat conditions.

DISCUSSION

The present investigation was designed to examine the possibility that Type A-scoring individuals would be more likely to cheat to achieve success than Type B-scoring students. This possibility was confirmed in a situation in which subjects performed a word-forming task and were either given or not given an opportunity to cheat. Results showed that Type A-scoring individuals were indeed more likely to cheat when they had the opportunity to do so, regardless of whether they competed against another person or performed alone.

Although cheating was not observed directly, several lines of research support the hypothesis that Type A-scoring students are more likely to cheat in some situations when given the opportunity. For example, Johnson (1981) showed that individuals with high achievement motivation are more likely than individuals with low achievement motivation to cheat on college examinations. Since this characteristic appears to be one of the central components of the Type A behavior pattern (Carver & Humphries, 1982; Matthews, 1982), it is logical to assume that Type A-scoring students would also be more likely to cheat to achieve success. In addition, Perry (1986) found that Type A-scoring students were more likely to violate traffic laws and consequently received more tickets for driving violations than Type B scorers.

It may be that, when Type A-scoring students are in situations in which their expectations for success cannot be reached by exerting additional effort, they will use other means. The present investigation provided such a situation. The expectation of success on the word-forming task was not possible given the time constraint. However, when Type A scorers were given the opportunity to cheat, they reported word-forming scores that were significantly higher than those of Type A scorers who were not given the opportunity to cheat. If cheating did not occur on the word-forming task, no difference should have been found between those groups.

In summary, a range of studies have shown that Type A-scoring individuals are more achievement-oriented than their Type B-scoring peers. Normally, Type A-scorers believe that by exerting sufficient effort they can overcome obstacles and reach their goals. The present findings suggest that in some situations Type

A-scoring students may use other means for achieving success especially when their expectations cannot be met simply by putting forth greater effort.

References

Brand, R. J. (1978). Coronary-prone behavior as an independent risk factor for coronary heart disease. In T. M. Dembroski, S. M. Weiss, J. L. Shields, S. G. Haynes, & M. Feinleib (Eds.). *Coronary-prone behavior.* (pp. 11–24) New York: Springer-Verlag.

Carver, C. S., & Humphries, C. (1982). Social psychology and the Type A coronary-prone behavior pattern. In G. S. Sanders & J. Suls (Eds.), *Social psychology of health and illness.* Hillsdale, NJ: Erlbaum. (pp. 33–64).

Cooper, S., & Peterson, C. (1980). Machiavellianism and spontaneous cheating in competition. *Journal of Research in Personality, 14,* 70–75.

Cooper, T., Detre, T., & Weiss, S. (1981). Coronary prone behavior and coronary heart disease: a critical review. *Circulation, 63,* 1199–1215.

Davis, S. F., Grover, C. A., Sadowski, C. J., Tramill, J. L., & Kleinhammer-Tramill, P. J. (1986). The relationship between the Type A behavior pattern and process versus impact achievement motivation. *Bulletin of the Psychonomic Society, 24,* 441–443.

Edwards, A. L. (1957). *Manual for the Edwards Personal Preference Schedule.* New York: Psychological Corp.

Friedman, M., & Rosenman, R. H. (1959). Association of specific overt behavior pattern with blood and cardiovascular findings. *Journal of the American Medical Association, 159,* 1286–1296.

Friedman, M., & Rosenman, R. H. (1974). *Type A behavior and your heart.* New York: Knopf.

Glass, D. C. (1977). *Behavior patterns, stress, and coronary disease.* Hillsdale, NJ: Erlbaum.

Glass, D. C. (1983). Behavioral, cardiovascular, and neuroendocrine responses. *International Review of Applied Psychology, 32,* 137–151.

Grimm, L. G., & Yarnold, P. R. (1984). Performance standards and the Type A behavior pattern. *Cognitive Therapy and Research, 8,* 59–66.

Hays, W. L. (1981). *Statistics.* (3rd ed.) New York: Holt, Rinehart & Winston.

Jenkins, C. D., Rosenman, R. H., & Zyzanski, S. J. (1974). Prediction of clinical heart disease by a test for the coronary-prone behavior pattern. *New England Journal of Medicine, 290,* 1271–1275.

Jenkins, C. D., Zyzanski, S. J., & Rosenman, R. H. (1979). *Manual for the Jenkins Activity Survey.* New York: Psychological Corp.

Johnson, P. B. (1981). Achievement motivation and success: Does the end justify the means? *Journal of Personality and Social Psychology, 40,* 374–375.

Kirmeyer, S. L., & Biggers, K. (1988). Environmental demand and demand engendering behavior: an observational analysis of the Type A pattern. *Journal of Personality and Social Psychology, 54,* 997–1005.

Manuck, S. B., Kaplan, J. R., & Matthews, K. A. (1986). Behavioral antecedents of coronary heart disease and atherosclerosis. *Arteriosclerosis, 6,* 2–14.

Matthews, K. A. (1982). Psychological perspectives on the Type A behavior pattern. *Psychological Bulletin, 91,* 293–323.

Matthews, K. A., & Haynes, S. G. (1986). Type A behavior pattern and coronary risk: Update and evaluation. *American Journal of Epidemiology, 123,* 923–960.

Matthews, K. A., & Saal, F. E. (1978). The relationship of the Type A coronary-prone behavior pattern to achievement, power, and affiliation motives. *Psychosomatic Medicine, 40,* 631–636.

Mettlin, C. (1976). Occupational careers and the prevention of coronary-prone behavior. *Social Sciences and Medicine, 10,* 367–372.

Ovcharchyn, C. A., Johnson, H. H., & Petzel, T. P. (1981). Type A behavior, academic aspirations, and academic success. *Journal of Personality, 49,* 248–256.

Perry, A. R. (1986). Type A behavior and motor vehicle driver's behavior. *Perceptual and Motor Skills, 63,* 875–878.

Sparacino, J., & Hansell, S. (1979). Physical attractiveness and academic performance: Beauty is not always talent. *Journal of Personality, 47,* 449–469.

Suls, J., Becker, M. A., & Mullen, B. (1981). Coronary-prone behavior, social insecurity and stress among college-aged adults. *Journal of Human Stress, 7,* 27–34.

Tang, T. L. (1988). Effects of Type A personality and leisure ethic on Chinese college students' leisure activities and academic performance. *Journal of Social Psychology, 128,* 153–164.

Waldron, I. (1978). Sex differences in the coronary-prone behavior pattern. In T. M. Dembroski, S. M. Weiss, J. L. Shields, S. G. Haynes, & M. Feinleib (Eds.), *Coronary-prone behavior.* (pp. 199–205) New York: Springer-Verlag.

Waldron, I., Hickey, A., McPherson, C., Butensky, A., Gruss, L., Overall, K., Schmader, A., & Wohlmuth, D. (1980). Type A behavior pattern: Relationship to variation in blood pressure, parental characteristics, and academic and social activities of students. *Journal of Human Stress, 6,* 16–27.

Waldron, I., Zyzanski, S. J., Shekelle, R. B., Jenkins, C. D., & Tannenbaum, S. (1977). The coronary-prone behavior pattern in employed men and women. *Journal of Human Stress, 3,* 2–19.

Questions for Discussion

1. This essay's title identifies the subject, but does little to motivate the audience. Would you recommend a different title? If so, why? If not, why not?
2. Do you think this article has a subordinate aim? If so, cite specific passages to support your answer. If not, explain how you would integrate a subordinate expressive or persuasive aim.
3. Notice the abundance of source citations, especially at the beginning of the article? What do you think of this technique? Does it clarify the subject? Does it establish the credibility of the authors? Explain your answer.
4. The authors display their major findings in a single table of information. Do you think other illustrations are necessary? If so, why? Identify specific tables or figures you would like to see included. If not, why not?
5. This article was written for a professional journal and its audience of psychology specialists. If the authors were revising this article for the general readership of a weekly news magazine, what changes would you recommend?

Opportunities for Writing

1. After interviewing a variety of academic majors, analyze the causes of cheating at your school. Why do some students cheat? Why don't all students cheat? When and where are students most likely to cheat? Write your essay as a special investigative article for your school newspaper.
2. Analyze the effects of cheating on students and teachers. How does cheating influence the teaching, testing, and grading practices of teachers? How does cheating influence the self-image of students? How does cheating change the relationship of students and teachers?

3. Using a questionnaire, compare and contrast the attitudes of a group of Type A-behavior students and a group of Type B-behavior students on the subject of cheating in college. Report the results of your research to your school's administrator of academic affairs.

Athenian Democracy

JOSIAH OBER AND CATHERINE VANDERPOOL

Josiah Ober and Catherine Vanderpool are involved in the Democracy 2500 Project, sponsored by the American School of Classical Studies at Athens. Ober is also professor of Greek history at Princeton University and author of Mass and Elite in Democratic Athens: Rhetoric, Ideology, and the Power of the People *(1989) as well as numerous books and articles on Greek history and archaeology. Vanderpool is director of U.S. Operations for the American School. She lectures and writes about Greek and Roman art and archaeology. In this essay, Ober and Vanderpool explain Athenian democracy, "a great political experiment" that began some 2500 years ago. This article appeared in* Prologue, *a publication of the National Archives and Records Administration. The authors, writing for a general readership, explain ideas and terms immediately within the text or in content notes at the end of their essay instead of using formal internal documentation and bibliographic references.*

Two thousand five hundred years ago, that is to say, sometime between July of 508 and July of 507 B.C., there occurred one of the most influential revolutions in the history of western civilization. In that year, the ordinary citizens of Athens rose en masse against a ruling clique of Athenian aristocrats and the foreign army of occupation supporting them. The spontaneous, leaderless uprising was successful. Some of the foreign soldiers were executed on the spot; others, along with the leader of the Athenian quislings, Isagoras, were expelled from the city-state. Suddenly and remarkably the people of Athens found themselves in control of their own political destiny—and they now had to decide what to do about it. What they eventually did was to lay the foundations for the world's first democracy—a government that has been studied, praised, and often condemned. Until the American and French revolutions of the late eighteenth century developed new democratic institutions, Athenian democracy was also universally regarded as the ultimate experiment with political freedom and equality.

Even today, Athens remains the best documented example of direct democracy in human history (in contrast to the representative democracy of many modern nations). The story of Athenian democracy, however, can only be partially told by the few and precious ancient texts that have survived the centuries—whether those of Thucydides, Plato, Aristotle, Herodotus, or others. But these, taken together with the material record obtained principally through extensive archaeological investigation, can re-create for us a vivid image of the ancient democracy that has greatly, if indirectly, influenced our own. Much of the history of Athenian democracy took place in and around the ancient political and commercial center of Athens, known as the Agora. Excavations of the Agora have also revealed much about early Athenian social structure.

At the time of the revolution, Athens was a *polis* (city-state) in central Greece, covering an area of approximately one thousand square miles and populated by some 150,000 persons. It shared many of the features that characterized other Greek city-states. Power lay, as it had for many generations, in the hands of a few large aristocratic families, their claim to political power and prestige based on extensive property holdings and their supposedly noble bloodlines. Outside this small group, the rest of the population played little direct role in the political life of the city.

Among the finds in the Agora, which in the early centuries of the first millennium B.C. served mainly as a cemetery, are grave goods from burials where the wealth and position of the deceased is reflected in gold jewelry, fine glass, and elegant pottery. One of the most curious finds, from a female burial of the mid-ninth century, is a terra-cotta chest with a lid decorated with five miniature structures thought to represent granaries. In turn, these granaries have been interpreted as a reference to the source of the family's wealth. Perhaps they numbered among the *pentekosiomedimnoi,* those Athenians whose property produced 500 *medimnoi,* equivalent to 730 bushels, of wheat or barley a year.

In addition to the "500 *medimnoi* people," the early-sixth-century constitution of Solon, known as the Lawgiver, recognized three other classes: the *hippeis* (knights), who could afford to maintain a horse and had land producing 300 *medimnoi* per year; the *zeugitai* (teamsters), who owned a pair of oxen for plowing and whose land produced 200 *medimnoi* per year; and the *thetes,* or common laborers. Perhaps we can read indirect reference to these additional classes in objects such as the *pyxis* (a round, lidded box) of the mid-eighth century B.C., that has three horses perched on the lid, recalling the *hippeis,* or a terra-cotta figure showing a pair of oxen and their driver, recalling the teamsters. One of the humblest items found, an iron pick, recalls the *thetes,* a class so poor and powerless that legal recognition was necessary to keep its members from being confused with, or even becoming, slaves.

A generation before the revolution of 508–507 B.C. the government had been taken over by a single man, Peisistratos, and his family. Peisistratos was known as a *tyrannos,* but the Greek word did not have the same connotations as does the modern English cognate, "tyrant." Although the portrayal of the Peisistratids in surviving literary sources is generally hostile, archaeological evidence shows even as they ruled, other members of the aristocracy continued to serve as archons (chief magistrates of the Athenian state).[1] Excavations in the Agora have uncovered a fragmentary inscription that preserves portions of the names of the archons during the 520s, including that of Kleisthenes, whose postrevolution reforms marked the beginning of democracy.

Albeit for ultimately selfish reasons, Peisistratos attempted to build up grass roots patriotism by focusing on Athenian uniqueness, instituting new national festivals and monumental building programs, and encouraging cultivation of the arts, both visual and literary. The Acropolis, increasingly the focus of religious activity, and the Agora, now focus of commercial and political activity, were the recipients of benefactions not only by Peisistratos himself but by members of his family. Evidence of the tribute paid by the tyrants to religious tradition is reflected, for example, in the Altar of the Twelve Gods, dedicated in

522–521 B.C., whose foundations have been uncovered in the Agora excavations. In addition to temples and altars, the Peisistratids also improved the city's infrastructure, donating utilitarian structures such as aqueducts and fountain houses.

Peisistratos worked to break the oppressive hold of the old aristocratic families on their dependents, which meant the effective liberation of many Athenians from the informal, but powerful, social bonds that tied them to the aristocrats. For this reason, the "tyrant" was probably quite popular with most nonaristocratic Athenians. But Peisistratos's sons, Hipparchos and Hippias, who took over as rulers of the *polis* after his death, were more capricious and failed to retain the loyalty of the ordinary citizens. Their diminishing popularity encouraged the old aristocratic families to try to overthrow the tyranny. The beginning of the end for the Peisistratids is vividly memorialized by a fragmentary inscription from the base of one of the most famous statues in the Agora. Preserved is the name "Harmodios" and the phrase "established their native land." Harmodios and his friend and companion Aristogeiton slew Hipparchos in 514 B.C., setting in motion a chain of events that ultimately led to the overthrow of the family. Almost immediately the two friends became symbols of the struggle against tyranny and were honored by statues in the Agora. With the help of Sparta, an extraordinarily powerful and conservative city-state in southern Greece, the Athenians expelled the last son of Peisistratos, Hippias, from Athens in 510 B.C.—two years before the revolution.

After the end of the tyranny, many aristocrats hoped for and expected a quick return to government as usual—that is, to the pre-tyranny days in which Athenian society and politics were dominated by a handful of powerful and wealthy families. Two leaders, Isagoras and Kleisthenes, quickly emerged and just as quickly became rivals for power. Isagoras had an immediate advantage—he was a close friend of Kleomenes, the leading king of Sparta. (Sparta, anomalously, was ruled by two kings and a council of elders.) Kleomenes had stayed at Isagoras's house during the military operations that ended in the expulsion of the Peisistratid tyrants, and it was whispered that the Spartan king had been allowed free access to Isagoras's wife. Be that as it may, Isagoras certainly had friends in high places, and his influential contacts gained him election as the chief archon—the most important officer in the Athenian government—for the year 508–507 B.C. Kleisthenes was initially flummoxed, but he soon struck back with a daring and original plan; he turned away from intra-elite politics and openly solicited the support of the ordinary citizens. Writing about a half century after the fact, the Greek historian Herodotus remarked that Kleisthenes set about to become the trusted comrade of the people and quickly began to overshadow his rival in Athenian politics.

10 Not to be outdone by his opponent's bold initiative, Isagoras responded by playing his trump card. He sent word of the unsettling developments to Kleomenes, who dispatched a herald to Athens ordering Kleisthenes into exile. Kleisthenes had no choice but to obey; Sparta was, after all, the dominant military state in Greece. But affairs in Athens were still unsettled. Kleomenes arrived in the city with a small army and proceeded to establish Isagoras and his friends as the new government of Athens. Kleomenes first expelled seven hundred prominent families thought to be a threat to Isagoras and then attempted to dissolve the Athenian advisory council. But here Isagoras and Kleomenes made a serious mistake. The councilmen (who remain anonymous in our sources) re-

sisted, and their brave resistance sparked the spontaneous uprising of the mass of Athenians. Isagoras and his allies fled to the Acropolis but surrendered after a three-day siege.

Immediately following the expulsion of Isagoras and the Spartans, the people of Athens recalled their comrade Kleisthenes. He was faced with a remarkable challenge—to create a system of government that would be acceptable to the revolution-inspired Athenian people and to have it operating smoothly before the Spartans inevitably returned to punish Athens for its insolent behavior. Kleisthenes' options were limited. The old hierarchical social order had been shattered by the double blow of a generation of tyranny and the revolution itself; there was no longer a viable tradition on which to build a new government. The people would not tolerate continued aristocratic rule, and tyranny had been discredited by the harsh reign of Hipparchos and Hippias. How then to restore legitimate political authority?

Kleisthenes' remarkable insight—and the origin of ancient democracy—was to build a new political order quite literally from the ground up. He divided the Athenian population into ten new tribes, effectively breaking up the centuries-old power structure. Each tribe was deliberately subdivided and gerrymandered so as to include people from different parts of Attica. The tribes were named after ten early Athenian heroes, who were ever after referred to as the Eponymous Heroes. The foundations of the Monument of the Eponymous Heroes have been excavated in the Agora just east of the Metroon (the state archives). Over sixteen meters long, the base supported bronze statues of the heroes.

The roots of Kleisthenes' new system lay in much smaller political units—the existing village and neighborhood communities that dotted the territory of Athens. Kleisthenes designated 140 of these little communities as demes *(demoi)*, which translates as "peoples." Each deme was to be a semi-independent political entity that would be responsible for its own internal government. The adult male members of each deme (on the average about one hundred to two hundred people) would be expected to meet regularly in an open assembly, at which every member had a vote, and everyone could speak his mind ("his" is precise, as women were never regarded as citizens of Athens or of any other Greek *polis*). Among the duties of the deme assembly was the "election" of new members—no one could be a citizen of the deme unless he had been voted in by the other members. Election was tremendously significant because deme membership was, from this period on, the basis of citizenship in the *polis* itself. Thus, overnight, the Athenian citizen body became a self-establishing body, and that body was responsible for its own membership.

Kleisthenes' new system called upon each deme to send a certain number of representatives (based on population) to an advisory council of five hundred citizens, fifty from each tribe. The council handled the day-to-day business of the government. At first, the selection of representatives may have been by election, but soon the demes adopted the method of an open lottery. Any citizen aged thirty or older who was willing to serve (and perhaps half or three-quarters of all Athenian citizens *did* eventually serve a term in the council) could put his name in the lottery. If his lot came up in the drawing, he was sent to the council. Councilmen could only serve two nonconsecutive annual terms, and most served only one. The councilmen met regularly in a special building on the west side of the Agora, the Bouleuterion. The earliest form of the council house appears to date from around 500 B.C. It served simultaneously as the state archives until the end of the fifth century, at which time the council moved to a new Bouleuterion, and the old building, now known as the Metroon, was dedicated entirely to archival purposes. Remains of the foundations of the early Bouleuterion have led to its reconstruction as a nearly square building, presumably filled with wooden benches. The inscription on a fragment of a marble basin found close by its foundation indicates that it belonged to the council; archaeologists speculate that it may have held water in which Athenians washed or dipped their hands (as a form of ritual purification) before entering any sacred place.

Administration of the council lay in the hands of a rotating executive committee, the *prytaneis,* each tribe's fifty councilmen serving as such for thirty-five or thirty-six days at a time. Headquartered in the Tholos, a round building next to the Bouleuterion, the *prytaneis* ate at public expense throughout their term of office. Fragments of the Tholos dining ware have turned up in excavations, clearly marked with the letters "DE," the first two letters of the word *demosion,* or public property.

The council's most important task was the preparation of the agenda for the national assembly, the much larger governing body made up of all Athenian citizens who cared to show up. Meetings of the assembly, held outdoors in a natural depression shaped like a theater and located on a ridge (the Pnyx) to the west of the Agora and the Acropolis, were remarkable affairs. In the fourth century B.C. (the period for which our sources are most detailed), the assembly, or *ekklesia,* met forty times each year. Six thousand to eight thousand men regularly attended, approximately 20–25 percent of the total citizen body. After a preliminary sacrifice to the state gods, a member of the *prytaneis,* selected by lot as "president for the day," would call the meeting to order. He announced the first item on the agenda, which could be anything from a change in the calendar of the state religion to the state of the city's food supply, welfare provisions for the orphaned and handicapped, or a declaration of war against a neighboring *polis.* The president then indicated the council's recommendation on the subject, if it had one to offer (sometimes it did not). In either case, he then opened the subject for discussion by asking, "Who among the Athenians wishes to speak?" At this point every one of the thousands of men in the audience had the chance to stand up and address the assembly for as long as two conditions pertained: his voice held out, and his fellow citizens were willing to listen to him. Addressing the assembly was a tough and potentially humiliating undertaking. When the assemblymen decided a speech was of excessive length, they simply hooted and jeered the speaker from the orator's stand.

After everyone who wished to speak had faced this public gauntlet, a vote was taken by counting raised hands. A simple majority determined the issue, and if it passed, the new decree immediately became Athenian policy. Thus, for example, if the assembly voted for war with Sparta, a state of war would immediately be declared. It was in this manner that *all* of the important business of the state was attended to; taxes were levied, alliances with other states were made or broken, and generals and other specialized officials were elected to annual terms of office. By ca. 390 B.C., the Athenians deemed it necessary to reimburse citizens for their attendance at deliberations of the *ekklesia*. Shortly following the devastating Peloponnesian War (431–404 B.C.), Athens was plagued by economic hardship. Many Athenians were impoverished in the postwar years, and taking an unpaid day off work imposed a real strain. In order to make it possible for working Athenians to fulfill their citizen duties, lead tokens were distributed to those attending the meeting and could be redeemed for first one, then two, and finally nine *obols* per day for certain meetings (an *obol* was the equivalent of one-sixth of a *drachma,* which equaled roughly one day's wage).

To the modern observer, perhaps the most unusual meetings of the assembly were those held to carry out an ostracism. Until the late fifth century B.C. when the procedure was abandoned, the Athenian citizens voted annually whether or not to hold an ostracism.[2] If the vote was positive, a date was set for the actual ceremony. On the designated day, every Athenian citizen was entitled to come to the Agora with a shard of pottery (*ostrakon*) on which he (or someone for him) had scratched the name of the man he thought most deserved banishment from the *polis*. At the end of the day, if a quorum of six thousand votes had been cast, the "winner," the man whose name was found on the most shards, was forced into exile for ten years. Among the powerful political figures of the fifth century thus eliminated were Kimon (son of Miltiades), the general who defeated the Persians at the river Eurymedon ca. 469 B.C., and Themistokles, the architect of Athenian naval power and the man responsible for successfully deploying the Athenian fleet against the Persians at Salamis in 480 B.C. In practical terms, those ostracized were invariably prominent politicians, men who frequently took it upon themselves to address the assembly on important affairs and who ran for major offices. The ostracism procedure ensured that political leadership in Athens was always a tenuous business and always subject to sharp and sudden reversals of fortune. Those Athenians who actively participated in the affairs of the *polis* also put themselves at the mercy of the people they hoped to lead, a people who held their leaders to almost impossibly high standards of conduct. In 406 B.C., for example, after a victory over the Spartan fleet at Arginusae, the Athenians, overstrained by the length and devastation of the Peloponnesian war, condemned six of the victorious generals to death for not picking up survivors.

Disputes between citizens that could not be resolved by private or public arbitration and crimes against society were normally resolved in the people's courts. A citizen who felt himself wronged or who believed that a crime had been committed would, in front of witnesses, challenge the malefactor to appear before a certain state magistrate at a certain time. In civil cases, the magistrate might require the disputants to appear before an official public arbitrator. In the fourth century B.C., every Athenian citizen who reached age sixty was expected to put his accumulated wisdom and experience to work by serving for one year as an arbitrator. The arbitrator would attempt to resolve the problem equitably, but if he failed to satisfy both parties, the evidence presented to him was sealed, and the case was forwarded to the people's courts. The Athenians were a notoriously litigious people, causing the comic playwright Aristophanes to joke, "The cicada sings for only a month, but the people of Athens are buzzing with lawsuits and trials their whole life long." Law courts were scattered throughout the city. A series of rooms excavated in the northeast corner of the Agora may have served as a law court from the late fifth century B.C., as suggested by finds of bronze ballots and a ballot box.

A jury, usually consisting of two hundred to five hundred men (although its size might occasionally reach twenty-five hundred), would be drawn from the list of approximately six thousand available jurors. As with the assemblymen, the jurors were for the most part ordinary working men chosen for a period of one year and (in the fourth century B.C.) asssigned to courts by an elaborate allotment machine. Jurors received compensation from the mid-fifth century B.C., when Perikles introduced a two-*obol* stipend for service. In the 420s, Kleon raised this to three *obols*. Their goal was to encourage participation of poorer men in the democratic process.[3]

To speed up trials and to keep them to a one-day limit, the Athenians timed speakers with a *klepsydra,* or water clock. Some clocks may have allowed only a few minutes of speaking time, but judging from speeches preserved in literary texts, the harangues could be of considerably greater length. The trial itself consisted of an officially timed speech by the plaintiff, followed by a speech of the same length by the defendant. Each party to the case had to speak for himself, at least in theory. There were no professional lawyers in Athens, although there were men willing to write a clever legal speech for a fee. Persuading an Athenian jury often required more than just the facts. A litigant might attempt to persuade jurors that he was a better citizen than his opponent—more public-spirited, more generous with his time and resources, and less offensive in his private life. Many jury trials (especially of rich and powerful men) were highly publicized contests in which political opponents competed for the respect and admiration of their fellow citizens. But a private citizen, unskilled in the arts of rhetoric, might be at a disadvantage in such a contest. Thus, occasionally, after speaking a few words, a litigant with a poor speaking voice would step aside and allow a friend to continue to plead his case.

After listening to the two speeches, the jury voted; all verdicts were in principle final. As in the assembly, a simple majority determined the issue; though in jury trials from the fifth century on, a secret ballot procedure was employed in the place of a show of hands. This was probably done to avoid undue influence by the powerful, revenge by relatives, or bribery of jurors. By the middle of the fourth century B.C., the secret voting procedure employed bronze ballots manufactured with an axle through the middle, half of them hollow and half solid. After all the evidence was presented, each juror, in full view of all, received one of each type of ballot. As they voted, jurors held their thumbs and forefingers over the ends of the axles (disguising which hand held which ballot), placing one into a receptacle for valid votes, the other into a waste receptacle. A hollow ballot indicated a vote for the plaintiff, a solid for the defendant.

The penalties levied in many categories of legal action were fixed by law, generally consisting of a fine, exile, or death. Rarely was long-term imprisonment prescribed as Athens had no formal prison system. While there was a jail in which to hold those who could not be released on bail, Athenians would probably find long-term imprisonment a waste of state resources, especially as exile was a viable option. In certain cases, however, no penalty was set by law, and a different procedure was used. If, after the first pair of speeches, the jury voted for the plaintiff, each litigant was given a second chance to address the court, this time to propose alternate penalties. The stakes could be very high. In the famous trial of Sokrates, who in 399 B.C. was charged with impiety and corrupting the youth of Athens, the prosecution called for the death penalty. Ordinarily the defendant (now officially guilty) would propose a stiff fine or possibly even exile. In his case, however, Sokrates proposed an ironic "penalty" of being feasted for life at state expense. As Athenian juries were required to choose one of the two alternatives, it is not surprising that Sokrates was penalized with death.

Trials could be equally problematic for the plaintiff. The Athenian judicial calendar was rather busy, and nuisance suits were looked upon with great disapproval. Thus, in many categories of legal action, if the plaintiff did not receive one-fifth of the jury votes cast (thus justifying his case), he could be severely fined. If he was incapable of paying the fine, he would be stripped of citizenship and forced into exile.

Kleisthenes' system of government, which was soon given the newly coined name *demokratia,* meaning "people power," was a startling success. As expected, the Spartans attacked the city-state in 506 B.C., but the Athenian army, mustered under the new political regime, faced down the invaders. Herodotus was impressed by this event and noted that before the revolution the Athenians were not a major power in the Greek world, but after the liberation, they were unstoppable. Indeed, democratic Athens went on to become the most powerful state in Greece, playing a key role in the successful Greek resistance to the great Persian invasion of 480 B.C. and subsequently creating the first and only great classical Greek empire in the Aegean. There is no doubt that Herodotus was right; this tremendous surge in Athens's ability to play a leading role in international affairs was quite directly a result of the democratic political order.

In the century following the reforms, Athens extended its power well beyond its borders and from mid-century experienced a peak of glory, prosperity, and renewal under the leadership of the statesman Perikles. Athens built up a powerful army and navy, which in organization and administration reflected the new political system. The *ekklesia* elected one general from each tribe per year, and at least in the early fifth century, the army as a whole was managed by the *polemarch,* or chief commander. The majority of the army consisted of armed *hoplites,* infantry soldiers wearing helmets, breastplates, and greaves (armor for the lower legs) and fighting with a shield and thrusting spear. The cavalry formed a smaller elite unit because of the expense of maintaining a mount, although the state itself paid a maintenance allowance to the owners after an annual inspection. The Athenian navy, comprising as many as four hundred ships and eighty thousand sailors during its peak, helped Athens dominate the eastern Mediterranean in the fifth century B.C. Many of the sailors, while citizens, were drawn from the poorer ranks of society. They served principally as oarsmen for the wooden warships known as *triremes,* each of which carried 170 rowers positioned on three banks of oars.

Although Athens and Sparta had cooperated against the Persians, the two city-states remained locked in a bitter rivalry. Peace was declared between Athens and Sparta in 446, giving Athens a chance to rebuild. The city and its temples had been burned by the Persians in 480 B.C., and the truce as well as additional funds provided from the opening of the silver mines and the seizure of the Delos Treasury gave Perikles the chance not only to repair the damage, but also to erect the Parthenon, Propylaea, and other buildings throughout the city. The peace, however, was short lived, and the renewed power struggle with Sparta would test the resiliency of the democracy.

In 431 B.C. war again erupted between Athens and Sparta; both city-states were by this time leaders of large confederacies; it was not just Athens versus Sparta but the Athenian empire versus the Spartan-led Peloponnesian League. The stakes were high; it soon became clear that the winner would dominate the whole of Greece. The Peloponnesian War, which lasted twenty-seven years, took a terrible toll on the Athenians; at least a quarter of the total population was wiped out in a few years by wartime plague, and battle deaths numbered in the tens of thousands. Modern estimates suggest that, by the end of the war, the male population of Athens may have been cut in half.

The war, which Athens eventually lost, also put a tremendous strain on the democracy. In 411 B.C., soon after Athens had suffered a ghastly reverse in Sicily, concerted terrorism by pro-oligarchy Athenians led to the temporary overthrow of the democracy. But the oligarchic government soon collapsed, and the democracy was restored. After the Spartan victory in 404 B.C., the victors imposed a new government administered by "The Thirty," a band of democracy-hating Athenian aristocrats, whose leader, Kritias, was a well-known follower of Sokrates. Once again, the democrats fought back successfully. A band of prodemocracy Athenians gathered a guerrilla army outside the city, challenged and defeated the military forces of The Thirty, took back the city, and in 403 B.C. reinstituted the democracy. For the next eight decades, the Athenians enjoyed a stable democratic government and maintained their independence against various external threats. The democracy was finally extinguished in 322 B.C., after Athens had been repeatedly defeated by the vastly superior military forces of Macedon—an imperial nation-state in northern Greece that was gigantic by the standards of the *polis*. Yet for centuries thereafter the memory of democracy contributed to periodic revolts by the Athenians against a succession of foreign masters. Whenever the Athenians managed to free themselves, they reinstated a democratic government.

A modern admirer of democratic Athens can point to a number of signal accomplishments. The Athenians created the first known complex society that proclaimed and actively maintained significant political equality. When Athenians entered the assembly or sat on a jury, the rich and the poor, the scion of the oldest family and the "nobody, son of nobody," were equals. When they raised their hands or dropped their juror's ballots, their votes had identical weight. Notably, this equality was achieved without the need to resort to an oppressive statist enforcement of social equality; there was no push by the democratic government to equalize property or wealth. Moreover, Athenian citizen society was famous for having the highest level of freedom of thought, speech, and behavior in the Greek world. Everybody knew that, as the orator Demosthenes put it, "you can praise Sparta in Athens, but not Athens in Sparta." As that comment suggests, freedom of speech extended to the freedom to criticize the Athenian form of government. Among the most outstanding products of Athenian literature produced under the democracy are works by Thucydides, Plato, and Aristotle, many of which are profoundly critical of the working of democracy. Finally, although there was no formal Athenian bill of rights, the practical workings of the democracy served to protect the essential dignity of the lowliest citizen from insult or violent outrage by those who were his superiors in strength, wealth, or political influence. Any Athenian could be tried for the crime of committing *hubris* against one of his fellows. *Hubris* generally meant verbal or physical assault but was never defined in the law code. Because it was up to the jurymen themselves to decide if some member of the aristocracy was using his influence in an unacceptable manner, elite Athenians were careful to avoid any sort of public arrogance that could be interpreted by a hostile jury as *hubris*. And so, Athenian citizenship provided security against the types of personal indignity that social inequality has often visited upon the poor and undistinguished elsewhere.

But if we honor Athen's successes, it is at the same time important to remember that the ideals and institutions on which Athenian society was based were far removed from those assumed by contemporary American society. Democratic Athens proved no less willing than other Greek states to commit ugly atrocities in times of war, and the Athenian empire of the fifth century was frankly exploitative. Many resident foreigners (*metics*) lived in Athens and were quite welcome to do so, yet few of them ever had the opportunity to become citizens. After 451 B.C., when Perikles' law restricting citizenship was passed, only those with both an Athenian father and mother could be brought before a deme assembly for consideration of membership. Before this decree, only the father was required to be an Athenian. Ironically, this law would later affect Perikles' own son, who was born of a foreign mother. Only with the express permission of the *ekklesia* could citizenship be granted to foreigners or the children of foreigners. And even then, to ensure that no rules had been bent or broken, "cleansings" were occasionally held in the demes, stripping some people of their ever-tenuous citizenship.

Athenian women enjoyed none of the equality and little of the freedom and dignity cherished by their citizen husbands. An Athenian woman was normally expected to avoid frequenting public places. Women who were forced by economic hardship into occupations such as ribbon-selling in the Agora were objects of scorn to others and shame to their families. Women had little or no voice in the choice of their husbands; a father or male guardian would arrange a suitable match, and the girl might see her husband for the first time at the betrothal. Further, she had only indirect control (at best) over her property, but if her husband divorced her, he was forced to return her dowry.

Slave ownership was legal and probably quite common (although exact figures do not exist) in the democratic state. Slaves were brought to Athens from all over the eastern Mediterranean and Black Sea regions. Some were Greeks taken by the Athenians as prisoners of war. Others were bought up by professional slave dealers from various peoples of eastern Europe, Asia, and northern Africa and sold on the open market in Athens and other Greek *poleis*. The conditions under which slaves worked, especially those purchased for the silver mines, were miserable to the extreme. Although there were laws against killing or hitting slaves, they were hardly free from abuse. A slave's testimony was allowed in an Athenian courtroom only on the condition that it had been given under torture; slaves who gave information without torture were assumed to be liars.

When celebrating the remarkable equality, openness, and dignity enjoyed by Athenian citizens, we must not forget that those citizens were a relatively small minority who jealously guarded their privileges against a more numerous and oppressed majority of noncitizens. To claim, however, that we have nothing to learn from this early, and in many ways still unique, experiment in direct democracy because Athenians had the moral standards of classical Greeks rather than of twentieth-century Americans, is at once anachronistic and ethnocentric.

Athenian democracy was a great political experiment, acknowledged by America's Founding Fathers and ultimately rejected in favor of a model based more on the Republic of Rome. It was feared that direct democracy had too few controls and might lead to "rabble" rule. Direct democracy was a system that evolved in what was, by modern standards, a small homogeneous state, where it was possible to travel from one end to the other, for the most part, in less than a day; where citizens could attend an assembly that met every ten days to pass laws; where the shared knowledge of the community and its inner workings permitted the citizens, in Aristotle's words, "to rule and be ruled in turns." The differences are easy to see; remarkable is the fact that 2,500 years later we can still recognize some common ground and respond (even if with mixed emotions) to the words of Perikles, who declared his city "an education to Greece," indeed, to the world.

Notes

1. There were a total of nine archons, or state magistrates, selected (by various means) each year. The first was "the" archon, sometimes called the "eponymous" archon because he gave his name to the year. For clarity, we have called this officer "chief archon." This was clearly a very powerful office before 508 B.C. (much less so afterwards and largely ceremonial by the time of Perikles). It was the office of "the" archon that some of the other aristocrats held under the Peisistratids. The second magistrate was the "king" archon. He was not actually a king but rather the head of the state religion. The third archon was the *polemarch,* or military leader. The remaining six archons were *thesmothetes,* or legal officials.
2. We do not know why ostracism was abandoned after the late fifth century B.C. Presumably it fell into disuse at least in part because its function was replaced by the legal action of *graphe paranomon,* which was the indictment of the proposer of an illegal or "uncustomary" decree.
3. The issue of pay in Athens is very complex; some workers could make a *drachma* for the days they worked, which may suggest to the modern mind that the workers would not give up a day's wage for lower-paying jury service. But the laborers did not work 365 days a year. We should also not immediately make the modernizing assumption that all Athenian actions were governed solely by "rational" economic motives. Serving on a jury was regarded as vitally important in protecting basic rights, was empowering, and probably was often a lot of fun. If we say that only the leisured citizens (nonworkers) served as jurors because the poorer men could not afford to, we must throw out the number six thousand potential jurors (for which there is good textual support), since there cannot have been that many leisure-class Athenians. All the evidence (gathered especially by M. M. Markle) suggests that we have every reason to suppose that most jurors fell between the leisured and the genuinely impoverished.

There may have been an overrepresentation by elderly men, but this cannot be proved. The dread that the wealthy felt of the courts is good evidence that poorer Athenians did in fact dominate the courts.

Questions for Discussion

1. What is the essay's subordinate aim? Cite specific passages to support your answer.
2. In the essay, the authors introduce and define a variety of Greek words. What is their purpose in doing so? What do you think of this technique? Is it appropriate? Is it necessary?
3. Do you think the authors establish themselves as credible sources of information? Explain your answer.
4. Do the authors do a satisfactory job of motivating the audience? If so, cite specific passages. If not, offer specific suggestions for revision.
5. Add appropriate headings to this essay. How do the headings influence your reading? Is the essay more or less effective?

Opportunities for Writing

1. Your school newspaper is running a series of articles on famous trials. For your contribution to this series, analyze the trial of Socrates. Why was he accused? Was he guilty? Why was he convicted?
2. Investigate the causes of the Peloponnesian War. Why did it start? When? Where? Why did it continue for a generation? Why did it stop?
3. Explain the meaning of the word *tyranny*. How has the meaning of this word changed from the days of ancient Greece? Address your essay to the membership of a local civil rights organization.

The Big New Mix

Renee Loth

Renee Loth is a writer for the Boston Globe, *contributing news articles, interviews, commentaries, and book reviews. In this essay, in which Loth presents statistics on how the demographics in the United States are changing, she considers the possible effects of this new "multiculturalism" on Americans in the twenty-first century. "A Big New Mix" appeared in* The Boston Globe Magazine *(October 12, 1991). As you read this article, see how Loth integrates her research material (e.g., statistics and quotations) into the text; notice also that she tags sources of information instead of using a formal system of documentation. Why do you think Loth presents knowledge by observation in this way?*

Given the implacable surge of Asian and Hispanic immigrants over the past decade, it might seem that we'll soon be celebrating Tet instead of Columbus Day and eating tacos on the Fourth of July—er, *Cinco de Mayo.* The ascendancy of English-only movements, the backlash against political correctness, and the dismantling of hiring quotas are all symptoms of a growing anxiety on the part of some "natives" that the 8.5 million immigrants expected in the 1990s will render the United States unrecognizable.

But demographers, who limit their study to just the statistics, are remarkably sanguine about the effect of massive in-migration on the dominant American culture. To these number crunchers, the past is prologue, and the past suggests that immigrants adjust to America more than the country adjusts to them.

The annealing powers of the melting pot are stronger than the will to retain separate ethnic identities, they say. With few exceptions, immigrants tend to intermarry, become fluent in English, and have smaller families with each succeeding generation. They leave the ghetto and move to the suburbs, leave the labor unions and strive to become managers, and drop their ethnic customs except on holidays. In the dry terminology of demographic science, they "regress toward the mean."

"The overwhelming number of people who emigrate want an American passport, not just the green card," says Christopher Jencks, professor of sociology and urban affairs at Northwestern University. Julian L. Simon, an economist at the University of Maryland, concurs: "They want to play baseball, not pachinko."

5   This is not to say that demographers don't anticipate stress and dislocation as the immigrant waves continue to wash over America. Although newcomers may be beneficial to the US economy as a whole, try telling that to the individual who loses his job to an immigrant willing to work for lower pay. As American blacks can attest, assimilation gets progressively harder as it moves through the barriers of ethnicity, religion, and race. Asians and Hispanics, who now account for 74 percent of all US immigration, must breach all three levels to join mainstream America.

Moreover, some believe that the trend toward multiculturalism could itself retard assimilation, as immigrants realize there is a benefit to retaining their ethnic distinctions. "To the extent that we have codified some of these groups, we may be preserving them," says Jeffrey Passel, director of the program for research on immigration policy at the Urban Institute, in Washington, D.C. Passel and others think that second-generation ethnics may resist assimilation because certain rights and privileges have been attached to the "new tribalism." Ironically, the very people who promote ethnic and racial separateness are often the fiercest opponents of discrimination.

The numbers suggest that the current flood of immigrants, as overwhelming as it may sometimes seem, will be easier to absorb than the so-called European migration that every right-thinking American now celebrates. Although the 656,000 legal immigrants who arrived in 1990 represent the largest single wave since 1924, it is but a fraction of the European migration when taken as a percentage of the US population. Although today's immigrants may seem uniquely "foreign," they are probably no more strange to us now than the Southern and Eastern Europeans were to the prevailing American culture at the turn of the century. And though the US Census does predict that Hispanics, blacks, and Asians eventually will outnumber whites in America, one widely used demographic model developed by the Urban Institute—which adjusts for falling fertility rates—doesn't show that occurring until 2090, a century away.

Leon Bouvier, a demographer at Tulane University, is a dissenting voice. He projects that America will become "a majority minority" nation by 2050, and within just 20 years in New York, California, and Texas. "It's a momentous shift, and to close your eyes to it can lead to enormous problems between groups," he says. Bouvier, who served on the US Select Commission on Immigration and Refugee Policy in 1980, advocates reducing immigration quotas to 450,000 a year, almost half the present level.

All of these projections come with the caveat that demography is an inexact science, its predictive purity corrupted by politics, human behavior, and other imponderables. Birth rates are dropping for all immigrant groups, but new child-friendly government tax breaks could interfere with the neat models. Congress periodically votes to "diversify" immigration quotas, correcting trends toward over-representation of one nationality or another. (Indeed, in 1986 Congress legalized 3 million mostly Hispanic immigrants in one sweeping amnesty period.)

Demographic definitions are quirky and ever-changing. Until 1980 the US Census considered people of Pakistani or Indian descent "white" but now counts them as Asian. World events can and probably will change the nature of the 120,000 political refugees admitted annually under current immigration laws. "If we believed the projections of 1914 for 1990," says Charles Keely, professor of international migration at Georgetown University, "we would be a country overrun by pizza parlors and delicatessens by now." No one predicted spring rolls.

We asked demographers, historians, and social scientists to envision America in the 21st century along social, economic, and political lines. Will English lose its unifying power to a Babel of foreign tongues? Will the growing numbers of Asians and Hispanics be reflected in political clout? Will the country resemble more a stew, with each ingredient melting into the whole; a parfait, with a clear hierarchy of distinct ingredients; or a salad, with all the elements tossed together but retaining their individual character?

Observers as diverse as historian Arthur Schlesinger and economist Robert J. Samuelson worry that the currently fashionable ethic of "celebrating differences" will atomize America, elevating the special interest above the national interest. Nowhere is that concern more acute than in the debate over bilingualism. Although it is not a new issue—in 1919 Theodore Roosevelt warned against becoming "dwellers in a polyglot boarding house"—the US Census does record an increase over the past 20 years in households in which English is not the dominant language spoken. Some Americans find this a threat, and English-only laws were passed in 17 states during the 1980s. Former US Sen. S. I. Hayakawa (R-California) has been pushing a constitutional amendment restricting bilingual education lest the United States become "another Quebec."

Most of our prognosticators doubt that America will become bilingual in the next century. "Speaking English will still be really important to success as an American concept," says Jencks. A kind of Canadian or Swiss-style pluralism, he says, is difficult to obtain in a country as large and media-sensitive as the United States. Not entirely in jest, Jencks adds: "Historically, the tradition is that people of low status have to learn the language of the high, so we may all have to learn Japanese."

One key difference between the European migrations and the current waves gives our experts pause, however. The migrations of the 1920s were interrupted, first by restrictive legislation, then by the Great Depression and World War II. That gave immigrants a "breather" in which to adapt to American culture. Today, by contrast, there is a continuous stream of fresh immigrants keeping the old-country customs, and language, alive.

15   Raul Yzaguirre is president of the National Council of la Raza, a Hispanic-rights group in Washington. He notes that his ancestors came to America in 1721, yet he still speaks Spanish. "History has shown that you cannot outlaw a language," he says. "You can't artificially impose a culture or try to oppress a culture. That's what's happening in the [former] Soviet Union right now."

Yzaguirre envisions a multilingual, multicultural America in the 21st century, with more Latin influence on music, art, politics, and popular culture. Hispanics will learn English, but the English language itself will "learn Spanish." More and more Spanish words will be incorporated into *Webster's*, he says, "just like 'pizza' and 'chutzpah.'"

Whether such piquancy is a good thing is largely a matter of taste. "For some people, one immigrant is too many," says Keely. "Dade County [Florida] goes ape when 40,000 Haitians show up. In New York City, that's a block party."

Julian Simon, author of *The Economic Consequences of Immigration,* thinks the new immigrants are a nearly unalloyed good: They'll stimulate the economy, improve the American standard of living, reverse the birth dearth, and provide for baby boomers in their old age.

"The more immigrants that come, the brighter our economic future is across the board," he says. "They mean a higher standard of living, greater productivity, better international competitiveness, and the only painless solution to the deficit. It's an extraordinary opportunity to achieve every one of our economic national goals at once."

20   More profound than the "browning of America," Simon notes, is its graying. The US Census projects that the over–65 population, currently around 26 million, will be 39 million by the year 2010 and 51 million by 2020. The Urban Institute model projects an average life expectancy in the year 2090 of 90.2 years, which is 14 more years of Social Security than the current average. Since most immigrants arrive when they are young and healthy, Simon believes they could be the needed relief to the burden of an aging US population.

Congress has helped out by passing an immigration law, which became effective October 1, that increases the quotas for managerial and high-tech workers from 58,000 a year to 140,000. Michael Hoefer, chief demographer for the US Immigration and Naturalization Service, explains that the new law also tries to address a pent-up demand for visas for the children and spouses of permanent residents, especially those from Mexico, the Philippines, and the Dominican Republic. In addition, it lowers barriers erected in 1965 to immigrants from Northern European countries, such as Ireland (thanks to congressmen Joseph Kennedy and Brian Donnolly).

Capitalism is one of the strongest assimilators known in the United States. Many women striving to climb the corporate ladder have found pressure to adopt "male" management styles to fit in comfortably. Similarly, most experts believe the corporate culture will subsume individual ethnic cultures, especially in white-collar jobs. "You have to be more traditional than traditional to be the first one through any of these doors," says Jencks, predicting relatively little diversity at the top. "It's part of the nature of corporate America to be homogenous."

Three crucial economic programs that eased assimilation for the children of European immigrants are missing today, however. Nothing worked better to assimilate second-generation immigrants in the 1940s than the FHA loan, the GI Bill, and the federal interstate highways program that helped create suburbia. "Those government programs had a great absorption impact," says Keely. "They allowed mixing of people, allowed access to education, and a great deal of economic prosperity."

For generations, politics served as a social escalator for Irish and Italian immigrants locked out of traditional avenues to wealth and power. In his cultural history of Massachusetts, *Bibles, Brahmins and Bosses,* Thomas O'Connor describes the practical value of political patronage in the early years of this century. "For many an Irish ward boss," he writes, "politics was an invaluable opportunity to provide effective help and assistance to his own people when they could not obtain what they needed from any other source." The needs were basic, he writes, but often unattainable: food, eyeglasses, pardons, jobs.

Today, the spoils system of politics is largely out of favor, or at least out of money, and the offspring of Irish and Italian machine pols have assimilated to WASPy suburbs and taken careers in banking. The new immigrants, especially Asians, have been somewhat slower to become politically active. For those who come from countries with little or no tradition in democracy, there is cultural resistance to political activism. It is difficult to imagine survivors of Pol Pot's killing fields having much enthusiasm for politics.

"It will be a long process for that refugee movement . . . to become savvy to the white political structure," says Andrew Buni, a history professor at Boston College who specializes in issues of immigration and ethnicity. Moreover, according to Hoefer, at the US Immigration Service, even though Asians have the highest naturalization rates of any immigrants, few of the post-Vietnam-era immigrants have been here for the seven years required to become citizens.

Like most ethnic groups, Asians are not monolithic. A Sony executive and a Vietnamese boat person may both be considered of Asian descent, but there the similarity ends. Cambodians, Vietnamese, Koreans, Hmong, and Laotians all speak different languages. "It's hard enough to get a coalition of Democrats together on something, let alone people whose language and customs and political alliances in their own worlds are vastly different from each other," says Professor Buni.

Nor can Hispanics be expected to vote in a singular way. Cuban-Americans tend to be very conservative and Mexicans rather liberal. George Bush won the "Hispanic" vote in Miami in 1988, but Michael Dukakis won the "Hispanic" vote in Texas. "It would be disingenuous to argue that we think exactly alike on the same issues," says Lisa Navarette, of the National Council of la Raza.

Ironically, one key to better political representation for minorities—legislative redistricting—argues against assimilation, since the new immigrants need to cluster together in a single district to elect one of their own successfully. Hispanic leaders say the fact that they are more assimilated than most blacks puts them at a disadvantage in the redistricting sweepstakes. "There is more mobility within the Hispanic community, and that has prevented Hispanic clout," says Navarette.

30   Mexico sent the greatest number of immigrants to America in the 1980s, accounting for 12 percent of the nation's newcomers, not counting undocumented aliens. All of our demographic models predict that the number of Hispanics will soon overtake that of blacks in America. But it takes more than demographics to win elections. Unless Hispanics improve their naturalization rates and start to vote—just 13 percent of Mexicans who entered the country in 1977 had become citizens by 1989, compared with 50 percent of Asian immigrants and 44 percent of Eastern Europeans—their political muscle will not be proportionate to their numbers.

Most of our demographers agree that nativist fears about the "wretched refuse" at our shores could be cooled significantly by a quick course in American history. Like many of his colleagues, the Urban Institute's Passel is struck by similarities between reactions to the current wave of immigration and the xenophobia prevalent at the turn of the century.

"Eighty years ago, at the peak of the last great wave of immigration, people were concerned that the new immigrants would never fit in, that they were bringing alien ideas, that they would never learn English," Passel says. "It's the grandchildren of those people who are saying those same things now."

Questions for Discussion

1. How important is this essay's persuasive aim? Is it as important as the essay's referential aim? Could this essay be classified as persuasive aim writing? Explain your answer.
2. This essay was written for the general readership of a daily newspaper. How might the author revise this essay for a specific audience of business managers? of immigration officials? of liberals? of conservatives?
3. What do you think of the ending? Is it appropriate? Is it effective? Why do you think it is or isn't?
4. How might the author integrate knowledge by participation? If she did, do you think the essay would be more or less effective? Why?
5. Explain the organization of the essay. Why is it organized the way it is?

Opportunities for Writing

1. Explain the procedure for becoming a naturalized citizen of the United States of America. How do individuals apply for citizenship? When? Where? Who is eligible?
2. Using interviews of naturalized and native citizens, compare and contrast their attitudes regarding immigrants. What similarities and differences do you notice?
3. Analyze the impact of a specific group of immigrants (e.g., Chinese, Italians) on America's food, literature, clothing, athletics, or language. How has this group of immigrants influenced America? Report the results of your research in a special article for the Independence Day issue of your local newspaper.

The Underdog Concept in Sport

JIMMY A. FRAZIER AND ELDON E. SNYDER

Jimmy A. Frazier and Eldon E. Snyder were both at Bowling Green State University in 1991, when this essay appeared in the Sociology of Sport Journal. *In this essay, Frazier and Snyder study the phenomenon of the underdog effect. They present and analyze data gathered from responses to a questionnaire that they designed, and they conclude that underdog status can increase spectator interest and support. The documentation style used in this study is APA.*

The tension and excitement of competitive sport is created by the indeterminacy of the contest that is based on an approximate equity between the contestants. Yet players and teams vary in competence and prestige, and those with less competence are frequently labeled as the underdog. While winning is valued, cross-cutting values often create sentiments for the underdog, that is, the desire for the underdog to overcome the inferior status and upset the favored opponent. Social support for the underdog reflects a utilitarian perspective that helps maintain an emotional interest in a contest; additionally, underdogs receive support from the social value of equity. At a microlevel, the underdog status is often used to increase the level of motivation and performance. Data gathered from university students are used to support the positions taken in the paper.

One of the fundamental characteristics of sport in western society is that it is a competitive activity, that is, the contestants are competing for a scarce goal—the prize, the victory, the win (the exception would be ties). This characteristic creates an uncertainty in game situations regarding the outcome, and this unpredictability is important in creating the tension and excitement for the participants and spectators. Caillois (1961) notes that to maintain the uncertainty in games, the contestants must be equated so each may have a chance to win. Indeed, "the game is no longer pleasing to one who, because he is too well trained or skillful, wins effortlessly and infallibly" (Caillois, 1961, p. 7). Similarly, Loy (1968) argues that the uncertain outcome is the primary factor in creating tension and excitement in any sports contest, and Goffman (1967), in his essay "Where the Action Is," notes the importance of chance-taking in producing thrills.

Additionally, Elias and Dunning (1986) argue that the uncertainty of sport creates the tension and excitement that is necessary for the survival of games and sports. Even the rules of games and sports are designed to maintain that tension and excitement by reducing the likelihood of unfair tactics and undue advantages by one contestant over the other. In Eliasian terminology, this process is described as maintaining the tone or the "tension-balance" of the game (see also Kew, 1990). In short, if one contestant is clearly superior to the other, there is no contest and no excitement, and boredom soon sets in.

Thus in sports we have handicaps, and competitive classifications based on experience, skill level, gender, age, height, weight, and size of school or competing units. And the rules of athletic contests may specify fewer sets in tennis, shorter distances for par in golf, and adjustments in equipment (e.g., size of the ball in basketball, different weights for the field events in track) for different ages and either sex in order to adapt to the assumed variations among contestants. Yet, despite these adjustments some individuals or teams compete against opponents of unequal ability or skill level. In other words, while some contestants will be approximately equal in their performance level, others will be more or less likely to achieve victory. It is in this context that we consider the concept of the underdog in sport and society.

In a competitive situation, the underdog is expected to lose the contest. The concept of the underdog is applied not only in sports but also in political campaigns as well as to the victims of political and social injustice. The term underdog appears to have originated in a popular 19th century song titled, "The Under-Dog in the Fight"; two stanzas of the song are,

> I know that the world, that the great big world
> Will never a moment stop
> To see which dog may be in the fault,
> But will shout for the dog on top.
> But for me, I shall never pause to ask
> Which dog may be in the right
> For my heart will beat, while it beats at all,
> For the under dog in the fight. (Hendrickson, 1987, p. 540)

5   As suggested by the original use of the term underdog, spectators, and fans, at least in American society, are thought to be predisposed to root for the underdog. Yet this assumption has remained unchallenged and unexamined by sociologists of sport. Nor has there been any attempt to incorporate this assumption into a general theory of spectatorship or motivation. In an exploratory way we address some of these concerns. In this paper we first introduce a macrotheoretical perspective of spectating; second, we present some relevant (though exploratory) data gathered from university students; third, a microperspective of motivation is introduced; and finally, some concluding thoughts on the underdog phenomenon are presented.

A Utilitarian Perspective: an Emotional Marketplace

We might proffer a utilitarian based model to explain the underdog effect. But assuming that spectators are hedonistic, that they seek the most rewarding situations, we might initially assume that unattached spectators would root only for athletes and teams most likely to win—for favorites. (We assume that many spectators will have long-term attachments to teams or athletes and will be respectively faithful to these sentimental attachments.) However, when favorites do lose, the situation is most unrewarding for the favorite's supporters. Perhaps spectators even lose face when they stake their reputation and judgment with a favored team that loses.

Therefore, rooting for the favorite is, on the whole, a poor emotional investment. For the unattached spectator, little excitement is gained when the favorite wins because this outcome was expected. And a loss by the favorite must certainly be felt that much more, coming when it was not expected. It would seem, then, that a true hedonist would root only for underdogs. If the underdog should win, the emotional investment is repaid with a good deal of excitement and emotional reward. If on the other hand the underdog loses, the spectator probably will not be particularly surprised and should not especially feel the loss. After all, the spectator knew he or she was rooting for an underdog.

All in all, an investment in an underdog is more rewarding in the emotional marketplace than an investment in a favorite. In summary, because it is unexpected, an underdog's victory is more satisfying than a favorite's and an underdog's loss is much less traumatic. Thus a utilitarian model would indeed predict the underdog effect.

It may well be that this type of reasoning has its value counterpart in the American notions of equity. If fans are guided by this value in their spectating, rooting for the underdog would be the logical product. In this view, the sympathies of unattached fans would lie with the team with the least prestige, the underdog. If the favored team were to win, the inequality in prestige between the teams would remain. But if the underdog wins, the underdog's prestige deficit will be mitigated, if not corrected completely. Interestingly, an underdog does not have to win, but just come close to winning, for its prestige to increase (in the form of a moral victory). To sum up, rooting for the underdog may be an expression in sport of the western ideal of equality. Perhaps fans want little more than to "even up the sides."

Too, one might even conceive of the underdog orientation as one of two opposing worldviews. In one worldview, inequality is seen as a necessity, while in the underdog worldview, inequalities are seen as unjust and needing correction. Some historians have asserted that history consists of the struggle between these two worldviews, with the two alternately and cyclically ascendant (see Schlesinger, 1986). One might even hypothesize that expressions of the underdog in sport (and other fields) would be relatively more common in those cycles when the underdog worldview was predominant. In any event, the underdog worldview can be discerned throughout history.

The history, literature, and mythology of American society and perhaps other western societies are, accordingly, replete with underdogs. David versus Goliath, the dragon slayers, Cinderella, the tortoise and the hare, the "Little Train That Could," the Horatio Alger novels, the "Log Cabin Presidents," the "Impossible Dream," and even the American Revolution all have elements of the underdog effect within them. These and many other examples certainly give dramatic credence to the idea that our cultural values might yield underdog effects within the institution of sport.

Of course, despite the cultural value of equity that seems to have existed for some time in American society, much of American history is in fact the story of inequality (and attempts to overcome such obstacles). Slavery, indentured servitude, the exclusively male franchise, poll taxes, the continuing oppression of minorities, women, gays and lesbians and the poor—all of these, and other shameful aspects of American history, illustrate that the value of equity has often been subverted by appeals to other beliefs (such as Americans' regard for group conformity and their appreciation of material wealth). Within sport, the win-at-any-cost mentality of some coaches, participants, and spectators indicates that equity can easily be disregarded in the pursuit of success. Similarly, recent military ventures in Vietnam, Grenada, Panama, and Iraq demonstrate that equity can easily be manipulated in ways that "justify" a superpower's intervention into the affairs of smaller, poorer nations.

In spite of these transgressions, though, an American value of equity certainly does exist. Indeed, many American movement ideologies—from abolitionism and populism to contemporary feminism and gay liberation—confront oppression and exploitation with calls for equity. Here, it is suggested that equity is the one value from a spectrum of available choices that American spectators use to legitimize their utilitarian based preferences for underdogs.

FINDINGS

In order to test some of these theoretical suggestions, a short questionnaire (see Figure 1) was administered to a convenience sample of 122 university students from a medium-sized university in the Midwest. Eighty-seven of these students were from introductory sociology courses while 35 were from an upper level sociology of sport class. Each student was presented with a scenario in which a highly favored Team A was meeting Team B, the underdog, in a best-of-seven series. Students were asked which team they would prefer to win (in the absence of any prior sentimental attachments); in addition, students were asked to explain their choice. In the second question, students were told that Team B has unexpectedly won the first three games of the series. Students were asked which team they preferred to win the next game only. In a final question, the students were told that the series was even at three games apiece. Again, students were asked whom they preferred to win the final and deciding game.

Of the 122 students, 99 (or 81.1%) originally said they preferred Team B, given no more knowledge than the fact that Team B was not favored. Yet in the second question, approximately half (49) of those 99 said they would switch their allegiance to Team A if Team B (the original underdog) were to win the first

---

Assume that in a play-off series Team A is highly favored to defeat Team B. If you *did not* have any attachments to either team, which team would you prefer to win the series?
Team A _____
Team B _____
Explain your choice:

Assume that during the play-offs between Team A (the favorite) and Team B, Team B wins the first three games in a best-of-seven series. Which team would you prefer to win the next game?
Team A _____
Team B _____
Explain your choice:

Assume the play-offs have progressed and each team has won three games. Which team would you prefer to win the final and deciding game?
TEAM A _____
TEAM B _____
Explain your choice:

Figure 1. Questionnaire used to determine preference for underdog vs. favorite

three games of the series. Of this group that did change their allegiance, 37 of 44 (5 of the 49 did not make a third choice) said they would change their preference again—back to Team B—if the series were to wind up tied at three games apiece.

As Table 1 indicates, there was little variation in the responses either by gender or by course level. Apparently such variables do not seriously affect the underdog preference. Indeed, none of the gender differences is statistically significant. And only one of the course-level differences approaches significance; there, students in a sociology of sport class were more likely than introductory sociology students to initially favor the underdog. One plausible explanation for this difference might be that students who are strongly involved in sport, presumably those in a sociology of sport class, have been better socialized into the norms for preferring sports underdogs. Of course more research is needed to investigate this suggestion.

If nothing else, these data show how pervasive and attractive is the notion of rooting for the underdog. Given the absence of attachments to teams or athletes, an overwhelming majority was drawn to the underdog. These data also point to how fluid the underdog label can be. Once underdog Team B had won three games, many respondents opted to root for Team A. Apparently Team A was, at least for some, the new underdog. One respondent wrote, "Team A has suddenly become the underdog. Throw out all of past records because the playoffs are a new season and Team B is on top."

But, as mentioned above, once Team A did catch up in the series, a majority returned to rooting for Team B. Apparently Team B had reclaimed its underdog status. Many of the explanations provided by the respondents spoke directly to the theoretical assertions made above. For example, many respondents emphasize the emotional payoff an investment (the utilitarian model) in the underdog can provide. One wrote, "The unexpected makes it more exciting. If the favored team always won, it would be far less exciting." Another said, "Because they are the underdog, it would be a better game, to see if there was a struggle for a win." And several alluded to the surprise value an underdog's win provides. One simply wrote, "If Team A was picked to win, then if Team B won, it would be a surprise." And another noted the lack of risk in rooting for the underdog: "It's fun to root for the underdog, even if they lose, it's not a big disappointment." One student mentioned a different pleasure that those who root for underdogs can

TABLE 1 STUDENT RESPONSES TO UNDERDOG QUESTIONNAIRE

	GENDER		CLASSES	
	Females	Males	Intro. soc.	Sport soc.
Initially favored the underdog (Team B)	55 of 69 79.7%	44 of 53 83.0%	67 of 87* 77.0%	32 of 35* 91.4%
Switched to new underdog (Team A)	25 of 55 45.5%	24 of 44 54.5%	30 of 67 44.8%	19 of 32 59.4%
Reverted to original underdog (Team B)	21 of 24† 87.5%	16 of 20† 80.0%	24 of 29† 82.8%	13 of 15† 86.7%

* This difference is significant at the $p = .07$ level.

† Five respondents did not answer this question.

enjoy: "I like to see the underdog win. It makes the series more exciting and dramatic. Plus I could 'ride' the fans of Team A."

Other respondents discussed rooting for the underdog in terms of the equity argument. Many implied they would be more satisfied with the underdog's victory because it would restore equity. One wrote, "By Team B winning, it will keep one group from getting too arrogant while lifting the confidence and pride of another group. It will keep the two teams closer to a happy medium." The same respondent explained switching allegiance to Team A after Team B took the first three games by saying, "It would be too embarrassing for both teams if Team B won in straight games."

In regard to the switch in allegiance, another explained, "The playoffs should be competitive, and the teams should have the same strength. It's more exciting when the teams are close and the series gets dragged out." And yet another said, "I would like it to be a close series. I wouldn't want either team to get blown out and embarrassed." Another wrote, "There's not enough drama in a sweep, even if Team B is a big underdog."

The common theme in these responses is that the spectators see the underdog as having the potential for pulling the upset and providing pleasure. In short, by creating an underdog, a special kind of tension and pleasurable excitement is evoked in an unexciting game situation. Hence, identification with the underdog is consistent with the tension-balance figuration discussed by Elias and Dunning (1986). And likewise, at least some spectators consciously relate their rooting for the underdog to cultural values of equality.

A Motivational Perspective

Utilizing a microlevel of analysis, if a team or person is an underdog in a competitive situation, this position may promote an increased incentive to overcome the odds. Hochschild (1983) postulates that people manage their feelings to achieve a particular level of performance or behavior. In sports, athletes engage in emotion to work through the mental and physical preparation for a contest. For example, Zurcher (1982) reported on the buildup of emotions prior to a football game, and Gallmeier (1987) examined the staging of emotions at professional hockey games. While the Zurcher and Gallmeier studies describe the dramaturgical aspects of staging and scripting of emotions in team sports, Snyder (1990) analyzed the feelings of individual performers, women gymnasts, prior to and during their meets.

Using the microframework of emotions, to be labeled as the underdog may be used as a means of emotionally psyching up for the event. That is, knowing that one is not expected to win may motivate the underdog to exert a greater effort to achieve victory. Thus the underdogs may play with abandon because they have nothing to lose. The following statements from our survey of students illustrate the motivational aspects of being an underdog:

> The advantage of being an underdog is that the favorites may be overconfident and they will leave themselves open to defeat. If they display this overconfidence, this might motivate the underdog to work harder.

The advantage of being an underdog is that this title gives added incentive to win. The underdog can win by effectively using this mental and emotional advantage to overcome superior athletic ability.

I would like to be an underdog. To overcome odds is the great American dream. This is depicted in movies like the Rocky series. The underdog status gives me the extra lift to win.

The underdog team must usually work harder and more efficiently to win any game, I enjoy seeing the underdog team win especially when the opposing team is heavily favored. It gives me a sense that anything can happen.

Conclusion

Given the prevalence of the underdog effect, further research might reveal social characteristics that influence the decision of spectators to root for the underdog athlete or team. Are there social class, subcultural, or intercultural differences that figure into the spectators' decisions as to which underdogs are most worthy of support? Our exploratory data indicate that the underdog role is evident in the minds of spectators who are not committed to either contestant.

Worth additional consideration is the question of how spectators at some contests are able, notwithstanding the potential emotional payoffs of preferring underdogs, to root for favorites. As noted above, we believe sentimental attachments to contestants may prevent many spectators from considering the utilitarian benefits of rooting for an underdog. But it is not clear how such sentiments are formed. The influence of geography, social stratification, family, and other variables on such attachments must therefore be studied. In like manner, the exact nature of viewing an event may alter the underdog effect, and this fact should be considered in future analysis. It may be that spectators' preferences are affected by paying admission or by joining a crowd of partisans. On the other hand, the experience of watching the game on television or listening to it on the radio may be affected by the preferences and allegiances of announcers.

We suspect that the underdog effect would be most evident in settings without any one-sided narration from fans or the media. Thus we would predict that the underdog effect would be better seen among spectators at a sparsely attended collegiate tennis match held at a neutral site than among spectators at a Notre Dame football game. Likewise, we would expect a purer underdog effect among viewers of a TV network baseball game with "objective" announcers than among viewers of a game called by local announcers.

We are suggesting that supporting the underdog, like sports gambling, provides a form of "action" (a game within the game) that satisfies a quest for excitement regarding the outcome of the contest. Indeed, this similarity between gambling and the underdog phenomenon is worthy of additional analysis. Guttmann (1986, p. 179) notes that "there are those who cannot enjoy a sports event if they have not bet on the outcome," and Smith (1990, p. 274) considers one of the appeals of sports gambling to be its ability "to relieve boredom and generate excitement."

Likewise, Goffman (1967) emphasizes the thrill of risk-taking that is inherent in gambling. To root for the underdog is to place one's sentiments on the team with the longest odds of winning. Consequently, as we have argued, this is a sure bet: It serves to enhance the level of excitement in the outcome of the contest while leaving the spectator with everything to gain and nothing to lose. True sports bettors will not necessarily place their bets on the underdog, however, unless the handicapper's odds are sufficient to attract money to the underdog. Apparently the desire to win some prize, however small, accounts for the tendency to bet on the contestant who is the prohibitive favorite (Eadington, 1976, p. 113).

Additionally, to support the underdog seems to have some legitimation from the western value of equity. Thus the mantle of "athletic hero" is often accorded those who overcome the odds of achieving their goal. However, we do not know whether this tendency is evident across many different cultures. Perhaps the support for the underdog is a reflection of the meritocratic ideology that anyone can make it to the top if they try hard enough. Thus the underdog concept may vary with the social structure of the society. At a microlevel, to be an underdog may increase the level of arousal and tension and thus promote an overall motivation to overcome the apparent superior opponent; or perhaps it decreases the motivation of the superior team or player due to their overconfidence.

The media frequently seek to use the underdog role as a way of promoting the level of interest in a contest between unequal opponents. In promoting a contest, the media entice viewers and readers to speculate about whether the upset can be pulled off, and if indeed this happens, the media will focus on the human interest associated with achieving the unlikely goal. In this process the underdog concept is commodified for the marketplace and becomes a part of the overall spectacle and theatrics of modern sport (see Sewart, 1987).

In conclusion, as we have emphasized, the fundamental attraction of a contest is the emotional excitement associated with the uncertainty of its outcome. If the contestants are of unequal caliber, the tension and excitement are reduced, perhaps to the point of boredom. By focusing attention on the underdog, a measure of excitement and action is returned to a potentially uninteresting event. In this respect the underdog role is a way of maintaining the core function of competitive events.

References

Caillois, R. (1961). *Man, play and games.* New York: The Free Press.
Eadington, W. (1976). *Gambling and society.* Springfield, IL: C.C Thomas.
Elias, N., & Dunning, E. (1986). The quest for excitement in leisure. In N. Elias & E. Dunning (Eds.), *Quest for excitement* (pp. 63–90). New York: Basil Blackwell.
Gallmeier, C. (1987). Putting on the game face: The staging of emotions in professional hockey. *Sociology of Sport Journal,* 4, 347–362.
Goffman, E. (1967). *Interaction ritual.* New York: Doubleday.
Guttmann, A. (1986). *Sports spectators.* New York: Columbia University Press.
Hendrickson, R. (1987). *The Facts on File encyclopedia of word and phrase origins.* New York: Facts on File Publications.
Hochschild, A. (1983). *The managed heart.* Berkeley: University of California Press.
Kew, F. (1990). The development of games: An endogenous explanation. *International Review for the Sociology of Sport,* 25, 251–267.

Loy, J. (1968). The nature of sport: A definitional effort. In J. Loy & G. Kenyon (Eds.), *Sport, culture, and society.* London: Collier-Macmillan.
Schlesinger, A.M. (1986). *The cycles of American history.* Boston: Houghton Mifflin.
Sewart, J. (1987). The commodification of sport. *International Review for the Sociology of Sport,* 22, 171–192.
Smith, G. (1990). Pools, parlays, and point spreads: A sociological consideration of the legalization of sports gambling. *Sociology of Sport Journal,* 7, 271–286.
Snyder, E.E. (1990). Emotion in sport: A case study of collegiate women gymnasts. *Sociology of Sport Journal,* 7, 254–270.
Zurcher, L. (1982). The staging of emotion: A dramaturgical analysis. *Symbolic Interaction,* 5, 1–22.

Questions for Discussion

1. This article was written for the specialized audience of a professional journal. How might the authors revise this article for the general readership of *Sports Illustrated?*
2. What do you think of the illustrations? Are more illustrations necessary? If so, identify specific tables or figures you would like to see. If not, explain why you think the two illustrations are sufficient.
3. Explain the organization of this essay. Why is it organized this way? Is the organization effective? Why do you think it is or isn't?
4. Notice that the authors discuss the political implications of their subject. What is their purpose in doing so? Does it contribute to their credibility? Does it clarify the subject? Does it motivate the audience?
5. How might the authors integrate knowledge by participation? Identify specific passages that could be revised.

Opportunities for Writing

1. Analyze your reasons for supporting a particular athlete or athletic team. How long have you supported this athlete or team? Why? Are you a faithful supporter or is your support variable? What either keeps you faithful or keeps you coming back?
2. Using a questionnaire like Frazier and Snyder's, analyze the underdog concept in politics. Are voters more or less likely to support a candidate perceived as the underdog?
3. For a special article in your school's newspaper, interview men and women athletes at your school to determine if athletes prefer to be perceived as favorites or as underdogs. Compare and contrast the attitudes of men and women athletes.
4. For a specific athletic contest, examine the media coverage given to the favorite and to the underdog. What kinds of things do commentators say about the favorite? What visual images of the favorite are displayed? How much time is given to coverage of the favorite? How does this coverage differ from that given to the underdog?

Communication Stereotypes
Is Interracial Communication Possible?

REBECCA LEONARD AND DON C. LOCKE

Rebecca Leonard and Don C. Locke are both on the faculty at North Carolina State University. Leonard is an associate professor and coordinator of advising in the Department of Speech Communication. Locke is Professor and Head of the Department of Counselor Education. "Communication Stereotypes: Is Interracial Communication Possible?" focuses on how the perceptions that blacks and whites have of each other prevent the two groups from "genuine interpersonal interactions." This essay was published in the Journal of Black Studies *(March 1993) and follows the APA style of documentation.*

If Blacks and Whites are ever to engage in genuine communication, many barriers or obstacles must be removed. One of the more pervasive hindrances to authentic interracial relations is stereotyping. Blacks and Whites hold a variety of stereotypes of each other, often negative, and these racial stereotypes have generally remained unchanged over the years.

Katz and Braly (1933) tackled the question of racial stereotypes early. They asked 100 White college students to choose from a prepared list of traits those that characterized certain racial groups. These Princeton University students characterized "Negroes" as superstitious, lazy, happy-go-lucky, ignorant, musical, ostentatious, very religious, stupid, physically dirty, naive, slovenly, and unreliable.

Eight years after the Katz and Braly study, Bayton (1946) suggested that, although several studies had been conducted in which White students were asked to assign traits to Blacks and other racial groups, few studies investigated how Blacks and other racial minorities viewed Whites. His study, conducted at Virginia State College, a Black school, questioned 100 students using the Katz and Braly list of traits. Bayton found that Black students characterized Whites as intelligent, industrious, scientifically minded, progressive, ambitious, peace loving, sportsmanlike, sophisticated, conceited, and neat. He also found that Black students shared many of the White stereotypes of Negroes. The Black students attributed traits to themselves such as musical, superstitious, very religious, happy-go-lucky, loud, lazy, progressive, imitative, intelligent, and faithful. Bayton (1946) concluded that "propaganda . . . has exerted a much greater influence than personal association" (p. 102) in the choices made by Black respondents. The Black students had apparently adopted the prevailing White attitude about their own race.

The Katz and Braly (1933) method was used again by Meenes (1943) at Howard University. Meenes, in an effort to determine if attitudes had changed over a 7-year period, surveyed Black Howard University students in 1935 and in 1942. He discovered that the Black student attitude toward White Americans, although similar in the 2 years tested, had become slightly more favorable. In the 1935 group, the students chose words such as *mercenary, deceitful,* and *boastful* to characterize Whites. But, in 1942, these words did not appear. However, both groups listed Whites as intelligent, materialistic, conceited, progressive, ambitious, industrious, and pleasure loving.

All of these studies used the original Katz and Braly list of 84 traits and were primarily concerned with general racial stereotypes. But Ogawa (1971) studied the communication stereotypes of 100 White UCLA students of Black, Mexican, and Japanese students in small discussion groups. Ogawa adjusted the original 84-word list of traits to include ethnic communication characteristics. Blacks were perceived as argumentative, emotional, aggressive, straightforward, critical, sensitive, ostentatious, defiant, hostile, open, responsive, and intelligent, in that order. Rich (1974) questioned "Black ghetto residents" about their perceptions of the communication behavior of Whites. Whites were seen as evasive, critical, conservative, ignorant, boastful, aggressive, arrogant, ostentatious, concealing, emotional, individualistic, and nonmilitant. Rich concluded:

> The stereotypes blacks hold of white communicators are so negative that, with the influence of selective perception reinforcing these negative views, productive interracial communication is rendered difficult, if not impossible, at times. The study also reveals a great lack of trust and empathy between blacks and whites in communication situations; the resultant interpersonal gap must be overcome if interracial communication is to occur without the disruption caused by antagonism and hostility. (pp. 61–62)

It is important to note that the two groups of subjects in these studies were quite different. Rich's subjects were Black ghetto residents, and Ogawa's were White students of UCLA. It appears that differences noted in the two lists of perceptions were caused by such factors as socioeconomic class, age, or geographical location, rather than race alone.

METHOD

In this study, subjects were asked to choose from a list of communication traits those that best characterized the communication behavior of the other racial group. Subjects were all college students and were attending school at either a predominantly Black (99%) or an integrated campus (93% White; 7% Black). Mean age of the Black respondents was 20.97 years, and of the White respondents 21.29 years. Of the 120 Black and 106 White respondents, 32 were freshmen, 62 sophomores, 57 juniors, and 75 seniors. The following research questions were posed:

1. What are Black college students' stereotypes of the communication behavior of Whites?
2. What are White college students' stereotypes of the communication behavior of Blacks?
3. Have perceptions of the communication traits of the other racial group changed since the Rich (1974) and Ogawa (1971) studies?
4. Has desegregation, with its assumed increased racial contact, produced a change in communication stereotypes?

The method used by Katz and Braly (1933) was once again followed in this study. The list used by Ogawa (1971) and by Rich (1974), which included 57 terms reflecting communication behavior, was adjusted by replacing terms that did not clearly describe communication (such as *conservative* and *imitative*) with more specific communication terms (such as *supportive* and *articulate*). The final list was composed of the 66 items contained in Table 1.

The following written instructions were given to the subjects:

> Read through the list of words below and circle which words seem to you typical of the communicative behavior of (White) (Black) Americans.

TABLE 1 LIST OF TERMS

Attentive	Organized	Directive
Hesitant	Alert	Passive
Intelligent	Straightforward	Evasive
Argumentative	Sensitive	Conventional
Critical	Perceptive	Persistent
Practical	Supportive	Ostentatious (showy)
Submissive	Agreeable	Considerate
Deceptive	Calm	Manipulative
Boastful	Quiet	Loud
Ignorant	Quarrelsome	Courteous
Witty	Dogmatic	Cooperative
Active	Arrogant	Noisy
Emotional	Concealing	Friendly
Efficient	Aggressive	Anxious
Smooth	Uninvolved	Hostile
Resistant	Imaginative	Reserved
Nondirective	Open	Talkative
Jovial	Individualistic	Rude
Inarticulate	Articulate	Defiant
Soft-spoken	Silent	Overbearing
Humble	Responsive	Demanding
Conforming	Unintelligible	Caring

When they completed their list of traits, subjects were asked to choose the 10 words from their list that they believed to be *most* representative of the communicative behavior of the other racial group.

RESULTS

Table 2 presents the 12 communication traits most frequently assigned to Blacks by White students (left column) and to Whites by Black students (right column). Whites most frequently chose the trait *loud* to describe the communication of Blacks. A total of 62% of the Whites chose that trait, far more than the next trait (*ostentatious,* 44%), and far more than the first traits on the other list (*demanding* and *manipulative,* 43% each). *Aggressive* (42%), *active* (41%), and *boastful* (37%) completed the top 5 traits assigned to Blacks. Two of the 12 top traits assigned to Blacks were words not included among the choices on Ogawa's checklist, *active* (ranked fourth) and *friendly* (ranked seventh). But of the 12 traits most frequently assigned to Blacks in this research, only 5 duplicated Ogawa's top list: *ostentatious, aggressive, straightforward, emotional,* and

TABLE 2 TWELVE MOST FREQUENTLY ASSIGNED TRAITS (RANK ORDERED)

	ASSIGNED TO BLACKS				ASSIGNED TO WHITES		
Rank	Trait	%	Ogawa %	Rank	Trait	%	Rich %
1.	Loud	62		1.	Demanding	43	
2.	Ostentatious	44	19	2.	Manipulative	43	
3.	Aggressive	42	32	3.	Organized	37	
4.	Active	41		4.	Rude	36	
5.	Boastful	37		5.	Critical	32	26
6.	Talkative	33		6.	Aggressive	31	22
7.	Friendly	32		7.	Arrogant	31	21
8.	Noisy	32		8.	Boastful	28	23
9.	Straightforward	32	26	9.	Hostile	26	
10.	Emotional	30	35	10.	Ignorant	25	24
11.	Argumentative	29	40	11.	Deceptive	23	
12.	Witty	29		12.	Noisy	23	

argumentative. The percentage of respondents to these terms varied considerably from that in the Ogawa study. For example, 40% of Ogawa's respondents listed *argumentative* as a Black communication trait, whereas only 29% of respondents in the present research assigned *argumentative* to Blacks. Only 19% of Ogawa's respondents listed *ostentatious,* whereas 44% of respondents in this study did. Forty-two percent of respondents in this study listed *aggressive,* 32% of Ogawa's did. Only 2 of the traits, *straightforward* and *emotional* varied little (32% and 26% for *straightforward,* and 30% and 35% for *emotional*).

Black students most frequently chose *demanding* and *manipulative* to describe Whites' communication behavior, both traits chosen by 43% of the Black respondents. Black students also perceived Whites as organized (37%), rude (36%), and critical (32%). Four of the top 12 traits assigned to Whites were not among the choices on the Rich (1974) checklist: *manipulative, demanding, organized,* and *deceptive.* In fact, the top 3 traits in this research were terms not used by Rich in her research. But 5 of this list of 12 were also on Rich's top 12 list: *critical* (32% this research, 26% Rich's research); *aggressive* (31%, 22%); *arrogant* (31%, 21%); *boastful* (28%, 23%,); and *ignorant* (25%, 24%). The percentages of respondents listing each of these traits were similar in the two studies.

Only three traits (*aggressive, boastful,* and *noisy*) appeared on both the Black and White lists. However, the rank order and percentage of respondents differed. *Aggressive* was 3rd on the list of traits assigned to Blacks, with 42% of the White students listing it as a Black communication trait. However, *aggressive* appeared 6th on the list of traits assigned to Whites, with 31% of the Black respondents choosing *aggressive* to describe Whites. *Boastful* was 5th on the list of traits given Blacks (37%) and 8th on the list of White traits (28%). *Noisy* appeared 8th on the list of traits assigned to Blacks (32%) and 12th on the list of traits assigned to Whites (23%).

The authors rated all 66 terms on the checklist as either threatening or nonthreatening. A word was rated as threatening if it implied potential danger, punishment, or intent to hurt or abuse. Words that were clearly opposite of these criteria or more neutral in meaning were considered nonthreatening words. Of the 12 communication traits most frequently assigned to Blacks, 6 (50%) were threatening (*loud, aggressive, boastful, noisy, emotional,* and *argumentative*). Six traits (50%) were nonthreatening (*ostentatious, active, friendly, witty, talkative,* and *straightforward*). For traits assigned to Whites, Black students selected 10 terms (83%) that the researchers had identified as threatening (*demanding, manipulative, rude, critical, arrogant, aggressive, boastful, hostile, deceptive,* and *noisy*). Two of the 12 traits assigned most frequently to Whites (17%) were nonthreatening (*organized* and *ignorant*).

Table 3 lists the 12 communication traits least frequently assigned to Blacks by White students (left column) and to Whites by Black students (right column), as well as the percentages of respondents choosing each trait. All traits appearing in either column were chosen by fewer than 8 respondents. Two terms, *calm* and *humble*, were not chosen by White respondents, and therefore appear as the two least assigned traits in the left column. Six traits appeared on both lists: *humble, silent, articulate, passive, quiet,* and *submissive*.

Only one threatening term appeared on either list of least assigned traits. *Dogmatic* was chosen by one White respondent and therefore appears third on the list of traits least assigned to Blacks.

Discussion

15   Black and White students perceived one another as aggressive, boastful, and noisy. A large percentage of White students saw Blacks as loud, a characteristic that did not appear on the list in the Ogawa (1971) study, nor was it among the traits frequently chosen by Blacks in this research to describe Whites. Apparently Whites' perceptions of the communication traits of Blacks have changed since Ogawa's study. Loud as a communication trait is not only a new choice, but it indicates a very strong impression. Sixty-two percent of White

TABLE 3 TWELVE LEAST FREQUENTLY ASSIGNED TRAITS (RANK ORDERED)

	ASSIGNED TO BLACKS			ASSIGNED TO WHITES	
Rank	**Trait**	**%**	**Rank**	**Trait**	**%**
1.	Calm	0	1.	Smooth	.008
2.	Humble	0	2.	Quiet	.02
3.	Dogmatic	.009	3.	Passive	.02
4.	Reserved	.009	4.	Silent	.02
5.	Silent	.009	5.	Humble	.02
6.	Articulate	.02	6.	Considerate	.03
7.	Efficient	.02	7.	Jovial	.04
8.	Conventional	.03	8.	Inarticulate	.04
9.	Passive	.03	9.	Submissive	.05
10.	Quiet	.04	10.	Articulate	.06
11.	Evasive	.05	11.	Imaginative	.06
12.	Submissive	.05	12.	Soft-spoken	.06

students chose *loud,* more than any other single trait on the checklist. Black students in this research perceived Whites as *manipulative* and *demanding,* terms that were not chosen by Whites to describe Blacks. These Black students also viewed Whites as quite different from Rich's (1984) subjects.

That *loud, manipulative,* and *demanding* are the top-ranked terms seems consistent with Myrdal's (1944) conclusions in his classic research on race, when he reported that Blacks often expressed anger when asked to interact with White people, and Whites expressed fear in similar circumstances. If Blacks are loud as an expression of anger, then Whites may fear them. If Whites, out of their fear, are manipulative and demanding, Blacks may respond with anger. Indeed, these emotional responses may reinforce each other in a circular manner. These reactions of fear and anger serve to keep Black and White communicators apart.

Of the terms chosen from both lists, 14 of the 24 (58%) reflected threat to the receiver. Only 4 of the 24 (17%) were nonthreatening. Obviously, Black and White students still perceive interracial interactions as potentially threatening. But Blacks perceived greater threat than did Whites, because 83% of the traits assigned to Whites were threatening, and only 50% of the traits assigned to Blacks were threatening. If Blacks and Whites predict interactions with persons of the other race will be abusive, punishing, and dangerous, then we cannot expect them to initiate interactions very frequently. Even when interactions are initiated, the participants are likely to be hesitant, reserved, and concealing.

The individual traits chosen in this research changed somewhat from the Rich (1974) and Ogawa (1971) studies. Only 5 of the top 12 traits assigned to each group duplicated the earlier results, and the order of appearance on the list also differed. But the overall sense of the descriptions remains generally negative and threatening, especially the Black respondents' perceptions of White's communication behavior. It seems that Whites hold a more favorable impression of the communication of the other group than do Blacks. For example, a large percentage of White students chose traits such as *friendly, talkative,* and *witty* to describe Blacks. But all of the top traits assigned to Whites were negative, except *organized.* Apparently, increased interracial contact in the past 20 years has had little effect on mutual perceptions. In fact, these data indicate that interracial perceptions are still generally negative and, as such, serve to keep Blacks and Whites from engaging in genuine interpersonal interactions.

Six of the 12 traits assigned least frequently to both Blacks and Whites were the same: *humble, silent, articulate, passive, quiet,* and *submissive.* Apparently neither group of respondents perceived the other as reticent, timid, or taciturn. In fact, as the previous discussion indicates, both Black and White students saw one another as not only verbose but also aggressive and noisy. The traits least frequently assigned to both groups support the impressions implied by the list of most frequently assigned traits.

Gibb's (1961) standard work on defensive and supportive communication climates gives us another framework within which to view interactions between Blacks and Whites. Gibb defined defensive communication as likely to occur "when an individual perceives threat or anticipates threat" (p. 141). Gibb then suggested six behaviors that he believed produced a defensive climate and six behaviors that he believed would contribute to a supportive climate, one that reduces defensiveness and therefore allows "the receivers [to] become better able to concentrate upon the structure, the content, and the cognitive meanings of the message" (p. 142). The six traits producing defensive climates are evaluation, control, strategy, neutrality, superiority, and certainty. Their counterparts, producing supportive climates, are description, problem orientation, spontaneity, empathy, equality, and provisionalism.

A large number of the top traits on both lists could be considered defensive communication traits, but more of these have been attributed to Whites by Blacks than to Blacks by Whites. Whites perceived Blacks as loud, aggressive, talkative, noisy, and argumentative—all behaviors associated with the defensive communication trait control. (*Argumentativeness* might also communicate certainty.) Whites also described Blacks as ostentatious and boastful, behaviors of superiority. Seven of the 12 traits that Whites assigned to Blacks fit into Gibb's (1961) concept of those that produce a defensive climate.

Ten of the top 12 communication traits assigned to Whites by Blacks are clearly of the defensive type: *demanding* (control and certainty), *manipulative* (strategy), *rude* (control), *critical* (evaluation), *aggressive* (control), *arrogant* (superiority), *boastful* (superiority), *hostile* (evaluation and control), *deceptive* (strategy), and *noisy* (control). Clearly, Blacks perceive a highly defensive climate when communicating or when thinking of communicating with Whites.

Few of the top 12 traits on either list could be defined as characteristics of a supportive climate. Blacks saw Whites as organized, a behavior that might be seen as one of problem orientation, the opposite of control. Gibb (1961) says that behaviors of thinking problems through in a clear and organized manner contribute to a supportive climate. Whites chose 3 terms in the top 12 traits assigned to Blacks, which can be seen as supportive: *friendly* (spontaneity and empathy), *emotional* (empathy), and *witty* (spontaneity). Whites apparently perceive Blacks in contradictory ways, as projecting both defensive and supportive climates, although more often defensive. But Blacks strongly expressed their impression of the defensive communication behaviors of Whites.

Mehrabian (1981) proposed an alternative way of viewing interactions in his three-dimensional model. One dimension of his communication model is that of immediacy, or liking and approach. "People approach what they like and avoid what they don't like" (Mehrabian, 1981, p. 22). Although Mehrabian focused primarily on nonverbal correlates of liking or disliking, there are implications of his liking metaphor in this research. Whites are unlikely to approach Blacks if they perceive their behavior as threatening and defensive, as the results of this research indicate. Conversely, Blacks, perceiving or anticipating a threat in interactions with Whites, will probably not approach Whites. With little immediacy or approach in their mutual behaviors, it is certain that Blacks and Whites will not perceive or experience liking of the other. The resultant communication, if indeed there is any, will probably be hostile or, at best, neutral. Few close and trusting relationships can result.

25   Although the conclusions from this research serve to answer the research questions posed, they also raise additional issues and concerns. For example, at what age were these stereotypes acquired? From what interactions or in what

settings were they acquired? Future research should assess the communication stereotypes in different age groups.

Far more important are questions regarding exactly what people do with their stereotypes, specifically, how they operationalize or implement their beliefs at school, at work, or in social situations. Stereotyped beliefs have implications beyond simply being manipulative, demanding, and loud. Is a person who is perceived as demanding likely to be perceived as trustworthy or honest? Is a person who is perceived as loud likely to be perceived as competent or likable? These communication stereotypes, translated into observable qualities, suggest far more important personality or character traits.

Another area of interest is the role of the self-fulfilling prophecy in viewing members of racial groups. Translation of the research data into practical situations might raise questions regarding the degree to which Whites are demanding and manipulative and the degree to which Blacks are loud. Reasonable requests by Whites might be perceived by Blacks as demanding. Likewise, reasonable noise levels might be perceived as loud by Whites. The stereotype becomes a handy device to confirm beliefs and expectations.

Is interracial communication possible? Are there insurmountable obstacles or barriers to genuine interracial communication? Although barriers still exist, acquiring knowledge of existing stereotypes is a major step in the process of developing interracial interactions. As in any interpersonal communication situation, participants in interracial interactions must be aware of the difficulties they face and be willing to confront them directly and honestly. Because interracial communication is desirable, both Black and White communicators must work to make it possible, despite the stereotypes inherent in the communication situation.

References

Bayton, J. A. (1946). The racial stereotypes of Negro college students. *Journal of Abnormal Social Psychology, 36,* 97–102.
Gibb, J. R. (1961). Defensive communication. *Journal of Communication, 11,* 141–48.
Katz, D., & Braly, K. (1933). Racial stereotypes of one hundred college students. *Journal of Abnormal Social Psychology, 28,* 280–290.
Meenes, M. (1943). A comparison of racial stereotypes of 1935 and 1942. *Journal of Social Psychology, 17,* 327–336.
Mehrabian, A. (1981). *Silent messages.* Belmont, CA: Wadsworth.
Myrdal, G. (1944). *An American dilemma.* New York: Harper & Brothers.
Ogawa, D. M. (1971). Small-group communication stereotypes of Black Americans. *Journal of Black Studies, 1,* 273–281.
Rich, A. L. (1974). *Interracial communication.* New York: Harper & Row.

Questions for Discussion

1. Do you consider the authors credible sources of information on this topic? Explain your answer.
2. What is the thesis of this article? How do the authors try to support their thesis? Is the supporting information sufficient? plausible? pertinent?

3. What is the subordinate aim of this essay? Cite specific passages to support your answer.
4. Notice the organization of this article: introduction and review of earlier studies, explanation of methods, report of results, and analysis and conclusions. Is this organization appropriate? Is it effective? How would you organize this information?
5. Is the final paragraph a satisfactory ending? If you think it is, explain why. If you think it isn't, explain how you would revise it.

Opportunities for Writing

1. Analyze race relationships as depicted on television. Focus your analysis on a particular type of television program (e.g., soap operas, game shows, situation comedies, police dramas). Compose your essay for the television section of your local newspaper.
2. After interviewing students from different racial groups, write a report for school administrators on the current state of race relations at your school. How do the students you interviewed perceive the situation? What similarities and differences do you notice? How representative are the students you interviewed?
3. Using Leonard and Locke's list of communication traits, analyze your communicative behavior. Which traits do you genuinely believe apply to you? Why? Give examples of times you have displayed such traits.
4. Trace the history of race relations within your community. Start your investigation by examining old issues of your local newspaper and by interviewing retired city officials. Has your community ever experienced racial tensions or violence? If so, when and why? If not, how has your community avoided such incidents?

Using Color Effectively
Designing to Human Specifications

GERALD M. MURCH

Gerald M. Murch received his doctorate in natural sciences (physics, physiology, and experimental psychology) from the University of Göttingen, West Germany. He has directed the Human Factors Research Group within the Applied Research Labs of Tektronix, Inc. In addition, Murch has also been professor of experimental psychology and director of the Human Color Vision Lab at Portland State University. In this article, Murch reviews some research on color, human perception, and human factors, and then offers some guidelines for its effective use in texts. Writing for a professional readership about a specialized subject, Murch integrates headings and figures into his text. "Using Color Effectively" appeared in Technical Communication *in 1985 and follows the style guidelines for the journal at that time by including superscript numbers in the text and notes at the end of the essay.*

The human visual system's capacity and capability to process color can be applied as design criteria for color displays. This paper reviews key elements in the visual domain of color, encompassing the visual, perceptual, and cognitive modes, and develops a series of recommendations for effective color usage based on these elements.

Color can be a powerful communication tool. Used properly, it can enhance the effectiveness of information. Improperly used, however, color can also seriously impair communication. Thus it is important to establish and follow some basic guidelines for effective color usage. Unfortunately, no one set of guidelines can cover all applications.

Up to now, color has been used almost exclusively in a qualitative rather than a quantitative fashion, i.e., showing that one item is "different from" another rather than displaying relationships of degree. A typical example would be color-coding each layer of a multilayer circuit board. Color serves to differentiate the layers but says nothing about their relationships. A simple quantitative extension of the multilayer circuit board might involve placing the layers in spectral order, with the first layer red, the second orange, and so on, following the popular mnemonic ROY G. BIV (red, orange, yellow, green, blue, indigo, violet). The demands for the proper use of color increase when color is used quantitatively to show progressing change.

Basically, effective color usage depends upon matching the physiological, perceptual, and cognitive aspects of the human visual system. This paper reviews some well documented aspects of these visual-system capacities and develops some basic principles that should allow us to improve graphics systems by using color properly.

Physiology of Color

In understanding how we see color, it is important to realize that color is not a physical entity. Color is a sensation, like taste or smell, that is tied to the properties of our nervous system.

Figure 1 shows the light wavelengths to which the human eye is sensitive, along with the corresponding color sensed. The color sensation results from the

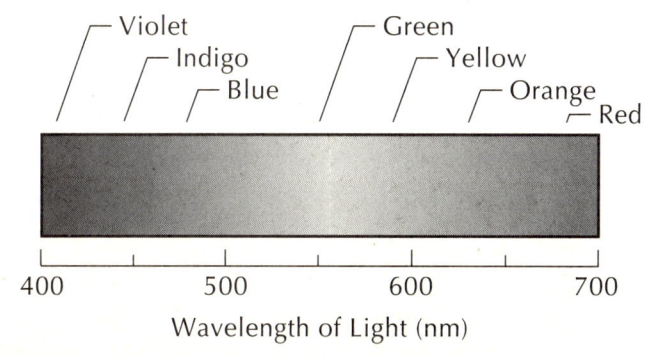

Figure 1. The color spectrum of human vision

interaction of light with a color-sensitive nervous system. Most importantly, individuals can have vastly different color-discrimination capabilities because of differences in the eye's lens, its retina, and other parts of the visual system.

The Lens

The lens of the human eye is not color corrected. This causes chromostereopsis, an effect that causes two pure colors at the same distance to appear to be at different distances. For most people, reds appear closer and blues more distant. In fact, short wavelengths—pure blue—always focus in front of the retina and thus appear defocused. This phenomenon is most noticeable at night when deep-blue signs seem fuzzy and out of focus, while other colors appear sharp.[1]

Lens transmissivity also has an effect. The lens absorbs almost twice as much energy in the blue region as in the yellow or red region. Also, a pigment in the retina's center transmits yellow while absorbing blue. The net result is a relative insensitivity to shorter wavelengths (cyan to deep blue) and enhanced sensitivity to longer wavelengths (yellows and oranges).[2]

As we grow older, lens yellowing increases, which makes us increasingly insensitive to blues. Similarly, aging reduces the transmittance of the eye's fluids, which makes colors appear less vivid and bright. Actually, age aside, there is normally a great deal of variation, with some people's eyes being very transparent and others' naturally yellowed. This variation alone contributes to differences in color sensitivities among individuals.[2]

The Retina

The human retina consists of a dense population of light-sensitive rods and cones. Rods are primarily responsible for night vision, while cones provide the initial element in color sensation.

Photopigments in the cones translate wavelength to color sensation. The range of sensation is determined by three photopigments—blue (445 nanometers, or nm), green (535 nm), and red (575 nm). Here, "red" is really a misnomer, because maximum sensitivity at 575 nm actually invokes the sensation of yellow.

Both photopigment and cone distribution vary over the retinal surface. Red pigment is found in 64% of the cones, green in 32%, and blue in about 2%. Additionally, the center of the retina, which provides detailed vision, is densely packed with cones but has no rods. Moving outward, the number of rods increases to eventual predominance; as a result, shapes appear unclear and colorless at the extreme periphery of vision.[3]

Because of the cone and photopigment distributions, we can detect yellows and blues farther into our peripheral vision than reds and greens. Also, the center of the retina, while capable of high acuity, is nearly devoid of cones having blue photopigment. This results in a "blue blindness' that causes small blue objects to disappear when they are fixated upon.[4]

For the eye to detect any shape of a specific color, an edge must be created by focusing the image onto the mosaic of retinal receptors. An edge is the basic element in perceiving form. It can be created by adjacent areas differing in brightness, color, or both. Edges guide the eye's accommodation mechanism, which brings images into focus on the retina. Recent research has shown, however, that edges formed by color difference alone with no brightness difference, such as a red circle centered on a large green square of equal brightness, are poor guides to accurate focusing. Such contours remain fuzzy.[5] For sharply focused images, it is necessary to combine both color and brightness differences.

Also, for photopigments to respond, a minimum level of light is required. Additionally, the response level depends on wavelength, with the visual system being most sensitive to the center of the spectrum and decreasingly sensitive at the spectral extremes. This means a blue or red must be of much greater intensity than a minimum-level green or yellow in order to be perceived. Similarly, equal-energy reds might not appear equally intense.[3]

After the Retina

The optic-nerve bundle leads from the photoreceptors at the back of the retina. Along the optic-nerve path, at the lateral geniculate body, the photo-receptor outputs recombine.[2] Figure 2 diagrams how this recombination takes place.

Notice in Figure 2 that the original retinal channels—red, green, and blue—form three new "opponent channels." One channel signals the red-to-green ratio, another the yellow-to-blue, and the third indicates brightness. Again, we find a bias against the blue photopigments, since the perception of brightness, and hence of edges and shapes, is signaled by the red and green photopigments. The exclusion of blue in brightness perception means that colors differing only in the amount of blue will not produce sharp edges.[5]

Neural organization into opponent channels has several other effects, too. The retinal color zones, which link opponent red with green and opponent yellow with blue, provide an example. Opponent-color linking precludes visually experiencing combinations of opposing colors—we cannot experience reddish green or yellowish blue.[2]

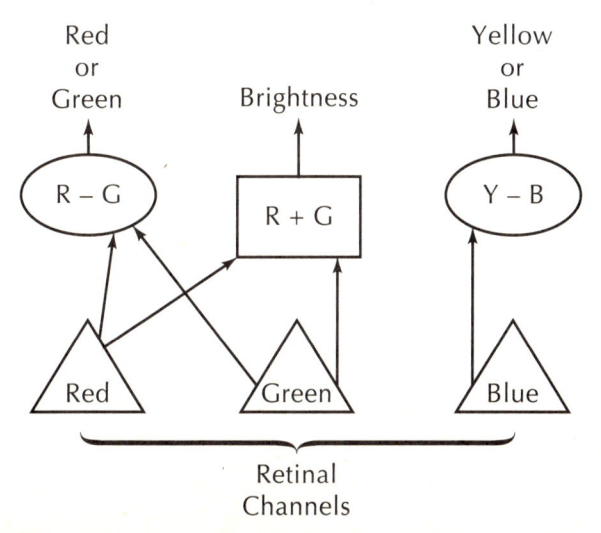

Figure 2. Processing of color input into opponent channels

Colorblindness

The term "colorblind" is an unfortunate summarization of the color deficiencies besetting only about 9% of the population, and only a tiny percentage of those deficiencies result in true blindness to color.[4]

Not all the causes of color-deficient vision are known; however, some are related to the cones and their photo-pigments. A rare form occurs when blue photopigment is missing. The best-known condition, however, is red-green deficiency, caused by the lack of either red or green photopigments. Lack of either photopigment causes the same color-discrimination problem; however, for people lacking red photopigment, long-wave stimuli appear much darker.

A more common case is that of photopigment-response functions deviating significantly from normal. In one form, the red photopigment peak lies very close to that of the green; whereas in another, green is shifted towards red. The net result is reduced ability to distinguish small color differences, particularly those of low brightness. Less extreme cases of response deviation, which occur regularly across the population in general, explain the common situation of two people differing on whether a given color is blue or green.[4]

PRINCIPLES OF PERCEPTION

20   Perception refers to the process of sensory experience. Although perception is most certainly a product of our nervous system, adequate information about the "higher order" function does not exist to describe perception in physiological terms. As a result, psychological methods must be relied on, the most valuable discipline being psychophysics. Psychophysics is a discipline that seeks to describe objectively how we experience the physical world around us.

Perception Is Nonlinear

Psychophysical research has shown that practically all perceptual experiences are nonlinearly related to the physical event. Figure 3 illustrates this by graphing perceived intensity versus physical intensity. The relationship is nearly logarithmic, with perceived intensity increasing as the logarithm of stimulus intensity.[6] We have all experienced this relationship on a more mundane level when switching intensities on a three-way lamp—the brightness increase from 50 to 100 watts appears greater than that from 100 to 150 watts.

Perception of Achromatic Color

White or achromatic light contains all the wavelengths to which the human eye responds. When such light strikes an object and all wavelengths are reflected equally, the color of the object is achromatic; that is, the object appears white, black, or some intermediate level of gray.

The lightness of the object depends on the amount of light reflected. An object reflecting 80% or more appears very light; it is white. Reflection of 3% or less results in the object appearing very dark (black). Various levels of gray ap-

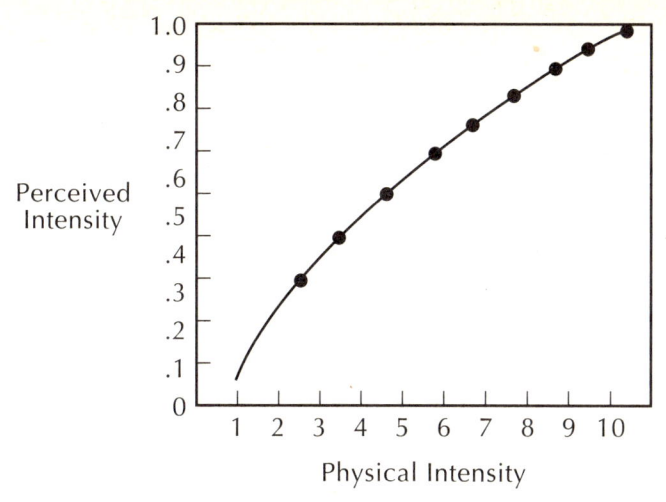

Figure 3. Perceived intensity as a function of physical intensity

pear in between, with lightness appearing to increase toward white as a logarithm of reflectance.[6]

Consider, for example, black, white, and gray automobiles. Each car reflects different amounts of light and, therefore, takes on a specific achromatic color. If the total amount of light illuminating the cars is increased, the lightness stays the same but the brightness increases. The white car stays white but becomes much brighter—perhaps even dazzling. Thus, lightness is a property of an object itself, but brightness depends upon the amount of light illuminating the object.

The most common example of all of this is black print on white paper. Changing illumination has little perceptual effect on the relative lightness of the paper or print, since the ratio of reflectance, or contrast, remains unchanged.

Perception of Chromatic Color

Objects that reflect or emit unequal distributions of wavelengths are said to be chromatic, i.e., to have a color. The color we sense derives from the physical attributes of the dominant wavelengths, the intensity of the wavelengths, and the number and proportion of reflected waves. Color identification also depends upon a multitude of learning variables, such as previous experiences with the object and association of specific sensations with color names. The sensation is also affected by the context in which the color occurs and the characteristics of the surrounding area or the colors of other objects.[7]

The study of the physical attributes of chromatic objects is always compounded by the experiences of the observer with colors in general. Because color perception is subjective, many of its aspects can be described only in the psychological dimensions of hue, lightness, saturation, and brightness.[8]

Hue is the sensation reported by observers exposed to wavelengths between approximately 380 and 700 nm. For the range between 450 and 480 nm, the predominant sensation reported is blue. Green is reported across a broader range of 500 to 550 nm, and yellow across a narrow band around 570 to 580 nm. Above

610 nm, most persons report the sensation of red. The best or purest colors—defined as those containing no trace of a second color—would indicate pure blue at about 470 nm, pure green at 505, and pure yellow at 575 nm.[4]

Hue, then, is the basic component of color. It is the primary determinant for the specific color sensation. Although hue is closely related to certain wavelengths, remember that hue is a psychological variable and wavelength a physical one. Although people with normal color vision will name a sector of the visual spectrum as red, disagreement will occur about the reddest red or where red becomes orange. Such disagreement reflects varying experiences with color as well as the intrinsic differences in the color mechanisms of each person's visual system.

Saturation is most closely related to the number of wavelengths contributing to a color sensation. As the band of wavelengths narrows, the resulting color sensation becomes more saturated—the wider the band, the less saturated the color.

Conceptually, a scale of saturation can be envisioned as extending from a pure hue, such as red, through less distinct variants of the hue, such as shades of pink, to a neutral gray in which no trace of the original hue is noticed. A measure of saturation discrimination can be obtained by starting with a neutral color and determining the amount of pure hue that must be added in order for the hue to become detectable. Figure 4 shows the results of such a study.[9]

In Figure 4, the abscissa indicates wavelength. The ordinate shows the proportion of pure hue that must be added to neutral color for the hue to become discernible. From this graph, it becomes obvious that substantial differences exist in our ability to detect color presence at different wavelengths. The largest amount of color required for detection is at the 570-nm stimulus. Such a yellow appears initially to be less saturated than any other pure hue and desaturates quickly as the wavelength distribution is broadened or as neutral colors are mixed with it.

Lightness, as mentioned previously, refers to the gamut of achromatic colors ranging from white through gray to black. By definition, achromatic colors are completely desaturated, since no trace of hue is present.

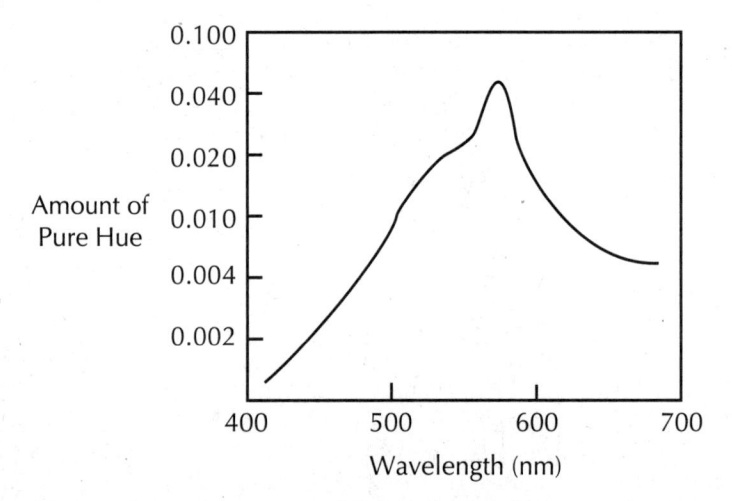

Figure 4. Perceived saturation at different wavelengths

Just as with achromatic colors, the lightness of a mixed color also depends on the reflectance of the surface under consideration—the higher the reflectance, the lighter the color. As might be anticipated, monochromatic colors do not all appear equal in lightness. Some hues appear lighter than others even though their reflectances are the same. If, for example, observers are shown a series of monochromatic lights of equal brightness and are asked to rate them for lightness, a relationship similar to that shown in Figure 4 results. A monochromatic color 570 nm appears much lighter than all other wavelengths, and the lightness decreases rapidly as the extremes of the visual spectrum are approached.[9]

Brightness is another aspect of color perception. Increasing the illumination of both achromatic and chromatic colors produces a qualitative change in appearance that ranges from dark to bright. However, separation of brightness from lightness is often difficult, since brighter colors invariably appear lighter as well.[6]

Consider broadband light shining on a series of equal-reflectance surfaces, each reflecting a very narrow band of wavelengths. At low illumination, the surfaces are first perceived as gray. Increasing the intensity allows dark and desaturated hues to become discernible, with mid-spectrum wavelengths (555 nm) becoming visible at lower intensity levels. As the intensity increases, a broader range of hues appears, with extremely long and short wavelengths visible only at high intensities.[3]

Colors in Context

Colors are also subject to contextual effects, in which adjacent colors influence one another. For example, a color on a dark background appears lighter and brighter than the same color on a light background. If a test field is neutral (gray) or dark and displayed on a colored background, the background induces color into the test field.[7] Red, for example, induces green into a neutral gray.

The size of a colored area also influences its perceptual properties. In general, small areas become desaturated and can show a shift in hue.[7] This creates problems when text is color coded, especially with blues and yellows, because they are susceptible to small-area color loss. Also, small areas of color can mix; red and green in smaller areas are eventually integrated by the visual system into yellow.

Individual Characteristics

Thus far, perception has been described in general terms as it applies to the typical human visual system. Yet all of us have our own perceptual idiosyncrasies that affect how we use color. For example, some people prefer highly saturated colors and others prefer muted tones.

It is important, too, to remember that color perception changes over time. We adapt to color with prolonged viewing. This results in an apparent softening of colors. As a result, there is a tendency to use highly saturated colors to offset adaptation. The unadapted viewer, however, sees the colors as highly saturated. Additionally, some research indicates that pure colors are visually fatiguing.[10]

Although we are still far from developing an aesthetics of color displays, some information has been compiled on color combinations that go well together and those that do not. Tables 1 and 2 present data from a study in which

Table 1 Best Color Combinations (N = 16)

Background	Thin Lines and Text	Thick Lines and Panels
White	Blue (94%) Black (63%) Red (25%)	Black (69%) Blue (63%) Red (31%)
Black	White (75%) Yellow (63%)	Yellow (69%) White (50%) Green (25%)
Red	Yellow (75%) White (56%) Black (44%)	Black (50%) Yellow (44%) White (44%) Cyan (31%)
Green	Black (100%) Blue (56%) Red (25%)	Black (69%) Red (63%) Blue (31%)
Blue	White (81%) Yellow (50%) Cyan (25%)	Yellow (38%) Magenta (31%) Black (31%) Cyan (31%) White (25%)
Cyan	Blue (69%) Black (56%) Red (37%)	Red (36%) Blue (50%) Black (44%) Magenta (25%)
Magenta	Black (63%) White (56%) Blue (44%)	Blue (50%) Black (44%) Yellow (25%)
Yellow	Red (63%) Blue (63%) Black (56%)	Red (75%) Blue (63%) Black (50%)
Overall Frequency of Selection	Black 25% White 20% Blue 20% Yellow 13% Red 11% Cyan 5% Magenta 4% Green 1%	Black 23% Blue 19% Red 17% Yellow 13% White 10% Magenta 7% Cyan 6.4% Green 4%

people were asked to pick the best and worst appearing colors on different backgrounds. Choices were made for both thin lines and for larger filled panels. The tables list those combinations preferred or rejected by at least 25% of the 16 subjects participating in the study. Obviously this is a small study sample, but it does represent the start of an understanding of the complex issue of color-display aesthetics.[11]

Cognitive Principles

The least understood area of effective color usage is how to capitalize on our modes of thinking about, and associating with, color. This area of study falls into the domain of cognitive ergonomics.

Despite the infancy of this area of human-factors study, some initial observations prove useful in effective color usage. An example involves the functional use of color stereotypes: red for warning, green for go, and yellow for at-

TABLE 2 Worst Color Combinations (N = 16)

Background	Thin Lines and Text	Thick Lines and Panels
White	Yellow (100%) Cyan (94%)	Yellow (94%) Cyan (75%)
Black	Blue (87%) Red (37%) Magenta (25%)	Blue (81%) Magenta (31%)
Red	Magenta (81%) Blue (44%) Green and Cyan (25%)	Magenta (69%) Blue (50%) Green (37%) Cyan (25%)
Green	Cyan (81%) Magenta (50%) Yellow (37%)	Cyan (81%) Magenta and Yellow (44%)
Blue	Green (62%) Red and Black (37%)	Green (44%) Red and Black (31%)
Cyan	Green (81%) Yellow (75%) White (31%)	Yellow (69%) Green (62%) White (56%)
Magenta	Green (75%) Red (56%) Cyan (44%)	Cyan (81%) Green (69%) Red (44%)
Yellow	White and Cyan (81%)	White (81%) Cyan (56%) Green (25%)

Overall Frequency of Selection

Cyan	24%	Cyan	23%
Green	18%	Yellow	17%
Yellow	16%	Green	16%
Magenta	11%	Magenta	12%
Red	10%	White	12%
White	8%	Blue	9%
Blue	8%	Red	7%
Black	3%	Black	2%

tention. Since we all have experience with these meanings, maintaining the relationship maps nicely into our expectations.

In color-coding graphed measurement data, variation of hue can quickly communicate important information. Portions of the data within a certain tolerance, or range limit, can be coded green; portions approaching a limit can be yellow; and excesses can be coded red. This procedure fits into the normal cognitive expectations.

For multiple graphs, where color is simply used for quick distinction between data, contrast is a big consideration. As a result, it is tempting to use red for one line and green for another. While this makes the data readily distinguishable, which is the goal, it can also bias an observer toward making some quality judgments about the data—the red data are bad or dangerous, the green are okay. Such biasing of the observer might not be what you intended. Similarly, the perceived magnitude of different colors varies. A red square will be perceived as being larger than a green one of identical size.[12]

Guidelines for Effective Color Usage

On the basis of the preceding discussion, some general guidelines for color usage can be stated. They are listed here according to the area of their derivation—physiological, perceptual, or cognitive.

Physiological Guidelines

Avoid the simultaneous display of highly saturated, spectrally extreme colors. Reds, oranges, yellows, and greens can be viewed together without refocusing, but cyan and blues cannot be easily viewed simultaneously with red. To avoid frequent refocusing and visual fatigue, extreme color pairs such as red and blue or yellow and purple should be avoided. However, desaturating spectrally extreme colors will reduce the need for refocusing.

Avoid pure blue for text, thin lines, and small shapes. Our visual system is just not set up for detailed, sharp, short-wavelength stimuli. However, blue does make a good background color and is perceived clearly out into the periphery of our visual field.

Avoid adjacent colors differing only in the amount of blue. Edges that differ only in the amount of blue will appear indistinct.

Older viewers need higher brightness levels to distinguish colors.

Colors change appearance as ambient light level changes. Displays change color under different kinds of ambient light—fluorescent, incandescent, or daylight. Appearance also changes as the light level is increased or decreased. On the one hand, a change occurs because of increased or decreased contrast, and on the other hand, because of the shift in the sensitivity of the eye.

The magnitude of a detectable change in color varies across the spectrum. Small changes in extreme reds and purples are more difficult to detect than small changes in other colors such as yellow and blue-green. Also, our visual system does not readily perceive changes in green.

Difficulty in focusing results from edges created by color alone. Our visual system depends on a brightness difference at an edge to effect clear focusing. Multicolored images, then, should be differentiated on the basis of brightness as well as of color.

Avoid red and green in the periphery of large-scale displays. Because of the insensitivity of the retinal periphery to red and green, these colors in saturated form should be avoided, especially for small symbols and shapes. Yellow and blue are good peripheral colors.

Opponent colors go well together. Red and green or yellow and blue are good combinations for simple displays. The opposite combinations—red with yellow or green with blue—produce poorer images.

For color-deficient observers, avoid single-color distinctions. Colors which differ only in the amount of red or green added or subtracted from the two other primaries may prove difficult to distinguish for certain classes of color-deficient observers.

Perceptual Guidelines

Not all colors are equally discernible. Perceptually, we need a large change in wavelength to perceive a color difference in some portions of the spectrum and a small one in other portions.

Luminance does not equal brightness. Two equal-luminance but different hue colors will probably appear to have different brightnesses. The deviations are most extreme for colors towards the ends of the spectrum (red, magenta, blue).

Different hues have inherently different saturation levels. Yellow in particular always appears to be less saturated than other hues.

Lightness and brightness are distinguishable on a printed copy, but not on a color display. The nature of a color display does not allow lightness and brightness to be varied independently.

Not all colors are equally readable or legible. Extreme care should be exercised with text color relative to background colors. Besides a loss in hue with reduced size, inadequate contrast frequently results when the background and text colors are similar.

Hues change with intensity and background color. When grouping elements on the basis of color, be sure that backgrounds or nearby colors do not change the hue of an element in the group. Limiting the number of colors and making sure they are widely separated in the spectrum will reduce confusion.

Avoid the need for color discrimination in small areas. Hue information is lost for small areas. In general, two adjacent lines of a single-pixel width will merge to produce a mixture of the two. Also, the human visual system produces sharper images with achromatic colors. Thus for fine detail, it is best to use black, white, and gray while reserving chromatic colors for larger panels or for attracting attention.

Cognitive Guidelines

Do not overuse color. Perhaps the best rule is to use color sparingly. The benefits of color as an attention getter, information grouper, and value assigner are lost if too many colors are used. Cognitive scientists have shown that the human mind experiences great difficulty in maintaining more than five to seven elements simultaneously, so it is best to limit displays to about six clearly discriminable colors.

Group related elements by using a common background color. Cognitive science has advanced the notion of set and preattentive processing. In this context, you can prepare or set the user for related events by using a common color code. A successive set of images can be shown to be related by using the same background color.

Similar colors connote similar meanings. Elements related in some way can convey that message through the degree in similarity of hue. The color range from blue to green is experienced as more similar than the gamut from red to green. Along these same lines, saturation level can also be used to connote the strength of relationships.

Use brightness and saturation to draw attention. The brightest and most highly saturated area of a color display immediately draws the viewer's attention.

Link the degree of color change to event magnitude. As an alternative to bar charts or tic marks on amplitude scales, one can portray magnitude changes with progressive steps of changing color. A desaturated cyan can be increased in saturation as the graphed elements increase in value. Progressively switching from one hue to another can be used to indicate passing critical levels.

Order colors by their spectral position. To increase the number of colors on a display requires imposing a meaningful order on the colors. The most obvious order is that provided by the spectrum with the mnemonic ROY G. BIV (red, orange, yellow, green, blue, indigo, violet).

Warm and cold colors should indicate action levels. Traditionally, the warm (long-wavelength) colors are used to signify action or the requirement of a response. Cool colors, on the other hand, indicate status or background information. Most people also experience warm colors advancing toward them—hence forcing attention—and cool colors receding or drawing away.

References

1. G. M. Murch, "Visual Accommodation and Convergence to Multi-chromatic Display Terminals," *Proceedings of the Society for Information Display* 24 (1983), pp. 67–72.
2. L. Hurvich, *Color Vision* (Sunderland, Mass.: Sinauer, 1981).
3. G. M. Murch, *Visual and Auditory Perception* (Indianapolis: Bobbs-Merrill, 1973).
4. R. Boynton, *Human Color Vision* (New York: Holt, Rinehart and Winston, 1980).
5. F. S. Fromme, "Improving Color CAD Systems for Users: Some Suggestions from Human Factors Studies," *IEEE Design and Test* (Feb. 1984), pp. 18–27.
6. L. M. Hurvich and D. S. Jameson, *The Perception of Brightness and Darkness* (Boston: Allyn and Bacon, 1966).
7. J. Walraven, *Chromatic Induction* (Utrecht, Holland: Elinkwisk, 1981).
8. G. M. Murch, "Perceptual Considerations of Color," *Computer Graphics World* 7 (1983), pp. 32–40.
9. G. S. Wasserman, *Color Vision* (New York: Wiley, 1978).
10. L. D. Silverstein, "Human Factors for Color Displays," *Society for Information Display Seminar* (San Diego, California, 1982).
11. G. M. Murch, "Physiological Principles for the Effective Use of Color," *IEEE Computer Graphics and Applications* (Nov. 1984), pp. 49–55.
12. W. S. Cleveland and R. McGill, "A Color-Caused Optical Illusion on a Statistical Graph," *The American Statistician* 37 (May 1983), pp. 101–105.

Questions for Discussion

1. This essay was written for technical writers and artists. How would this essay differ if it were written for advertising directors? automotive engineers? newspaper editors? fashion designers? architects? Identify specific changes you think would be necessary.
2. Do the tables and figures contribute to your understanding of the subject? Explain your answer.
3. This essay has no summarizing or concluding paragraphs. Do you like the ending? If so, why? If not, compose the ending you believe is necessary.

4. Identify the thesis of the essay. Where is it located? How does the author clarify and develop the thesis?
5. In explaining his subject, the author uses a lot of technical terminology (e.g., chromatic, achromatic). Is this technical terminology appropriate? Is it necessary?

Opportunities for Writing

1. Explain the various meanings typically associated with specific colors in the United States (e.g., red signals danger). How did such meanings come to be associated with the colors? Address your essay to a foreign visitor.
2. Investigate people's favorite and least favorite color combinations. After reviewing the existing studies of this subject, show subjects a variety of color combinations and record their likes and dislikes. In a magazine published by your local science museum and distributed to museum visitors, report the results of your research.
3. Discuss the various processes of full-color printing. What are the similarities and differences among the processes? How does full-color printing differ from black-and-white printing? How is it similar? Compose your essay for a special display on printing processes at your local library.

Knowledge by Participation and Observation

Friends, Good Friends—and Such Good Friends

Judith Viorst

A professional writer, Judith Viorst graduated from Rutgers University and the Washington Psychoanalytic Institute. Among her published works are volumes of poetry, children's books, and essays, including Sad Underwear and Other Complications *(1995),* If I Were in Charge of the World and Other Worries *(1981),* Alexander and the Terrible, Horrible, No Good, Very Bad Day *(1972),* The Tenth Good Thing About Barney *(1971), and* People and Other Aggravations *(1969). "Friends, Good Friends—and Such Good Friends" identifies the different kinds of friendship and friends that we may have; to develop her catalog of the various types, Viorst uses both knowledge by participation and observation. This essay first appeared in Viorst's regular column in* Redbook.

Women are friends, I once would have said, when they totally love and support and trust each other, and bare to each other the secrets of their souls, and run—no questions asked—to help each other, and tell harsh truths to each other (no, you can't wear that dress unless you lose ten pounds first) when harsh truths must be told.

Women are friends, I once would have said, when they share the same affection for Ingmar Bergman, plus train rides, cats, warm rain, charades, Camus, and hate with equal ardor Newark and Brussels sprouts and Lawrence Welk and camping.

In other words, I once would have said that a friend is a friend all the way, but now I believe that's a narrow point of view. For the friendships I have and the friendships I see are conducted at many levels of intensity, serve many different functions, meet different needs and range from those as all-the-way as the friendship of the soul sisters mentioned above to that of the most nonchalant and casual playmates.

Consider these varieties of friendship:

1. Convenience friends. These are women with whom, if our paths weren't crossing all the time, we'd have no particular reason to be friends: a next-door neighbor, a woman in our car pool, the mother of one of our children's closest friends or maybe some mommy with whom we serve juice and cookies each week at the Glenwood Co-op Nursery.

Convenience friends are convenient indeed. They'll lend us their cups and silverware for a party. They'll drive our kids to soccer when we're sick. They'll take us to pick up our car when we need a lift to the garage. They'll even take our cats when we go on vacation. As we will for them.

But we don't, with convenience friends, ever come too close or tell too much; we maintain our public face and emotional distance. "Which means," says Elaine, "that I'll talk about being overweight but not about being depressed. Which means I'll admit being mad but not blind with rage. Which means that I might say that we're pinched this month but never that I'm worried sick over money."

But which doesn't mean that there isn't sufficient value to be found in these friendships of mutual aid, in convenience friends.

2. Special-interest friends. These friendships aren't intimate, and they needn't involve kids or silverware or cats. Their value lies in some interest jointly shared. And so we may have an office friend or a yoga friend or a tennis friend or a friend from the Women's Democratic Club.

"I've got one woman friend," says Joyce, "who likes, as I do, to take psychology courses. Which makes it nice for me—and nice for her. It's fun to go with someone you know and it's fun to discuss what you've learned, driving back from the classes." And for the most part, she says, that's all they discuss.

"I'd say that what we're doing is *doing* together, not being together," Suzanne says of her Tuesday-doubles friends. "It's mainly a tennis relationship, but we play together well. And I guess we all need to have a couple of playmates."

I agree.

My playmate is a shopping friend, a woman of marvelous taste, a woman who knows exactly *where* to buy *what,* and furthermore is a woman who always knows beyond a doubt what one ought to be buying. I don't have the time to keep up with what's new in eyeshadow, hemlines and shoes and whether the smock look is in or finished already. But since (oh, shame!) I care a lot about eyeshadows, hemlines and shoes, and since I don't *want* to wear smocks if the smock look is finished, I'm very glad to have a shopping friend.

3. Historical friends. We all have a friend who knew us when . . . maybe way back in Miss Meltzer's second grade, when our family lived in that three-room flat in Brooklyn, when our dad was out of work for seven months, when our brother Allie got in that fight where they had to call the police, when our sister married the endodontist from Yonkers and when, the morning after we lost our virginity, she was the first, the only, friend we told.

The years have gone by and we've gone separate ways and we've little in common now, but we're still an intimate part of each other's past. And so whenever we go to Detroit we always go to visit this friend of our girlhood. Who knows how we looked before our teeth were straightened. Who knows how we talked before our voice got un-Brooklyned. Who knows what we ate before we learned about artichokes. And who, by her presence, puts us in touch with an earlier part of ourself, a part of ourself it's important never to lose.

"What this friend means to me and what I mean to her," says Grace, "is having a sister without sibling rivalry. We know the texture of each other's lives. She remembers my grandmother's cabbage soup. I remember the way her uncle played the piano. There's simply no other friend who remembers those things."

4. Crossroads friends. Like historical friends, our crossroads friends are important for *what was*—for the friendship we shared at a crucial, now past, time of life. A time, perhaps, when we roomed in college together; or worked as eager young singles in the Big City together; or went together, as my friend Elizabeth and I did, through pregnancy, birth and that scary first year of new motherhood.

Crossroads friends forge powerful links, links strong enough to endure with not much more contact than once-a-year letters at Christmas. And out of respect for those crossroads years, for those dramas and dreams we once shared, we will always be friends.

5. Cross-generational friends. Historical friends and crossroads friends seem to maintain a special kind of intimacy—dormant but always ready to be revived—and though we may rarely meet, whenever we do connect, it's personal and intense. Another kind of intimacy exists in the friendships that form across generations in what one woman calls her daughter-mother and her mother-daughter relationships.

Evelyn's friend is her mother's age—"but I share so much more than I ever could with my mother"—a woman she talks to of music, of books and of life. "What I get from her is the benefit of her experience. What she gets—and enjoys—from me is a youthful perspective. It's a pleasure for both of us."

I have in my own life a precious friend, a woman of 65 who has lived very hard, who is wise, who listens well; who has been where I am and can help me understand it; and who represents not only an ultimate ideal mother to me but also the person I'd like to be when I grow up.

In our daughter role we tend to do more than our share of self-revelation; in our mother role we tend to receive what's revealed. It's another kind of pleasure—playing wise mother to a questing younger person. It's another very lovely kind of friendship.

6. Part-of-a-couple friends. Some of the women we call our friends we never see alone—we see them as part of a couple at couples' parties. And though we share interests in many things and respect each other's views, we aren't moved to deepen the relationship. Whatever the reason, a lack of time or—and this is more likely—a lack of chemistry, our friendship remains in the context of a group. But the fact that our feeling on seeing each other is always, "I'm *so* glad she's here" and the fact that we spend half the evening talking together says that this too, in its own way, counts as a friendship.

(Other part-of-a-couple friends are the friends that came with the marriage, and some of these are friends we could live without. But sometimes, alas, she married our husband's best friend; and sometimes, alas, she *is* our husband's best friend. And so we find ourselves dealing with her, somewhat against our will, in a spirit of what I'll call *reluctant* friendship.)

7. Men who are friends. I wanted to write just of women friends, but the women I've talked to won't let me—they say I must mention man-woman

friendships too. For these friendships can be just as close and as dear as those that we form with women. Listen to Lucy's description of one such friendship:

"We've found we have things to talk about that are different from what he talks about with my husband and different from what I talk about with his wife. So sometimes we call on the phone or meet for lunch. There are similar intellectual interests—we always pass on to each other the book that we love—but there's also something tender and caring too."

In a couple of crises, Lucy says, "he offered himself for talking and for helping. And when someone died in his family he wanted me there. The sexual, flirty part of our friendship is very small—but *some*—just enough to make it fun and different." She thinks—and I agree—that the sexual part, though small, is always *some*, is always there when a man and a woman are friends.

It's only in the past few years that I've made friends with men, in the sense of a friendship that's *mine,* not just part of two couples. And achieving with them the ease and the trust I've found with women friends has value indeed. Under the dryer at home last week, putting on mascara and rouge, I comfortably sat and talked with a fellow named Peter. Peter, I finally decided, could handle the shock of me minus mascara under the dryer. Because we care for each other. Because we're friends.

There are medium friends, and pretty good friends, and very good friends indeed, and these friendships are defined by their level of intimacy. And what we'll reveal at each of these levels of intimacy is calibrated with care. We might tell a medium friend, for example, that yesterday we had a fight with our husband. And we might tell a pretty good friend that this fight with our husband made us so mad that we slept on the couch. And we might tell a very good friend that the reason we got so mad in that fight that we slept on the couch had something to do with that girl who works in his office. But it's only to our very best friends that we're willing to tell all, to tell what's going on with that girl in his office.

30 The best of friends, I still believe, totally love and support and trust each other, and bare to each other the secrets of their souls, and run—no questions asked—to help each other, and tell harsh truths to each other when they must be told.

But we needn't agree about everything (only 12-year-old girl friends agree about *everything*) to tolerate each other's point of view. To accept without judgment. To give and to take without ever keeping score. And to *be* there, as I am for them and as they are for me, to comfort our sorrows, to celebrate our joys.

Questions for Discussion

1. How do sources of information contribute to this essay? How would this essay differ if it were written using only knowledge by participation?
2. Notice the ordering of the different types of friends. Why are the types assigned this order? Why are the types numbered? How would you have ordered the types of friends?
3. What is the thesis of the essay? Do you think the author does a satisfactory job of supporting the thesis? Why or why not?
4. This essay was written for a women's magazine. How might the author revise this essay for a men's magazine? What specific changes would you recommend?

5. How does the writer try to motivate the audience? Cite specific passages to support your answer.

Opportunities for Writing

1. Compare and contrast your friendships with men versus your friendships with women. Do you notice more similarities or differences? How typical do you think your experience is? Address your analysis to the membership of a local women's or men's organization.
2. After interviewing people from a variety of occupations, offer guidelines for making and keeping friends on the job. What are the secrets of success? What are the potential pitfalls to avoid? Write your essay for the employee newsletter at your place of work.
3. Your school newspaper is soliciting articles on the subject of friendship for its Valentine's Day issue. Using a questionnaire, analyze the similarities and differences among men and women regarding their definitions of friendship. What is a friendship? How is it initiated? How is it developed? How does a friendship differ from a romantic relationship?

An Architect Who Takes Stairways One Step at a Time

RICHARD WOLKOMIR

Richard Wolkomir wrote this essay for The Smithsonian, *to which he is a frequent contributor. He interviewed architect John Templer, the "stair master" of Georgia Tech University. Templer, author of* The Staircase *(MIT, 1992) and* The Staircase: Studies of Hazards, Falls, and Safer Design *(MIT, 1992), has spent the past 25 years studying the history, aesthetics, and safety of stairs. Wolkomir's other publications include articles for* Omni, Reader's Digest, *and* National Wildlife.

Ever since John Templer saw his sister-in-law fall down a flight of stairs at New York City's Lincoln Center, he has been seeking the perfect staircase. "Stairs are one of the most dangerous manufactured objects," he tells me with genuine concern.

But stairs can offer stunning flights of architectural fancy, too. And they are part of our collective consciousness. In Genesis, Jacob dreamed he saw angels going up and down a ladder to heaven. That is in our memory bank, along with Rhett Butler sweeping Scarlett O'Hara off her feet and carrying her up the stairs of their Atlanta mansion. Bedimpled Shirley Temple tap-danced down another celluloid staircase. And Hollywood also gave us two generations of tights-clad Fairbankses, swinging swords on the stairs of make-believe castles. In Victorian England, "upstairs" and "downstairs" were social directions. And jumbled in our memories with stairway nursery rhymes and nonsense-like "As I was going up the stair/I met a man who wasn't there" and the '70s pop hit "Stairway to Heaven"—are tragedies, such as fabric designer Laura Ashley's fall to her death on a stairway.

Nobody knows more about stairs than John Templer, an architect at the Georgia Institute of Technology. He has pondered stairs for 23 years. And he is the author of *The Staircase*, a recently published two-volume tome from MIT Press on the design and history of the staircase, which he traces back to its invention by the prehistoric human foot. Neolithic people climbed steep slopes by bracing their feet against roots and rocks. Eventually, these footholds were worn into permanent steps. Such "land stairs" still exist in the stepped streets of old Italian towns, and are used by people and donkeys. At New Mexico's Sky City, the Pueblo Indians carved steps down a steep rock face to a pool that supplied water.

Some Stone Age Einstein took the stair a step further by cutting down a tree trunk, notching footholds into its sides and leaning it against a wall to be climbed. Templer says West Africa's Dogon people still use such climbing poles, and so do Panamanian villagers. The USS *Constitution*, moored in Boston Harbor, has a climbing pole to reach its bowsprit.

Climbing poles evolved into "straight-flight" staircases, which go up in an undeviating flow of steps. Later came the helical stair, a springlike spiral. Later still, designers invented the composite stair, in which straight or helical flights end at landings, with new flights angling off in different directions.

Stairs are utilitarian, for getting up or down. But they can be striking, too. Among Templer's favorites are the Spanish Steps, built in Rome in the late 1600s and early 1700s. "They flow down the hill like a waterfall, with all sorts of rivulets and ripples and changes of direction," he says. And the landings are as significant as the steps: "They are places for the street vendors, fashion models and photographers; for people to meet, to embrace, to play and to look."

Templer calls stairs "architectural theater." But beauty can be treacherous. In fact, it was a fall, although not his own, that first got him fired up over stairs. When he was a graduate student at Columbia University in Manhattan, a worried citizen telephoned the architecture school with a question: Why did so many people leaving the Metropolitan Opera House at Lincoln Center fall down the front steps? Nobody knew. Templer looked for clues in the university's architectural library. Little, he found, had been written about stairs or stair safety. "All that night the idea of stairs ran through my mind," says Templer, who is a tall man, with a swirl of white hair and a British accent.

Eventually, he did figure out what was wrong at the Met: "People would come out, sodden from hours of Wagner, walk across the plaza jammed with pretzel and popcorn vendors and theatergoers, and never see the stairs because they're so shallow and wide—down they'd go." He took his wife, an artist, on a field trip to the Met, along with her sister. His sister-in-law missed a step and fell.

"I decided this would be a great subject for a doctoral thesis," says Templer. He went on to explore his stairs topic, earned his PhD in architecture and soon learned how apt his choice had been. In a call to his adviser at Columbia he learned that the distinguished architect had just fallen down a flight of subway stairs and broken his leg.

Templer took up the quest for the perfect stairway with renewed dedication. "There are so many bad stairs—they vastly overwhelm the good stairs." In fact, stairway falls are epidemic. In the United States alone, at least 4,000 people die every year from injuries suffered in stair falls. Another two million Americans are hurt badly enough in stairway falls to require a physician or at least one day's recuperation. "Perhaps stairs should carry a message from the Surgeon General, warning that they may be dangerous to health," says Templer.

He has put his decades of research to work in his own Atlanta home, which he designed: the central stairway—a stunning half-circular upward curl—emulates an automobile's padded dashboard. The handrail is softened with foam, covered with leather. "It's like the steering wheel on a good car—you get a strong grip, and if you fall it won't hurt you," he explains. The carpeted treads are padded with foam, too. Also, the treads are alternately colored dark and light, so that each step's edge is clear. And the proportions are optimal, direct from the lab: risers 7 inches high, treads 11 inches deep. All edges are rounded. Even the stairway's graceful curl makes it safer.

"It used to be assumed that circular stairs were automatically more dangerous, but statistics show they're actually safer," Templer says. "That's because they're a little more difficult to walk on, so you're more cautious, and you also can't fall so far."

One reason for the slip-and-fall epidemic is that today's stair proportions date back to 1675, when the director of France's Royal Academy of Architecture, François Blondel, concocted a formula linking stair geometry to the human gait: 2 × riser + tread = 24 inches (25.5 in today's inches). One of the formula's drawbacks is that, for unusually high or low risers, it requires treads that are extremely narrow or extremely wide.

"Walking on a stair requires skill, like playing with a bat and a ball," says Templer. "If eye-brain-arm coordination is always perfect, we can slug the ball solidly every time, but we're imperfect and sometimes we fail." One reason for pratfalls is that our descending and ascending gaits differ. Going down, shorter risers and deeper treads would be better because descent requires a moment when the body is balanced on one leg, the foot up on its toes, as the other foot reaches down for the tread below. It is an awkward—even dangerous—moment. Our bodies can be ungainly contraptions. And if a high riser forces the forward foot too far down, we can lose our balance and easily topple. As Dante noted in *The Divine Comedy,* the worst thing about hell is that all the steps have different dimensions.

15   Finding the perfect stairway, esthetically and functionally, is for Templer "a kind of designer's philosopher's stone." One elusive goal is a slip-proof stair. Building codes generally call for nonslip or nonskid surfaces, but that is not specified in detail. Meanwhile, society has no standards at all for the slipperiness of shoe soles and heels. And when rain or spilled drinks wet a stair tread, the surface friction instantly changes.

Slipperiness is not the only problem with which stair researchers are wrestling. For instance, John Templer's studies have shown how our gait on a stairway is influenced by the riser-tread geometry. Ascending, risers from 6.3 to 8.9 inches cause fewer missteps. Lower risers mean the stair has more risers and so more opportunities for tripping. But descending is safer with risers that are only 4.6 to 7.2 inches high. Templer suggests a compromise: risers about 7 inches high.

Tread depth is important, too. The narrower the tread the more we twist our feet sideways as we descend, so that more of the sole will rest on the tread, giving us a more secure base. Meanwhile, average foot length has increased since

Blondel's time in the 17th century. Templer calculates that a tread should be no less than 11 inches deep to accommodate the modern foot, while many building codes call for 10 inches or less.

Stairs must also provide space for the body, including room to bob and weave as we ascend or descend. And so designers must consider traffic flow in figuring a stairway's width. When we use a stair we require an ellipse of surrounding space, widest at our shoulders. The minimum width of a two-lane stairway should be 56 inches, while 69 inches would be more comfortable.

Illumination is important, too—one study showed that 95 percent of household stairways are too dim. And there are handrail questions, such as where they should be placed. One laboratory set up trick stairs with steps that unexpectedly collapsed, forcing hapless volunteers to grasp wildly for a handrail to keep from tumbling. After 830 science-induced trips and falls, researchers concluded that the ideal railing height is around 35.6 inches.

John Templer has probed how we use stairways by studying, Sherlock Holmes-style, the paths our shoes erode into steps over centuries. It is, he says, like following the "spoor of animals." He has observed these human trails in stone steps up the side of a medieval building in Orvieto, Italy, and in Manhattan subway entrances. He found a stone stairway slanting down a waterfront embankment in St. Augustine, Florida, that is so narrow, thousands of walkers have had to put their feet in the same spots, creating shoe-shaped hollows in the steps.

When starting up or down a stairway, Templer has found, we first give it a "conceptual scan," to check out its configuration and any dangers, such as junior's roller skates. Once we have established a "cognitive model" of the stairway, we are ready to start, on the assumption that we know what to expect. Sometimes we assume wrongly—stairs may be irregular—and that can trip us up. To ward off such surprises, we give the stairway a "monitoring scan" every seven steps or so. But distractions can throw us—a view that suddenly opens up or too many martinis. Sometimes we don't see a stairway ahead and experience "unintentional use of steps." Down we go.

Once we start tumbling, it's almost too late. By 190 milliseconds into the fall, we have already dropped seven inches. We are flailing, about to become a human Slinky. Every 2,222 times we use a stair, we have a noteworthy misstep. Women fall more frequently than men, but boys under the age of 14 fall more often than girls of the same age. And you are more likely to take a tumble if you are single. Go figure.

Stairs, Templer says, "remain some of the most dangerous artifacts in our environment." One reason is that building safety has no official watchdog. "We have relatively safe cars, roads and airplanes because of the Department of Transportation, but no equivalent federal agency considers research in building safety as their primary game." Also, building codes used in various regions of the country cling to the ancient riser-tread standards, usually a riser of about 8.5 inches and a tread that is 9.5 inches deep.

A few years ago, based on Templer's and others' research, one of the codes that govern construction in the Northeast was revised to the safer 7-inch riser and 11-inch-deep tread. But the National Association of Home Builders got the change reversed. "They argued that there was no proof the 7–11 standard was safer and that it greatly increased the cost of housing," says Templer sadly, adding that he figures the new stair standard would add only 12 square feet to a house's size.

Research shows that many of the great stairs of history are dangerous. Still, as architectural creations, they can be impressive, with reverberations in our unconscious. Templer traces his fascination with stairs to an old house in the English countryside, where he lived as a child. He was born in 1928 in Oxford, but until age 3 he was raised in Kenya, where his father, a British civil servant, was chief forester. Then his parents sent their children back to England for schooling. Templer lived with his grandmother and his grandfather, an Anglican priest at an ancient Norman church. He grew up in the rambling Georgian rectory, with input for the future architect's data banks: a grand stairway and also a back stairway to the attic, where the servants lived.

After World War II, Templer's family relocated to South Africa, and he enrolled at the University of Natal as an engineering student. He found himself wandering the city, idly studying buildings. It dawned on him that he should switch to architecture. After earning an undergraduate degree, he went on to graduate studies at Columbia, where he became smitten with stairs.

His first interest was safety. But he quickly became fascinated with the esthetics of stairs and their history. He discovered that, early in their evolution, stairs and their kid brother, the ladder, were serious weapons of war. In Egyptian writing, the image of a ladder meant "siege." Pueblo Indians pulled up the ladders to their cliffside villages to keep out enemies. At Mesa Verde, in Colorado, the villagers carved a permanent stair into the cliff face with an ingenious twist: unless you knew the correct foot and hand with which to start your climb, you finished hanging in space, unable to enter the village because the hand you had free to reach up for the final grip was on the wrong side of your body. In medieval European castles, to reach the first floor you often had to climb a stairway that could easily be destroyed to keep out attackers. Or the entrance stairway was positioned so that defenders on the walls could pepper it with rocks or pour boiling oil down onto it.

Stairs had peaceful uses, of course. Designers learned to adjust stairway dimensions to control human movement. Templer explains that ancient workaday stairs, like today's, had high risers and small treads to hurry people along. Ceremonial stairs had smaller risers and deeper treads to promote a pensive gait.

To get a bead on such tricks, he has scouted Europe, armed with a ruler. At Vaux-le-Vicomte, the chateau completed in 1661 outside Paris for the lord high treasurer, who immediately afterward went to jail for embezzlement, Templer found that treads on a stairway descending into the main garden deepen as you go down. The aim, he believes, was to force arriving dignitaries into "an increasingly stately pace," at the risk of breaking an occasional royal neck.

Status stairs came into their own in the medieval period with the helical staircase. Building circular stairs requires advanced technical skills, and it was the rise of medieval crafts guilds that revved up the market. A classic helical stairway, at the abbey of St. Gilles du Gard, near Arles, had star quality: craftsmen from across Europe made pilgrimages to see it. Rich people showed off by putting helical stairs in their mansion towers.

In the Renaissance, many designers favored composite stairways of interconnected flights angling off from landings. At first, these complex stairways were used to add pizzazz to the era's grand gardens. But the designs soon invaded mansions and palaces, too. Designers experimented with stairs that clung to a wall on only one side, and then stairs with no walls at all. For Florence's Laurentian Library, Michelangelo created a freestanding grand stairway, with smaller flights going up along each flank. The secondary stairways showed off the central flight's monumentality. And uniformed footmen could stand on them, holding lanterns.

Stairs have served as theater seats, too, and as stages for public events. In Venice, the Scala dei Giganti (Stairs of the Giants) of the Doge's Palace were designed as the stage for the coronation of Leonardo Loredan. By the 1500s, a newly installed doge would sit regally at the top of the stairway to receive guests, who had to haul themselves up the flight to greet their new leader in an appropriately breathless state.

After the American and French revolutions, palaces were passé. The new hot spots were public buildings like museums or opera houses. And with ordinary Joes and Janes now thronging into government halls and other large buildings, stairs still had to be monumental—not to underscore the grandeur of kings and dukes but to handle the crowds. "Stair capacity became as important as location and effect," says Templer. And several 19th-century disasters—such as the 1876 fire at Brooklyn's Convoy Theatre, in which 283 people died—added to the importance of another stairway function, as fire escape.

Meanwhile, stairs have always had a purely esthetic side. They give architects a chance to experiment with diagonal lines, which Templer says have "shock value." He cites the Pompidou Center in Paris, where a suspended exterior escalator undulates diagonally up the building's face like an anaconda. Helical stairs offer curves. Renaissance architects in France and Germany even prefigured the discovery of the molecular structure of DNA by designing stairways in the form of a double helix.

Renaissance architects were entranced with the analogy between steps and flowing water. They began to incorporate fountains into garden stairways or send water gushing along a flue down a stairway's center. By the Baroque period, at the Royal Palace at Caserta, in Italy, the real stairs were dwarfed by a huge water stair running down their center, the immense liquid steps receding to the horizon. In a different mood, the designers of the 1600s became playful with water at Villa Torrigiani, near Siena. There the host could wait until his lady guests in their satins and silks were descending the stairway into his garden and then turn on fountains hidden in the steps. He could direct these spurts to hound the women into fleeing this way and that among the flowers.

When they weren't playing water pranks, Baroque designers might fiddle with the balustrades, the railings running alongside the stairs, turning them into fanciful shapes. Balustrades of the vestibule stairway at the Palazzo dell'Università, built in 1623 in Genoa, end in lifesize carved lions that seem to be braced against slipping down the final seven steps. At Prince Eugene's town palace in Vienna, sculptures of Atlas and Hercules strain to hold up the archways over the stairs, risking herniation. The balustrade at the Mirabell Palace in Salzburg is a frothy stone evocation of waves in which cherubs cavort, and where any stairway climber seeking a handhold is out of luck. By the 1800s, when Charles Garnier designed the Paris Opéra's foyer staircase as a kind of second stage where theatergoers might pose and preen, he could announce, "the Opéra is the staircase."

Today we might have to say "the skyscraper is the elevator" or "the shopping mall is the escalator." New materials like plastics and poured concrete let architects continue to experiment with stairs, making flights that seem inspired by Tinkerbell. John Templer points to Brasilia's Palace of the Arches, where Oscar Niemeyer designed freestanding concrete stairs—free of balustrades or railings—that twist upward as if levitated by helium.

"Structural pyrotechnics," says Templer.

For the stairstruck, the quest is neverending. At a new Harvard University art building, says Templer, an architect has created yet another stairway in the modern no-hands mode. Or so he has heard. He sounds wistful.

"I'd love to see that!"

Questions for Discussion

1. In this essay, which information is knowledge by participation and which is knowledge by observation?
2. Notice the frequency of direct quotations. What do you think of this technique? What is the author trying to accomplish by using direct quotations? Does he achieve his objective?
3. What is the essay's subordinate aim? Cite specific passages to support your answer.
4. What do you think of the ending? Is it appropriate? Is it effective? Why do you think it is or isn't?
5. Do you like the title? Why or why not? What other titles are possible for this essay?

Opportunities for Writing

1. Analyze the stairs in a building you often visit. Is it straight-flight, helical, or composite? How often do people trip? Do people trip more often while ascending or while descending? Report the results of your research to the owner of the building.
2. Compare and contrast straight-flight staircases and helical staircases. Using personal experience, interviews, and existing studies, specifically address issues of safety and cost. Are people more or less cautious on helical stairs? Do people trip more or less often on straight-flight stairs? Are helical stairs more or less expensive to build? Are straight-flight stairs more or less difficult to build?
3. Investigate the causes and effects of a specific accident at your school. When and where did the accident occur? Why? How serious were the injuries? Have similar accidents occurred previously? If so, how often? Could similar accidents be avoided? How? Write your essay as a special investigative article for your school newspaper.
4. Investigate the safety of a specific architectural item (e.g., doors). What are the different types (e.g., hinged, sliding, and revolving doors)? What are the hazards associated with each type? Compose your essay for a special display on architecture at a local museum

The Mind of the Puzzler

ROBERT J. STERNBERG AND JANET E. DAVIDSON

Robert J. Sternberg and Janet E. Davidson are both psychologists. Sternberg is a professor of psychology at Yale University and the author of several books on creativity and intelligence, such as Defying the Crowd: Cultivating Creativity in a Culture of Conformity *(1995) and* Metaphors of Mind: Conceptions of the Nature of Intelligence *(1990). He has also edited or co-edited over a dozen books, including* The Encyclopedia of Human Intelligence *(1994). In addition to their collaboration on this article published in* Psychology Today, *Sternberg and Davidson co-edited* The Nature of Insight *(1995) and* Conceptions of Giftedness *(1986). When this article was published in* Psychology Today, *Davidson was a Yale psychology graduate student. In "The Mind of the Puzzler," Sternberg and Davidson present "the literature on problem-solving" and conduct a study "to measure the relationship between performance on insight problems and scores on standard intelligence tests."*

Before departing from San Francisco on a flight to New York recently, a colleague of ours picked out some reading to test his wits. A professor of some accomplishment, he expected to make short work of the problems in *Games for the Superintelligent, More Games for the Superintelligent,* and *The Mensa Genius Quiz Book.* By the time he crossed the Rocky Mountains, however, he had realized that he was neither a genius nor, as *The Genius Quiz Book* puts it, "a secret superbrain who doesn't even know it." By the time he crossed the Mississippi River, he knew that he wasn't "superintelligent," either.

More often than not, the puzzles stumped him. How could two men play five games of checkers and each win the same number of games without any ties? He couldn't figure it out. How could you plant a total of 10 trees in five rows of four trees each? He drew several diagrams, and none of them worked. But he couldn't put the books down.

Our colleague wasn't alone in his frustration. Mental puzzles, whose appeal must be limited to the relatively intelligent, have nevertheless been a staple of the publishing industry for years. Martin Gardner's mathematical puzzles, from the monthly column he used to write for *Scientific American,* have been collected in 10 different books, with total sales of more than half a million copies. *Solve It, Games for the Superintelligent,* and *More Games for the Superintelligent,* all by James Fixx, have together sold nearly one million copies.

Puzzles can certainly be fun, and great ego boosters for those who eventually get the right answers. According to James Fixx, many people use mental puzzles to "strengthen their thought processes" and to "tune up their minds." Others use them to test or measure their own intelligence. In fact, *More Games* and *The Mensa Genius Quiz Book* actually contain what are suppposed to be short IQ tests.

Many of the problems in these books require flashes of insight or "leaps of logic" on the part of the solver, rather than prior knowledge or laborious computation. We wondered just how people approach such puzzles—which are commonly called insight problems—and whether they provide a valid measure of a person's intelligence. To answer these questions, we examined the literature on problem-solving, and then conducted a mini-experiment to measure the relationship between performance on insight problems and scores on standard intelligence tests.

On the basis of our research, we identified three types of intellectual processes that, separately or together, seem to be required in solving most insight problems: the ability to select and "encode" information—that is, to understand what information is relevant to solving the problem, and how it is relevant; the ability to combine different and seemingly unrelated bits of useful information; and the ability to compare the problem under consideration with problems previously encountered. For example, in solving the problem of the checker players, faulty encoding would lead one to assume that the two men were playing each other. Correctly combining the facts that there were no ties and that each player won the same number of games should lead one to conclude that they couldn't be playing each other.

Similarly, to plant 10 trees in five rows of four trees each, one must get away from the idea of making the five rows parallel. People who are accustomed to thinking in geometric terms will usually imagine several other kinds of patterns, until they hit on the correct one:

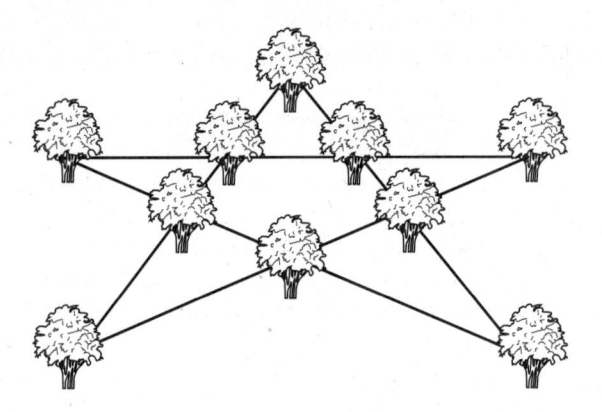

The literature on how people solve insight problems is meager, and includes almost no reports on research relating solution of these problems to intelligence. One of the few studies of this sort was done in 1965 by Norman Maier and Ronald Burke at the University of Michigan. Maier and Burke compared people's scores on a variety of aptitude tests with their skill at solving the "hat-rack problem." The problem calls on them to build a structure, sufficiently stable to support a man's overcoat, using only two long sticks and a C-clamp. The opening of the clamp is wide enough so that the two sticks can be inserted and held together securely when the clamp is tightened. Participants are placed in a small room and are asked to build a hat rack in the center of the room. The solution is shown on the following page.

When the researchers compared people's ability to solve the hat-rack problem with their scores on the Scholastic Aptitude Test, the correlations were all trivial. In other words, whatever insight people needed to build the hat rack seemed to be unrelated to their scores on standardized intelligence tests. Burke and Maier concluded that the abilities needed to solve insight problems may be different from those required to solve problems of the kinds found on such tests. Their study is of limited value, however: They used only one problem, and scored the responses only in terms of "right" or "wrong."

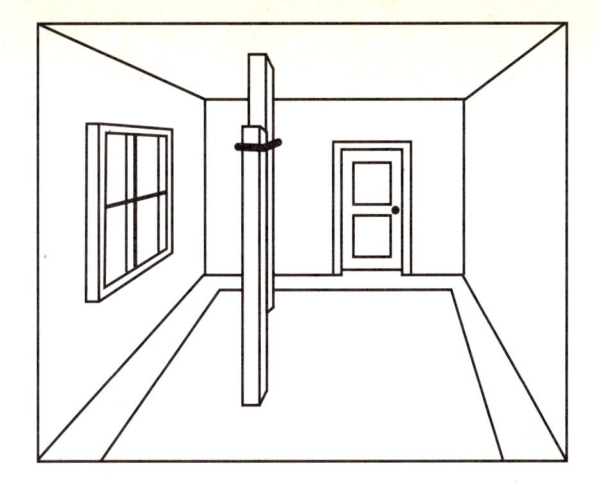

We did find in the literature some theoretical basis for the lack of relationship between intelligence and performance on the hat-rack problem. Kjell Raaheim, a psychologist at the University of Bergen, in Norway, wrote in *Problem Solving and Intelligence* that "it is unreasonable to expect intelligence to be an important factor of success in solving tasks which are totally unfamiliar to the individual facing them." According to Raaheim, problems will best measure intelligence if they present a situation that is *intermediate* in its degree of familiarity to a problem-solver. Problems presenting situations that are either too familiar or too unfamiliar will provide poorer measures of a person's intelligence.

In an ingenious set of experiments, Robert Weisberg and Joseph Alba, of Temple University, asked people to solve a set of insight problems. One was the familiar nine-dot problem, in which they were shown a three-by-three array of nine equally spaced dots and asked to connect the nine dots using four straight lines without lifting pencil from paper. The solution requires an approach similar to that used to plant the five rows of trees.

What is unique about Weisberg and Alba's study is that participants were actually given the insight they needed to solve the problem: They were told that it could be solved only by drawing the lines beyond the boundaries formed by the dots. Still, even after they were given the relevant insights, people in this study had considerable difficulty in solving the problem. Weisberg and Alba interpreted the results as suggesting that such problems may not really measure insight, but rather problem-specific prior knowledge. Our interpretation is a bit different. As we see it, subjects not only needed to know that they could draw the lines outside the boundaries; they also had to know how to combine what went outside the dots with what went inside. Performance on these insight problems therefore might not correlate with performance on intelligence-test problems.

Even though classic insight problems may not truly measure insight alone, we believed that problems could be found that do provide fairly accurate measures of insight, and that performance on such problems would be correlated with intelligence as it is typically measured by standardized tests.

To test this view, we compiled a set of 12 insight problems from a number of popular books. The problems vary in difficulty, in trickiness, and in the number of possible approaches that can be taken to reach a solution.

We recruited 30 people from the New Haven area by means of a newspaper advertisement that invited them to take part in a problem-solving experiment at Yale. Though not selected by scientific criteria, our small sample—19 men and 11 women—represented a fairly typical cross-section of urban residents, with a wide range of ages, occupations, and educational backgrounds. None were connected with Yale.

First, we gave them a standard IQ test (the Henmon-Nelson Test of Mental Ability), including questions of vocabulary, math, and reasoning. None of the problems were quite like our insight problems. A typical reasoning problem, for example, might require the person to solve an analogy such as: CAR is to GASOLINE as HUMAN is to (a. OIL b. ENERGY c. FOOD d. FUEL); or a number series such as: 3, 7, 12, 18,—? (a. 24 b. 25 c. 26 d. 27). The IQ test problems were multiple-choice, whereas the insight problems we used required people to generate their own answers.

The average IQ score of our sample on this test was 112, 12 points above the national average. (Elevated average IQs are typical in such experiments, since those who volunteer for studies on problem-solving are likely to be of above-average intelligence. People with very low IQs may not read newspapers, and probably wouldn't volunteer for experiments on problem-solving even if they do.)

Second, we gave our subjects a deductive-reasoning test on nonsense syllogisms, such as "All trees are fish. All fish are horses. Therefore, all trees are horses. Please indicate whether the conclusion is logically valid or not." (This one is.) Third, in a test of inductive reasoning, we presented our subjects with five sets of letters (for example, NOPQ, DEFL, ABCD, HIJK, UVWX) and asked them to choose the set that was based on a rule different from the rule used as a basis for the other sets.

We included these two specific tests, as well as the more general IQ test, to judge the accuracy of a prediction we had made: If our problems genuinely measured insight, they should be more highly correlated with the inductive test, which requires one to go beyond the information given, than with the deductive test, which merely requires one to analyze the given information and draw the proper conclusion. Normal arithmetic or logic problems, for example, require primarily deductive rather than inductive reasoning skills.

Our subjects found the insight problems fun but sometimes frustrating, since the items varied considerably in difficulty. The easiest item, answered correctly by 73 percent of our sample, was this:

"Next week I am going to have lunch with my friend, visit the new art gallery, go to the Social Security office, and have my teeth checked at the dentist's. My friend cannot meet me on Wednesday; the Social Security office is closed weekends; the art gallery is closed Tuesday, Thursday, and weekends; and the dentist has office hours only on Tuesday, Friday, and Saturday. What day can I do everything I have planned?" Reaching the answer (Friday) is easy because one can simply check off which days don't work.

The hardest item, answered correctly by only 7 percent of our subjects, was: "A bottle of wine cost $10. The wine was worth $9 more than the bottle. How much was the bottle worth?" People probably had a hard time coming up with the answer (50 cents) because they misunderstood the word 'more.'

The average score on our insight problem test was 4.4 correct out of 12, or roughly 37 percent. The individual scores ranged from a low of one to a high of 10, with no difference between the average scores of the men and the women. The times people spent solving the problems ranged from 11 minutes to 47 minutes, with an average of 28 minutes.

When we examined the relationship between scores on the set of 12 insight problems and scores on the mental-ability tests, we found relatively high correlations between the insight-problem scores and the scores on the tests of IQ (.66 on a scale from zero to one, on which a correlation of zero means no relationship, and a correlation of one means a perfect relationship) and inductive reasoning (.63), and only a moderate correlation with the scores on the test of deductive reasoning (.34). (All of the correlations were statistically significant.) These correlations suggest that performance on insight problems does provide a good index of intelligence, and that such performance may be more closely related to inductive than to deductive reasoning.

We then looked at the relationship between the test scores and time spent on the insight problems, and found that people who spent the most time working on the problems tended to have a higher number of correct solutions, and higher IQ scores. (The correlation between time spent and number of insight problems correctly solved was .62. The correlation between time spent and IQ was .75, which is remarkably high.) Why did smart people take longer on this task? Although we can only speculate, we suspect it is because they became more absorbed in the problems and more motivated to solve them. Our observations suggested that the less bright people either were too quick to choose the seemingly obvious but wrong answers on trick questions, or simply didn't know how to get started on the tougher problems and gave up more quickly.

When we looked at the correlations between the test scores on the insight problems and the scores on the standardized intelligence test, we found that the problems varied considerably in their validity as indicators of IQ. The problem of which day to schedule a lunch date with a friend had almost no correlation with IQ; the problem that proved to be the best predictor of IQ score was the following:

"Water lilies double in area every 24 hours. At the beginning of the summer there is one water lily on a lake. It takes 60 days for the lake to become covered with water lilies. On what day is the lake half covered?" To find the answer, people must realize that since the water lilies double in area every 24 hours, the lake will be half covered on the 59th day in order to be completely covered on the 60th.

What made some items better measures of IQ than others? We discovered two patterns among the "good" and "bad" indicators of IQ that we thought were striking, at least as preliminary hypotheses.

The best indicators of IQ seemed to be those problems that presented both relevant and irrelevant information: The key to success was the ability to distinguish necessary information from unnecessary. For example, people with high

IQs tended to realize that "water lilies double in area every 24 hours" was an important clue to solving this problem. People with low IQs frequently ignored this information and tried to solve the problem by dividing the 60 days by two.

Our interpretation of performance on the problems supports the theory that the ability to detect and use clues embedded in the context of what one reads plays an important role in solving verbal problems. When reading a test—whether it is a newspaper, a science book, or a verbal or arithmetic problem—much of the information may be irrelevant to one's needs; often the hard part is figuring out what is relevant, and how it is relevant.

The problems that proved to be poor indicators of IQ were the "trick" problems in which errors were due primarily to misreading the problem situation—fixing on the apparent question rather than on the actual question. Take the following problem: "A farmer has 17 sheep. All but nine break through a hole in the fence and wander away. How many are left?" People making errors generally failed to comprehend exactly what "all but nine" meant; many assumed that the nine had escaped and thus subtracted that number from 17 to get the number of sheep that remained behind.

If, as we have shown, insight problems do provide a good measure of intellectual ability—at least when they require one to make inductive leaps beyond the given data and when they require one to sift out relevant from irrelevant information—we must ask: Just what is insight? The reason that others have not found any common element in the various insights they have studied is that no one model works for all cases. We have identified three basic kinds of cognitive processes or insightful performance, one or more of which may be required to solve a given problem:

Selective Encoding, or processing of information. This kind of insight occurs when one perceives in a problem one or more facts that are not immediately obvious. Earlier, we referred to the importance of being able to sort out relevant from irrelevant information. This skill can provide the solver with a basis for selective encoding.

35   Consider the following problem: "If you have black socks and brown socks in your drawer, mixed in the ratio of 4 to 5, how many socks will you have to take out to make sure of having a pair the same color?" Subjects who failed to realize that "mixed in the ratio of 4 to 5" was irrelevant information consistently came up with the wrong solution. (The correct answer: three.) In the hat-rack problem, noticing the relevance of the floor and ceiling as elements in the problem is also an example of selective encoding.

Selective Combination. This type of insight takes place when one sees a way of combining unrelated (or at least not obviously related) elements, as one must do in the following problem: "With a seven-minute hourglass and an 11-minute hourglass, what is the simplest way to time the boiling of an egg for 15 minutes?" Our subjects had all of the necessary facts, but they had to figure out how to combine the two timers to measure 15 minutes. In the hat-rack problem, figuring out how to combine the use of the floor, ceiling, C-clamp, and two sticks constitutes a similar insight of selective combination.

Selective Comparison. This kind of insight occurs when one discovers a nonobvious relationship between new and old information. It is here that analogy, metaphor, and models come into play. In the hat-rack problem, for example, one might think of how a pole lamp can be stabilized by wedging it between the floor and ceiling of a room, and how the same principle could be used in the construction of a hat rack.

Consider another type of selective comparison: If someone doesn't know a word on a vocabulary test, he can often figure out its definition by thinking of words he does know that have the same word stems. For example, if he doesn't know the word 'exsect,' he might be able to guess its meaning by thinking of a word that has the same prefix (such as 'extract,' where *ex* means out) and a word that has the same root (such as 'dissect,' where *sect* means cut). This information might help him realize that 'exsect' means 'to cut out.'

We emphasize the critical role of selection in each kind of information-processing. In Selective Encoding, one must choose elements to encode from the often numerous and irrelevant bits of information presented by the problem; the trick is to select the right elements. In Selective Combination, there may be many possible ways for the encoded elements to be combined or otherwise integrated; the trick is to select the right way of combining them. In Selective Comparison, new information must be related to one or more of many possible old pieces of information. There are any number of analogies or relations that might be drawn; the trick is to make the right comparison or comparisons. Thus, to the extent that there is a communality in the three kinds of insight, it appears to be in the importance of selection to each kind.

We believe that much of the confusion in the past and present literature on problem-solving stems from a failure to recognize the existence of and differences among these three kinds of insight, which together seem to account for the mental processes that have been labeled as insight, and which are involved in everything from solving problems in puzzle books to making major scientific breakthroughs.

Although we have focused on the importance of insight in problem-solving—and also in intelligence—insight alone is not enough to solve problems. Certain other essential ingredients exist, including:

Prior Knowledge. Even apparently simple problems often require a store of prior knowledge for their solution; complex problems can require a vast store of such knowledge. Consider the problem of the seven-minute and 11-minute hourglasses, and how to time a 15-minute egg. If people have used hourglass timers before, and can remember that they can turn them over at any point, the knowledge will certainly help.

Executive Processes. These are the processes used to plan, monitor, and evaluate one's performance in problem-solving. To start with, one must first study the problem carefully, in order to figure out exactly what question is being asked.

Another executive process involves monitoring one's solution process (keeping track of what one has done, is doing, and still needs to do) and then switching strategies if one isn't making progress. Sometimes it helps to try a new approach if an old one doesn't work.

Motivation. Really challenging problems often require a great deal of motivation on the part of the solver. Successful problem-solvers are often those who simply are willing to put in the necessary effort. Indeed, in our mini-study we found that the better problem-solvers were more persevering than the poorer ones.

Style. People approach problems with different cognitive styles. In particular, some tend to be more impulsive and others more reflective. It seems to us—although we have no hard experimental evidence to support our view—that the most successful problem-solvers are those who manage to combine both impulsive and reflective styles. We do not believe that most people follow just one style or the other. Rather, at certain points in the problem-solving process, people act on impulse; at other times, they act only after great reflection. The hard part is knowing which style will pay off at which point in solving problems.

Successful problem-solving involves a number of different abilities. For many problems, one kind of insight may provide a key to a quick solution. But we believe that most problems are like the apartment doors one finds in some of our larger cities: They have multiple locks requiring multiple keys. Without combining different kinds of insights, as well as prior knowledge, executive processes, motivation, and style, the problems remain locked doors, waiting for the clever solver to find the right set of keys.

Questions for Discussion

1. Which passages constitute knowledge by participation? Which constitute knowledge by observation? Notice that the authors don't always cite sources of information for knowledge by observation. Does this omission damage their credibility? Explain your answers.
2. Add appropriate headings to this essay. How do the headings influence your reading? Is the essay more or less effective without the headings?
3. What is the purpose of the opening narrative? Is it appropriate? Is it necessary? Why or why not?
4. What is the essay's subordinate aim? Cite specific passages to support your answer.
5. Do the illustrations contribute to your understanding of the essay? Are more illustrations necessary? If so, identify specific tables or figures you would like to see. If not, explain why you think the authors included only two illustrations.

Opportunities for Writing

1. Compare and contrast inductive and deductive reasoning. How does each correlate with problem-solving ability? with intelligence? with creativity?
2. Using the puzzles mentioned in this essay, examine the problem-solving abilities of five friends. What does your research reveal about their individual abilities? Are you surprised by the findings? Why?
3. Using interviews of teachers, analyze the impact of intelligence testing on classroom teaching. Does such testing influence the expectations of teachers regarding their students? Is intelligence testing a positive or negative influence on teaching? Address your essay to a local organization of teachers.
4. Trace the history of intelligence testing. Who originally identified the IQ? How was IQ determined? How is it determined today? Compose your essay as a special article for your local newspaper.

Luis Jimenez's Outdoor Sculptures Slow Traffic Down

Chiori Santiago

Chiori Santiago lives in Berkeley, California, where she is writing a book on Caribbean-American musicians. In this essay, which was published in The Smithsonian, *Santiago interviews artist Jimenez to learn more about him and his fiberglass sculptures. When reading this article, notice how Santiago weaves quotations from Jimenez and descriptions of his sculptures into her narration (i.e., what she sees and thinks as it happens).*

Luis Jimenez is tooling down the main drag of El Paso, Texas, acting as tour guide to his past. We're on our way to San Jacinto Plaza in the old downtown, where he plans to install one of his fanciful sculptures later this year. But all he can think of at the moment are the signs in front of the 7-Elevens and furniture showrooms and Chinese eateries that line Mesa Street. The signs are ubiquitous plastic boxes, or worse, garish computerized light screens that elbow their way into one's field of vision like an ill-mannered tourist. To Jimenez, that's what they represent—interlopers in a bygone world of elegance and artistry.

Neon signs with lots of punch

"My father made signs that were individual works of great imagination," Jimenez says, navigating traffic past a lot filled with new cars. "Right here was the Fiesta Drive-In. It had a neon sign that he made of a woman dancing in a flamenco skirt in front of two guys sitting on the ground wearing sombreros. With each flash of light in the circuit, her dress would appear to go higher and higher, until at the end the guys' hats would fly up in the air." He chuckles. "That was typical of my dad's signs—lots of action and color. He gave El Paso a personality in the 1950s and '60s, and now it's all gone. When the plastic boxes came in, they killed neon. He couldn't compete pricewise."

The drive-in's fiesta dancer may be in marquee heaven, but the legacy of his father's neon sign shop lives on in Luis Jimenez's art. When he was enlisted by the business at age 6, Jimenez never suspected it was the start of an apprenticeship in public sculpture. Today, Jimenez's own *Fiesta Dancers,* a nine-foot-high fiberglass tribute to the passionate folkloric *jarabe* dance of Mexico, is a kind of Technicolor postcard, a greeting to travelers from Tijuana as they cross the border into San Diego. His muscular, highly colored, larger-than-life figures occupy other equally prominent niches on U.S. terrain. The hunched shoulders of his *Sodbuster* follow a plow down the main street of Fargo, North Dakota; a bronze coyote howls mournfully in the sculpture garden of the Albuquerque Museum; and his fearless *Vaquero* clings to a wild bronco in front of the Smithsonian's National Museum of American Art in Washington, D.C. Other works by Jimenez are currently on view in a group exhibition, "La Frontera/The Border," which is at the downtown branch of the Museum of Contemporary Art in San Diego from March 5 through May 22.

"To a certain extent, my outdoor pieces are performing the same function as a sign," Jimenez muses. "They're giving the place a sense of identity.

Certainly, when they put up the *Vaquero,* they were proclaiming: 'Hey, we're in an old Greek Revival building, but what we're showing inside is really a lot more adventurous.' "

5   Jimenez's pieces are signposts marking elements of 20th-century culture. But his art-historical roots go far deeper. "He's a major contemporary sculptor whose works reflect the idealized imagery of Michelanglo, the Greeks and the Romans," says Ellen Landis, who is assembling a major retrospective of Jimenez's work to open next year at the Albuquerque Museum. "Yet his pieces are exceptionally relevant to current social problems; Luis's images are so universal it's easy for the populace to relate to them."

Certainly, Jimenez's pieces make reference to those stalwarts of the sculptural tradition: the equestrian statue, the Pietà, the figurative monument. Except, rather than using the traditional materials of marble and bronze, he molds his high-energy tableaus in fiberglass, the material of boat hulls and hot rods, painted in a riotous car-buff palette of Mexicali red, school-bus yellow and Capri blue. And Jimenez chooses to raise unconventional subjects to the level of famous generals and laureled men of letters. He immortalizes the overlooked and long forgotten: the immigrants who nightly wade the Rio Grande toward its northern bank; the Mexican ranch hands who were the West's original cowboys; or the alligators that once drew scores of Sunday visitors to El Paso's town square.

The town square is, in fact, our next stop, and as Jimenez walks toward it, he's the picture of a self-made man, tall and energetic at 52. A multicolored welder's cap covers his thick gray hair, and his sartorial taste declares his status as a working man; he favors paint-stained jeans and T-shirts. But as we near our destination he is a boy once again, not much bigger than his 5-year-old son, Orion, who tags along. He remembers this place as La Plaza de los Lagartos—Alligator Plaza—the starting point for weekend jaunts with his grandmother. After looking at the thrilling knurled beasts, they'd head across the border to visit the bird markets and vegetable stands of Mexico.

The walkway that joins El Paso with its Mexican neighbor, Juárez, is just 12 blocks or so from here, and in terms of culture and commerce this is where the border disappears. Old men rest in the shade, their creased brown faces hidden by straw brims; passers-by wave at friends with a shout of *"¿Qué pasa, hombre?"* Two women with the long black braids and patterned skirts worn by Guatemalan mountain people mull the contents of their plastic shopping bags. There's a multitude of life in the square, but no alligators. Today, only a chunky blue-tiled fountain marks the scene where the animals lived; it is said that a local dentist used to sneak into the pond at midnight to clean the beasts' teeth. Eventually, they were moved to a zoo, perhaps more for their own safety than the public's.

Jimenez, as he does in most of his public art, intends to resurrect history by bringing back the alligators, this time as a playful fountain built of frolicking fiberglass beasts. The commission is something of an epiphany for Jimenez, his first opportunity to stamp his esthetic on the hometown that holds his bittersweet past. "It was a tough city to grow up in if you were Mexican, not unlike being in South Africa," he says. "The majority of the population was Mexican or Chicano, but their traditions were slighted. I have very mixed feelings about El Paso."

Jimenez's grandmother and father crossed the border into El Paso's "Segundo Barrio" illegally in 1924; his father didn't obtain citizenship until after Jimenez was born. Luis sr. was an ambitious man, with a street fighter's tenaciousness that would enable him to eventually own the sign shop at which he'd started as an employee. He was also an artist frustrated by poverty—he'd won a national art contest in the 1930s, but Depression-era cutbacks erased the expected prize scholarship. Consequently, he maintained unrelentingly high standards for his sons. Jimenez mentions this as he pulls his car in front of the abandoned Crystal Cleaners on Wyoming Street. We stare up at a huge white polar bear that still stands guard overhead, and Jimenez remembers his 6-year-old self pressed into service to slap wet concrete onto the animal's metal frame. The task seemed impossibly huge, but the boy was less frightened by the size of the job than by his father's demands.

There were rewards, too: journeys to Mexico to see the vibrant art in its museums, so different from dull El Paso, where his favorite artworks were the government-sponsored 1930s murals in the federal courthouse and elsewhere. These sweeping, idealized vistas of westward development would influence

Jimenez in a way that he wouldn't understand until much later. When he entered college he would defy his father and switch majors from architecture to art, a move that meant the younger Jimenez had to pay his own tuition. Jimenez's mother, Alicia, lives just a few blocks from Crystal Cleaners, not far from where Luis grew up. We step in. She greets her son with a kiss, admonishes him for his tattered clothing, shoos her Chihuahua out of the way and proudly points out the early Jimenez works scattered around the floor of the entryway. They are abstract, Henry Moore-ish forms carved of oak and mesquite, whatever the young artist could pick up around the neighborhood. One of them demonstrates his budding penchant for brazenness. On a conventional, stylized carving of a Madonna and Child, he's imposed a pair of pendant breasts.

Alicia Jimenez sighs as she remember her son's decision not to follow his father into the sign business. "You see how he looks now, with his pants falling down and his shirt untucked? He used to look so nice. Wait, I'll show you." She disappears into a bedroom, emerging a moment later clutching a fading snapshot. "See? This is just after he went to New York."

In the picture is Jimenez at 26, posed before a wall full of drawings. He wears a dark suit and tie, and his mouth is a straight line in a square, determined face. After the unequal turf of El Paso, "New York City was a totally level playing field," Jimenez recalls. "Being Chicano didn't mean much; I became a Latino." Away from the racial limitations of Texas, he could develop an individual voice and yet see himself as part of a larger national culture. It was a heady time; he apprenticed himself to sculptor Seymour Lipton, worked for the Head Start program and organized street dances for the city's Youth Board. He didn't have much money, but he could afford a room in SoHo where entertainment was free: a number of musicians lived nearby, and the sounds of all-night jam sessions often wafted up and down the street.

In the meantime, Jimenez was experimenting with three-dimensional form. "Perhaps because of the experience of working in the sign shop, I realized early on that I wanted to do it all—paint, draw, work with wood, metal, clay. Sculpture allows you to do that." His images were those of 1960s pop culture, chosen for their familiarity and shock value. He made buxom blondes like *California Chick,* demolition derby cars, overweight sun worshipers. They were images of a society in the thrall of machinery, with its humanity out of control: his best-known early works include *American Dream* (1967), which depicts a Volkswagen making love to a woman (it is owned by the Hirshhorn & Museum Sculpture Garden), and *Barfly* (1969), portraying the Statue of Liberty as a lushly degenerate beer drinker. The pieces were thin and flimsy—he was pinching pennies and skimping on material, mixing resins, aluminum powder and pigments rather than investing in expensive commercial finishes—but the sculpture was developing an energy that was hard to ignore.

The visual language he grew up with

15   "Using fiberglass was a logical decision." he comments. "The material carries the same baggage as the images. It's not a 'high art' material. People have asked me if I choose garish colors for their shock value. But I like those colors. It has to do with personal taste, and that varies from culture to culture." Indeed,

a good deal of Jimenez's visual language is pure Segundo Barrio, with references to *cholos'* tattoos, plaster saints, black velvet paintings of fantastic beasts and wanton women, ceramic ashtrays in the shape of cacti. "Yeah, it's all that stuff," he says. "My working-class roots have a lot to do with it; I want to create a popular art that ordinary people can relate to as well as people who have degrees in art. That doesn't mean it has to be watered down. My philosophy is to create a multilayered piece, like Hemingway's *Old Man and the Sea*. The first time I read it, it was an exciting adventure story about fishing. The last time, I was deeply moved."

Getting his first show required a Segundo Barrio chutzpah, too. At the end of one long afternoon in 1969, after he'd been refused by every exhibit space he'd visited, he pulled his truck in front of the Leo Castelli Gallery where director Ivan Karp, he'd heard, was sympathetic to emerging artists. Finding no one in the empty space, Jimenez decided to carry the three sculptures he had in the truck inside, as if he were selling nothing more than Fuller brushes. When Karp finally emerged from a back room, he was first astounded by the stranger's nerve, then taken by the work. He couldn't show it, he said, but perhaps the Graham Gallery would. The folks at Graham Gallery did, although they weren't confident about selling it. To their surprise, the work not only attracted attention, but artist and art patron Alfonso Ossorio agreed to purchase enough of it to enable the gallery to underwrite Jimenez's first solo show. "I was just very lucky; things happened pretty quickly after that," he says. Even Hilton Kramer, at that time the *New York Times'* notoriously grumpy critic, gave his second show at Graham high marks. Then, just as he was riding the crest of Eastern acceptance, Jimenez decided it was time to move on.

"I did all right in New York but I felt rooted in the Southwest," he says. "I missed the connection to the land." So, in 1972 he drove his truck west to Roswell, New Mexico, where collector Donald Anderson had agreed to set him up in a studio and fund production of his first two large-scale sculptures. Based on the old government murals that had impressed him as a boy, they are glossy, high-voltage interpretations of the mythic West. They pay tribute to Indian buffalo hunters, Spanish cowboys and longhorn steers—essentially, species headed for extinction—in unsentimental cartoon colors that convey their place in a pantheon of romantic heroes.

Rodeo, bronco, corral—*all Spanish words*

In 1979 Jimenez won his first public commission, which was to be a cast of *Vaquero* for Houston's Moody Park. "I wanted to do something about Texas, and the early studies for that piece were straight cowboys, a fairly obvious image," he says. "As I got more involved, and because I do have a social agenda for the work, I realized that cowboys had come out of the Mexican experience." He ticks off evidence in the archaeology of language: *rodeo, bronco* and *corral* are all Spanish words; *vaquero,* of course, means "cowboy."

"I realized that we just got left out of history. Making *Vaquero* acknowledges the contribution Mexicans and Mexican-Americans made toward popular American imagery."

On another level, the piece is a comment on equestrian sculpture. "There's a whole tradition around the position of the horse's legs," Jimenez explains. "If all four feet are down, the person died in his sleep. One front foot up means he died in battle. Well, two back feet in the air didn't mean anything. So putting the vaquero on a bucking bronco was a way of breaking with tradition."

It's Jimenez's lusty attack on hidebound themes that invigorates his work and makes it so universally accessible. The corollary of a democratic art, however, is that the public has an equal right to complain about it. When *Vaquero* was temporarily installed in Scottsdale, Arizona, gallery owners deemed it inappropriate and tried to have it removed. "What [they] seem to want is . . . something inoffensive, generic, forgettable . . . Muzak in metal," shot back Richard Nilsen, columnist for the *Arizona Republic*. Then, after the piece went into Moody Park, says Jimenez, some public officials criticized the gun-toting figure as an advocate of violence. "You wouldn't think of taking the gun away from a statue of Robert E. Lee, but a gun in the hand of a Mexican becomes dangerous."

There have been other flaps. In 1983, residents of Albuquerque's Old Town neighborhood protested the commission of *Southwest Pieta,* Jimenez's interpretation of the classic Romeo-and-Juliet tragedy of Aztec lovers Popocatepetl and Princess Ixtaccihuatl. But some misunderstood it. "Critics, who say it depicts the aftermath of a rape of an Indian maiden by a Spanish conquistador, say it is offensive to those of Spanish heritage," reported the *Albuquerque Tribune*. Chicano residents of the city's Martineztown, on the other hand, fought hard to have the sculpture installed there, which was done in 1988. And in Pittsburgh, says Jimenez with some relish, a local politician denounced *Steelworker* as an "ugly guy" as it was being put up outdoors at a 1990 festival. "But after it was installed, people came to lay flowers at the base. It was an image that hit a raw nerve."

"There's a lot of pathos and joy in his work, and when the two come together you have mixed emotions," comments Ellen Landis. "That can be hard for people."

The confrontational quality of his art simply reproduces the reality Jimenez sees around him—which isn't always comfortable. At home in Hondo, New Mexico, where he now lives in rural solitude in a converted WPA-era schoolhouse with his wife, Susie, and their three children, he is surrounded by the continuous drama of life grappling with death. Peacocks in the yard sometimes get attacked by the dog. During early-morning walks, the family may stop to examine the remains of a road kill or to watch a group of ravens chase a marauding hawk from their aerial territory. Scattered among the art at his home are the skulls of small creatures, the shards of past civilizations and other things he has picked up. The reverberations find their way into Jimenez's work as what writer Annette DiMeo Carlozzi calls "a dense encyclopedia of iconographic detail."

25 "I guess most of my work ends up being about predator-prey relationships," Jimenez says, "with Man just one more predator in the chain." He falls silent during the five-minute commute from his home on one side of Hondo to his workshop, in an old apple-processing warehouse, on the other. "Of course, the animals may be getting back at us," he says suddenly. "Oscar had to get his car repaired four times this year after deer jumped in front of him after dark."

"Oscar" is Oscar Macias, one of a battery of assistants who help Jimenez turn out his long list of commissions. As we walk toward the shop, Spanish love songs float out to greet us. *"Enamorado-o-o-o,"* sighs a crooner, full blast, over the radio. Inside, the place bustles. Macias has the nose of a tiny mustang—a maquette for a proposed 30-foot-high sculpture for the new international airport in Denver—clamped in a vise; he smooths its snout with strokes of a chisel. His brother Jose Luis works on a sculpture base, while on a loading dock outside Jesus Medina reinforces the mold for another casting of *Fiesta Dancers*. A finished casting of the piece stands nearby, the man tall and proud, his buxom partner confronting him with a loose-lipped grin, their unpainted alabaster-white forms rising toward the sun.

Pressing each fistful of clay into place

For each commissioned piece, Jimenez reserves the right to make five castings for his own use in addition to an artist's proof. That would add up to a tremendous body of work dotted around the country, except the process is prohibitively slow. It calls for construction of a steel armature, over which a clay form takes shape. Jimenez insists on pressing each fistful of clay into place himself. He tried having assistants do some of the basic work but found it impossible for others to duplicate the imprint of the artist's hands. "I ended up taking off most of the clay that they put on," he says.

Fiberglass is shaped over the clay form to make a master mold used to cast each sculpture. For each casting, pieces of fiberglass are applied in layers to the inside of the mold, building up each section of sculpture. After it's released from the mold and sanded, Jimenez goes to work with a spray gun, applying layers of acrylic urethane ("the same finish used on jet aircraft," he says) to give his pieces the luster of a low-rider fender.

With the individual attention involved, it's not surprising that his commissioners often wait embarrassingly long stretches for his public pieces. The alligators for El Paso's town square, for example, pose half-finished in clay in his studio right now, several years overdue. The setbacks may be legitimate—Jimenez underwent four major operations last year to deal with continuing problems from a childhood eye injury—but that doesn't make some clients less impatient. One off them threatened to fine him $500 a day when a project went overtime. "But I have to do it right," Jimenez says. "Once they understand that they're getting a one-of-a-kind piece, they back off. It's not like pulling a print out of a drawer."

Besides, there's the matter of artistic impulse. When it comes right down to it, "an artist doesn't want to be in the same position as a sign painter, where you're just doing manual labor," he says. "To make it fun, you've got to get near the edge, you've got to get the adrenaline going, you've got to push it to the point where you're going to lose it, because that's what makes it exciting. Like those alligators; I've changed them so radically from the original drawing by now that I don't have anything to go by anymore. I've just got to make them work."

Perhaps tonight Jimenez will spend some endless, painful hours pacing around the sculpture that towers over him, threatening to engulf him. He'll decide where to press the clay, how to wrestle his demons to the ground. For now, he locks up the apple shed at sundown and drives home, where his Appaloosa waits to be fed, where his children will clamber onto his lap, where he'll take in some of the life that he'll breathe into his work tomorrow. Behind him, the figures of *Fiesta Dancers* cavort on the loading dock in Brobdingnagian splendor, surprising the midnight drivers along Highway 70.

Questions for Discussion

1. How would this essay differ if it were written using only knowledge by participation? Would it be more or less effective? Explain your answer.
2. How does the author try to motivate the audience? Does she do a satisfactory job? Why or why not?
3. Do the headings clarify the organization of the essay? If so, how? If not, how would you revise the headings?
4. How does the author try to establish credibility on this subject? How might she reinforce this credibility?
5. Notice the frequency of direct quotations. Do you think this technique is effective here? If so, how does it contribute to the essay? If not, how would you revise the essay?

Opportunities for Writing

1. Analyze the work of a specific sculptor. What are the characteristics of his or her work? What materials does he or she prefer? What are his or her typical methods? Compose your essay for a special exhibit of this sculptor's works at a local art gallery.
2. Using a questionnaire, analyze the impact of public sculptures on your community. What do people in your community think of the sculptures? How do such sculptures contribute to the quality of life in your community? Report the results of your research to your city council.
3. Explain the process for creating a fiberglass sculpture. What materials and instruments are required? What are the steps involved?
4. Compose a special article for your local newspaper to explain the process for commissioning public art in your community. Who decides that such art is necessary? Who chooses the artist? How?

The Bambi Syndrome

MATT CARTMILL

Educated at Pomona College and the University of Chicago, Matt Cartmill is a professor of anatomy and biological anthropology at Duke University Medical Center and the co-editor of The American Journal of Physical Anthropology. *"The Bambi Syndrome" traces the history of the original story by Felix Salten and analyzes the effect that Walt Disney's resulting animated film* Bambi *has had on American perceptions of animals and hunting. This essay is Cartmill's adaptation from his* A View to a Death in the Morning: Hunting and Nature Through History *(1993) and appeared in* Natural History, *a magazine published by the American Museum of Natural History.*

Prospects look bleak for America's hunters. Only about 12 percent of Americans still hunt, and the percentage seems to be dwindling year by year. In 1982, Americans spent 109,000 hours hunting on U.S. public lands; by 1990, the figure had dropped to less than half that.

Part of this change probably reflects the shrinking population of small-town America, where hunting has always been a part of the rural way of life. But public attitudes are changing, too. Although most of us still think it all right to hunt for meat, many people oppose hunting for trophies or recreation. One poll shows that almost a third of all Americans feel sport hunting should be illegal. And that feeling is being promoted by organized antihunters, who are hard at work circulating petitions and propaganda, pressing for new laws and regulations to limit hunting, and even running through the woods in front of hunters to scare off their prey.

Each side in this confrontation sees the other as a congregation of lunatics. Pro-animal activists regard hunters as macho gun nuts eager to prove their manhood by drilling anything that moves. For their part, hunters view their opponents as sentimental fluffheads, who dream of the natural world as a happy Eden and idealize wild animals as little innocent people in bunny suits.

Many hunters blame this antihunting sentiment on Walt Disney. A lot of hunting writers seem to think it all began with the 1942 release of *Bambi* and that if this film and certain other Disney products could somehow be suppressed, opposition to hunting would evaporate. Warren Page, a former editor of *Field and Stream*, expressed this view in a 1973 speech:

> In this country we have undergone an entire generation of brainwashing. Not only our kids but our wives, our brothers, our mothers, our cousins, our brothers-in-law have for twenty-five years been subjected to constant film and TV presentations of the Disney myth. In the Wonderful World of Disney . . . the lion and the lamb love one another and only man is the bastard in the black hat . . . whose chief aim is the spilling of Bambi's blood. Now this is the Bambi Syndrome. The Disney films may not have started out that way, but once it became clear that sentimentality and outright anthropomorphism would make money, that's the way the films went . . . . They deliberately misinform viewers of basic biological facts.

5   Bambi bashing pervades the defensive protests of today's embattled outdoorsmen. "Too many antihunters believe in the Bambi quality of animals," writes sports columnist Jim Wilson. "Those animals don't procreate or eliminate wastes or eat one another, they gaily romp and play their lives away. . . . These people never knew or don't want to know that death is as quotidian in the wild as sucking air in and blowing it out."

The hunters are surely right about one thing: for all its saccharine sweetness and childish whimsy, Disney's *Bambi* is probably the most effective piece of antihunting propaganda ever made. It had a wide and deep influence on modern attitudes toward hunting, wildlife, and the wilderness.

The Bambi myth was the creation of an ambitious young Hungarian writer named Siegmund Salzmann, who came to Vienna in the mid-1880s in search of fame and fortune. Changing his Jewish-sounding name to Felix Salten, he began turning out volume after volume of plays, stories, and criticism and quickly became a major force in Viennese literary circles. Salten's life, like those of many middle-class Viennese, seethed with public and private contradictions. A pillar of Establishment propriety on the surface, he was also the secret author of a notorious pornographic novel, *The Memoirs of Josephine Mutzenbacher*. An aristocratically contemptuous critic of American society and culture, he was also a Rotarian and the German translator of the long-running Broadway hit *Abie's Irish Rose*. He liked to go hunting with Hapsburg aristocrats and even owned a private hunting preserve of his own just outside of Vienna. But he was also an ardent animal lover, and his hunting experiences led him to produce a masterpiece of antihunting sentiment.

Salten's novel *Bambi: A Forest Life* appeared in 1924. Written in the decaying capital of the defeated and dismembered Hapsburg empire, in an intellectual atmosphere dominated by Freudian gloom and the increasingly hysterical voices of artistic and political extremists, the book radiates a cold aura of pessimism. "Death is the central theme of *Bambi*," writes sportsman-conservationist George Reiger. "Something fears dying, or does die in terrible agony, in almost every chapter." The forest world that Salten describes in sometimes exquisitely poetic prose provides a backdrop of intense color and beauty in front of which his animal characters suffer and bleed and limp and die awful, uncomprehending deaths. Some of those deaths result from disease or predation, but these natural evils seem trivial compared with the terrors inflicted on the animals by the satanic two-legged demigod they call Him with a capital H. The young roebuck Bambi finds himself dodging bullets within seconds after his first glimpse of a human, and he staggers through the book watching one after another of his friends and relatives fall to hunters' guns.

Although Salten's tame animals revere humans as gods and the wild animals abominate them as demons, they all acknowledge human dominion over nature. "No one can escape Him," says one forest creature after another throughout Salten's book. "He kills what He wants. . . . He can do anything." "I worship Him, I serve Him," yelps a dog to a maimed fox. "He's all-powerful. He's above all of you. . . . Everything that lives or grows comes from Him." At the end of the book, this delusion is dispelled for Bambi when his dying father takes him to view the corpse of a murdered poacher. Bambi thereby learns the great secret: *Homo sapiens* is only another dying animal, and the governance of the world lies elsewhere.

10   The English translation of *Bambi* appeared in 1928. The translator was the young Whittaker Chambers, who had joined the Communist party not long before and was later to become famous as Richard Nixon's star witness in the Alger Hiss case. The English novelist and Nobelist John Galsworthy, a virulent opponent of hunting, contributed a foreword to the translation, calling Salten's book "a little masterpiece." Reviewers were ecstatic. "The author," wrote John Chamberlain in the *New York Times,* "has given us the life story of a forest deer, and Felix Salten's comprehension of the entire universe as well . . . . Throw away your Spinozan tomes on pantheism and read *Bambi*."

Salten's books would probably be as little read nowadays as Spinoza's were it not for another event in 1928. That September in a New York recording studio, a young film maker named Walt Disney managed to get a sound recording of "Turkey in the Straw" synchronized with the movements of a cartoon mouse. As a result of this cinematic breakthrough, Bambi's name was going to become virtually synonymous with "deer," although neither Disney nor Salten expected it yet.

Walt Disney was born in Chicago in 1901. When he was five years old, his family left the city and moved to a farm in Missouri. Disney always remembered the four years he spent on that farm as the happiest part of his childhood, and the idyllic farmyard and the animal friends he made there turn up again and again in his films. Significantly, one of his few unpleasant memories of the place involved hunting.

When Disney's family arrived, they found the farm overrun with rabbits, and Walt crept into the fields with his older brother Roy to watch them in their springtime mating rituals. Charmed and excited by all the March-hare antics, Walt spent the next few days memorializing them in his very first cartoons: childish sketches of cottontails playing peekaboo in the grass. But when Roy next returned to the fields, he brought along his air rifle and shot the biggest buck bunny he saw. Walt dissolved in tears when Roy broke the thrashing rabbit's neck, and he refused to touch the rabbit stew their mother served up that evening. The contrast that this incident embodied between innocent animal desire and malign human contrivance was to recur in several Disney films. He would impress that love-and-death opposition on the world with particular force in *Bambi*.

Disney began his film career making animated ads in Kansas City. Moving to Hollywood in 1923, he pressed toward heights that no one before him had dreamed of reaching with animation. Starting from the crude drawing and barnyard humor of the first Mickey Mouse cartoons in 1928, Disney and his artists took less than a decade to learn how to inspire pity and terror, as well as laughter, with a twelve-per-second flow of talking-animal caricatures. Everybody, including the intellectuals, went wild over the results. "A great many people," gushed film critic Gilbert Seldes in 1937, "consider Disney as the great satirist of the machine age."

Bambi posed serious challenges even for the Disney studio. The Disney cartoon animals of the 1930s had rounded outlines and a rubbery consistency, which made them easier to draw and gave their movements the conviction of exaggeration. They were drawn as bipeds with human hands, so that the animators could use gestures to express the characters' emotions. When Disney selected *Bambi* for his second animated feature, he knew that these habits had to be abandoned. What Salten was saying about life, death, suffering, and God could not be put in the mouth of a cartoon deer that looked like Clarabelle Cow with antlers. To give the animated deer the potential for tragedy, an unprecedentedly realistic set of drawing conventions had to be developed. The *Bambi* animators were told that they could use whatever human expressions they could impose upon the stiff, elongated face of a deer, but human-looking postures and movements were forbidden. The animators gritted their teeth and began imagining themselves into the bodies of deer, learning to express human feelings with shifts in weight support and gait patterns, with head and neck posture, with flicks of the ears and tail.

Work on the script began in 1937. The first story treatments were frivolous pastiches of cornball dialogue and Silly Symphony sight gags. But during 1938 and 1939, as the clouds of war gathered in Europe and the Pacific, the script drafts grew increasingly tense and despairing and began to center on human cruelty and violence. On September 1, 1939, the day that German tanks struck across the Polish border and plunged Europe into World War II, the film's story editor Perce Pearce announced that all predators other than *Homo sapiens* had to be excised from the script. "There's nobody swooping down and eating someone else and their one common enemy is Man. That's the conflict there—and keep it simple."

The first reasonably complete script treatment for *Bambi* that survives was written near the end of 1939. It is saturated with bitter detestation of human beings and their weaponry. The fawns Bambi and Faline are shot at (but missed) as they play in a sunny meadow. The deer gather for a colloquium on human depravity. "Whenever man comes into the forest, there's nothing but fear!" cry the animals. "He kills without mercy!" Bambi's mother declares her faith in the possibility of human love. A little later, she and Bambi are stalked by a hunter. They flee, but a shot rings out; we see her jerk in midleap and fall dead. As Bambi wanders the forest crying for his lost mother, he hears what he thinks is her voice and runs toward it joyously—to discover a hunter with a deer call, who shoots him. Bleeding and gasping with pain, Bambi staggers back to the thicket where he was born. He begins calling for his mother again and falls down, apparently dead. His anxious father arrives to watch over him until the unconscious fawn begins to breathe once more.

Humans reenter the forest after Bambi has grown into an antlered buck. Hunting dogs run in the vanguard, praising human omnipotence and tearing cornered animals to bits. Friend Hare, the prototype of Thumper, intercepts a bullet and dies at Bambi's feet, murmuring, "I don't understand—What have I ever done to Them?" After a fire set by the intruders devastates the forest, Bambi's father leads him through the smoldering ashes to a man's charred cadaver, revealing the great secret of *Homo sapiens'* animal nature. The film ends in a scene of rebirth, with the forest sprouting anew and Bambi glimpsing Faline with two newborn fawns.

In succeeding drafts, the script grew simpler and sweeter, and the animals' assessments of the human condition were deleted one by one, until no dialogue remained to establish their superstitious awe of humanity. The climactic scene with the cooked cadaver was reluctantly dropped from the film in the last stages of production, and with it went the last vestiges of Salten's attempted reconciliation of human beings with nature. The only remaining discussion of the human presence is Bambi's question, "What happened, Mother? Why did we all run?" and Mother's slow, portentous response: "Man . . . was in the forest."

20   The prickly uncertainties of Salten's novel are replaced in the film by the crystalline simplicities of myth. Deer biology is distorted to fit the familiar symbolic cycle of the agricultural year, like John Barleycorn, Bambi is born and sows his seed in the spring and is cut down in the autumn. Christian symbolism pervades the film's opening scenes. After the adoring animals finish hailing the birth of the young prince and depart, the camera pulls back to show mother and child nestled in a thorny thicket—a tableau that story editor Pearce referred to as "that madonnalike picture"—while a remote, godlike father looks down from a heavenly crag.

Contemporary psychoanalytic gimmicks also made their way into *Bambi*. The first English translation of Jung's *Archetypes of the Collective Unconscious* appeared in 1939. Late in that year, the Disney conception of Faline abruptly changed from a shy fawn to a teasing, seductive minx who repeatedly shows up as a double of Bambi's reflection in the water. All this bears a suspiciously minute resemblance to Jung's description of his "anima" archetype. Freudian motifs are also prominent in the film. As one might expect of an intellectual in Freud's Vienna, Salten had put plenty of Oedipal conflict into his book, and the Disney people picked up on it. Bambi's film father is strong, scary, and forbiddingly distant, and the tension between them is resolved only by the wrenching death of Bambi's mother. The film portrays the natural world as a realm of peace and beauty, saturated with innocent love in all its varieties. The amorous warmth of this sylvan pastorale is enhanced by the animals' permanently dilated pupils, like those of a Renaissance courtesan on belladonna. The sole source of discord in the magic forest is the human presence, which manifests itself as a wave of mad slaughter and ecological catastrophe. The Freudian opposition between the instincts of life and death is equated throughout the film with the symbolic opposition of humanity to nature, and no possible resolution of the conflict is hinted at.

Conflict between humanity and nature is mirrored even in the film's musical score. Like *Fantasia, Bambi* is essentially a silent movie: a wordless, rhythmical ballet performed to an orchestral accompaniment. (The final script contains less than a thousand spoken words.) The alienation of the human species from the natural order is symbolized by barring the human presence completely from the universal dance. Human beings are represented only by ominous, lurching music that—unlike the rest of the score—is unaccompanied by onscreen choreography.

All these psychological and symbolic devices chugging away in Disney's *Bambi*—its archetypal characters, its Freudian machineries, its invocations of Christian and pagan mythology, its perfectly choreographed universal dances of all things not human, its A-B-A architecture silently proclaiming the eternal recurrence of nature, its superbly executed animation, its occasionally breathtaking visual beauty, and its despairing subliminal consciousness of the implacable onrush of World War II—give the movie the force of a sledgehammer for many viewers, despite its pervasive and repellent cuteness. "I came out of *Bambi* on my hands and knees," recalled director Richard Williams in a 1989 interview. Reviewing *Bambi* when it was rereleased in 1988, critic Roger Ebert described it as "a parable of sexism, nihilism, and despair, portraying absentee fathers and passive mothers in a world of death and violence," and called it unsuitable for young and impressionable children.

The first attack on *Bambi* by America's outdoorsmen came in 1942 from Raymond J. Brown, the editor of *Outdoor Life.* Denouncing the movie as "the worst insult ever offered in any form to American sportsmen," Brown complained that *Bambi* showed hunters engaging in such unsportsmanlike practices as killing a doe and hunting deer with dogs. Now hunters' attacks on *Bambi* are, if anything, more strident and insistent, but they no longer criticize it as a slur on the honor of sportsmen. The line commonly encountered nowadays is that the movie is nature-fakery, a fantastic distortion of the facts about the behavior of wild beasts, and that children who see it are misled into a foolish sentimentalism about wildlife.

25
American hunters, who tend to cluster toward the political right, have also picked up the scent of Marxism and atheism in *Bambi*. In a 1980 article in *Field and Stream,* George Reiger argues that Salten wrote *Bambi* out of a pious liberal revulsion against the carnage of World War I, and Chambers was attracted to it because of his Marxist inability "to accept the impersonal realities of nature." But in Reiger's eyes, what Disney himself "and his staff of little helpers" are guilty of is not Marxism but blasphemy—specifically mockery of Christ. Reiger complains that "in Disney's version, once Bambi is raised in status from mere deer to Jesus Whitetail Superstar, man's hunting of deer becomes a crime comparable to the persecution of Christ."

Is there any truth in what these writers say about the Bambi syndrome and its importance? Certainly none of the things that hunters object to in the film originated with Disney. The vision of the wilderness as an Eden and of man as a destructive intruder into the harmony of nature extends back into classical and medieval thinking. Wounded deer have for centuries personified injured innocence. They are common symbols of the crucified Christ in medieval literature; one fourteenth-century German poet described Jesus as a hunted stag "whose hoof is stained with blood, for He ransomed us at so great a price." Moral indignation over hunting flared up now and then even in antiquity and has become steadily more commonplace in Western culture since the Renaissance. The notion that all this is Walt Disney's fault is wishful thinking on the part of Reiger, Page, and other outdoorsmen.

Yet if Disney did not invent the symbolism that portrays hunted deer as ravished maidens and martyred Princes of Peace, he gave it a mass audience, an irresistible graphic expression, and a mythical embodiment that it would not otherwise have had. Bambi has become emblematic of deer in general. Stand for an hour or two in front of a deer pen at a zoo; some child or its mother is sure to point to a deer and exclaim, "Look! Bambi!" (I have heard the name applied to sika, axis, white-tailed and mule deer, as well as to various more or less gracile antelopes, up to and including the big, cowlike nilgai of India.) Even some jocular hunters like to call their quarry "Bambis." Bambi seems to be on his way to becoming a lower-case noun, as his predecessor Reynard the Fox did in the French language.

As the stereotypic deer, Bambi symbolizes all those things we associate with deer, including doe-eyed innocence, wilderness, and the natural order. (When James Watt became U.S. Secretary of the Interior, editorial cartoons showed the forest animals shouting, "Run, Bambi, Run!" and comedian Mark Russell announced that Bambi was leaving for Canada.) Some historians of forestry think that the forest-fire sequence in *Bambi* was what drove the U.S. Forest Service to launch a no-burn policy two years later. *Bambi* also had an important influence as the prototype for Disney's True-Life Adventures of the 1950s. Two central conventions of those pioneering wildlife films derive from *Bambi*. One is the eternal recurrence, in which a final return to the starting place marks one round of nature's ancient and unchanging cycle. The other is the exclusion of the human image from the picture—and, by implication, from the kingdom of nature.

Even hunters fall prey to the Bambi syndrome. One ex-hunter interviewed by the writer John Mitchell for his book *The Hunt* admitted that his attitude was changed by his two daughters, who "got the idea every deer is named Bambi. And I began to wonder what is sport and what isn't." In the last paragraphs of his book, Mitchell tells of the moment when he gets his own first buck centered in his rifle's sights. Suddenly, he stops, ejects his cartridge, and collapses, trembling uncontrollably after staring into "the eyes—the huge glistening eyes that had torn my own away from the cross hairs on the shoulder." In a 1982 *Smithsonian* article, Mitchell frankly blamed his shakes on *Bambi:* "Walt Disney got to me early .... I wept for Bambi when the huntsmen slew its mamma; yet today I count deer slayers among my closest friends, and ... occasionally join them afield, bearing arms. But I have never shot a deer, or at one."

30   *Bambi* and other Disney films had a profound impact on American attitudes toward hunting, wildlife, and nature. Today, fifty-one years since the first release of *Bambi,* they continue to have a similar impact on children and adults alike, and their influence is sure to be strengthened by the video-

tape revolution that has put copies of these movies into millions of American homes. These Disney products have been influential not only because they are effective theater but also because they express thoughts that we are predisposed to think for other reasons. Much of their force derives from our vision of the natural world as a special, mystical realm from which human beings are alienated by their culture and technology. That vision was not dreamed up in the Disney studios. It has deep roots in the Romantic rebellion against scientific materialism, and its branches extend into just about every aspect of twentieth-century thought, from psychoanalysis to postmodernism.

Ironically, that same vision is also central to hunting as we define and understand it. The line we draw between the human world and nature is what separates wild from domestic animals and thereby distinguishes the hunter's craft from the butcher's. When hunters say, as many do, that they go hunting to restore their sense of oneness with nature, they are at bottom expressing the same sort of sentimental reverence for "nature" that underlies the Bambi syndrome.

Questions for Discussion

1. Explain the organization of this essay. Why is it organized the way it is? How would you organize this essay? Why?
2. Do you think the author does a satisfactory job of identifying his sources of information? Why or why not?
3. Does the author establish himself as a credible source of information on this subject? Cite specific passages to support your answer.
4. How important is the essay's persuasive aim? Is it as important as the essay's referential aim? Could this essay be classified as persuasive aim writing? Why or why not?
5. This essay was written for the general readership of a magazine published by the American Museum of Natural History. If the author were revising this essay for a specialized audience of film critics, how might he proceed? What particular changes would you recommend?

Opportunities for Writing

1. Offer your analysis of Disney's *Bambi*. How does it portray animals? How does it portray human beings? Citing your personal experience, discuss the impact of the film on viewers. Address your essay to the membership of a local animal rights organization.
2. In a special essay for the movie section of your local newspaper, compare and contrast early Disney animated films such as *Snow White, Dumbo,* and *Pinnochio* with later animated films such as *Beauty and the Beast, Aladdin,* and *The Lion King.* Do you notice more similarities or differences? Why?
3. Using a questionnaire, examine the attitudes of students at your school toward hunting. Which students like hunting? Why? Which students dislike hunting? Why? Report the results of your investigation in a memo to the director of your school's recreation program.

Peach Preserves and "A New Texas"

A Rhetorical Analysis of the Inaugural Addresses of "Ma" Ferguson and Ann Richards

Linda Hatchel

Linda Hatchel teaches at McLennan Community College in Waco, Texas. In this essay, Hatchel analyzes the inaugural gubernatorial addresses by the only two women elected to that office in Texas: "Ma" Ferguson in 1925 and Anne Richards in 1991. This essay appeared in the journal English in Texas *and follows the MLA documentation style.*

On January 15, 1991, Texas inaugurated its 45th governor, Ann Willis Richards. She, however, is not the first female governor of Texas. That distinction belongs to "Ma" Ferguson, inaugurated on January 25, 1925, as the 28th Texas governor.

Miriam Amanda "Ma" Ferguson ran for the office when her husband, recently impeached Governor James E. Ferguson, proposed his wife's name after he failed to win legal authorization to run for governor in 1924. He directed her campaign and wrote her speeches, including the inaugural address. A curious agreement between Texas voters and the Fergusons was well publicized. Even though Mrs. Ferguson would be the elected governor, her husband would actually make most of the gubernatorial decisions. Indeed, after she was elected, he moved his desk into the governor's office beside hers.

Ann Richards, on the other hand, makes her own policies and decisions. Although her inaugural speech was a collaborative effort of several of her key personnel, she also contributed to its writing, even adding her own comments during the actual delivery. (In fact, a note to the reader appears at the beginning of the printed text: "Governor Richards frequently deviates from her prepared remarks.") A proven administrator and politician, Richards supervises the state government through direct intervention.

Despite the difference in leadership philosophy, the primary theme of each inaugural address calls for Texans to cooperate, a popular "god term" for discourse such as this. The aim of discourse for each address is to initiate unity between the diverse factions of the state. Although both governors communicate effectively, each employs a distinct style. Textual analysis reveals the rhetorical effectiveness of each address.

5   Although the theme of cooperation is presented in both addresses, given the differing norms of the 1920s and the 1990s, one would expect the presentation to be quite different. Ferguson's speech creates the public image of "Ma" as a peacemaker, an ideal for which the citizens of Texas were looking. This image is evoked early in her first inaugural address when she delivers an enthymeme in a tone that a mother might direct toward recalcitrant children as she addressed members of Congress: "I hope and pray that there is to be that friendly co-operation on the part of each.... One good way to establish this relation is for each department to recognize and respect the rights and powers of the other."

Ferguson's election to the governorship was taken, at least by her and by her supporters, as a signal from the people of Texas that they still supported her husband. She implicitly expresses this view near the beginning of her address: "In assuming the duties of the governorship to which I have been called by the people of Texas, I find myself overwhelmed with the feeling of gratitude and responsibility." Later, she continues this allusion when she says, "The people have spoken. Their verdict is plain." The verdict, of course, was that her husband was innocent of all impeachment charges. Presumably, she and her husband were trusting that the divided legislators would recognize voter support for the Fergusons and, as a consequence, stop opposing the obvious will of the people.

To reinforce the theme of cooperation, Ferguson then shifts pronoun usage from first person singular to first person plural, moving responsibility from the voters to the government: "We are all humble servants of a great people and we must do our best for the common good."

After stating that all must work together, she then admits her "inexperience in governmental affairs" and asks "the advice and counsel of others." This statement implies that she is asking for her husband's advice. She further suggests that perhaps asking for advice "would not be a bad idea for others to adopt, even though their training and learning may be more than mine."

Ferguson's husband, when writing this speech, has competently slipped into a feminine rhetorical persona as he has his wife ask for help. This gender-based language, used during an era when independent or assertive women were not well accepted, served two purposes. First, the expected female characteristic of acknowledging weakness and asking for advice would help her to maintain the proper female behavior. The second purpose, and we can almost see Mr. Ferguson chuckling, is that he in effect has just had his wife admit that she will be asking for and needing his help. He then has her suggest to the rest of the Congress that they do the same.

Continuing with this theme of cooperation, Ferguson employs a metaphoric picture of laborers (most probably both legislators and the people of Texas) working together: "What Texas needs more than anything else at this time, is a strong pull, a steady pull, and a pull all together." Although the noun "pull" occurs three times within this one sentence, the emphasis is not necessarily on the noun but on the modifiers "strong," "steady," and "all together." The sound experience of the stronger letter combination of *st* overshadows the softer consonant *p* of the noun *pull*, underscoring the theme of the speech in which Mr. Ferguson portrays the new administration, headed in actuality by himself, as strong and steady, in spite of having a woman for governor. Knowing that a struggle faces them, he emphasizes the gravity of the problems with the next sentence: "In this way we may climb the hill of difficulties that confront us." The plural pronoun again is used inclusively.

The next paragraph again refers to their difficulties, using polysyndeton for emphasis in the phrase, "the turmoil and strife and passions of the hour," with the nouns separated by the conjunctions. This phrase then segues into a plea to turn to God for help: "I am praying for this administration to be one of progress in matters spiritual as well as material." By this reference to the spiritual, "Ma" Ferguson gains more credibility as she affirms that she is strong in her faith.

Thus, "Ma" accomplished two purposes in her inaugural address in 1925: (1) to present the female governor as credible and acceptable and (2) to reiterate that her husband would, in actuality, have the final authority in the state government. If these premises were accepted, the only logical thing for Texans to do would be to come together in the spirit of team work.

Ann Richards, the current governor of Texas, succeeds equally with her inaugural speech. Richards also pleads for cooperation; however, rather than admonishing voters as she would children, she assumes partial ownership of the problem and points out the consequences of not resolving the problem amicably. First, throughout most of her address, she uses the first person plural pronoun *we* to suggest the image of many working as one. Second, the assertive tone of the one paragraph that deals directly with this issue is less like Ferguson's maternal lecture and more like the firm hand of a leader who will tolerate nothing less: "And if tomorrow, we begin with the understanding that government must stop telling people what they want . . . and start listening to the people and hearing what the people need, we will make government mean something good in people's lives."

This paradigm of a rhetorically well crafted, accessible political address is simple in language and syntax, and not burdened with complex, detailed ideas. Short, simply constructed sentences dominate the address. The short paragraphs, often one sentence long, allow Richards an opportunity to pause, insert her own spur-of-the-moment comments, or accept applause from the audience. We must remember, also, that the address was presented outside over a public address system. Because of the outdoor acoustics, more complex sentences would have been lost before the audience could hear the words of a lengthy thought pattern.

15   The first sentence in Richards' welcome, her exordium, begins the theme of cooperation that she repeats throughout the address: "Welcome to the first day of the new Texas." She then welcomes "the official representatives of thirty-five countries and the governors of the four Mexican border states" who attended the inauguration. After extending to them an invitation to visit "often in the capitol," she begins her theme of cooperation as she looks forward to "working cooperatively with your governments and to excellent relationships with your people." To identify with the visiting dignitaries, many of whom were from Spanish-speaking countries, she welcomes them in Spanish, *"¡Bienvenidos, mis amigos!"* This acknowledgment is presumably intended to help her deal with the international relations inevitable for a border state, to help her domestic relations with her constituents who rely on foreign trade, and to help her with the many Texans who have a cultural heritage from these countries to the south of Texas.

The theme of a cooperative New Texas blends linguistically with the idea of that New Texas being made up of "the people of Texas." After stating that "we are reclaiming the Capitol for the people of Texas," for emphasis she reiterates this idea: "We say proudly that the people of Texas are back." This is closely followed by, "Today, the historians will record . . . a new administration." The term "new administration" draws together the two images of a "New Texas" made up of the "people of Texas."

Unlike Ferguson's address, which was centered on the vindication of her husband, Richards' address is filled with many references to schoolchildren.

The futuristic middle section of her address begins, "Twenty, fifty, one hundred years from now, schoolchildren will open their textbooks—or perhaps, switch on their video texts—and they will see a picture." Using this frame, she presents all that she hopes to accomplish as a way to benefit those children, beginning with the brief narrative discourse, "They will see us standing proudly on this bright winter noon. . . . Those children will read that on January 15th, 1991, a woman named Ann W. Richards took the oath of office as the 45th Governor of Texas." This image of the children reading from textbooks occurs again: "Today, the headline has been written . . . but the pages are blank. Tomorrow, we begin filling in the pages. . . . Today, we have a vision of a Texas where *every* child receives an education." Returning to this image of children reading, in the closing peroration she concludes, "I want us to be able to look forward . . . to see a small child with a textbook. . . . I want us to know that what we started here will reach out across time to that child." Interestingly, she begins with the plural children but concludes with a rhetorical focus on the symbolic singular child, allowing the audience to picture more easily one child representing all children.

Technically, Richards' address is also unified through parallelism. The phrase, "the people of Texas," has been used several times to indicate a "New Texas." The image of the children reading their history books allows her to establish an accessible parallel structure using "Today" and "Tomorrow" and then to combine this with the theme of cooperation today to benefit tomorrow. "Today" is used as the first word of three one-sentence paragraphs within the opening: "Today is a day of celebration"; "Today, we marched up Congress Avenue"; "Today, the historians will record that a new administration began." The last sentence introduces the idea of working together for the future: "Today, the headline has been written. . . . Tomorrow, we begin filling in the pages." This complementation strategy first centers on the words "Today" and "Tomorrow" and then expands, through the addition of structurally parallel clauses, to become the phrases "Today, we have a vision of a Texas" and "Tomorrow, we must build that Texas." This alternating anaphora appears four times. Much of the parallel structure and repetition is a necessary code for effective delivery to the large audience, straining physically to understand what she is saying over the outdoor public address system.

One of the longest paragraphs uses another parallel structure, actually a series of short clauses introduced with the conjunction *where,* in a statement of "public philosophy." As explained by political rhetoric critic Dante Germino, the term, "public philosophy," indicates a system of commonly held beliefs with which none would disagree even though individually each is free to disagree about the method of achieving these ideals (3). In the written text of Richards' address, a verbal pause is elliptically indicated between each clause for more effective delivery:

> Today, we have a vision of a Texas where the government treats every citizen with respect and dignity and honesty . . . where consumers are protected . . . where business is nurtured and valued . . . where good jobs are plentiful . . . where those in need find compassion and help . . . where every decision is measured against a high standard of ethics and true commitment to the public trust.

20   The audience is rhetorically coaxed to listen cooperatively and agree. Richards' "New Texas" becomes the embodiment of that universal public philosophy.

The theme of cooperation is also emphasized by Richards' use of the first person plural pronoun, used the same way that Ferguson used it. However, unlike Ferguson, Richards draws specific attention to that pronoun in her conclusion: "I want us to be able to look back together and say—not he, not she, not me—but *WE* came to this moment." This parallel use of the negative and singular pronouns also emphasizes the final unity of the plural pronoun.

The last image is of the child sitting at a desk, reading about "the year of our Lord nineteen hundred and ninety-one" and the "new era" that "began in Texas."

Thus, although both female governors of Texas have diverse administrative philosophies, both began their gubernatorial reigns with rhetorically effective inaugural addresses, accomplishing their purposes. Ferguson's purpose was to let the people know that her husband would, in most instances, direct the governor's office as he had done in the past. Nothing would change. Richards' address was more of a celebration of the return of a government responsive to the people. Both, however, thematically call for all citizens and elected officials to join in a spirit of cooperation and end divisive, often partisan quarreling.

After the ceremonies of inauguration day, "Ma" Ferguson went back to her kitchen and continued making her famous peach preserves. Ann Richards began making changes, paving the way for a New Texas.

Works Cited

Germino, Dante. *The Inaugural Addresses of American Presidents: The Public Philosophy and Rhetoric Series* funded by the John and Mary R. Markle Foundation 7. New York: University Press of America, 1984.

"Inaugural Address by Gov. Miriam A. Ferguson Before Forty-Third Legislature." *Ferguson Forum* 19 Jan. 1933: 1.

Richards, Ann, et al. "Remarks of Governor Ann Richards on the Occasion of the Inauguration January 15, 1991." Austin, Texas.

Questions for Discussion

1. This essay was written for English teachers. How might it differ if it were written for history teachers? high school students? your local newspaper?
2. What do you think of the opening paragraph? How would you start this essay?
3. What is the thesis of the essay? Does the author support the thesis using sufficient, plausible, and pertinent information? If so, cite specific passages. If not, identify necessary revisions.
4. Do you think the title is effective? Does it clarify the subject? Does it motivate the audience? Explain your answer.
5. Is the author a credible source of information on this subject? Why or why not?

Opportunities for Writing

1. Analyze a major policy speech by a political candidate. What is the theme of this speech? How does it develop this theme? Consider specific rhetorical techniques such as polysyndeton, anaphora, metaphor, and parallel structure. Address your essay to a rival candidate.
2. Compare and contrast the administrations of "Ma" Ferguson and Ann Richards? What did each accomplish as governor of Texas? How is or was each perceived by the voters? by political rivals? by historians?
3. Identify and explain the origins of the inaugural address. When and where did this practice start? Why? Compose your essay as the introduction to a book of famous inaugural addresses.

Alma's Bedside Ghost
Or the Importance of Cultural Similarity

MARINA OPPENHEIMER

Marina Oppenheimer is a psychotherapist in South Miami. In this article, Oppenheimer explains and analyzes how diagnosis and culture are related, using the case of one of her patients, Alma, to illustrate her point. The author uses two notes at the end of the essay to indicate that she has maintained her patients' confidentiality. "Alma's Bedside Ghost" was published in the Hispanic Journal of Behavioral Sciences *and follows the APA documentation style.*

Cultural similarity between client and therapist is a significant variable in the successful outcome of therapy. People from different cultures do not only speak different languages, but also have different (sometimes opposing) perceptions of reality. Values, moral and social codes, and the meaning of pathology can often only be understood within the parameters of the patient's culture. This article describes the case of a severely depressed Hispanic patient who started improving only after she was able to reframe her depression within the context of her Latino spiritist beliefs. During therapy, her belief in the supernatural was not labeled pathological. The therapist, also a Hispanic, accepted the client's references to "intranquil spirits" as a way of dealing with painful issues within some Latino cultures. This is an example of how cultural affinity between client and therapist is often a necessary tool in therapy.

How significant is the psychotherapist's cultural background in the successful outcome of therapy? The positive aspects of the intraethnic therapeutic dyad have long been the focus of academic controversy. Most experts in cross-cultural psychology agree that a therapeutic alliance is more easily established when client and therapist share the same language and a similar cultural background (e.g., Fuller-Torrey, 1986; Munoz, 1979).

Experts in other fields of knowledge, such as sociology and linguistics, have also supported the thesis that culture molds our perception of reality.

Linguist Benjamin Whorf, among others, contends that different linguistic groups have different cognitive structures (Fuller-Torrey, 1986).

Skeptics, on the other hand, note that cultural similarity in the therapeutic dyad has many drawbacks. They cite, for instance, the fact that therapists can be blind to dysfunctional behavior in their clients just because their common culture sanctions it (Munoz, 1979). For example, a male Latino therapist could justify a Hispanic husband's lack of cooperation with his wife's domestic chores because many Latin men consider housework to be "women's stuff." Because living conditions in the United States are different from those in Latin America, this therapist is not only ignoring the wife's overload and humiliation, but is also missing an important goal of therapy (i.e., to help his clients learn new and more adaptive behaviors).

Despite these obvious pitfalls, few experts will dispute that clients feel more comfortable with therapists who share their language and culture. Not only are some words untranslatable, but feelings of loneliness, anger or frustration sometimes make sense only within a specific culture. We have to be familiar with the role the extended family plays in the life of Hispanic people to understand why a Latino client, who may be happily married and have many friends in the United States, still feels lonely.

5   This is also the case with Latino clients who believe in the supernatural, and who project the cause of their illness onto external factors (Abad, Ramos, & Boyce, 1974; Comas-Diaz, 1981) with which Anglo therapists are often unfamiliar. Sometimes, Latino clients (especially in the lower socioeconomic strata) will confront their therapists with beliefs that fate or the deceased are in control of their lives. Western psychotherapists, with their heavy emphasis on insight and personal responsibility for behavior (Fuller-Torrey, 1986; Ruiz & Langrod, 1976) may diagnose such clients as psychotic. In this case, a Latino therapist may know better.

This is what I learned from treating Alma,[1] a Cuban woman who was suffering from major depression. She had almost given up on life after 12 years of unsuccessful therapy when she walked into my office.

Alma is a 67-year-old Cuban widow now living with her octogenarian parents. She was referred to our adult day treatment program by her latest psychiatrist who was treating her for major depression. When she showed up for an intake interview at my office, my first impression was that she was not appropriate for the program. Alma had walked into the room with a walker. She stared blankly at me and had difficulties concentrating on my questions. She would give me very concrete one-word answers and would then fall into a stupor for several seconds. Her difficulty in signing her treatment authorization form made me wonder if she was suffering from an organic mental disorder.

I would soon discover how wrong I was. Alma's case would prove to be a lesson on the wonders that cultural similarity between patient and therapist can sometimes achieve. Despite Alma's withdrawn attitude, I had sensed during the intake interview that she was making an effort to communicate with me. Months later, she would tell me that my touch of Hispanic familiarity at that time had motivated her to attend my group after 12 years of unsuccessful treatments with non-Latino therapists and psychiatrists. She was probably referring to the fact that both of us had used similar verbal and nonverbal codes (Sue, 1981).

Alma started coming to our groups under pressure from her eldest son, who firmly believed that his mother needed more therapy and fewer antidepressant drugs. For several months she sat passively, not participating in the group's activities. She sometimes fell asleep during the sessions. When awake, Alma's recurrent theme in therapy was that her life was over and only death could save her from her suffering. When I asked her if she had contemplated suicide, she answered that self-inflicted death is never an option for a Catholic. However, it was obvious that Alma was a desperate woman who seemed to reject every attempt from the group to help her.

Over time, however, I managed to learn that she was born in Cuba; had come to the United States in the early sixties fleeing from Fidel Castro's Communist regime; had lost her husband in an automobile accident in Miami when she was 40 years old; had raised her two children with the help of her mother, and was married to another Cuban man for only 8 months. Shortly after her divorce Alma had moved into her parents' home, gradually falling into a major depression.

But there was something intriguing about Alma: Despite her negativity and her apathy, she never missed a session, except twice when she had strong back pains (which I suspected were psychogenic in nature). Her firm attendance to my group kept me going.

As time went by, Alma became even more apathetic. It was already summer, and I had to tell the group that I was about to go on vacation. As I had anticipated, they felt distraught, but seemed reassured when I told them that I would be back in a couple of weeks. When Alma left the session that day, her eyes as emotionless as always, I wondered if I could ever reach her soul.

On my return, I learned that Alma had been readmitted into a hospital after an acute episode of depression. During my absence she had decompensated, totally neglecting her appearance and withdrawing even more from her environment. I called her family to find out whether she would return to the group. I was told that as soon as she was discharged, she would come back to our program. I was relieved.

A few weeks later, she showed up. After welcoming her back, I asked her if she knew what had precipitated her crisis. To my surprise, she said: "You took a vacation, and I took a vacation too." I was amazed. This was her first sign of attachment to me in 4 months of three-times-a-week therapy. I felt elated. All those hours had not been in vain after all. I had succeeded at least in building a bridge between us. Now, there was hope for recovery.

Then, one day shortly thereafter, I was handed by accident the key to Alma's mystery. The group's conversation had drifted away from the usual topics, shifting towards the death of our loved ones. One of the members of the group, a high-functioning, 96-year-old Puerto Rican lady named Maria,[2] said that, in order to go on with their lives, the living need to detach from the deceased.

"However," she added, "it's different when somebody dies in an accident, because they don't realize that they are dead, and keep haunting the living. These souls feel very frustrated because they don't know that we can't see them nor hear them. They don't understand why we don't pay any attention to them."

Maria was referring to the so-called intranquil spirits (*espíritus intranquilos*) who, according to Latino spiritism, are unsettled for having, among other things, died suddenly (Comas-Diaz, 1981).

I held my breath. Suddenly, for the first time ever, I detected a sparkle of life in Alma's eyes. She nodded. I looked at her, and encouraged her to talk.

"What Maria says is true," Alma started. "I sometimes feel that my husband is with me in the house."

She looked around the room, as if afraid somebody would laugh at her. Nobody did. She went on.

"When I go to sleep at night, he sits on my bed."

"How do you know?" I asked her in a whisper. "Do you see him?"

"Of course not!" she retorted. "I just know it. Even my second husband knew. He used to tell me that our marriage would not last because my first husband was always around. And it didn't."

That was it. With a few words the group had broken Alma's spell—the spell that had kept her soul a prisoner for so long. Her well-guarded secret, which she had never disclosed to her non-Latino therapists or psychiatrists in the past 12 years had lost its power. What our group had done was define Alma's disorder with words that made sense to her (Fuller-Torrey, 1986), a dead husband whose soul kept haunting her. From then on Alma could not stop talking. Her words came pouring out as if there would be no tomorrow. She was transfigured. She had finally become the Alma I had perceived between the lines during our first session together. And while I listened to her, I remembered the tales of supernatural beings my grandfather used to tell me when I was a child in Argentina. The language and the feeling of awe were the same.

The following day Alma opened the session stating that she had not slept that well in a very long time. She had brought some pictures of her family to share with the group: her husband, the house they had bought together, their children, the Christmas parties. . . . She could not stop talking. The thoughts that had been bottled up for so long kept coming out like a broken dam.

As is characteristic in many Hispanic patients, when the catharsis was over, Alma asked the group to give her concrete advice on how to detach from her deceased husband. He had been the source of her depression for too long. The group, that included several believers in Afro-Cuban religions blended into Catholicism, suggested that she ask God to make her husband understand that he was dead. And so she did. Alma started praying every night so that her husband's soul—the intranquil spirit—could finally go to rest, and she could be set free.

For many Hispanic Roman Catholics, Catholicism is just one aspect of their religion. They also believe in religious-healing cults such as spiritism in Puerto Rico, santeria in Cuba, and witchcraft in other Latin American countries, whose rituals they often mix with Catholic ceremonies (Fuller-Torrey, 1986; Ruiz & Langrod, 1976). In Cuba, for instance, the Roman Catholic Church allows parishioners to bring dolls embodying Yemaya—the Goddess of the Rivers—or Chango—the God of War—to Church. Cuban Church officials have stated that antagonizing African healing ceremonies would drive many of their countrymen away from Catholicism (Bolivar-Arostegui, 1990).

Folk healers play in the life of some Hispanics the same role as psychotherapists in Western society: they help clients understand their conflicts and they prescribe a treatment (Fuller-Torrey, 1986). And if clients believe that the treatment will be successful, their expectation often proves to be a self-fulfilling prophecy (Fuller-Torrey, 1986). It is conceivable that if Alma had consulted a santero, besides a psychiatrist, to get rid of her depression, she may have improved many years ago.

Such was my encounter with Alma. Although she still attends my group, she is also taking an English course for Hispanics. The walker is long gone, and so is the back pain. Her goal now is to lose some weight, buy herself a new wardrobe and move out of her parents' home. As for her social life, she started attending a Hispanic social club, where she has already met some friends. Even her signature has changed. Her handwriting doesn't look like an earthquake anymore.

When Alma told me that she felt like a new woman, I warned her that she might suffer a relapse. She answered that if she did, it did not really matter. Her journey within the group had taught her a valuable lesson: that life is spelled in the present tense. Implicit was the message that her husband's ghost had ceased to exist.

Conclusion

Alma's case makes me wonder what would have happened if she had once again landed at a non-Latino therapist's office. Would she have risked disclosing that her dead husband sat on her bedside? And if she had, what would have been the diagnosis? Would she have been labeled psychotic? Would she have spent the rest of her life misdiagnosed as a chronic patient?

As shown in this case, diagnosis has a lot to do with culture (Ibrahim, 1991). When the group told Alma that her husband's intranquil spirit was keeping her a prisoner, they diagnosed her disorder with a terminology that made sense to her and that she could readily accept (Fuller-Torrey, 1986; Ruiz and Langrod, 1976). The same thing happened with the treatment they suggested: ask God to make the intranquil spirit realize that he was no longer alive. As a therapist, I didn't dispute the group's explanation of her disorder (Comas-Diaz, 1981). On the contrary, I decided that my role was to help Alma regain control of her life no matter how. And she was able to do so because for the first time in the past 12 years, she was given opportunity to deal with her depression within the parameters of her own culture.

Notes

1. In the case example, the identifying data have been altered to protect clients' confidentiality.
2. In the case example, the identifying data have been altered to protect clients' confidentiality.

References

Abad, V., Ramos, J., & Boyce, E. (1974). A model for delivery of mental health services to Spanish speaking minorities. *American Journal of Orthopsychiatry, 44,* 584–595.

Bolivar-Arostegui, N. (1990). *Los orishas en Cuba.* La Habana: Ediciones Union.

Comas-Diaz, L. (1981) Puerto-Rican espiritismo and psychotherapy. *American Journal of Orthopsychiatry, 51,* 635–645.

Fuller-Torrey, E. (1986). *Witchdoctors and psychiatrists: The common roots of psychotherapy and its future.* Northdale, NJ: Jason Aronson.

Ibrahim, F. A. (1991). Contribution of cultural worldview to generic counseling and development. *Journal of Counseling & Development, 70,* 13–19.

Munoz, J. A. (1979). Difficulties of a Hispanic-American psychotherapist in the treatment of Hispanic-American patients. *American Journal of Orthopsychiatry, 51,* 646–653.

Ruiz, P., & Langrod, J. (1976). The role of folk healers in community mental health services. *Community Mental Health Journal, 12,* 392–398.

Sue, D. (1981). *Counseling the culturally different: Theory and practice.* New York: Wiley.

Questions for Discussion

1. How might this essay differ if it were written using only knowledge by participation? Would it be more or less effective? Why?
2. This essay starts with a question and proceeds to answer it. Do you like this technique? Why or why not?
3. Would headings clarify the organization? If so, compose appropriate headings for this essay. If not, explain why you think headings are unnecessary.
4. How important is the essay's persuasive aim? Is it as important as the essay's referential aim? Could this essay be classified as persuasive aim writing? Explain your answer.
5. This essay was written for a specific audience of psychology professionals. If the author were revising this essay for a women's magazine, what specific changes would you recommend?

Opportunities for Writing

1. Explain the *santería* of Cuba? What are the principles of this religion? Who practices it? What are its origins? Write your essay for a special exhibit at your school on religions of the world.
2. Distribute a questionnaire at your school regarding belief in ghosts. Who believes in ghosts? Who doesn't? Are particular religious groups or academic majors more or less likely to believe in ghosts? Why?
3. Interview local psychologists to identify the psychotherapeutic services available within your community. Which services are available? Which services are unavailable? Why? Using this information, compose a brochure to be distributed to new residents of your community.
4. Explain the theories of Benjamin Whorf regarding the influence of language on thinking. What are Whorf's theories? How are Whorf's theories received by language and psychology researchers?

The Man Who Cries Wolf

FRED H. HARRINGTON

An ethologist, Fred H. Harrington studies animal behavior. In "The Man Who Cries Wolf," the author tells about his research collaboration with L. David Mech, a member of the U.S. Fish and Wildlife Service, and reports his discoveries about timber wolf packs' responses to his howling to them over a two-year period in Superior National Forest in Minnesota. This essay was published in the magazine Natural History.

The winter night was perfect for howling. The air was cold and motionless. Light, fluffy snow blanketed the ground, cushioning my steps as I edged closer to the wolf pack. Best of all, a full moon hung in the clear black sky, illuminating my way and perhaps stirring a few primordial howls within the wolves. Soon I came across wolf tracks that crossed the road and headed toward a spruce bog. I tried to follow, but at every third step I broke through the crust and was left floundering midthigh in powdery snow. I stopped trying to walk, set my microphone on its tripod, and switched on my tape recorder. Then I howled.

Within seconds, a pack of radio-collared wolves answered. For nearly a minute the spruce woods reverberated with a cacophony of yips, yaps, and yowls, anchored by an occasional low bass note. Finally, the wolves' reply ended with a series of staccato, barklike yaps.

At the time, I was studying timber wolf howling in Superior National Forest in northeastern Minnesota. Working in conjunction with L. David Mech, of the U.S. Fish and Wildlife Service, I was trying to test a theory that howling plays a role in the establishment and maintenance of wolf pack territories. Each night I searched a vast network of logging roads from an antenna-equipped truck, patiently listening for radio signals from wolves Dave had radio-collared.

Populating the forest were about forty packs of wolves, each occupying some twenty-five to one hundred square miles. Under normal conditions, a pack could satisfy all its needs within an area that size—there would be an adequate number of dens, for example, and sufficient prey throughout the year. Virtually every square mile in the forest was claimed by at least one pack, so at the edges of adjacent territories, a one- or two-mile-wide overlapping strip was shared. If at all possible, these overlapping areas were typically avoided by neighboring packs and were thus underused compared with the packs' exclusive territories. Lone wolves accordingly found these areas relatively safe and therefore made frequent use of them. And since the packs tended to stay in their own areas, they rarely met one another or even crossed the path of a lone wolf.

Observing all this led me to wonder if wolves communicate to maintain this quiltlike pattern. So each night I would set out by truck in search of a radio-collared wolf. Once I located one, I would drive as close to the animal as the road allowed. Then I'd howl.

Most animal-vocalization studies use playbacks of recorded calls to provoke live responses. My studies had started that way too. Using several different taped howls, I had attempted playbacks but had been plagued by poor fidelity and equipment failure. My tape recorder, for instance, became very sluggish as the temperature dropped toward freezing. When the speed of the machine slowed, pups' voices deepened and they began to sound like adults. Adult howls took on an unearthly quality that can only be compared to the moaning of lost souls in a horror film. So after three months with no success, I dumped the playback gear and developed my own personal howl.

Getting a howl that fooled the wolves, I soon discovered, was not at all difficult. After learning to maintain enough wind to sustain a loud, six-second howl, I soon developed a standard series of five howls, which I used for the rest of the study. By this time I had been in the field four months and had not heard a single wolf howl. Soon, however, the wolves began to reply to me, and when I left the forest two years later, nearly five hundred of my howls had evoked some sort of vocal reply.

Once I knew my howls were being interpreted as those of an intruding wolf, I was ready to force encounters with packs and then note the conditions under which they replied.

A pack's responses, I learned, could be divided into two major categories based on their howling. If a pack responded by howling, it nearly always stood its ground. (Only 3 percent of the time did the pack reply and then retreat.) If it kept quiet, it either stayed put or it fled. Thus, if there is a message to a pack's reply, it probably reads, "We are a wolf pack, we are here, and we intend to stay here." Implicit in this message is the threat that "if you get closer, we might attack."

Of course, there could be a good deal of bluff involved in a reply. I soon found out that there were times when packs would turn tail and run if an intruder ignored their replies and continued to close in. I also learned that if an encounter does occur, a pack's actual response might depend on a quick appraisal of the odds.

When a pack did not reply, it retreated about a third of the time. These retreats ranged from a fraction of a mile to more than a mile. Dave Mech and I watched one small retreat in progress. I was on the ground, howling to a pack about a mile away, while Dave watched from a circling aircraft as the pack rested on a frozen lake. When I howled, one wolf leaped up and appeared to bark once or twice, perhaps to arouse the rest of the pack. Within minutes the wolves retreated from the open ice and into the woods north of the lake, where they lay down again, less than a mile from shore. Now that the wolves knew my location, and had placed a lake between us, they would have ample warning if I moved closer. In addition, fresh scent from urination, defecation, feet, and bodies would act as an additional olfactory warning.

One probable reason why packs don't forcibly evict intruders is that direct physical encounters carry the risk of severe injury or even death. Dave has now watched several direct encounters between packs, and in each case at least one animal was seriously wounded.

Howling thus serves the pack as a long-distance defense system. Wolves may be able to hear howls from as far away as five miles, making them aware of one another's locations long before an accidental encounter can take place. Once aware of a neighboring pack's position, a pack can avoid traveling into an area where a chance meeting would be likely.

Packs typically tried to avoid other packs that were too far away to be seen. The reason for this seemed clear: encounters between packs could be dangerous if one pack turned out to be larger. Once two packs could see each other, they would quickly discover which had the advantage of size, and usually the larger pack would chase after the smaller. We haven't been able to determine, however, whether the smaller pack flees first, thus drawing the chase, or whether the larger pack attacks the smaller first.

When a pack does reply, it may "hope" the intruder will go away. But that doesn't always happen. On an increasing number of occasions, both Dave Mech in Minnesota and researchers elsewhere have watched packs leave their territories and invade those of their neighbors. In some cases, the intruders seemed content merely to filch a deer or moose, eat it hurriedly, and return to their own territory. But other intrusions were different. The invading packs picked up the residents' trail and excitedly followed it, not repelled by the residents' scent, as might normally be expected. In several cases in Minnesota, the intruders pressed on until they had located the residents and attacked them. Most of these incursions resulted in at least one mortally wounded resident. What motivated these attacks is unknown.

This introduces the crux of a pack's howling dilemma. If a pack howls and its neighbors answer, and if each pack is content to leave the other alone, then the howling has served its function: a potentially destructive encounter has been averted. But if one pack intent on attack howls and the other answers, then the second pack has given away its location and has facilitated its potential demise. This may explain why packs only answered me on half of the occasions on which I howled.

On each howling occasion, I tried to note various kinds of information, such as where I was in relation to the territory edge or center, whether the pack was traveling or stationary; whether it was at a den, a rendezvous site, or out hunting; whether the pups were present; and which adults were there. Despite my sketchy data, a number of striking patterns emerged, which fleshed out an answer to the howl or not to howl question.

If replying to intruders carries the risk of attack, then wolves should expect to reap benefits that make the risk worth taking. One such benefit is the advantage of staying put. For the most part, wolves have no overriding reason to stay put. They can afford to get up, move off, and start hunting again, rather than risk an attack. But if a site contains an important resource, such as their favorite prey or their pups, there is no incentive to move.

Just one of the large ungulates that wolves hunt in Minnesota can keep the average pack well fed for a few days to a week or more. The typical wolf needs about four to eight pounds of meat each day to survive. An adult male moose provides about 725 pounds of edible meat, enough to fuel a pack of six wolves for two to four weeks. Packs are understandably reluctant to leave their kills.

But the kills get old, their meat and marrow are consumed, and soon nothing but hair, bones, and pieces of hide remain. When a pack was ready to move on, howls to them often resulted in a silent retreat. Thus an interesting pattern developed at kills. The freshest of largest kills were associated with the highest reply rates. I located one pack feeding on a six- to seven-month-old fawn that had been killed less than four hours before. It replied to my howls nine times in less than one and a half hours. When I returned the following day, the pack was still there but refused to answer any of my howls. It was gone when I checked again a few hours later, leaving nothing but the fawn's lower jawbone.

Pups also tie a pack to a specific site, but for a much longer period. Once out of the den at three to four weeks of age, the pups spend the next three to four months at rendezvous sites, where they grow and mature as rapidly as the adults can keep them supplied with food. During this period, the pups become increasingly capable of traveling but still cannot match the endurance of an adult. Should danger threaten while the pups are near the den, they can scamper back into it and take refuge. But most rendezvous sites lack such havens and the pups are more exposed to danger, making them more dependent on protection by the adults.

Packs are therefore quite vocal at rendezvous sites. For each pack I studied, the highest reply rates were obtained at rendezvous sites during the summer. One pack replied on all twenty-four nights I howled to it in July and August, while another replied on seventeen of twenty nights in July and on all thirty-two howling sessions in August.

During these pack replies, the pups readily joined in. Pups are accustomed to replying to packmates on their return to the rendezvous site. I found that when pups were left alone, they frequently approached me when I howled near the rendezvous site. On one occasion a pup traveled nearly half a mile toward me. It was panting and whimpering when it crashed through the brush a few feet away. Once it caught my scent it circled around me, still looking for the phantom adult wolf it was so anxious to meet. When I couldn't hear it anymore, I howled, and within seconds the pup came panting and whimpering toward me again. To the pups I must have seemed one of the pack's adults, coming back to the rendezvous site with food and perhaps in the mood to play.

The adults, however, made no such errors in identification. To them, I was an intruder and a real threat to their pups. Therefore, replying to my howls was a serious matter. If I pressed the pack by continuing to howl, the adults led the pups several hundred feet away, giving up some ground rather than endanger the pups in a fight.

As their pups grew and developed, however, packs became less and less responsive. Sometimes in late November or early December, by which time pups had been traveling with the adults for some two months, packs were unlikely to reply unless they were camped at a kill. Because the pups were now very mobile, there was no need to stay on their account. Silence, and perhaps retreat, might be the best response to an intruder's howling. Accordingly, in December and January, replies came sporadically. If a pack had just made a kill, I could expect a day or two of replies before the pack clammed up. But I soon discovered that more than kills or pups influenced a pack's decision about replying.

When the breeding season approached in late February, reply rates went up for all my study packs; kills at that time made no difference in responses. With the increased production of reproductive hormones at the onset of the breeding season, there is a parallel rise in aggressiveness. Within the pack, wolves of the same sex jealously compete for the privilege of mating. This aggression is directed toward strangers as well. Most fatality-producing encounters between packs occur during the mating season, when the dominant wolves seem unwilling to tolerate a threat to their status from any corner. But the breeding season ends even more suddenly than it begins, and as aggressiveness wanes, the number of replies to howling plummets. By April, a month after mating activity had ceased, replies were extremely difficult to elicit.

One last factor seemed to influence the pack's decision whether to reply—its size. One pack of seven to twelve wolves replied twice as frequently as a smaller pack with four to six members. This was true at kill sites, around rendezvous sites, and elsewhere in the packs' territories. Being in a group appears to make wolves more confident in replying to an intruder's threat. As the size of the group increases, individuals become bolder and therefore more likely to reply.

Such group support seems to make larger packs more aggressive than smaller ones. They are accordingly more likely to trespass into neighboring territories, to attack their neighbors, and to chase away any strangers they encounter in their own territories. When deer were in short supply recently in Minnesota's Superior National Forest, packs were occasionally forced to trespass in order to find food. Most were content to make brief forays into alien territory and returned home quickly after finishing their filched kills. One pack of four to six members played this form of Russian roulette once too often; the dominant male was killed when the pack was detected and confronted by the residents. But one of the largest packs, numbering nearly a dozen, trespassed repeatedly during this time and prospered.

In my two years of howling, I had some close encounters with the wolves and experienced moments of fear when the mythology about the animals took over and my imagination got the better of me. But only on seven of more than four hundred occasions did a single wolf leave the pack and approach me. Even these approaches happened only when I continued to howl after the wolves had given me one or more vocal indications of their original position.

Another thing. Even after tearing apart my data in as many ways as I could, I was never able to make any connection between wolf howls and the phases of the moon. I found that especially comforting. Why should wolves pay more attention to the moon than to their families, their food, and their foes?

Questions for Discussion

1. What was the author's purpose in choosing this title? What other titles could you give this essay?
2. How important is this essay's expressive aim? Could this essay be classified as expressive aim writing? Cite specific passages to support your answer.
3. Are you satisfied with the way the author identifies sources of information? Is this technique effective? Is it appropriate?
4. Why is the essay organized the way it is? How would you organize this essay?
5. Do you think a table of statistical findings is necessary? Explain your answer.

Opportunities for Writing

1. Analyze the image of the wolf in children's stories. Why is the wolf usually characterized as evil? Compose your essay for a special exhibit on children's stories at your local library.
2. Using a questionnaire, analyze the attitudes of people in your community regarding wolves. Why are people afraid or unafraid of wolves? How did people develop their attitudes?
3. Analyze job opportunities available through the U.S. Fish and Wildlife Service. What kinds of jobs are available? How many? When? Where? Who is eligible? How do individuals apply? Call or write the agency for pertinent information and interview officers of the Fish and Wildlife Service. Report the results of your research in a flier to be distributed to interested students at your school's career counseling office.
4. Explain the process of fitting wolves with radio-collars. What materials are required? How are the wolves fitted? Who authorizes and subsidizes such research? Why? Address your essay to a local animal rights organization.

The Indian Image

JANE AND MICHAEL STERN

Jane and Michael Stern analyze the changing image of Native Americans in this essay. "The Indian Image" is taken from these coauthors' book Way Out West *(1993). Together the Sterns have written nineteen books, including* Roadfood, Elvis World, *and* The Encyclopedia of Bad Taste. *Considered leading authorities on America's roadside culture, they have also published articles in such popular magazines as* The New Yorker, The Atlantic Monthly, *and* GQ.

In 1907, the American Indian became the best-known Western advertising image prior to the Marlboro cowboy. It was that year that the Santa Fe Railroad issued the first of its annual calendars, featuring paintings of Native Americans engaged in tribal activities or simply looking august and exotic. Hundreds of thousands of these calendars, meant to be enchanting invitations to come visit the Southwest, were sent free throughout the land each year for more than three quarters of a century. The railroad had tickets to sell, and the Indians on the calendars (as well as in advertising) proved to be a powerful lure. "The Santa Fe Indian," T. C. McLuhan wrote in her enlightening book about the impact of the railroad on Southwest Indian life, *Dream Tracks* (1985), "possessed an aura of glamour. An intangibility. An ineffable essence.... Simplicity. Freedom. Nobility." Even before that first calendar, the Indian image had become a symbol of the West, and it has remained a symbol ever since—so powerful that it has obscured the reality of Indian life.

The true story of America's native peoples, and of what happened to them as the West was won—and as their lands were lost—has been called this nation's great unfinished business. It is a story that is grand and colorful, gilded with lofty ideals, stained by wave upon wave of unspeakable tragedy, and almost always tinged by fear and fascination—and misunderstanding—on the part of white people. "Why do you call us Indians?" a tribesman asked Pilgrim missionary John Eliot in 1646. As Robert F. Berkhofer, Jr., points out in *The White Man's Indian* (1978), there were some two thousand different cultures in North America when white people arrived; each saw itself as separate and distinct. But the newcomers lumped them all together and misnamed them, simply because Columbus thought he had landed somewhere near India.

(The proper name for indigenous Americans is still very much an issue. Some tribal spokespeople prefer "Native American," which is technically correct. For the most part, though, Native Americans we have encountered in our travels still frequently use the term "Indian," at least when talking to outsiders. Among themselves they aren't likely to use either "Indian" or "Native American"; instead, "Navajo," "Choctaw," "Cherokee," etc., are the words that really tell a listener who they are. Some tribes are even battling these labels. A faction of Navajos want to shed the word *Navajo,* which was derived from the Spanish term *Apaches de Navajó* [*Navajó* was the Spanish name for what is now northern New Mexico and Arizona], and return to what they used to call themselves—*Diné,* meaning simply "people." The former Papagos—also a Spanish name, meaning bean people—who live in the Sonoran desert south of

Phoenix, Arizona, have already officially reclaimed the more traditional name of Tohono O'odham, meaning desert people.)

One reason for tribal interest in reclaiming original names is that the rest of America has always felt free to appropriate the names, as well as the likeness, of indigenous peoples for products of all kinds—from Red Man chewing tobacco to Crazy Horse beer, Navajo Van Lines to Chevrolet Apache trucks and Jeep Cherokee station wagons. High school, college, and professional sports teams traditionally adopt names such as "Indians," "Braves," and "Chiefs" for their connotation of never-say-die ferocity; in the last few years, the Atlanta Braves fans' rallying gesture—the tomahawk chop—has become a sore point among many Native Americans and their sympathizers, who see it as a disrespectful cliché. (Actually, a freehand chop was originally devised in the early 1980s at Florida State to cheer on the university's Seminoles; it became a Braves' trademark in 1991 only after a foam-bedding salesman named Paul Braddy began marketing foam tomahawks.)

5   For Indians, it hasn't necessarily been a wonderful thing that their image—however exalted, ferocious, or magical—has veiled their existence as human beings. One original obstacle to perceiving the native people of this continent as equal beings was that the United States was founded on a firm belief in natural law, at a time when nature and all things close to it were thought to hold the key to truth and virtue. "Nature itself had become holy," wrote William H. Goetzmann and William N. Goetzmann in their book *The West of the Imagination* (1986). "Primitive people [were equated with] nature and nature's laws, thus making them, in their grand simplicity, the people closest to God." So while the natives of America represented a problem to be reckoned with—they had to be evicted from their homelands for westward settlement to proceed—they also took on a role in white people's eyes as nature's truest surrogates. The complexities and refinement of their ancient cultures notwithstanding, Indians became the U.S.A.'s own race of "noble savages." They were considered primitive, and therefore linked to the earth and wise in the ways of cosmic law.

James Fenimore Cooper's Leatherstocking Tales, *Last of the Mohicans* in particular, helped crystallize this sentimental image in print—of a heroic race doomed by the onslaught of civilization. George Catlin, originally of Philadelphia, realized it on canvas in lyric paintings that depicted the Indians of the West (and of the East) as a glorious breed of people, enveloped in nature's dignity; in his words: "their long arms in orisons of praise to the Great Spirit in the sun, for the freedom and happiness of their existence." Writing about the red man he painted, he described him as a being "in the innocent simplicity of nature, in the full enjoyment of the luxuries which God has bestowed upon him . . . happier than kings and princes can be, with his pipe and little ones about him." He described his subjects as "Lords of the forest" and "Nature's proudest, noblest men," and the West they inhabited as "the great and almost boundless garden spot of the earth."

To Catlin, the Indian was a vanishing idol, a baleful victim of the march of civilization. He wrote, "From the towering cliffs of the Rocky Mountains, the luckless savage will turn back his swollen eyes on the illimitable hunting grounds from which he has fled; and there contemplate, like Caius Marius on the ruins of Carthage, their splendid desolation."

Catlin was so disturbed by the awful effects of settlement on Indians and their land that as early as 1842 he wishfully imagined the West being transformed into a kind of huge nature preserve, where Indians, like an endangered species, would be protected. It would become "a *magnificent park,* where the world could see for ages to come the native Indian in his classic attire, galloping his wild horse, with sinewy bow, and shield and lance, amid the fleeting herds of elk and buffaloes . . . A *nation's Park,* containing man and beast, in all the wild and freshness of their nature's beauty."

The enduring influence of Henry Wadsworth Longfellow's epic poem "Song of Hiawatha," published in 1855, was due in great measure to its setting in the past, on the verge of the coming of the white man. Its Indians (who lived in the East) were not a roadblock standing in the way of manifest destiny, but a simple, happy people living in harmony with the earth . . . and gladly welcoming the black-robed missionary who comes to convert them to Christianity at the end. Written in drumbeat meter like a legend chanted around a campfire, the poem's idyllic descriptions of the ways of the Ojibways and Dakotas cast a nostalgic spell so powerful that even as a very real policy of bloody extirpation was being waged by the United States against intransigent natives, thousands of schoolchildren learned to give recitations of the poem—to honor America's first people. Young white students dressed in dyed feather headdresses and mock buckskin, and delivered their verse complete with an elaborate system of hand signals to indicate a wigwam, a rising moon, and baby Hiawatha being rocked in his linden cradle "safely bound with reindeer sinews." The most oft-repeated part of the heroic tale was from the section titled "Hiawatha's Childhood":

> By the shores of Gitche Gumee,
> By the shining Big-Sea-Water,
> Stood the wigwam of Nokomis,
> Daughter of the Moon, Nokomis.
> Dark behind it rose the forest,
> Rose the black and gloomy pine trees,
> Rose the firs with cones upon them;
> Bright before it beat the water,
> Beat the clear and sunny water,
> Beat the shining Big-Sea-Water.

10   By the time Buffalo Bill Cody began to mythologize the frontier in his Wild West shows in 1883, it was impossible to envision the West remaining wild any longer. The frontier was on the verge of being "closed." The West had been won, Indian resistance had been broken, and with rare exception, the surviving Indians had surrendered. "Some of my best friends were Indians," Buffalo Bill once boasted, speaking in the past tense; and out of friendship—as well as showmanship—he made them part of his spectacle. Along with longhorn cows, buffalo, coyotes, and cowboys, Indians became featured players in the exhilarating pageant of the frontier that originally defined the pop-culture West.

Most of the Indians employed in the Wild West show were Dakota Sioux, and thanks in part to their role in Buffalo Bill's pageant, they became *the* symbolic

Indians of North America. It was the Sioux who camped in circles of white tepees (their word was *tipi*), who painted their ponies for war, who smoked peace pipes, and who wore spectacular eagle-feather headdresses, fringed buckskin shirts, and beaded moccasins. To many people unaware of the diversity of Native American cultures, they formed the basis for the singular image of the American Indian.

And of course under the direction of Buffalo Bill, who knew that audiences would not spend money freely to see peaceable natives sitting together in equanimity, they did their best to yelp and cavort and behave like wild Indians were supposed to do. They chased after a covered wagon train, ululating and wielding their tomahawks, and in a grand melodramatic finale, they massed as an army of feathered savages and re-created "Custer's Last Charge" (the word *stand* was then considered too defeatist), including battle with the U.S. Cavalry on horseback, hand-to-hand knife and fistfights, and a chilling climactic moment when a Sioux brave reached down to take the scalp of General George Armstrong Custer. Imagine the awe and horror audiences felt when, immediately after this blood-curdling mayhem, Hunkpapa Sioux chief Sitting Bull—the very man who had directed the massacre of Custer's troops less than ten years earlier—rode out before them, in full-feather regalia. Many in the audience took the opportunity to jeer Sitting Bull as Custer's murderer.

After one season with the Wild West show, in 1885, Sitting Bull (a U.S. government captive since 1881) was allowed to go to the Standing Rock Sioux reservation in Dakota; Buffalo Bill Cody—with whom he had become fast friends—gave him a gray horse from the show to keep. It was a trick horse that had been trained to sit and wave its hooves in the air at the report of a gun. In 1890, at the height of the Ghost Dance frenzy (a belief that spread through many Western reservations that wild—but peaceful—dancing would soon bring forth an Indian Messiah who would renew the buffalo herds, restore Indians to their land, and make white men vanish), Major General Nelson Miles ordered the rearrest of Sitting Bull for fomenting the allegedly subversive cult. (It was a trumped-up charge; in fact, Sitting Bull was skeptical of Ghost Dancing.) When police arrived, more than a hundred Ghost Dancers rallied to protect the venerable chief; in the confusion, shots were fired. At the sound of the guns, Sitting Bull's horse began to perform its theatrical dance—sitting on its haunches and waving a hoof in the air as it had learned to do in the Wild West show: an unsettling coda to the image white men had created for the vanquished chief. The Sioux leader, whom police later accused of resisting arrest, took a bullet and fell dead. But his horse continued to perform in the midst of the melee—stunning onlookers who thought the horse itself had been seized with the Ghost Dance spirit.

Even before the Ghost Dance cult animated the Plains reservation dwellers and became a catalyst for the final awful massacre at Wounded Knee in the Badlands in 1890, the Indian wars had come to a symbolic close in the Southwest when Apache leader Geronimo surrendered for the last time in 1886 in Skeleton Canyon on the Arizona–New Mexico border. Geronimo, who was already notorious as the "Tiger of the Southwest" for his ability to wage guerrilla war and to elude capture, became the most famous Apache in America. After serving time at hard labor in Florida, Geronimo was allowed to appear in Pawnee Bill's Wild West show, where he was billed as "the worst

Indian that ever lived." Outfitted in flamboyant eagle-feather headdress, he rode before the crowds in a Locomobile touring car, gunning down a live buffalo from the passenger seat—a performance advertised as "The Last Buffalo Hunt." Never mind that, as a Chiricahua Apache of the Southwest mountains, it is likely Geronimo had never shot a buffalo and had never worn head-feathers. He had become the supreme image of an Indian on the warpath, and that image, in the popular mind, necessarily included a warbonnet as well as a wake of dead buffalo.

15   Indians soon became one of the prime tourist attractions in the Southwest. Subdued on reservations and no longer an obstacle to settlement, they still carried a whiff of danger, which provided the traveler with the kind of wild game-park thrill George Catlin had once imagined. Beyond their curiosity value as an only recently defeated enemy, Indians were also intriguing because of their crafts skills. The opening of Hotel El Tovar at the rim of the Grand Canyon in 1904 provided visitors not only with a close-up view of nature, but with a view of America's natural people—Indians—making jewelry at Hopi House, a crafts studio built by the Fred Harvey Company just across the way from the hotel. In Albuquerque, Harvey's Alvarado Hotel opened an entire room devoted to the display (and sale) of native pottery, baskets, jewelry, and rugs.

In 1926, encouraged by the success of El Tovar and tour buses that took tourists around the rim of the Grand Canyon, the Santa Fe Railway, in conjunction with the Fred Harvey Company, introduced "Indian Detours." Now someone traveling coast-to-coast by rail could pay extra and stop in Winslow, Albuquerque, or Santa Fe for a guided excursion into Indian country. Groups of Detourists stepped off the train and boarded elongated Packard Harveycars with eleven upholstered swivel seats and broad Pullman-style windows for two- or three-day trips. Each car was driven by a cowboy-mechanic in a ten-gallon hat and riding boots, and each was hosted by a specially trained "courier," who was a college-educated white woman in an Indian velvet shirt and silver concha belt. According to company literature, the couriers all had supplemented their education with "special training on archaeological and ethnological history." Their job was to make the trip an experience that brought travelers so close to Indians they could touch them:

> Greeting guests upon arrival by train, it is thereafter their privilege to fill the pleasant dual role of hostesses as well as guides. Couriers' friendships with representative Indians in many pueblos assure their guests of intimate glimpses of Indian life not otherwise obtainable.

Just as movies consummated the transformation of cowboy from hired man to folk hero, they further flattened the Indian image into a familiar stereotype. Hollywood's Indians were based primarily on the whooping Sioux of the Wild West shows, and while silver-screen red men have ranged from tragic innocents to bloodthirsty demons, certain aspects of their role in movies have been consistent: Indians are always symbolic of something, and they are usually clichés, outfitted in what Ralph and Natasha Friar, in their book *The Only Good Indian* (1972), described as the "instant Indian kit" of buckskin and warbonnet, with tomahawk and bow and arrow. They all live in tepees, pound drums, ride beautiful pinto ponies, and communicate in an elementary language of grunts and hand signs. They are simple people—simple and happy or simple and wicked, depending on what the plot requires.

In the 1950s Hollywood's image of Indians began to change. Starting with Delmer Daves's *Broken Arrow* (1950), about a white man in love with an Apache girl (played by Debra Paget, not an Apache), it became more common to see Indians depicted as innocent victims rather than scalp-hunting fiends. A number of red men had always been featured trusty sidekicks, such as the Lone Ranger's Tonto or Little Beaver (played by juvenile Robert Blake), the junior companion of Wild Bill Eliott as Red Ryder, and of course, there were plenty of comic characters, such as Chief Thunderthud and Princess Summerfall Winterspring on television's "Howdy Doody." But after *Broken Arrow,* such movies as Robert Aldrich's *Apache* (1954) and Douglas Sirk's *Taza, Son of Cochise* (1955) actually purported to deal with the Indian question as a troubling issue in need of solutions; both movies set forth a policy of peaceful coexistence.

Indians were the subject of a great cultural vogue starting in the late 1960s, thanks mostly to hippies, who liked to see themselves as tribal sorts of people. Headbands, moccasins, body paint, and turquoise jewelry were all adopted by flower children as symbols of their closeness to North America's original tribes. Wearing beads became "a symbolic rejection of a corrupt society and a return to the communal values of American Indians," announced Columbia University student rebel Ted Kaptchuk in a 1968 *Eye* magazine fashion story. In *Flashing on the Sixties* (1987), which includes an account of the New Buffalo hippie commune in New Mexico, Lisa Law wrote, "The Indians of the Taos Pueblo helped the New Buffaloers by being friends and teachers, and the young Indians in turn gained self respect when they saw other men with long hair."

In 1971 the Raiders (formerly Paul Revere and the Raiders) hit the top of the *Billboard* chart with "Indian Reservation (The Lament of the Cherokee Reservation Indian)," about the sad fate of Native Americans forced to live on reservations. Originally written by John D. Loudermilk in 1963 and recorded by Don Fardon in England, it became a monster hit in the United States—the biggest-selling single in Columbia Records' history to that date. Two years later Cher went native in Bob Mackie beads and buckskin for her "Sonny and Cher Comedy Hour" on television, and had a number one hit with "Half-Breed," a socially conscious song with an Indian theme.

As national shame over the Vietnam war escalated, the cause of Indians became a favorite one among many concerned people in the entertainment business, who saw parallels between the U.S. government policies toward the indigenous people of the American West and those of Southeast Asia. Starting in 1970 for about a half-dozen years, Hollywood produced dozens of diligently pro-Indian, anti-Army pictures. Setting the tone for many, *Soldier Blue* (1970), billed as "the most brutal and liberating, the most honest American film ever made," dramatized the Army's 1864 Sand Creek slaughter of Indians. According to director Ralph Nelson, it was meant to parallel the My Lai incident in Vietnam, and it is, even today, shocking in its depiction of senseless bloodshed (mostly by whites against Indians). It featured a plaintive title song written and performed by Cree activist and folk singer Buffy Sainte-Marie; however—as usual—the Indians in the movie were mostly anonymous, and all the major roles were played by whites (including Candice Bergen and Peter Strauss). Another 1970 picture, *A Man Called Horse,* was scrupulous in its attempt at realism, including dialogue spoken in Lakota Sioux; nevertheless, *The BFI Companion to the Western* quotes the Native American newspaper *Akwesasne Notes* about it: "Same old savage stereotype. White actors playing cigar store Indians." Reportedly the Sioux who allowed the film to be made on their reservation became "the laughing stock of Indian America."

Chief Dan George, an actor from the Tse-lal-watt tribe of British Columbia, provided audiences with another perspective on Native Americans in the 1970s: he was smart and he had a sense of humor. First as Old Lodge Skins in the savage history lesson *Little Big Man* (1970, from the novel by Thomas Berger), and then as Lone Watie, Clint Eastwood's traveling companion in the resonant epic *The Outlaw Josey Wales* (1976), he provided both films with unexpected tenderness. George's addition of intellectual whimsy to the Indian image has been echoed in many films since, perhaps most effectively in *Thunderheart* (1992), about an earnest FBI agent (Val Kilmer) who comes to terms with his mystical Indian heritage while solving a murder. Spiritual as its plot may be, *Thunderheart* is notable for the pranks and fun enjoyed by its Indian supporting cast—Graham Greene as a witty tribal cop and Chief Ted Thin Elk as a shrewd old Sioux medicine man who's addicted to television shows and who always seems to be hoodwinking Kilmer.

The traditional image of Indians has broadened tremendously thanks to many popular books with Indian characters and themes, from the bestselling historical novel *Sacajawea* to the embarrassingly successful book of bogus Native American maxims, *The Education of Little Tree.* Novels and nonfiction by Tony Hillerman, Louise Erdrich, and Michael Dorris, the latter two of Native American descent, have created compelling alternatives to old stereotypes, but probably the most influential recent pop-culture portrayal of Indians was a movie—*Dances with Wolves* (1990). After a decade in which Indians hadn't been seen much on screen, director-star Kevin Costner revived the ultra-noble image in an Academy Award–winning movie that *U.S. News & World Report* declared the catalyst for a new era of "Native American chic." Costner's romantic parable extolled the Lakota Sioux as a loving, peaceful, loyal, emotionally expressive, ecologically responsible, and joyous culture who find themselves besieged by U.S. soldiers who are nothing but evil predators. As Union officer Dunbar, Costner is so smitten with the Sioux that he changes sides and joins them, even falls in love with one (who happens to be a white woman raised by them, thus allowing the plot to dodge the issue of intermarriage); when they name him Dances with Wolves, he declares that he knows for the first time who he really is. Audiences loved the three-hour fable, which, along with Clint Eastwood's *Unforgiven* (1992), is credited with resurrecting the Western genre.

We recently stumbled across a Western scene that said a lot about the enduring power of the stereotyped Indian image in contemporary life. In Window Rock, Arizona, headquarters of the Navajo nation, there is an immense red-rock arch shaped like a portal that rises up above the sandstone buildings that house tribal offices and the federal Bureau of Indian Affairs. It is an awesome natural sight, but when we came to town in the spring of 1992, it was not possible to get near it because a television commercial was being filmed in front of it. Surrounded by lights, reflectors, a camera, a microphone boom, and about a dozen crew members in T-shirts and jeans, a Navajo stood with the rock formation rising up behind him. He was a very handsome old man wearing a velvet blouse and draped in a spectacular suite of Navajo silver and turquoise necklaces. The camera crew had recruited him for the occasion, hiring him for his noble appearance. When he was cued, he looked into the camera and spoke in a voice that quivered with portent, delivering his single line over and over again, perhaps three dozen times, until he said it exactly the way the director wanted. "In nature, all things are balanced," the red man repeated, each time holding up a perfumed loofah sponge you can buy at your favorite department store.

25   We asked one of the crew members about the commercial being filmed. He explained that the concept behind it was to emphasize the sponge's closeness to the earth. An Indian was chosen to deliver the message, he said, because "They're more in touch with nature than anybody else."

Questions for Discussion

1. Do you think the opening paragraph is effective? Explain why you think it is or isn't.
2. Do you think that headings would contribute to the clarity of this essay? If so, add appropriate headings. If not, explain why you think headings are unnecessary.
3. Which passages of this essay constitute knowledge by participation? Would this essay be more or less effective without this information?
4. Why do the authors include a quotation from "Song of Hiawatha"? Do you think the quotation achieves their objective? Explain your answer.
5. Which passages of this essay do you consider necessary to support the thesis? Justify your answer.

Opportunities for Writing

1. Using interviews, investigate your family's knowledge of Indians. How did your family acquire this knowledge: through participation or through observation? How has television, films, or literature influenced their knowledge?
2. Design a questionnaire to solicit the opinions of students at your school regarding the adoption of Indian names and images by high school, college, and professional sports teams. Do students consider this practice disrespectful? Why or why not? Does opinion differ according to racial or ethnic group? In a guest editorial for your school newspaper, discuss the findings of your questionnaire.
3. After examining a representative sample of major newspapers and popular magazines, analyze the characterization of Indians in newspaper and magazine advertising. How often are Indian images used? How are Indians portrayed? With what products and services are Indians associated?

4. Where did the idea of the "noble savage" begin? To which groups of people was the term or idea first applied? How has it since been used in art, literature, and popular culture?

Gender Bias and the 1992 Summer Olympic Games
An Analysis of Television Coverage

CATRIONA T. HIGGS AND KAREN H. WEILLER

Catriona T. Higgs and Karen H. Weiller teach, research, and write about physical education. Higgs is an associate professor and chair of physical education at Slippery Rock University, and Weiller is an assistant professor of physical education at the University of North Texas. These coauthors analyze the 1992 Summer Olympics, by examining specific differences in the way men and women athletes and events were covered by NBC. In this essay, which was published in the Journal of Sport & Social Issues, *Higgs and Weiller present their data according to APA documentation style, using internal parenthetical citations and a list of references at the end of the article.*

This study provides a quantitative and qualitative analysis of NBC's coverage of sports that held competitions for both women and men during the 1992 Olympic Games. The study presents results of the broadcast time devoted to women's and men's basketball, volleyball, gymnastics, swimming/diving, track and field, and other sports. The analysis examines qualitative differences in portrayals of female and male athletes. The analysis of each sport evaluated announcers' use of strength and weakness descriptors to characterize women and men athletes and the nature of the narratives used to describe women and men competitors. The study finds that although women were given greater coverage in individuals sports, that coverage was divided into shorter and more heavily edited segments. In addition, commentators relied on gender marking, biased and ambivalent reporting, and a focus on personalities as opposed to athletic abilities when covering women's sports.

Mass media often influence their audiences through biased accounts that are premised on a distorted construction of reality (Altheide & Snow, 1979; Harris & Hills, 1993). Following Altheide and Snow's (1979) theory of media logic, Duncan and Brummett (1987) argue that televised narrative accounts of sporting events shape our interpretations about sport in a way that meets the needs of the medium, but do so in a way that affects our sensemaking not only about sport but about its competitors and their relative social power. Thus media coverage of important events such as the Olympic Games can be influential in shaping inaccurate perceptions of women and men and their roles in sport and society.

The use of narrative or story in television is particularly appealing to audiences, as stories allow viewers to identify with those being portrayed. The power of the televised sport can be most clearly seen "when announcers go far beyond the bounds of merely reporting the action to forcing the spectator into the form of narrative" (Duncan & Brummett, 1987, p. 170). The concept of narrative is used compellingly to frame perceptions of events, providing drama, human interest, and appeal necessary to attract and keep viewers. One frequent way this can be done is to provide a personal accounting of an athlete's life in order to "weave an interesting tale" (Duncan & Brummett, 1987, p. 170). Such involving devices help narratives about sport take on a heightened sense of excitement as the sport epic unfolds. Narrative is used persuasively to lure viewers into maintaining interest so they will return for the next "episode" of sporting competition (Harris & Hills, 1993).

According to Duncan and Brummett (1987), three central features dominate the televised sport narrative: interchangeable stock characters, repeatable formulaic plots, and themes stressing competition and conflict. These contribute to a media logic that allows featured athletes to be viewed as consistent and stable in their caricature, yet allows them to often be "cast into agonistic forms . . . of competition and conflict" (p. 170). Uncertainty of outcome and future conflict potential helps make total closure fleeting and dramatic appeal intense (Harris & Hills, 1993). Further, messages about competition in these narratives often reinforce inequities in power and gender relations (Kinkema & Harris, 1992).

These inequities, seen in both television imagery and narrative, help construct a hegemonic masculinity, an ideology legitimizing what Humberstone (1990) calls the "reproduction of patriarchal gender relations in society" (p. 202). Previous studies (Duncan, 1986; Jacobs & Real, 1986; Weiller & Higgs, 1993) have documented the underrepresentation of women in media coverage of the Olympic Games. Limited televised coverage of women's team sport competition has been noted by a variety of authors (Duncan & Hasbrook, 1988; Weiller & Higgs, 1993). Coverage of such team sports is important because issues of power and control are central to maintaining the naturalness of male dominance (Birrell, 1984). Further, as Sabo (1985) suggests, coverage of women's team sports are important because they help break stereotypes of women holding ancillary positions by showing them in active leadership and decision-making roles.

Yet, even as the media cover women competing in team sports that reflect concepts of strength, dominance, and power, the coverage often tends to subvert these effects by providing women's sports with less air time, fewer comments denoting strength, and unfortunately consistent gender marking of events. The coverage of women's sports is often further denigrated in importance by a heightened focus on the athletes' personal lives, a media logic strategy aimed at creating human interest and appeal to viewers (Duncan, 1993). This study seeks to compare the extent and quality of media biases in gender portrayal found in earlier studies by examining differences in the televised coverage of female and male athletes engaged in the same sports during the 1992 Summer Olympic Games in Barcelona.

METHOD

NBC televised 86 hours of Olympic coverage in summer 1992. Sixty hours (70% of total coverage) were randomly taped and a content analysis was conducted on only those segments that featured same-sport activities for men and women. Time constraints and resources limited the researchers to 60 hours of taped material; however, relative randomness was assured by taping the events at various times in the day/evening coverage. Quantitative analysis measured the running time of coverage devoted to women and men in the same sports.

Qualitative analysis focused on one characteristic of television's media logic: the narrative. Qualitative analysis can often reveal characteristics unseen in a simple quantitative accounting. To better understand the media logic, researchers examined adjectives used by commentators to describe male and female athletes and themes stressed by commentators in the course of weaving narratives about the events.

RESULTS

Of the 60 hours of taped material, 40 hours and 40 minutes, or 68%, were devoted to same-sport activities, with 56% of that time devoted to the coverage of male athletes versus 44% for female athletes. The same-sport events analyzed were the following team and individual activities: basketball, volleyball, gymnastics, swimming, diving, track and field, cycling, rowing, and kayaking. Table 1 shows the amount of coverage that NBC allotted for each of these same-sport events.

With 44% of the same-sport air time, women were relatively well represented in NBC's coverage of the Olympic Games. Given the historical lack of media representation of women in worldwide sporting events, the amount of coverage was encouraging. However, it is important to assess those sports in which females were most featured. As the quantitative data show, the highest percentage of coverage for women occurred in gymnastics (84%), cycling (60%), tennis (67%), and rowing (67%). These activities are individual in nature and reflect a traditional view of women in sports. The coverage of the two major team sports, basketball and volleyball, demonstrated a disproportionate amount of time devoted to men in these "power" events. Women's team sports received considerably less coverage than did the men's.

TABLE 1 SAME-SPORT TIME RESULTS

Sport	% Male	% Female	Total Time
Basketball	74	26	18:23
Volleyball	75	25	3:05
Gymnastics	16	84	5:48
Swimming	48	52	3:35
Diving	44	56	2:11
Track/field	63	37	9:10
Cycling	40	60	:52
Tennis	33	67	:18
Kayaking	81	9	:27
Rowing	33	67	:12

Note: Time is shown in hours (left of colon) and minutes (right of colon).

Basketball

10 In these data, the denial of power was most evident in the women's basketball and volleyball competitions. Intense focus on the U.S. "Dream Team" dominated the coverage of basketball. In fact, the Dream Team dominated the 1992 Olympic coverage more so than any other event or any other year. As a result, the quantity and quality of production in the men's and women's games showed vast differences, and the generalizability of results presented here should be evaluated in light of the uniqueness of the Dream Team situation.

Time Differentials   Spectators of men's games were treated to six games versus four for the women. The average time segment of men's games was 1 hour and 15 minutes as compared to 32 minutes for women's games. Halves were shown in their entirety for each of the men's games, whereas in the women's games, commentators often (three times per game) returned to the studio for updates on other events. Each men's game was previewed by commentators, with the average preview being 12 minutes in length. Each women's game was joined "in progress" or was previewed as players' names were being announced.

Gender Differentials   Slow-motion replays, gender marking, and commentators' use of adjective differentials were found to be relatively imbalanced. Slow-motion replays were shown more often in the men's games (16/game) than in the women's (9/game). Verbal and on-screen statistics were more evident in the men's games than in the women's (men: verbal, 35/game and on-screen, 20/game; women: verbal, 26/game and on-screen, 6/game). Although these figures suggest vast differences, the differences in actual air time devoted to men's and women's games needs to be taken into account.

Beyond these quantifiable differences, gender marking was evident throughout the games. The women's events were presented as the "U.S. Women's Team," whereas men's events were most often (85%) billed as the "U.S. Olympic Team." Constant references to the Dream Team were made by commentators during women's games. For example, the men's team was referred to 31 times during the games played by the women, with the women's team mentioned only 4 times during men's games.

Gender marking by the use of the "infantile" first name (see Duncan, Messner, Williams, & Jensen, 1990) in this event would, however, be expected as many of the NBA players were already household names, often recognizable by their nicknames. The women's team essentially comprised college players who had yet to receive the same level of exposure. Thus, not surprisingly, first-name descriptors were more often used in the men's games (85%) than in the women's (62%), in contrast to previous studies (Duncan et al., 1990).

15 **Strength/Weakness Descriptors**   Commentators' use of adjectives to describe the strengths and weaknesses of men and women differed considerably. In describing the men's games, commentators used 185 descriptors of strength, such as "strongly aggressive in his rebounding," "strong passing team," and "strong powerful drive to the basket." In describing the women's games, com-

mentators used 68 descriptors of strength and 15 descriptors denoting weaknesses. Comments suggested ambivalence, such as "she's a strong rebounder, but her shooting skills are weak" and "she powered through the pick and roll only to throw up a weak shot." The use of a strength descriptor followed by a qualifying inept descriptor was a common feature of the women's coverage.

Narratives The narratives offered by male commentators to describe the men's games exemplified the themes of competition, conflict, and the American ideology of winning and domination. Coverage of the Dream Team versus Croatia game opened with the following statement: "The whole world was awed by their spectacular show. They look to complete their glorious run to the gold. Croatia comes up against the greatest team ever to be assembled in history." Even though no such narrative was provided in the women's game, this is understandable as this comment was made during the men's gold medal game.

Volleyball

As with basketball, depictions of power were heavily geared toward the men's competition. It should be noted that the success of the men's 1984 and 1988 Olympic volleyball teams probably contributed to the amount of coverage given the 1992 team by NBC.

Time Differentials The majority (75%) of the coverage in this sport (2:18) was devoted to men, compared with 25% (47 minutes) devoted to women. The average time segment of men's volleyball was 16 minutes and 23 seconds compared with 7 minutes and 52 seconds for the women's games.

Gender Differentials In the limited coverage, segments shown in the women's games were constantly gender marked: "U.S. women's team," "women players," and "women athletes." Women's first names were used 85% of the time, compared with 62% for men, supporting Duncan et al.'s (1990) concept of a "hierarchy of naming." The word "kills" to indicate a successful spike/serve by the players was mentioned 37 times in the men's games with such phrases as "he's a killing machine," "he kills a jump serve," and "brutally kills that one." The same commentators used the word "kills" only 7 times in the women's games, preferring such phrases as "did she get some heat on that one" and "what a banger."

Strength/Weakness Descriptors Strength descriptors in both events outweighed weakness descriptors (men 63/4; women 26/3). Although the data show relatively similar numbers in terms of weakness descriptors, strength descriptors in men's games far outweighed those for the women by 37, or 41%. Although perhaps a relatively minor point, these figures still define the power base in this popular team sport.

Narratives Narratives in the men's and women's games revealed a strong distinction in presentation of male dominance and strength in this team sport competition. Narratives surrounding the men's games were filled with strong images of the gold medal teams of 1984 and 1988, defining a group described as "the best team in the world for eight years." One prominent example in gender distinction concerned the portrayal of one woman athlete as a "beauty." During the U.S. versus the Netherlands game, commentators ridiculed the athletes by discussing this Dutch player's appearance in the Dutch version of *Penthouse* magazine. The comment began, "She's featured this month in the Dutch edition of *Penthouse*. . . " followed by a pause, and then laughingly "Of course, it's only a sport interview." The woman's appearance was then commented on, leaving the audience with no doubt that this athlete could probably have appeared in *Penthouse* as a centerfold.

As evidenced by the overwhelming focus on the men's basketball and volleyball team sport competitions, audiences were left to wonder about the viability of women's team events as legitimate competition. Rather, viewers were presented with either an ambivalent representation or qualified support for the female athletes' performances. In contrast to team sports such as basketball and volleyball, media portrayals of individual sports for women have relied on a more familiar "ideal" of femininity: the Cinderella of the sport world. This portrayal was evident in both a quantitative and qualitative analysis of NBC's coverage of individual Olympic sports.

Gymnastics

Time Differentials Of the 5 hours and 48 minutes devoted to gymnastics coverage, women's events were featured 84% of the time (5:08), whereas men's gymnastics was only featured 16% of the time (40 minutes). The average segment time for the women's coverage was 24 minutes and only 11 minutes for the men.

Gender Differentials First-name descriptors were used frequently in the women's events. Female athletes were referred to by their first name 46 times versus only 10 times for the males. Although these figures appear to suggest a wide disparity, it is necessary to keep in mind time differences in which men's and women's gymnastics were featured. In the over 5 hours of televised women's gymnastics, the descriptor "girl" was used 37 times. During the 40 minutes of men's gymnastics competition, the word "boy" was never mentioned, albeit in many cases the ages of the men and women competing were comparable.

Inconsistencies in portrayal were evident throughout the events. Slow-motion sequences in the women's events highlighted the skills of the gymnasts competing and camera angles deftly focused on the intense emotion of the sport. Opening sequences for both compulsory and all-around competition in the women's event involved evocative shots, filters over camera lenses to enhance light, and music that was played to enhance images presented. Visual images were inconsistent with verbal commentary. Audiences saw difficult and daring moves on the uneven bars, yet commentators provided listeners with such phrases as "those long beautiful legs," "the beautiful lady," and "the painted bird" instead of focusing on the difficulty of the event. An incongruence between the delightful female image and the intense, competitive athlete was present. Ambivalence in the comments used to describe the athletes was found to be as commonplace as the true female stereotype. The following comments reflect this ambivalence: "where strength and beauty combine," "pretty Kim Zmeskal showing her muscle in Barcelona," and "she is as terrific an athlete as she is gorgeous." It is these kinds of inconsistencies that could leave audiences with an ambivalent attitude toward the event.

Strength/Weakness Descriptors Verbal attributions of strength and weakness contrasted sharply. In discussing the female gymnasts, 30 descriptors suggested strength, compared with 110 suggesting weakness—a ratio of 1/3.66—whereas the men were portrayed with 60 descriptors of strength and 8 of weakness—a ratio of 7.5/1. These data further the notion of the power of male gymnasts versus the grace and beauty of the female gymnasts.

Narratives The women's gymnastic competition was framed by an emotional narrative that painted an exotic and dramatic picture of the event, typical of television's coverage of a women's gymnastics event. Opening montages were filled with images of young gymnasts "aspiring to be what they had become," thus fulfilling society's image of the complete and fulfilled Cinderella. The most articulate and flowery descriptions used to open the event included such phrases as "a lifetime of dedication to the mats at Barcelona," "her parents traded her childhood for dreams," and "for the first time the world met the Cinderella of gymnastics whose dreams are as fragile as the body that carries them." One Russian gymnast was portrayed as furthering the Cinderella image; commentators described her as "the goddess of gymnastics—the Bella Russian Swan."

Commentators in the women's event focused heavily on "weaving an interesting tale" (Duncan & Brummett, 1987). As competition proceeded, commentators began to weave a tale of both the distraught and downtrodden female gymnast and the triumphant heroine. A segment on the same Russian athlete delved into a personal accounting of the effect her coach's suicide had had on the gymnast. Commentators focused on a particular gymnast who had fallen off the beam in team competition and had made it to the individual event only because another competitor had been injured. Audiences were repeatedly subjected to this gymnast's fall off the beam, and cameras focused on her tears. Upon winning the individual all-around medal, this gymnast was hailed as a heroine triumphing over adversity. She was described as "the little girl who wanted nothing more than to be the best." Male commentators discussed one female athlete's dream of becoming a model and highlighted another whose wonderful grandmother learned to drive in order to take her to the gym. Such blatant comments on athletes' personal lives as well as their stature demeans their intensity and importance. It is interesting to note that the narrative in the men's competition focused only on the gymnasts' "power" and athleticism. No references in the limited time coverage focused on their personal lives.

Swimming and Diving

Time Differentials   Swimming and diving proved to be the most equitably covered events. Women's swimming was presented for 1 hour and 52 minutes (52% of total coverage) and men's for 1 hour and 45 minutes (48% of total coverage). Segment lengths were also equitable, with the average time allocation for women being 6 minutes and 13 seconds and for men 7 minutes and 43 seconds. Women's events in diving were shown for 1 hour and 14 minutes (56% of total coverage) and the men's for 53 minutes (44% of the total coverage). Although the amount of coverage in both diving and swimming were comparable for male and females, diving was more equitably presented, whereas differentials in coverage of swimming were considerable.

Gender Differentials   Both ambivalent and blatant sexist comments were used consistently to describe the women swimmers. These included "a powerhouse of a swimmer is only a 16-year-old school girl," "her powerful strong kick," "she really burns up the pool," "she's much prettier now with long hair—that other look didn't become her," "our first look at the babe of summer [referring to Summer Sanders]—she's got a face that says it all," and "she's got the looks, but does she have what it takes to win?" Both male and female divers were described by words such as "graceful," "superb," and "aesthetic."

In swimming, the word "girl" was used 15 times, whereas the word "boy" was never mentioned. Summer Sanders was constantly referred to as "the babe" or "the glamour girl of swimming." No such similar references were made for the male swimmers. In diving, the word "girl" was used 10 times. There was no use of the word "boy" during the men's competition, even though there were young divers competing. During the swimming competition, women were primarily referred to by their first name (37 times) and men by both first name and surname (34 times). Men's swimming events were not gender marked, whereas the women's events were introduced with "women" in the title.

Strength/Weakness Descriptors   More strength than weakness descriptors were used to describe men's swimming events (47/4) compared with the women's (33/6). Strength/weakness ratios in diving were almost identical for men and women competitors: 46/21 for men and 49/23 for women. Both of these represent more equitable coverage.

Narratives   Narratives of the swimming events showed dramatic contrasts in characterizations of male and female athletes. As much of the swimming coverage was mixed, contrasts between the commentary was easier to discern than in other events. Sexist comments framed the narrative of the women's events, with commentators often referring to the women athletes as "girls" and focusing on their personal appearance and age. The men's events contrasted sharply, with the focus on power, ability, and strength.

In diving, athletes appeared to be covered in a more androgynous manner than in any other event. Perhaps this was an artifact of this specific coverage, or perhaps it was reflective of the skill and grace necessary for both men and women to compete in this event.

Track and Field

Time Differentials Disparity was noted in the amount of coverage devoted to men and women. Of the 9 hours and 10 minutes, men were featured for 5 hours and 47 minutes (63%), whereas women were featured for 3 hours and 23 minutes (37%). In men's events, initial rounds as well as semifinals and finals were covered, whereas in women's events, only the semifinals and finals were featured. The women's marathon was extensively covered, with 43 minutes shown. However, one commentator made much of the "mountain that would only admit the bravest and the strongest." A 3-minute segment on Gabrielle Strauss, the Swiss marathoner who struggled to finish the 1984 marathon, was shown to emphasize "how difficult this event is for women."

Gender Differentials Overt sexist comments were made by commentators. Whereas he was the "Michelangelo of the event," she was the "chief fashion plate of the Olympic Games." Perhaps the most marked differential in coverage was reflected in the 4 × 100 meter relay event. Both the U.S. women and men won their event; however, the commentary in the interview, which featured both teams, hardly emphasized the strength of both the male and female athletes. In his interview with both teams, the commentator joked to the women that "he was not used to being around fast women" but said to the men, "Boy, I wished I had the speed of one of these guys when I was playing football."

Narratives Women athletes' personal lives were used by commentators to create a more interesting story. In the 100 meter event audiences were told that "Gwen Torrance has a new focus in her life with her baby." In the 200 meter event, viewers were informed that Gail Devers "gets up early with her husband to train." Repeatedly, commentators focused on the women athletes' appearance. Comments such as "she has the prettiest nails in the competition" and "she's a little too chunky for this event" reflected those made throughout the event.

Cycling, Tennis, Kayaking, and Rowing

Only 1 hour and 49 minutes was devoted to these four sports. In cycling, 60% of the coverage was devoted to women and 40% to men. Only 18 minutes of tennis was featured, with 67% devoted to women and 33% devoted to men. Meaningful analysis of these sports was difficult due to the limited coverage.

With the sole exception of diving, women in individual events were marginalized and trivialized in their depiction in television coverage. Narratives focused heavily on their personal lives or on diminishing their acceptability as strong and effective athletes. Male athletes, however, were framed as competitive and powerful.

Discussion

It has been characteristic of the mass media to present men's and women's sporting events in different ways (Duncan, 1986; Duncan & Hasbrook, 1988; Duncan et al., 1990; Harris & Hills, 1993; Weiller & Higgs, 1993), thus shaping preferred texts for audiences to negotiate. Narratives help to maintain interest in sport as a social commodity by adding pleasure to the television spectator's experience of watching a sporting event (Condit, 1989; Fiske, 1987; Harris & Hills, 1993). Yet many aspects of the televised sport narrative may reinforce messages that enhance male hegemony in sport as well as in other spheres of everyday life (Lembo & Tucker, 1990).

The findings here reinforce those of other studies that have examined Olympic coverage (Birrell, 1984; Duncan et al., 1990; Duncan & Hasbrook, 1988; Sabo, 1985; Weiller & Higgs, 1993). In an earlier study, Jacobs and Real (1986) reported that of the 56 hours of coverage of the 1984 Winter Olympics by ABC, 77% of air time was devoted to men's events and 23% to women's events. Even when removing sports in which only men were featured (e.g., ice hockey), Jacobs and Real still found a disparity in the amount of coverage devoted to men and women (56% and 44%, respectively). Although results of the present study suggest that the quantitative discrepancies may not be so great today, many qualitative differences in television's coverage of men's and women's sports remain. In particular, our findings suggest the following:

1. Although women were actually featured for a longer time period in 6 of the 10 sports presented in this study, these sports were not only individual ones but ones in which it has been considered appropriate for females to participate.
2. Same-sport activities often featured gender marking of women's events, sexist descriptors, biased commentary, and continued to show women in shorter time segments.
3. Ambivalent reporting of female athletes was most noticeable in diving, gymnastics, and swimming, with fewer ambivalent representations in basketball and volleyball.
4. Analysis of the narratives revealed that in women's events the drama focused more on the personalities of the athletes than on the competition.

Although ambivalent portrayals of female athletes were frequent, the results here suggest there are some meaningful changes under way. In NBC's coverage of the 1992 Summer Olympic Games, there was movement toward more positive and equitable coverage of women athletes. Still, the overall results from this study suggest that true media equity is yet to be achieved.

The Olympic Games, as the elite in the amateur sport world, are viewed by millions of individuals of all ages. What is viewed by people as consensus views of the athletic abilities of women carries over into other spheres of life. Because of the limitations of this study, we cannot answer just how much these qualitative differences in the coverage of women's and men's events affect spectators' ideological sensibilities. These questions need to be examined from spectators' perspectives. However, our results do suggest that much work needs to be done in addressing systematic qualitative differences in television coverage given to women's and men's sports, and that, in the meantime, there is reason to worry about audience sensemaking about the athletic abilities and limitations of women and men.

References

Altheide, D. L, & Snow, R. P. (1979). *Media logic.* Beverly Hills, CA: Sage.
Birrell, S. (1984). Separatism as an issue in women's sport. *Arena Review, 8*(2), 21–29.
Condit, C. M. (1989). The rhetorical limits of polysemy. *Critical Studies in Mass Communication, 3,* 189–206.
Duncan, M. C. (1986). A hermeneutic of spectator sport: The 1976 and 1984 Olympic Games. *Quest, 38*(1), 50–77.
Duncan, M. C. (1993). Representation and the gun that points backwards. *Journal of Sport & Social Issues, 17,* 42–46.
Duncan, M. C., & Brummett, B. (1987). The mediation of spectator sport. *Research Quarterly, 58,* 168–177.
Duncan, M. C., & Hasbrook, C. (1988). Denial of power in televised woman's parts. *Sociology of Sport Journal, 5,* 1–21.
Duncan, M. C., Messner, M. A., Williams, W., & Jensen, K. (1990). *Gender stereotyping in televised sports.* Los Angeles: Amateur Athletic Foundation.
Fiske, J. (1987). *Television culture.* London: Routledge & Kegan Paul.
Harris, J., & Hills, L. A. (1993). Telling the story: Narrative in newspaper accounts of a men's collegiate basketball tournament. *Research Quarterly for Exercise & Sport, 64,* 108–121.
Humberstone, B. (1990). Warriors or wimps. Creating alternative forms of physical education. In M. Messner & J. Sabo (Eds.), *Sport, men and the gender order* (pp. 202–204). Champaign, IL: Human Kinetics.
Jacobs, V., & Real, M. (1986). *Ritual analysis: The global Olympic event.* Report no.341304 for UNESCO, Global Understanding. San Diego, CA: San Diego State University, Department of Telecommunication and Film.
Kinkema, K. M., & Harris, J. C. (1992). Sport and the mass media. *Exercise and Sport Science Review, 20,* 127–159.
Lembo, R., & Tucker, K. W. (1990). Cultures, television and opposition. Rethinking cultural studies. *Critical Studies in Mass Communication, 1,* 97–116.
Sabo, D. (1985). Sport, patriarchy and male identity: New questions about men and sport. *Arena Review, 9*(2),1–30.
Weiller, K., & Higgs, C. T. (1993). Gender differentials in televised sport: The 1980's and beyond. *Pennsylvania Journal for Health, Physical Education, Recreation and Dance, 63*(3), 22–25.

Questions for Discussion

1. This essay was written for a professional journal. If the authors were revising their essay for *Sports Illustrated,* would you give the essay a different title? If so, why? What title would you give it? If not, why not? What do you like about this title?

2. How do the authors try to establish their credibility? Do you think the authors are biased? Cite specific passages to support your answer.
3. What is the thesis of the essay? Are you satisfied with the evidence supporting the thesis? Is it sufficient, plausible, and pertinent? Explain your answer.
4. Which passages of this essay would be more effective if displayed as a table or figure? Using a specific passage, design a table or figure to exemplify your answer.
5. What do you think of the closing paragraph? Is it effective? If you think it is, explain why. If you think it isn't, offer specific suggestions for a revised closing paragraph.

Opportunities for Writing

1. Analyze the television coverage of a specific sports competition involving both men and women athletes (e.g., tennis or gymnastics). Like Higgs and Weiller, consider such issues as time differentials, gender differentials, strength/weakness descriptors, and narratives. Compose your essay for the television page of your local newspaper.
2. Using copies of your school's old yearbooks and newspapers, trace the history of women's intercollegiate sports at your school. How did the women's program start? How has it developed over the years?
3. Compare and contrast your attitudes toward men and women athletes. Which men athletes do you admire? Why? Which women athletes do you admire? Why?
4. Analyze the impact of sexist stereotypes on women athletes at your school. In your investigation, interview both the athletes themselves and their coaches. Do sexist stereotypes damage their self-confidence and diminish community support? How are sexist stereotypes communicated at your school? Report the results of your research to appropriate school administrators.

Amphibian Alarm
Just Where Have All the Frogs Gone?

BETH LIVERMORE

Beth Livermore lives and writes in New York City. Her articles have appeared in such popular magazines as Psychology Today, Self, *and* Sea Frontiers. *She has addressed a wide variety of subjects in her writing, from sea manatees and water pollution to t'ai chi fitness and curry cuisine. "Amphibian Alarm" focuses on an inexplicable phenomenon: the vanishing amphibians in the United States. Notes Livermore: "Amphibians are among the oldest creatures on Earth. They evolved more than 350 million years ago and shared their steamy swamps with dinosaurs." This essay was published in* The Smithsonian.

Their eyes bulge, their mouths are ludicrously wide, their fat bellies glisten, their voices are a joke. To some they are synonyms for ugly, but frogs and toads are surprisingly beloved. Mark Twain gave us "The Celebrated Jumping Frog of Calaveras County," Kenneth Grahame wrote Mr. Toad a prominent role in the *The Wind in the Willows,* and for graying adults who grew up on the Smiling Pool stories of Thornton Burgess, a pond is not a pond without the *chug-a-rum* of a bullfrog. It is no accident that they figure prominently in children's stories: How many youngsters have marveled at tadpoles metamorphosing into frogs? How many little boys have come home from a day in the fields with a frog in their pocket? Countryfolk still gig frogs from boats at night, but teenage animal-rights activists increasingly refuse to dissect frogs in their high school biology classes, on the grounds that amphibians are sentient beings, too. Gardeners turn a flowerpot upside down, knock a hole in one side and set it in the dirt, hoping it will become home for a toad that will feast on herbivorous insects. Many more of us equate a frog on its lily pad with the contentment that somehow eludes us.

Now it appears frogs may be fading away, like a number of species of migratory birds. In many parts of the world, a good frog is hard to find. Ponds that once echoed to the crystal plinking of peepers in spring and the tuba riffs of bullfrogs in summer are silent. Nothing plunks into the water as an intruder moves along the shore. Even the biologists whose business it is to know where to find frogs are hard-pressed to locate any. In the past several years herpetologists, the biologists who specialize in amphibians and reptiles, have come to realize that many species are simply disappearing. And no one knows why.

Interviews with biologists on two continents brought the problem home to me. In the Pacific Northwest, I went on a collecting trip with ecologist Andrew Blaustein of Oregon State University at Corvallis. Rather, we tried to collect. Only after half a dozen stops did we finally come up with a single toad, the catch of the day, and that from a roadside puddle. For decades Corvallis scientists have ventured into the nearby Cascade Range to collect amphibians, and it was as easy as falling off a lily pad: frogs and toads lined the shorelines. "We'd go home with dozens after just a few hours," said Blaustein.

About five years ago, however, Blaustein and his colleagues began having to make two and three trips over Tombstone Pass to fill their needs. "Now we feel lucky to go home with anything," he said, placing the warty western toad into an empty cooler. "It's weird. There's no obvious reason for this."

5   Indeed. We had visited several of Blaustein's favorite hunting grounds. Nothing, other than the lack of amphibians, seemed to be wrong with them. Lost Lake, our first stop, looked healthy. Sedges feathered the shoreline. Damselflies, their wings like spun glass, danced among a dazzling array of butterflies. In the center of the lake, which dries to mud come summer, thousands of inch-long toadlets popped up and down.

According to Blaustein there should have been millions. Two years earlier, 50 percent of two million fertilized eggs never hatched. The year before, nearly 100 percent of the million eggs produced lay dead in a gooey white mat. And now only a few thousand had hatched. "We've monitored Lost Lake for 11 years," Blaustein told me. "There has never been more than 5 percent mortality."

The second site was equally idyllic and equally troubling. Lily pads and silver logs sat devoid of web-toed feet. Nothing moved. "Two years in a row Cascades frogs laid eggs here; they hatched into tadpoles, they did fine for a few weeks, and then they completely disappeared," recalled Blaustein, stirring the water idly with an empty net. The site has been studied since 1975. "Nothing like this has ever happened before." Only after half a dozen more stops did we find our toad. "That's not just inconvenient, it's scary. The massive egg mortality and the disappearance of larvae are unprecedented in Oregon." Now Blaustein looks for clues. Like hundreds of other biologists around the globe, he thinks that ailing amphibian populations may reflect the sickly state of their environments—and our world.

Blaustein is not alone. At the first World Congress of Herpetology, held in 1989 in Canterbury, England, scientists from all over the world swapped similar stories and concerns. David Bradford of the University of California said yellow-legged frogs had vanished from 37 of the 38 ponds where he had studied them ten years earlier. Michael Tyler from the University of Adelaide in Australia had not seen a gastric brooding frog, which raises its young in its stomach, since 1980. Martha Crump of the University of Florida in Gainesville said the golden toad, native to Costa Rica's Monteverde Cloud Forest Reserve, had virtually disappeared.

Alarm gave rise to an emergency workshop the following February in Irvine, California. More stories surfaced: frogs, toads and other amphibians have vanished from parts of Denmark, Nova Scotia, Peru and Panama. Places as different as the Swiss Alps and the wetlands of India are missing species. In all, 16 countries, representing five continents, reported massive dips and die-offs among their amphibians. The implications are profound.

10   Amphibians are among the oldest creatures on Earth. They evolved more than 350 million years ago and shared their steamy swamps with dinosaurs. "If they disappear now, after all of that time, there's something to be concerned about," says biologist David Wake, director of the Museum of Vertebrate Zoology at the University of California at Berkeley. In addition, amphibians are a vital link in the food chain: larvae eat plants and/or animals, and predatory adults consume a wide spectrum of creatures; reptiles, birds, fish and mammals, in turn, eat them.

Moreover, it may be that amphibians signal environmental stress earlier than do most other organisms. Most have dual habitats, thereby risking exposure to both water-based and land-based contaminants and predators. They have permeable skin that interacts with water, air and dirt. They lack feathers and hair, so small increases in ultraviolet radiation may cause immediate damage. Many biologists say that amphibians are the canaries in the global coal mine.

Herein lies the debate. Cautious observers point out that much of the evidence is anecdotal. "That's not the kind of evidence that a quantitative ecologist would feel comfortable with," says biologist Peter Morin, of Rutgers University in New Jersey. Furthermore, critics assert that little is known about the biology and behavior of most species. So, determining whether an extinction is natural or induced by mankind is, at best, difficult. In addition, what may look like an extinction could instead be a temporary absence because of hibernation or dormancy. "You'd need about a hundred years of data to know what is 'normal,'" says Joseph H. K. Pechmann, coauthor of a 12-

year study at the University of Georgia's Savannah River Ecology Laboratory in South Carolina. His investigations show wild fluctuations but overall stability.

Adding to the uncertainty, amphibians in some areas are doing quite well. Penn State biologist Blair Hedges, who has worked in the West Indies for the past ten years, reports: "Within the past two years we have heard or observed all 28 species of frog ever known to have occurred at those sites. In fact, we just added two species." The cane toad has overrun southeastern Queensland in Australia. And then there are places where both vanishing and stable species live side by side. For example, thriving wood frog and declining northern leopard frog colonies reside in the same area of the Rocky Mountains.

Still, even skeptics believe that the question of decline is worth investigating. "I'm not saying that people shouldn't study the problem. I'm saying they should do it rigorously and using a protocol that you can apply from one place to the next so that you can compare results," says Morin. Others call for immediate action. "If you wait for the final word—definitive research—there may not be anything left to study," says Russell Mittermeier, president of Conservation International in Washington, D.C. "When it comes to problems of this magnitude, I'm in favor of jumping to conclusions." A number of herpetologists, a generally conservative bunch, appear to agree with him.

15   In December 1990 the International Union for the Conservation of Nature and Natural Resources (IUCN) assigned its Species Survival Commission to create a task force to explore the problem. "Out of this request came the Declining Amphibian Populations Task Force," says James Vial, the international coordinator. "We're applying a SWAT team approach to the problem. We want to get in there, figure out what's going on and get out as fast as possible."

His office is located in the Environmental Protection Agency's research laboratory in Corvallis—just down the road from the Blaustein team. "But this is an international group," he says, diagraming the family tree on a chalkboard. The world will be divided into working groups. He has already assigned chiefs of staff to more than 40 groups in 30 countries. Each group will evaluate the health of local populations and probe peculiarities. He will enter the resulting information into a "Frog Log" database, which will be available to scientists worldwide.

The Australian work group sent 600,000 questionnaires to its citizenry for population data. Scientists working in Panama and Costa Rica have met to coordinate their work and to prepare a proposal for future joint studies. A team at the Smithsonian's National Museum of Natural History is developing a protocol for worldwide data collection. "It will be a complete, self-contained manual for scientists, fish-and-game people, environmental consultants—anyone interested in quantifying amphibian populations," says coauthor Roy McDiarmid. He hopes it will lead to more reliable data.

Biologists are looking for probable causes as well as measuring declines. When the European Herpetological Society (SEH) met in Budapest last fall, an IUCN committee added another 14 species to an already crowded list of threatened frogs and toads. "Habitat destruction and landscape planning are the major threats to these species," the SEH said. Most of the damage in Europe was done long ago and is not as visible today as it is in Central and South America, where daily destruction of rain forest may be wiping out frogs faster than they can be identified. But some is recent. "Before World War II, white storks sat on every rooftop in many German towns," said Ulrich Joger, an SEH officer. After the war, development swept through Germany. "Now you never see them anymore," he said wistfully. "They feed mainly on frogs."

In some areas the German government has dug new ponds and transferred populations of frogs and toads. But it also stocks them with fish, and all too often the frogs are soon gone. French biologist Alain Dubois told me that fish planting was also common in the natural lakes of Europe. He had discovered a subspecies of newt in what was then Yugoslavia: "There were thousands of them in 1978." A few years later he sent a student to collect samples. No more newts. Instead, the student found introduced trout. In France goldfish gobble frog eggs from ponds and lakes, he said. "People bring them home from holiday and don't know what to do with them, so they dump them into the nearest pond. Zap! The frogs are gone."

Dubois is assistant director of the Musée National d'Histoire Naturelle in Paris and general secretary of the International Society for the Study and Conservation of Amphibians. I had to ask him how much the French passion for grenouille—frogs' legs—was affecting the decline of frog populations. "It may contribute to the problem," he conceded. It was in the 1950s that demand began to exceed the local supply of the species *Rana esculenta* (the common name is "edible frog," even though most frogs are edible). In the '90s the majority of frogs' legs sold in France are those of Asian bullfrogs imported from Indonesia and Bangladesh. "Today France consumes 3,000 to 4,000 [metric] tons of frogs' legs each year," said Dubois. "That's about ten times more than 20 years ago." (It takes at least 20,000 frogs to make up a metric ton.)

These days the Asian bullfrog is becoming increasingly more difficult to find. Some scientists suspect that many of the so-called Bangladesh frogs are actually being smuggled from India, where exports were banned in 1987 because insects were getting out of control. India has been forced to introduce a new frog species and increase the use of insecticides.

Dubois leaned toward me. "Do you want to discuss anything else?" he asked, a little annoyed. "There are a lot of other things to consider," he said. Indeed, predation does not explain the mysterious die-off of clutches of frog eggs in the protected Fountainbleau forest, south of Paris. In fact, the most confounding disappearances of amphibians are those occurring in preserves and parks worldwide, where hunting, fishing and farming are prohibited. Some scientists believe the most important factors in this mystery are still to be unveiled. Among the favored hypotheses: acid rain, global warming, pathogens and increased ultraviolet radiation.

To learn about the first of these, I headed to Penn State and a symposium titled "Habitat Acidity and Amphibian Decline." A joint meeting of the Society for the Study of Amphibians and Reptiles and the Herpetologists' League heard eight hours of papers that appeared to indicate that acid deposition (by rain or snow or in dry form) hurt many, but not all, amphibians. Frogs and toads are most vulnerable early in life. One study showed that their eggs, when bathed in slightly acidic water, either die or produce deformed tadpoles. Several others showed that increased acidity can slow growth rates in frogs, which means trouble for species that breed in temporary ponds and must mature before the water evaporates. Still other evidence indicated that highly acidic water kills frog sperm.

There are exceptions, however. Some Eastern amphibians, such as the New Jersey Pine Barrens frog, show little effect. One explanation proposed at the symposium: genetic adaptation. Scientists theorize that these frogs may have evolved in their boggy, acidic habitat to avoid competition. Swedish biologist Claes Andren, of the University of Goteborg, presented evidence that a population of moor frogs exposed to high acidity for approximately 15 generations showed increased adaptation to acidic conditions. But this sort of adaptation does not help frog populations that are suddenly exposed to greater acidity.

Some scientists argued that acid rain is not a reasonable explanation for frogs' disappearance at high altitudes because precipitation is less acid there. Melting snowbanks, however, can produce a "pulse" of accumulated acidity in just a few hours. And this pulse flushes into lakes and ponds in the spring just as frogs, toads and salamanders are mating—the most crucial time in their life cycle.

The slightest warming of the globe could have a major effect on amphibians. Many scientists believe that any warming will bring changes in precipitation patterns as well. And even without global warming, of course, there are wide fluctuations in precipitation from year to year and decade to decade. Even small differences in the amount or timing can spell doom for animals that depend on water for survival and reproduction. Amphibians need a reliable water source because their permeable skins leak body fluids rapidly and need to be kept moist for proper respiration. Frogs and toads must have water to lay and fertilize their eggs; tadpoles need water for development and growth.

An example of weather change as disaster was offered by Richard Wyman, director of the Edmund Niles Huyck Preserve and Biological Research Station in Rensselaerville, New York. In 1988 he studied breeding patterns of the yellow-spotted salamander in south-central New York. Traditionally, males journey to ponds during the first spring rain, just after the ground defrosts. Females migrate the next rainy day. That year, 23 days of dry weather followed the male pilgrimage. When the females finally made their way to the pond, most of the males had already moved on.

"Five of the 12 driest months on record and six of the ten warmest years since 1855 have occurred during the 1980s," said Wyman. Climatologists expect global warming to cause continental interiors to be drier, and droughts more intense. There is also some evidence that another predicted effect of global warming is happening now: the climatic and ecological conditions to which animals and plants have adapted may be moving northward at 300 to 600 miles per century.

On the telephone to Costa Rica I learned that biologist Alan Pounds, who lives and works in the Monteverde Cloud Forest Reserve, thinks a disruption of the water cycle probably played a role in the sudden disappearance of the golden toad and other species in his area. In 1988 the University of Florida's Martha Crump spotted just one golden toad. Last spring Pounds found no golden toads, no yellow-and-black harlequin frogs and just a few lime-green glass frogs. "Everything seems less abundant," he said.

Between the 1987 and 1988 breeding seasons, Pounds says, the number of golden toads and harlequin frogs observed declined by 99 percent. He notes that there is evidence that the population crashes of these two species may be linked to the unusually warm, dry conditions in 1986 and 1987. These climatic effects, combined with changes in groundwater levels caused by deforestation outside the Monteverde Reserve, may have been too great for the animals to withstand. Pounds adds that the last time harlequin frogs were censused in the 1980s, they were stressed from lack of moisture. Thus he does not rule out the idea of pathogens possibly having affected the stressed animals.

In Oregon, Andrew Blaustein had talked about the third general explanation for the apparent worldwide drop in amphibian populations: an increase in the ultraviolet (UV) radiation reaching Earth's surface. The flux has been increasing as the ozone layer 30 miles up has thinned, not only over Antarctica but, to a lesser degree, everywhere. This kind of exposure harms plants and animals, including humans. In Antarctica, biologists found that UV radiation damages the DNA of some phytoplankton, microscopic plants growing in the ocean. In 1975 an Oregon State University biologist had discovered that toad eggs and tadpoles (his sample had come from Lost Lake) are very sensitive to increased radiation in the middle of the ultraviolet range, commonly referred to as UV-B. (This is the same range that does the most serious damage to human skin.) Reports of frog loss seem to come more often from higher altitudes and latitudes than from lower altitudes and the tropics.

Blaustein thinks the correlation is worth investigating. So in spring of the past two years he filled a plastic jug with frog eggs from Lost Lake before the die-offs and reared them in his laboratory, away from direct sunlight. The tadpoles, raised in water from the lake, developed normally. Blaustein and his team are currently surveying 70 historically rich frog ponds to document their overall population status. He is preparing to conduct laboratory and field experiments to see how various levels of UV affect developing amphibian larvae, reproductive endocrinology and adult behavior in amphibians.

A colleague of Blaustein's, John B. Hays, has been trying to find whether frog and toad eggs can repair damage to their DNA caused by high levels of UV radiation. For nearly a year, Blaustein has delivered wild amphibians to Hays, an agricultural chemist, who removes eggs and oocytes, precursors to eggs, from them. "With those extracts we can measure two different kinds of DNA repair activity," said Hays. "The standard lab frog, *Xenopus laevis,* or African clawed frog, has a tremendous capacity to repair UV damage." If the same holds true for their wild cousins, UV may be acquitted of local egg clutch die-offs.

I left this world of test tubes and microscopes to say goodbye to the toad that Blaustein and I had caught for Hays earlier in the day. It would be killed as part of his research. Many a frog and toad have died for human benefit. Indians used the skin secretions of poison-arrow frogs to tip their darts. Frogs' legs gave us an understanding of electrical nerve impulses as well as gourmet dining. Those African clawed frogs have recently offered up clues to cystic fibrosis and Parkinson's disease. But as I walked down the hall, I found myself thinking not of their utility but of how much poorer the world would be without those unhandsome guardians of pond and garden. I made my goodbyes, shut the cooler top and headed for home.

Questions for Discussion

1. Notice the frequency of direct quotations. What is the author's purpose in using direct quotations? Is this technique effective? Why do you think it is or isn't?
2. How would this essay differ if it were written using only knowledge by participation? How would it differ if it were written using only knowledge by observation?
3. How important is this essay's expressive aim? Could this essay be classified as expressive aim writing? Explain your answer.
4. What do you think of the opening paragraph. Why do you think the author starts the essay this way? Is this opening effective?
5. Do you think the organization of the essay is clear? If so, cite specific passages that serve to clarify the organization. If not, identify specific revisions that you think might clarify the organization.

Opportunities for Writing

1. Investigate the condition of your region's frog population by interviewing local biologists. Which species of frogs are native to your region? Are species disappearing? Is the frog population thriving? Report the results of your research to the membership of a local conservation organization.
2. Using a questionnaire, investigate the public's knowledge of amphibians. How much do people know about the environmental role played by amphibians? Do people appreciate the significance of a declining amphibian population? Which groups of people know the most about amphibians? Which groups know the least? Why? Compose a detailed discussion of your findings and offer a copy to the high school science teachers in your community.
3. Create a flier that explains (without using technical language) how to preserve a local frog habitat. List the dos and don'ts and discuss their impact on the survival of the frog population. Ask your local zoo if it would be willing to distribute your flier.

PART THREE

READING PERSUASIVE AIM WRITING

Persuasive aim writing is important in virtually every field of endeavor. Persuasive texts attempt to influence readers to change (or consider changing) attitudes or actions regarding a subject.

Newspaper ads, sales letters, coupons, and a host of other documents are constant reminders that all texts can be considered, to some degree, persuasive. As is true of expressive and referential aim texts, a persuasive text may have subordinate aims. That is, ads, sales letters, and coupons may have a dominant persuasive aim, yet they may also inform us about new products or services, thus revealing a subordinate referential aim. If these documents also include personal anecdotes about how these products or services have significantly impressed specific users, they may also reflect an expressive aim.

How writers and readers come to know about their subjects (participation, observation, or both) undoubtedly affects or shapes the way in which these people write about or interpret persuasive writing. Let's look at a few examples of how writers might shift among these three kinds of knowing.

If, for instance, a writer evaluates a new restaurant, he or she might focus exclusively on a particular dining experience to compose a review. If a writer composes a position statement for a political candidate, he or she might survey public opinion, interview specialists, and study government documents for information. And if you as a writer were proposing a solution to the rising crime rate in your hometown, you might refer to your experience as a victim as well as various newspaper and magazine articles reporting on the issue.

When reading these different articles, you would want to consider questions such as the following, based on the different combinations of aims and knowing: Who is the author? What kind of knowing does the author use? What kind of information has the author woven into the essay? Is the information in the essay pertinent, accurate, and complete? Based on the existing evidence, does the author seem credible? Why?

In addition, you would want to know about the following aspects of persuasive aim writing, aspects that provide you background and concepts with which to interpret, analyze, and evaluate that writing.

Using Adversarial and Conciliatory Persuasion

The tone and sense of urgency or forcefulness in a persuasive text are often the result of how an author perceives his or her objective. For example, when the writer's objective is to prove that his or her opinion is the only appropriate opinion on the subject, it is called *adversarial persuasion.* No compromise is possible. This is a rhetorical situation of winners and losers. In *conciliatory persuasion,* however, compromise is possible. The writer's objective is to bring together opposing sides to decide a given issue. As you read different kinds of persuasive texts, you'll find it useful to see how the "attitude" corresponds to the adversarial or conciliatory intent of those texts.

Establishing Credibility

Establishing credibility is vital to effective persuasion because if a reader doubts a writer's credibility, the persuasive force is lost. By exhibiting knowledge of the subject and basic integrity (called *ethos),* writers characterize themselves as both authoritative and trustworthy. Writers could, for example, establish their credibility by listing their qualifications to write on a given subject.

Identifying with the audience is also a way that writers establish their credibility. If a writer and his or her readers think alike about a given subject, readers will be more likely to trust this writer's opinion.

Self-criticism might also be incorporated, especially if readers are hostile or suspicious. For example, writers might admit to a change of mind on a given subject or acknowledge that they don't know everything about a subject. In this way, writers demonstrate their ability to take as well as give criticism. Also, revealing a change of heart or point of view can suggest that writers are open-minded and reasonable, not narrow and fixed, in their thinking.

Offering Claims and Evidence

Persuasive aim writing that evaluates a subject, takes a position, and proposes solutions to problems has a main idea—a thesis, be it explicit or implicit. For this kind of writing, the thesis is an assertion or *claim.* How can you find claims in texts? Basically, claims are often introduced by the word *therefore* or by words with the meaning of *therefore,* such as *thus, hence, so, consequently, as a consequence,* and *as a result.* Evidence is often introduced by the word *because* or by words with the meaning of *because,* such as *since, for, as, inasmuch as,* and *due to.*

To determine whether or not a writer's claim is logical, you consider if the evidence presented is sufficient, plausible, and pertinent (called *logos*). In addition, you examine the relationship of the evidence to the claim for its validity: Is the claim a direct consequence of the evidence? And has the writer considered and answered possible objections to the claim? As you can see, knowing how to recognize claims enables you to locate and critically assess the thesis and supporting evidence in a persuasive aim text.

MOTIVATING READERS

In order for persuasive writing to be effective, readers have to do more than just acknowledge that the writer is credible and that his or her claim is logical. They have to make the writer's claim their own in some sense; that is, readers have to feel themselves as somehow being involved in or affected by the discussion (called *pathos*).

To achieve their persuasive aim, writers might try to demonstrate that your approval of the claim is essential because of the size, severity, or urgency of the issue. In order to emphasize size or severity, writers might discuss the likely impact of the issue either on you or on groups or individuals important to you, appealing either to your self-interest or to your sense of altruism. In order to emphasize urgency, writers emphasize either that the situation is deteriorating quickly or that the opportunity to address the issue is immediate and limited.

Writers will also try to assure you of your ability to approve the claim. Often, readers believe themselves to be the wrong people to approve a claim. They imagine that the people likely to adopt a given evaluation, position, or proposal are somehow different—more or less educated, experienced, sophisticated, liberal, or conservative. A writer might try to dispel this impression, emphasizing your similarity to other people who approve of his or her claim. Writers must also demonstrate that the cost of approving the claim is justified, again appealing either to your self-interest or to your sense of altruism.

Different types of evidence and techniques will serve to motivate your audience:

Statistics are often perceived as decisive and unambiguous.
Examples make ideas easier to remember by linking a specific object to a generalized claim.
Narratives dramatize and personalize ideas, making an evaluation, position, or proposal easier to understand.
Illustrations make ideas vivid and easily accessible.
Quotations associate ideas with the words of important, famous, or credible people.
Similes and metaphors associate a claim with objects or ideas that are more familiar to an audience. Similes are explicit comparisons, using the words *like* or *as;* metaphors are implicit comparisons.
Questions and directions encourage audiences to participate in the composition of a claim.

Using Persuasive Information and Techniques Ethically

Writers might try to persuade you without proving their claims logically and without establishing their credibility or honestly earning your trust, trying instead to convince you by appealing only to your emotions. It is your responsibility as a careful reader to detect instances when persuasive information and techniques are used in such a way. For example, consider a letter promising "last rites arrangements" (i.e., funeral services, mortician's services, plot selection, and so on) that is sent to residents at old-age homes. Recipients of this letter are urged to send cash installments, along with a description of their funeral preferences, to this particular "insurance" company in confidence. After all, the letter explains, the advantage of this company is that by participating in this plan "you alleviate your family's financial and emotional burden at a time when they are mourning their loss." Moreover, "our plan assures that your funeral will be the way *you* want it to be," states the letter. Upon receipt of the last payment, the company will forward the contract and confirmation of the plans and arrangements. Note that no specifics are arrived at or put into writing before all payments have been made.

This correspondence is an example of an unethical sales letter, designed to prey on senior citizens. Such rhetorical practices as this one are considered unethical—deception rather than persuasion. Instead of using evidence (logos) and credibility (ethos) to persuade, this letter appeals to readers' emotions (pathos) to convince them to part with their money in exchange for "security" when they die.

Granted, all persuasive texts include emotional appeals, to some degree. But texts that contain information to arouse pathos (emotional appeals such as fear, joy, pain, happiness, guilt, sadness) should strive for balance by also providing logos (logical appeals or evidence and good reasons) and ethos (ethical appeals or credibility and integrity). In other words, whenever a writer motivates you, he or she will necessarily arouse emotions. Arousing emotions to motivate readers is appropriate and ethical, but substituting emotions for logical evidence to prove a claim is inappropriate and unethical. It is your responsibility as a critical reader to be sure the writer is fulfilling his or her ethical obligations as a writer.

Organized by ways of knowing, the following essays reveal how writers try to integrate the characteristics of persuasive aim writing. The essays evaluate subjects, declare positions, and propose solutions, while incorporating subordinate expressive and referential aims.

Asking the questions in the Guide to Critical Reading can help you to direct your planning, translating, and reviewing processes as well as to examine the various essays from a content, function/feature, and rhetorical perspective. Explore also the internal and external influences on your reading processes. In this section, learning to examine persuasive aim writing—newspaper articles, magazine editorials, research studies, literary arguments, position papers, problem-solution essays—with a critical eye is an essential element of your reading repertoire.

Knowledge by Participation

The Outlaw Princesses

Terence Rafferty

Terence Rafferty is a film critic for The New Yorker, *where this essay first appeared. In "The Outlaw Princesses," Rafferty reviews* Thelma & Louise, *a box office hit "about a couple of women who go off in search of a little personal space and discover that they have to keep going and going and going to find a space that's big enough." As you read this review, consider how the critic advances his discussion of the movie's plot and main characters while also evaluating them, the director, and the scriptwriter. What effect does this review have on you as a moviegoer? If you have seen this film before, do you agree with Rafferty's critique? If you haven't seen* Thelma & Louise, *do you want to see it now?*

Ridley Scott's *Thelma & Louise* is a crazily overstuffed Hollywood entertainment. Its heroines, played by Geena Davis (Thelma) and Susan Sarandon (Louise), are a couple of Arkansas women who set out for a weekend in the mountains and wind up speeding through the Southwest, on the run from the law. Following the tradition of movie outlaws, they're headed for the Mexican border; they cross a fair number of state lines, and genre lines, on the way. The act that puts the women on this reckless course is a murder. To get themselves in the mood for their carefree weekend, Thelma and Louise stop off at a roadside honky-tonk, where Thelma, elated at the prospect of a few days' freedom from her obnoxious husband, Darryl (Christopher McDonald), allows herself to be picked up by a smooth-talking cracker named Harlan (Timothy Carhart). After whooping it up on the dance floor for a while, Thelma, feeling sick, heads for the parking lot, and Harlan tries to rape her; Louise shoots him dead. They hop in Louise's convertible and flee the scene, because Louise is sure that the police won't believe the women's version of events; she thinks that Thelma's flirtatious behavior in the roadhouse would cast doubt on the story of attempted rape. Louise makes this radical decision, to go on the lam rather than face the skepticism of the authorities, instantaneously and with unanswerable conviction. For the audience, the moment requires a leap of faith that is far greater than the one

337

the cops would have to make in order to believe the women's story. And it's only the first of a series of leaps that the script, by Callie Khouri, forces us to make if we want to stay with these unlikely desperadoes on their wild ride. The women have plenty of opportunities to turn back, but the movie is designed to keep pushing them farther and farther out there—past the point of no return, into the vanishing point of a vast Western landscape, and, finally, over the edge of the world.

Essentially, *Thelma & Louise* is an outlaw fantasy, and a mighty shameless one. The feminist justification that Khouri's script provides for the heroines' behavior doesn't make their actions any less preposterous: the characters would probably be more believable if the movie provided fewer explanations of their motives—if it allowed us to see their mad dash to the border as purely irrational (in the manner of, say, a Patricia Highsmith novel). The way the script is constructed, we sometimes feel, unfortunately, that the feminist ideas are being used opportunistically, just to keep the narrative moving—that every time Thelma and Louise have a chance to give themselves up, a man does something horrible and strengthens their conviction that they're better off on the run. The funny thing about *Thelma & Louise* is that you can recognize the crudeness of the script's devices and still have an awfully good time. The dopey ideas do at least give the picture some momentum: the heroines' flight is fueled (however implausibly) by impulses that are more powerful than the usual road-movie anomie. The movie has the hellbent energy of a drive-in exploitation picture, and it's eventful—it isn't just figures drifting dazedly through alienating landscapes. Thelma and Louise are lively, voluble good old girls, and they're not given to brooding; they keep each other's spirits up. The audience's, too. Davis and Sarandon are so vivid and likable that they carry us past the plot's most obvious contrivances; a little disbelief seems a small price to pay for being allowed to remain in their company.

Davis has the flashier role. Thelma is totally oppressed by her loud-mouthed, beer-swilling, gold-chain-wearing husband, an irredeemable male-chauvinist goon. Despite her grim servitude to this pig, she manages to be pretty cheerful, in a girlish, spacey way. She seems never to have grown up; when she sneaks off, without telling Darryl, for her weekend with Louise, she giggles wickedly, like a teenager who has put one over on her parents. It's a wonderful role for Geena Davis: she gets to show off her (proven) talent for dizzy comedy, and to go through lots of emotional changes besides. In her best scenes, she does both at once. After a one-night stand with a sexy young hitchhiker (Brad Pitt, who has the sullen handsomeness—and the white cowboy hat—of the country singer Dwight Yoakam), Thelma sashays into the motel coffee shop with a big goofy grin on her face and tells Louise, "I finally understand what all the fuss is about." Davis's silly rapture makes this a classic scene, a sweetly funny image of sexual bliss. Throughout the movie, Davis's large, changeable features and her lanky frame serve the character beautifully; she seems to combine the malleability of a cartoon character—which isn't inappropriate here—with a kind of long-limbed Western grace. She gets terrific vocal effects, too: she produces a lovely comic music out of laughs and shouts and drawls. Davis is spectacular, but Sarandon, whose character has a less extreme emotional range, is every bit as good. Louise, a fortyish diner waitress who's involved with a kindhearted but unreliable musician (Michael Madsen), is steadier, world-wearier, and more practical than her young friend. She has a been-there look about her, and she doesn't trust people much; she's always scolding Thelma for striking up conversations with strangers. (And her suspiciousness always turns out to be justified.) In many scenes, Sarandon plays straight person to Davis, and does it with the skill and good humor of an extremely confident actress. She trains a penetrating, no-nonsense stare on her companion's antics; her looks of affectionate disbelief often mirror the audience's reactions. And when she breaks down and laughs, giving in to the craziness around her, her abandon is infectious. Sarandon holds our attention by not betraying her character's emotions too readily. Her held-in quality makes an effective contrast to Davis's overflowing exuberance, and it has its own power, too; in a sense, Sarandon's mysterious straight-ahead intensity is what propels the story forward.

There's an exhilarating ease and intuitiveness in the way these actresses work together; we feel, and share, their pleasure in surprising each other. *Thelma & Louise* is at its best in its most casual, most aimless-seeming moments, in the dawdling intervals between "important" scenes, while the women are just zipping down the highway and trying to figure out what to do next. (Or why they did what they did last. They often seem as dumbfounded by the story as the audience is.) And Ridley Scott provides an abundance of moments like these: scenes in which the women tease each other or get on each other's nerves or sing along with the car radio, as their hair blows all over their faces. The camera lingers on Davis and Sarandon as if it couldn't get enough of them: Scott seems to want to show us what they look like in every kind of light and every kind of mood. The director's entranced gaze slows down the rhythm of the narrative; quite a lot happens in this movie, but it has a leisurely, expansive air. Scott—the director of *The Duellists, Alien,* and *Blade Runner*—is known for his striking, even overpowering, visual style: the compositions in his films are meticulous, shiny, and elaborately textured. They frequently look too good to be true, and Scott has sometimes been seen as just another member of a school of filmmakers who developed a slick, manipulative craft in the British advertising industry—directors like Alan Parker (*Midnight Express* and *Mississippi Burning*), Adrian Lyne (*Flashdance* and *Fatal Attraction*), and Ridley's brother Tony Scott (*Top Gun* and *Days of Thunder*). Ridley Scott isn't really that kind of filmmaker, though. He has never been a cynical manipulator of audience reactions. He's a romantic, and rather an innocent and credulous one, at that, investing everything he works on with the passion and enthusiasm of an imaginative child. His images have a true believer's intensity, and if they're not always persuasive it's perhaps because Scott isn't terribly selective about what he believes in.

5 His fabulist's sensibility does wonders for *Thelma & Louise.* He dances attendance on the outlaw princesses who are his heroines, and treats every stage of their journey as an occasion for awe. Truck stops, mesas, motel pools, deserted country roads, messy kitchens, and the packed ladies' room of the honky-tonk all have a hyper-real gleam to them, a luminous expressiveness. When Thelma and Louise are on the road, the movie has the look of a mirage, a jeweled shimmer that keeps us half hypnotized. (The trance is broken periodically by the intrusion of banal plot mechanics: cutaways to the police investigation, under the direction of a sympathetic cop played by Harvey Keitel. These are the movie's clumsiest scenes; we can feel Scott's impatience to get back to the women.) Scott's love of the women and the landscape doesn't quite transform

Khouri's gimmicky, rabble-rousing script into something profound, but it has the welcome effect of softening the hard edges of the story; it gives the whole movie a pleasantly dreamy quality. In the end, *Thelma & Louise* seems less a feminist parable than an airy, lyrical joke about a couple of women who go off in search of a little personal space and discover that they have to keep going and going and going to find a space that's big enough.

Questions for Discussion

1. What is the author's claim? Is the evidence for the claim sufficient, plausible, and pertinent? Cite specific passages to support your answer.
2. How does the author establish his credibility to discuss this subject? Does he display his knowledge and integrity? identify with the audience? practice self-deprecation?
3. How might the author integrate knowledge by observation? How might this information establish credibility, support the claim, and motivate the audience?
4. Do you have to be familiar with *Thelma & Louise* to appreciate this essay or consider it convincing? Explain your answer.
5. Is this essay adversarial or conciliatory persuasion? Cite specific passages to support your answer.

Opportunities for Writing

1. Compose a movie review for your school newspaper. Don't evaluate a movie you've already seen: choose a movie you'd like to see and go to see it with the intention of reviewing it. What do you like about the movie? What do you dislike? On balance, would you recommend this movie to your friends?
2. Evaluate this and other published reviews of *Thelma & Louise*. With which critics do you agree? With which do you disagree? Why? Do the reviews contribute to your understanding and appreciation of this movie?
3. In a letter to the Motion Picture Association of America, declare your position on the MPAA rating system: G, PG, PG–13, R, NC–17. Does this rating system allow viewers to make appropriate entertainment choices? Does it encourage moviemakers to practice self-censorship? Is the meaning of each of the ratings clear? Do you consider the R rating for *Thelma & Louise* appropriate?

It Is Time to Stop Playing Indians

ARLENE B. HIRSCHFELDER

Born in Chicago, Arlene B. Hirschfelder went to Brandeis University, the University of Chicago, and Columbia University. Her study of American history contributed to her interest and participation in Indian affairs. She has been a staff member of the Association on American Indian Affairs since 1969 and serves as a consultant on education for American Indians. In addition, her writing deals with Indian affairs. The author of six books and numerous articles, Hirschfelder received the Carter G. Woodson Book Award and a Western Heritage Book Award for her book Happily May I Walk: American Indians and Alaska Natives *(1986). In "It Is Time to Stop Playing Indians," which first appeared in the* Los Angeles Times, *Hirschfelder calls for an end to product, behavior, and language "stereotypes that, whether deliberately or inadvertently, denigrate Indian cultures and people."*

It is predictable. At Halloween, thousands of children trick-or-treat in Indian costumes. At Thanksgiving, thousands of children parade in school pageants wearing plastic headdresses and pseudo-buckskin clothing. Thousands of card shops stock Thanksgiving greeting cards with images of cartoon animals wearing feathered headbands. Thousands of teachers and librarians trim bulletin boards with Anglo-featured, feathered Indian boys and girls. Thousands of gift shops load their shelves with Indian figurines and jewelry.

Fall and winter are also the seasons when hundreds of thousands of sports fans root for professional, college and public school teams with names that summon up Indians—"Braves," "Redskins," "Chiefs." (In New York State, one out of eight junior and senior high school teams call themselves "Indians," "Tomahawks" and the like.) War-whooping team mascots are imprinted on school uniforms, postcards, notebooks, tote bags and car floor mats.

All of this seems innocuous; why make a fuss about it? Because these trappings and holiday symbols offend tens of thousands of other Americans—the Native American people. Because these invented images prevent millions of us from understanding the authentic Indian America, both long ago and today. Because this image-making prevents Indians from being a relevant part of the nation's social fabric.

Halloween costumes mask the reality of high mortality rates, high diabetes rates, high unemployment rates. They hide low average life spans, low per capita incomes and low educational levels. Plastic war bonnets and ersatz buckskin deprive people from knowing the complexity of Native American heritage—that Indians belong to hundreds of nations that have intricate social organizations, governments, languages, religions and sacred rituals, ancient stories, unique arts and music forms.

5   Thanksgiving school units and plays mask history. They do not tell how Europeans mistreated Wampanoags and other East Coast Indian peoples during the 17th century. Social studies units don't mention that, to many Indians, Thanksgiving is a day of mourning, the beginning of broken promises, land theft, near extinction of their religions and languages at the hands of invading Europeans.

Athletic team nicknames and mascots disguise real people. Warpainted, buckskin-clad, feathered characters keep the fictitious Indian circulating on decals, pennants and team clothing. Toy companies mask Indian identity and trivialize sacred beliefs by manufacturing Indian costumes and headdresses, peace pipes and trick-arrow-through-the-head gags that equate Indianness with playtime. Indian figures equipped with arrows, guns and tomahawks give youngsters the harmful message that Indians favor mayhem. Many Indian people can tell about children screaming in fear after being introduced to them.

It is time to consider how these images impede the efforts of Indian parents and communities to raise their children with positive information about their heritage. It is time to get rid of stereotypes that, whether deliberately or inadvertently, denigrate Indian cultures and people.

It is time to bury the Halloween costumes, trick arrows, bulletin-board pin-ups, headdresses and mascots. It has been done before. In the 1970s, after student protests, Marquette University dropped its "Willie Wampum," Stanford University retired its mascot, "Prince Lightfoot," and Eastern Michigan University and Florida State modified their savage-looking mascots to reduce criticism.

It is time to stop playing Indians. It is time to abolish Indian images that sell merchandise. It is time to stop offending Indian people whose lives are all too often filled with economic deprivation, powerlessness, discrimination and gross injustice. This time next year, let's find more appropriate symbols for the holiday and sports seasons.

Questions for Discussion

1. Is this essay adversarial or conciliatory persuasion? Which do you think would be more effective?
2. Does the author anticipate and answer objections to the claim? If you think she does, cite specific passages. If you think she doesn't, assess the impact of this omission.
3. How does the writer try to motivate her audience? Does she emphasize the size, severity, or urgency of the issue?
4. This essay was written for a daily newspaper. How might the author revise this essay for a specific audience of advertising executives or school administrators?
5. Notice the repetition of the words "It is time to . . ." in the final paragraphs of the essay. What is the purpose of this repetition? Do you think this technique is effective?

Opportunities for Writing

1. In a letter to the owner of the Atlanta Braves, the Cleveland Indians, the Kansas City Chiefs, or the Washington Redskins, give your opinion of the adoption of Indian names and images by professional sports teams. Do you think this practice is disrespectful? Why or why not?
2. Write a letter to appropriate school administrators urging institution of a Native American Studies program at your school: that is, a series of interdisciplinary courses that would examine the histories and traditions of America's native peoples.
3. Write a review of the television program *Doctor Quinn: Medicine Woman*. In your review, focus on the characterization of the Indians. Does this program offer a realistic portrait of Indian traditions and practices? Does it encourage stereotyping? Explain your evaluation.

Farewell to Fitness

MIKE ROYKO

A newspaper columnist, Mike Royko was born in Chicago and, since beginning his career in 1956, has been a writer for different Chicago newspapers. Since 1984, Royko has had a regular column in the Chicago Tribune. *Over the years, he has received recognition for his commentaries: Heywood Broun Award (1986); Pulitzer Prize (1972); H. L. Mencken Award (1981); Ernie Pyle Award (1982); Medal for Service to Journalism, University of Missouri School of Journalism (1979); Lifetime Achievement Award, National Press Club (1990); Best Newspaper Columnist in America, Washington Journalism Review (1975, 1987, 1988, 1990); Chicago Press Club Journalism Hall of Fame (1980). In "Farewell to Fitness," Royko takes a position: he vows to renounce "the physical fitness craze." This persuasive essay is autobiographical, and the information is gained exclusively from personal experience and reflection—from knowledge by participation.*

At least once a week, the office jock will stop me in the hall, bounce on the balls of his feet, plant his hands on his hips, flex his pectoral muscles and say: "How about it? I'll reserve a racquetball court. You can start working off some of that. . . ." And he'll jab a finger deep into my midsection.

It's been going on for months, but I've always had an excuse: "Next week, I've got a cold." "Next week, my back is sore." "Next week, I've got a pulled hamstring." "Next week, after the holidays."

But this is it. No more excuses. I made one New Year's resolution, which is that I will tell him the truth. And the truth is that I don't want to play racquetball or handball or tennis, or jog, or pump Nautilus machines, or do push-ups or sit-ups or isometrics, or ride a stationary bicycle, or pull on a rowing machine, or hit a softball, or run up a flight of steps, or engage in any other form of exercise more strenuous than rolling out of bed.

This may be unpatriotic, and it is surely out of step with our muscle-flexing times, but I am renouncing the physical-fitness craze.

5   Oh, I was part of it. Maybe not as fanatically as some. But about 15 years ago, when I was 32, someone talked me into taking up handball, the most punishing court game there is.

From then on it was four or five times a week—up at 6 AM, on the handball court at 7, run, grunt, sweat, pant until 8:30, then in the office at 9. And I'd go around bouncing on the balls of my feet, flexing my pectoral muscles, poking friends in their soft guts, saying: "How about working some of that off? I'll reserve a court," and being obnoxious.

This went on for years. And for what? I'll tell you what it led to: I stopped eating pork shanks, that's what. It was inevitable. When you join the physical-fitness craze, you have to stop eating wonderful things like pork shanks because they are full of cholesterol. And you have to give up eggs benedict, smoked liverwurst, Italian sausage, butter-pecan ice cream, Polish sausage, goose-liver paté, Sara Lee cheesecake, Twinkies, potato chips, salami-and-Swiss-cheese sandwiches, double cheeseburgers with fries, Christian Brothers brandy with a Beck's chaser, and everything else that tastes good.

Instead, I ate broiled skinless chicken, broiled whitefish, grapefruit, steamed broccoli, steamed spinach, unbuttered toast, yogurt, eggplant, an apple for dessert and Perrier water to wash it down. Blahhhhh!

You do this for years, and what is your reward for panting and sweating around a handball-racquetball court, and eating yogurt and the skinned flesh of a dead chicken?

—You can take your pulse and find that it is slow. So what? Am I a clock?

—You buy pants with a narrower waistline. Big deal. The pants don't cost less than the ones with a big waistline.

—You get to admire yourself in the bathroom mirror for about 10 seconds a day after taking a shower. It takes five seconds to look at your flat stomach from the front, and five more seconds to look at your flat stomach from the side. If you're a real creep of a narcissist, you can add another 10 seconds for looking at your small behind with a mirror.

That's it.

Wait, I forgot something. You will live longer. I know that because my doctor told me so every time I took a physical. My fitness-conscious doctor was very slender—especially the last time I saw him, which was at his wake.

But I still believe him. Running around a handball court or jogging five miles a day, eating yogurt and guzzling Perrier will make you live longer.

So you live longer. Have you been in a typical nursing home lately? Have you walked around the low-rent neighborhoods where the geezers try to survive on Social Security?

If you think living longer is rough now, wait until the 1990s, when today's Me Generation potheads and coke sniffers begin taking care of the elderly (today's middle-aged joggers). It'll be: "Just take this little happy pill, gramps, and you'll wake up in heaven."

It's not worth giving up pork shanks and Sara Lee cheesecake.

Nor is it the way to age gracefully. Look around at all those middle-aged jogging chicken-eaters. Half of them tape hairpieces to their heads. That's what comes from having a flat stomach. You start thinking that you should also have hair. And after that comes a facelift. And that leads to jumping around a disco floor, pinching an airline stewardess and other bizarre behavior.

I prefer to age gracefully, the way men did when I was a boy. The only time a man over 40 ran was when the cops caught him burglarizing a warehouse. The idea of exercise was to walk to and from the corner tavern, mostly to. A well-rounded health-food diet included pork shanks, dumplings, Jim Beam and a beer chaser.

Anyone who was skinny was suspected of having TB or an ulcer. A fine figure of a man was one who could look down and not see his knees, his feet or anything else in that vicinity. What do you have to look for, anyway? You ought to know if anything is missing.

A few years ago I was in Bavaria, and I went to a German beer hall. It was a beautiful sight. Everybody was popping sausages and pork shanks and draining quart-sized steins of thick beer. Even so often they'd thump their magnificent bellies and smile happily at the booming sound that they made.

Compare that to the finish line of a marathon, with all those emaciated runners sprawled on the grass, tongues hanging out, wheezing, moaning, writhing, throwing up.

If that is the way to happiness and a long life, pass me the cheesecake.

25   May you get a hernia, Arnold Schwarzenegger. And here's to you, Orson Welles.

Questions for Discussion

1. Does the author establish credibility on this subject? In which passages does he display his knowledge and integrity, identify with the audience, or practice self-deprecation?
2. How does the author motivate his readers to approve his claim? Does he appeal to their self-interest or sense of altruism?
3. Notice the frequency of short sentences. What do you think of the author's writing style? Is it effective? Is it appropriate?
4. How important is this essay's expressive aim? Is it as important as the persuasive aim? Could this essay be classified as expressive aim writing?
5. Would this essay be more or less effective if it was written using knowledge by observation? Explain your answer.

Opportunities for Writing

1. Weigh the advantages and disadvantages of a fitness-conscious lifestyle. In your evaluation, consider the findings of existing research as well as the opinions of people of different ages. Do people who exercise live longer or have a better quality of life? Do the advantages of a fitness-conscious lifestyle outweigh the disadvantages?
2. Recommend to a friend a specific type of exercise such as jogging, handball, tennis, aerobics, or weightlifting. Why do you especially like this type of exercise? Why do you think this type of exercise is superior to others?
3. Propose a solution for America's poor eating habits. How do you teach people to avoid high-fat and high-cholesterol foods? How do you encourage people to eat more fruits and vegetables?

Inside the Home

JILL FRAWLEY

Jill Frawley is a registered nurse who, in this essay, writes about the substandard conditions for the sick and elderly in nursing homes. From her personal experience at one "long-term-care facility (nursing home)" owned by a big corporation, Frawley urges readers with elderly relatives in these "homes" to realize that there may be a dramatic difference between the appearance (concerned, gentle, and competent caregivers) and reality (overworked, untrained, and inattentive caregivers) in these institutions. Frawley's experience and conscience compel her to speak up ("I confess my participation in these crimes. I can't keep this secret any longer"). As you read, try to identify the factual and emotional evidence used to support her claims.

I'm just one little nurse, in one little "care facility." Each shift I work, I carry in my soul a very big lie. I leave my job, and there aren't enough showers in the world to wash away my rage, my frustration, my impotence.

The long-term-care facility (nursing home) I work for is owned by a corporation that owns nursing homes throughout the country. Giving corporations like this control over the quality of medical care is handing over control to the fox. Every chicken in the coop knows there is no hope—only the ticking away of a life devoid of dignity or even minimal respect.

I watch the videos they show to new employees during "orientation." Smiling people spout corporate policy and speak of "guest relations." They tell us we are special; we are going to participate in a rewarding job. Elderly people in the video are dressed nicely; they are coherent and grateful for the help the staff member has time to give. We sign the attendance sheet: We saw it; now we know what "guest relations" means. It means to act in front of the families so that they think everything is okay.

The truth is ugly; I confess it in a burst of desperation. The elderly lie in feces and urine because there is only one aide for thirty patients. Eventually, they get changed abruptly—too fast, too harshly. They cry out in confused terror. Doors are closed to "protect their privacy"—but really so no one will see. The covers get flung back. It's evening bed check. The old person is shoved from one side of the bed to the other. He tries to protest; he thinks something bad is happening. Whip out the soiled underpad, wipe him, throw the covers over him . . . on to the next body.

5   No time for mouth care; sometimes no time for showers; never time to hold someone's hand even for a moment. Aides feed the helpless two spoonfuls of pureed stuff, dripping down chins; no time to wait for them to swallow. It gets charted: "Resident didn't eat much tonight." She loses weight; she gets more frail as each day passes. The food is so bad I can't begin to describe it. The cook is young and doesn't care much; if I complain, he gets mad. One resident asks me for a cup of hot water so she can use the instant soup in her drawer. She can't eat the cold, badly cooked stuff that is on her tray. Slow starvation is hard to get used to.

Why is there only one aide on these halls night after night? Most employees don't stay. They can't stand being flung into jobs that are too hard, too horrid, for too little money. The ones that do stay have given up complaining. They shut their eyes and ears and do the best they can. They have children to support, no education, are caught by life in such a way that quitting would intensify their own suffering and not alleviate anyone else's.

We're always short-staffed. We know it's to save money. One tired aide does a double shift, straining to do a job it takes two people to do correctly. I guess when you make four dollars and something an hour, it takes working double shifts (that's sixteen hours) to make enough to live on. Tired people get impatient, make mistakes, take shortcuts. A nurse calls in sick. That means one nurse does three halls. One nurse to pass out medicines for eighty residents.

Patients are dropped or fall. My coworkers agree that it's a widespread practice to chart this to avoid problems. Every incident report I have ever seen states that the patient or resident was "found on the floor" or appeared to have bruises or skin tears of "unknown" origin. When there's no time to turn the bedridden every two hours, skin breaks down and ulcers develop. The elderly get skin tears and bruises because they are fragile, but also because there is no time to handle them gently. Again, we chart carefully so there is no blame. We let our old ones die for many reasons. Sometimes it is because of sickness; sometimes it is from neglect.

The admissions director is a nice lady. She lives uneasily with her task. She tells anxious families not to worry, that the facility will be like a second home to their relative. She tells them what they want to hear. The families go away determined to believe everything will be fine. Secretly, they are relieved that they won't have to deal with dementia, incontinence, or the total dependency of a senile elder.

The silence is ominous in the evening. Nothing to do; no place to go. The residents sit and wait for death. The staff is ground down in despair and hopelessness. The guys at corporate headquarters must be patting each other on the back about the profits they're making.

It got bad at the place I work. Too many unhappy people; too much barely controlled anger always close to erupting. A corporate spokesperson was sent from headquarters to listen to grievances. He listened, this quiet, intelligent man who had been to our facility before. I asked some of my fellow workers why they weren't going to speak out. "It doesn't do any good," was the response. "He's been coming for three or four years. Nothing changes." I went; I spoke out; they were right. Nothing changes.

The elderly suffer quietly. They are afraid they will be punished if they speak up for themselves. Most of them can't speak for themselves. They just want to escape this hell. I do too. They need a place to stay; I need a job. We're trapped.

I am one little nurse, in one little care facility, living with this terrible secret. If they knew I was telling on them, I wouldn't have a job. What about my rent? What about my needs? But I need to tell. I confess to my participation in these crimes. I can't keep this secret any longer.

If you have an elderly relative in a facility:

1. Visit at odd hours.
2. Visit at mealtime.
3. Don't believe what the staff tells you.
4. Ask questions.
5. Don't worry if small items are missing. Petty theft is not serious. Abuse is.
6. Make sure your relative is clean.
7. Notice if your relative is losing weight.
8. Check your relative's skin for bruises.
9. Let "them" know you are watching.
10. Be polite to staff, but raise hell with the administrator or the director of nursing. Though they are just employees and will tell you what you want to hear, it's worth a try.
11. Contact local ombudsmen if you can't get results. If that doesn't work, contact the state regulatory agency.
12. Complain to headquarters or whoever owns the facility.

13. Don't allow yourself to be blackmailed by veiled threats of being forced to move your relative.
14. Don't give up; wear them down.

Questions for Discussion

1. What do you think of the opening paragraph? Does it diminish or reinforce the author's credibility? Why?
2. Is the evidence supporting the claim sufficient, plausible, and pertinent? Explain your answer.
3. Do you think the organization of this essay is effective? If so, why? If not, how would you organize this essay?
4. Does the author anticipate and answer objections to the claim? In this essay, is it necessary to do so? Why or why not?
5. The author closes this essay with a list of proposed solutions. Do you like this closing? Are the solutions explained to your satisfaction? How would you close this essay?

Opportunities for Writing

1. Voice your opinion on the ownership of nursing homes. Interview the directors of several local facilities and review existing research on this subject. Do you think nursing homes ought to be nonprofit institutions? Why or why not?
2. After visiting a local nursing home and speaking to residents and their families, evaluate the quality of care provided by this facility. What are the strengths and weaknesses of this facility? Would you choose this facility for a member of your family who required long-term care?
3. Write a letter to the governor of your state proposing new regulations for nursing homes. How do you achieve adequate staffing of such facilities? How do you insure the safety and dignity of residents? How do you avoid unqualified administrators, insensitive nurses, and untrained aides?
4. Evaluate the organization for which you work. What are the things you like and dislike about this organization? Are you asked to do things that you consider unethical or illegal? Would you recommend this organization to others?

I, Too, Am a Good Parent

Dorsett Bennett

Dorsett Bennett is an attorney in Roswell, New Mexico. In this essay about the dilemma of child custody, he asks "that those judges who make these critical decisions re-examine their attitudes and prejudices against placing children with fathers." As a lawyer, divorcé, and father who lost custody of his children, Bennett bases his evidence on personal experience. "I, Too, Am a Good Parent" appeared in the Newsweek *regular column "My Turn" on July 4, 1994. Attorneys have a reputation for using "legalese" when they write and speak about court-related matters, but Bennett avoids this tendency. Why do you think he does?*

Divorce is a fact of modern life. A great number of people simply decide that they do not wish to stay married to their spouse. A divorce is not a tremendously difficult situation unless there are minor children born to the couple. If there are no minor children you simply divide the assets and debts. But you cannot divide a child. The child needs to be placed with the appropriate parent.

In my own case, my former wife chose not to remain married to me. That is her right and I do not fault her decision. My problem is that I do not believe it is her right to deny me the privilege of raising our children. Some fathers want to go to the parent/teacher conferences, school plays, carnivals and to help their kids with homework. I have always looked forward to participating on a daily basis in my children's lives. I can no longer enjoy that privilege—the children live with their mother, who has moved to a northern Midwest state.

I tried so hard to gain custody of my children. I believe the evidence is uncontradicted as to what an excellent father (and more important, parent) I am. My ex-wife is a fairly good mother, but unbiased opinions unanimously agreed I was the better parent. Testimonials were videotaped from witnesses who could not attend the out-of-state custody hearing. I choose to be a father. When I was 3 years old, my own father left my family. While I've loved my father for many years, I did and still do reject his parental pattern.

A couple of centuries ago, a father and mother might have shared equally in the care and raising of children above the age of infancy. But with the coming of the Industrial Revolution the father went to work during the day, leaving the full-time care of the young to the mother, who stayed at home. It was easier to decide who should get child custody under those circumstances. That would be true today even if the mother were put into the position of working outside the home after the divorce.

5   Now, the majority of married mothers are in the workplace—often because the family needs the second income to survive. With the advent of the working mother, we have also seen a change in child care. Not only have we seen an increase in third-party caregivers, there is a decided difference in how fathers interact with their children. Fathers are even starting to help raise their children. I admit that in a great many families there is an uneven distribution of child-care responsibilities. But there are fathers who do as much to raise the children as the mother, and there are many examples where men are full-time parents.

But, because we have this past history of the mother being the principal child caregiver, the mother has almost always been favored in any contested child-custody case. The law of every state is replete with decisions showing that the mother is the favored custodial parent. The changes in our lifestyles are now being reflected in our laws. In most, if not all, states, the legislature has recognized the change in child-care responsibilities and enacted legislation that is gender blind. The statutes that deal with child custody now say that the children should be placed with the parent whose care and control of the child will be in the child's best interest.

This legislation is enlightened and correct. Society has changed. We no longer bring up our children as we did years ago. But it is still necessary to have someone make the choice in the child's best interest if the parents are divorcing and cannot agree on who takes care of the kids. So we have judges to make that enormous decision.

The state legislature can pass laws that say neither parent is favored because of their gender. But it is judges who make the ultimate choice. And those judges are usually *older males* who practiced law during the time when mothers were the favored guardians under the law. These same judges mostly come from a background where mothers stayed home and were the primary caregivers. By training and by personal experience they have a strong natural bias in favor of the mother in a child-custody case. That belief is regressive and fails to acknowledge the changed realities of our present way of life. Someone must be appointed to render a decision when parents cannot agree. I would ask that those judges who make these critical decisions re-examine their attitudes and prejudices against placing children with fathers.

After the videotaped testimony was completed, one of my lawyers said he had "never seen a father put together a better custody case." "But," he asked me, "can you prove she is unfit?" A father should not be placed in the position of having to prove the mother is unfit in order to gain custody. He should not have to prove that she has two heads, participates in child sacrifice or eats live snakes. The father should only have to prove that he is the more suitable parent.

10 Fathers should not be discriminated against as I was. It took me three years to get a trial on the merits in the Minnesota court. And Minnesota has a law directing its courts to give a high priority to child-custody cases. What was even worse was that the judge seemed to ignore the overwhelming weight of the evidence and granted custody to my ex-wife. At the trial, her argument was, "I am their mother." Other than that statement she hardly put on a case. Being the mother of the children was apparently deemed enough to outweigh evidence that all the witnesses who knew us both felt I was the better parent; that those witnesses who knew only me said what an excellent parent I was; that our children's behavior always improved dramatically after spending time with me; that my daughter wished to live with me, and that I had a better child-custody evaluation than my wife.

So I say to the trial judges who decide these cases: "Become part of the solution to this dilemma of child custody. Don't remain part of the problem." It is too late for me. If this backward way of thinking is changed, then perhaps it won't be too late for other fathers who should have custody of their children.

Questions for Discussion

1. In the closing paragraph, the author declares "It is too late for me." What is the author's purpose in making this admission?
2. This essay was written for a weekly news magazine but specifically addresses divorce trial judges: "So I say to the trial judges who decide these cases: 'Become part of the solution to this dilemma of child custody. Don't remain part of the problem.'" Why does the author choose this magazine to address this audience?

3. Would you characterize this essay as adversarial or conciliatory persuasion? Cite specific passages to support your answer.
4. Notice the following 73-word sentence: "Being the mother of the children was apparently deemed enough to outweigh evidence that all the witnesses who knew us both felt I was the better parent; that those witnesses who knew only me said what an excellent parent I was; that our children's behavior always improved dramatically after spending time with me; that my daughter wished to live with me, and that I had a better child-custody evaluation than my wife." Do you think this sentence is effective? If so, why? If not, how would you revise this sentence?
5. This essay displays both expressive and referential subordinate aims. Why? What do the expressive passages contribute to the essay? What do the referential passages contribute to the essay?

Opportunities for Writing

1. Declare your position on the child-custody laws of your state. Do the laws require revising? Why or why not? Cite specific cases to reinforce your position.
2. In a letter to the newspaper, assess the record of local trial judges regarding child-custody cases How often are mothers awarded custody? How often are fathers awarded custody? Do you perceive evidence of bias?
3. Consider a local child-custody case. You might know the family personally, or you might have heard about the case on television or read about it in the newspaper. If possible, visit the courtroom and observe the trial proceedings. Before listening to the judge's decision, decide which parent you believe ought to be awarded custody. Explain your decision as you would if you were addressing the parents and their lawyers.
4. In a letter to the principal of your high school, recommend the introduction of a family studies course: that is, a course that teaches students how to manage the responsibilities of being a husband or wife, a father or mother. Cite your personal experience: how do you think you or your high school friends would have benefited from such a course?

Knowledge by Observation

The "Bleaching Syndrome"
Implications of Light Skin for Hispanic American Assimilation

RONALD E. HALL

Ronald E. Hall received his doctorate from Atlanta University and is on the faculty in the Department of Social Work at the University of St. Thomas in St. Paul, Minnesota. Considered the leading scholar on skin color and its psychological impact on people of color, Hall testified as an expert witness in the trial Morrow v. Internal Revenue Service, the first case of its kind in the United States. He has recently published a book, Color Complex, *on this subject. "The 'Bleaching Syndrome'" first appeared in the* Hispanic Journal of Behavioral Sciences *(August 1994) and follows APA style.*

Light skin is an ideal in the United States because it is indicative of the dominant mainstream population. For Hispanic Americans whose skin reflects a range of colors, this causes distress. In their efforts to assimilate via a domination model, they are forced to internalize norms that conflict with that range. A result is the "bleaching syndrome," manifested in the preference for light skin where applicable. The alternative causes them to suffer depression and other mental health disorders. Only by adhering to the internalization of norms that idealize their population in toto can Hispanic Americans assimilate fully without incident.

The ethnic landscape in the United States comprises one of the most diverse civilizations ever. The descendants of Europeans, Africans, Asians, and others have made significant contributions. Unfortunately, all have not shared equally in its greatness. In spite of the diversity in the United States, skin color for some remains an obstacle to full or structural assimilation. As it pertains to Hispanic Americans (i.e., Cubans, Dominicans, Puerto Ricans, etc.), this fact is critical. They alone, among the various ethnic groups, are characterized by a rainbow of skin colors and diverse physical attributes. This means that for some of them the process of assimilation can be a rewarding experience because the influences of cultural domination may be overcome. For others, it may be painful. The same influences may all but completely deny those with dark skin the opportunity to assimilate successfully. The "bleaching syndrome" reflects an effort on the part of such dark-skinned Hispanic Americans to overcome the negative forces of domination. For light-skinned Hispanic Americans as well, it is not altogether irrelevant for they are more often the blood relatives of those on whom the culture of the United States places a stigma.

According to the domination model of assimilation (Kitano, 1985), Hispanic Americans in the United States are regarded as minorities. Their most salient feature is cutaneo-chroma (Hall, 1990), henceforth referred to as skin color. In the United States, skin color may have an effect on every aspect of life, including job placement, earnings, and, most important, self-concept (Vontress, 1970). It is a "master status" that distinguishes dark-skinned Hispanic Americans from the mainstream population of the United States. So potent is this master status that it has recently become the ground for legal suits between persons of light and dark skin color but of the same ethnic group (Hiskey, 1990; *Morrow v. Internal Revenue Service,* 1990). Resorting to legal tactics is an indication that assimilation for Hispanic Americans has been particularly painful given the psychologically conflicting implications of skin color. That is, they have internalized the culture but, unlike members of the mainstream society, are prohibited from structural or full assimilation into it (Rabinowitz, 1978). Their willingness to do so reflects an effort to improve their quality of life and live out "the American Dream." In doing so, even dark-skinned Hispanic Americans may develop a disdain for dark skin because the disdain is an expression of the dominant culture. Dark skin is regarded by the various institutions as an obstacle that bars Hispanic Americans from fully assimilating. This reality has resulted in acute conflict. To reduce such conflict and at the same time enable assimilation, some have manifested the bleaching syndrome. Furthermore, because degree of assimilation closely correlates with the phenotype of the mainstream population (i.e., skin color), light skin has emerged as one of the most critical ideals relative to degree of assimilation (Reuter, 1969). It is acted out socially by Hispanic Americans in their use of light skin as a point of reference to assure full assimilation into the mainstream of society.

The existence of the bleaching syndrome is historically rooted in the old "beauty" creams and folk preparations used by dark-skinned Hispanic Americans to make their skin lighter. According to *Webster's Ninth New Collegiate Dictionary,* "bleach" is a verb meaning to remove color or to make white. A "syndrome" consists of a grouping of symptoms (i.e., behaviors that occur in conjunction and make up a recognizable pattern). In combination, historical folklore and English terminology literally define the bleaching syndrome. It is also a metaphor. Its relevancy to the preferred domination model of assimilation in the United States is universal. The syndrome is applicable wherever domination exists. When applied to Hispanic Americans, its existence is substantiated in a most dramatic fashion, for they as a group have had to internalize skin-color ideals that are often radically inconsistent with the outward appearances of a significant number of their brethren (Levine & Padilla, 1980). Furthermore, the distress they suffer is exacerbated by the general lack of tolerance in the United States for its growing diversity and for persons who are dark-skinned. The effort, then, on the part of dark-skinned persons to assimilate and simultaneously bring about a reduction in their psychological conflict is made possible by their obsession with a "bleached" ideal. It is most evident in the Hispanic American's selection of marital partners, which closely resembles that of African Americans. No other aspect of social phenomena is more revealing.

Assimilation theory without domination views the selection of marital partners as an indicator that race (i.e., skin color) is not a barrier to full acceptance. An alternate approach, hypergamy, sees marriage as a function of inequality in dominant and racially stratified cultures (Shinagawa & Pang, 1988). For Hispanic Americans who manifest the bleaching syndrome, marriage then becomes a vehicle for the exchange of status characteristics. On that basis, higher status dark-skinned Hispanic Americans are then regarded as ineligible for marriage by light-skinned persons of equally high or higher status. Hypergamy is thus a consequence of the status disparity between persons with light and dark skin. If a marriage between two such persons does occur, it will require a disproportionate exchange of assets to compensate for the stigma associated with the assimilation of the dark-skinned spouse. When the prospects of marriage serve no purpose, the eventuality of mental health problems such as depression may follow (Roberts & Roberts, 1982).

5   As a social phenomenon, the bleaching syndrome is not unprecedented. It is the legacy of such theoretical concepts as "dramaturgy" (Adler, Adler, & Fantana, 1987), "looking glass self" (Cooley, 1902), and the more recent "cool pose" (Majors & Billson, 1992). Perhaps W.E.B. DuBois, a sociologist, was one of the first scholars in the United States to specifically acknowledge the problems of Hispanic Americans who must assimilate into the mainstream of society. He studied the problem and labeled it "double consciousness" (cf. Myrdal, 1944). The implication of this double consciousness was that the ideal of light skin was extremely potent. It required anyone with dark skin to assume a passive social demeanor in order not to offend further the light-skinned mainstream population. Survival and the possibility of structural assimilation were greatly enhanced commensurate with the ability to defer. Knowing this, Hispanic Americans evolved a "bleached" presentation of self separate from who they were within their own communities. This peculiar social phenomenon did not go unnoticed by social workers. Sometime following the death of DuBois, Norton (1993), a social worker who recognized the importance of the person-in-the-environment approach, developed the concept of the "dual perspective." Similar to the double consciousness theory of DuBois, dual perspective is a response to the domination model of assimilation. It is the process used by some Hispanic Americans to simultaneously perceive, understand, and compare the values, attitudes, and behavior of the larger social system with those of the immediate family and community system (Norton, 1983). Given the nature of duality, both theories suggest an identity, perhaps valued, separate from the ideal. In this respect, the bleaching syndrome differs. It is linear in progression and best illustrated as a scale constructed on the basis of the "double" and "dual" models. At one end is an identity for Hispanic Americans as defined by the mainstream of society—perhaps less valued. At the other end is the bleached

ideal as defined by the mainstream of society—perhaps more valued. Those who aspire to assimilate via the domination model invest their efforts in reaching the bleached ideal. This means that they will value and internalize all aspects of the mainstream culture—including the idealizations of light skin color—at the expense of their culture. By engaging in such efforts, they expect full assimilation into the society and the quality of life that goes with it. These Hispanic Americans have been referred to by scholars as "coconuts"—brown on the outside and white on the inside (Kitano, 1985).

The bleaching syndrome is germane to assimilation in the United States and its obsession with light skin. It was brought about by the colonization and naturalization of large numbers of Hispanics by the United States for various historical reasons. As a result of this activity, Hispanic Americans internalized light skin as an ideal point of reference because they were powerless to contest the influence of the dominant mainstream population. This internalization has resulted in conflict because light skin is immediately and undeniably verified upon sight. It is not only applied by the mainstream population to assess the assimilation potential of groups, but by groups to assess the assimilation potential of individual members as well (Myrdal, 1944). For Hispanic Americans, it is reflected not only in how they perceive attractiveness in one another or who they decide to marry but also in other life choices where skin color may be subjectively applied. The entire process, although it can be, is not necessarily a malicious act. Such a striking revelation may occur between light- and dark-skinned members of the same group, such as Hispanic Americans; between light- and dark-skinned members of different groups, such as Hispanic and Asian Americans; and between Hispanic Americans and the mainstream population.

The internalization of light skin as a point of reference among Hispanic Americans in the selection of marital partners reflects a behavioral manifestation of the bleaching syndrome. In toto, it is an effective, albeit ultimately pathological, method used for assimilation that predisposes Hispanic Americans to mental distress. There are, however, Hispanic Americans who, for whatever reasons, do not manifest the bleaching syndrome. They are under the same pressure to assimilate but are unable to reduce the resulting problems. Their suffering is characterized by mental health-related ailments verified in research as depression (Roberts & Roberts, 1982).

A substantial population of Hispanic Americans who experience mental health problems due to the domination model of assimilation is located in the United States. Like African Americans, Hispanic Americans vary greatly in skin color, from Caucasian light to the African dark. This variation has led some to believe that Hispanic Americans are not necessarily very distinct in skin color (Korzenny & Schiff, 1987). Similar to the experiences of African Americans, Hispanic Americans' experience with the conflict caused by efforts to assimilate is associated with light skin. This is a well-established fact that began in the colonial era with the arrival of the dominant light-skinned visitors who had just begun to migrate en masse from Europe via exploration expeditions (Montalvo, 1987). Their ability to impose their norms upon the indigenous people they encountered was long lasting and not without consequence. For Hispanic Americans today, the legacies of those norms exist in their standard of living and the frequency of depression that is associated with variations in their skin color. This fact was verified recently quite by accident (Relethford, Stern, Gaskill, & Hazuda, 1983).

A team of scholars had assembled to study diabetes among Mexican Americans. They used a spectrophotometer to measure the skin color of their subjects. Their research revealed that the skin color of the subjects in the sample became progressively lighter as the team moved from the low-income barrios to the more affluent San Antonio suburbs (Relethford et al., 1983). In a later study, Arce, Murgia, and Frisbie (1987) found a correlation between light skin among Hispanics and higher levels of income and education. Additionally, the same researchers discovered that those Hispanic Americans with darker skin reported significantly more discrimination, implying increased difficulty, than their lighter skinned counterparts. Those who had darker skin were perceived as more sinister and less attractive on that basis. Particularly for Hispanic American males, this would imply that the experience of assimilation via domination is similar to that of African Americans. Furthermore, the same ideal for marriage and attractiveness appear to cause conflict as well (Levine & Padilla, 1980). For example, Puerto Ricans are a group composed of "black, white, and mixed" people. In comparison to other Hispanic ethnics, their members are some of the darkest in skin color. Their rate of marriage to members of the mainstream population is also the lowest among Hispanic Americans (Wagenheim & deWagenheim, 1973).

When Hispanic Americans cannot use the bleaching syndrome to enable assimilation, the incidence of depression increases in relation to the darkness of skin color (Codina & Montalvo, 1992). This is a fact regardless of the person's education, family income, or command of the English language (Codina & Montalvo, 1992). But perhaps what is most striking is that the group's assimilation experience is differentiated by gender. According to research, a certain class of Hispanic American women born in the United States is not psychologically conflicted by the ideal of light skin in the same way that Hispanic American males are (Maldonado & Cross, 1977). This is especially peculiar given the fact that women tend to be valued for the way they look as opposed to men, who may be more valued for their ability to earn. A possible explanation for this phenomenon may have to do with the greater likelihood of Hispanic American males interacting with the discriminating mainstream population vis-à-vis the role of bread-winner. However, consistent with the ideal of light skin, Vargas-Willis and Cervantes (1987) found that conflict led Hispanic American women who were accorded position and status in their native land to experience depression after they immigrated to the United States. Their depression brought about by assimilation pressure is evident, but the reasons differ. If they are light-skinned, such women once they immigrate may be associated with the dark-skinned minority class because of their immigration and language. Due to their light skin and other features characteristic of the mainstream population, they may be rejected particularly by employers as not dark enough to receive minority status for a job. Their depression then, unlike that of Hispanic Americans who are darker, may be borne out of ambiguity. They may be privy to the racial slurs and ethnic jokes and at the same time expected to be loyal to the darker-skinned Hispanic American community. Additionally, many members of that community express some resentment that such persons seem to overcome their minority status with greater ease than should be expected. This expression is further cause for depression and similar to the experience of African Americans who claim biracial heritage. For both, the experience of assimilation is affected by the implications of domination vis-à-vis light skin for assimilation.

According to the aforementioned research, there is definite reason to suspect a relationship exists between a subject's skin color and the incidence of psyche-related ailments in the United States. It may be the cause of depression among both dark-skinned and light-skinned Hispanic Americans, albeit for different reasons. Their inability to reduce the psychic conflict brought on by the domination model of assimilation makes them susceptible. For others, the bleaching syndrome may enable a temporary progression toward assimilation. Its symptomatology is much less striking than depression but no less critical. It is maintained among other criteria by the use of light skin as an ideal point of reference in the selection of marital partners and in other significant life choices. Such persons are not in the best of mental health, but they are reasonably functional. Unlike Hispanic Americans who succumb to the stresses of depression, those who function by way of the bleaching syndrome affect the evolvement of familial and other systems vital to mental health and full assimilation. Their internalization of light skin as an ideal is ultimately pathological and can only ensure a continuation of the domination model as the sole means of assimilation into the mainstream of society.

The bleaching syndrome is not a required response to the influences of cultural domination in a diverse society such as the United States. Hispanic Americans, and other people of color, do have a choice. They may elect to celebrate their various hues of skin color and from that create their own ideal points of reference. Ultimately, this will facilitate assimilation and discourage the negative influences of cultural domination. It can be their unique gift to the culture and help move civilization to its next level.

References

Adler, P., Adler, P., & Fontana, A. (1987). Everyday life in sociology. *Annual Review of Sociology, 13,* 217–235.

Arce, C., Murgia, E., & Friabie, W. (1987). Phenotype and the life chances among Chicanos. *Hispanic Journal of Behavioral Sciences, 9,* 19–32.

Codina, E., & Montalvo, F. (1992). *Chicano phenotype and depression.* Unpublished manuscript, Our Lady of the Lakes University, Worden School of Social Services, San Antonio, TX.

Cooley, C. (1902). *Human nature and the social order.* New York: Scribner.

Hall, R. E. (1990). The projected manifestations of aspiration, personal values, and environmental assessment cognates of cutaneo-chroma (skin color) for a selected population of African-American (Doctoral dissertation, Atlanta University, 1989). *Dissertation Abstracts International, 50,* 3363A.

Hiskey, M. (1990, February 1). Boss: Skin hue, firing unrelated. *Atlanta Journal-Constitution*, pp. 1, 4.

Kitano, H. (1985). *Race relations*. Englewood Cliffs, NJ: Prentice-Hall.

Korzenny, F., & Schiff, E. (1987). Hispanic perceptions of communication discrimination. *Hispanic Journal of Behavioral Sciences, 9,* 33–48.

Levine, E. S., & Padilla, A. M. (1990). *Crossing cultures in therapy.* Monterey, CA: Brooks/Cole.

Majors, R., & Bilson, J. (1992). *Cool pose.* New York: Lexington.

Maldonado, M., & Cross, W. (1977). Today's Chicano refutes the stereotype. *College Student Journal, 11,* 146–152.

Montalvo, F. (1987). Skin color and Latinos: The origins and contemporary patterns of ethnoracial ambiguity among Mexican Americans and Puerto Ricans (monograph). San Antonio, TX: Our Lady of the Lake University.

Morrow v. Internal Revenue Service, 742 F. Supp. 670 (N.D. Ga. 1990).

Myrdal, G. (1944). *An American dilemma.* New York: Harper & Row.

Norton, D. (1983). Black family life patterns: The development of self and cognitive development of Black children. In Gloria J. Powell (Ed.), *The psychosocial development of minority group children* (pp. 181–193). New York: Brunner/Mazel.

Norton, D. (1993). Diversity, early socialization, and temporal development: The dual perspective revisited. *Social Work, 38*(1), 82–90.

Rabinowitz, H. (1978). *Race relations in the urban south.* New York: Oxford University Press.

Relethford, J., Stern, M., Gaskill, S., & Hazuda, H. (1983). Social class, admixture, and skin color variation among Mexican Americans and Anglo Americans living in San Antonio, Texas. *American Journal of Physical Anthropology, 62,* 97–102.

Reuter, E. (1969). *The mulatto in the United States.* New York: Haskell House.

Roberts, R. E., & Roberts, C. R. (1982). Marriage, work and depressive symptoms among Mexican Americans. *Hispanic Journal of Behavioral Sciences, 4,* 199–221.

Shinagawa, L., & Pang, G. (1988). Intraethnic, and interracial marriages among Asian-Americans in California, 1980. *Berkeley Journal of Sociology, 33,* 95–114.

Vargas-Willis, G., & Cervantes, R. (1987). Consideration of psychosocial stress in the treatment of the Latina immigrant. *Hispanic Journal of Behavioral Sciences, 9,* 315–329.

Vontress, C. (1970). Counseling Black. *Personnel and Guidance Journal, 48,* 713–719.

Wagenheim, K., & de Wagenheim, O. (1973). *The Puerto Ricans.* Garden City, NY: Doubleday.

Questions for Discussion

1. Do you think this essay has a persuasive aim? Or is it chiefly referential? Cite specific passages to support your answer.
2. What is the author's claim? How does he support this claim? Is the evidence sufficient, plausible, and pertinent?
3. Notice that the author quotes the dictionary for definitions of the words *bleach* and *syndrome.* What do you think of this technique? What other techniques are available for defining words?
4. Do you think this essay would be more or less effective if it included headings? If more effective, compose appropriate headings. If less effective, explain why you think headings are unnecessary.

Opportunities for Writing

1. Write a letter to your family offering your thoughts on skin color. How important is skin color to you? Does it influence your choice of friends? Would it influence your choice of a spouse? Discuss the ethical, social, emotional, and financial implications of your opinion.
2. Evaluate television commercials for their promotion of the ideal of light skin color. Over a period of a week, watch television at different times of the day, recording and analyzing each commercial you see. Are the characters in the commercials chiefly of a light skin color? Are characters with light skin colors portrayed more positively than characters with dark skin colors? Is light skin color portrayed as especially desirable? Which commercials do you consider especially sensitive or insensitive to skin color biases? Write a letter to a sponsor, reporting the results of your research and urging continuation or correction of its advertising practices.
3. Propose to school administrators a special investigation of the "bleaching syndrome" on your campus. Are light-skinned students, faculty, and administrators more easily assimilated than dark-skinned students, faculty, and administrators? In your proposal, identify appropriate information sources and methods of investigation. Devise a schedule and budget for your proposed research project. Emphasize the gravity and feasibility of your investigation of this issue.

The Data Game

Cynthia Crossen

Cynthia Crossen is a writer and editor at The Wall Street Journal, *specializing in news and feature articles. In "The Data Game," she examines product information and research about different foods and argues that we consumers beware: "Unless and until a study has been replicated, it should be looked on with care. . . ." This essay, adapted from her book* Tainted Truth, *appeared in the June 1994 issue of* The Washington Monthly.

> The year: 2173. Two scientists talk about a man who has just been roused from a 200-year sleep.
>
> "For breakfast, he requested something called wheat germ, organic honey, and tiger's milk."
>
> "Oh, yes, those were the charmed substances that some years ago were felt to contain life-preserving properties."
>
> "You mean there was no deep fat, no steak or cream pie or hot fudge?"
>
> "Those were thought to be unhealthy, precisely the opposite of what we now know to be true."
>
> "Incredible."
>
> —Woody Allen, *Sleeper*

People know how to discount some kinds of information. We usually would not take too seriously a claim by the maker of Quick 'n Crispy Crinkle Cut Fries that "In a nationwide taste test, you preferred the crispiness of Quick 'n Crispy Crinkle Cut Fries, 3 to 1." Similarly, when the *National Examiner* publishes a story saying, "You can slash your cholesterol level [as much as 30 percent], strengthen your heart and add years to your life with a daily can of 7-Up," many people would, rightly, not stop taking their cholesterol medication. We tend to give more weight to surveys, studies, and polls reported in the *New England Journal of Medicine, Time, The New York Times,* the network news shows, or *The Wall Street Journal.* Yet even forums like these have been slow to recognize how dubious is much of the research they publish.

People know enough to be suspicious of some numbers in some contexts, but we are at the mercy of others. We have little personal experience or knowledge of the topics of much modern research, and the methodologies are incomprehensibly arcane. Nevertheless, we respect numbers, and we cannot help believing them. Numbers bring a sense of rationality to complex decisions—the ones we used to make with common sense, experience, and intelligence.

Yet more and more of the information we use to buy, elect, advise, acquit, and heal has been created not to expand our knowledge but to sell a product or advance a cause. If the results of the research contradict the sponsor's agenda, they will routinely be suppressed. Researchers have become secretive and their sponsors greedy. The media, which can usually get the raw numbers if they want them, are stingy with data because data are boring, and many journalists are themselves innumerate.

For example: If there were two things about food that we knew for sure, it was that milk was good for children and chocolate was bad. Studies found the opposite. Surely wine, cigarettes, and paté are harmful to your health. Studies have shown the reverse. For years, whole wheat bread was thought to be better than white. No, says a study. Studies found that oat bran was good for the heart, then not good, then good. Apple a day? A study showed apples cause cancer. Hundreds of studies have exonerated coffee; hundreds have damned it.

5 While most of the financing for food research comes from the government, private interests with financial stake in the outcome of the studies are paying a growing share. State and federal government financing for colleges and universities to do research and development has flattened in recent years, while the amount of financing from industry has increased dramatically. In 1981, industry contributed $292 million to schools for research; by 1991, that figure had jumped to more than $1.2 billion. The theory is that if the companies may profit from the research, and they often do, the companies should pay for it. Many food researchers must choose: research funded by an interested party or no research at all.

However complex and compromised, food research commands an astonishing loyalty from consumers, resulting in alarming shifts of behavior from study to study. A study showing that the paté-consuming French have healthier hearts actually increased sales of the fatty spread in the U.S. While most people would not rush out to take an experimental drug after one small study demonstrated its effectiveness, vast numbers of people will eat or not eat a food based on a single study. That is why studies have become such a big part of the food business.

Research about food has contributed many truths to the world, resulting in longer, healthier lives for those who follow its path. Woody Allen's futuristic fantasy notwithstanding, it is unquestionably true that more fruits and vegetables and less animal fat than Americans typically eat is good. Yet beyond some broad strokes of knowledge, there is little agreement about how coffee, oat bran, margarine, wine, and nuts, just to name a few, affect human bodies.

There is no truth about food so sacred that it cannot be challenged by research. In fact, the more the study defies common wisdom, the more likely it is to enjoy wide acclaim. Consider these surprises of recent years:

- "Milk is the number one health hazard facing young children," wrote a Santa Rosa, California, doctor in support of a new report by the Physicians Committee for Responsible Medicine. The report, released at a widely covered news conference in September 1992, cited a recent study in the *New England Journal of Medicine* about milk contributing to juvenile diabetes. Despite its vaguely neutral name, the committee is actually a pressure group of mostly vegetarians who oppose animal research and support animal welfare groups.
- White bread will not make you gain weight and, when used in a high-fiber diet, is an okay nutritional choice, reported the Cooper Institute for Aerobic Research. Its sponsor for the study: the makers of Wonder Bread. The research: inconclusive, to say the least. The 118 subjects were divided into four groups. One ate their normal diet; one group added four slices of low-calorie bread to their daily diet; one added eight slices of low-calorie bread; and a forth added eight slices of regular bread. This ended after a mere eight weeks. Predictably, no one in the study gained or lost significant weight, but the researchers said they *believed* the bread eaters would have lost weight if the study continued. The study was reported by the Associated Press.
- Chocolate may actually prevent cavities, reported a newsletter from the Princeton Resource Center, citing a study about how tannins in cocoa inhibit plaque formation. The group also published reports of a study about how sticky snacks like caramel actually dissolve faster than starchy foods like potato chips. This research "should dispel myths that foods perceived as 'sticky' or 'chewy' pose the greatest threat of dental decay," said the center, which is financed by M&M/Mars.

The nutrition study, like a political poll, is a machine with a thousand knobs. Turning any one of them a notch, even well within ethical limits, will dramatically change the outcome of the study. When studies differ, there are many legitimate-sounding—and possibly legitimate—reasons. But the flood of deliberately contradictory studies insures there will be no definitive proof of anything. If a study contradicts another study's position, buyers of research can simply commission more studies. They cannot be absolutely certain the new studies will confirm their position, but they know the researchers whose labs have produced agreeable results. "Usually associations that sponsor research have a fairly good idea what the outcome will be," said Joseph Hotchkiss of Cornell University. "Or they won't fund it."

COFFEE TALK

10   There is probably no food on earth that has been as widely studied to so little effect as caffeine, the world's most popular drug. Several times a year, a new study about the effects of caffeine, usually studied in the form of coffee, is published to great media fanfare. The studies, which are often reported as though they are the first and last word on the subject, are in fact absurdly contradictory and would be funny if the media and consumers did not embrace them so fervently. "Coffee Study Finds Heavy Drinking Boosts Heart Risk," announced *The Wall Street Journal* in March 1990. Six months later, the *Journal* revisited the coffee question. "Coffee Study Finds No Link to Heart Illness," it reported, noting the earlier study and saying "controversy about coffee's effect on health probably will continue."

The hundreds, perhaps thousands, of studies on coffee have taught scientists a few things about it. For most people, coffee stimulates the nervous system, makes their muscles more resilient, and gives them a heady feeling of concentration and power. But there is much scientists do not know. Despite thousands of studies on coffee's effects on virtually every organ in the body, scientists still cannot completely rule out links to heart disease, cancer, infertility, breast cysts, and a dozen other maladies. Dueling studies suggest there may be associations—or there may not.

"You can never prove a negative," said George E. Boecklin, president of the National Coffee Association of U.S.A., the industry's trade group, which has certainly done its best, financing and publicizing studies that acquit coffee of all serious crimes.

In studying food, researchers have a choice between using animals and humans. As subjects, both are imperfect. Food research on mice or rats is flawed because animals have different physiologies and life expectancies: 30 months versus 70 years. One Food and Drug Administration study showed that when pregnant rats were fed the equivalent of 56 to 87 cups of strong coffee at one time, some of the offsprings' toes were deformed or missing. Human studies involving some 15,000 women, however, have found no association between caffeine and birth defects.

Human beings would be perfect subjects for research on human health. But unlike rats, people cannot be forced to do what they are supposed to do, and some of them lie about it. Ask a thousand men and women what they ate yesterday, and the answers will be inaccurate blends of what they should, could, and would have eaten. Even dietitians who have been subjects of nutritional studies say they are tempted to lie about the steak, potato chips, or ice cream they ate in private.

15   To study long-term effects of a food, especially on diseases that can take decades to develop, like cancer, scientists need 20 years. But they find coffee addicts reluctant to give up their drug for 20 years for the sake of science. Studies on substances strongly suspected of being killers are even tougher to analyze. Scientists cannot assign half of their subjects to smoke a pack of cigarettes a day.

To further complicate the picture, every human being is different. Some people can smoke a pack a day and live to 100. Others have never picked up a cigarette but die of lung cancer at 30. Sulfite, a food additive used in wine, fruits, and vegetables, is perfectly benign to all but a few people; when those few are exposed to it, they die.

Too, coffee is not just caffeine. It is different types and ages of beans roasted at very high temperatures, releasing other chemicals. It is brewed in different ways—boiling, dripping, percolating. It can be caffeinated or not. Like people, no two pots of coffee are exactly alike. And where does moderate coffee drinking cross into heavy coffee drinking? Four cups a day? Eight? Twelve? For that matter, what is a cup? Five ounces? Six ounces? Eight ounces?

People who drink coffee also tend to have other health habits that may cause the problems blamed on coffee. The coffee drinker is also more likely to smoke, to eat pork and potato chips and to exercise less than someone who doesn't drink coffee. For whatever reason, coffee is associated with risk taking, at least where health is concerned. One study even found that heavy coffee drinkers tend to be less likely to wear seat belts. So how can scientists ever know whether the thing that is killing people is the coffee or the doughnuts?

With so many variables involved, it is no wonder there is an endless stream of coffee studies, each proving or ruling out ever smaller chunks of the mosaic: "Caffeine, moderate alcohol intake, and risk of fractures of the hip and forearm in middle-aged women" was the tide of one 1991 study. As each new study arrives, newspapers and airwaves crackle with an excitement usually associated with major news events: "Caffeine Not Harmful to Health"; "Coffee's 'Perk-me-up' Effect Confirmed in Study"; "Coffee each Day Keeps Asthma Away in Italy." Such guileless enthusiasm for each coffee study is one reason scientists love to work on caffeine. So widely consumed is the addictive drug that if even a tiny association between it and disease was established, many lives could be saved and scientific careers made.

20   The National Coffee Association is an active player in the caffeine study game. It commissions its own research, and it trumpets other research that supports the business goals of the association members. When a critical study is published, the association quickly reacts, issuing news releases complete with critical comments from "independent experts." "The coffee industry is incredibly powerful," said Dr. Robert Superko, who did some coffee research at Stanford University. "Once you get on their bad side, they have a very heavy hammer." Superko believes the industry shapes coffee research by choosing which studies to fund partly based on its hopes, rather than scrutinizing the study design with a cool, objective eye. And industry financing, said Superko, "indeed affects the way you publish the results. The coffee industry puts pressure on you to do it their way."

George Boecklin of the coffee association said that is not true. The only reason the association gets involved in financing research, he continued, is because otherwise it would look as though it had its "head in the sand." The research is done by respected institutions that are given "no strings attached" grants, Boecklin said. But the association's credibility is doubtful, at least insofar as the way they use research to further their self-interested goals.

During the cholesterol mania of the 1980s, for example, many researchers turned their attention to the subject of coffee and cholesterol. Some earlier studies had suggested a link between heart disease and coffee, but just what that link was remained a mystery. Could it be cholesterol?

After having put out brushfires over cancer, birth defects and heart disease, the coffee association was clearly worried about this new threat to the already depressed coffee business. The association invited several experts in the field of cholesterol and clinical trials to submit proposals for a study on the subject. Dr. Roy Fried's proposal won the financing.

Fried, then a research fellow at Johns Hopkins, received more than $200,000 from the coffee association to do his study. Fried designed a study of the effects of drinking filtered coffee (the brewing method most Americans now prefer) on cholesterol levels. Fried and his fellow researchers first asked 100 male subjects to give up coffee for eight weeks to wash out their systems. Then the men were randomly assigned to one of four groups: Drink four cups (24 ounces) of regular coffee a day; drink four cups of decaffeinated coffee a day; drink two cups of regular coffee; and drink no coffee at all. The results: The cholesterol levels of the men who drank four cups a day of regular coffee rose. But the silver lining was that both their "good" and "bad" cholesterol levels seemed to have risen, canceling out any significantly increased risk of heart disease.

"We concluded that, based on the study, drinking modest amounts of filtered coffee does raise cholesterol, but that itself wouldn't increase the risk of heart disease," Fried said. His study was published on February 12, 1992, in the *Journal of the American Medical Association.*

Although the only *positive* result of the study was that coffee increased cholesterol, both the coffee association and the media found the *negative* results more interesting: "Study Refutes Link Between Coffee, High Cholesterol," said the *Minneapolis Star.* "Coffee is off the hook again," said the *Phoenix Gazette.* Meanwhile, the coffee association's fact sheet said: "Most studies involving U.S.-style filter-brewed coffee, including the 1992 study published in the *Journal of the American Medical Association,* have not found the association between . . . coffee and increased risk of cholesterol-related heart disease. Importantly, the *JAMA* study . . . controlled for diet, exercise and smoking, all known contributing factors for heart disease."

Fried's study was far from conclusive, however. The subjects were all men, and all but seven were white; the experiment lasted only four months (whereas many people drink coffee for most of a lifetime); the study was not double-blinded, which meant the subjects knew what they were drinking; and the maximum amount of coffee anyone drank was four cups a day, while many other studies tested more than four cups a day.

FOOD FIGHTS

It is almost impossible for average consumers to sort through studies like these and know what they should be eating and drinking. Unfortunately, most Americans do not have ready access to the studies and would not know how to decipher them if they did. Even relatively lucid scientific studies contain lines like "The final analysis was based on a 'pre protocol' basis since the study objective was to test a dose-response relationship of B-glucan on serum lipids." Most members of the media are ill-equipped to judge a technical study. Even if the science hasn't been explained or published in a U.S. journal, the media may jump on a study if it promises entertainment for the readers or viewers. And if the media jump, that is good enough for many Americans.

So what is to be done? A good rule is to keep in mind that a study may hint at an emerging truth, and possibly offer a diverting bit of entertainment, but in general that is all it is—a hint and a diversion. Unless and until a study has been replicated, it should be looked on with care—the experiments proving the existence of cold fusion, still unreplicated, being a good example. To establish something as widely accepted as the belief that smoking causes lung cancer took decades, and the evidence came from many different threads of research—animal studies, human studies, epidemiological studies.

30   Beware of research and researchers calling themselves independent. Independent often just means there are many paying clients instead of one; it does not mean that there is no financial incentive to provide agreeable results. Similarly, the word "nonprofit" means little in assessing the credibility of a study; nonprofit researchers still count on a regular paycheck.

The tacit acceptance of untruth in daily life eats away at belief in right and wrong. If nothing is true, how can one solution be better than another? Progress stalls. "We should fuss, we should be indignant," wrote Ivan Preston about disinformation in advertising. "We should call the advertisers phonies, or bullshitters, or harassers, when we think that's what they are. . . . We should not allow our own silence to be one of the reasons why things stay the same." It is time to reclaim our numbers, our truth.

Questions for Discussion

1. How does the author try to establish credibility on this subject? Cite specific passages to support your answer.
2. Do you consider this essay adversarial or conciliatory persuasion? Explain your answer.
3. What do you think of the opening quotation from Woody Allen's *Sleeper*? Why does the author start the essay this way? Is this opening effective? If you think it is, explain why. If you think it isn't, explain how you would start this essay.
4. How might the author integrate knowledge by participation? Would such information make the essay more or less effective?
5. While the author briefly mentions research on milk, white bread, and chocolate, she focuses chiefly on studies of coffee to exemplify a common deficiency of food research that she perceives. Why does she choose to focus on studies of coffee? How representative is this example?

Opportunities for Writing

1. Locate a newspaper article on food research. Does the article characterize the research as "the first and last word on the subject" or does it emphasize the limitations of the research? Does the article identify the source of funding? Does it describe the research methods and variables? Write a letter to the editor of the newspaper, offering your evaluation of this article.

2. Declare your position on the funding of food research. Is it ethical for food companies to sponsor food research at colleges and universities? Does this practice lead to biased findings?
3. Review the existing research on a specific food item such as milk, white bread, chocolate, or wine. What are the competing claims regarding potential risks and benefits? Which studies do you consider valid and reliable?

The Motherhood Myth

BETTY ROLLIN

Betty Rollin was a stage and television actress before starting as a writer at Vogue *in 1964. From 1965 to 1971, she was a contributor for* Look. *She is the author of several books, including* Last Wish *(1985),* Am I Getting Paid for This? *(1982), and* First, You Cry *(1976). She is known for her commentaries on the changing roles of women. In this essay, first published in 1970 in* Look, *Rollin takes a stand against a popular myth, "the idea that having babies is something that all normal women instinctively want and need and will enjoy doing."*

Motherhood is in trouble, and it ought to be. A rude question is long overdue: Who needs it? The answer used to be (1) society and (2) women. But now, with the impending horrors of overpopulation, society desperately *doesn't* need it. And women don't need it either. Thanks to the Motherhood Myth—the idea that having babies is something that all normal women instinctively want and need and will enjoy doing—they just *think* they do.

The notion that the maternal wish and the activity of mothering are instinctive or biologically predestined is baloney. Try asking most sociologists, psychologists, psychoanalysts, biologists—many of whom are mothers—about motherhood being instinctive: it's like asking department store presidents if their Santa Clauses are real. "Motherhood—instinctive!" shouts distinguished sociologist/author Dr. Jessie Bernard. "Biological destiny? Forget biology! If it were biology, people would die from not doing it."

"Women don't need to be mothers any more than they need spaghetti," says Dr. Richard Rabkin, a New York psychiatrist. "But if you're in a world where everyone is eating spaghetti, thinking they need it and want it, you will think so too. Romance has really contaminated science. So-called instincts have to do with stimulation. They are not things that well up inside of you."

"When a woman says with feeling that she craved her baby from within, she is putting into biological language what is psychological," says University of Michigan psychoanalyst and motherhood-researcher Dr. Frederick Wyatt. "There are no instincts," says Dr. William Goode, president-elect of the American Sociological Association. "There are reflexes, like eye-blinking, and drives, like sex. There is no innate drive for children. Otherwise, the enormous cultural pressures that there are to reproduce wouldn't exist. There are no cultural pressures to sell you on getting your hand out of the fire."

5   There are, to be sure, biologists and others who go on about biological destiny, that is, the innate or instinctive goal of motherhood. (At the turn of the cen-

tury, even good old capitalism was explained by a theorist as "the *instinct* of acquisitiveness.") And many psychoanalysts will hold the Freudian view that women feel so rotten about not having a penis that they are necessarily propelled into the child-wish to replace the missing organ. Psychoanalysts also make much of the psychological need to repeat what one's parent of the same sex has done. Since every woman has a mother, it is considered normal to wish to imitate one's mother by being a mother.

There is, surely, a wish to pass on love if one has received it, but to insist women must pass it on in the same way is like insisting that every man whose father is a gardener has to be a gardener. One dissenting psychoanalyst says, simply, "There is a wish to comply with one's biology, yes, but we needn't and sometimes we shouldn't." (Interestingly, the woman who has been the greatest contributor to child therapy and who has probably given more to children than anyone alive is Dr. Anna Freud, Freud's magnificent daughter, who is not a mother.)

Anyway, what an expert cast of hundreds is telling us is, simply, that biological *possibility* and desire are not the same as biological *need*. Women have childbearing equipment. To choose not to use the equipment is no more blocking what is instinctive than it is for a man who, muscles or no, chooses not to be a weight lifter.

So much for the wish. What about the "instinctive" *activity* of mothering? One animal study shows that when a young member of a species is put in a cage, say, with an older member of the same species, the latter will act in a protective, "maternal" way. But that goes for both males and females who have been "mothered" themselves. And studies indicate that a human baby will also respond to whoever is around playing mother—even if it's father. Margaret Mead and many others frequently point out that mothering can be a fine occupation, if you want it, for either sex. Another experiment with monkeys who were brought up without mothers found them lacking in maternal behavior toward their own offspring. A similar study showed that monkeys brought up without other monkeys of the opposite sex had no interest in mating—all of which suggests that both mothering and mating behavior are learned, not instinctual. And, to turn the cart (or the baby carriage) around, baby ducks who lovingly follow their mothers seemed, in the mother's absence, to just as lovingly follow wooden ducks or even vacuum cleaners.

If motherhood isn't instinctive, when and why, then, was the Motherhood Myth born? Until recently, the entire question of maternal motivation was academic. Sex, like it or not, meant babies. Not that there haven't always been a lot of interesting contraceptive tries. But until the creation of the diaphragm in the 1880's, the birth of babies was largely unavoidable. And, generally speaking, nobody really seemed to mind. For one thing, people tend to be sort of good sports about what seems to be inevitable. For another, in the past, the population needed beefing up. Mortality rates were high, and agricultural cultures, particularly, have always needed children to help out. So because it "just happened" and because it was needed, motherhood was assumed to be innate.

Originally, it was the word of God that got the ball rolling with "Be fruitful and multiply," a practical suggestion, since the only people around then were Adam and Eve. But in no time, supermoralists like St. Augustine changed the tone of the message: "Intercourse, even with one's legitimate wife, is unlawful and wicked where the conception of the offspring is prevented," he, we assume, thundered. And the Roman Catholic position was thus cemented. So then and now, procreation took on a curious value among people who viewed (and view) the pleasures of sex as sinful. One could partake in the sinful pleasure, but feel vindicated by the ensuing birth. Motherhood cleaned up sex. Also, it cleaned up women, who have always been considered somewhat evil, because of Eve's transgression ("... but the woman was deceived and became a transgressor. Yet woman will be saved through bearing children ... ," I Timothy, 2:14–15), and somewhat dirty because of menstruation.

And so, based on need, inevitability, and pragmatic fantasy—the Myth *worked,* from society's point of view—the Myth grew like corn in Kansas. And society reinforced it with both laws and propaganda—laws that made woman a chattel, denied her education and personal mobility, and madonna propaganda that she was beautiful and wonderful doing it and it was all beautiful and wonderful to do. (One rarely sees a madonna washing dishes.)

In fact, the Myth persisted—breaking some kind of record for long-lasting fallacies—until something like yesterday. For as the truth about the Myth trickled in—as women's rights increased, as women gradually got the message that it was certainly possible for them to do most things that men did, that they live longer, that their brains were not tinier—then, finally, when the really big news rolled in, that they could choose whether or not to be mothers—what happened? The Motherhood Myth soared higher than ever. As Betty Friedan made oh-so-clear in *The Feminine Mystique,* the '40's and '50's produced a group of ladies who not only had babies as if they were going out of style (maybe they were) but, as never before, they turned motherhood into a cult. First, they wallowed in the aesthetics of it all—natural childbirth and nursing became maternal musts. Like heavy-bellied ostriches, they grounded their heads in the sands of motherhood, only coming up for air to say how utterly happy and fulfilled they were. But, as Mrs. Friedan says only too plainly, they weren't. The Myth galloped on, moreover, long after making babies had turned from practical asset to liability for both individual parents and society. With the average cost of a middle-class child figured conservatively at $30,000 (not including college), any parent knows that the only people who benefit economically from children are manufacturers of consumer goods. Hence all those gooey motherhood commercials. And the Myth gathered momentum long after sheer numbers, while not yet extinguishing us, have made us intensely uncomfortable. Almost all of our societal problems, from minor discomforts like traffic to major ones like hunger, the population people keep reminding us, have to do with there being too many people. And who suffers most? The kids who have been so mindlessly brought into the world, that's who. They are the ones who have to cope with all of the difficult and dehumanizing conditions brought on by overpopulation. They are the ones who have to cope with the psychological nausea of feeling unneeded by society. That's not the only reason for drugs, but, surely, it's a leading contender.

Unfortunately, the population curbers are tripped up by a romantic, stubborn, ideological hurdle. How can birth-control programs really be effective as long as the concept of glorious motherhood remains unchanged? (Even poor old Planned Parenthood has to euphemize—why not Planned Unparenthood?) Particularly among the poor, motherhood is one of the few inherently positive institutions that are accessible. As Berkeley demographer Judith Blake points out, "Poverty-oriented birth control programs do not make sense as a welfare measure . . . as long as existing pronatalist policies . . . encourage mating, pregnancy, and the care, support, and rearing of children." Or, she might have added, as long as the less-than-idyllic child-rearing part of motherhood remains "in small print."

Sure, motherhood gets dumped on sometimes: Philip Wylie's Momism got going in the '40's and Philip Roth's *Portnoy's Complaint* did its best to turn rancid the chicken-soup concept of Jewish motherhood. But these are viewed as the sour cries of a black humorist here, a malcontent there. Everyone shudders, laughs, but it's like the mouse and the elephant joke. Still, the Myth persists. Last April, a Brooklyn woman was indicted on charges of manslaughter and negligent homicide—eleven children died in a fire in a building she owned and criminally neglected—"But," sputtered her lawyer, "my client, Mrs. Breslow, is a mother, a grandmother, and a great-grandmother!"

15   Most remarkably, the Motherhood Myth persists in the face of the most overwhelming maternal unhappiness and incompetence. If reproduction were merely superfluous and expensive, if the experience were as rich and rewarding as the cliché would have us believe, if it were a predominantly joyous trip for everyone riding—mother, father, child—then the going everybody-should-have-two-children plan would suffice. Certainly, there are a lot of joyous mothers, and their children and (sometimes, not necessarily) their husbands reflect their joy. But a lot of evidence suggests that for more women than anyone wants to admit, motherhood can be miserable. ("If it weren't," says one psychiatrist wryly, "the world wouldn't be in the mess it's in.")

There is a remarkable statistical finding from a recent study of Dr. Bernard's, comparing the mental illness and unhappiness of married mothers and single women. The latter group, it turned out, was both markedly less sick and overtly more happy. Of course, it's not easy to measure slippery attitudes like happiness. "Many women have achieved a kind of reconciliation—a conformity," says Dr. Bernard,

> that they interpret as happiness. Since feminine happiness is supposed to lie in devoting one's life to one's husband and children, they do that; so *ipso facto,* they assume they are happy. And for many women, untrained for independence and "processed" for motherhood, they find their state far preferable to the alternatives, which don't really exist.

Also, unhappy mothers are often loath to admit it. For one thing, if in society's view not to be a mother is to be a freak, not to be a *blissful* mother is to be a witch. Besides, unlike a disappointing marriage, disappointing motherhood cannot be terminated by divorce. Of course, none of that stops such a woman from expressing her dissatisfaction in a variety of ways. Again, it is not only she who suffers but her husband and children as well. Enter the harridan housewife, the carping shrew. The realities of motherhood can turn women into terrible people. And, judging from the 50,000 cases of child abuse in the U.S. each year, some are worse than terrible.

In some cases, the unpleasing realities of motherhood begin even before the beginning. In *Her Infinite Variety,* Morton Hunt describes young married women pregnant for the first time as "very likely to be frightened and depressed, masking these feelings in order not to be considered contemptible. The arrival of pregnancy interrupts a pleasant dream of motherhood and awakens them to the realization that they have too little money, or not enough space, or unresolved marital problems . . . ."

The following are random quotes from interviews with some mothers in Ann Arbor, Mich., who described themselves as reasonably happy. They all had positive things to say about their children, although when asked about the best moment of their day, they *all* confessed it was when the children were in bed. Here is the rest:

> Suddenly I had to devote myself to the child totally. I was under the illusion that the baby was going to fit into my life, and I found that I had to switch my life and my schedule to fit *him*. You think, "I'm in love, I'll get married, and we'll have a baby." First there's two, then three, it's simple and romantic. You don't even think about the work . . . .
>
> You never get away from the responsibility. Even when you leave the children with a sitter, you are not out from under the pressure of the responsibility. . . .
>
> I hate ironing their pants and doing their underwear and they never put their clothes in the laundry basket . . . . As they get older, they make less demands on our time because they're in school, but the demands are greater in forming their values . . . . Best moment of the day is when all the children are in bed . . . . The worst time of the day is 4 P.M., when you have to get dinner started, the kids are tired, hungry and crabby—everybody wants to talk to you about *their* day . . . your day is only half over.
>
> Once a mother, the responsibility and concern for my children became so encompassing . . . . It took me a great deal of will to keep up other parts of my personality. . . . To me, motherhood gets harder as they get older because you have less control . . . . In an abstract sense, I'd have several . . . . In the nonabstract, I would not have any . . . .
>
> I had anticipated that the baby would sleep and eat, sleep and eat. Instead, the experience was overwhelming. I really had not thought particularly about what motherhood would mean in a realistic sense. I want to do *other* things, like to become involved in things that are worthwhile—I don't mean women's clubs—but I don't have the physical energy to go out in the evenings. I feel like I'm missing something . . . the experience of being somewhere with people and having them talking about something—something that's going on in the world.

Every grownup person expects to pay a price for his pleasures, but seldom is the price as vast as the one endured "however happily" by most mothers. We have mentioned the literal cost factor. But what does that mean? For middle-class American women, it means a life style with severe and usually unimagined limitations; i.e., life in the suburbs, because who can afford three bedrooms in the city? And what do suburbs mean? For women, suburbs mean other women and children and leftover peanut-butter sandwiches and car pools and seldom-seen husbands. Even the Feminine Mystiqueniks—the housewives who finally admitted that their lives behind brooms (OK, electric brooms) were driving them crazy—were loath to trace their predicament to their children. But it is simply a fact that a childless married woman has no child-work and little housework. She can live in a city, or, if she still chooses the suburbs or the country, she can leave on the commuter train with her husband if she wants to. Even the most ardent job-seeking mother will find little in the way of great opportunities in Scarsdale. Besides, by the time she wakes up, she usually lacks both the preparation for the outside world and the self-confidence to get it. You will say there are plenty of city-dwelling working mothers. But most of those women do additional-funds-for-the-family kind of work, not the interesting career kind that takes plugging during childbearing years.

Nor is it a bed of petunias for the mother who does make it professionally. Says writer-critic Marya Mannes:

> If the creative woman has children, she must pay for this indulgence with a long burden of guilt, for her life will be split three ways between them and her husband and her work . . . . No woman with any heart can compose a paragraph when her child is in trouble . . . . The creative woman has no wife to protect her from intrusion. A man at his desk in a room with closed door is a man at work. A woman at a desk in any room is available.

Speaking of jobs, do remember that mothering, salary or not, is a job. Even those who can afford nurses to handle the nitty-gritty still need to put out emotionally. "Well-cared-for" neurotic rich kids are not exactly unknown in our society. One of the more absurd aspects of the Myth is the underlying assumption that, since most women are biologically equipped to bear children, they are psychologically, mentally, emotionally, and technically equipped (or interested) to rear them. Never mind happiness. To assume that such an exacting, consuming, and important task is something almost all women are equipped to do is far more dangerous and ridiculous than assuming that everyone with vocal chords should seek a career in the opera.

A major expectation of the Myth is that children make a not-so-hot marriage hotter, or a hot marriage, hotter still. Yet almost every available study indicates that childless marriages are far happier. One of the biggest, of 850 couples, was conducted by Dr. Harold Feldman of Cornell University, who states his finding in no uncertain terms: "Those couples with children had a significantly lower level of marital satisfaction than did those without children." Some of the reasons are obvious. Even the most adorable children make for additional demands, complications, and hardships in the lives of even the most loving parents. If a woman feels disappointed and trapped in her mother role, it is bound to affect her marriage in any number of ways: she may take out her frustrations directly on her husband, or she may count on him too heavily for what she feels she is missing in her daily life.

". . . You begin to grow away from your husband," says one of the Michigan ladies. "He's working on his career and you're working on your family. But you both must gear your lives to the children. You do things the children enjoy, more than things you might enjoy." More subtle and possibly more serious is what motherhood may do to a woman's sexuality. Often when the stork flies in, sexuality flies out. Both in the emotional minds of some women *and* in the minds of their husbands, when a woman becomes a mother, she stops being a woman. It's not only that motherhood may destroy her physical attractiveness, but its madonna concept may destroy her *feelings* of sexuality.

And what of the payoff? Usually, even the most self-sacrificing of maternal self-sacrificers expects a little something back. Gratified parents are not unknown to the Western world, but there are probably at least just as many who feel, to put it crudely, shortchanged. The experiment mentioned earlier—where the baby ducks followed vacuum cleaners instead of their mothers—indicates that what passes for love from baby to mother is merely a rudimentary kind of object attachment. Without necessarily feeling like a Hoover, a lot of women become disheartened because babies and children are not only not interesting to talk to (not everyone thrills at the wonders of da-da-ma-ma talk) but they are generally not empathetic, considerate people. Even the nicest children are not capable of empathy, surely a major ingredient of love, until they are much older. Sometimes they're never capable of it. Dr. Wyatt says that often, in later years particularly, when most of the "returns" are in, it is the "good mother" who suffers most of all. It is then she must face a reality: The child—the appendage with her genes—is not an appendage, but a separate person. What's more, he or she may be a separate person who doesn't even like her—or whom she doesn't really like.

25   So if the music is lousy, how come everyone's dancing? Because the motherhood minuet is taught freely from birth, and whether or not she has rhythm or likes the music, every woman is expected to do it. Indeed, she *wants* to do it. Little girls start learning what to want—and what to be—when they are still in their cribs. Dr. Miriam Keiffer, a young social psychologist at Bensalem, the Experimental College of Fordham University, points to studies showing that

> at six months of age, mothers are already treating their baby girls and boys quite differently. For instance, mothers have been found to touch, comfort, and talk to their females more. If these differences can be found at such an early stage, it's not surprising that the end product is as different as it is. What as surprising is that men and women are, in so many ways, similar.

Some people point to the way little girls play with dolls as proof of their innate motherliness. But remember, little girls are *given* dolls. When Margaret Mead presented some dolls to New Guinea children, it was the boys, not the girls, who wanted to play with them, which they did by crooning lullabies and rocking them in the most maternal fashion.

By the time they reach adolescence, most girls, unconsciously or not, have learned enough about role definition to qualify for a master's degree. In general, the lesson has been that no matter what kind of career thoughts one may entertain, one must, first and foremost, be a wife and mother. A girl's mother is usually her first teacher. As Dr. Goode says, "A woman is not only taught by society to have a child; she is taught to have a child who will have a child." A woman who has hung her life on the Motherhood Myth will almost always reinforce her young married daughter's early training by pushing for grandchildren. Prospective grandmothers are not the only ones. Husbands, too, can be effective sellers. After all, they have the Fatherhood Myth to cope with. A married man is *supposed* to have children. Often, particularly among Latins, children are a sign of potency. They help him assure the world—and himself—that he is the big man he is supposed to be. Plus, children give him both immortality (whatever that means) and possibly the chance to become more in his lifetime through the accomplishments of his children, particularly his son. (Sometimes it's important, however, for the son to do better, but not *too* much better.)

Friends, too, can be counted on as myth-pushers. Naturally one wants to do what one's friends do. One study, by the way, found a correlation between a woman's fertility and that of her three closest friends. The negative sell comes into play here, too. We have seen what the concept of non-mother means (cold, selfish, unwomanly, abnormal). In practice, particularly in the suburbs, it can mean, simply, exclusion—both from child-centered activities (that is, most activities) and child-centered conversations (that is, most conversations). It can also mean being the butt of a lot of unfunny jokes. ("Whaddya waiting for? An immaculate conception? Ha ha.") Worst of all, it can mean being an object of pity.

In case she's escaped all those pressures (that is, if she was brought up in a cave), a young married woman often wants a baby just so that she'll (1) have something to do (motherhood is better than clerk/typist, which is often the only kind of job she can get, since little more has been expected of her and, besides, her boss also expects her to leave and be a mother); (2) have something to hug and possess, to be needed by and have power over; and (3) have something to *be*—e.g., a baby's mother. Motherhood affords an instant identity. First, through wifehood, you are somebody's wife; then you are somebody's mother. Both give not only identity and activity, but status and stardom of a kind. During pregnancy, a woman can look forward to the kind of attention and pampering she may not ever have gotten or may never otherwise get. Some women consider birth the biggest accomplishment of their lives, which may be interpreted as saying not much for the rest of their lives. As Dr. Goode says, "It's like the gambler who may know the roulette wheel is crooked, but it's the only game in town." Also, with motherhood, the feeling of accomplishment is immediate. It is really much faster and easier to make a baby than paint a painting, or write a book, or get to the point of accomplishment in a job. It is also easier in a way to shift focus from self-development to child development—particularly since, for women, self-development is considered selfish. Even unwed mothers may achieve a feeling of this kind. (As we have seen, little thought is given to the aftermath.) And, again, since so many women are underdeveloped as people, they feel that, besides children, they have little else to give—to themselves, their husbands, to their world.

You may ask why then, when the realities do start pouring in, does a woman want to have a second, third, even fourth child? OK, (1) just because reality is pouring in doesn't mean she wants to *face* it. A new baby can help bring back some of the old illusions. Says psychoanalyst Dr. Natalie Shainess, "She may view each successive child as a knight in armor that will rescue her from being a 'bad unhappy mother.'" (2) Next on the horror list of having no children, is having one. It suffices to say that only children are not only OK, they even have a high rate of exceptionality. (3) Both parents usually want at least one child of each sex. The husband, for reasons discussed earlier, probably wants a son. (4) The more children one has, the more of an excuse one has not to develop in any other way.

What's the point? A world without children? Of course not. Nothing could be worse or more unlikely. No matter what anyone says in *Look* or anywhere else, motherhood isn't about to go out like a blown bulb, and who says it should? Only the Myth must go out, and now it seems to be dimming.

The younger-generation females who have been reared on the Myth have not rejected it totally, but at least they recognize it can be more loving to children not to have them. And at least they speak of adopting children instead of bearing them. Moreover, since the new nonbreeders are "less hung-up" on ownership, they seem to recognize that if you dig loving children, you don't necessarily have to own one. The end of the Motherhood Myth might make available more loving women (and men!) for those children who already exist.

When motherhood is no longer culturally compulsory, there will, certainly, be less of it. Women are now beginning to think and do more about development of self, of their individual resources. Far from being selfish, such development is probably our only hope. That means more alternatives for women. And more alternatives means more selective, better, happier, motherhood—and childhood and husbandhood (or manhood) and peoplehood. It is not a question of whether or not children are sweet and marvelous to have and rear; the question is, even if that's so, whether or not one wants to pay the price for it. It doesn't make sense any more to pretend that women need babies, when what they really need is themselves. If God were still speaking to us in a voice we could hear, even He would probably say, "Be fruitful. Don't multiply."

Questions for Discussion

1. The author could have integrated knowledge by participation, referring to her own experience as either a mother or a nonmother. Why do you think she doesn't do so? What impact would such information have on her credibility?
2. Consider the way the author identifies her information sources. Do you always know which information is coming from which source? Do you consider this method of citing sources satisfactory? If so, why? If not, why not?
3. What is the subordinate aim of this essay? Cite specific passages to support your answer.
4. How does the author try to motivate the audience? Does she emphasize the size, severity, or urgency of the issue?
5. In addition to citing various statistics and professional opinions, the author incorporates direct quotations from five Michigan mothers. What is her purpose in doing so? What is your opinion of this evidence?

Opportunities for Writing

1. In a letter to a friend, weigh the advantages and disadvantages of having children. Consider financial, psychological, and social factors. Do you recommend having children?
2. Evaluate the "Fatherhood Myth." Is having children critical to a man's identity? Is it a sign of virility? Does it offer immortality? Examine biological and psychological studies of fatherhood. Interview fathers and nonfathers for their insights. Compose your essay as a special article for the Father's Day issue of your local newspaper.
3. Review the characterization of nonmothers on television. Focus your review on either comedies or dramas. How often are women depicted

as nonmothers? How are nonmothers typically portrayed? Positively or negatively? Why? Give examples to support your review.
4. After interviewing a variety of mothers on the subject of motherhood, propose a solution to a specific issue that is often troubling to mothers.

Murder, Inc.

ROBERT SHERRILL

Robert Sherill was born in Frogtown, Georgia and attended Pepperdine University and the University of Texas. A journalist and editor, Sherrill investigates and writes about controversial subjects. Among his works are The Oil Follies of 1970–1980: How the Petroleum Industry Stole the Show *(1983);* Edward M. Kennedy of Massachusetts *(1976);* The Saturday Night Special and Other Guns *(1973);* Military Justice Is to Justice as Military Music Is to Music *(1970). In "Murder, Inc.," reprinted from* Grand Street *(Spring 1986), Sherrill declares that corporation executives who, for the sake of profit, knowingly allow dangerous products to be marketed could be guilty of murder. The author cites information gained by observation in order to support his position.*

There are something over fifteen hundred men and women on the death rows of America. Given the social context in which they operated, one might reasonably assume that they were sentenced to be executed not because they are murderers but because they were inefficient. Using guns and knives and the usual footpad paraphernalia, they dispatched only a few more than their own number. Had they used asbestos, mislabeled pharmaceutical drugs and devices, defective autos, and illegally used and illegally disposed chemicals, they could have killed, crippled, and tortured many thousands of people. And they could have done it without very much fuss.

Corporate criminals, as we all know, live charmed lives. Not until 1978 had a corporation ever been indicted for murder (Ford Motor Company, which was acquitted), and not until 1985 had corporate executives ever been brought to trial for murder because of the lethal mischief done by their company.

The executives who made history last year were the president, plant manager, and plant foreman of Film Recovery Systems Corporation, a ratty little silver-rendering operation in Elm Grove Village outside Chicago. The silver was recovered by cooking used X-ray films in vats of boiling cyanide. Film Recovery hired mostly illegal immigrants, who were afraid to protest working conditions so foul that they made employees vomit and faint. The illegals were preferred also because they couldn't read much English and would not be spooked by the written warnings on the drums of cyanide. To make doubly sure that fright wouldn't drive workers away, management had the skull-and-crossbones signs scraped off the drums. Although the antidote for cyanide poisoning is cheap and easy to obtain, Film Recovery Systems didn't keep any on hand.

So it came to pass that Stefan Golab, a sixty-one-year-old illegal immigrant from Poland, took too hefty a lungful of cyanide fumes and died. Charged with murder on the grounds that they had created such unsafe working conditions as to bring about "a strong probability of death and great bodily harm," the three officials were convicted and sentenced to twenty-five years in prison.

5   Will executives at other villainous corporations be similarly charged and convicted? Don't bet on it. In this instance the law was applied so properly, so rightly, so common-sensically that one would be foolish to expect such usage to appear again soon. It was a sort of Halley's Comet of Justice.

The idea of treating corporate murderers as just plain murderers strikes many people as excessive. Some lawyers who cautiously approved the conviction in principle said they were afraid it would confuse people generally because a bald murder charge is usually associated with a bullet in the gut or an ice pick in the neck, and nice people would have a hard time adapting the charge to the way things are sometimes accomplished in the front office. Speaking for this timid viewpoint, Alan Dershowitz, Harvard's celebrated criminal law specialist, said he thought the Film Recovery case showed we need a new category of crime. "We should have one that specifically reflects our condemnation of this sort of behavior," he said, "without necessarily assimilating it into the most heinous forms of murder"–as if the St. Valentine's Day massacre were any more heinous than Bhopal.

During the trial, the Illinois prosecutor accused the defendants of "callousness, disregard of human lives, and exposing people to dangerous products all for the sake of profits." No wonder the verdict has been so modestly praised. If that's enough to rate a murder charge, our whole commercial system is at risk. If it were to become the rule, we could look forward to a lineup of accused corporate executives extending out the courthouse and around the block several times. Since there is no statute of limitations on murder, prosecutors would be obliged to charge those executives at Firestone who, a few years back, allegedly killed and injured no telling how many people by flooding the market with ten million tires they knew to be defective; and the executives at Ford who sent the Pinto into circulation knowing its gas tank was so poorly designed that a rear-end collision could turn the car into a fire trap (several dozen men, women, and children were burned alive). From the pharmaceutical fraternity would come such as Dr. William Shedden, former vice-president and chief medical officer for Eli Lily Research Laboratories, who recently pleaded guilty to fifteen criminal counts relating to the marketing of Oraflex, an arthritis drug that the Food and Drug Administration says has been "possibly" linked to forty-nine deaths in the United States and several hundred abroad, not to mention the hundreds who have suffered nonfatal liver and kidney failure. Seems as how the folks at Lilly, when they sought approval from the FDA, forgot to mention that the drug was already known to have killed at least twenty-eight people in Europe. (Shedden was fined $15,000; Lilly, which earned $3.1 billion in 1984, was fined $25,000.) And let's be sure to save an early murder indictment for those three sly dogs at SmithKline Beckman Corporation who whizzed their product, Selacryn, through the FDA without mentioning that it had caused severe liver damage in some patients in France. False labels were used to peddle it in this country, where it has been linked to thirty-six deaths and five hundred cases of liver and kidney damage.

Now comes a ripple of books that, were there any justice, would put a dozen or so hangdog executives in the dock. Three of the books make particularly persuasive cases. Paul Brodeur's *Outrageous Misconduct: The Asbestos Industry on Trial* (Pantheon) is an account of how the largest manufacturer of asbestos products, Manville Corporation (previously known as Johns-Manville Corporation), and other asbestos companies committed over the years what one plaintiff's attorney called "the greatest mass murder in history," which is possibly true if one means industrial mass murder, not political. People who regularly inhale asbestos fibers are likely to die, or at least be crippled, from the lung disease called asbestosis or the even worse (at least it sounds worse) mesothelioma. It sometimes takes twenty to thirty years for asbestosis to appear, so a measure of the slaughter from it is somewhat vague. But the best experts in the field, which means Dr. Irving J. Selikoff and his staff at the Mount Sinai Hospital in New York City, estimate that aside from the many thousands who have died from asbestos diseases in the past, there will be between eight and ten thousand deaths from asbestos-related cancer each year for the next twenty years. These deaths are not accidental. Manville et al. knew exactly what they were doing. Brodeur's book is mainly an account of how the asbestos companies, though they claimed to be ignorant of the deadly quality of their product until a study by Dr. Selikoff was released in 1964, had for forty years known about, and had suppressed or disregarded, hundreds of studies that clearly showed what asbestos was doing to the people who inhaled it. Did the companies even care what was happening? Typically, at a Manville asbestos mine in Canada, company doctors found that of seven hundred and eight workers, only four—who had worked there less than four years—had normal lungs. Those who were dying of asbestosis were not told of their ailment.

The other two books, Susan Perry and Jim Dawson's *Nightmare: Women and the Dalkon Shield* (Macmillan) and Morton Mintz's *At Any Cost: Corporate Greed, Women, and the Dalkon Shield* (Pantheon), remind me of what Dr. Jules Amthor said to my favorite detective: "I'm in a very sensitive profession, Mr. Marlowe. I'm a quack." The murderous quackery of the Dalkon Shield, an intrauterine device, was committed by A. H. Robins, a company that should have stuck to making Chap Stick and Sergeant's Flea & Tick Collars, and left birth-control gadgets to those who knew how to make them properly. These two books should convince anyone, I think, that compared to the fellows at A. H. Robins, the Film Recovery executives were pikers when it came to showing disregard for human lives for the sake of profits. Profits were plentiful, that's for sure. A. H. Robins sold more than 4.5 million Dalkon Shields worldwide (2.8 million in the United States) for $4.35 each; not bad for a device that cost only twenty-five cents to produce. The death count among women who wore the shield still isn't complete; the last I heard it was twenty. But wearers of the shield also have reported stillbirths, babies with major congenital defects, punctured uteri, forced hysterectomies, sterilization from infection, and various tortures and illnesses by the thousands—some generous portion, we may presume, of the 9,230 lawsuits that A. H. Robins has settled out of court. And as both books make clear, the company launched the Dalkon Shield fully aware of the shield's dangers, sold it with false advertising, kept on selling it for several years after the company knew what its customers were going through, and pulled a complicated cover-up of guilt.

10 Dershowitz is right in one respect: corporate murderers are not like your typical killer on death row. Corporate murderers do not set out to kill. There's no profit in that. They are simply willing to accept a certain amount of death and physical torment among their workers and customers as a sometimes necessary byproduct of the free enterprise system. Mintz has uncovered a dandy quote from history to illustrate this attitude. When it was suggested to Alfred P. Sloan, Jr., president of General Motors circa 1930, that he should have safety glass installed in Chevrolets, he refused with the explanation, "Accidents or no accidents, my concern in this matter is a matter of profit and loss."

The Sloan spirit is everywhere. Brodeur quotes from a deposition of Charles H. Roemer, once a prominent New Jersey attorney who handled legal matters for the Union Asbestos and Rubber Company. Roomer reveals that around 1942, when Union Asbestos discovered a lot of its workers coming down with asbestos disease, he and some of Union Asbestos's top officials went to Johns-Manville and asked Vandiver Brown, Manville's attorney, and Lewis Brown, president of Manville, if their physical examination program had turned up similar results. According to Roemer, Vandiver Brown said, in effect, Sure, our X-rays show many of our workers have that disease, but we don't tell them they are sick because if we did, they would stop working and sue us. Roemer recalled asking, "Mr. Brown, do you mean to tell me you would let them work until they dropped dead?" and Brown answering, "Yes, we save a lot of money that way."

Saving money, along with making money, was obviously the paramount objective of A. H. Robins, too. This was evident from the beginning, when Robins officials learned—*six months before marketing the device nationally*—that the Dalkon Shield's multifilament tail had a wicking tendency and could carry potentially deadly bacteria into the uterus. Did the company hold up marketing the shield until it could be further tested and made safe? No, no. That would have meant a delay, for one thing, in recovering the $750,000 they had paid the shield's inventors. Though Robins knew it was putting its customers in great jeopardy, it hustled the shield onto the market with promotional claims that it was "safe" and "superior" to all other intrauterine devices; and never, during the four years the shield was on the market, did A. H. Robins conduct wicking studies of the string. The shield's promotional literature, by the way, was a classic example of phony drugstore hype. A. H. Robins claimed the shield kept the pregnancy rate at 1.1 percent; the company was well aware that the shield allowed at least a 5 percent pregnancy rate, one of the most slipshod in the birth-control business. A. H. Robins also advertised that the device could be easily inserted in "even the most sensitive woman," although in fact many doctors, before inserting the shield, had to give patients an anesthetic, and many women were in pain for months.

Not long after the shield went on the market, Wayne Crowder, one of the few heroes in this sorry tale, a quality-control engineer at Chap Stick, which manufactured many of the shields for its parent firm, rejected ten thousand of them because he was convinced the strings could wick bacteria. His boss overruled him with the remark, "Your conscience doesn't pay your salary." Crowder also suggested a method for stopping the wicking, but his technique was rejected because it would have cost an extra five cents per device. Crowder kept on complaining (he would ultimately be fired as an irritant) and he finally stirred Daniel French, president of Chap Stick, to convey Crowder's criticisms to the home office. French was told to mind his own business and not worry about the safety of the shield, which prompted him to go into the corporate soft-shoe routine he knew would please. He wrote A. H. Robins: "It is not the intention of Chap Stick Company to attempt any unauthorized improvements in the Dalkon Shield. My only interest in the Dalkon Shield is to produce it at the lowest possible price and, therefore, increase Robins' gross profit level."

Of course, when thousands of women begin dying, screaming, cursing, and suing, it gets a little difficult to pretend that all is well with one's product, but for more than a decade A. H. Robins did its best, never recalling the gadget, never sending a warning to doctors about possible deadly side effects, and continuing to the last—continuing right up to the present even after losing hundreds of millions of dollars in lawsuits—to argue that the shield is just hunkydory. The A. H. Robins school spirit was beautifully capsulated by one of its officials who told the *National Observer,* "But after all, we are in business to sell the thing, to make a profit. I don't mean we're trying to go out and sell products that are going to be dangerous, fatal, or what have you. But you don't put all the bad things in big headlines."

15   Where is the corporate executive who will not savor the easy insouciance of "or what have you"?

One of the more fascinating characteristics of corporate murderers is the way these fellows cover up their dirty work. They are really quite bold and successful in their deviousness. When one considers how many top officials there are at places like Manville and Robins, and when one assumes (obviously naïvely) among the lot of them surely there must be at least one or two with a functioning conscience, the completeness of their cover-ups is indeed impressive. Which isn't to say that their techniques are very sophisticated. They simply lie, or hide or burn the incriminating material. When the litigation flood began to break over Manville Corporation in the late 1960s, the asbestos gang began thwarting their victims' attorneys by claiming certain Manville executives couldn't give depositions because they were dead (when they were very much alive), by refusing to produce documents ordered by the court, and by denying that certain documents existed when in fact they did. A. H. Robins was just as expert at that sort of thing. According to Mintz, "Thousands of documents sought by lawyers for victims of the Dalkon Shield sank from sight in suspicious circumstances. A few were hidden for a decade in a home basement in Tulsa, Oklahoma. Other records were destroyed, some admittedly in a city dump in Columbus, Indiana, and some allegedly in an A. H. Robins furnace. And despite court orders, the company did not produce truckloads of documents for judicial rulings on whether the women's lawyers could see the papers."

A. H. Robins's most notorious effort at a cover-up ultimately failed, thanks to one Roger Tuttle, a classic example of what can happen when the worm turns.

Tuttle was an attorney for A. H. Robins in the early 1970s. He says that immediately after the company lost its first Dalkon Shield lawsuit, his superiors ordered him (they deny it) to search through the company's files and burn every document that he thought might be used against A. H. Robins in future lawsuits—documents that, in Tuttle's words, indicated "knowledge and complicity, if any, of top officials in what at that stage of the game appeared to be a grim situation." Unfortunately for the company, Tuttle did not fully obey orders. He took possession of some of the juiciest documents and kept them. Just why he rebelled isn't clear. Perhaps it was because Tuttle, a plain little guy who admits he isn't the smartest attorney in the world, was tired of having his employers push him around, which they often did. He says he did it because he was ashamed that "I personally lacked the courage" to challenge the order and "I wanted some sop for my own conscience as an attorney." Whatever his motivation, Tuttle sat on the purloined files for nearly ten years. He moved on to other jobs, finally winding up, a born-again Christian, on the Oral Roberts University law faculty. Watching the Dalkon Shield trials from afar, troubled by the plaintiffs' inability to cope with A. H. Robins's cover-up, Tuttle finally decided to step forward and provide the material their attorneys needed for the big breakthrough.

A lucky windfall like that is the only way victims can overcome the tremendous imbalance in legal firepower. In the way they muster defense, corporate murderers bear no resemblance to the broken-down, half-nuts, penniless drifters on death row, dozens of whom have no attorney at all. Corporate killers are like the Mafia in the way they come to court with a phalanx of attorneys. They are fronted by the best, or at least the best known. Griffin Bell, President Carter's Attorney General, has been one of A. H. Robins's attorneys.

There are two other significant differences between corporate killers and the habitués of death rows. In the first place, the latter generally did not murder as part of doing business, except for the relatively few who killed coincidental to a holdup. They did not murder to protect their rackets or territory, as the Mafia does, and they did not murder to exploit a patent or to increase production and sales, as corporate murderers do. One judge accused A. H. Robins officials of taking "the bottom line as your guiding beacon and the low road as your route." Killing for the bottom line has probably not sent a single murderer to death row anywhere. In the second place, most of the men and women on death row were lonely murderers. No part of society supported what they did. But just as the Mafia can commit murder with impunity only because it has the cooperation of police and prosecutors, so too corporate murderers benefit from the collusion of respectable professions, particularly doctors (who, for a price, keep quiet), and insurance companies (who, to help Manville, did not reveal what their actuarial tables told about the risks to asbestos workers; and, for Robins, worked actively backstage to conceal the Dalkon Shield's menace to public health), and government agencies who are supposed to protect public health but look the other way.

It was an old, and in its way valid, excuse that Film Recovery's officials gave the court: "We were just operating like other plants, and none of the government health and safety inspectors who dropped around—neither the Elm Grove Village Public Health Department nor the Environmental Protection

Agency—told us we shouldn't be letting our workers stick their heads in vats of boiling cyanide." They were probably telling the truth. That's the way health and safety regulators have usually operated.

Brodeur tells us that a veritable parade of government inspectors marched through the Pittsburgh Corning asbestos plant in Tyler, Texas, over a period of six and a half years without warning the workers that the asbestos dust levels were more than twenty times the maximum recommended for health safety. One Department of Labor official later admitted he had not worn a respirator when inspecting the plant because he did not want to excite the workers into asking questions about their health. Though the Public Health Service several times measured the fallout of asbestos dust, never did it warn the workers that the stuff was eating up their lungs. Finally things got so bad at Tyler that federal inspectors, forced to bring charges against the owners for appalling infractions of health standards, recommended that they be fined $210. Today the men and women who worked in that plant (since closed) are dying of lung cancer at a rate five times greater than the national average.

The most impressive bureaucratic collusion A. H. Robins received was, not surprisingly, from the Food and Drug Administration. When trial attorneys brought evidence that the Dalkon Shield's rotting tail strings were endangering thousands of women and asked FDA officials to remove the device from the market, the agency did nothing. When the National Women's Health Network petitioned the FDA for a recall—paid for by Robins—that would remove the shield from all women then wearing it, the FDA did nothing. For a full decade it pretended to be helpless.

There is one more significant difference between the people on death row and the corporate murderers: the former sometimes say they are sorry; the latter never do. Midway through 1985, Texas executed Charles Milton, thirty-four, because when he stuck up a liquor store the owner and his wife wrestled Milton for the gun, it went off, and the woman died. Shortly before the state killed him with poison, Milton said, "I am sorry Mrs. Denton was killed in the struggle over the gun." There. He said it. It wasn't much, but he said it. And that's more than the folks at Manville have ever said about the thousands of people they killed with asbestos. When it comes to feeling no remorse, A. H. Robins doesn't take a back seat to anybody. In a famous courtroom confrontation between Federal Judge Miles W. Lord and three A. H. Robins officials, including company president E. Claiborne Robins, Jr., Judge Lord asked them to read silently to themselves a long reprimand of their actions. The most scathing passage, quoted both by Mintz and by Perry and Dawson, was this:

> Today as you sit here attempting once more to extricate yourselves from the legal consequences of your acts, none of you has faced up to the fact that more than nine thousand women [the figure two years ago (in 1984)] have made claims that they gave up part of their womanhood so that your company might prosper. It is alleged that others gave their lives so you might so prosper. And there stand behind them legions more who have been injured but who had not sought relief in the courts of this land....
>
> If one poor young man were by some act of his—without authority or consent—to inflict such damage upon one woman, he would be jailed for a good portion of the rest of his life. And yet your company, without warning to women, invaded their bodies by the millions and caused them injuries by the thousands. And

when the time came for these women to make their claims against your company, you attacked their characters. You inquired into their sexual practices and into the identity of their sex partners. You exposed these women—and ruined families and reputations and careers—in order to intimidate those who would raise their voices against you. You introduced issues that had no relationship whatsoever to the fact that you planted in the bodies of these women instruments of death, of mutilation, of disease.

Judge Lord admitted that he did not have the power to make them recall the shield but he begged them to do it on their own: "You've got lives out there, people, women, wives, moms, and some who will never be moms. . . . You are the corporate conscience. Please, in the name of humanity, lift your eyes above the bottom line."

It was a pretty stirring piece of writing (later, when Judge Lord got so pissed off he read it aloud, they say half the courtroom was in tears), and the judge asked them if it had had any impact on them.

Looking sulky, they just stared at him and said nothing.

A few weeks later, at A. H. Robins's annual meeting, E. Claiborne Robins, Jr., dismissed Lord's speech as a "poisonous attack." The company did not recall the shield for another eight months.

Giving deposition in 1984, Ernest L. Bender, Jr., senior vice-president for corporate planning and development, was asked if he had ever heard an officer or employee say he or she was "sorry or remorseful about any infection that's been suffered by any Dalkon Shield wearer." He answered, "I've never heard anyone make such remarks because I've never heard anyone that said the Dalkon Shield was the cause."

What punishment is fitting for these fellows?

If they are murderers, why not the death sentence? Polls show that 84 percent of Americans favor the death penalty, but half think the penalty is unfairly applied. Let's restore their faith by applying justice equally and poetically. In Georgia recently it took the state two 2,080 volts spaced over nineteen minutes to kill a black man who murdered during a burglary. How fitting it would be to use the same sort of defective electric chair to execute, for example, auto manufacturers and tire manufacturers who knowingly kill people with defective merchandise. In Texas recently it took the state executioners forty minutes to administer the lethal poison to a drifter who had killed a woman. Could anything be more appropriate than to tie down drug and device manufacturers who have killed many women and let slow-witted executioners poke around their bodies for an hour or so, looking for just the right blood vessel to transport the poison? At a recent Mississippi execution, the prisoner's protracted gasping for breath became such an ugly spectacle that prison authorities, in a strange burst of decorum, ordered witnesses out of the death chamber. That sort of execution for Manville executives who specialized in spreading long-term asphyxiation over thousands of lives would certainly be appropriate.

But these things will never happen. For all our popular declarations of democracy, most Americans are such forelock-tugging toadies that they would be horrified to see, say, Henry Ford II occupying the same electric chair that cooked black, penniless Alpha Otis Stephens.

Nor will we incarcerate many corporate murderers. Though some of us with a mean streak may enjoy fantasizing the reception that our fat-assed corporate killers would get from some of their cellmates in America's more interesting prisons—I like to think of the pious chaps from A. H. Robins spending time in Tennessee's notorious Brushy Mountain Prison—that is not going to happen very often either, the precedent of Film Recovery to the contrary notwithstanding. The Film Recovery trio had the misfortune of working for a crappy little corporation that has since gone defunct. Judges will not be so stern with killers from giant corporations.

So long as we have an army of crassly aggressive plaintiff attorneys to rely on, however, there is always the hope that we can smite the corporations and the men who run them with a punishment they probably fear worse than death or loss of freedom: to wit, massive loss of profits. Pamela C. Van Duyn, whose use of the Dalkon Shield at the age of twenty-six destroyed one Fallopian tube and critically damaged the other (her childbearing chances are virtually nil), says: "As far as I'm concerned, the last dime that is in Claiborne Robins's pocket ought to be paid over to all the people that have suffered." Author Brodeur dreams of an even broader financial punishment for the industry he hates:

> When I was a young man, out of college in 1953, I went into the Army Counterintelligence Corps and went to Germany, where I saw one of the death camps, Dachau. And I saw what the occupational army had done to Dachau. They had razed it, left the chimneys standing, and the barbed wire as a monument—quite the same way the Romans left Carthage. What I would do with some of these companies that are nothing more or less than killing grounds would be to sell their assets totally, reimburse the victims, and leave the walls as a reminder—just the way Dachau was—that a law-abiding and decent society will not tolerate this kind of conduct.

He added, "I know perfectly well that this is not going to happen in the private enterprise system."

How right he is. The laws, the court system, federal and state legislature, most of the press, the unions—most of the establishment is opposed to applying the final financial solution to killer corporations.

As it became evident that juries were inclined to agree with Mrs. Van Duyn's proposal to wring plenty of money from A. H. Robins, the corporation in 1985 sought protection under Chapter 11 of the Federal Bankruptcy Code. It was a sleazy trick they had picked up from Manville Corporation, which had declared bankruptcy in August 1982. Although both corporations had lost hundreds of millions in court fights, neither was actually in financial trouble. Indeed, at the time it copped out under Chapter 11, Manville was the nation's 181st largest corporation and had assets of more than $2 billion. Bankruptcy was a transparent ploy—or, as plaintiff attorneys put it, a fraudulent abuse and perversion of the bankruptcy laws—but with the connivance of the federal courts it is a ploy that has worked. Not a penny has been paid to the victims of either corporation since they declared bankruptcy, and the 16,500 pending lawsuits against Manville and the five thousand lawsuits pending against A. H. Robins (those figures are climbing every day) have been frozen.

Meanwhile, companies are not even mildly chastised. Quite the contrary. Most major newspapers have said nothing about Manville's malevolent cover-up but have clucked sympathetically over its courtroom defeats. *The New York Times* editorially seemed to deplore the financial problems of the asbestos industry almost as much as it deplored the industry's massacre of workers: "Asbestos is a tragedy, most of all for the victims and their families but also for the companies, which are being made to pay the price for decisions made long ago." Senator Gary Hart, whose home state, Colorado, is corporate headquarters for Manville, pitched in with legislation that would lift financial penalty from the asbestos companies and dump it on the taxpayers. And in Richmond, Virginia, corporate headquarters for the makers of the Dalkon Shield, civic leaders threw a banquet for E. Claiborne Robins, Sr. The president of the University of Virginia assured Robins that "Your example will cast its shadow into eternity, as the sands of time carry the indelible footprint of your good works. We applaud you for always exhibiting a steadfast and devoted concern for your fellow man. Truly, the Lord has chosen you as one of His most essential instruments."

After similar encomiums from other community leaders, the top man behind the marketing of the Dalkon Shield was given the Great American Tradition Award.

Questions for Discussion

1. How does the author try to motivate his audience? Cite specific passages to support your answer.
2. Twice the author uses language that might be considered offensive (i.e., *pissed off* and *fat-assed*). Why do you think he chooses such words? Is this technique effective? Is it appropriate?
3. This essay is adversarial persuasion. How might the author revise this essay to make it more conciliatory? What specific changes do you think would be necessary?
4. Explain the organization of this essay. Why is it organized the way it is?
5. The final paragraph of the essay describes E. Claiborne Robins, Sr. receiving the Great American Tradition Award. What is your opinion of this ironic ending? What is the author's purpose in ending the essay this way? Do you think the ending is effective?

Opportunities for Writing

1. Write a letter to the chief executive officer of a company that you believe manufactures a dangerous product. How is this product dangerous? What do you want the company to do about it?
2. Evaluate the health and safety record of a local company. Interview current and former employees. Examine pertinent newspaper articles. Does this company provide a safe working environment?

3. Write a review of either Paul Brodeur's *Outrageous Misconduct: The Asbestos Industry on Trial;* Susan Perry and Jim Dawson's *Nightmare: Women and the Dalkon Shield;* or Morton Mintz's *At Any Cost: Corporate Greed, Women, and the Dalkon Shield.* Is the book a credible source of information? Did you enjoy reading it?
4. Declare your position on the issue of executive misconduct. Do you believe that corporate executives ought to be personally liable for creating unsafe working conditions that injure employees or for producing defective products that injure customers? Why or why not?

Knowledge by Participation and Observation

Fenimore Cooper's Literary Offenses

Mark Twain (Samuel Langhorne Clemens)

Samuel Langhorne Clemens (1835–1910) was born in Florida, Missouri, and spent much of his adolescence in Hannibal, Missouri. In 1863, Clemens began using Mark Twain as his pen name and wrote newspaper reports, essays, short stories, and novels about life, times, and people as he knew them. Among his best known works are A Connecticut Yankee in King Arthur's Court *(1889),* The Adventures of Huckleberry Finn *(1885),* Life on the Mississippi *(1883),* The Prince and the Pauper *(1877), and* The Adventures of Tom Sawyer *(1876). In the following selection written in 1895, Twain evaluates James Fenimore Cooper's* The Deerslayer *and* The Pathfinder.

> The Pathfinder *and* The Deerslayer *stand at the head of Cooper's novels as artistic creations. There are others of his works which contain parts as perfect as are to be found in these, and scenes even more thrilling. Not one can be compared with either of them as a finished whole.*
>
> *The defects in both of these tales are comparatively slight. They were pure works of art.*
>
> —Prof. Lounsbury
>
> *The five tales reveal an extraordinary fulness of invention.*
>
> *. . . One of the very greatest characters in fiction, Natty Bumppo. . . .*
>
> *The craft of the woodsman, the tricks of the trapper, all the delicate art of the forest, were familiar to Cooper from his youth up.*
>
> —Prof. Brander Matthews
>
> *Cooper is the greatest artist in the domain of romantic fiction yet produced by America.*
>
> —Wilkie Collins

It seems to me that it was far from right for the Professor of English Literature in Yale, the Professor of English Literature In Columbia, and Wilkie Collins to deliver opinions on Cooper's literature without having read some of it. It would have been much more decorous to keep silent and let persons talk who have read Cooper.

Cooper's art has some defects. In one place in *Deerslayer,* and in the restricted space of two-thirds of a page, Cooper has scored 114 offenses against literary art out of a possible 115. It breaks the record.

There are nineteen rules governing literary art in the domain of romantic fiction—some say twenty-two. In *Deerslayer* Cooper violated eighteen of them. These eighteen require:

1. That a tale shall accomplish something and arrive somewhere. But the *Deerslayer* tale accomplishes nothing and arrives in the air.
2. They require that the episodes of a tale shall be necessary parts of the tale, and shall help to develop it. But as the *Deerslayer* tale is not a tale, and accomplishes nothing and arrives nowhere, the episodes have no rightful place in the work, since there was nothing for them to develop.
3. They require that the personages in a tale shall be alive, except in the cases of corpses, and that always the reader shall be able to tell the corpses from the others. But this detail has often been overlooked in the *Deerslayer* tale.
4. They require that the personages in a tale, both dead and alive, shall exhibit a sufficient excuse for being there. But this detail also has been overlooked in the *Deerslayer* tale.
5. They require that when the personages of a tale deal in conversation, the talk shall sound like human talk, and be talk such as human beings would be likely to talk in the given circumstances, and have a discoverable meaning, also a discoverable purpose, and a show of relevancy, and remain in the neighborhood of the subject in hand, and be interesting to the reader, and help out the tale, and stop when the people cannot think of anything more to say. But this requirement has been ignored from the beginning of the *Deerslayer* tale to the end of it.
6. They require that when the author describes the character of a personage in his tale, the conduct and conversation of that personage shall justify said description. But this law gets little or no attention in the *Deerslayer* tale, as Natty Bumppo's case will amply prove.
7. They require that when a personage talks like an illustrated, gilt-edged, tree-calf, hand-tooled, seven-dollar Friendship's Offering in the beginning of a paragraph, he shall not talk like a negro minstrel in the end of it. But this rule is flung down and danced upon in the *Deerslayer* tale.
8. They require that crass stupidities shall not be played upon the reader as "the craft of the woodsman, the delicate art of the forest," by either the author or the people in the tale. But this rule is persistently violated in the *Deerslayer* tale.
9. They require that the personages of a tale shall confine themselves to possibilities and let miracles alone; or, if they venture a miracle, the

author must so plausibly set it forth as to make it look possible and reasonable. But these rules are not respected in the *Deerslayer* tale.
10. They require that the author shall make the reader feel a deep interest in the personages of his tale and in their fate; and that he shall make the reader love the good people in the tale and hate the bad ones. But the reader of the *Deerslayer* tale dislikes the good people in it, is indifferent to the others, and wishes they would all get drowned together.
11. They require that the characters in a tale shall be so clearly defined that the reader can tell beforehand what each will do in a given emergency. But in the *Deerslayer* tale this rule is vacated.

In addition to these large rules there are some little ones. These require that the author shall

12. *Say* what he is proposing to say, not merely come near it.
13. Use the right word, not its second cousin.
14. Eschew surplusage.
15. Not omit necessary details.
16. Avoid slovenliness of form.
17. Use good grammar.
18. Employ a simple and straightforward style.

Even these seven are coldly and persistently violated in the *Deerslayer* tale. Cooper's gift in the way of invention was not a rich endowment; but such as it was he liked to work it, he was pleased with the effects, and indeed he did some quite sweet things with it. In his little box of stage-properties he kept six or eight cunning devices, tricks, artifices for his savages and woodsmen to deceive and circumvent each other with, and he was never so happy as when he was working these innocent things and seeing them go. A favorite one was to make a moccasined person tread in the tracks of the moccasined enemy, and thus hide his own trail. Cooper wore out barrels and barrels of moccasins in working that trick. Another stage-property that he pulled out of his box pretty frequently was his broken twig. He prized his broken twig above all the rest of his effects, and worked it the hardest. It is a restful chapter in any book of his when somebody doesn't step on a dry twig and alarm all the reds and whites for two hundred yards around. Every time a Cooper person is in peril, and absolute silence is worth four dollars a minute, he is sure to step on a dry twig. There may be a hundred handier things to step on, but that wouldn't satisfy Cooper. Cooper requires him to turn out and find a dry twig; and if he can't do it, go and borrow one. In fact, the Leather Stocking Series ought to have been called the Broken Twig Series.

5   I am sorry there is not room to put in a few dozen instances of the delicate art of the forest, as practiced by Natty Bumppo and some of the other Cooperian experts. Perhaps we may venture two or three samples. Cooper was a sailor—a naval officer; yet he gravely tells us how a vessel, driving toward a lee shore in a gale, is steered for a particular spot by her skipper because he knows of an *undertow* there which will hold her back against the gale and save her. For just pure woodcraft, or sailorcraft, or whatever it is, isn't that neat? For several years Cooper was daily in the society of artillery, and he ought to have noticed that when a cannon-ball strikes the ground it either buries itself or skips a hundred

feet or so; skips again a hundred feet or so—and so on, till finally it gets tired and rolls. Now in one place he loses some "females"—as he always calls women—in the edge of a wood near a plain at night in a fog, on purpose to give Bumppo a chance to show off the delicate art of the forest before the reader. These mislaid people are hunting for a fort. They hear a cannon-blast, and a cannon-ball presently comes rolling into the wood and stops at their feet. To the females this suggests nothing. The case is very different with the admirable Bumppo. I wish I may never know peace again if he doesn't strike out promptly and *follow the track* of that cannon-ball across the plain through the dense fog and find the fort. Isn't it a daisy? If Cooper had any real knowledge of Nature's ways of doing things, he had a most delicate art in concealing the fact. For instance: one of his acute Indian experts, Chingachgook (pronounced Chicago, I think), has lost the trail of a person he is tracking through the forest. Apparently that trail is hopelessly lost. Neither you nor I could have guessed out the way to find it. It was very different with Chicago. Chicago was not stumped for long. He turned a running stream out of its course, and there, in the slush in its old bed, were that person's moccasin-tracks. The current did not wash them away, as it would have done in all other cases—no, even the eternal laws of Nature have to vacate when Cooper wants to put up a delicate job of woodcraft on the reader.

We must be a little wary when Brander Matthews tells us that Cooper's books "reveal an extraordinary fulness of invention." As a rule, I am quite willing to accept Brander Matthews's literary judgments and applaud his lucid and graceful phrasing of them; but that particular statement needs to be taken with a few tons of salt. Bless your heart, Cooper hadn't any more invention than a horse; and I don't mean a high-class horse, either; I mean a clothes-horse. It would be very difficult to find a really clever "situation" in Cooper's books, and still more difficult to find one of any kind which he has failed to render absurd by his handling of it. Look at the episodes of "the caves"; and at the celebrated scuffle between Maqua and those others on the table-land a few days later; and at Hurry Harry's queer water-transit from the castle to the ark; and at Deerslayer's half-hour with his first corpse; and at the quarrel between Hurry Harry and Deerslayer later; and at—but choose for yourself; you can't go amiss.

If Cooper had been an observer his inventive faculty would have worked better; not more interestingly, but more rationally, more plausibly. Cooper's proudest creations in the way of "situations" suffer noticeably from the absence of the observer's protecting gift. Cooper's eye was splendidly inaccurate. Cooper seldom saw anything correctly. He saw nearly all things as through a glass eye, darkly. Of course a man who cannot see the commonest little everyday matters accurately is working at a disadvantage when he is constructing a "situation." In the *Deerslayer* tale Cooper has a stream which is fifty feet wide where it flows out of a lake; it presently narrows to twenty as it meanders along for no given reason, and yet when a stream acts like that it ought to be required to explain itself. Fourteen pages later the width of the brook's outlet from the lake has suddenly shrunk thirty feet, and become "the narrowest part of the stream." This shrinkage is not accounted for. The stream has bends in it, a sure indication that it has alluvial banks and cuts them; yet these bends are only thirty and fifty feet long. If Cooper had been a nice and punctilious observer he would have noticed that the bends were oftener nine hundred feet long than short of it.

Cooper made the exit of that stream fifty feet wide, in the first place, for no particular reason; in the second place, he narrowed it to less than twenty to accommodate some Indians. He bends a "sapling" to the form of an arch over this narrow-passage, and conceals six Indians in its foliage. They are "laying" for a settler's scow or ark which is coming up the stream on its way to the lake; it is being hauled against the stiff current by a rope whose stationary end is anchored in the lake; its rate of progress cannot be more than a mile an hour. Cooper describes the ark, but pretty obscurely. In the matter of dimensions "it was little more than a modern canal-boat." Let us guess, then, that it was about one hundred and forty feet long. It was of "greater breadth than common." Let us guess, then, that it was about sixteen feet wide. This leviathan had been prowling down bends which were but a third as long as itself, and scraping between banks where it had only two feet of space to spare on each side. We cannot too much admire this miracle. A low-roofed log dwelling occupies "two-thirds of the ark's length"—a dwelling ninety feet long and sixteen feet wide, let us say—a kind of vestibule train. The dwelling has two rooms—each forty-five feet long and sixteen feet wide, let us guess. One of them is the bedroom of the Hutter girls, Judith and Hetty; the other is the parlor in the daytime, at night it is papa's bedchamber. The ark is arriving at the stream's exit now, whose width has been reduced to less than twenty feet to accommodate the Indians—say to eighteen. There is a foot to spare on each side of the boat. Did the Indians notice that there was going to be a tight squeeze there? Did they notice that they could make money by climbing down out of that arched sapling and just stepping aboard when the ark scraped by? No, other Indians would have noticed these things, but Cooper's Indians never notice anything. Cooper thinks they are marvelous creatures for noticing, but he was almost always in error about his Indians. There was seldom a sane one among them.

The ark is one hundred and forty feet long; the dwelling is ninety feet long. The idea of the Indians is to drop softly and secretly from the arched sapling to the dwelling as the ark creeps along under it at the rate of a mile an hour, and butcher the family. It will take the ark a minute and a half to pass under. It will take the ninety-foot dwelling a minute to pass under. Now, then, what did the six Indians do? It would take you thirty years to guess, and even then you would have to give it up, I believe. Therefore, I will tell you what the Indians did. Their chief, a person of quite extraordinary intellect for a Cooper Indian, warily watched the canal-boat as it squeezed along under him, and when he had got his calculations fined down to exactly the right shade, as he judged, he let go and dropped. And *missed the house!* That is actually what he did. He missed the house, and landed in the stern of the scow. It was not much of a fall, yet it knocked him silly. He lay there unconscious. If the house had been ninety-seven feet long he would have made the trip. The fault was Cooper's, not his. The error lay in the construction of the house. Cooper was no architect.

10   There still remained in the roost five Indians. The boat has passed under and is now out of their reach. Let me explain what the five did—you would not be able to reason it out for yourself. No. 1 jumped for the boat, but fell in the water astern of it. Then No. 2 jumped for the boat, but fell in the water still farther astern of it. Then No. 3 jumped for the boat, and fell a good way astern of

it. Then No. 4 jumped for the boat, and fell in the water *away* astern. Then even No. 5 made a jump for the boat—for he was a Cooper Indian. In the matter of intellect, the difference between a Cooper Indian and the Indian that stands in front of the cigarshop is not spacious. The scow episode is really a sublime burst of invention; but it does not thrill, because the inaccuracy of the detail throws a sort of air of fictitiousness and general improbability over it. This comes of Cooper's inadequacy as an observer.

The reader will find some examples of Cooper's high talent for inaccurate observation in the account of the shooting-match in *The Pathfinder.*

> A common wrought nail was driven lightly into the target, its head having been first touched with paint.

The color of the paint is not stated—an important omission, but Cooper deals freely in important omissions. No, after all, it was not an important omission; for this nailhead is *a hundred yards from* the marksmen, and could not be seen by them at that distance, no matter what its color might be. How far can the best eyes see a common house-fly? A hundred yards? It is quite impossible. Very well; eyes that cannot see a house-fly that is a hundred yards away cannot see an ordinary nail head at that distance, for the size of the two objects is the same. It takes a keen eye to see a fly or a nail-head at fifty yards—one hundred and fifty feet. Can the reader do it?

The nail was lightly driven, its head painted, and game called. Then the Cooper miracles begin. The bullet of the first marksman chipped an edge of the nail-head; the next man's bullet drove the nail a little way into the target—and removed all the paint. Haven't the miracles gone far enough now? Not to suit Cooper; for the purpose of this whole scheme is to show off his prodigy, Deerslayer-Hawkeye-Long-Rifle-Leather-Stocking-Pathfinder-Bumppo before the ladies.

> "Be all ready to clench it, boys!" cried out Pathfinder, stepping into his friend's tracks the instant they were vacant. "Never mind a new nail; I can see that, though the paint is gone, and what I can see I can hit at a hundred yards, though it were only a mosquito's eye. Be ready to clench!"
>
> The rifle cracked, the bullet sped its way, and the head of the nail was buried in the wood, covered by the piece of flattened lead.

There, you see, is a man who could hunt flies with a rifle, and command a ducal salary in a Wild West show today if we had him back with us.

The recorded feat is certainly surprising just as it stands; but it is not surprising enough for Cooper. Cooper adds a touch. He has made Pathfinder do this miracle with another man's rifle; and not only that, but Pathfinder did not have even the advantage of loading it himself. He had everything against him, and yet he made that impossible shot; and not only made it, but did it with absolute confidence, saying, "Be ready to clench." Now a person like that would have undertaken that same feat with a brick-bat, and with Cooper to help he would have achieved it, too.

Pathfinder showed off handsomely that day before the ladies. His very first feat was a thing which no Wild West show can touch. He was standing with the group of marksmen, observing—a hundred yards from the target, mind; one Jasper raised his rifle and drove the center off the bull's-eye. Then the Quartermaster fired. The target exhibited no result this time. There was a laugh.

"It's a dead miss," said Major Lundie. Pathfinder waited an impressive moment or two; then said, in that calm, indifferent, know-it-all way of his, "No, Major, he has covered Jasper's bullet, as will be seen if anyone will take the trouble to examine the target."

Wasn't it remarkable! How *could* he see that little pellet fly through the air and enter that distant bullet-hole? Yet that is what he did; for nothing is impossible to a Cooper person. Did any of those people have any deep-seated doubts about this thing? No; for that would imply sanity, and these were all Cooper people.

> The respect for Pathfinder's skill and for his *quickness and accuracy of sight* [the italics are mine] was so profound and general, that the instant he made this declaration the spectators began to distrust their own opinions, and a dozen rushed to the target in order to ascertain the fact. There, sure enough, it was found that the Quartermaster's bullet had gone through the hole made by Jasper's, and that, too, so accurately as to require a minute examination to be certain of the circumstance, which, however, was soon clearly established by discovering one bullet over the other in the stump against which the target was placed.

They made a "minute" examination; but never mind, how could they know that there were two bullets in that hole without digging the latest one out? For neither probe nor eyesight could prove the presence of any more than one bullet. Did they dig? No; as we shall see. It is the Pathfinder's turn now; he steps out before the ladies, takes aim, and fires.

But, alas! here is a disappointment; an incredible, an unimaginable disappointment—for the target's aspect is unchanged; there is nothing there but that same old bullet-hole!

> "If one dared to hint at such a thing." cried Major Duncan, "I should say that the Pathfinder has also missed the target!"

20   As nobody had missed it yet, the "also" was not necessary; but never mind about that, for the Pathfinder is going to speak.

> "No, no, Major," said he, confidently, "that *would* be a risky declaration. I didn't load the piece, and can't say what was in it; but if it was lead, you will find the bullet driving down those of the Quartermaster and Jasper, else is not my name Pathfinder."
>
> A shout from the target announced the truth of this assertion.

Is the miracle sufficient as it stands? Not for Cooper. The Pathfinder speaks again, as he "now slowly advances towards the stage occupied by the females":

> "That's not all, boys, that's not all; if you find the target touched at all. I'll own to a miss. The Quartermaster cut the wood, but you'll find no wood cut by that last messenger."

The miracle is at last complete. He knew—doubtless *saw*—at the distance of a hundred yards—that his bullet had passed into the hole *without fraying the edges*. There were now three bullets in that one hole—three bullets embedded processionally in the body of the stump back of the target. Everybody knew this—somehow or other—and yet nobody had dug any of them out to make sure. Cooper is not a close observer, but he is interesting. He is certainly always that, no matter what happens. And he is more interesting when he is not noticing what he is about than when he is. This is a considerable merit.

The conversations in the Cooper books have a curious sound in our modern ears. To believe that such talk really ever came out of people's mouths would be to believe that there was a time when time was of no value to a person who thought he had something to say; when it was the custom to spread a two-minute remark out to ten; when a man's mouth was a rolling-mill, and busied itself all day long in turning four-foot pigs of thought into thirty-foot bars of conversational railroad iron by attenuation; when subjects were seldom faithfully stuck to, but the talk wandered all around and arrived nowhere; when conversations consisted mainly of irrelevancies, with here and there a relevancy, a relevancy with an embarrassed look, as not being able to explain how it got there.

Cooper was certainly not a master in the construction of dialogue. Inaccurate observation defeated him here as it defeated him in so many other enterprises of his. He even failed to notice that the man who talks corrupt English six days in the week must and will talk it on the seventh, and can't help himself. In the *Deerslayer* story he lets Deerslayer talk the showiest kind of book-talk sometimes, and at other times the basest of base dialects. For instance, when someone asks him if he has a sweetheart, and if so, where she abides, this is his majestic answer:

> "She's in the forest—hanging from the boughs of the trees, in a soft rain—in the dew on the open grass—the clouds that float about in the blue heavens—the birds that sing in the woods—the sweet springs where I slake my thirst—and in all the other glorious gifts that come from God's Providence!"

25 And he preceded that, a little before, with this:

> "It consarns me as all things that touches a fri'nd consarns a fri'nd."

And this is another of his remarks:

> "If I was Injin born, now, I might tell of this, or carry in the scalp and boast of the expl'ite afore the whole tribe; or if my inimy had only been a bear"

—and so on.

We cannot imagine such a thing as a veteran Scotch Commander-in-Chief comporting himself in the field like a windy melodramatic actor, but Cooper could. On one occasion Alice and Cora were being chased by the French through a fog in the neighborhood of their father's fort:

> "*Point de quartier aux coquins!*" cried an eager pursuer, who seemed to direct the operations of the enemy.
>
> "Stand firm and be ready, my gallant 60ths!" suddenly exclaimed a voice above them; "wait to see the enemy; fire low, and sweep the glacis."
>
> "Father! father!" exclaimed a piercing cry from out the mist; "it is I! Alice! thy own Elsie! spare, O! save your daughters!"
>
> "Hold!" should the former speaker, in the awful tones of parental agony, the sound reaching even to the woods, and rolling back in solemn echo. "'Tis she! God has restored me my children! Throw open the sally-port; to the field, 60ths, to the field! pull not a trigger, lest ye kill my lambs! Drive off these dogs of France with your steel!"

Cooper's word-sense was singularly dull. When a person has a poor ear for music he will flat and sharp right along without knowing it. He keeps near the tune, but it is *not* the tune. When a person has a poor ear for words, the result is a literary flatting and sharping; you perceive what he is intending to say, but you also perceive that he doesn't *say* it. This is Cooper. He was not a word-musician. His ear was satisfied with the *approximate* word. I will furnish some circumstantial evidence in support of this charge. My instances are gathered from half a dozen pages of the tale called *Deerslayer*. He uses "verbal," for "oral"; "precision," for "facility"; "phenomena," for "marvels"; "necessary," for "predetermined"; "unsophisticated," for "primitive"; "preparation," for "expectancy"; "rebuked," for "subdued"; "dependent on," for "resulting from"; "fact," for "condition"; "fact," for "conjecture"; "precaution," for "caution"; "explain," for "determine"; "mortified," for "disappointed"; "meretricious," for "factitious"; "materially," for "considerably"; "decreasing," for "deepening"; "increasing," for "disappearing"; "embedded," for "enclosed"; "treacherous," for "hostile"; "stood," for "stooped"; "softened," for "replaced"; "rejoined," for "remarked"; "situation," for "condition"; "different," for "differing"; "insensible," for "unsentient"; "brevity," for "celerity"; "distrusted," for "suspicious"; "mental imbecility," for "imbecility"; "eyes," for "sight"; "counteracting," for "opposing"; "funeral obsequies," for "obsequies."

There have been daring people in the world who claimed that Cooper could write English, but they are all dead now—all dead but Lounsbury. I don't remember that Lounsbury makes the claim in so many words, still he makes it, for he says that *Deerslayer* is a "pure work of art." Pure, in that connection, means faultless—faultless in all details—and language is a detail. If Mr. Lounsbury had only compared Cooper's English with the English which he writes himself—but it is plain that he didn't; and so it is likely that he imagines until this day that Cooper's is as clean and compact as his own. Now I feel sure, deep down in my heart, that Cooper wrote about the poorest English that exists in our language, and that the English of *Deerslayer* is the very worst that even Cooper ever wrote.

I may be mistaken, but it does seem to me that *Deerslayer* is not a work of art in any sense; it does seem to me that it is destitute of every detail that goes to the making of a work of art; in truth, it seems to me that *Deerslayer* is just simply a literary *delirium tremens*.

30   A work of art? It has no invention; it has no order, system, sequence, or result; it has no lifelikeness, no thrill, no stir, no seeming of reality; its characters are confusedly drawn, and by their acts and words they prove that they are not the sort of people the author claims that they are; its humor is pathetic; its pathos is funny; its conventions are—oh! indescribable; its love-scenes odious; its English a crime against the language.

Counting these out, what is left is Art. I think we must all admit that.

Questions for Discussion

1. Do you have to be familiar with Cooper's novels in order to appreciate this review or consider it convincing? Explain your answer.
2. How does the author establish his credibility as a reviewer? Cite specific passages to support your answer.
3. This essay is adversarial persuasion. Why do you think the author chooses this way to write his review? How would this review differ if it were conciliatory persuasion? What particular changes would be necessary?

4. Would this review have more or less impact without the final paragraph? Explain your answer.
5. Notice the author's use of exaggeration (e.g., "needs to be taken with a few tons of salt"), oxymoron (e.g., "splendidly inaccurate"), and understatement (e.g., "Cooper's art has some defects"). How often does the author use each of these techniques? Why? What do these techniques contribute to the review?

Opportunities for Writing

1. Write a review of James Fenimore Cooper's *Last of the Mohicans*. In your review, emphasize Cooper's writing ability. Decide if you think he is as terrible a writer as Mark Twain claims. Do library research to identify literary critics who support your position. Aim your review at college students who have never read this book. Tell them why they should or shouldn't read it.
2. Write a review of a novel you genuinely disliked reading. Why did you dislike this novel? Who does like it? Why? Address your evaluation to the individual (e.g., a teacher or friend) who asked you to read this novel.
3. Write a review of Mark Twain's *The Adventures of Tom Sawyer*, *The Prince and the Pauper*, *The Adventures of Huckleberry Finn*, or *A Connecticut Yankee in King Arthur's Court*. In your review, consider Twain's 18 rules of fiction. Does he obey or violate the rules?

Letter from Birmingham Jail

MARTIN LUTHER KING, JR.

Born in Atlanta, Georgia, Martin Luther King, Jr. (1929–1968) was a Baptist minister and civil rights leader. King attended Morehouse College, Crozer Theological Seminary, and Boston University, where he earned his doctorate in systematic theology. A powerful orator, King was a guiding force in the passage of the Civil Rights Act (1964), which called for desegregation in schools, and of the Voting Rights Act (1966), which helped African Americans exercise their right to vote without impediment. One of his most memorable speeches was delivered in August 1963 at the Lincoln Memorial in Washington, D.C. Known as his "I Have a Dream" speech, it served to motivate and mobilize civil rights efforts in the United States. In 1964, King won the Nobel Peace Prize.

"Letter from Birmingham Jail" was written on April 16, 1963, four months before he made his famous address in Washington. King wrote in response to a letter written by eight Alabama clergymen and published in Birmingham newspapers on April 12, calling for "Negro citizens" to stop their "unwise and untimely" demonstrations; both letters are reprinted here. "Injustice anywhere is a threat to justice everywhere," writes King.

We the undersigned clergymen are among those who, in January, issued "An Appeal for Law and Order and Common Sense," in dealing with racial problems in Alabama. We expressed understanding that honest convictions in racial matters could properly be pursued in the courts, but urged that decisions of those courts should in the meantime be peacefully obeyed.

Since that time there has been some evidence of increased forbearance and a willingness to face facts. Responsible citizens have undertaken to work on various problems which cause racial friction and unrest. In Birmingham, recent public events have given indication that we all have opportunity for a new constructive and realistic approach to racial problems.

However, we are now confronted by a series of demonstrations by some of our Negro citizens, directed and led in part by outsiders. We recognize the natural impatience of people who feel that their hopes are slow in being realized. But we are convinced that these demonstrations are unwise and untimely.

We agree rather with certain local Negro leadership which has called for honest and open negotiation of racial issues in our area. And we believe this kind of facing of issues can best be accomplished by citizens of our own metropolitan area, white and Negro, meeting with their knowledge and experience of the local situation. All of us need to face that responsibility and find proper channels for its accomplishment.

Just as we formerly pointed out that "hatred and violence have no sanction in our religious and political traditions," we also point out that such actions as incite to hatred and violence, however technically peaceful those actions may be, have not contributed to the resolution of our local problems. We do not believe these days of new hope are days when extreme measures are justified in Birmingham.

We commend the community as a whole, and the local news media and law enforcement officials in particular, on the calm manner in which these demonstrations have been handled. We urge the public to continue to show restraint should the demonstrations continue, and the law enforcement officials to remain calm and continue to protect our city from violence.

We further strongly urge our own Negro community to withdraw support from these demonstrations, and to unite locally in working peacefully for a better Birmingham. When rights are consistently denied, a cause should be pressed in the courts and in negotiations among local leaders, and not in the streets. We appeal to both our white and Negro citizenry to observe the principles of law and order and common sense.

Signed by:

C. C. J. Carpenter, D.D., LL.D., *Bishop of Alabama*
Joseph A. Durick, D.D., *Auxiliary Bishop, Diocese of Mobile, Birmingham*
Rabbi Milton L. Grafman, *Temple Emanu-El, Birmingham, Alabama*
Bishop Paul Hardin, *Bishop of the Alabama-West Florida Conference of the Methodist Church*
Bishop Nolan B. Harmon, *Bishop of the North Alabama Conference of the Methodist Church*
George M. Murray, D.D., LL.D., *Bishop Coadjutor, Episcopal Diocese of Alabama*

Edward V. Ramage, *Moderator, Synod of the Alabama Presbyterian Church in the United States*
Earl Stallings, *Pastor, First Baptist Church, Birmingham, Alabama*

April 16, 1963

My Dear Fellow Clergymen:

While confined here in the Birmingham city jail, I came across your recent statement calling my present activities "unwise and untimely." Seldom do I pause to answer criticism of my work and ideas. If I sought to answer all the criticisms that cross my desk, my secretaries would have little time for anything other than such correspondence in the course of the day, and I would have no time for constructive work. But since I feel that you are men of genuine good will and that your criticisms are sincerely set forth, I want to try to answer your statement in what I hope will be patient and reasonable terms.

I think I should indicate why I am here in Birmingham, since you have been influenced by the view which argues against "outsiders coming in." I have the honor of serving as president of the Southern Christian Leadership Conference, an organization operating in every southern state, with headquarters in Atlanta, Georgia. We have some eighty-five affiliated organizations across the South, and one of them is the Alabama Christian Movement for Human Rights. Frequently we share staff, educational and financial resources with our affiliates. Several months ago the affiliate here in Birmingham asked us to be on call to engage in a nonviolent direct-action program if such were deemed necessary. We readily consented, and when the hour came we lived up to our promise. So I, along with several members of my staff, am here because I was invited here. I am here because I have organizational ties here.

But more basically, I am in Birmingham because injustice is here. Just as the prophets of the eighth century B.C. left their villages and carried their "thus saith the Lord" far beyond the boundaries of their home towns, and just as the Apostle Paul left his village of Tarsus and carried the gospel of Jesus Christ to the far corners of the Greco-Roman world, so am I compelled to carry the gospel of freedom beyond my own home town. Like Paul, I must constantly respond to the Macedonian call for aid.

Moreover, I am cognizant of the interrelatedness of all communities and states. I cannot sit idly by in Atlanta and not be concerned about what happens in Birmingham. Injustice anywhere is a threat to justice everywhere. We are caught in an inescapable network of mutuality, tied in a single garment of destiny. Whatever affects one directly, affects all indirectly. Never again can we afford to live with the narrow, provincial "outside agitator" idea. Anyone who lives inside the United States can never be considered an outsider anywhere within its bounds.

You deplore the demonstrations taking place in Birmingham. But your statement, I am sorry to say, fails to express a similar concern for the conditions that brought about the demonstrations. I am sure that none of you would want to rest content with the superficial kind of social analysis that deals merely with effects and does not grapple with underlying causes. It is unfortunate that demonstrations are taking place in Birmingham, but it is even more unfortunate that the city's white power structure left the Negro community with no alternative.

In any nonviolent campaign there are four basic steps: collection of the facts to determine whether injustices exist; negotiation; self-purification; and direct action. We have gone through all these steps in Birmingham. There can be no gainsaying the fact that racial injustice engulfs this community. Birmingham is probably the most thoroughly segregated city in the United States. Its ugly record of brutality is widely known. Negroes have experienced grossly unjust treatment in the courts. There have been more unsolved bombings of Negro homes and churches in Birmingham than in any other city in the nation. These are the hard, brutal facts of the case. On the basis of these conditions, Negro leaders sought to negotiate with the city fathers. But the latter consistently refused to engage in good-faith negotiation.

Then, last September, came the opportunity to talk with leaders of Birmingham's economic community. In the course of the negotiations, certain promises were made by the merchants—for example, to remove the stores' humiliating racial signs. On the basis of these promises, the Reverend Fred Shuttlesworth and the leaders of the Alabama Christian Movement for Human Rights agreed to a moratorium on all demonstrations. As the weeks and months went by, we realized that we were the victims of a broken promise. A few signs, briefly removed, returned; the others remained.

As in so many past experiences, our hopes had been blasted, and the shadow of deep disappointment settled upon us. We had no alternative except to prepare for direct action, whereby we would present our very bodies as a means of laying our cases before the conscience of the local and the national community. Mindful of the difficulties involved, we decided to undertake a process of self-purification. We began a series of workshops on nonviolence, and we repeatedly asked ourselves: "Are you able to accept blows without retaliating?" "Are you able to endure the ordeal of jail?" We decided to schedule our direct-action program for the Easter season, realizing that except for Christmas, this is the main shopping period of the year. Knowing that a strong economic-withdrawal program would be the by-product of direct action, we felt that this would be the best time to bring pressure to bear on the merchants for the needed change.

Then it occurred to us that Birmingham's mayoral election was coming up in March, and we speedily decided to postpone action until after election day. When we discovered that the Commissioner of Public Safety, Eugene "Bull" Connor, had piled up enough votes to be in the run-off we decided again to postpone action until the day after the run-off so that the demonstrations could not be used to cloud the issues. Like many others, we waited to see Mr. Connor defeated, and to this end we endured postponement after postponement. Having aided in this community need, we felt that our direct-action program could be delayed no longer.

10   You may well ask: "Why direct action? Why sit-ins, marches and so forth? Isn't negotiation a better path?" You are quite right in calling for negotiation. Indeed, this is the very purpose of direct action. Nonviolent direct action seeks to create such a crisis and foster such a tension that a community which has constantly refused to negotiate is forced to confront the issue. It seeks so to dramatize the issue that it can no longer be ignored. My citing the creation of tension as part of the work of the nonviolent-resister may sound rather shocking.

But I must confess that I am not afraid of the word "tension." I have earnestly opposed violent tension, but there is a type of constructive, nonviolent tension which is necessary for growth. Just as Socrates felt that it was necessary to create a tension in the mind so that individuals could rise from the bondage of myths and half-truths to the unfettered realm of creative analysis and objective appraisal, so must we see the need for nonviolent gadflies to create the kind of tension in society that will help men rise from the dark depths of prejudice and racism to the majestic heights of understanding and brotherhood.

The purpose of our direct-action program is to create a situation so crisis-packed that it will inevitably open the door to negotiation. I therefore concur with you in your call for negotiation. Too long has our beloved Southland been bogged down in a tragic effort to live in monologue rather than dialogue.

One of the basic points in your statement is that the action that I and my associates have taken in Birmingham is untimely. Some have asked: "Why didn't you give the new city administration time to act?" The only answer that I can give to this query is that the new Birmingham administration must be prodded about as much as the outgoing one, before it will act. We are sadly mistaken if we feel that the election of Albert Boutwell as mayor will bring the millennium to Birmingham. While Mr. Boutwell is a much more gentle person than Mr. Connor, they are both segregationists, dedicated to maintenance of the status quo. I have hope that Mr. Boutwell will be reasonable enough to see the futility of massive resistance to desegregation. But he will not see this without pressure from devotees of civil rights. My friends, I must say to you that we have not made a single gain in civil rights without determined legal and nonviolent pressure. Lamentably, it is an historical fact that privileged groups seldom give up their privileges voluntarily. Individuals may see the moral light and voluntarily give up their unjust posture; but, as Reinhold Niebuhr has reminded us, groups tend to be more immoral than individuals.

We know through painful experience that freedom is never voluntarily given by the oppressor; it must be demanded by the oppressed. Frankly, I have yet to engage in a direct-action campaign that was "well timed" in the view of those who have not suffered unduly from the disease of segregation. For years now I have heard the word "Wait!" It rings in the ear of every Negro with piercing familiarity. This "Wait" has almost always meant "Never." We must come to see, with one of our distinguished jurists, that "justice too long delayed is justice denied."

We have waited for more than 340 years for our constitutional and God-given rights. The nations of Asia and Africa are moving with jetlike speed toward gaining political independence, but we still creep at horse-and-buggy pace toward gaining a cup of coffee at a lunch counter. Perhaps it is easy for those who have never felt the stinging darts of segregation to say, "Wait." But when you have seen vicious mobs lynch your mothers and fathers at will and drown your sisters and brothers at whim; when you have seen hate-filled policemen curse, kick and even kill your black brothers and sisters; when you see the vast majority of your twenty million Negro brothers smothering in an airtight cage of poverty in the midst of an affluent society; when you suddenly find your tongue twisted and your speech stammering as you seek to explain to your six-year-old daughter why she can't go to the public amusement park that has just been advertised on television, and see tears welling up in her eyes when she is told that Funtown is closed to colored children, and see ominous clouds of inferiority beginning to form in her little mental sky, and see her beginning to distort her personality by developing an unconscious bitterness toward white people; when you have to concoct an answer for a five-year-old son who is asking: "Daddy, why do white people treat colored people so mean?"; when you take a cross-country drive and find it necessary to sleep night after night in the uncomfortable corners of your automobile because no motel will accept you; when you are humiliated day in and day out by nagging signs reading "white" and "colored"; when your first name becomes "nigger," your middle name becomes "boy" (however old you are) and your last name becomes "John," and your wife and mother are never given the respected title "Mrs."; when you are harried by day and haunted by night by the fact that you are a Negro, living constantly at tiptoe stance, never quite knowing what to expect next, and are plagued with inner fears and outer resentments; when you are forever fighting a degenerating sense of "nobodiness"—then you will understand why we find it difficult to wait. There comes a time when the cup of endurance runs over, and men are no longer willing to be plunged into the abyss of despair. I hope, sirs, you can understand our legitimate and unavoidable impatience.

15 You express a great deal of anxiety over our willingness to break laws. This is certainly a legitimate concern. Since we so diligently urge people to obey the Supreme Court's decision of 1954 outlawing segregation in the public schools, at first glance it may seem rather paradoxical for us consciously to break laws. One may well ask: "How can you advocate breaking some laws and obeying others?" The answer lies in the fact that there are two types of laws: just and unjust. I would be the first to advocate obeying just laws. One has not only a legal but a moral responsibility to obey just laws. Conversely, one has a moral responsibility to disobey unjust laws. I would agree with St. Augustine that "an unjust law is no law at all."

Now, what is the difference between the two? How does one determine whether a law is just or unjust? A just law is a man-made code that squares with the moral law or the law of God. An unjust law is a code that is out of harmony with the moral law. To put it in the terms of St. Thomas Aquinas: An unjust law is a human law that is not rooted in eternal law and natural law. Any law that uplifts human personality is just. Any law that degrades human personality is unjust. All segregation statutes are unjust because segregation distorts the soul and damages the personality. It gives the segregator a false sense of superiority and the segregated a false sense of inferiority. Segregation, to use the terminology of the Jewish philosopher Martin Buber, substitutes an "I–it" relationship for an "I–thou" relationship and ends up relegating persons to the status of things. Hence, segregation is not only politically, economically and sociologically unsound, it is morally wrong and sinful. Paul Tillich has said that sin is separation. Is not segregation an existential expression of man's tragic separation, his awful estrangement, his terrible sinfulness? Thus it is that I can urge men to obey the 1954 decision of the Supreme Court, for it is morally right; and I can urge them to disobey segregation ordinances, for they are morally wrong.

Let us consider a more concrete example of just and unjust laws. An unjust law is a code that a numerical or power majority group compels a minority group to obey but does not make binding on itself. This is *difference* made legal.

By the same token, a just law is a code that a majority compels a minority to follow and that it is willing to follow itself. This is *sameness* made legal.

Let me give another explanation. A law is unjust if it is inflicted on a minority that, as a result of being denied the right to vote, had no part in enacting or devising the law. Who can say that the legislature of Alabama which set up that state's segregation laws was democratically elected? Throughout Alabama all sorts of devious methods are used to prevent Negroes from becoming registered voters, and there are some counties in which, even though Negroes constitute a majority of the population, not a single Negro is registered. Can any law enacted under such circumstances be considered democratically structured?

Sometimes a law is just on its face and unjust in its application. For instance, I have been arrested on a charge of parading without a permit. Now, there is nothing wrong in having an ordinance which requires a permit for a parade. But such an ordinance becomes unjust when it is used to maintain segregation and to deny citizens the First-Amendment privilege of peaceful assembly and protest.

20   I hope you are able to see the distinction I am trying to point out. In no sense do I advocate evading or defying the law, as would the rabid segregationist. That would lead to anarchy. One who breaks an unjust law must do so openly, lovingly, and with a willingness to accept the penalty. I submit that an individual who breaks a law that conscience tells him is unjust, and who willingly accepts the penalty of imprisonment in order to arouse the conscience of the community over its injustice, is in reality expressing the highest respect for law.

Of course, there is nothing new about this kind of civil disobedience. It was evidenced sublimely in the refusal of Shadrach, Meshach and Abednego to obey the laws of Nebuchadnezzar, on the ground that a higher moral law was at stake. It was practiced superbly by the early Christians, who were willing to face hungry lions and the excruciating pain of chopping blocks rather than submit to certain unjust laws of the Roman Empire. To a degree, academic freedom is a reality today because Socrates practiced civil disobedience. In our own nation, the Boston Tea Party represented a massive act of civil disobedience.

We should never forget that everything Adolf Hitler did in Germany was "legal" and everything the Hungarian freedom fighters did in Hungary was "illegal." It was "illegal" to aid and comfort a Jew in Hitler's Germany. Even so, I am sure that, had I lived in Germany at the time, I would have aided and comforted my Jewish brothers. If today I lived in a Communist country where certain principles dear to the Christian faith are suppressed, I would openly advocate disobeying that country's antireligious laws.

I must make two honest confessions to you, my Christian and Jewish brothers. First, I must confess that over the past few years I have been gravely disappointed with the white moderate. I have almost reached the regrettable conclusion that the Negro's great stumbling block in his stride toward freedom is not the White Citizen's Councilor or the Ku Klux Klanner, but the white moderate, who is more devoted to "order" than to justice; who prefers a negative peace which is the absence of tension to a positive peace which is the presence of justice; who constantly says: "I agree with you in the goal you seek, but I cannot agree with your methods of direct action"; who paternalistically believes he can set the timetable for another man's freedom; who lives by a mythical concept of time and who constantly advises the Negro to wait for a "more convenient season." Shallow understanding from people of good will is more frustrating than absolute misunderstanding from people of ill will. Lukewarm acceptance is much more bewildering than outright rejection.

I had hoped that the white moderate would understand that law and order exist for the purpose of establishing justice and that when they fail in this purpose they become the dangerously structured dams that block the flow of social progress. I had hoped that the white moderate would understand that the present tension in the South is a necessary phase of the transition from an obnoxious negative peace, in which the Negro passively accepted his unjust plight, to a substantive and positive peace, in which all men will respect the dignity and worth of human personality. Actually, we who engage in nonviolent direct action are not the creators of tension. We merely bring to the surface the hidden tension that is already alive. We bring it out in the open, where it can be seen and dealt with. Like a boil that can never be cured so long as it is covered up but must be opened with all its ugliness to the natural medicines of air and light, injustice must be exposed, with all the tension its exposure creates, to the light of human conscience and the air of national opinion before it can be cured.

25 In your statement you assert that our actions, even though peaceful, must be condemned because they precipitate violence. But is this a logical assertion? Isn't this like condemning a robbed man because his possession of money precipitated the evil act of robbery? Isn't this like condemning Socrates because his unswerving commitment to truth and his philosophical inquiries precipitated the act by the misguided populace in which they made him drink hemlock? Isn't this like condemning Jesus because his unique God-consciousness and never-ceasing devotion to God's will precipitated the evil act of crucifixion? We must come to see that, as the federal courts have consistently affirmed, it is wrong to urge an individual to cease his efforts to gain his basic constitutional rights because the quest may precipitate violence. Society must protect the robbed and punish the robber.

I had also hoped that the white moderate would reject the myth concerning time in relation to the struggle for freedom. I have just received a letter from a white brother in Texas. He writes: "All Christians know that the colored people will receive equal rights eventually, but it is possible that you are in too great a religious hurry. It has taken Christianity almost two thousand years to accomplish what it has. The teachings of Christ take time to come to earth." Such an attitude stems from a tragic misconception of time, from the strangely irrational notion that there is something in the very flow of time that will inevitably cure all ills. Actually, time itself is neutral; it can be used either destructively or constructively. More and more I feel that the people of ill will have used time much more effectively than have the people of good will. We will have to repent in this generation not merely for the hateful words and actions of the bad people but for the appalling silence of the good people. Human progress never rolls in on wheels of inevitability; it comes through the tireless efforts of men willing to be co-workers with God, and without this hard work, time itself becomes an ally of the forces of social stagnation. We must use time creatively, in the knowledge that the time is always ripe to do right. Now is the time to make real the promise of democracy and transform our pending national elegy into a creative psalm of brotherhood. Now is the time to lift our national policy from the quicksand of racial injustice to the solid rock of human dignity.

You speak of our activity in Birmingham as extreme. At first I was rather disappointed that fellow clergymen would see my nonviolent efforts as those of an extremist. I began thinking about the fact that I stand in the middle of two opposing forces in the Negro community. One is a force of complacency, made up in part of Negroes who, as a result of long years of oppression, are so drained of self-respect and a sense of "somebodiness" that they have adjusted to segregation; and in part of a few middle-class Negroes who, because of a degree of academic and economic security and because in some ways they profit by segregation, have become insensitive to the problems of the masses. The other force is one of bitterness and hatred, and it comes perilously close to advocating violence. It is expressed in the various black nationalist groups that are springing up across the nation, the largest and best-known being Elijah Muhammad's Muslim movement. Nourished by the Negro's frustration over the continued existence of racial discrimination, this movement is made up of people who have lost faith in America, who have absolutely repudiated Christianity, and who have concluded that the white man is an incorrigible "devil."

I have tried to stand between these two forces, saying that we need emulate neither the "do-nothingism" of the complacent nor the hatred and despair of the black nationalist. For there is the more excellent way of love and nonviolent protest. I am grateful to God that, through the influence of the Negro church, the way of nonviolence became an integral part of our struggle.

If this philosophy had not emerged, by now many streets of the South would, I am convinced, be flowing with blood. And I am further convinced that if our white brothers dismiss as "rabble-rousers" and "outside agitators" those of us who employ nonviolent direct action, and if they refuse to support our nonviolent efforts, millions of Negroes will, out of frustration and despair, seek solace and security in black-nationalist ideologies—a development that would inevitably lead to a frightening racial nightmare.

30 Oppressed people cannot remain oppressed forever. The yearning for freedom eventually manifests itself, and that is what has happened to the American Negro. Something within has reminded him of his birthright of freedom, and something without has reminded him that it can be gained. Consciously or unconsciously, he has been caught up by the *Zeitgeist,* and with his black brothers of Africa and his brown and yellow brothers of Asia, South America and the Caribbean, the United States Negro is moving with a sense of great urgency toward the promised land of racial justice. If one recognizes this vital urge that has engulfed the Negro community, one should readily understand why public demonstrations are taking place. The Negro has many pent-up resentments and latent frustrations, and he must release them. So let him march; let him make prayer pilgrimages to the city hall; let him go on freedom rides—and try to understand why he must do so. If his repressed emotions are not released in nonviolent ways, they will seek expression through violence; this is not a threat but a fact of history. So I have not said to my people: "Get rid of your discontent." Rather, I have tried to say that this normal and healthy discontent can be channeled into the creative outlet of nonviolent direct action. And now this approach is being termed extremist.

But though I was initially disappointed at being categorized as an extremist, as I continued to think about the matter I gradually gained a measure of satisfaction from the label. Was not Jesus an extremist for love: "Love your enemies, bless them that curse you, do good to them that hate you, and pray for them which despitefully use you, and persecute you." Was not Amos an extremist for justice: "Let justice roll down like waters and righteousness like an everflowing stream." Was not Paul an extremist for the Christian gospel: "I bear in my body the marks of the Lord Jesus." Was not Martin Luther an extremist: "Here I stand; I cannot do otherwise, so help me God." And John Bunyan: "I will stay in jail to the end of my days before I make a butchery of my conscience." And Abraham Lincoln: "This nation cannot survive half slave and half free." And Thomas Jefferson: "We hold these truths to be self-evident, that all men are created equal. . . ." So the question is not whether we will be extremists, but what kind of extremists we will be. Will we be extremists for hate or for love? Will we be extremists for the preservation of injustice or for the extension of justice? In that dramatic scene on Calvary's hill three men were crucified. We must never forget that all three were crucified for the same crime—the crime of extremism. Two were extremists for immorality, and thus fell below their environment. The other, Jesus Christ, was an extremist for love, truth and goodness, and thereby rose above his environment. Perhaps the South, the nation and the world are in dire need of creative extremists.

I had hoped that the white moderate would see this need. Perhaps I was too optimistic; perhaps I expected too much. I suppose I should have realized that few members of the oppressor race can understand the deep groans and passionate yearnings of the oppressed race, and still fewer have the vision to see that injustice must be rooted out by strong, persistent and determined action. I am thankful, however, that some of our white brothers in the South have grasped the meaning of this social revolution and committed themselves to it. They are still all too few in quantity, but they are big in quality. Some—such as Ralph McGill, Lillian Smith, Harry Golden, James McBride Dabbs, Ann Braden and Sarah Patton Boyle—have written about our struggle in eloquent and prophetic terms. Others have marched with us down nameless streets of the South. They have languished in filthy, roach-infested jails, suffering the abuse and brutality of policemen who view them as "dirty nigger-lovers." Unlike so many of their moderate brothers and sisters, they have recognized the urgency of the moment and sensed the need for powerful "action" antidotes to combat the disease of segregation.

Let me take note of my other major disappointment. I have been so greatly disappointed with the white church and its leadership. Of course, there are some notable exceptions. I am not unmindful of the fact that each of you has taken some significant stands on this issue. I commend you, Reverend Stallings, for your Christian stand on this past Sunday, in welcoming Negroes to your worship service on a nonsegregated basis. I commend the Catholic leaders of this state for integrating Spring Hill College several years ago.

But despite these notable exceptions, I must honestly reiterate that I have been disappointed with the church. I do not say this as one of those negative critics who can always find something wrong with the church. I say this as a minister of the gospel, who loves the church; who was nurtured in its bosom;

who has been sustained by its spiritual blessings and who will remain true to it as long as the cord of life shall lengthen.

When I was suddenly catapulted into the leadership of the bus protest in Montgomery, Alabama, a few years ago, I felt we would be supported by the white church. I felt that the white ministers, priests and rabbis of the South would be among our strongest allies. Instead, some have been outright opponents, refusing to understand the freedom movement and misrepresenting its leaders: all too many others have been more cautious than courageous and have remained silent behind the anesthetizing security of stained-glass windows.

In spite of my shattered dreams, I came to Birmingham with the hope that the white religious leadership of this community would see the justice of our cause and, with deep moral concern, would serve as the channel through which our just grievances could reach the power structure. I had hoped that each of you would understand. But again I have been disappointed.

I have heard numerous southern religious leaders admonish their worshipers to comply with a desegregation decision because it is the law, but I have longed to hear white ministers declare: "Follow this decree because integration is morally right and because the Negro is your brother." In the midst of blatant injustices inflicted upon the Negro, I have watched white churchmen stand on the sideline and mouth pious irrelevancies and sanctimonious trivialities. In the midst of a mighty struggle to rid our nation of racial and economic injustice, I have heard many ministers say: "Those are social issues, with which the gospel has no real concern." And I have watched many churches commit themselves to a completely otherworldly religion which makes a strange, un-Biblical distinction between body and soul, between the sacred and the secular.

I have traveled the length and breadth of Alabama, Mississippi and all the other southern states. On sweltering summer days and crisp autumn mornings I have looked at the South's beautiful churches with their lofty spires pointing heavenward. I have beheld the impressive outlines of her massive religious-education buildings. Over and over I have found myself asking: "What kind of people worship here? Who is their God? Where were their voices when the lips of Governor Barnett dripped with words of interposition and nullification? Where were they when Governor Wallace gave a clarion call for defiance and hatred? Where were their voices of support when bruised and weary Negro men and women decided to rise from the dark dungeons of complacency to the bright hills of creative protest?"

Yes, these questions are still in my mind. In deep disappointment I have wept over the laxity of the church. But be assured that my tears have been tears of love. There can be no deep disappointment where there is not deep love. Yes, I love the church. How could I do otherwise? I am in the rather unique position of being the son, the grandson and the greatgrandson of preachers. Yes, I see the church as the body of Christ. But, oh! How we have blemished and scarred that body through social neglect and through fear of being nonconformists.

There was a time when the church was very powerful—in the time when the early Christians rejoiced at being deemed worthy to suffer for what they believed. In those days the church was not merely a thermometer that recorded the ideas and principles of popular opinion; it was a thermostat that transformed the mores of society. Whenever the early Christians entered a town, the people in power became disturbed and immediately sought to convict the Christians for being "disturbers of the peace" and "outside agitators." But the Christians pressed on, in the conviction that they were "a colony of heaven," called to obey God rather than man. Small in number, they were big in commitment. They were too God-intoxicated to be "astronomically intimidated." By their effort and example they brought an end to such ancient evils as infanticide and gladiatorial contests.

Things are different now. So often the contemporary church is a weak, ineffectual voice with an uncertain sound. So often it is an archdefender of the status quo. Far from being disturbed by the presence of the church, the power structure of the average community is consoled by the church's silent—and often even vocal—sanction of things as they are.

But the judgment of God is upon the church as never before. If today's church does not recapture the sacrificial spirit of the early church, it will lose its authenticity, forfeit the loyalty of millions, and be dismissed as an irrelevant social club with no meaning for the twentieth century. Every day I meet young people whose disappointment with the church has turned into outright disgust.

Perhaps I have once again been too optimistic. Is organized religion too inextricably bound to the status quo to save our nation and the world? Perhaps I must turn my faith to the inner spiritual church, the church within the church, as the true *ekklesia* and the hope of the world. But again I am thankful to God that some noble souls from the ranks of organized religion have broken loose from the paralyzing chains of conformity and joined us as active partners in the struggle for freedom. They have left their secure congregations and walked the streets of Albany, Georgia, with us. They have gone down the highways of the South on tortuous rides for freedom. Yes, they have gone to jail with us. Some have been dismissed from their churches, have lost the support of their bishops and fellow ministers. But they have acted in the faith that right defeated is stronger than evil triumphant. Their witness has been the spiritual salt that has preserved the true meaning of the gospel in these troubled times. They have carved a tunnel of hope through the dark mountain of disappointment.

I hope the church as a whole will meet the challenge of this decisive hour. But even if the church does not come to the aid of justice, I have no despair about the future. I have no fear about the outcome of our struggle in Birmingham, even if our motives are at present misunderstood. We will reach the goal of freedom in Birmingham and all over the nation, because the goal of America is freedom. Abused and scorned though we may be, our destiny is tied up with America's destiny. Before the pilgrims landed at Plymouth, we were here. Before the pen of Jefferson etched the majestic words of the Declaration of Independence across the pages of history, we were here. For more than two centuries our forebears labored in this country without wages; they made cotton king; they built the homes of their masters while suffering gross injustice and shameful humiliation—and yet out of a bottomless vitality they continued to thrive and develop. If the inexpressible cruelties of slavery could not stop us, the opposition we now face will surely fail. We will win our freedom because the sacred heritage of our nation and the eternal will of God are embodied in our echoing demands.

45   Before closing I feel impelled to mention one other point in your statement that has troubled me profoundly. You warmly commended the Birmingham police force for keeping "order" and "preventing violence." I doubt that you would

have so warmly commended the police force if you had seen its dogs sinking their teeth into unarmed, nonviolent Negroes. I doubt that you would so quickly commend the policemen if you were to observe their ugly and inhumane treatment of Negroes here in the city jail; if you were to watch them push and curse old Negro women and young Negro girls; if you were to see them slap and kick old Negro men and young boys; if you were to observe them, as they did on two occasions, refuse to give us food because we wanted to sing our grace together. I cannot join you in your praise of the Birmingham police department.

It is true that the police have exercised a degree of discipline in handling the demonstrators. In this sense they have conducted themselves rather "nonviolently" in public. But for what purpose? To preserve the evil system of segregation. Over the past few years I have consistently preached that nonviolence demands that the means we use must be as pure as the ends we seek. I have tried to make clear that it is wrong to use immoral means to attain moral ends. But now I must affirm that it is just as wrong, or perhaps even more so, to use moral means to preserve immoral ends. Perhaps Mr. Connor and his policemen have been rather nonviolent in public, as was Chief Pritchett in Albany, Georgia, but they have used the moral means of nonviolence to maintain the immoral end of racial injustice. As T. S. Eliot has said: "The last temptation is the greatest treason: To do the right deed for the wrong reason."

I wish you had commended the Negro sit-inners and demonstrators of Birmingham for their sublime courage, their willingness to suffer and their amazing discipline in the midst of great provocation. One day the South will recognize its real heroes. They will be the James Merediths, with the noble sense of purpose that enables them to face jeering and hostile mobs, and with the agonizing loneliness that characterizes the life of the pioneer. They will be old, oppressed, battered Negro women, symbolized in a seventy-two-year-old woman in Montgomery, Alabama, who rose up with a sense of dignity and with her people decided not to ride segregated buses, and who responded with ungrammatical profundity to one who inquired about her weariness: "My feets is tired, but my soul is at rest." They will be the young high school and college students, the young ministers of the gospel and a host of their elders, courageously and nonviolently sitting in at lunch counters and willingly going to jail for conscience' sake. One day the South will know that when these disinherited children of God sat down at lunch counters, they were in reality standing up for what is best in the American dream and for the most sacred values in our Judaeo-Christian heritage, thereby bringing our nation back to those great wells of democracy which were dug deep by the founding fathers in their formulation of the Constitution and the Declaration of Independence.

Never before have I written so long a letter. I'm afraid it is much too long to take your precious time. I can assure you that it would have been much shorter if I had been writing from a comfortable desk, but what else can one do when he is alone in a narrow jail cell, other than write long letters, think long thoughts and pray long prayers?

If I have said anything in this letter that overstates the truth and indicates an unreasonable impatience, I beg you to forgive me. If I have said anything that understates the truth and indicates my having a patience that allows me to settle for anything less than brotherhood, I beg God to forgive me.

50   I hope this letter finds you strong in the faith. I also hope that circumstances will soon make it possible for me to meet each of you, not as an integrationist or a civil-rights leader but as a fellow clergyman and a Christian brother. Let us all hope that the dark clouds of racial prejudice will soon pass away and the deep fog of misunderstanding will be lifted from our fear-drenched communities, and in some not too distant tomorrow the radiant stars of love and brotherhood will shine over our great nation with all their scintillating beauty.

Yours for the cause of Peace and Brotherhood,
Martin Luther King, Jr.

Questions for Discussion

1. Notice the author's use of metaphors (e.g., "a tunnel of hope through the dark mountain of disappointment"). What other metaphors does the author use? Why? What is his purpose in using metaphors?
2. Consider the following 310-word sentence:
   "But when you have seen vicious mobs lynch your mothers and fathers at will and drown your sisters and brothers at whim . . . then you will understand why we find it difficult to wait."
   Why does the author choose to write such a long sentence? How does the parallelism of this sentence (i.e., the repetition of "when . . . ") contribute to his purpose?
3. This essay is organized as a point-by-point refutation of the clergy's opposing opinions. Why does the author choose to organize his essay this way?
4. In this letter, the author uses a variety of techniques to establish his credibility. Why does he consider it necessary to do so? Identify the various techniques he uses. Cite specific passages that exemplify the techniques. Which technique do you consider most effective? Why?
5. In this letter, which information is knowledge by participation? Which is knowledge by observation? Why does the author use both types of knowledge to write this letter? To establish credibility? To support the claim? To motivate the audience?

Opportunities for Writing

1. In a letter to the editor of your school newspaper, voice your opinion on the issue of civil disobedience. Do you believe people have a "moral responsibility to disobey unjust laws"?
2. Evaluate Martin Luther King, Jr.'s leadership of the Southern Christian Leadership Conference. What were his most important achievements? What mistakes did he make? What can today's civil rights leaders learn from your evaluation?
3. Assess the principle of nonviolence. Which do you consider more effective: violent or nonviolent demonstrations? Support your answer by citing appropriate examples.

4. To support interracial communication at your school, propose a special series of programs on the life of Martin Luther King, Jr. Identify appropriate speakers, activities, and displays, and estimate the resulting costs. Address your proposal to school administrators, urging their approval of the necessary funding.

Warning: Sports Stars May Be Hazardous to Your Health

JASON DEPARLE

Jason DeParle is a professional writer and editor of The Washington Monthly. *This essay, "Warning: Sports Stars May Be Hazardous to Your Health," first appeared in* The Washington Monthly *in September 1989. DeParle takes a stand against the tobacco industry's practice of "sponsoring" sporting events and athletes. To argue his position, the author presents three consequences that result from the "marriage of cigarettes and sports." His discussion of these consequences includes knowledge by both participation and observation. In writing this article, DeParle received research assistance from Daniel Mirvish, John Larew, John Heilemann, Michael Carolan, and Anita Bose.*

In case you missed it, this year's press guide to the Women's International Tennis Association is an impressive volume. Its 456 glossy pages bear tribute to what the guide immodestly calls "one of the greatest success stories of the modern sports world"—how women's tennis stepped from obscurity into the limelight of the Virginia Slims circuit, where this year players will compete for more than $17 million in prize money. Just twenty years ago, the nation's best women tennis players languished before small crowds on high school courts. Now, the guide says, with their own massage therapists and "state-of-the-art forecasting system," they've become "synonymous with style."

They're synonymous with wealth, too: Chris Evert's $8.6 million in lifetime earnings places her a distant second to Martina Navratilova's $14 million. But most of all, they're synonymous with fine physical form. Sprinkled throughout the media guide are photos of athletes in peak physical condition: Manuela Maleeva bends "low for a forehand volley," "Hana Mandlikova intently awaits a return," "Gabriela Sabatini puts to use her 'smashing' backhand."

Those of us less physically gifted than Hana Mandlikova can't help but envy the strength in her legs, power in her arms, and stamina in her lungs as she pauses, racket poised, before exploding into her backhand. It's precisely the rareness of these qualities that brings us to admire her so, and to pause a moment when looking at her picture. Because as Hana Mandlikova intently awaits a return, she does so in front of a big sign that says "Virginia Slims"—a product not known for promoting the powers of heart and lung that lie at the center of her trade. In fact, throughout the guide—not to mention the nation's sports pages and television broadcasts—we find these stars showcasing their enviable talents in front of cigarette ads. The bold corporate logo of the Virginia Slims series emphasizes the bond: a woman, sassy and sleek, holds a racket in one hand and a cigarette in the other.

This is odd. Tennis champions, after all, are models of health, particularly the health of heart and lungs, where endurance is essential. And cigarette smoking, as the Surgeon General recently reminded, "is the chief avoidable cause of death in our society"—death, more precisely, from heart and lung disease.

Struck by this seeming contradiction, I called Renee Bloch Shallouf, whom the guide lists as Media Services Manager for the players union, and asked if she, too, was impressed with the incongruity. "I think I'll defer this one over to Virginia Slims," she said. "They're the sponsor. We're just the players union. All I can do is give you a personal opinion."

"What is your personal opinion?"

"Noo—hoooo," she said, keeping the answer to herself.

Shallouf ended the conversation by saying, "If I find somebody opinionated—someone willing to give their opinion—around here, I'll call you."

Turning back to the media guide, I flipped to the section marked "Virginia Slims Personnel," and, to my surprise, found a familiar face on the page. There, bearing the impressive title of "Director, Worldwide Operations," was Anne Person, a college classmate of mine. Perhaps she would have some thoughts on the compatibility of tennis and tobacco. But, though she answers a phone at Philip Morris headquarters, she said she was only a "consultant" and that she worked "only on the tennis end." As for her thoughts about tobacco, she said, "I just can't do it. I don't choose to do it.... Regarding the tobacco issue, I don't choose to share my opinions." She suggested I call Steve Weiss, the manager of media relations for Philip Morris, U.S.A.

When I did, Weiss sounded astonished. He said he found the question—is there a contradiction between the vigor of athletics and the disease caused by cigarettes?—a breach of journalistic ethics. "Are you editorializing?" he said. "I disagree with your premises.... You're saying that cigarette smoking causes a disease? Can I ask you something? Is that your opinion? That's a very opinionated statement. I'd appreciate a little more openmindedness.... I disagree with a journalist who calls and issues a very opinionated statement, when the credo of journalism is balance, fairness, and accuracy." He referred me to the code of reportorial probity, as articulated by the professional society, Sigma Delta Chi.

We backed up and started again.

Q: Does smoking lead to disease?

A: "I'm not a doctor. I would leave that to more informed individuals."

Q: Is the Surgeon General an informed individual?

A: "I think the Surgeon General is but one voice among many in the continuing debate about cigarette smoking."

On it went for about an hour, a stock recitation of the Philip Morris line. Or almost—there was a momentary point of diversion. Insisting that Philip Morris was not trying to make cigarettes seem glamorous, Weiss said, "We don't ask any of our players to smoke. *I doubt many, if any, do.*"

Hmmm . . . and why is that?

Pause.

Then, growing agitated, Weiss said, "That's their choice. You have to ask them. I'm not qualified to answer that. I am absolutely not qualified to say what anybody does or does not do. *I'm retracting that, Jason. . . .*"

At that point, Weiss's voice took on the tin echo of a speaker phone. "*I want you to know that I'm recording this conversation,*" he said.

SMOKES ILLUSTRATED

The fit athletes of the Virginia Slims circuit who swat balls in front of cigarette ads, in a tournament named for a cigarette brand, pocketing large sums from a cigarette company's largesse, are but a small subset of the great marriage of sports and tobacco. A large and growing number of sports now lend their athletes' credibility as fine physical specimens to the tobacco companies, whose products, by the Surgeon General's estimate, kill about 1,000 people a day. Cigarette manufacturers exploit sporting events in a variety of ways, ranging from such old-fashioned strategies as stadium advertising to the virtual invention of eponymous sports, like Winston Series Drag Racing or Marlboro Cup horseracing. When the pitchmen of Philip Morris say, "You've come a long way baby," they could very well be congratulating themselves; their success in co-opting the nation's health elite to promote a product that leads to an array of fatal diseases is extraordinary.

But they couldn't have done it alone. For starters, they needed the cooperation of the athletes, and, with a few praiseworthy exceptions, they've gotten it. When Billie Jean King set out 20 years ago to find a sponsor for women's tennis, she may have needed Philip Morris as much as it needed her. But these days, she and the other stars of women's tennis have actually had to fight off other corporate sponsors who would welcome the chance to take over. The tobacco companies have also needed the help of sports journalists, and, again, they've gotten it. The daily papers have been silent. The big magazines, like *Sports Illustrated,* are thick with tobacco ads and thin on tobacco critics. And the networks have been perfectly happy to show an infield decked with Marlboro banners, race cars painted with Marlboro signs, officials wearing Marlboro logos—while pretending that cigarette ads are still banned from the air.

The marriage of cigarettes and sports has at least three insidious consequences. The first, and perhaps most troubling, is that it obscures the connection of cigarettes and disease, subliminally and perhaps even consciously. Quick: speak the words "Virginia Slims" and what do you see? A) Chris Evert, or B) the cancer ward? If you answered A)—and most people do—then Philip Morris has you right where it wants you. (The recognition of this power is why the soccer star Pele won't pose near cigarette signs.) The second troubling fact about cigarettes' tryst with sport is that it allows them to penetrate the youth market. Cigarette spokesmen self-righteously insist they have no such goal. But tobacco companies desperately need teen smokers for the simple reason that few people start smoking once they are adults; and there's scarcely anyone more glamorous to a teenager than a star athlete. The third reason why cigarettes' infiltration of athletics is bad is that it circumvents the ban on television ads. Previously, cigarette companies had to hire actors to play athletes in their commercials, but now they've got the real thing.

EMPHYSEMA SLIMS

For those keeping moral score, cigarettes' involvement with aerobic sports, like tennis and soccer, is probably the most indefensible, since the respiratory fitness those sports require and represent is precisely what cigarettes deprive people of. That is, race car drivers can smoke and drive, but soccer stars certainly can't smoke and sprint. That doesn't mean race car drivers are welcome to promote cigarettes, of course. Their ties to tobacco endanger the public health by continuing to make cigarettes seem glamorous to kids, and by keeping the cigarette signs on T.V.

For leads on many of the following items, I am indebted to Dr. Alan Blum, a Baylor physician whose anti-smoking research and protests (like the staging of an "Emphysema Slims") makes him the Don King of the anti-smoking world:

Soccer Besides the world's most enviable lungs, soccer offers cigarettes two other advantages: wild overseas popularity at a time when American tobacco companies are stepping up their Third World trade, and a growing popularity among American youth.

Camel cigarettes, manufactured by R.J. Reynolds, was one of four major sponsors of the 1986 World Cup in Mexico City. Among the privileges it received in return was the chance to post four seven-meter Camel signs next to the field, where the worldwide television audience of 650 million for the final game alone could see them.

A brochure by ISL Marketing, a firm that handles World Cup marketing, explains: "The launch of their Camel Filters in Mexico was arranged to coincide with World Cup 86. . . . The team of Camel girls was stationed at each stadium distributing free samples. . . . Sponsorship of World Cup 86 provided Camel with a golden profile that reflected its product image of independence, masculinity, and adventure."

Earlier in the decade, RJR even tried to field its own World Cup club. In sponsoring the 1983 "Winston Team America Series," it compiled an all-star team and held a 30-game series against the pros in major stadiums across the country. During halftime, fans joined a contest to kick a ball through the "o" in a Winston sign.

Baseball Cigarette companies have ads in 22 of the 24 Major League ballparks in the United States, typically in spots that enhance broadcast coverage. The camera near the visiting team dugout at Shea Stadium, for instance, which is used to capture men leading off first base, frames the player with the Marlboro sign in left-center. At Fenway Park in Boston, a sign for the Jimmy Fund for cancer research, a favorite Red Sox charity, hangs above the right field bleacher. So does a Marlboro sign.

Skiing For about eight years, until last season. Loew's sponsored the Newport Ski Weekend, which offered half-price lift tickets in exchange for cigarette boxes. Philip Morris invites skiers at a number of Western resorts to take the "Marlboro Challenge," a plunge down a timed race course festooned with Marlboro flags.

In the 1983–84 season, RJR's brand, Export A, became the official sponsor of the Canadian Ski Association, which oversees the country's major competitions. The company's original contract called for "the exclusive right ... to identify itself or its products (including name, logo, and colours) on: flags, poles, course markers, scoreboards, award presentations, start banners ... all buildings, podiums, backdrops...." To be sure no one missed the point, the contract added: "The Association shall use its best efforts to have the events telecast on national network television."

But the Canadian skiers rebelled, with some refusing to accept league trophies. The contract was modified following the protest, and the controversy led finally to a ban on all tobacco advertising in Canada. Ken Read, who represented Canada twice in Olympic skiing and is now a broadcaster, was among the leaders of the protest. "I think it's inappropriate for a cigarette to sponsor any sporting event—period," he said. "It's incompatible with the objective of sport—to promote a healthy lifestyle."

I asked Read what he thought about the cigarette companies' argument that they're only promoting brand loyalty and, therefore, not encouraging kids to smoke. "That's absolute garbage," he said. "When you're using sports as a tool, you're influencing youth."

Horse racing Rather than take over an existing horse race, in 1973 Philip Morris simply went out and created one from scratch: the nationally-televised Marlboro Cup, which it sponsored until 1987.

In a interview with *The Daily Racing Form,* Ellen Merlo, director of marketing promotions at Philip Morris, explained the event's appeal: "First, it has created enormous visibility for Marlboro. There are newspaper stories leading up to and following the race that mention the Marlboro name frequently, and this is excellent exposure. Secondly the image of horse racing and the imagery of the Marlboro Man campaign seem to have reinforced each other. The man on the horse theme is central to both, and we feel it has worked well as a partnership."

Autoracing Since 1971, RJR has been the chief sponsor of NASCAR's premier circuit, the $18 million, 29-race Winston Cup Series. This is a sport that has other problems besides cigarette sponsorship, of course—such as encouraging 16-year-olds to play Richard Petty on the interstate. As they do, the word "Winston" may quickly come to mind: one of the races is called the Winston 500; another is simply known as The Winston. The driver who accumulates the most points during the season wins the $1 million Winston Cup. The driver who wins three of the top four races wins a bonus called, accurately, the Winston Million—you get the idea.

"We're in the cigarette business. We're *not* in the sports business. We *use* sports as an avenue for advertising our products...." said Wayne Robertson, an RJR executive, in a trade journal. "We can go into an area where we're marketing an event, measure sales during the event and measure sales after the event, and see an increase in sales."

If this list seems lengthy, don't forget it omits the Vantage Golf Scoreboard, Salem Pro-Sail races, Lucky Strike bowling, the Winston Rodeo, Benson & Hedges on Ice, and any number of other cigarette-sponsored sports. It also omits Camille Duvall, champion water skier and the cover girl for the current issue of *Philip Morris Magazine,* where the company that insists its interest in athletes has nothing to do with glamour, describes her as "gorgeous—swimsuit issue, pack-it-in-Paulina, no-exaggeration, gorgeous."

Those who think that tobacco's conquest of sport is complete, however, can take heart—according to the *Chicago Sun-Times,* Philip Morris recently lost the $12,000 sponsorship of the U.S. boomerang team to an anti-smoking group called Doctors Ought to Care, which is run by Alan Blum. Philip Morris "promised us all kinds of publicity," the team captain, Eric Shouffer, told the newspaper. "If we'd wear big Philip Morris logos on our chest, they told us we'd be on 'Good Morning America' and so on."

It wasn't just conscience that governed the team's decision, Shouffer said, but practical considerations, too: One member is an asthmatic "who falls over dead when he gets near smokers."

THE MAN WITH THE COUGH

Lung cancer, which is almost always fatal, is a curiously polite disease. It glides through the body, making itself at home but careful not to cause a fuss. The chest may be its harbor but it can sail wherever the bloodstream goes, and it explores the body at leisure. It can list south toward the groin, or tack its way north to the brain; it can stretch out yawning on beaches of bone marrow. It is lazy and can afford to be. It is confident. It announces itself at the time of its choosing. One day, it knocks.

By then, the average man—or, increasingly, woman—hasn't been feeling his usual robust self for three month or so. He's 55 or 60 years old, and has been smoking most of his life, but never had any problems as a result. It was just a cough at first, with a bit of mucous, and sure to go away in another week. Then the mucous disappeared, but the cough kept hanging on. His appetite began to slow.

Let's have a look, the physician says. Though there's something oddly reassuring about the touch of his cold stethoscope on the patient's chest and back, it's less reassuring to be directed in front of the X-ray machine. There is something there, the doctor reports—pneumonia, maybe—but he's careful not to sound too alarmed. It might be nothing that 10 days of antibiotics can't cure. Ten days later, when the cough and the spot on the X-ray have endured, it's time for another look.

The word cancer *has been there all along, but no one's wanted to say it. And with good reason—from the time it first gets uttered, the average lung cancer patient will live less than three years. Perhaps the doctor will say it first: The purpose of the biopsy, he explains, is "to rule out cancer." A phrase like "let's not get worried until we know what we're dealing with" will almost certainly follow. We're just going to remove a small piece of tissue, the physician says; you can expect some discomfort.*

Draped in a soft blue gown, the man with the cough gets wheeled into a 65-degree room, where a surgeon snakes an optic fiber down his throat and snatches a piece of lung. A pathologist slices the sample, using one portion to prepare a quick slide and saving the rest for future tests. In the waiting room, there is a human community—wife, children, friends from work, grandchildren perhaps—that is connected through nerves and fears, or, maybe, prayers. The initial indication may come as quickly as 15 minutes, but final confirmation can take three or four days—itself a sample of the waiting that will fill future months. Time seems to stop until the word arrives.

If the word is something like squamous cell carcinoma—*lung cancer*—*there will begin a difficult discussion indeed.*

HACKING HAGS

Whether or not the figure of 1,000 deaths a day presents tobacco companies with a moral challenge, it certainly presents them with an economic one: how to replace the thousands of people their products kill each week. To some extent, cigarette companies have been losing the war. In 1965, 40 percent of American adults smoked; by 1987, this figure had dropped off to 29 percent. But while cigarette consumption is declining, it's declining least among blacks, women, high school drop-outs, blue-collar workers, and other groups whose members tend to lead more difficult lives. The more marginal one's status in society, the more likely one is to smoke.

Since 1971, when the ban on televised cigarette ads took effect, the cigarette companies' efforts to reach their target audiences have grown more complicated. The story of the ad ban is an interesting one in itself, and perhaps its most salient moral is that, despite the immense wealth and power of the tobacco companies, there is, in fact, much that one person can do. In this case, the person was John Banzhaf, a 26-year-old law school graduate. Noting the saturation of TV with cigarette ads, he sent off a three-page letter to the Federal Communications Commission, arguing that the Fairness Doctrine required broadcasters to give anti-smoking groups their say. To nearly everyone's surprise, the FCC agreed, announcing in 1967 that henceforth broadcasters should air one anti-smoking spot for every three or four cigarette commercials.

Anti-smoking groups took to the air with an inordinate amount of creativity. Though television viewers were still being blitzed with ads that showed happy smokers in vigorous poses, now they received other visions too: a Marlboro-like man, bursting boldly through the saloon doors, only to collapse in a fit of coughs; a wrinkled hag on a respirator, cigarette in hand, asking, "Aren't I sexy?" Though still outnumbered, these hacking, wincing images of death began to register: cigarette consumption declined in each of the next four years. The cigarette companies weren't just losing the battle; through the Fairness Doctrine they were subsidizing the other side's artillery. In 1970, they went to Congress to say they wanted out.

The withdrawal wasn't as easy as it might seem, however. If one company withdrew its ads, it ceded an advantage to its competitors; if all withdrew at once, they were subject to antitrust reprisals for collusion. What they needed was an order: ban us, they asked. Perhaps the constituency least pleased by this prospect was the broadcasters, who were then banking about $250 million a year in tobacco ad revenues. Though Congress finally passed the ban over broadcasters' objections, the TV executives, to whom the the term "conscience-stricken" could not fairly be applied, did win a soothing concession: the ban didn't take effect until midnight on January 1, 1971—after the commercial-thick bowl games were aired.

Cigarette strategists now had to contend with a more complicated world. They still needed to saturate the culture with the idea that smoking leads to happiness, but television, their most powerful weapon, seemed off limits. *Seemed* is the operative word here. By channeling some of that $250 million ad budget into sports sponsorship, cigarette companies were right back on the air. Consider the timing: Virginia Slims, born 1971; Winston Cup racing, born 1971; Marlboro Cup horse racing, born 1973. Sports sponsorship has become such a spectacular success that by now all kinds of corporations want in—the John Hancock Bowl, the Mazda Gator Bowl. "We have a waiting list for inside billboards," says Jane Allen, who works in the marketing department of the Charlotte Motor Speedway. "Everybody in the business knows it's because of TV coverage."

A Cardinal Sins

But tobacco's problems extended beyond the TV ban, and sports was only part of the answer. Since 1964, the industry had been stuck with the Surgeon General's warnings and increasingly vocal criticisms of their products. What the tobacco industry needed was friends, and its strategy for finding them was sound: it decided to buy them. Donning the mask of philanthropy, the tobacco companies have courted not only athletes but ballerinas, modern dancers, jazz musicians, museum curators, unions, civil rights groups, feminists, religious leaders—almost anyone with a glimmer of uprightness and a use for cash. The Guggenheim Museum. The Joffrey Ballet. The Whitney.

The purpose of this fevered gift-giving has been to divert the public's attention from what tobacco companies really do: lure people, particularly young ones, into buying a highly addictive drug, which, if used as intended, courts death. In this, they are no different than crack peddlers. The Surgeon General has likened the addictive powers of nicotine to those of heroin and cocaine: all of them create psychological and *physical* cravings; each causes a chemical reaction that makes the body want more. As anyone understands who's watched someone they care for try to quit, the pack-a-day smoker "chooses" his habit as freely as the cocaine addict chooses his. Cocaine and heroin inflict their damage more quickly; but cigarettes kill more widely. It is cigarettes, not cocaine, that cause about 390,000 deaths each year according to C. Everett Koop.

In respectable society today, cocaine peddlers are objects of scorn. But cigarette peddlers are jauntily strolling the halls of their latest museum exhibits. The tobacco companies need this false status as respectable corporations in order to survive. If the world saw them as the drug pushers they are, Congress would ban their ads, if not their product, and Drug Czars would join the fray. By accepting tobacco sponsorship, the country's singers, dancers, curators, and the like help ensure this doesn't happen. While accepting the Devil's money may be defensible if you give nothing in return, the recipients of tobacco largesse have given something very precious indeed, the one thing the cigarette sellers could never earn on their own: respect.

Thus comes Philip Morris beneficiary Alvin Ailey, writing the Surgeon General last year to call tobacco executives "enlightened . . . generous patrons," and to argue that, "A nation has a cultural health as well as a physical health." Thus comes Terrence Cardinal Cooke to say a prayer at a cigarette-sponsored display of Vatican art, leading one Philip Morris vice president to boast, "We're probably the only cigarette company on this earth to be blessed by a cardinal."

While tobacco's been busy assembling this circle of courtiers, athletes aren't just any members of the court. Their unique evocation of health, access to television, and influence on teenagers makes them especially prized, and a report this year by the Surgeon General adds extra emphasis to the point about youth: "The uptake of smoking is now a phenomenon that occurs almost entirely during the teenage years. . . ."

Tobacco spokesmen have a way of sounding positively wounded when someone suggests they're scheming to entice the young—the Tobacco Institute even funds an anti-teenage smoking program. It's not advertising or athletes that cause teenagers to start smoking, but "peer pressure," says Steve Weiss, the Philip Morris spokesman and ethics buff. As if peer pressure were something that filtered down through the ozone layer and had nothing to do with race cars and tennis stars.

METS TO RJR: DROP DEAD

Of course, cigarette companies couldn't co-opt athletics if athletics wasn't willing to be co-opted. For the most part, that willingness consists not of active promotion but of silence, which is just as necessary to the cigarette salesmen's success. Imagine how many baseball fans, teenage and adult, would get the message if Darryl Strawberry held a press conference to denounce the indecency the Marlboro sign lends to the Shea Stadium outfield. Or better yet, trotted out with a paint brush to cover it up. What could the Mets management do? Bench him?

While Strawberry's probably valuable enough to get away with it on his own, lots of lesser players aren't. Alone, that is. But imagine if the entire Mets roster signed a petition, refusing to play the 1990 season under the Marlboro banner—refusing to donate their authority as athletes, TV stars, and teen idols to the nation's number one health hazard. Look northward, New York Mets! The Canadian skiers told RJR to drop dead—you can, too!

What the athletes need is a little leadership, and one place where you might hope to find it is the office of Dr. Bobby Brown, the American League president, former New York Yankee, and *cardiologist*. In 1985, Alan Blum, the anti-smoking activist, wrote to Brown and suggested he do something to remove cigarette ads from stadiums. Brown wrote back a nothing-I-can-do letter ("legally permitted," "forced to recognize an individual's rights") promising serenely that, "This is an ongoing problem, however, that we will continue to address."

I called Brown recently to see how the progress was coming. Major League Baseball, after all, forbids athletes from smoking in uniform—why can't it forbid them from playing in front of cigarette billboards? Isn't the purpose of the uniform ban to keep baseball players from promoting cigarettes? Brown couldn't have been more disingenuous: he said he didn't know the reason athletes were forbidden to smoke in uniform, just that it was on the books and he didn't feel compelled to change it.

As for billboards, Brown agreed that "anytime you have advertising, the tobacco companies think you have a chance of increasing sales—that's why they're doing it." To remove them, however, would be "unrealistic," since tobacco companies could still advertise elsewhere, such as in subways. Maybe even Brown didn't want to hear himself offer this explanation, however, because he began to sound annoyed. "Who are you, sir?" he asked. "Who funds you?" When I suggested that subways might not pack the prestige of Major League Baseball, and, anyway, someone needed to take the first step, he got angrier. "It's *unrealistic* for tobacco ads to be removed from baseball parks," he said. Then he hung up.

Most athletes can probably claim to have given the issue little thought (some too convincingly). Brown at least can claim that he's not actively soliciting the billboards, just shrugging his shoulders while others do. But I'd like to know what people like Billie Jean King, Chris Evert, and Martina Navratilova—athletes who have thought it over, and pledged the cigarette companies their fidelity—can claim, but they aren't returning phone calls on the issue.

65 "I believe in free enterprise," King said in 1983, on one of the few times she's been publicly quizzed on her tobacco ties (significantly, it wasn't a journalist but an anti-smoking activist who asked the question). King went on to say that "Personally, I hate cigarette smoking. I hate cigarettes. Ninety-five percent of the girls do"—as though this excuses her prominent role in their promotion over the past two decades, as though this justifies her taking the court against Bobby Riggs in 1973 dressed in Virginia Slims colors, with Virginia Slims sequins on her chest. What she's saying is this: Let someone else get lung cancer; it won't be me; and I'll get rich and famous in the process.

In the two decades that King's been selling Philip Morris her image of vigor—she not only played Riggs, remember, she beat him—lung cancer has overtaken breast cancer as a leading cause of women's death. And what are King & Co. doing about it now? Continuing to coo about how "loyal" Philip Morris has been, while rebuffing a bid by Proctor & Gamble last year to take over the women's tour.

Pam Shriver's career earnings are $3.9 million. "I don't feel bad at all about looking somebody in the eye and saying, 'Virginia Slims is our sponsor,' cause they're a great sponsor," she said in 1986. "Too bad they're a cigarette."

THE TISSUES' REVENGE

The average American smoker consumes about 7,000 cigarettes a year. If he inhales each one six times—a modest estimate—then 42,000 jet streams a year travel down his throat and into his lungs and out his mouth and nose, bathing the tissues of the respiratory tract in clouds of smoke and nicotine. Lung cancer is the tissues' revenge. Sometime, somehow, a cell rebels and begins to divide. One cell becomes two, the two become four, the four become eight, and the cancer is off and racing.

If lung cancer is caught in an early stage, that is, if it's anatomically confined, there's a chance it can be surgically removed. But the disease rarely gives itself away before spreading so far that surgery is no longer an option. Back from biopsy, then, the man with the cough will have two options. The type of lung cancer known as "small cell" may respond to chemotherapy, although the response, even when complete—driving the cancer from all medical detection— almost never stays that way.

Doctors know how to kill cancer cells. The problem is what they call the "therapeutic-to-toxic ratio"—how to kill cancer cells without killing other cells too. During chemotherapy, the patient will almost surely succumb to wild fits of vomiting. His hair will fall out. His body will go limp. For days afterwards he may feel too exhausted to lift himself from bed. If the process works and the cancer goes into retreat, chemotherapy can earn the patient a modest extension of life.

The second type of lung cancer, known, straightforwardly enough, as "non smallcell lung cancer," does not respond to chemotherapy. It may respond to radiation. When it's time for the bombardment to begin, the patient will stretch out beneath a linear accelerator—a hulking structure that, resembling a 10-foot microscope, hunches over his form. When technicians turn on the switch, a 12.5 ton medical marvel will send between 180 and 300 "rad" burning into the diseased cells. A tumor the size of a cubic centimeter—the size, say, of a bouillon cube—will contain about a billion cancerous cells. If treatment kills a billion minus one, the patient is still left with a fatal disease, for the one that survives will continue to divide.

Breast cancer, testicular cancer, prostate cancer, and others have all been known to succumb to the linear accelerator's might. But lung cancer rarely loses. Within five years of diagnosis, 87 percent of those afflicted can expect to be dead.

Lying on the table, the man with the cough feels nothing. Only the tension of waiting.

'A LOOPHOLE'

Just as it takes a certain physiological culture for cancer to conquer a lung, it takes a certain journalistic one for tobacco to conquer sports. And sports journalists, for the most part, have provided it. The major components of this culture are indifference ("I just report the news; I don't make it") and rationalization ("It's a legal product; people can make their own choices")—with a generous sprinkling of publisher's greed, in the form of cigarette ads. Relish for a moment the thought of a Sam Donaldson of sport trailing Chris Evert and you get a sense of how vulnerable athletes would be to a determined inquiry: "Ms. Evert, lung cancer has just surpassed breast cancer as a killer of women; why do you display your athletic talents in front of that Virginia Slims banner? Don't you care about the welfare of women? Does money mean that much to you?"

And it's not as though sports journalists can't see what's going on. As Lydia Stephans, programming manager for ABC Sports, said, "I'm sure that's why Virginia Slims put up that money—so they could get that recognition, the association with sports and health. Otherwise why would they want to pump millions of dollars into sports? They can't do it by putting a commercial on the TV. They used to show people sailing around smoking cigarettes. So now they do it through sports. . . . On their half, I think it's clever. They've found a loophole."

As for the dailies, no one who has walked past the sports desk of an average American newspaper is likely to confuse it for a breeding ground of social reform. The idea that they have a moral obligation to speak out against tobacco's role in sport is likely to strike many sportswriters as about as compelling as their obligation to champion educational reform in Zambia. For lots of them, it's just not on the radar.

"We haven't done the piece you're doing. It's a legitimate story. I'm glad you're doing it," said Leonard Shapiro, sports editor at *The Washington Post,* who was more thoughtful about the topic than most of the journalists I spoke to. "Maybe it's become such an ingrained part of our culture, it's something we don't even notice."

What are the sports editors' options? One strategy might just be to rename the event. When Ellen Merlo of Philip Morris brags about "the newspaper stories leading up to and following the race that mention the Marlboro name frequently," sportswriters could decide that henceforth the "Marlboro Cup" will just become "The Cup." (Newspapers routinely make such judgments about proper editorial content, screening out, say, obscenity.) Failing that, how about a big "Surgeon General's Warning: Smoking Causes Lung Cancer, Heart Disease, Emphysema, and May Complicate Pregnancy" slapped on the photos of the tourney?

The sportswriter who, by chance, does develop a Donaldson complex on the issue isn't likely to find great encouragement from above. For one, a number of newspapers have actually allied themselves as co-sponsors of cigarette-backed sporting events. *The Houston Chronicle, The Houston Post, The Boston Herald,* and the *Los Angeles Times* have all joined Philip Morris as backers of Virginia Slims events, while the *Atlanta Journal* joins RJR in financing the Atlanta Journal 500.

AD MEN

80   More to the point is a basic fact of American journalism: Publishers like the income from cigarette ads, and few are likely to regard an anti-tobacco crusade as a boon to business. Not many will respond as forthrightly as Mark Hoop, publisher of the *Twin Cities Reader,* who flatly fired the reporter whose preview of the Kool Jazz Festival pointed out that Duke Ellington had died of lung cancer. (When later asked by ABC News if he'd really said, "If we have to fly to Louisville, Kentucky and crawl on bended knees and beg the cigarette company not to take their ads out of our newspaper, we'll do that," Hoop said, "True.") But those with a subtler touch will still find a way to communicate that inordinate crusading on the issue does not enhance journalists' career advancement.

While actual cigarette advertising in many papers is modest, it's not so modest that publishers are anxious to lose it. (A recent 12-page advertising supplement for Marlboro Grand Prix racing in *The New York Times Magazine* cost close to $300,000, according to the *Times*'s advertising department.) And the conglomerate nature of cigarette ownership may mean that other ad revenues are also at stake: RJR's holdings include Nabisco, Del Monte, and Kentucky Fried Chicken, while Philip Morris controls those of Seven-Up, the Miller Brewing Company, and General Foods, makers of Jell-O, Maxwell House, Tang, Oscar Mayer, and so forth. Let no one mistake the point—the cigarette companies haven't been shy about exercising this clout. After the advertising firm Saatchi & Saatchi produced a recent anti-smoking commercial for Northwest Airlines, RJR pulled its *$70 million* Nabisco account.

The media's own conglomerate status means it has more than one flank exposed. Denunciations of RJR in *The Washington Post* could mean fewer ads for Camels, Oreos, and Smirnoff in *Newsweek,* just as an attack on Virginia Slims in *The New York Times* could lead to the end of the $900,000 of tobacco ads that appeared last year in its wholly-owned *Tennis* magazine. Obviously, both the *Post* and *Times* have had unkind words for tobacco; but neither can claim to have provided the kind of unforgiving coverage that tobacco has earned with a product that *every two years* kills more Americans than have died in all the wars of this century.

And that's just the daily press. For a sense of how cigarette revenues have shaped the attitudes of the magazine world, consider the views of George Gross, executive vice president of the Magazine Publishers of America. He recently went before Congress to warn that restrictions on cigarette advertising could lead to a surge in smoking, since "the prominent health warnings now carried in all magazine tobacco advertising will not be seen by millions of readers." Now there's an original argument.

Meanwhile, a 1986 study by the University of Michigan School of Public Health found that no other category of magazines—fashion, politics, general-interest, and so forth—relies more heavily on tobacco ads than do sports magazines. On the average, tobacco provided 11.3 percent of the sports journals' income, down slightly from 14.0 in 1976—but up impressively from pre-ad ban days of 1966, when it was only 2.1 percent. *Sports Illustrated,* the industry giant, weighed in at 11.3 percent—or $27 million.

THE DANGERS OF MILK

What kinds of inhibitions might such revenues induce? It's certainly fair to say that *Sports Illustrated,* itself part of a larger Time, Inc. empire full of cigarette ads, hasn't brought an exceptionally skeptical view to the issue of tobacco and sports. "It's a fringe thing," says Peter Carry, the magazine's executive editor. In 1977, the magazine did find space for "Chaws," a nine-page celebration of chewing tobacco by an array of baseball stars. Sample? "I'll stick a chaw in my mouth and everything seems to get a little brighter," said pitcher Rick Reuschel.

Meanwhile, one could suggest that *Sports Illustrated* has been less than zealous in publishing alternative points of view. Ask Greg Connolly, a Massachusetts dentist hired by Major League baseball to help athletes quit chewing tobacco. In 1986, Connolly says he contacted the magazine and offered to write a piece about the program. He said that two different editors, including baseball editor Steve Wulf, warned him that higher-ups might find a possible "conflict of interest" with advertisers, but Wulf told him to try it nonetheless. Connolly turned it in, but the piece never ran.

So what—maybe Connolly can't write. But that wasn't the explanation that Wulf gave Howard Wolinsky, a *Chicago Sun-Times* medical writer, when Wolinsky asked what happened. Wolinsky says Wulf told him, "based on common sense, magazines do not like to upset their advertisers by publishing stories that are negative on an advertised product." When I called Wulf he confirmed that he had warned Connolly about possible conflicts of interest, and he acknowledged the conversation with Wolinsky. He said he was speaking to Wolinsky about magazines in general, not *Sports Illustrated,* which he said "does not let its advertisers dictate its editorial content." His fears about the possible conflict of interest, he said, "turned out not to be the case. The sole reason it didn't run was for editorial purposes."

Judging from another *Sports Illustrated* article, the magazine seems to think that tobacco isn't just a "fringe" issue in sports but also in health. In 1983, the magazine ran a 10-page article deploring the sad state of "fitness" in America, explaining how poor diet and a lack of exercise contribute to heart disease and general ill health. The article doesn't exactly ignore tobacco. Cigarettes show up twice. First the magazine argues, "The problem is not only too little exercise—the culprits in the case of children include TV and, recently, video games—but too many cigarettes, too many calories and a diet far too rich in salt and saturated fats . . . ." Next, it advises "'lifestyle' changes, such as cutting out cigarettes . . . . *Just as important* is the need to 'engineer' more activity into daily life. Use stairs instead of elevators. Leave your car at the far end of the parking lot . . . ." (Emphasis added.)

With the messy little business of cigarettes put behind, the magazine turned a tarter tongue toward a real social blight: sweetened water. The Los Angeles public pools were offering free admission to "to children producing wrappers from Kool-Aid packages," the authors said. "Of course, the appropriateness of such an association with Kool-Aid, a product not ordinarily thought of as promoting fitness, might be questioned." Imagine how heartless those Kool-Aid peddlers are! Of all the things to push on kids! The writers went on to document another crass exercise of corporate power, blasting the National Dairy Council for "disseminating educational material on nutrition that pointedly neglects to suggest that readers might want to restrict their intake of eggs, whole milk, butter." Why the dairy council even gave those milk pamphlets to kids! Rascals! Have they no shame?

The same issue that emphasized the dangers of elevators and eggs more than Marlboros, Camels, or Winstons, happened to have ten pages of cigarette advertising. Among the ads was a two-page spread from the Tobacco Institute, which asked "Is cigarette advertising a major reason why kids smoke?" and answered, "No." When I asked Jerry Kirshenbaum, the fitness article's co-author, how the ethics of that ad compared to the Dairy Council's plug for milk, he said, "I really don't think I want to discuss this any further."

Interestingly, *Sports Illustrated* did run a very hard-hitting article last year on beer's effect on sports, which shows the magazine hasn't just simply tuned out on moral issues. (See Monthly Journalism Award, November 1988.) Beer's involvement in sport, through sponsorship and advertising, led the magazine "to wonder just what kind of cultural hypocrisy is going on when Americans relentlessly insist on immersing sport—our most wholesome, most admired, even (sometimes) most heroic institution—in a sea of intoxicating drink." SI suggested that this was "cynical, ironic, immoral, hypocritical . . ." The magazine's beer-ad revenues in 1988 were $6.3 million—significant, but far short of tobacco's $35 million. And perhaps equally significant, beer companies don't feel as imperilled, and hence, as vindictive, as cigarette makers do.

Carry, the executive editor and a former smoker, said that quitting was one of the hardest things he'd ever done. But as far as tobacco's involvement with sports, "I would say on the level of the world's evils, I would say it ranks pretty low."

THE 150 M.P.H. MARLBORO

While it would certainly help if *Sports Illustrated* saved its righteous indignation for Kools instead of Kool-Aid, the tobacco companies have friends in even higher places—television. It was the broadcasters, remember, who did their level best to keep cigarette commercials on the air. These days, televised tennis and auto-racing doesn't sell cigarette ads but does sell equally lucrative car ads and truck ads and beer ads instead.

The small group of network executives who control the nation's sports programming have unique power where tobacco and athletics are concerned. If the heads of CBS, ABC, and NBC simply turned on the TV, saw the whirl of Marlboro cars, flags, and banners, and said, "Hey, that's a cigarette ad—don't show it," the game would be over. Without the magnifying effects of broadcast coverage, tobacco's 20-year outbreak of sports fever would meet its antibiotic. (To protect themselves from losing a competitive advantage to some less scrupulous, upstart station, the networks could seek a ruling from the FCC, pointing out tobacco's circumvention of the law. And, of course, the FCC needn't be shy; it could always instigate an investigation itself.) A few "sports" might go under, at least in their present forms. Then again, if the Winston Cup can't exist without Winston, then isn't it more cigarette ad than sport, after all?

The media employees who wait for the executives to move are likely to wait a long time. To push the process along, a little unity would help. Just as baseball players, acting together, could bring the necessary pressure to bear on ballparks, writers and producers can put pressures on the media corporations. Acting alone, the reporter who condemns cigarette ads may get branded an "activist" and sent to write obits. Joining together, the top 50 reporters at the *Times* or the *Post* or ABC could exercise real pressure—particularly if they said they were willing to take a cut in pay equal, on a percentage basis, to the loss in revenue, as long as the executives and shareholders did the same.

Judging from my recent discussions with sports broadcasters, however, the dangers of such an outbreak of moral zeal seem slight. It's certainly not expected at CBS, where CEO Larry Tisch happens to wear a second hat as chairman of the board of Loew's, owners of Lorillard Tobacco, makers of Kents, Newports, and Trues. The new anti-tobacco policy isn't on the horizon at ESPN either, where RJR/Nabisco owns 20 percent.

At ABC, Lydia Stephans, the programmer with a clear-eyed view of tobacco's clever loophole, argued that there's little the networks can do. If they didn't broadcast sporting events with cigarette ads, she said, there wouldn't be any left to broadcast—which is sort of the point. "I'm basically neutral," she said.

The fervor at NBC wasn't much greater. I asked Doug Kelly, an NBC spokesman, how the network deals with the tobacco ads that line scoreboards and racetrack infields. He called back a few days later to explain that "we only show the part that shows the scoreboard." Kelly did concede that it was hard to get a tight shot of the Indy 500, which NBC also broadcasts, at least one that would crop the Marlboro sign off the racecar's hood. When I asked if all those 150 m.p.h. cigarette signs didn't violate at least the spirit of the ad ban, Kelly's tone became distinctly less friendly. "I'm not going to comment on that," he said.

"Is that K-e-l-l-y?" I asked in parting.

"No, it's s-p-o-k-e-s-m-a-n," he said. "I prefer to be known as an NBC spokesman. It's not our policy to identify our spokesmen here."

It's too bad that Pete Axthelm doesn't have a spokesman. It's not that he's been any more complicit in the promotion of cigarettes and sports than most other big-name sports writers. He hasn't. But the more loudly he defended the marriage of the two, the more embarassing it became to listen, and the more so because he seemed like a terrifically nice guy.

This, remember, is a man who's been at the top of the profession that should be chasing cigarettes from sports:

"Obviously, I can be criticized since we all make our outrageous salaries as a result of tobacco and beer advertising, so I know I'm setting myself up," he began. "I have to keep coming back to the thing with our Constitution—free rights, free markets, whatever."

And if kids look to athletes as role models? Well, that's their fault, Axthelm said. "What we really should be striving for is not to have athletes conform to more rules, but to have our kids realize that athletes are *not* role models," he said. (Philip Morris, no doubt, would be happy to sponsor another educational program, to help kids kick the hero-worship habit.)

Virginia Slims? "What I recall is the general slogan, 'You've come a long way, baby,' as being a good thing for women," he said. "I'm a feminist."

Q: "Isn't one of the areas in which women are achieving parity lung cancer?"

A: "I don't want to comment on that."

By the end of the conversation, Axthelm began to sound concerned. Perhaps, finally, he was as unconvinced by his own defense of the cigarette companies as I was. While Bobby Brown dealt with his lack of good answers by slamming down the phone, and Doug Kelly dealt with it by seeking anonymity, at least Axthelm stayed on the line. But the more he talked, the more his answers turned back against him: "I just don't want to be set up as an idiot," he said. "Don't set me up after a lung cancer paragraph and say, 'Virginia Slims has done a lot for women.'"

SIXTY PACK-YEARS

There's an odd sign on the door to one of the cancer wards at the Bethesda Naval Hospital. It lets visitors know that the "smoking lounge is located on 6 center." Not long ago, Dr. Paul Sperduto, an oncologist at the National Cancer Institute, escorted me onto the NCI ward and pulled the medical chart of a patient, who, four years ago, coughing, had gone to see his doctor. "Metastatic small cell lung cancer to the left neck, mediastinum, right hilum, and liver," Dr. Sperduto said. "That's definitely *not curable."*

But the mere fact of the patient's presence at such a sophisticated facility indicated he'd been luckier than most. If he hadn't been chosen for a government study, he probably wouldn't have been there. His chart tagged him as lucky, too. Under sophisticated "cancer management," his disease had disappeared twice, adding a few years to his life.

The first bout of management began in 1985 with the onset of chemotherapy, monthly for eight consecutive months—four or five days of chemicals followed by a week or so of vomiting and exhaustion; rest and repeat. It seemed to work. By July 1986, a CT scan could no longer find the lump in his chest. Cancer management then called for a round of brain radiation, since the disease is known to sojourn there.

By December 1987, it was back, and four more months of chemotherapy began, this time with different chemicals. Again the cancer fled. "That's great," Dr. Sperduto said. "Relatively speaking." Six months later, in September, 1988, it returned. This time, the cancer managers tried the experimental therapy called In Vitro Best Regimen. They sent a piece of the patient's lung into the lab, grew his disease in petri dishes, and sprinkled them with competing chemicals, to see which seemed to work best. Cytoxan won. And into his veins it went, over the course of five monthly cycles. It was now January 1989, and nothing was happening. The cancer held firm.

Another experiment began—a monoclonal antibody, the discovery of which had earned a researcher a Nobel Prize. That didn't work either. The cancer now appeared throughout his chest and liver. In March, a tumor in the throat wouldn't let him swallow. The cancer managers radiated it down. In April, the pain medicine was locking his bowels. The physicians reduced his dosage—good for the bowels, bad for the pain. Next came an electrolyte imbalance, which brings more vomiting and the possibility of seizures. The chemotherapy, meanwhile, had caused a "peripheral neuropathy," the sensation of burning in the patient's arms and legs. When I met him in July, the man with the lucky chart, a former auto mechanic now 58 years old, was back for more treatment.

Cancer doctors speak not in years but in pack-years, and this man's number was 60: one-and-a-half packs of Lucky Strikes a day, times forty years, beginning at age 15. "My father smoked, both my brothers smoked," he said. "At that age, it makes you feel like you're a big man. . . . Of course, my daughters have always been after me to stop. They smoke now, too. Now I'm trying to get them to stop. The oldest one sent away for that Cigarrest, or whatever you call it. But her husband smokes too. She said it didn't work."

It was quiet in his room. He spoke in a monotone, with no peaks of anger or dips of despair. He wasn't mad, he said—not at Lucky Strikes, not at the disease, not at the clumps of hair that keep falling out "all over the bed and all over the pillow." He'd had a full life, he said, and Dr. Sperduto nodded in support: his patient had been married for 33 years, with three daughters, and four grandchildren. By the time we said goodbye, all three of us knew he'd be dead by Christmas.

Driving out of the hospital, we passed an advertisement on the side of a city bus. It showed an athletic young woman, diving into a pool. "Salem," it said. "The Refreshest."

Questions for Discussion

1. Why does the author choose to write this essay as adversarial persuasion? Would conciliatory persuasion be more or less effective?
2. Notice how the author speaks directly to the readers (e.g., "In case you missed it . . . "). What do you think of this technique? What is the author's purpose in using this technique?
3. This essay was written for the readers of *The Washington Monthly,* a magazine of news and opinion. How might the author revise the essay if he were addressing readers of *Advertising Age,* a magazine for advertising executives? What changes would you recommend? What are the potential pitfalls of addressing this particular audience on this particular subject?
4. Is the author a credible source of information on this subject? If so, why? How does he achieve credibility? If not, what might he do to establish his credibility?
5. Do you think the evidence supporting the claim is sufficient, plausible, and pertinent? Why do you think it is or isn't? Cite specific passages to support your answer.

Opportunities for Writing

1. Write a letter to your favorite professional athlete, urging him or her to avoid all associations with cigarettes and cigarette companies. Cite appropriate statistics to support your position.
2. Voice your opinion on the subject of cigarette advertising. Do you think it ought to be illegal? Why or why not? Consider the legal, financial, medical, and ethical implications of your position.
3. Propose a new policy to officials at your school regarding cigarette smoking. In designing your policy, interview smokers and nonsmokers, faculty and students. Discuss possible objections to your proposal.
4. Evaluate the impact of corporate sponsorship on professional sports. Focus your evaluation on a specific sport. Review television and radio commercials as well as newspaper, magazine, and billboard advertising. What are the advantages and disadvantages of corporate sponsorship for both athletes and spectators?

Sexism in English
A 1990s Update

ALLEEN PACE NILSEN

Alleen Pace Nilsen was educated at Brigham Young University, American University, and the University of Iowa. She is currently a professor and administrator at Arizona State University. Her publications include Literature for Today's Young Adults *(1993) as well as articles for* English Journal *and* College English, *major professional journals pub-*

lished by the National Council of Teachers of English. She also served as co-editor of English Journal. In this essay, a revised version of "Sexism in English: A Feminist View," first published in Female Studies VI *in 1972, Nilsen compiles and analyzes English words and usages in order to "see what it could tell me about sexism." This linguist finds that the "language a culture uses is telltale evidence of the values and beliefs of that culture." Using knowledge by participation and observation, Nilsen not only recounts her research process but also argues three points that illustrate how her linguistic evidence (words and their denotations and connotations) reveal bias against women (sexism).*

Twenty years ago I embarked on a study of the sexism inherent in American English. I had just returned to Ann Arbor, Michigan, after living for two years (1967–1969) in Kabul, Afghanistan, where I had begun to look critically at the role society assigned to women. The Afghan version of the *chaderi* prescribed for Moslem women was particularly confining. Few women attended the American-built Kabul University where my husband was teaching linguistics because there were no women's dormitories, which meant that the only females who could attend were those whose families happened to live in the capital city. Afghan jokes and folklore were blatantly sexist; for example, this proverb: "If you see an old man, sit down and take a lesson; if you see an old woman, throw a stone."

But it wasn't only the native culture that made me question women's roles; it was also the American community. Nearly 600 Americans lived in Kabul, mostly supported by U.S. taxpayers. The single women were career secretaries, school teachers, or nurses. The three women who had jobs comparable to the American men's jobs were textbook editors with the assignment of developing reading books in Dari (Afghan Persian) for young children. They worked at the Ministry of Education, a large building in the center of the city. There were no women's restrooms so during their two-year assignment whenever they needed to go to the bathroom they had to walk across the street and down the block to the Kabul Hotel.

The rest of the American women were like myself—wives and mothers whose husbands were either career diplomats, employees of USAID, or college professors teaching at Kabul University. These were the women who were most influential in changing my way of thinking because we were suddenly bereft of our traditional roles. Servants worked for $1.00 a day and our lives revolved around supervising these men (women were not allowed to work for foreigners). One woman's husband grew so tired of hearing her stories that he scheduled an hour a week for listening to complaints. The rest of the time he wanted to keep his mind clear to focus on working with his Afghan counterparts and with the president of the University and the Minister of Education. He was going to make a difference in this country, while in the great eternal scheme of things it mattered little that the servant stole the batteries out of the flashlight or put chili powder instead of paprika on the eggs.

I continued to ponder this dramatic contrast between men's and women's work, and when we finished our contract and returned in the fall of 1969 to the University of Michigan in Ann Arbor I was surprised to find that many other women were also questioning the expectations that they had grown up with. I attended a campus women's conference, but I returned home more troubled than ever. Now that I knew housework was worth only a dollar a day, I couldn't take it seriously, but I wasn't angry in the same way these women were. Their militancy frightened me. I wasn't ready for a revolution, so I decided I would have my own feminist movement. I would study the English language and see what it could tell me about sexism. I started reading a desk dictionary and making notecards on every entry that seemed to tell something about male and female. I soon had a dog-eared dictionary, along with a collection of notecards filling two shoe boxes.

5   Ironically, I started reading the dictionary because I wanted to avoid getting involved in social issues, but what happened was that my notecards brought me right back to looking at society. Language and society are as intertwined as a chicken and an egg. The language that a culture uses is telltale evidence of the values and beliefs of that culture. And because there is a lag in how fast a language changes—new words can easily be introduced, but it takes a long time for old words and usages to disappear—a careful look at English will reveal the attitudes that our ancestors held and that we as a culture are therefore predisposed to hold. My notecards revealed three main points. Friends have offered the opinion that I didn't need to read the dictionary to learn such obvious facts. Nevertheless, it was interesting to have linguistic evidence of sociological observations.

WOMEN ARE SEXY; MEN ARE SUCCESSFUL

First, in American culture a woman is valued for the attractiveness and sexiness of her body, while a man is valued for his physical strength and accomplishments. A woman is sexy. A man is successful.

A persuasive piece of evidence supporting this view are the eponyms—words that have come from someone's name—found in English. I had a two-and-a-half-inch stack of cards taken from men's names, but less than a half-inch stack from women's names, and most of those came from Greek mythology. In the words that came into American English since we separated from Britain, there are many eponyms based on the names of famous American men: bartlett pear, boysenberry, diesel engine, franklin stove, ferris wheel, gatling gun, mason jar, sideburns, sousaphone, schick test, and winchester rifle. The only common eponyms taken from American women's names are *Alice blue* (after Alice Roosevelt Longworth), bloomers (after Amelia Jenks Bloomer) and *Mae West jacket* (after the buxom actress). Two out of the three feminine eponyms relate closely to a woman's physical anatomy, while the masculine eponyms (except for *sideburns* after General Burnsides) have nothing to do with the namesake's body, but instead honor the man for an accomplishment of some kind.

Although in Greek mythology women played a bigger role than they did in the biblical stories of the Judeo-Christian cultures and so the names of goddesses are accepted parts of the language in such place names as Pomona from the goddess of fruit and Athens from Athena, and in such common words as *cereal* from Ceres, *psychology* from Psyche, and *arachnoid* from Arachne, the same tendency to think of women in relation to sexuality is seen in the eponyms aphrodisiac from Aphrodite, the Greek name for the goddess of love and beauty, and *venereal disease,* from Venus, the Roman name for Aphrodite.

Another interesting word from Greek mythology is *Amazon.* According to Greek folk etymology, the *a* means "without" as in *atypical* or *amoral* while *mazon* comes from *mazos* meaning *breast* as still seen in *mastectomy.* In the Greek legend, Amazon women cut off their right breasts so that they could better shoot their bows. Apparently, the storytellers had a feeling that for women to play the active "masculine" role that the Amazons adopted for themselves, they had to trade in part of their femininity.

This preoccupation with women's breasts is not limited to ancient stories. As a volunteer for the University of Wisconsin's *Dictionary of American Regional English (DARE),* I read a western trapper's diary from the 1830s. I was to make notes of any unusual usages or language patterns. My most interesting finding was that he referred to a range of mountains as *The Teats,* a metaphor based on the similarity between the shapes of the mountains and women's breasts. Because today we use the French wording, *The Grand Tetons,* the metaphor isn't as obvious, but I wrote to mapmakers and found the following listings: *Nippletop* and *Little Nipple Top* near Mt. Marcy in the Adirondacks; *Nipple Mountain* in Archuleta County, Colorado; *Nipple Peak* in Coke County, Texas; *Nipple Butte* in Pennington, South Dakota; *Squaw Peak* in Placer County, California (and many other locations); *Maiden's Peak* and *Squaw Tit* (they're the same mountain) in the Cascade Range in Oregon; *Mary's Nipple* near Salt Lake City, Utah; and *Jane Russell Peaks* near Stark, New Hampshire.

Except for the movie star Jane Russell, the women being referred to are anonymous—it's only a sexual part of their body that is mentioned. When topographical features are named after men, it's probably not going to be to draw attention to a sexual part of their bodies but instead to honor individuals for an accomplishment. For example, no one thinks of a part of the male body when hearing a reference to Pike's Peak, Colorado, or Jackson Hole, Wyoming.

Going back to what I learned from my dictionary cards, I was surprised to realize how many pairs of words we have in which the feminine word has acquired sexual connotations while the masculine word retains a serious businesslike aura. For example, a *callboy* is the person who calls actors when it is time for them to go on stage, but a *callgirl* is a prostitute. Compare *sir* and *madam. Sir* is a term of respect while *madam* has acquired the specialized meaning of a brothel manager. Something similar has happened to *master* and *mistress.* Would you rather have a painting by *an old master* or *an old mistress*?

It's because the word *woman* had sexual connotations as in "She's his woman," that people began avoiding its use, hence such terminology as *ladies room, lady of the house,* and *girls' school* or *school for young ladies.* Feminists, who ask that people use the term *woman* rather than *girl* or *lady,* are rejecting the idea that *woman* is primarily a sexual term. They have been at least partially successful in that today *woman* is commonly used to communicate gender without intending implications about sexuality.

I found 200 pairs of words with masculine and feminine forms, for example, *heir/heiress, hero/heroine, steward/stewardess, usher/usherette,* etc. In nearly all such pairs, the masculine word is considered the base with some kind of a feminine suffix being added. The masculine form is the one from which compounds are made; for example, from *king/queen* comes *kingdom* but not *queendom,* from *sportsman/sportslady* comes *sportsmanship* but not *sports/ladyship.* There is one—and only one—semantic area in which the masculine word is not the base or more powerful word. This is in the area dealing with sex and marriage. When someone refers to a *virgin,* a listener will probably think of a female unless the speaker specifies *male* or uses a masculine pronoun. The same is true for *prostitute.*

15   In relation to marriage, there is much linguistic evidence showing that weddings are more important to women than to men. A woman cherishes the wedding and is considered a bride for a whole year, but a man is referred to as a groom only on the day of the wedding. The word *bride* appears in *bridal attendant, bridal gown, bridesmaid, bridal shower,* and even *bridegroom. Groom* comes from the Middle English *grom,* meaning "man," and in this sense is seldom used outside of a wedding. With most pairs of male/female words, people habitually put the masculine word first, *Mr. and Mrs., his and hers, boys and girls, men and women, kings and queens, brothers and sisters, guys and dolls,* and *host and hostess,* but it is the *bride and groom* who are talked about, not the *groom and bride.*

The importance of marriage to a woman is also shown by the fact that when a marriage ends in death, the woman gets the title of *widow.* A man gets the derived title of *widower.* This term is not used in other phrases or contexts, but *widow* is seen in *widowhood, widow's peak,* and *widow's walk.* A *widow* in a card game is an extra hand of cards, while in typesetting it is an extra line of type.

How changing cultural ideas bring changes to language is clearly visible in this semantic area. The feminist movement has caused the differences between the sexes to be downplayed, and since I did my dictionary study two decades ago the word *singles* has largely replaced such sex specific and value-laden terms as *bachelor, old maid, spinster, divorcee, widow,* and *widower.* And in 1970, I wrote that when a man is called *a professional* he is thought to be a doctor or a lawyer, but when people hear a woman referred to as *a professional* they are likely to think of a prostitute. That's not as true today because so many women have become doctors and lawyers that it's no longer incongruous to think of women in those professional roles.

Another change that has taken place is in wedding announcements. They used to be sent out from the bride's parents and did not even give the name of the groom's parents. Today, most couples choose to list either all or none of the parents' names. Also, it is now much more likely that both the bride and groom's picture will be in the newspaper, while a decade ago only the bride's picture was published on the "Women's" or the "Society" page. Even the traditional wording of the wedding ceremony is being changed. Many officials now pronounce the couple "husband and wife" instead of the old "man and wife," and they ask the bride if she promises "to love, honor, and cherish," instead of "to love, honor, and obey."

WOMEN ARE PASSIVE; MEN ARE ACTIVE

The wording of the wedding ceremony also relates to the second point that my cards showed, which is that women are expected to play a passive or weak role while men play an active or strong role. In the traditional ceremony, the official asks "Who gives the bride away?" and the father answers "I do." Some fathers answer "Her mother and I do," but that doesn't solve the problem inherent in the question.

The idea that a bride is something to be handed over from one man to another bothers people because it goes back to the days when a man's servants, his children, and his wife were all considered to be his property. They were known by his name because they belonged to him and he was responsible for their actions and their debts.

20   The grammar used in talking or writing about weddings as well as other sexual relationships shows the expectation of men playing the active role. Men *wed* women while women *become* brides of men. A man *possesses* a woman; he *deflowers* her; he *performs;* he *scores;* he *takes away* her virginity. Although a woman can *seduce* a man, she cannot offer him her virginity. When talking about virginity, the only way to make the woman the actor in the sentence is to say that "She lost her virginity," but people lose things by accident rather than by purposeful actions and so she's only the grammatical, not the real-life, actor.

The reason that women tried to bring the term *Ms.* into the language to replace *Miss* and *Mrs.* relates to this point. Married women resented being identified only under their husband's names. For example, when Susan Glascoe did something newsworthy she would be identified in the newspaper only as Mrs. John Glascoe. The dictionary cards showed what appeared to be an attitude on the part of editors that it was almost indecent to let a respectable woman's name march unaccompanied across the pages of a dictionary. Women were listed with male names whether or not the male contributed to the woman's reason for being in the dictionary or in his own right was as famous as the woman. For example, Charlotte Brontë was identified as Mrs. Arthur B. Nicholls, Amelia Earhart as Mrs. George Palmer Putnam, Helen Hayes as Mrs. Charles MacArthur, Jenny Lind as Mme. Otto Goldschmit, Cornelia Otis Skinner as the daughter of Otis, Harriet Beecher Stowe as the sister of Henry Ward Beecher, and Edith Sitwell as the sister of Osbert and Sacheverell. A very small number of women got into the dictionary without the benefit of a masculine escort. They were rebels and crusaders: temperance leaders Frances Elizabeth Caroline Willard and Carry Nation, women's rights leaders Carrie Chapman Cart and Elizabeth Cady Stanton, birth control educator Margaret Sanger, religious leader Mary Baker Eddy, and slaves Harriet Tubman and Phillis Wheatley.

Etiquette books used to teach that if a woman had *Mrs.* in front of her name, then the husband's name should follow because *Mrs.* is an abbreviated form of *Mistress* and a woman couldn't be a mistress of herself. As with many arguments about "correct" language usage, this isn't very logical because *Miss* is also an abbreviation of *Mistress.* Feminists hoped to simplify matters by introducing *Ms.* as an alternative to both *Mrs.* and *Ms.,* but what happened is that *Ms.* largely replaced *Miss* to became a catchall business title for women. Many married women still prefer the title *Mrs.,* and some resent being addressed with the term *Ms.* As one frustrated newspaper reporter complained, "Before I can write about a woman, I have to know not only her marital status but also her political philosophy." The result of such complications may contribute to the demise of titles which are already being ignored by many computer programmers who find it more efficient to simply use names, for example, in a business letter, "Dear Joan Garcia," instead of "Dear Mrs. Joan Garcia," "Dear Ms. Garcia," or "Dear Mrs. Louis Garcia."

The titles given to royalty provide an example of how males can be disadvantaged by the assumption that they are always to play the more powerful role.

In British royalty, when a male holds a title, his wife is automatically given the feminine equivalent. But the reverse is not true. For example, a *count* is a high political officer with a *countess* being his wife. The same is true for a *duke* and a *duchess* and a *king* and a *queen*. But when a female holds the royal title, the man she marries does not automatically acquire the matching title. For example, Queen Elizabeth's husband has the title of *prince* rather than *king*, but if Prince Charles should become king while he is still married to Lady or Princess Diana, she will be known as the queen. The reasoning appears to be that since masculine words are stronger, they are reserved for true heirs and withheld from males coming into the royal family by marriage. If Prince Phillip were called *King Phillip*, it would be much easier for British subjects to forget where the true power lies.

The names that people give their children show the hopes and dreams they have for them, and when we look at the differences between male and female names in a culture we can see the cumulative expectations of that culture. In our culture girls often have names taken from small, aesthetically pleasing items, for example, *Ruby, Jewel,* and *Pearl. Esther,* and *Stella* mean "star," *Ada* means "ornament," and *Vanessa* means "butterfly." Boys are more likely to be given names with meanings of power and strength; for example, *Neil* means "champion," *Martin* is from Mars, the God of War, *Raymond* means "wise protection," *Harold* means "chief of the army," *Ira* means "vigilant," *Rex* means "king," and *Richard* means "strong king."

25   We see similar differences in food metaphors. Food is a passive substance just sitting there waiting to be eaten. Many people have recognized this and so no longer feel comfortable describing women as "delectable morsels." However, when I was a teenager, it was considered a compliment to refer to a girl (we didn't call anyone a *woman* until she was middle-aged) as *a cute tomato, a peach, a dish, a cookie, honey, sugar, or sweetie-pie.* When being affectionate, women will occasionally call a man *honey or sweetie,* but, in general, food metaphors are used much less often with men than with women. If a man is called *a fruit,* his masculinity is being questioned. But it's perfectly acceptable to use a food metaphor if the food is heavier and more substantive than that used for women. For example, pinup pictures of women have long been known as *cheesecake,* but when Burt Reynolds posed for a nude centerfold the picture was immediately dubbed *beefcake,* that is, *a hunk of meat.* That such sexual references to men have come into the general language is another reflection of how society is beginning to lessen the differences between their attitudes toward men and women.

Something similar to the *fruit* metaphor happens with references to plants. We insult a man by calling him a *pansy,* but it wasn't considered particularly insulting to talk about a girl being a *wallflower,* a *clinging vine,* or a *shrinking violet,* or to give girls such names as *Ivy, Rose, Lily, Iris, Daisy, Camellia, Heather,* or *Flora.* A plant metaphor can be used with a man if the plant is big and strong, for example, Andrew Jackson's nickname of *Old Hickory.* Also, the phrases *blooming idiots* and *budding geniuses* can be used with either sex, but notice how they are based on the most active thing a plant can do, which is to bloom or bud.

Animal metaphors also illustrate the different expectations for males and females. Men are referred to as *studs, bucks,* and *wolves* while women are referred to with such metaphors as *kitten, bunny, beaver, bird, chick,* or *lamb.* In the 1950s, we said that boys went *tomcatting,* but today it's just *catting around* and both boys and girls do it. When the term *foxy,* meaning that someone was sexy, first became popular it was used only for girls, but now someone of either sex can be described as *a fox.* Some animal metaphors that are used predominantly with men have negative connotations based on the size and/or strength of the animals, for example, *beast, bullheaded, jackass, rat, loanshark,* and *vulture.* Negative metaphors used with women are based on smaller animals, for example, *social butterfly, mousy, catty,* and *vixen.* The feminine terms connote action, but not the same kind of large-scale action as with the masculine terms.

Women Are Connected with Negative Connotations, Men with Positive Connotations

The final point that my notecards illustrated was how many positive connotations are associated with the concept of masculine, while there are either trivial or negative connotations connected with the corresponding feminine concept. An example from the animal metaphors makes a good illustration. The word shrew taken from the name of a small but especially vicious animal was defined in my dictionary as "an ill tempered scolding woman," but the word *shrewd* taken from the same root was defined as "marked by clever, discerning awareness" and was illustrated with the phrase "a shrewd businessman."

Early in life, children are conditioned to the superiority of the masculine role. As child psychologists point out, little girls have much more freedom to experiment with sex roles than do little boys. If a little girl acts like a *tomboy,* most parents have mixed feelings, being at least partially proud. But if their little boy acts like a *sissy* (derived from *sister*), they call a psychologist. It's perfectly acceptable for a little girl to sleep in the crib that was purchased for her brother, to wear his hand-me-down jeans and shirts, and to ride the bicycle that he has outgrown. But few parents would put a boy baby in a white and gold crib decorated with frills and lace, and virtually no parents would have their little boy wears his sister's hand-me-down dresses, nor would they have their son ride a girl's pink bicycle with a flower-bedecked basket. The proper names given to girls and boys show this same attitude. Girls can have "boy" names—*Chris, Craig, Jo, Kelly, Shawn, Teri, Toni,* and *Sam*—but it doesn't work the other way around. A couple of generations ago, *Beverley, Frances, Hazel, Marion,* and *Shirley* were common boys' names. As parents gave these names to more and more girls, they fell into disuse for males, and some older men who have these names prefer to go by their initials or by such abbreviated forms as *Haze* or *Shirl.*

When a little girl is told to *be a lady,* she is being told to sit with her knees together and to be quiet and dainty. But when a little boy is told to *be a man* he is being told to be noble, strong, and virtuous—to have all the qualities that the speaker looks on as desirable. The concept of manliness has such positive connotations that it used to be a compliment to call someone a *he-man,* to say that he was doubly a man. Today, many people are more ambivalent about this term and respond to it much as they do to the word *macho.* But calling someone a *manly man* or a *virile man* is nearly always meant as a compliment. *Virile* comes from the Indo-European *vir* meaning "man," which is also the basis of *virtuous*. Contrast the positive connotations of both *virile* and *virtuous* with the negative connotations of *hysterical*. The Greeks took this latter word from their name for *uterus* (as still seen in *hysterectomy*). They thought that women were the only ones who experienced uncontrolled emotional outbursts and so the condition must have something to do with a part of the body that only women have.

Differences between positive male connotations and negative female connotations can be seen in several pairs of words which differ denotatively only in the matter of sex. *Bachelor* as compared to *spinster* or *old maid* has such positive connotations that women try to adopt them by using the term *bachelor-girl* or *bachelorette*. *Old maid* is so negative that it's the basis for metaphors: pretentious and fussy old men are called *old maids* as are the leftover kernels of unpopped popcorn and the last card in a popular children's game.

Patron and *matron* (Middle English for *father* and *mother*) have such different levels of prestige that women try to borrow the more positive masculine connotations with the word *patroness,* literally "female father." Such a peculiar term came about because of the high prestige attached to *patron* in such phrases as *a patron of the arts* or *a patron saint*. *Matron* is more apt to be used in talking about a woman in charge of a jail or a public restroom.

When men are doing jobs that women often do, we apparently try to pay the men extra by giving them fancy titles; for example, a male cook is more likely to be called a *chef* while a male seamstress will get the title of *tailor*. The Armed Forces have a special problem in that they recruit under such slogans as "The Marine Corps builds men!" and "Join the Army! Become a Man." Once the recruits are enlisted, they find themselves doing much of the work that has been traditionally thought of as "women's work." The solution to getting the work done and not insulting anyone's masculinity was to change the titles as shown below:

waitress	orderly
nurse	medic or corpsman
secretary	clerk-typist
assistant	adjutant
dishwasher or kitchen helper	KP (kitchen police)

Compare *brave* and *squaw*. Early settlers in America truly admired Indian men and hence named them with a word that carried connotations of youth, vigor, and courage. But they used the Algonquin's name for "woman," and over the years it developed almost opposite connotations to those of *brave*. *Wizard* and *witch* contrast almost as much. The masculine *wizard* implies skill and wisdom combined with magic, while the feminine *witch* implies evil intentions combined with magic. Part of the unattractiveness of both *witch* and *squaw* is that they have been used so often to refer to old women, something with which our culture is particularly uncomfortable, just as the Afghans were. Imagine my surprise, when I ran across the phrases *grandfatherly advice* and *old wives' tales* and realized that the underlying implication is the same as the Afghan proverb about old men being worth listening to while old women talk only foolishness.

Other terms that show how negatively we view old women as compared to young women are *old nag* as compared to *filly, old crow* or *old bat* as compared to *bird,* and being *catty* as compared to being *kittenish.* There is no matching set of metaphors for men. The chicken metaphor tells the whole story of a woman's life. In her youth she is a *chick.* Then she marries and begins *feathering her nest.* Soon she begins feeling *cooped up,* so she goes to *hen parties* where she *cackles* with her friends. Then she has her *brood,* begins to *henpeck* her husband, and finally turns into *an old biddy.*

I embarked on my study of the dictionary not with the intention of prescribing language change but simply to see what the language would tell me about sexism. Nevertheless, I have been both surprised and pleased as I've watched the changes that have occurred over the past two decades. I'm one of those linguists who believes that new language customs will cause a new generation of speakers to grow up with different expectations. This is why I'm happy about people's efforts to use inclusive language, to say *he or she* or *they* when speaking about individuals whose names they do not know. I'm glad that leading publishers have developed guidelines to help writers use language that is fair to both sexes and I'm glad that most newspapers and magazines list women by their own names instead of only by their husbands' names and that educated and thoughtful people no longer begin their business letters with "Dear Sir" or "Gentlemen" but instead use a memo form or begin with such salutations as "Dear Colleagues," "Dear Reader," or "Dear Committee Members." I'm also glad that such words as *poetess, authoress, conductress,* and *aviatrix* now sound quaint and old fashioned and that *chairman* is giving way to *chair* or *head, mailman* to *mail carrier, clergyman* to *clergy,* and *stewardess* to *flight attendant.* I was also pleased when the National Oceanic and Atmospheric Administration bowed to feminist complaints and in the late seventies began to alternate men's and women's names for hurricanes. However, I wasn't so pleased to discover that the change did not immediately erase sexist thoughts from everyone's mind as shown by a headline about Hurricane David in a 1979 New York tabloid, "David Rapes Virgin Islands." More recently, a similar metaphor appeared in a headline in the *Arizona Republic* about Hurricane Charlie, "Charlie Quits Carolinas, Flirts with Virginia."

What these incidents show is that sexism is not something existing independently in American English or in the particular dictionary that I happened to read. Rather, it exists in people's minds. Language is like an x-ray in providing visible evidence of invisible thoughts. The best thing about people being interested in and discussing sexist language is that as they make conscious decisions about what pronouns they will use, what jokes they will tell or laugh at, how they will write their names, or how they will begin their letters, they are forced to think about the underlying issue of sexism. This is good because as a problem that begins in people's assumptions and expectations, it's a problem that will be solved only when a great many people have given it a great deal of thought.

Questions for Discussion

1. What is the purpose of the essay's opening narrative? Does it serve to establish the author's credibility? Does it serve to motivate the audience?

2. Could you classify this essay as expressive aim writing? Could you classify it as referential aim writing?
3. Is the author's claim explicit or implicit? Cite specific passages to support your answer. Would the essay be more effective if the claim were implicit or explicit?
4. Is the evidence to support the claim sufficient? Is it excessive? Why do you think it is or isn't?
5. Does the author anticipate and answer objections to the claim? If you think she does, cite specific passages. If you think she doesn't, assess the impact of this omission.

Opportunities for Writing

1. Evaluate your favorite magazine on its usage of sexist language. Look at several issues for sexist headlines such as "David Rapes Virgin Islands" or sexist wording such as "chairman." Is this magazine doing a satisfactory job of avoiding sexist language?
2. Write a letter to the editor of your school or local newspaper, proposing a revised policy regarding "inclusive" language. Do you think inclusive language is necessary or unnecessary?
3. Give your opinion of the following words as applied to women: *babe, bitch, broad, chick, dish, fox, girl.* Do you consider such words offensive? Explain to a friend why such words are appropriate or inappropriate.

The Language of Discretion

AMY TAN

Amy Tan was born in Oakland, California, and attended San Jose State University and Dominican College. She is the author of Moon Lady *(1992),* The Kitchen God's Wife *(1991), and* The Joy Luck Club *(1989), as well as numerous short stories and essays. In this essay, Tan argues that we shouldn't attribute characteristics to people based solely on the language (i.e., words and phrases) that they use. "The Language of Discretion" appeared in* About Language: A Reader for Writers *(1992). Tan uses both knowledge by participation and observation to shape her arguments.*

At a recent family dinner in San Francisco, my mother whispered to me: "Sausau [Brother's Wife] pretends too hard to be polite! Why bother? In the end, she always takes everything."

My mother thinks like a *waixiao,* an expatriate, temporarily away from China since 1949, no longer patient with ritual courtesies. As if to prove her point, she reached across the table to offer my elderly aunt from Beijing the last scallop from the Happy Family seafood dish.

Sau-sau scowled. *"B'yao, zhen b'yao!"* (I don't want it, really I don't) she cried, patting her plump stomach.

"Take it! Take it!" scolded my mother in Chinese.

"Full, I'm already full," Sau-sau protested weakly, eyeing the beloved scallop.

"Ai!" exclaimed my mother, completely exasperated. "Nobody else wants it. If you don't take it, it will only rot!"

At this point, Sau-sau sighed, acting as if she were doing my mother a big favor by taking the wretched scrap off her hands.

My mother turned to her brother, a high-ranking communist official who was visiting her in California for the first time: "In America a Chinese person could starve to death. If you say you don't want it, they won't ask you again forever."

My uncle nodded and said he understood fully: Americans take things quickly because they have no time to be polite.

I thought about this misunderstanding again—of social contexts failing in translation—when a friend sent me an article from the *New York Times Magazine* (24 April 1988). The article, on changes in New York's Chinatown, made passing reference to the inherent ambivalence of the Chinese language.

Chinese people are so "discreet and modest," the article stated, there aren't even words for "yes" and "no."

That's not true, I thought, although I can see why an outsider might think that. I continued reading.

If one is Chinese, the article went on to say, "One compromises, one doesn't hazard a loss of face by an overemphatic response."

My throat seized. Why do people keep saying these things? As if we truly were those little dolls sold in Chinatown tourist shops, heads bobbing up and down in complacent agreement to anything said!

I worry about the effect of one-dimensional statements on the unwary and guileless. When they read about this so-called vocabulary deficit, do they also conclude that Chinese people evolved into a mild-mannered lot because the language only allowed them to hobble forth with minced words?

Something enormous is always lost in translation. Something insidious seeps into the gaps, especially when amateur linguists continue to compare, one-for-one, language differences and then put forth notions wide open to misinterpretation: that Chinese people have no direct linguistic means to make decisions, assert or deny, affirm or negate, just say no to drug dealers, or behave properly on the witness stand when told, "Please answer yes or no."

Yet one can argue, with the help of renowned linguists, that the Chinese are indeed up a creek without "yes" and "no." Take any number of variations on the old language-and-reality theory stated years ago by Edward Sapir: "Human beings . . . are very much at the mercy of the particular language which has become the medium for their society . . . . The fact of the matter is that the 'real world' is to a large extent built up on the language habits of the group."*

This notion was further bolstered by the famous Sapir-Whorf hypothesis, which roughly states that one's perception of the world and how one functions in it depends a great deal on the language used. As Sapir, Whorf, and new carriers of the banner would have us believe, language shapes our thinking, channels

---

*Edward Sapir, *Selected Writings*, ed. D.G. Mandelbaum (Berkeley and Los Angeles, 1949).

us along certain patterns embedded in words, syntactic structures, and intonation patterns. Language has become the peg and the shelf that enables us to sort out and categorize the world. In English, we see "cats" and "dogs"; what if the language had also specified *glatz,* meaning "animals that leave fur on the sofa," and *glotz,* meaning "animals that leave fur and drool on the sofa"? How would language, the enabler, have changed our perceptions with slight vocabulary variations?

And if this were the case—of language being the master of destined thought—think of the opportunities lost from failure to evolve two little words, *yes* and *no,* the simplest of opposites! Ghengis Khan could have been sent back to Mongolia. Opium wars might have been averted. The Cultural Revolution could have been sidestepped.

There are still many, from serious linguists to pop psychology cultists, who view language and reality as inextricably tied, one being the consequence of the other. We have traversed the range from the Sapir-Whorf hypothesis to est and neurolinguistic programming, which tell us "you are what you say."

I too have been intrigued by the theories. I can summarize, albeit badly, ages-old empirical evidence: of Eskimos and their infinite ways to say "snow," their ability to *see* the differences in snowflake configurations, thanks to the richness of their vocabulary, while non-Eskimo speakers like myself founder in "snow," "more snow," and "lots more where that came from."

I too have experienced dramatic cognitive awakenings via the word. Once I added "mauve" to my vocabulary I began to see it everywhere. When I learned how to pronounce *prix fixe,* I ate French food at prices better than the easier-to-say *à la carte* choices.

But just how seriously are we supposed to take this?

Sapir said something else about language and reality. It is the part that often gets left behind in the dot-dot-dots of quotes: ". . . No two languages are ever sufficiently similar to be considered as representing the same social reality. The worlds in which different societies live are distinct worlds, not merely the same world with different labels attached."

When I first read this, I thought, Here at last is validity for the dilemmas I felt growing up in a bicultural, bilingual family! As any child of immigrant parents knows, there's a special kind of double bind attached to knowing two languages. My parents, for example, spoke to me in both Chinese and English; I spoke back to them in English.

"Amy-ah!" they'd call to me.

"What?" I'd mumble back.

"Do not question us when we call," they scolded me in Chinese. "It is not respectful."

"What do you mean?"

"Ai! Didn't we just tell you not to question?"

To this day, I wonder which parts of my behavior were shaped by Chinese, which by English. I am tempted to think, for example, that if I am of two minds on some matter it is due to the richness of my linguistic experiences, not to any personal tendencies toward wishy-washiness. But which mind says what?

Was it perhaps patience—developed through years of deciphering my mother's fractured English—that had me listening politely while a woman announced over the phone that I had won one of five valuable prizes? Was it respect—pounded in by the Chinese imperative to accept convoluted explanations—that had me agreeing that I might find it worthwhile to drive seventy-five miles to view a time-share resort? Could I have been at a loss for words when asked, "Wouldn't you like to win a Hawaiian cruise or perhaps a fabulous Star of India designed exclusively by Carter and Van Arpels?"

And when this same woman called back a week later, this time complaining that I had missed my appointment, obviously it was my type A language that kicked into gear and interrupted her. Certainly, my blunt denial—"Frankly I'm not interested"—was as American as apple pie. And when she said, "But it's in Morgan Hill," and I shouted, "Read my lips. I don't care if it's Timbuktu," you can be sure I said it with the precise intonation expressing both cynicism and disgust.

It's dangerous business, this sorting out of language and behavior. Which one is English? Which is Chinese? The categories manifest themselves: passive and aggressive, tentative and assertive, indirect and direct. And I realize they are just variations of the same theme: that Chinese people are discreet and modest.

Reject them all!

If my reaction is overly strident, it is because I cannot come across as too emphatic. I grew up listening to the same lines over and over again, like so many rote expressions repeated in an English phrase-book. And I too almost came to believe them.

Yet if I consider my upbringing more carefully, I find there was nothing discreet about the Chinese language I grew up with. My parents made everything abundantly clear. Nothing wishy-washy in their demands, no compromises accepted: "Of course you will become a famous neurosurgeon," they told me. "And yes, a concert pianist on the side."

In fact, now that I remember, it seems that the more emphatic outbursts always spilled over into Chinese: "Not that way! You must wash rice so not a single grain spills out."

I do not believe that my parents—both immigrants from mainland China—are an exception to the modest-and-discreet rule. I have only to look at the number of Chinese engineering students skewing minority ratios at Berkeley, MIT, and Yale. Certainly they were not raised by passive mothers and fathers who said, "It is up to you, my daughter. Writer, welfare recipient, masseuse, or molecular engineer—you decide."

And my American mind says, See, those engineering students weren't able to say no to their parents' demands. But then my Chinese mind remembers: Ah, but those parents all wanted their sons and daughters to be *pre-med.*

Having listened to both Chinese and English, I also tend to be suspicious of any comparisons between the two languages. Typically, one language—that of the person doing the comparing—is often used as the standard, the benchmark for a logical form of expression. And so the language being compared is always in danger of being judged deficient or superfluous, simplistic or unnecessarily complex, melodious or cacophonous. English speakers point out that Chinese is extremely difficult because it relies on variations in tone barely discernible to the human ear. By the same token, Chinese speakers tell me English is extremely difficult because it is inconsistent, a language of too many broken rules, of Mickey Mice and Donald Ducks.

Even more dangerous to my mind is the temptation to compare both language and behavior *in translation*. To listen to my mother speak English, one might think she has no concept of past or future tense, that she doesn't see the difference between singular and plural, that she is gender blind because she calls my husband "she." If one were not careful, one might also generalize that, based on the way my mother talks, all Chinese people take a circumlocutory route to get to the point. It is, in fact, my mother's idiosyncratic behavior to ramble a bit.

Sapir was right about differences between two languages and their realities. I can illustrate why word-for-word translation is not enough to translate meaning and intent. I once received a letter from China which I read to non-Chinese-speaking friends. The letter, originally written in Chinese, had been translated by my brother-in-law in Beijing. One portion described the time when my uncle at age ten discovered his widowed mother (my grandmother) had remarried—as a number three concubine, the ultimate disgrace for an honorable family. The translated version of my uncle's letter read in part:

> In 1925, I met my mother in Shanghai. When she came to me, I didn't have greeting to her as if seeing nothing. She pull me to a corner secretly and asked me why didn't have greeting to her. I couldn't control myself and cried, "Ma! Why did you leave us? People told me: one day you ate a beancake yourself. Your sister-in-law found it and sweared at you, called your names. So . . . is it true?" She clasped my hand and answered immediately. "It's not true, don't say what like this." After this time, there was a few chance to meet her.

"What!" cried my friends. "Was eating a beancake so terrible?"

Of course not. The beancake was simply a euphemism; a ten-year-old boy did not dare question his mother on something as shocking as concubinage. Eating a beancake was his equivalent for committing this selfish act, something inconsiderate of all family members, hence, my grandmother's despairing response to what seemed like a ludicrous charge of gluttony. And sure enough, she was banished from the family, and my uncle saw her only a few times before her death.

While the above may fuel people's argument that Chinese is indeed a language of extreme discretion, it does not mean that Chinese people speak in secrets and riddles. The contexts are fully understood. It is only to those on the *outside* that the language seems cryptic, the behavior inscrutable.

I am, evidently, one of the outsiders. My nephew in Shanghai, who recently started taking English lessons, has been writing me letters in English. I had told him I was a fiction writer, and so in one letter he wrote, "Congratulate to you on your writing. Perhaps one day I should like to read it." I took it in the same vein as "Perhaps one day we can get together for lunch." I sent back a cheery note. A month went by and another letter arrived from Shanghai. "Last one perhaps I hadn't writing distinctly," he said. "In the future, you'll send a copy of your works for me."

I try to explain to my English-speaking friends that Chinese language use is more *strategic* in manner, whereas English tends to be more direct; an American business executive may say, "Let's make a deal," and the Chinese manager may reply, "Is your son interested in learning about your widget business?" Each to his or her own purpose, each with his or her own linguistic path. But I hesitate to add more to the pile of generalizations, because no matter how many examples I provide and explain, I fear that it appears defensive and only reinforces the image: that Chinese people are "discreet and modest"—and it takes an American to explain what they really mean.

Why am I complaining? The description seems harmless enough (after all, the *New York Times Magazine* writer did not say "slippery and evasive"). It is precisely the bland, easy acceptability of the phrase that worries me.

I worry that the dominant society may see Chinese people from a limited—and limiting—perspective. I worry that seemingly benign stereotypes may be part of the reason there are few Chinese in top management positions, in mainstream political roles. I worry about the power of language: that if one says anything enough times—in *any* language—it might become true.

Could this be why Chinese friends of my parents' generation are willing to accept the generalization?

"Why are you complaining?" one of them said to me. "If people think we are modest and polite, let them think that. Wouldn't Americans be pleased to admit they are thought of as polite?"

And I do believe anyone would take the description as a compliment—at first. But after a while, it annoys, as if the only things that people heard one say were phatic remarks: "I'm so pleased to meet you. I've heard many wonderful things about you. For me? You shouldn't have!"

These remarks are not representative of new ideas, honest emotions, or considered thought. They are what is said from the polite distance of social contexts: of greetings, farewells, wedding thank-you notes, convenient excuses, and the like.

It makes me wonder though. How many anthropologists, how many sociologists, how many travel journalists have documented so-called "natural interactions" in foreign lands, all observed with spiral notebook in hand? How many other cases are there of the long-lost primitive tribe, people who turned out to be sophisticated enough to put on the stone-age show that ethnologists had come to see?

And how many tourists fresh off the bus have wandered into Chinatown expecting the self-effacing shopkeeper to admit under duress that the goods are not worth the price asked? I have witnessed it.

"I don't know," the tourist said to the shopkeeper, a Cantonese woman in her fifties. "It doesn't look genuine to me. I'll give you three dollars."

"You don't like my price, go somewhere else," said the shopkeeper.

"You are not a nice person," cried the shocked tourist, "not a nice person at all!"

"Who say I have to be nice," snapped the shopkeeper.

"So how does one say 'yes' and 'no' in Chinese?" ask my friends a bit warily.

And here I do agree in part with the *New York Times Magazine* article. There is no one word for "yes" or "no"—but not out of necessity to be discreet. If anything, I would say the Chinese equivalent of answering "yes" or "no" is dis*crete,* that is, specific to what is asked.

Ask a Chinese person if he or she has eaten, and he or she might say *chrle* (eaten already) or perhaps *meiyoi:* (have not).

Ask, "So you had insurance at the time of the accident?" and the response would be *dwei* (correct) or *meiyou* (did not have).

Ask, "Have you stopped beating your wife?" and the answer refers directly to the proposition being asserted or denied: stopped already, still have not, never beat, have no wife.

What could be clearer?

As for those who are still wondering how to translate the language of discretion, I offer this personal example.

My aunt and uncle were about to return to Beijing after a three-month visit to the United States. On their last night I announced I wanted to take them out to dinner.

"Are you hungry?" I asked in Chinese.

"Not hungry," said my uncle promptly, the same response he once gave me ten minutes before he suffered a low-blood-sugar attack.

"Not too hungry," said my aunt. "Perhaps you're hungry?"

"A little," I admitted.

"We can eat, we can eat," they both consented.

"What kind of food?" I asked.

"Oh, doesn't matter. Anything will do. Nothing fancy, just some simple food is fine."

"Do you like Japanese food? We haven't had that yet," I suggested. They looked at each other.

"We can eat it," said my uncle bravely, this survivor of the Long March.

"We have eaten it before," added my aunt. "Raw fish."

"Oh, you don't like it?" I said. "Don't be polite. We can go somewhere else."

"We are not being polite. We can eat it," my aunt insisted.

So I drove them to Japantown and we walked past several restaurants featuring colorful plastic displays of sushi.

"Not this one, not this one either," I continued to say, as if searching for a Japanese restaurant similar to the last. "Here it is," I finally said, turning into a restaurant famous for its Chinese fish dishes from Shandong.

"Oh, Chinese food!" cried my aunt, obviously relieved.

My uncle patted my arm. "You think Chinese."

"It's your last night here in America," I said. "So don't be polite. Act like an American."

And that night we ate a banquet.

Questions for Discussion

1. Do you think the title of this essay is effective? If so, why? If not, what other title would you recommend for this essay?
2. How important is this essay's expressive aim? Do you think this essay could be classified as expressive aim writing?
3. Do you think the ending is appropriate? What is the author's purpose in ending the essay this way?
4. How would this essay differ if it were written using only knowledge by participation? Which passages would be omitted? How important is

that information? Does that information establish the author's credibility, support the claim, or motivate the audience?
5. Notice the frequency of dialogue. What do you think of this technique? Is it effective here? How does it influence your reading of this essay?

Opportunities for Writing

1. Write a letter to city officials proposing a special program to honor the contributions of Chinese people to the local community. Identify a specific date and location for the program, appropriate award recipients, estimated costs, and possible program sponsors.
2. Write a review of a movie, focusing on its characterization of Chinese people. Does this movie offer a realistic portrait of Chinese traditions and practices? Does it encourage stereotyping? Explain your evaluation.
3. Using a questionnaire, assess the knowledge of 100 students at your school regarding the history, geography, politics, and languages of China. In a letter to the editor of your school newspaper, discuss the positive or negative implications of your findings.

From a Native Daughter

HAUNANI-KAY TRASK

Haunani-Kay Trask, a native Hawaiian, was educated at the University of Wisconsin. She is a professor of Hawaiian Studies, the director of the Center for Hawaiian Studies at the University of Hawaii at Manoa, and author of Eros and Power: The Promise of Feminist Theory *(1986). In "From a Native Daughter," Trask argues that Western historians have not and cannot tell the history of Hawaiian people, land, native stories, and language. "They must come," she contends, "as American Indians suggested long ago, to understand the land. Not in the Western way, but in the indigenous way, the way of living within and protecting the bond between people and 'āina [stories]." While her knowledge by participation is strong, Trask bolsters it with additional sources (i.e., consider her academic bibliography and ability to integrate research). This essay first appeared in* The American Indian and the Problem of History *and uses a variation of the APA style.*

> *E noi'i wale mai no ka haole, a,*
> *'a'ole e pau na hana a Hawai'i 'imi loa*
> *Let the haole freely research us in detail*
> *But the doings of deep delving Hawai'i*
> *will not be exhausted.*
>
> —Kepelino, 19th-century Hawaiian historian

Aloha kākou. Let us greet each other in friendship and love. My given name is Haunaniokawēkiu o Haleakalā, native of *Hawai'i Nei*. My father's family is from the *'āina* (land) of Kaua'i, my mother's family from the *'āina* of Maui. I reside today among my native people in the community of *Waimānalo*.

I have lived all my life under the power of America. My native country, Hawai'i, is owned by the United States. I attended missionary schools, both

Catholic and Protestant, in my youth, and I was sent away to the American mainland to receive a "higher" education at the University of Wisconsin. Now I teach the history and culture of my people at the University of Hawai'i.

When I was young the story of my people was told twice: once by my parents, then again by my school teachers. From my 'ohana (family), I learned about the life of the old ones: how they fished and planted by the moon; shared all the fruits of their labors, especially their children; danced in great numbers for long hours; and honored the unity of their world in intricate genealogical chants. My mother said Hawaiians had sailed over thousands of miles to make their home in these sacred islands. And they had flourished, until the coming of the *haole* (whites).

At school, I learned that the "pagan Hawaiians" did not read or write, were lustful cannibals, traded in slaves, and could not sing. Captain Cook had "discovered" Hawai'i and the ungrateful Hawaiians had killed him. In revenge, the Christian god had cursed the Hawaiians with disease and death.

5   I learned the first of these stories from speaking with my mother and father. I learned the second from books. By the time I left for college, the books had won out over my parents, especially since I spent four long years in a missionary boarding school for Hawaiian children.

When I went away I understood the world as a place and a feeling divided in two: one *haole* (white), and the other *kānaka* (native). When I returned ten years later with a Ph.D., the division was sharper, the lack of connection more painful. There was the world that we lived in—my ancestors, my family, and my people—and then there was the world historians described. This world, they had written, was the truth. A primitive group, Hawaiians had been ruled by bloodthirsty priests and despotic kings who owned all the land and kept our people in feudal subjugation. The chiefs were cruel, the people poor.

But this was not the story my mother told me. No one had owned the land before the *haole* came; everyone could fish and plant, except during sacred periods. And the chiefs were good and loved their people.

Was my mother confused? What did our *kūpuna* (elders) say? They replied: did these historians (all *haole*) know the language? Did they understand the chants? How long had they lived among our people? Whose stories had they heard?

None of the historians had ever learned our mother tongue. They had all been content to read what Europeans and Americans had written. But why did scholars, presumably well-trained and thoughtful, neglect our language? Not merely a passageway to knowledge, language is a form of knowing by itself; a people's way of thinking and feeling is revealed through its music.

10   I sensed the answer without needing to answer. From years of living in a divided world, I knew the historian's judgment: *There is no value in things Hawaiian; all value comes from things haole.*

Historians, I realized, were very like missionaries. They were a part of the colonizing horde. One group colonized the spirit; the other, the mind. Frantz Fanon had been right, but not just about Africans. He had been right about the bondage of my own people: "By a kind of perverted logic, [colonialism] turns to the past of the oppressed people, and distorts, disfigures, and destroys it" (1968:210). The first step in the colonizing process, Fanon had written, was the deculturation of a people. What better way to take our culture than to remake our image? A rich historical past became small and ignorant in the hands of Westerners. And we suffered a damaged sense of people and culture because of this distortion.

Burdened by a linear, progressive conception of history and by an assumption that Euro-American culture flourishes at the upper end of that progression, Westerners have told the history of Hawai'i as an inevitable if occasionally bittersweet triumph of Western ways over "primitive" Hawaiian ways. A few authors—the most sympathetic—have recorded with deep-felt sorrow the passing of our people. But in the end, we are repeatedly told, such an eclipse was for the best.

Obviously it was best for Westerners, not for our dying multitudes. This is why the historian's mission has been to justify our passing by celebrating Western dominance. Fanon would have called this missionizing, intellectual colonization. And it is clearest in the historian's insistence that pre-*haole* Hawaiian land tenure was "feudal"—a term that is now applied, without question, in every monograph, in every schoolbook, and in every tour guide description of my people's history.

From the earliest days of Western contact my people told their guests that *no one* owned the land. The land—like the air and the sea—was for all to use and share as their birthright. Our chiefs were *stewards* of the land; they could not own or privately possess the land any more than they could sell it.

15 But the *haole* insisted on characterizing our chiefs as feudal landlords and our people as serfs. Thus, a European term which described a European practice founded on the European concept of private property—feudalism—was imposed upon a people halfway around the world from Europe and vastly different from her in every conceivable way. More than betraying an ignorance of Hawaiian culture and history, however, this misrepresentation was malevolent in design.

By inventing feudalism in ancient Hawai'i, Western scholars quickly transformed a spiritually-based, self-sufficient economic system of land use and occupancy into an oppressive, medieval European practice of divine right ownership, with the common people tied like serfs to the land. By claiming that a Pacific people lived under a European system—that the Hawaiians lived under feudalism—Westerners could then degrade a successful system of shared land use with a pejorative and inaccurate Western term. Land tenure changes instituted by Americans and in line with current Western notions of private property were then made to appear beneficial to the Hawaiians. But in practice, such changes benefited the *haole,* who alienated the people from the land, taking it for themselves.

The prelude to this land alienation was the great dying of the people. Barely half a century after contact with the West our people had declined in number by eighty percent. Disease and death were rampant. The sandalwood forests had been stripped bare for international commerce between England and China. The missionaries had insinuated themselves everywhere. And a debt-ridden Hawaiian king (there had been no king before Western contact) succumbed to enormous pressure from the Americans and followed their schemes for dividing up the land.

This is how private property land tenure entered Hawai'i. The common people, driven from their birthright, received less than one percent of the land. They starved while huge *haole*-owned sugar plantations thrived.

And what had the historians said? They had said that the Americans "liberated" the Hawaiians from an oppressive "feudal" system. By inventing a false feudal past, the historians justify—and become complicitous in—massive American theft.

20 Is there "evidence"—as historians call it—for traditional Hawaiian concepts of land use? The evidence is in the sayings of my people and in the words they wrote more than a century ago, much of which has been translated. However, historians have chosen to ignore any references here to shared land use. But there *is* incontrovertible evidence in the very structure of the Hawaiian language. If the historians had bothered to learn our language (as any American historian of France would learn French) they would have discovered that we show possession in two ways: through the use of an "a" possessive, which reveals acquired status, and through the use of an "o" possessive, which denotes inherent status. My body (*ko 'u kino*) and my parents (*ko'u mākua*), for example, take the "o" form; most material objects, such as food (*ka'u mea'ai*) take the "a" form. But land, like one's body and one's parents, takes the "o" possessive (*ko'u 'āina*). Thus, in our way of speaking, land is inherent to the people; it is like our bodies and our parents. The people cannot exist without the land, and the land cannot exist without the people.

Every major historian of Hawai'i has been mistaken about Hawaiian land tenure. The chiefs did not own the land: they *could not* own the land. My mother was right and the *haole* historians were wrong. If they had studied our language they would have known that no one owned the land. But was their failing merely ignorance, or simple ethnocentric bias?

No, I did not believe them to be so benign. As I read on, a pattern emerged in their writing. Our ways were inferior to those of the West, to those of the historians' own culture. We were "less developed," or "immature," or "authoritarian." In some tellings we were much worse. Thus, Gavan Daws (1968), the most famed modern historian of Hawai'i, had continued a tradition established earlier by missionaries Hiram Bingham (1848) and Sheldon Dibble (1909), by referring to the old ones as "thieves" and "savages" who regularly practiced infanticide and who, in contrast to "civilized" whites, preferred "lewd dancing" to work. Ralph Kuykendall (1938), long considered the most thorough if also the most boring of historians of Hawai'i, sustained another fiction—that my ancestors owned slaves, the outcast *Kauwā*. This opinion, as well as the description of Hawaiian land tenure as feudal, had been supported by respected sociologist Andrew Lind (1938).* Finally, nearly all historians had refused to accept our

---

*See also Fornander (1878–85). Lest one think those sources antiquated, it should be noted that there exist only a handful of modern scholarly works on the history of Hawai'i. The most respected are those by Kuykendall (1938) and Daws (1968), and a social history of the twentieth century by Lawrence Fuchs (1961). Of these, only Kuykendall and Daws claim any knowledge of pre-*haole* history, while concentrating on the nineteenth century. However, countless popular works have relied on these two studies which, in turn, are themselves based on primary sources written in English by extremely biased, anti-Hawaiian Westerners such as explorers, traders, missionaries (e.g., Bingham [1848] and Dibble [1909]), and sugar planters. Indeed, a favorite technique of Daws's—whose *Shoal of Time* is the most acclaimed and recent general history—is the lengthy quotation without comment of the most racist remarks by missionaries and planters. Thus, at one point, half a page is consumed

(Continued on p. 447)

genealogical dating of over one hundred generations in Hawai'i. They had, instead, claimed that our earliest appearance in Hawai'i could only be traced to A.D. 700. Thus at least seven hundred years of our history were repudiated by "superior" Western scholarship. Only recently have archeological data confirmed what Hawaiians had said these many centuries (Tuggle, 1979).

Suddenly the entire sweep of our written history was clear to me. I was reading the West's view of itself through the degradation of my own past. When historians wrote that the king owned the land and the common people were bound to it, they were saying that ownership was the only way human beings in their world could relate to the land, and in that relationship, some one person had to control both the land and the interaction between humans.

And when they said that our chiefs were despotic, they were telling of their own society, where hierarchy always results in domination. Thus any authority or elder is automatically suspected of tyranny.

And when they wrote that Hawaiians were lazy, they meant that work must be continuous and ever a burden.

And when they wrote that we were promiscuous, they meant that love-making in the Christian West is a sin.

And when they wrote that we were racist because we preferred our own ways to theirs, they meant that their culture needed to dominate other cultures.

And when they wrote that we were superstitious, believing in the *mana* of nature and people, they meant that the West has long since lost a deep spiritual and cultural relationship to the earth.

And when they wrote that Hawaiians were "primitive" in their grief over the passing of loved ones, they meant that the West grieves for the living who do not walk among their ancestors.

For so long, more than half my life, I had misunderstood this written record, thinking it described my own people. But my history was nowhere present. For we had not written. We had chanted and sailed and fished and built and prayed. And we had told stories through the great blood lines of memory: genealogy.

To know my history, I had to put away my books and return to the land. I had to plant taro in the earth before I could understand the inseparable bond between people and 'āina. I had to feel again the spirits of nature and take gifts of plants and fish to the ancient altars. I had to begin to speak my language with our elders and leave long silences for wisdom to grow. But before anything else, I had to learn the language like a lover so that I could rock within her and lay at night in her dreaming arms.

---

with a "white man's burden" quotation from an 1886 *Planter's Monthly* article ("It is better for the colored man of India and Australia that the white man rules, and it is better here that the white man should rule . . . ," etc., p. 213). Daws's only comment is "The conclusion was inescapable." To get a sense of such characteristic contempt for Hawaiians, one has but to read the first few pages, where Daws refers several times to the Hawaiians as "savages" and "thieves" and where he approvingly has Captain Cook thinking, "It was a sensible primitive who bowed before a superior civilization" (p. 2). See also—among examples too numerous to cite—his glib description of sacred *hula* as a "frivolous diversion," which, instead of work, the Hawaiians "would practice energetically in the hot sun for days on end . . . their bare brown flesh glistening with sweat" (pp. 65–66). Daws, who repeatedly displays an affection for descriptions of Hawaiian skin color, taught Hawaiian history for some years at the University of Hawai'i; he now holds the Chair of Pacific History at the Australian National versity's Institute of Advanced Studies.

There was nothing in my schooling that had told me of this, or hinted that somewhere there was a longer, older story of origins, of the flowing of songs out to a great but distant sea. Only my parents' voices, over and over, spoke to me of a Hawaiian world. While the books spoke from a different world, a Western world.

And yet, Hawaiians are not of the West. We are of *Hawai'i Nei,* this world where I live, this place, this culture, this *'āina.*

What can I say, then, to Western historians of my place and people? Let me answer with a story.

A while ago I was asked to share a panel on the American overthrow of our government in 1893. The other panelists were all *haole.* But one was a *haole* historian from the mainland who had just published a book on what he called the American anti-imperialists. He and I met briefly in preparation for the panel. I asked him if he knew the language. He said no. I asked him if he knew the record of opposition to our annexation to America. He said there was no real evidence for it, just comments here and there. I told him that he didn't understand and that at the panel I would share the evidence. When we met in public and spoke, I said this:

> There is a song much loved by our people. It was sung when Hawaiians were forbidden from congregating in groups of more than three. Addressed to our imprisoned Queen, it was written in 1898, and tells of Hawaiian feelings for our land against annexation. Listen to our lament:
>
> | | |
> |---|---|
> | Kaulana na pua o'o Hawai'i | Famous are the children of Hawai'i |
> | Kūpa'a mahope o ka 'āina | Who cling steadfastly to the land |
> | Hiki mai ka 'elele o ka loko 'ino | Comes the evil-hearted with |
> | Palapala 'ānunu me ka pākaha | A document greedy for plunder |
> | Pane mai Hawai'i moku o Keawe | Hawai'i, island of Keawe, answers |
> | Kokua na hono a'o Pi'ilani | The bays of Pi'ilani [of Maui, Moloka'i, and Lana'i] help |
> | Kāko'o mai Kaua'i o Mano | Kaua'i of Mano assists |
> | Pau pu me ke one o Kakuhihewa | Firmly together with the sands of Kakuhihewa |
> | 'A'ole a'e kau i ka pūlima | |
> | Maluna o ka pepa o ka 'enemi | Do not put the signature |
> | Ho'ohui 'āina kū'ai hewa | On the paper of the enemy |
> | I ka pono sivila a'o ke kānaka | Annexation is wicked sale |
> | | Of the civil rights of the Hawaiian people |
> | Mahope mākou o Lili'ulani | We support Lili'uokalani |
> | A loa'a 'e ka pono o ka 'āina | Who has earned the right to the land |
> | Ha'ina 'ia mai ana ka puana | The story is told |
> | 'O ka po'e i aloha i ka 'āina | Of the people who love the land |

This song, I said, continues to be sung with great dignity at Hawaiian political gatherings. For our people still share the feelings of anger and protest that it conveys.

But our guest, the *haole* historian, answered that this song, although beautiful, was not evidence of either opposition or of imperialism from the Hawaiian perspective.

Many Hawaiians in the audience were shocked at his remarks, but, in hindsight, I think they were predictable. They are the standard response of the historian who does not know the language and has no respect for its memory.

Finally, I proceeded to relate a personal story, thinking that surely such a tale could not want for authenticity since I myself was relating it. My *tūtū* (grandmother) had told my mother who had told me that at the time of annexation (1898) a great wailing went up throughout the islands, a wailing of weeks, a wailing of impenetrable grief, a wailing of death. But he remarked again, this too is not evidence.

And so, history goes on, written in long volumes by foreign people. Whole libraries begin to form, book upon book, shelf upon shelf.

At the same time, the stories go on, generation to generation, family to family.

Which history do Western historians desire to know? Is it to be a tale of writings by their own countrymen, individuals convinced of their "unique" capacity for analysis, looking at us with Western eyes, thinking about us within Western philosophical contexts, categorizing us by Western indices, judging us by Judeo-Christian morals, exhorting us to capitalist achievements, and finally, leaving us an authoritative-because-Western record of their complete misunderstanding?

All this has been done already. Not merely a few times, but many times. And still, every year, there appear new and eager faces to take up the same telling, as if the West must continue, implacably, with the din of its own disbelief.

But there is, as there has been always, another possibility. If it is truly our history Western historians desire to know, they must put down their books, and take up our practices. First, of course, the language. But later, the people, the *'āina,* the stories. Above all, in the end, the stories. Historians must listen, they must hear the generational connections, the reservoir of sounds and meanings.

They must come, as American Indians suggested long ago, to understand the land. Not in the Western way, but in the indigenous way, the way of living within and protecting the bond between people and *'āina.*

This bond is cultural, and it can be understood only culturally. But because the West has lost any cultural understanding of the bond between people and land, it is not possible to know this connection through Western culture. This means that the history of indigenous people cannot be written from within Western culture. Such a story is merely the West's story of itself.

Our story remains unwritten. It rests within the culture, which is inseparable from the land. To know this is to know our history. To write this is to write of the land and the people who are born from her.

Cumulative Bibliography

Bingham, Hiram (1848). *A Residence of Twenty-one Years in the Sandwich Islands.* 2nd ed. New York: Converse.

Daws, Gavan (1968). *Shoal of Time: A History of the Hawaiian Islands.* Toronto and New York: Macmillan.

Dibble, Sheldon (1909). *History of the Sandwich Islands.* Honolulu: Thrum.

Fanon, Frantz (1968). *The Wretched of the Earth*. New York: Grove, Evergreen Edition.

Fornander, Abraham (1878–85). *An Account of the Polynesian Race: Its Origin and Migrations and the Ancient History of the Hawaiian People to the Times of Kamehameha I*. 3 vols. Vol. 1. London: Trübner.

Fuchs, Lawrence (1961). *Hawaii Pono: A Social History*. New York: Harcourt, Brace and World.

Kuykendall, Ralph S. (1938). *The Hawaiian Kingdom, 1778–1854*. Honolulu: Univ. of Hawaii Press.

Lind, Andrew (1938). *An Island Community: Ecological Succession in Hawaii*. New York: Greenwood.

Tuggle, H. David (1979). "Hawaii." In *The Prehistory of Polynesia*. Ed. Jesse D. Jennings. Pp. 167–99. Cambridge, Mass.: Harvard Univ. Press.

Questions for Discussion

1. How does the author establish credibility on this subject? Which techniques do you consider especially effective? Why?
2. How is this essay organized? Do you think headings would clarify the organization? If you do, add appropriate headings to the essay. If you don't, explain why headings are unnecessary.
3. Do you think this essay is adversarial or conciliatory persuasion? If adversarial, how might it be revised to be more conciliatory? If conciliatory, how might it be revised to be more adversarial?
4. Do you think this essay would be more or less effective if it were written without knowledge by participation? Which passages would be omitted?
5. Notice the series of six sentences beginning "And when they . . . ." What do you think of this repetition? What is the author trying to achieve through this technique? Is it effective?

Opportunities for Writing

1. Weigh the advantages and disadvantages for Hawaii of its annexation by the United States. Has Hawaii benefited from this annexation? If so, how? If not, why not?
2. Write a review of a television program that has a Hawaiian setting. In your evaluation, focus on the depiction of Hawaiians. Does it characterize Hawaiians as a primitive people? Does it display their dignity, variety, complexity, and humanity?
3. Write a review of Daws's *Shoal of Time: A History of the Hawaiian Islands* or Kuykendall's *The Hawaiian Kingdom, 1778–1854*. Is this book a credible source of information? Why do you think it is or isn't?

Give Children the Vote

VITA WALLACE

Vita Wallace is a professional writer and violinist who lives in Philadelphia. In "Give Children the Vote," Wallace argues that "the right of citizens under 19 to vote not be de-

nied or abridged on account of age." Wallace uses knowledge by observation (legal cases, history, statistics) combined with knowledge by participation to define the problem and develop her solution to it. *This essay first appeared in the* The Nation *on October 14, 1991.*

I first became interested in children's rights two years ago, when I learned that several states had passed laws prohibiting high school dropouts from getting driver's licenses. I was outraged, because I believe that children should not be forced to go to school or be penalized if they choose not to, a choice that is certainly the most sensible course for some people.

I am what is called a home schooler, I have never been to school, having always learned at home and in the world around me. Home schooling is absolutely legal, yet as a home schooler, I have had to defend what I consider to be my right to be educated in the ways that make the most sense to me, and so all along I have felt sympathy with people who insist on making choices about how they want to be educated, even if that means choosing not to finish high school. Now this choice is in jeopardy.

Since first learning about the discriminatory laws preventing high school dropouts from getting driver's licenses that have been passed by some state legislatures, I have done a lot of constitutional and historical research that has convinced me that children of all ages must be given the same power to elect their representatives that adults have, or they will continue to be unfairly treated and punished for exercising the few legal options they now have, such as dropping out of high school.

Most people, including children themselves, probably don't realize that children are the most regulated people in the United States. In addition to all the laws affecting adults, including tax laws, children must comply with school attendance laws, child labor laws, and alcohol and cigarette laws. They are denied driver's licenses because of their age, regardless of the dropout issue: they are victims of widespread child abuse; and they are blatantly discriminated against everywhere they go, in libraries, restaurants, and movie theaters. They have no way to protect themselves: Usually they cannot hire lawyers or bring cases to court without a guardian, and they are not allowed to vote.

5   The child labor and compulsory schooling laws were passed by well-meaning people to protect children from exploitation. Child labor laws keep children from being forced to work, and compulsory schooling allows all children to get an education. But the abolition of slavery in 1865 didn't end the exploitation of black people. They needed the right to vote and the ability to bring lawsuits against their employers. Children need those rights too. Without them, laws that force children to go to school and generally do not allow them to work may be necessary to prevent exploitation, but they also take away children's rights as citizens to life, liberty, and the pursuit of happiness. In my case, the compulsory education laws severely limited my right to pursue the work that is important to me (which is surely what "the pursuit of happiness" referred to in the Declaration of Independence).

I am 16 now, still not old enough to vote. Like all children, then, the only way I can fight for children's rights is by using my freedom of speech to try to convince adults to fight with me. While I am grateful that I have the right to speak my mind, I believe that it is a grave injustice to deny young people the most effective tool they could have to bring about change in a democracy. For this reason, I suggest that the right of citizens under 18 to vote not be denied or abridged on account of age.

Many people argue that it would be dangerous to let loose on society a large group of new voters who might not vote sensibly. They mean that children might not vote for the right candidates. The essence of democracy, however, is letting people vote for the wrong candidates. Democratic society has its risks, but we must gamble on the reasonableness of all our citizens, because it is less dangerous than gambling on the reasonableness of a few. That is why we chose to be a democracy instead of a dictatorship in the first place.

As it is, only 36 to 40 percent of adults who are eligible to vote actually vote in nonpresidential years, and about 25 percent of the population is under 18. As you can see, our representatives are elected by a very small percentage of our citizens. That means that although they are responsible *for* all of us, they are responsible *to* only a few of us. Politicians usually do all they can to keep that few happy, because both voters and politicians are selfish, and a politician's reelection depends on the well-being of the voters. Large segments of society that are not likely or not allowed to vote are either ignored or treated badly because of this system. It would be too much to expect the few always to vote in the interests of the many. Under these circumstances, surely the more people who vote the better, especially if they are of both sexes and of all races, classes and ages.

People also claim that children are irresponsible. Most of the teenagers who act irresponsibly do so simply because they are not allowed to solve their problems in any way that would be considered responsible—through the courts or legislature. They fall back on sabotage of the system because they are not allowed to work within it.

10   Some people believe that children would vote the way their parents tell them to, which would, in effect, give parents more votes. Similarly, when the Nineteenth Amendment was passed in 1920, giving women the vote, many people thought women would vote the way their husbands did. Now women are so independent that the idea of women voting on command seems absurd. The Nineteenth Amendment was a large part of the process that produced their independence. I think a similar and equally desirable result would follow if children were allowed to vote. They are naturally curious, and most are interested in the electoral process and the results of the elections even though they are not allowed to vote. Lacking world-weary cynicism, they see, perhaps even more clearly than their elders, what is going on in their neighborhoods and what is in the news.

Suffragist Belle Case La Follette's comment that if women were allowed to vote there would be a lot more dinner-table discussion of politics is as true of children today. More debate would take place not only in the home but among children and adults everywhere. Adults would also benefit if politics were talked about in libraries, churches, stores, laundromats, and other places where children gather.

People may argue that politicians would pander to children if they could vote, promising for instance that free ice cream would be distributed every day. But if kids were duped, they would not be duped for long. Children don't like to be treated condescendingly.

Even now, adults try to manipulate children all the time in glitzy TV ads or, for example, in the supposedly educational pamphlets that nuclear power advocates pass out in school science classes. Political candidates speak at schools, addressing auditoriums full of captive students. In fact, schools should be no more or less political than workplaces. Children are already exposed to many different opinions, and they would likely be exposed to even more if they could vote. The point is that with the vote, they would be better able to fight such manipulation, not only because they would have the power to do so but because they would have added reason to educate themselves on the issues.

What I suggest is that children be allowed to grow into their own right to vote at whatever rate suits them individually. They should not be forced to vote, as adults are not, but neither should they be hindered from voting if they believe themselves capable, as old people are not hindered.

15   As for the ability to read and write, that should never be used as a criterion for eligibility, since we have already learned from painful past experience that literacy tests can be manipulated to ensure discrimination. In any case, very few illiterate adults vote, and probably very few children would want to vote as long as they couldn't read or write. But I firmly believe that, whether they are literate or not, the vast majority of children would not attempt to vote before they are ready. Interest follows hand in hand with readiness, something that is easy to see as a home schooler but that is perhaps not so clear to many people in this society where, ironically, children are continually taught things when they are not ready, and so are not interested. Yet when they are interested, as in the case of voting, they're told they are not yet ready. I think I would not have voted until I was 8 or 9, but perhaps if I had known I could vote I would have taken an interest sooner.

Legally, it would be possible to drop the voting-age requirements. In the Constitution, the states are given all powers to set qualifications for voters except as they defy the equal protection clause of the Fourteenth Amendment, in which case Congress has the power to enforce it. If it were proved that age requirements "abridge the privileges or immunities of citizens of the United States" (which in my opinion they do, since people born in the United States or to U.S. citizens are citizens from the moment they are born), and if the states could not come up with a "compelling interest" argument to justify a limit at a particular age, which Justices Potter Stewart, Warren Burger, and Harry Blackmun agreed they could not in *Oregon v. Mitchell* (the Supreme Court case challenging the 1970 amendment to the Voting Rights Act that gave 18-year-olds the vote), then age requirements would be unconstitutional. But it is not necessary that they be unconstitutional for the states to drop them. It is within the power of the states to do that, and I believe that we must start this movement at the state level. According to *Oregon v. Mitchell*, Congress cannot change the qualifications for voting in state elections except by constitutional amendment, which is why the Twenty-sixth Amendment setting the voting age at 18 was necessary. It is very unlikely that an amendment would pass unless several states had tried eliminating the age requirement and had good results. The experience of Georgia and Kentucky, which lowered their age limits to 18, helped to pass the Twenty-sixth Amendment in 1971.

Already in our country's history several oppressed groups have been able to convince the unoppressed to free them. Children, who do not have the power to change their situation, must now convince the adults who do to allow them that power.

Questions for Discussion

1. Notice that the title clearly identifies the claim of this essay. What do you think of this technique? Is it effective? Why do you think it is or isn't?
2. In the sixth paragraph of the essay, the author reveals that she is 16, legally still a child. Why doesn't she reveal this information earlier? Why doesn't she reveal this information later?
3. After proposing that children be given the right to vote, the author dedicates the remainder of the essay to the discussion and refutation of possible objections. Why do you think she does so?
4. What is the subordinate aim of this essay? Is it expressive or referential? Cite specific passages to support your answer.
5. This essay was written for a politically liberal magazine. How would this essay differ if it were written for a politically conservative magazine? How might the author try to establish credibility, support the claim, or motivate the audience?

Opportunities for Writing

1. Weigh the merits of child labor laws. What are the advantages and disadvantages of such laws for both employers and employees, for both adults and children?
2. Declare your position on compulsory schooling laws. Do you think such laws are necessary?
3. In a letter to the students of a local high school, solicit their support of your favorite political candidate. Specifically encourage their cooperation in the distribution of campaign literature door-to door a week prior to election day. Discuss the candidate's positions on issues important to high school students: address the students' self-interest as well as their sense of altruism.
4. Prepare a report for your city council representative, proposing action on a citywide curfew law for all residents under age 18. Should your city council pass, modify, or repeal such a law? Evaluate the curfew laws of surrounding communities as well as cities of comparable size to yours. What is their record of success or failure with such laws? What are the advantages and disadvantages of such laws?

Why Mow: The Case Against Lawns

MICHAEL POLLAN

Michael Pollan works at Harper's Magazine *as an executive editor. He has written articles for magazines such as* Vogue, The New York Times Magazine, *and* House & Garden. *"Why Mow: The Case Against Lawns" first appeared in* The New York Times Magazine *and is a chapter in* Second Nature: A Gardener's Education *(1991), Pollan's book on nature and gardening. In this essay, Pollan explains the problems that lawns create and offers a solu-*

tion: turn lawns into gardens. Notice how the author integrates personal experience and information from sources such as Frederick Law Olmsted and Frank J. Scott. Find the knowledge by observation sources in this essay and highlight this material with a pen or by adding a marginal comment. Afterward, consider the amount of information that Pollan has incorporated from outside sources. Are you surprised by what you've found?

Anyone new to the experience of owning a lawn, as I am, soon figures out that there is more at stake here than a patch of grass. A lawn immediately establishes a certain relationship with one's neighbors and, by extension, the larger American landscape. Mowing the lawn, I realized the first time I gazed into my neighbor's yard and imagined him gazing back into mine, is a civic responsibility.

For no lawn is an island, at least in America. Starting at my front stoop, this scruffy green carpet tumbles down a hill and leaps across a one-lane road into my neighbor's yard. From there it skips over some wooded patches and stone walls before finding its way across a dozen other unfenced properties that lead down into the Housatonic Valley, there to begin its march south to the metropolitan area. Once below Danbury, the lawn—now purged of weeds and meticulously coiffed—races up and down the suburban lanes, heedless of property lines. It then heads west, crossing the New York border; moving now at a more stately pace, it strolls beneath the maples of Scarsdale, unfurls across a dozen golf courses, and wraps itself around the pale blue pools of Bronxville before pressing on toward the Hudson. New Jersey next is covered, an emerald postage stamp laid down front and back of ten thousand split levels, before the broadening green river divides in two.

One tributary pushes south, and does not pause until it has colonized the thin, sandy soils of Florida. The other dilates and spreads west, easily overtaking the Midwest's vast grid before running up against the inhospitable western states. But neither flinty soil nor obdurate climate will impede the lawn's march to the Pacific: it vaults the Rockies and, abetted by a monumental irrigation network, proceeds to green great stretches of western desert.

Nowhere in the world are lawns as prized as in America. In little more than a century, we've rolled a green mantle of grass across the continent, with scarcely a thought to the local conditions or expense. America has more than fifty thousand square *miles* of lawn under cultivation, on which we spend an estimated $30 billion a year—this according to the Lawn Institute, a Pleasant Hill, Tennessee, outfit devoted to publicizing the benefits of turf to Americans (surely a case of preaching to the converted).

5   Like the interstate highway system, like fast-food chains, like television, the lawn has served to unify the American landscape; it is what makes the suburbs of Cleveland and Tucson, the streets of Eugene and Tampa, look more alike than not. According to Ann Leighton, the late historian of gardens, America has made essentially one important contribution to world garden design: the custom of "uniting the front lawns of however many houses there may be on both sides of a street to present an untroubled aspect of expansive green to the passer-by." France has its formal, geometric gardens, England its picturesque parks, and America this unbounded democratic river of manicured lawn along which we array our houses.

It is not easy to stand in the way of such a powerful current. Since we have traditionally eschewed fences and hedges in America (looking on these as Old World vestiges), the suburban vista can be marred by the negligence—or dissent—of a single property owner. This is why lawn care is regarded as such an important civic responsibility in the suburbs, and why the majority will not tolerate the laggard. I learned this at an early age, growing up in a cookie-cutter subdivision in Farmingdale, Long Island.

My father, you see, was a lawn dissident. Whether owing to laziness or contempt for his neighbors I was never sure, but he could not see much point in cranking up the Toro more than once a month or so. The grass on our quarter-acre plot towered over the crew-cut lawns on either side of us and soon disturbed the peace of the entire neighborhood.

That subtle yet unmistakable frontier, where the closely shaved lawn rubs up against a shaggy one, is a scar on the face of suburbia, an intolerable hint of trouble in paradise. The scar shows up in *The Great Gatsby,* when Nick Carraway rents the house next to Gatsby's and fails to maintain his lawn according to West Egg standards. The rift between the two lawns so troubles Gatsby that he dispatches his gardener to mow Nick's grass and thereby erase it.

Our neighbors in Farmingdale displayed somewhat less class. "Lawn mower on the fritz?" they'd ask. "Want to borrow mine?" But the more heavily they leaned on my father, the more recalcitrant he became, until one summer—probably 1959, or 1960—he let the lawn go altogether. The grass plants grew tall enough to flower and set seed; the lawn rippled in the breeze like a flag. There was beauty here, I'm sure, but it was not visible in this context. Stuck in the middle of a row of tract houses on Long Island, our lawn said *turpitude* rather than *meadow,* even though strictly speaking that is what it had become.

10   That summer I felt the hot breath of the majority's tyranny for the first time. No one said anything now, but you could hear it all the same: *Mow your lawn or get out.* Certain neighbors let it be known to my parents that I was not to play with their children. Cars would slow down as they drove by. Probably some of the drivers were merely curious: they saw the unmowed lawn and wondered if someone had left in a hurry, or perhaps died. But others drove by in a manner that was unmistakably expressive, slowing down as they drew near and then hitting the gas angrily as they passed—pithy driving, the sort of move that is second nature to a Klansman.

We got the message by other media, too. Our next-door neighbor, a mild engineer who was my father's last remaining friend in the development, was charged with the unpleasant task of conveying the sense of the community to my father. It was early on a summer evening that he came to deliver his message. I don't remember it all (I was only four or five at the time), but I can imagine him taking a highball glass from my mother, squeaking out what he had been told to say about the threat to property values, and then waiting for my father—who next to him was a bear—to respond.

My father's reply could not have been more eloquent. Without a word he strode out to the garage and cranked up the rusty old Toro for the first time since fall; it's a miracle the thing started. He pushed it out to the curb and then started back across the lawn to the house, but not in a straight line: he swerved right, then left, then right again. He had cut an *S* in the high grass. Then he made an *M*, and finally a *P.* These are his initials, and as soon as he finished writing them he wheeled the lawn mower back to the garage, never to start it up again.

I wasn't prepared to take such a hard line on my new lawn, at least not right off. So I bought a lawn mower, a Toro, and started mowing. Four hours every Saturday. At first I tried for a kind of Zen approach, clearing my mind of everything but the task at hand, immersing myself in the lawn-mowing here-and-now. I liked the idea that my weekly sessions with the grass would acquaint me with the minutes details of my yard. I soon knew by heart the exact location of every stump and stone, the tunnel route of each resident mole, the address of every anthill. I noticed that where rain collected white clover flourished, that it was on the drier rises that crabgrass thrived. After a few weekends I had a map of the lawn in my head as precise and comprehensive as the mental map one has of the back of one's hand.

The finished product pleased me too, the fine scent and the sense of order restored that a new-cut lawn exhales. My house abuts woods on two sides, and mowing the lawn is, in both a real and metaphorical sense, how I keep the forest at bay and preserve my place in this landscape. Much as we've come to distrust it, the urge to dominate nature is a deeply human one, and lawn mowing answers to it. I thought of the lawn mower as civilization's knife and my lawn as the hospitable plane it carved out of the wilderness. My lawn was a part of nature made fit for human habitation.

15   So perhaps the allure of lawns is in the genes. The sociobiologists think so: they've gone so far as to propose a "Savanna Syndrome" to explain our fondness for grass. Encoded in our DNA is a preference for an open grassy landscape resembling the short-grass savannas of Africa on which we evolved and spent our first few million years. This is said to explain why we have remade the wooded landscapes of Europe and North America in the image of East Africa.

Such theories go some way toward explaining the widespread appeal of grass, but they don't really account for the American Lawn. They don't, for instance, account for the keen interest Jay Gatsby takes in Nick Carraway's lawn, or the scandal my father's lawn sparked in Farmingdale. Or the fact that, in America, we have taken down our fences and hedges in order to combine our lawns. And they don't even begin to account for the unmistakable odor of virtue that hovers in this country over a scrupulously maintained lawn.

If any individual can be said to have invented the American lawn, it is Frederick Law Olmsted. In 1868, he received a commission to design Riverside, outside Chicago, one of the first planned suburban communities in America. Olmsted's design stipulated that each house be set back thirty feet from the road and it proscribed walls. He was reacting against the "high deadwalls" of England, which he felt made a row of homes there seem "as of a series of private madhouses." In Riverside, each owner would maintain one or two trees and a lawn that would flow seamlessly into his neighbors', creating the impression that all lived together in a single park.

Olmsted was part of a generation of American landscape designer-reformers who set out at midcentury to beautify the American landscape. That it needed beautification may seem surprising to us today, assuming as we do that the history of the landscape is a story of decline, but few at the time thought otherwise. William Cobbett, visiting from England, was struck at the "out-of-door slovenliness" of American homesteads. Each farmer, he wrote, was content with his "shell of boards, while all around him is as barren as the sea beach . . . though there is no English shrub, or flower, which will not grow and flourish here."

The land looked as if it had been shaped and cleared in a great hurry—as indeed it had: the landscape largely denuded of trees, makeshift fences outlining badly plowed fields, tree stumps everywhere one looked. As Cobbett and many other nineteenth-century visitors noted, hardly anyone practiced ornamental gardening; the typical yard was "landscaped" in the style southerners would come to call "white trash"—a few chickens, some busted farm equipment, mud and weeds, an unkempt patch of vegetables.

20   This might do for farmers, but for the growing number of middle-class city people moving to the "borderland" in the years following the Civil War, something more respectable was called for. In 1870, Frank J. Scott, seeking to make Olmsted's ideas accessible to the middle class, published the first volume ever devoted to "suburban home embellishment": *The Art of Beautifying Suburban Home Grounds,* a book that probably did more than any other to determine the look of the suburban landscape in America. Like so many reformers of his time, Scott was nothing if not sure of himself: "A smooth, closely shaven surface of grass is by far the most essential element of beauty on the grounds of a suburban house."

Americans like Olmsted and Scott did not invent the lawn; lawns had been popular in England since Tudor times. But in England, lawns were usually found only on estates; the Americans democratized them, cutting the vast manorial greenswards into quarter-acre slices everyone could afford. Also, the English never considered the lawn an end in itself: it served as a setting for lawn games and as a backdrop for flower beds and trees. Scott subordinated all other elements of the landscape to the lawn; flowers were permissible, but only on the periphery of the grass: "Let your lawn be your home's velvet robe, and your flowers its not too promiscuous decoration."

But Scott's most radical departure from Old World practice was to dwell on the individual's responsibility to his neighbors. "It is unchristian," he declared, "to hedge from the sight of others the beauties of nature which it has been our good fortune to create or secure." One's lawn, Scott held, should contribute to the collective landscape. "The beauty obtained by throwing front grounds open together, is of that excellent quality which enriches all who take part in the exchange, and makes no man poorer." Like Olmsted before him, Scott sought to elevate an unassuming patch of turfgrass into an institution of democracy.

With our open-faced front lawns we declare our like-mindedness to our neighbors—and our distance from the English, who surround their yards with "inhospitable brick wall, topped with broken bottles," to thwart the envious gaze of the lower orders. The American lawn is an egalitarian conceit, implying that there is no reason to hide behind fence or hedge since we all occupy the same middle class. We are all property owners here, the lawn announces, and that suggests its other purpose: to provide a suitably grand stage for the proud display of one's own house. Noting that our yards were organized "to capture the admiration of the street," one garden writer in 1921 attributed the popularity of open lawns to our "infantile instinct to cry 'hello!' to the passer-by, to lift up our possessions to his gaze."

Of course the democratic front yard has its darker, more coercive side, as my family learned in Farmingdale. In specifying the "plain style" of an unembellished lawn for American front yards, the midcentury designer-reformers were, like Puritan ministers, laying down rigid conventions governing our relationship to the land, our observance of which would henceforth be taken as an index of our character. And just as the Puritans would not tolerate any individual who sought to establish his or her own back-channel relationship with the divinity, the members of the suburban utopia do not tolerate the homeowner who establishes a relationship with the land that is not mediated by the group's conventions.

25   The parallel is not as farfetched as it might sound, when you recall that nature in America has often been regarded as divine. Think of nature as Spirit, the collective suburban lawn as the Church, and lawn mowing as a kind of sacrament. You begin to see why ornamental gardening would take so long to catch on in America, and why my father might seem an antinomian in the eyes of his neighbors. Like Hester Prynne, he claimed not to need their consecration for his actions; perhaps his initials in the front lawn were a kind of Emerald Letter.

Possibly because it is this common land, rather than race or tribe, that makes us all Americans, we have developed a deep distrust of individualistic approaches to the landscape. The land is too important to our identity as Americans to simply allow everyone to have his own way with it. And once we decide that the land should serve as a vehicle of consensus, rather than an arena of self-expression, the American lawn—collective, national, ritualized, and plain—begins to look inevitable.

After my first season of lawn mowing, the Zen approach began to wear thin. I had taken up flower and vegetable gardening, and soon came to resent the four hours that my lawn demanded of me each week. I tired of the endless circuit, pushing the howling mower back and forth across the vast page of my yard, recopying the same green sentences over and over: "I am a conscientious homeowner. I share your middle-class values." Lawn care was gardening aimed at capturing "the admiration of the street," a ritual of consensus I did not have my heart in. I began to entertain idle fantasies of rebellion: Why couldn't I plant a hedge along the road, remove my property from the national stream of greensward and do something else with it?

The third spring I planted fruit trees in the front lawn, apple, peach, cherry, and plum, hoping these would relieve the monotony and begin to make the lawn productive. Behind the house, I put in a perennial border. I built three raised beds out of old chestnut barnboards and planted two dozen different vegetable varieties. Hard work though it was, removing the grass from the site of my new beds proved a keen pleasure. First I outlined the beds with string. Then I made an incision in the lawn with the sharp edge of a spade. Starting at one end, I pried the sod from the soil and slowly rolled it up like a carpet. The grass made a tearing sound as I broke its grip on the earth. I felt a little like a pioneer subduing the forest with his ax; I daydreamed of scalping the entire yard. But I didn't do it—I continued to observe front-yard conventions, mowing assiduously and locating all my new garden beds in the back yard.

The more serious about gardening I became, the more dubious lawns seemed. The problem for me was not, as it was for my father, the relation to my neighbors that a lawn implied; it was the lawn's relationship to nature. For however democratic a lawn may be with respect to one's neighbors, with respect to nature it is authoritarian. Under the mower's brutal indiscriminate rotor, the landscape is subdued, homogenized, dominated utterly. I became convinced that lawn care had about as much to do with gardening as floor waxing or road paving. Gardening was a subtle process of give and take with the landscape, a search for some middle ground between culture and nature. A lawn was nature under culture's boot.

30   Mowing the lawn, I felt that I was battling the earth rather than working it; each week it sent forth a green army and each week I beat it back with my infernal machine. Unlike every other plant in my garden, the grasses were anonymous, massified, deprived of any change or development whatsoever, not to mention any semblance of self-determination. I ruled a totalitarian landscape.

Hot, monotonous hours behind the mower gave rise to existential speculations. I spent part of one afternoon trying to decide who, in the absurdist drama of lawn mowing, was Sisyphus. Me? A case could certainly be made. Or was it the grass, pushing up through the soil every week, one layer of cells at a time, only to be cut down and then, perversely, encouraged (with fertilizer, lime, etc.) to start the whole doomed process over again? Another day it occurred to me that time as we know it doesn't exist in the lawn, since grass never dies or is allowed to flower and set seed. Lawns are nature purged of sex and death. No wonder Americans like them so much.

And just where *was* my lawn, anyway? The answer's not as obvious as it seems. Gardening, I had come to appreciate, is a painstaking exploration of place; everything that happens in my garden—the thriving and dying of particular plants, the maraudings of various insects and other pests—teaches me to know this patch of land intimately, its geology and microclimate, the particular ecology of its local weeds and animals and insects. My garden prospers to the extent I grasp these particularities and adapt to them.

Lawns work on the opposite principle. They depend for their success on the *overcoming* of local conditions. Like Jefferson superimposing one great grid over the infinitely various topography of the Northwest Territory, we superimpose our lawns on the land. And since the geography and climate of much of this country is poorly suited to turfgrasses (none of which are native), this can't be accomplished without the tools of twentieth-century industrial civilization—its chemical fertilizers, pesticides, herbicides, and machinery. For we won't settle for the lawn that will grow here; we want the one that grows *there,* that dense springy supergreen and weed-free carpet, that Platonic ideal of a lawn we glimpse in the ChemLawn commercials, the magazine spreads, the kitschy sitcom yards, the sublime links and pristine diamonds. Our lawns exist less here than there; they drink from the national stream of images, lift our gaze from the real places we live and fix it on unreal places elsewhere. Lawns are a form of television.

Need I point out that such an approach to "nature" is not likely to be environmentally sound? Lately we have begun to recognize that we are poisoning ourselves with our lawns, which receive, on average, more pesticide and herbicide per acre than just about any crop grown in this country. Suits fly against the national lawn-care companies, and interest is kindled in "organic" methods of lawn care. But the problem is larger than this. Lawns, I am convinced, are a symptom of, and a metaphor for, our skewed relationship to the land. They teach us that, with the help of petrochemicals and technology, we can bend nature to our will. Lawns stoke our hubris with regard to the land.

What is the alternative? To turn them into gardens. I'm not suggesting that there is no place for lawns *in* these gardens or that gardens by themselves will right our relationship to the land, but the habits of thought they foster can take us some way in that direction.

Gardening, as compared to lawn care, tutors us in nature's ways, fostering an ethic of give and take with respect to the land. Gardens instruct us in the particularities of place. They lessen our dependence on distant sources of energy, technology, food, and, for that matter, interest.

For if lawn mowing feels like copying the same sentence over and over, gardening is like writing out new ones, an infinitely variable process of invention and discovery. Gardens also teach the necessary if rather un-American lesson that nature and culture can be compromised, that there might be some middle ground between the lawn and the forest—between those who would complete the conquest of the planet in the name of progress and those who believe it's time we abdicated our rule and left the earth in the care of its more innocent species. The garden suggests there might be a place where we can meet nature halfway.

Probably you will want to know if I have begun to practice what I'm preaching. Well, I have not ripped out my lawn entirely. But each spring larger and larger tracts of it give way to garden. Last year I took a half acre and planted a meadow of black-eyed Susans and oxeye daisies. In return for a single annual scything, I am rewarded with a field of flowers from May until frost.

The lawn is shrinking, and I've hired a neighborhood kid to mow what's left of it. Any Saturday that Bon Jovi, Twisted Sister, or Van Halen isn't playing the Hartford Civic Center, this large blond teenaged being is apt to show up with a forty-eight-inch John Deere mower that shears the lawn in less than an hour. It's $30 a week, but he's freed me from my dark musings about the lawn and so given me more time in the garden.

Out in front, along the road where my lawn overlooks my neighbors', and in turn the rest of the country's, I have made my most radical move. I built a split rail fence and have begun to plant a hedge along it—a rough one made up of forsythia, lilac, bittersweet, and bridal wreath. As soon as this hedge grows tall and thick, my secession from the national lawn will be complete.

Anything then is possible. I *could* let it all revert to meadow, or even forest, except that I don't go in for that sort of self-effacement. I could put in a pumpkin patch, a lily pond, or maybe an apple orchard. And I could even leave an area of grass. But even if I did, this would be a very different lawn from the one I have now. For one thing, it would have a frame, which means it could accommodate plants more subtle and various than the screaming marigolds, fierce red salvias, and musclebound rhododendrons that people usually throw into the ring against a big unfenced lawn. Walled off from the neighbors, no longer a tributary of the national stream, my lawn would now form a distinct and private space—become part of a garden rather than a substitute for one.

Yes, there might well be a place for a small lawn in my new garden. But I think I'll wait until the hedge fills in before I make a decision. It's a private matter, and I'm trying to keep politics out of it.

Questions for Discussion

1. What do you think of the following simile: "if lawn mowing feels like copying the same sentence over and over, gardening is like writing out new ones"? Why does the author compare mowing and gardening to copying and writing? What other similes for mowing and gardening might be appropriate?
2. Notice the allusions to characters from American literature, specifically Jay Gatsby and Nick Carraway from *The Great Gatsby* and Hester Prynne from *The Scarlet Letter*. What do such allusions indicate about the author's intended audience? Are the allusions necessary? What is the author's purpose in making such allusions?
3. How important is this essay's expressive aim? Do you think this essay is appropriately classified as persuasive aim writing? Cite specific passages to support your answer.
4. Would headings contribute to the clarity of this essay? If so, add appropriate headings. If not, explain why headings are unnecessary.
5. Do you think the essay would be more or less effective without the final two paragraphs (i.e., if the essay stopped at the following sentence: "As soon as this hedge grows tall and thick, my secession from the national lawn will be complete")? Explain your answer.

Opportunities for Writing

1. Write a letter to the Environmental Protection Agency to voice your opinion of lawn fertilizers and pesticides. Interview botanists and entomologists. Review the available research on this issue. Are lawn fertilizers and pesticides necessary? Are existing regulations effective? Are new regulations required?
2. Assess the advantages and disadvantages of gardening as a hobby. Cite your personal experience and interview friends and neighbors. Consider financial, nutritional, environmental, physical, and psychological issues.
3. Submit a proposal to your local city council for a community-wide tree-planting program. Discuss the details of your proposal. Emphasize the environmental benefits and the aesthetic improvement to the city. Acknowledge the potential costs of raking and disposing of leaves.
4. Evaluate the lawns of your neighborhood. Which do you consider attractive? Why? Which do you consider unattractive? Why? How important are lawns to the image and reputation of your neighborhood?

Sensationalism Versus News of the Moral Life
Making the Distinction

KAREN L. SLATTERY

Karen L. Slattery is a media researcher and teaches at Marquette University. In "Sensationalism Versus News of the Moral Life: Making the Distinction," Slattery defines the problem that journalists encounter when deciding to present sensational news stories; in her discussion, she distinguishes between two types of sensational news: necessary stories "for a community's moral health" and sensational news "for its own sake." She concludes her article by offering some guidelines that professionals can use in determining ethically whether or not to cover these kinds of stories. This essay was published in the Journal of Mass Media Ethics, *and all citations conform to the APA style.*

On September 3, 1992, the news rocked the Barney Street neighborhood in Wilkes-Barre, Pennsylvania. Sometime after 1:00 AM, the last time anyone had checked on the sleeping child, three-year-old Joelle Donovan disappeared from her grandmother's house. During the long daylight hours that followed, her family and neighbors helped police search the neighborhood for the blond, blue-eyed little girl.

The following day, the family's worst fears were realized. Joelle Donovan's tiny body was discovered in a plastic bag in a nearby creek. An autopsy revealed she had been molested and strangled. Shortly after the child's body was found, authorities arrested one of the searchers and charged him with first degree murder. He was Michael Bardo, Joelle Donovan's 23-year-old uncle. Bardo confessed to the crime. The parolee had earlier served a prison term for raping another child, who was also a family member.

The murder story dominated the local television news. Coverage focused on neighborhood reaction to the news of the child's death. The responses ranged from placing flowers and stuffed animals at the site where the child was found, to tears and expressions of disbelief, to angry threats from neighbors who traveled to nearby Nanticoke to watch as authorities hauled Bardo into jail. The coverage touched on investigations into why the parolee was allowed to stay in his mother's home with young children present, including the child he had earlier raped. There were also stories about the poor living conditions within the grandmother's home, the response of social workers to the crime, child custody hearings, and the like (Joelle Donovan Stories, 1992).

News coverage of this sort is routinely described as sensational. Sensationalism, as defined by Mott (1962), usually takes the form of stories about "crimes, disasters, sex scandals, and monstrosities" and stimulates "unwholesome emotional responses in the average reader" (p. 442). Critics scold the news media for dishing up this sort of coverage and the audience for being interested. Press sensationalism is harmful they argue, because it violates social boundaries of decency and respect (Dickson, 1988; Taylor-Flemming, 1992) and edges out more important public affairs reporting (Adams, 1978).

At the same time, however, others claim that sensational news coverage serves a useful purpose within the community (Franke, 1985; Hofstetter & Dozier, 1986). Of particular interest here is the argument that sensational news plays a role in the maintenance of a community's moral boundaries (Stevens, 1985).

The primary purpose of this article is to explore and extend the claim that there is a moral dimension to sensational news. If one considers that the citizens of the community are also its moral agents, then a convincing argument can be made that news coverage of the type surrounding the Donovan murder is vital to the moral health of the community. Albeit lurid and detailed, the Donovan stories pointed to a moral monster in that community's midst. Journalists documented the neighborhood's response to the news, one of visible pain and moral outrage. Subsequent coverage touched on matters requiring the community's notice. Some stories reported on circumstances that may have fostered the violent crime. Others focused attention on the vexing problem of releasing into the community prisoners who have been punished but not rehabilitated. The coverage also raised questions about who protects children when their families cannot. Clearly, any effort to downplay the unfortunate event and its implications by insisting it be discussed in polite terms or, worse yet, not at all, would have ignored pressing moral issues requiring the community's attention and, perhaps, action.

If it is true that some news coverage, casually labeled sensational, is vital to the moral health of the community, then it would appear that such coverage is justified. But this argument also raises questions about when and how to responsibly cover stories traditionally associated with sensationalism. In an effort to further responsible journalism, a second goal of this article is to suggest a method journalists can use to determine if coverage of a specific detail of a story or the story as a whole is morally justifiable.

The article is organized as follows: First, scholarship related to the problem of press sensationalism is presented in order to bring its moral dimension into sharper relief. Second, a distinction is drawn between news that is labeled sensational, but which is necessary for a community's moral health, and news that is sensational for its own sake. Finally, a method is offered to determine whether covering a topic historically associated with sensationalism is morally problematic.

At the outset, several assumptions are made about the audience. Citizens of a democracy clearly have a political interest in the community because their government determines, in part, how they will live. But no less important is their moral interest in the community because moral standards govern behavior within a social context.

This study further assumes that the news readers and viewers are rational human beings, with needs for information "about matters such as risks, alternatives, and consequences of what's being reported" (Klaidman & Beauchamp, 1987, p. 33). Their information needs are not limited solely to matters of political consequence; they reflect moral concerns as well (Ferre, 1988).

Finally, for the purpose of this research, Nord's definition of news will be used. According to Nord (1990), news is about public occurrences and public events. It is public in that it is reported and has public meaning.

The Moral Dimension of Sensationalism

Support for the claim that sensationalism has a moral dimension can be found in the scholarship related to other dimensions of the sensationalism construct, including topic, treatment, intent, and effect. The topic and treatment dimensions help to identify sensationalism, whereas the intent and effect dimensions allow questions to be raised about the purpose and consequences of such coverage. The intent and effect dimensions are also useful concepts, as will be discussed, in determining whether such topics ought to be covered and if so, how.

Topic and Treatment

Sensational topics are fairly consistent across historical time lines. A reading of the literature suggests they fall into several categories: cultural taboos, natural and manmade disasters, and unexplained phenomena. Sensational topics appearing in the 16th- and 17th-century news, for example, included murder, theft, prostitution, vanity, lust, and drinking on Sunday (Stephens, 1985). News of fires, shipwrecks, droughts, untimely deaths, murders, executions, war, piracy, epidemics, and witchcraft appeared in the 17th- and early 18th-century Puritan press (Nord, 1990). Copeland (1992) reported coverage of such topics as sexual encounters, suicide, rape, monsters, vampires, jilted lovers, revenge, and the evils of alcohol in South Carolina newspapers in the 1720s. Similar topics appeared in the press in the 1800s (Franke, 1985; Olasky, 1985; Shaw & Slater, 1985). Sensational topics in the modern news media include stories about crime, violence, natural disasters, accidents, and fires (Adams, 1978).

Sensational stories, as identified in these studies, reflect themes of right and wrong and good and evil, as well as themes of the unknown or unexpected. Most represent threats to the moral and/or physical well-being of the community and its members. One can reasonably expect such stories to be of interest to an audience. The primary focus of the remainder of this essay will be on news coverage that is related to the moral well-being of the community.

Treatment is an issue because sensational topics can be treated in a non-sensational fashion (Franke, 1978), and, likewise, topics not necessarily sensational can be sensationalized through treatment. Sensational treatment relates to the surface features of news presentation, such as lurid headlines and explicit photographs, elements that began evolving in the 19th and early 20th centuries. Other indicators include (but are not limited to): sensory details (Franke, 1985), descriptive adjectives (Nordin, 1979), and fear-inducing statements, loaded words, and the overemphasis of story in terms of placement and length (Gorney, 1992). Unlike topics, which are fairly easy to identify and categorize, indicators of sensational treatment are often subjective and dependent on historical context for interpretation.

Intent

Intent calls attention to the journalist's purpose in producing sensational news. Intent is difficult to measure, so much of the research related to this dimension has involved speculation. Scholars commonly link sensationalism to the media's desire to make money (Copeland, 1992; Emery & Emery, 1984; Stevens, 1991) or to satisfy the audience's desire for entertainment or titillation (Copeland, 1992; Kobre, 1969; Stevens, 1991). Scholars have also linked journalistic intent to a perceived moral underpinning of sensational news, particularly as it relates to religion.

Olasky (1985) studied news practices in late 19th-century Texas, noting that many editors were orthodox Christians. An analysis of their rhetoric, he argued, suggested that some editors believed theirs was a Christian mission and the press should work for "the glory of God" (p. 97). Against that backdrop, he drew parallels between the sensational news stories in the Texas press and stories containing similar themes in the Bible.

Nord (1990) convincingly argued that early American journalism was rooted in the Puritan religion. Touching on news of crime and punishment, fires, witchcraft and the like, but focusing primarily on reports of disasters and unexplained phenomena, Nord theorized that early New England news was selected and purveyed as evidence of God's intervention in human affairs. Nord further argued that as secular forces supplanted religion in the 18th century, news lost its meaning. Society was left with news as convention, and the patterns of "unusual occurrences" that were once important are now only interesting.

Nord's argument must be reassessed if we are to continue our discussion of the moral dimension of news. He is correct in saying that religion no longer plays a dominant role in the interpretation of news, but it does not follow from this premise that news is meaningless. Western philosophy informs us that religion, as a set of moral tenets, is but one way of accounting for moral behavior. Theoretical normative ethics outlines other systems, including those which focus on consequences or ends (teleological), rules or duties (deontological), and on the person of the moral agent (virtue). When the issue of intent is removed from Nord's narrower perspective of religion and reframed in a broader moral context, it is possible to once again begin discussing the meaning of news as it relates to matters of right and wrong. Those stories historically related to sensationalism, that is, murders, executions, sexual encounters, suicide, rape, alcoholism, violence, and the like, become meaningful as the moral community identifies, maintains, or attempts to renegotiate its moral standards. Such subjects touch the core of our moral existence.

When reframed in a larger moral context, new questions about intent can be raised: How are the decisions of those who decide what constitutes news in this culture influenced by issues of good or bad, right or wrong, justice or injustice? Much of the research on applied journalism ethics centers on moral standards within the profession (Anderson, 1987) and focuses on the nature of individual decisions or moral choices in the face of specific circumstances (Marion & Izard, 1986; Ziesenis, 1991). The relation between the news professional as a member of a moral community and the shape or nature of news as we know it has yet to be articulated.

Effect

The effects of sensationalism are closely tied to intent, and are often discussed by scholars in economic terms (Emery & Emery, 1984; Ryu, 1982) or as they relate to prurient interests or entertainment (Nordin, 1979). In contrast, other scholarship suggests sensational news advances the moral discourse of a community and can bring about social reform by encouraging self-examination of the community's moral standards.

Stevens (1985) framed sensationalism in the context of deviance theory and argued that coverage of stories involving murder, separation, and divorce, for example, force readers to reconsider moral boundaries. Sensationalism stimulates gossip, according to Nordin (1979), and one function of gossip is evaluative (Levin & Arluke, 1987). Gossip as evaluation may be one mechanism by which the members of a community reevaluate social values and moral boundaries.

Sensational news coverage has led to social reform (Kobre, 1969), an effect Franke (1985) links to intent. According to Franke, some turn-of-the century journalists consciously used sensory details to put life into reports that called attention to pressing social problems, including the conditions in tenements, prisons, and asylums. These stories, he insisted, deserved "as much praise as censure" (p. 73).

Franke's work points to an interesting relationship between sensationalism and the moral behavior of the community as a whole. Such coverage can be interpreted as enabling the larger community to raise and answer questions about the appropriateness of its attitudes and behavior toward its members. What kind of society, for example, would allow its poor and disadvantaged to live in diseased, filthy tenements? Its children to labor 16 hours a day in factories? Just as press sensationalism enabled the newly minted mass society to begin forging a moral identity, present-day sensational coverage, in part, forces a continuation of that process. When faced with the grim details of the gas leak in Bhopal, India, for example, what kind of community, we must ask, can turn its head without asking who is responsible, what can be done to help, and what steps should be taken to ensure that such a tragedy does not happen again?

The scholarship on the problem of sensationalism, then, suggests that some of the news that is considered sensational serves the purpose of keeping the public's finger on the pulse of the moral community. Cleansing the news of all that is labeled sensational is undesirable because some of the news casually tagged sensational, however unwholesome, is really news of the moral life. The difficulty of the journalist rests in distinguishing between news of the moral life and that which is sensational for its own sake. Once the distinction is made, the problem of responsibly covering issues or topics historically associated with sensationalism can be addressed. But before turning to that discussion of news of the moral life versus sensationalism qua sensationalism, it is necessary to consider the purpose of journalism in a democratic society, for it is from that purpose that journalism gets its warrant.

SENSATIONALISM AND THE RESPONSIBLE JOURNALIST

The social responsibility theory of the press holds that the news media are obliged to offer news that will enlighten the citizens of a democracy (Siebert, Peterson, &

Schramm, 1974). Framers of the theory did not object to publishing stories regarding sensational topics per se, citing "night-club murders, race riots, strike violence, and quarrels among public officials" as examples (Commission on Freedom of the Press, 1947, p. 55). However, they did object to the media's preoccupation with such incidents, arguing that overemphasis would deprive the citizen of the "[public affairs-related] information and discussion he needs to discharge his responsibilities to the community" (Commission on Freedom of the Press, 1947, p. 56).

Because citizens need information about the political life to participate in a democracy, and news of the moral life to participate in the moral community, the task facing journalists is one of balance. The responsible journalist or news organization must determine the appropriate blend of public affairs coverage and news of the moral life that will allow citizens to make informed decisions about both the political and moral environments in which they live. To achieve that balance, the journalist must necessarily distinguish between the news, which reflects matters of significance to the moral community, and sensationalism, which causes moral harm, that is, pernicious sensationalism.

For the purpose of this study, news of the moral life is defined as news of occurrences or events related to the standards a community embraces to regulate the social behavior of its members. Such coverage is developed to reflect broader, more general themes of good and evil, right and wrong, and justice and injustice. News of the moral life is central to the affirmation or renegotiation of moral boundaries within the community. Thus, when journalists as moral agents discharge their responsibility to inform the public of the day's events, and the day's events include a topic or issue that is particularly discouraging in its nature and gruesome in its detail, as in the Joelle Donovan story described earlier, charges of entertaining or pandering to the public's baser instincts may be misplaced.

Pernicious sensationalism, however, is defined as coverage of events or issues that are also tied to the community's moral standards, but which have been removed from their broader moral context. Such stories are packaged as isolated incidents and presented as matters lacking moral consequence. In the face of such coverage, news of the moral life loses its significance.

30   Consider the case in Iowa, reported by station KWWL-TV, regarding the fate of Lieutenant Russ Halley, a soldier who was killed in Vietnam in 1965 and whose body was returned home in a sealed casket (Russ Halley Stories, 1991). After an extensive check of medical and military records, members of his family feared the government had lied about what had happened to the soldier; they suspected that someone else might have been buried in Halley's place, or that the grave might, in fact, be empty. Following a quarter of a century of uncertainty, the family decided to have the body exhumed for examination.

The television station's subsequent coverage took unfair advantage of the viewers' legitimate interest in a subject that is tied to the moral well-being of the community—in this case, the government's treatment of families of the war dead. The reporter chose to frame the coverage within the context of the actual exhumation. In one story, for instance, he explained the family's concerns as viewers watched video of the casket being pulled out of the ground and transported to a mortuary. Another report focused on the casket being opened at the mortuary as family members observed. The reporter showed the medical examiners opening the casket lid, struggling to lift the body bag out, the soldier's wife watching, and so forth, building up a good deal of suspense about who was actually in the coffin. After putting the audience through the entire grisly process, stopping just short of showing the corpse, the reporter informed viewers that the soldier in question was indeed in the casket. The audience was left to surmise that the government had not lied or deliberately tried to cover a mistake.

The reporting was manipulative, attracting attention by foregrounding details of the exhumation while backgrounding the moral and political issues surrounding the story. It was noted during the coverage, for example, that the Halley family was one of a number of families around the country with questions about the fate of loved ones reportedly killed in Vietnam. Rather than spending precious news time on the details of the corpse identification, the time could have been better spent developing related issues, for example, what steps, if any, the military planned to take to relieve the fears of other families with questions similar to those raised by Lt. Halley's family? What steps should the military take? Questions regarding the obligation of the community, and its military, to the families of those who fight wars in its name might also have been addressed. As handled, the Halley coverage trivialized questions of considerable importance to both the moral and political communities, and robbed the audience of an opportunity to engage in the discussion of serious matters. Unlike the Donovan story described earlier, the Halley coverage sacrificed the moral dimension of the story for the sake of sensational detail.

Bok's Test of Publicity

Not surprisingly, news that is properly of interest to the moral community is often labeled sensational. It shares characteristics used to describe sensationalism (e. g., violent, grotesque, distasteful) because it reflects violations of cultural or social taboos. But there is a crucial distinction: The purpose of such coverage is not to appeal to prurient interests or to entertain; rather, it is to point to a wrong, an injustice or to a social evil, that is, a matter requiring the community's notice.

To determine if coverage of a topic routinely associated with sensationalism is morally problematic, the journalist must, in the end, answer the critical question of intent. An audience can suspect or infer motives, but it can make no confident claim about the reporter's purpose. Only the journalist can accurately judge whether the story is being covered in order to pander to an audience, or because it reflects a legitimate moral concern.

When considering intent, a responsible journalist must ask if the justification for covering a sensational story can survive a "test of publicity." The test, borrowed from Bok (1989), is designed to weigh "various excuses advanced for disputed choices" (p. 92). The test requires that the rationale for a choice be capable of defense to a wide audience of critical and reasonable persons. No one can be excluded on principle, according to Bok. A necessary assumption, of course, is that the "reasonable person" understands the process of weighing and balancing conflicting moral principles so that a responsible decision can be made.

Such a test demands that journalists ask appropriate questions regarding the moral implications of news traditionally considered sensational. Is there a defensible reason for printing or broadcasting the story? Is the grim tale the result of a particular policy that warrants reconsideration? Are media following up on those issues? Is community action required? If such questions were honestly asked and answered, one suspects, the present level of sensationalism in news would decline considerably. Justifications offered for many stories would fail the test.

Consider, for example, the rationale offered by a Milwaukee, Wisconsin television station for airing an exclusive interview with a 6-year-old sexual assault victim (Assault victim, 1992). The news announcer stressed to the audience that the purpose of the interview, which focused on the details of the encounter and the parents' grief, was to point out that the family knew and trusted the alleged molester, a babysitter, and the same thing could happen to any family. The announcer also insisted that the station was airing the interview without concealing the child's identity at the request of the parents, who did not want anyone else to "experience their agony." The parents said the child "did nothing wrong."

The reasons offered may all be true, but the station's justification for broadcasting the story fails on two counts. Driving home the problem of sexual assault in such an intense and graphic way was unnecessary. The community, well aware of the damage caused by such incidents, was already acting on its responsibilities to the child; the suspect's trial was about to begin. Further, the news organization blatantly ignored its obligation to prevent harm by protecting the youngster, even though her parents decided she should tell her story publicly. Distraught parents may not understand the possible harm in such publicity, but journalists are obliged to be aware of the potential damage caused by the invasion of privacy and to act accordingly. The cost of airing the child's interview heavily outweighed any conceivable benefit that might have been gained.

CONCLUSION

Sensationalism qua sensationalism is a destructive force that exacts a tremendous social price. A preoccupation with sensationalism for its own sake obscures news of moral interest to the community, and related issues that require community action may not be acted upon. Individuals involved in such stories often suffer from violations of privacy, manipulation, or a journalist's lack of good taste. Unfortunately, responsible journalists are often painted with the same brush as those who ignore professional moral standards; all suffer a loss of respect. An emphasis on negative news has also been tied to heightened perceptions of fear among audience members (Blackman & Hornstein, 1977) and negative images of the community (Galician & Vestre, 1987). And, as noted earlier, democratic processes are compromised when a government is not under careful scrutiny and is free to do as it wishes.

However, it is also argued that a press which reflects a community back to itself must necessarily cover news of the moral life, however discouraging. The topics normally associated with sensationalism, properly addressed, stimulate debate on issues of moral significance to the community. Such discussions provide a foundation for decisions that are related to the nature of life in the moral community, and they are central to its vitality. When considering how to treat a topic historically associated with sensationalism, or whether to cover it at all, the thoughtful journalist will consider his or her editorial decisions in light of such professional standards as fairness and good taste, along with questions of intent and effect. The responsible journalist will also ask whether the justification for covering the story can pass a test of publicity. Together, these elements allow judgments to be made regarding the appropriateness of the proposed coverage.

Finally, if the journalist has chosen a topic of importance to the moral community, has successfully defended the coverage against the test of publicity, and has portrayed the topic accurately, then that journalist may claim to have acted responsibly, regardless of the labels others might apply to the product of his or her effort.

Notes

1. The terms "news media" and "press" are used interchangeably and are meant to include the concept of broadcast news.
2. From a moral standpoint, not all news organizations are obligated to consider matters of balance in the same way. Olen (1988) suggests that an organization which pledges to present the news of the day, without bias, is obliged to refrain from excess when reporting sensational news. Tabloids, like the *National Enquirer*, for example, violate no covenant by indulging in sensationalism since they have made no promise to do otherwise.

References

Adams, W. (1978). Local public affairs content of TV news. *Journalism Quarterly, 55*(4), 690–695.

Anderson, D. (1987). How managing editors view and deal with ethical issues. *Journalism Quarterly, 64*(2), 341–345.

Assault victim. (1992, November 6). WVTV, Milwaukee, Wisconsin. Nine o'clock newscast.

Blackman, J., & Hornstein, H. (1977). Newscasts and the social actuary. *Public Opinion Quarterly, 41,* 295–313.

Bok, S. (1989). *Lying: Moral choice in public and private life.* New York: Random House.

Commission on Freedom of the Press. (1947). *A free and responsible press: A general report on mass communication.* Chicago: University of Chicago Press.

Copeland, D. (1992, August 5–8). *Melancholy accidents and deplorable news: Sensationalism and the South Carolina Gazette, 1732–1738.* Paper presented to the History Division of the Association for Education in Journalism and Mass Communication, Montreal, Canada.

Dickson, S. (1988). The "golden mean" in journalism. *Journal of Mass Media Ethics, 3*(1), 33–37.

Emery, E., & Emery, M. (1984). *The press and America: An interpretive history of the mass media.* Englewood Cliffs, NJ: Prentice-Hall.

Ferre, J. (1988). Grounding an ethics of journalism. *Journal of Mass Media Ethics, 3*(1), 18–27.

Franke, W. (1978). An argument in defense of sensationalism: Probing the popular and historical concept. *Journalism History, 5*(3), 70–73.

Franke, W. (1985). Sensationalism and the development of 19th-century reporting: The broom sweeps sensory details. *Journalism History, 12*(3–4), 80–85.

Galician, M., & Vestre, N. (1987). Effects of "good news" and "bad news" on television newscast image and community image. *Journalism Quarterly, 64*(2/3), 399–405, 525.

Gorney, C. (1992). Numbers versus pictures: Did network television sensationalize Chernobyl coverage? *Journalism Quarterly, 69*(2), 455–465.

Hofstetter, C., & Dozier D. (1986). Useful news, sensational news: Quality, sensationalism and local TV news. *Journalism Quarterly, 63*(4), 815–820, 853.

Joelle Donovan stories. (1992, September 3–8). WBRE-TV, Wilkes-Barre, PA. WNEP-TV and WYOU-TV, Scranton, PA. Early and late newscasts.

Klaidman, S., & Beauchamp, T. (1987). *The virtuous journalist.* New York: Oxford University Press.

Kobre, S. (1969). *Development of American journalism.* Dubuque, IA: Brown.

Levin, J., & Arluke, A. (1987). *Gossip: The inside scoop.* New York: Plenum.

Marion, G., & Izard, R. (1986). The journalist in life-saving situations: Detached observer or good samaritan? *Journal of Mass Media Ethics, 1*(2), 61–67.

Mott, F. (1962). *American journalism.* New York: Macmillan.

Nord, D. (1990). Teleology and news: The religious roots of American journalism, 1630–1730. *Journal of American History, 77*(1), 9–38.

Nordin, K. (1979). The entertaining press: Sensationalism in eighteenth-century Boston newspapers. *Communication Research, 6*(3), 295–320.

Olasky, M. (1985). Late 19th-century Texas sensationalism: Hypocrisy or biblical morality? *Journalism History, 12*(3–4), 96–100.

Olen, J. (1988). *Ethics in journalism.* Englewood Cliffs, NJ: Prentice-Hall.

Russ Halley stories. (1991, September 9, 10). KWWL-TV, Waterloo, IA. Early and late newscasts.

Ryu, J. (1982). Public affairs and sensationalism in local TV news programs. *Journalism Quarterly, 59*(1), 74–78, 137.

Shaw, D., & Slater, J. (1985). In the eye of the beholder? Sensationalism in American press news, 1820–1860. *Journalism History, 12*(3–4), 86–91.

Siebert, F., Peterson, T., & Schramm, W. (1974). *Four theories of the press.* Urbana, IL: University of Illinois Press.

Stephens, M. (1985). Sensationalism and moralizing in 16th and 17th-century newsbooks and news ballads. *Journalism History, 12*(3–4), 92–95.

Stevens, J. (1985). Social utility of sensational news: Murder and divorce in the 1920s. *Journalism Quarterly, 62*(1), 53–58.

Stevens, J. (1991). *Sensationalism and the New York press.* New York: Columbia University Press.

Taylor-Flemming, A. (1992, September 4). Essay: Public screening (Woody Allen and Mia Farrow and a look at private lives being made public). *MacNeil/Lehrer Newshour.* New York: WNET.

Ziesenis, E. (1991). Suicide coverage in newspapers: An ethical consideration. *Journal of Mass Media Ethics, 6,* 234–244.

Questions for Discussion

1. In this essay, which information is knowledge by participation? Is this information necessary?
2. What is the purpose of the opening narrative? Are the grisly details (e.g., "tiny body was discovered in a plastic bag") necessary?
3. In the introduction, the author explicitly identifies the essay's purpose and organization: "The primary purpose of this article is . . ." and "The article is organized as follows. . . ." What do you think of this technique? Do you consider it appropriate? Explain your answer.
4. This essay was written for the specialized readership of a professional journal on media ethics. How might this essay be revised for the general audience of a daily newspaper? What specific changes would you recommend? Would illustrations be appropriate?

5. How does the author establish credibility? How does she support the claim? How does she motivate the audience to approve the claim?

Opportunities for Writing

1. Review the television coverage of a specific crime. Was the coverage fair and judicious? Was it biased and exploitative? Before writing your review, interview television news people, television viewers, and (if possible) friends or family of the victim and the accused.
2. Write a letter to the editor of your local newspaper regarding its coverage of local crime stories. Is the newspaper's coverage thorough and necessary? Is it excessive and gratuitous?
3. Propose to the news director of a local television station that he or she revise the station's policy on coverage of automobile accidents. In your proposal, identify coverage you consider appropriate and inappropriate. Is it appropriate to show damaged vehicles? survivors receiving medical aid? dead bodies? Is it appropriate to interview survivors? police and fire officials? families of victims? Emphasize the benefits of your proposal for both the station itself and the community it serves.

The Killing Game

JOY WILLIAMS

Joy Williams is a novelist, short-story writer, and essayist. Among her published works are Escapes *(1990),* Taking Care *(1982),* Breaking and Entering *(1981), and* State of Grace *(1973). In this essay, the author takes a firm stand against sport hunting. Williams uses her own understanding of hunting, complemented by comments from hunters and information from various publications for hunters in order to develop her arguments. "The Killing Game" was originally published in* Esquire, *to which she is a frequent contributor.*

Death and suffering are a big part of hunting. A big part. Not that you'd ever know it by hearing hunters talk. They tend to downplay the killing part. To kill is to put to death, extinguish, nullify, cancel, destroy. But from the hunter's point of view, it's just a tiny part of the experience. *The kill is the least important part of the hunt,* they often say, or, *Killing involves only a split second of the innumerable hours we spend surrounded by and observing nature . . .* For the animal, of course, the killing part is of considerably more importance. José Ortega y Gasset, in *Meditations on Hunting,* wrote, *Death is a sign of reality in hunting. One does not hunt in order to kill; on the contrary, one kills in order to have hunted.* This is the sort of intellectual blather that the "thinking" hunter holds dear. The conservation editor of *Field & Stream,* George Reiger, recently paraphrased this sentiment by saying, *We kill to hunt, and not the other way around,* thereby making it truly fatuous. A hunter in West Virginia, one Mr. Bill Neal, blazed through this philosophical fog by explaining why he blows the toes off tree raccoons so that they will fall down and be torn apart by his dogs. *That's the best part of it. It's not any fun just shooting them.*

Instead of monitoring animals—many animals in managed areas are tagged, tattooed, and wear radio transmitters—wildlife managers should start hanging telemetry gear around hunters' necks to study their attitudes and listen to their conversations. It would be grisly listening, but it would tune out for good the *suffering as sacrament* and *spiritual experience* blather that some hunting apologists employ. *The unease with which the good hunter inflicts death is an unease not merely with his conscience but with affirming his animality in the midst of his struggles toward humanity and clarity,* Holmes Rolston III drones on in his book *Environmental Ethics*.

There is a formula to this in literature—someone the protagonist loves has just died, so he goes out and kills an animal. This makes him feel better. But it's kind of a sad feeling-better. He gets to relate to Death and Nature in this way. Somewhat. But not really. Death is still a mystery. Well, it's hard to explain. It's sort of a semireligious thing . . . Killing and affirming, affirming and killing, it's just the cross the "good" hunter must bear. The bad hunter just has to deal with postkill letdown.

Many are the hunter's specious arguments. Less semireligious but a long-standing favorite with them is the vegetarian approach: you eat meat, don't you? If you say no, they feel they've got you—you're just a vegetarian attempting to impose your weird views on others. If you say yes, they accuse you of being hypocritical, of allowing your genial A&P butcher to stand between you and reality. The fact is, the chief attraction of hunting is the pursuit and murder of animals—the meat-eating aspect of it is trivial. If the hunter chooses to be *ethical* about it, he might cook his kill, but the meat of most animals is discarded. Dead bear can even be dangerous! A bear's heavy hide must be skinned at once to prevent meat spoilage. With effort, a hunter can make okay chili, *something to keep in mind,* a sports rag says, *if you take two skinny spring bears.*

5   As for subsistence hunting, please . . . Granted that there might be one "good" hunter out there who conducts the kill as spiritual exercise and two others who are atavistic enough to want to supplement their Chicken McNuggets with venison, most hunters hunt for the hell of it.

For hunters, hunting is fun. Recreation is play. Hunting is recreation. Hunters kill for play, for entertainment. They kill for the thrill of it, to make an animal "theirs." (The Gandhian doctrine of nonpossession has never been a big hit with hunters.) The animal becomes the property of the hunter by its death. Alive, the beast belongs only to itself. This is unacceptable to the hunter. *He's yours . . . He's mine . . . I decided to . . . I decided not to . . . I debated shooting it, then I decided to let it live . . .* Hunters like beautiful creatures. A "beautiful" deer, elk, bear, cougar, bighorn sheep. A "beautiful" goose or mallard. Of course, they don't stay "beautiful" for long, particularly the birds. Many birds become rags in the air, shredded, blown to bits. *Keep shooting till they drop!* Hunters get a thrill out of seeing a plummeting bird, out of seeing it crumple and fall. *The big pheasant folded in classic fashion.* They get a kick out of "collecting" new species. *Why not add a unique harlequin duck to your collection?* Swan hunting is satisfying. *I let loose a three-inch Magnum. The large bird only flinched with my first shot and began to gain altitude. I frantically ejected the round, chambered another, and dropped the swan with my second shot. After retrieving the bird I was* amazed by its size. The swan's six-foot wingspan, huge body, and long neck made it an impressive trophy. Hunters like big animals, trophy animals. A "trophy" usually means that the hunter doesn't deign to eat it. Maybe he skins it or mounts it. Maybe he takes a picture. *We took pictures, we took pictures.* Maybe he just looks at it for a while. The disposition of the "experience" is up to the hunter. He's entitled to do whatever he wishes with the damn thing. It's dead.

Hunters like categories they can tailor to their needs. There are the "good" animals—deer, elk, bear, moose—which are allowed to exist for the hunter's pleasure. Then there are the "bad" animals, the vermin, varmints, and "nuisance" animals, the rabbits and raccoons and coyotes and beavers and badgers, which are disencouraged to exist. The hunter can have fun killing them, but the pleasure is diminished because the animals aren't "magnificent."

Then there are the predators. These can be killed any time, because, hunters argue, they're predators, for godssakes.

Many people in South Dakota want to exterminate the red fox because it preys upon some of the ducks and pheasant they want to hunt and kill each year. They found that after they killed the wolves and coyotes, they had more foxes than they wanted. The ring-necked pheasant is South Dakota's state bird. No matter that it was imported from Asia specifically to be "harvested" for sport, it's South Dakota's state bird and they're proud of it. A group called Pheasants Unlimited gave some tips on how to hunt foxes. *Place a small amount of larvicide* [a grain fumigant] *on a rag and chuck it down the hole . . . The first pup generally comes out in fifteen minutes . . . Use a .22 to dispatch him . . . Remove each pup shot from the hole. Following gassing, set traps for the old fox who will return later in the evening . . .* Poisoning, shooting, trapping—they make up a sort of sportsman's triathlon.

10   In the hunting magazines, hunters freely admit the pleasure of killing to one another. *Undeniable pleasure radiated from her smile. The excitement of shooting the bear had Barb talking a mile a minute.* But in public, most hunters are becoming a little wary about raving on as to how much fun it is to kill things. Hunters have a tendency to call large animals by cute names—"bruins" and "muleys," "berry-fed blackies" and "handsome cusses" and "big guys," thereby implying a balanced jolly game of mutual satisfaction between the hunter and the hunted—*Bam, bam, bam, I get to shoot you and you get to be dead.* More often, though, when dealing with the nonhunting public, a drier, businesslike tone is employed. Animals become a "resource" that must be "utilized." Hunting becomes "a legitimate use of the resource." Animals become a product like wool or lumber or a crop like fruit or corn that must be "collected" or "taken" or "harvested." Hunters love to use the word *legitimate*. (Oddly, Tolstoy referred to hunting as "evil legitimized.") *A legitimate use, a legitimate form of recreation, a legitimate escape, a legitimate pursuit.* It's a word they trust will slam the door on discourse. Hunters are increasingly relying upon their spokesmen and supporters, state and federal game managers and wildlife officials, to employ the drone of a solemn bureaucratic language and toss around a lot of questionable statistics to assure the nonhunting public (93 per-

cent!) that there's nothing to worry about. The pogrom is under control. The mass murder and manipulation of wild animals is just another business. Hunters are a tiny minority, and it's crucial to them that the millions of people who don't hunt not be awakened from their long sleep and become antihunting. Nonhunters are okay. Dweeby, probably, but okay. A hunter *can respect the rights* of a nonhunter. It's the "antis" he despises, those *misguided, emotional, not-in-possession-of-the-facts, uninformed zealots who don't understand nature . . . Those dime-store ecologists cloaked in ignorance and spurred by emotion . . . Those doggy-woggy types, who under the guise of being environmentalists and conservationists are working to deprive him of his precious right to kill.* (Sometimes it's just a *right;* sometimes it's a *God-given* right.) Antis can be scorned, but nonhunters must be pacified, and this is where the number crunching of wildlife biologists and the scripts of *professional resource managers* come in. Leave it to the professionals. They know what numbers are the good numbers. Utah determined that there were six hundred sandhill cranes in the state, so permits were issued to shoot one hundred of them. Don't want to have too many sandhill cranes. California wildlife officials reported "sufficient numbers" of mountain lions to "justify" renewed hunting, even though it doesn't take a rocket scientist to know the animal is extremely rare. (It's always a dark day for hunters when an animal is adjudged *rare.* How can its numbers be "controlled" through hunting if it scarcely exists?) A recent citizens' referendum prohibits the hunting of the mountain lion in perpetuity—not that the lions aren't killed anyway, in California and all over the West, hundreds of them annually by the government as part of the scandalous Animal Damage Control Program. Oh, to be the lucky hunter who gets to be an official government hunter and can legitimately kill animals his buddies aren't supposed to! Montana officials, led by K. L. Cool, that state's wildlife director, have definite ideas on the number of buffalo they feel can be tolerated. Zero is the number. Yellowstone National Park is the only place in America where bison exist, having been annihilated everywhere else. In the winter of 1988, nearly six hundred buffalo wandered out of the north boundary of the park and into Montana, where they were immediately shot at point-blank range by lottery-winning hunters. It was easy. And it was obvious from a video taken on one of the blow-away-the-bison days that the hunters had a heck of a good time. The buffalo, Cool says, threaten ranchers' livelihoods by doing damage to property—by which he means, I guess, that they eat the grass. Montana wants zero buffalo; it also wants zero wolves.

Large predators—including grizzlies, cougars, and wolves—are often the most "beautiful," the smartest and wildest animals of all. The gray wolf is both a supreme predator and an endangered species, and since the Supreme Court recently affirmed that ranchers have no constitutional right to kill endangered predators—apparently some God-given rights are not constitutional ones—this makes the wolf a more or less lucky dog. But not for long. A small population of gray wolves has recently established itself in northwestern Montana, primarily in Glacier National Park, and there is a plan, long a dream of conservationists, to "reintroduce" the wolf to Yellowstone. But to please ranchers and hunters, part of the plan would involve immediately removing the wolf from the endangered-species list. Beyond the park's boundaries, he could be hunted as a "game animal" or exterminated as a "pest." (Hunters kill to hunt, remember, except when they're hunting to kill.) The area of Yellowstone where the wolf would be restored is the same mountain and high-plateau country that is abandoned in winter by most animals, including the aforementioned luckless bison. Part of the plan, too, is compensation to ranchers if any of their far-ranging livestock is killed by a wolf. It's a real industry out there, apparently, killing and controlling and getting compensated for losing something under the Big Sky.

Wolves gotta eat—a fact that disturbs hunters. Jack Atcheson, an outfitter in Butte, said, *Some wolves are fine if there is control. But there never will be control. The wolf-control plan provided by the Fish and Wildlife Service speaks only of protecting domestic livestock. There is no plan to protect wildlife . . . There are no surplus deer or elk in Montana . . . Their numbers are carefully managed. With uncontrolled wolf populations, a lot of people will have to give up hunting just to feed wolves. Will you give up your elk permit for a wolf?*

It won't be long before hunters start demanding compensation for animals they aren't able to shoot.

Hunters believe that wild animals exist only to satisfy their wish to kill them. And it's so easy to kill them! The weaponry available is staggering, and the equipment and gear limitless. *The demand for big boomers has never been greater than right now,* Outdoor Life *crows, and the makers of rifles and cartridges are responding to the craze with a variety of light artillery that is virtually unprecedented in the history of sporting arms . . .* Hunters use grossly overpowered shotguns and rifles and compound bows. They rely on four-wheel-drive vehicles and three-wheel ATVs and airplanes . . . *He was interesting, the only moving, living creature on that limitless white expanse. I slipped a cartridge into the barrel of my rifle and threw the safety off . . .* They use snowmobiles to run down elk, and dogs to run down and tree cougars. It's easy to shoot an animal out of a tree. It's virtually impossible to miss a moose, a conspicuous and placid animal of steady habits . . . *I took a deep breath and pulled the trigger. The bull dropped. I looked at my watch: 8:22. The big guy was early. Mike started whooping and hollering and I joined him. I never realized how big a moose was until this one was on the ground. We took pictures . . .* Hunters shoot animals when they're resting . . . *Mike selected a deer, settled down to a steady rest, and fired. The buck was his when he squeezed the trigger. John decided to take the other buck, which had jumped up to its feet. The deer hadn't seen us and was confused by the shot echoing about in the valley. John took careful aim, fired, and took the buck. The hunt was over . . .* And they shoot them when they're eating . . . *The bruin ambled up the stream, checking gravel bars and backwaters for fish. Finally he plopped down on the bank to eat. Quickly, I tiptoed into range . . .* They use decoys and calls . . . *The six point gave me a cold-eyed glare from ninety steps away. I hit him with a 130-grain Sierra boat-tail handload. The bull went down hard. Our hunt was over . . .* They use sex lures . . . *The big buck raised its nose to the air, curled back its lips, and tested the scent of the doe's urine. I held my breath, fought back the shivers, and jerked off a shot. The 180-grain spire-point bullet caught the buck high on the back behind the shoulder and put it down. It didn't get up . . .* They use walkie-talkies, binoculars, scopes . . . *With my 308 Browning BLR, I steadied the 9X cross hairs on the front of the bear's massive shoulders and squeezed. The bear cartwheeled backward for fifty yards . . . The second Federal Premium 165-grain bullet found its mark. Another shot anchored the bear for good* . . . They bait deer with corn. They spread popcorn on golf courses for Canada geese and they douse meat baits with fry grease and honey for bears . . . *Make the baiting site redolent of inner-city doughnut shops.* They use blinds and tree stands and mobile stands. They go out in groups, in gangs, and employ "pushes" and "drives." So many methods are effective. So few rules apply. It's fun! . . . *We kept on repelling the swarms of birds as they came in looking for shelter from that big ocean wind, emptying our shell belts* . . . A species can, in the vernacular, be *pressured by hunting* (which means that killing them has decimated them), but that just increases the fun, the *challenge.* There is practically no criticism of conduct within the ranks . . . *It's mostly a matter of opinion and how hunters have been brought up to hunt* . . . Although a recent editorial in *Ducks Unlimited* magazine did venture to primly suggest that one should *not fall victim to greed-induced stress through piggish competition with others.*

But hunters are piggy. They just can't seem to help it. They're overequipped . . . insatiable, malevolent, and vain. They maim and mutilate and despoil. And for the most part, they're inept. Grossly inept.

Camouflaged toilet paper is a must for the modern hunter, along with his Bronco and his beer. Too many hunters taking a dump in the woods with their roll of Charmin beside them were mistaken for white-tailed deer and shot. Hunters get excited. They'll shoot anything—the pallid ass of another sportsman or even themselves. A Long Island man died last year when his shotgun went off as he clubbed a wounded deer with the butt. Hunters get mad. They get restless and want to fire! They want to use those assault rifles and see foamy blood on the ferns. Wounded animals can travel for miles in fear and pain before they collapse. Countless gut-shot deer—*if you hear a sudden, squashy thump, the animal has probably been hit in the abdomen*—are "lost" each year. "Poorly placed shots" are frequent, and injured animals are seldom tracked, because most hunters never learned how to track. The majority of hunters will shoot at anything with four legs during deer season and anything with wings during duck season. Hunters try to nail running animals and distant birds. They become so overeager, so *aroused,* that they misidentify and misjudge, spraying their "game" with shots but failing to bring it down.

The fact is, hunters' lack of skill is a big, big problem. And nowhere is the problem worse than in the new glamour recreation, bow hunting. These guys are elitists. They doll themselves up in camouflage, paint their faces black, and climb up into tree stands from which they attempt the penetration of deer, elk, and turkeys with modern, multiblade, broadhead arrows shot from sophisticated, easy-to-draw compound bows. This "primitive" way of hunting appeals to many, and even the nonhunter may feel that it's a "fairer" method, requiring more strength and skill, but bow hunting is the cruelest, most wanton form of wildlife disposal of all. Studies conducted by state fish and wildlife departments repeatedly show that bow hunters wound and fail to retrieve as many animals as they kill. An animal that flees, wounded by an arrow, will most assuredly die of the wound, but it will be days before he does. Even with a "good" hit, the time elapsed between the strike and death is exceedingly long. *The rule of thumb has long been that we should wait thirty to forty-five minutes on heart and lung hits, an hour or more on a suspected liver hit, eight to twelve hours on paunch hits, and that we should follow immediately on hindquarter and other muscle-only hits, to keep the wound open and bleeding,* is the advice in the magazine *Fins and Feathers.* What the hunter does as he hangs around waiting for his animal to finish with its terrified running and dying hasn't been studied—maybe he puts on more makeup, maybe he has a highball.

Wildlife agencies promote and encourage bow hunting by permitting earlier and longer seasons, even though they are well aware that, in their words, *crippling is a by-product of the sport,* making archers pretty sloppy for elitists. The broadhead arrow is a very inefficient killing tool. Bow hunters are trying to deal with this problem with the suggestion that they use poison pods. These poisoned arrows are illegal in all states except Mississippi *(Ah'm gonna get ma deer even if ah just nick the little bastard),* but they're widely used anyway. You wouldn't want that deer to suffer, would you?

The mystique of the efficacy and decency of the bow hunter is as much an illusion as the perception that a waterfowler is a refined and thoughtful fellow, a *romantic aesthete,* as Vance Bourjaily put it, equipped with his faithful Labs and a love for solitude and wild places. More sentimental drivel has been written about bird shooting than any other type of hunting. It's a soul-wrenching pursuit, apparently, the execution of birds in flight. Ducks Unlimited—an organization that has managed to put a spin on the word *conservation* for years—works hard to project the idea that duck hunters are blue bloods and that duck stamps with their pretty pictures are responsible for saving all the saved puddles in North America. *Sportsman's conservation* is a contradiction in terms (We protect things now so that we can kill them later) and is broadly interpreted (Don't kill them all, just kill most of them). A hunter is a conservationist in the same way a farmer or a rancher is: he's not. Like the rancher who kills everything that's not stock on his (and the public's) land, and the farmer who scorns wildlife because "they don't pay their freight," the hunter uses nature by destroying its parts, mastering it by simplifying it through death.

[20] George ("We kill to hunt and not the other way around") Reiger, the conservationist-hunter's spokesman (he's the best they've got, apparently), said that the "dedicated" waterfowler will shoot other game "of course," but *we do so much in the same spirit of the lyrics, that when we're not near the girl we love, we love the girl we're near.* (Duck hunters practice tough love.) The fact is, far from being a "romantic aesthete," the waterfowler is the most avaricious of all hunters ... *That's when Scott suggested the friendly wager on who would take the most birds* ... and the most resistant to minimum ecological decency. Millions of birds that managed to elude shotgun blasts were dying each year from ingesting the lead shot that rained down in the wetlands. Year after year, birds perished from feeding on spent lead, but hunters were "reluctant" to switch to steel. They worried that it would impair their shooting, and ammunition manufacturers said a changeover would be "expensive." State and federal officials had to weigh the poisoning

against these considerations. It took forever, this weighing, but now steel-shot loads are required almost everywhere, having been judged "more than adequate" to bring down the birds. This is not to say, of course, that most duck hunters use steel shot almost everywhere. They're traditionalists and don't care for all the new, pesky rules. Oh, for the golden age of waterfowling, when a man could measure a good day's shooting by the pickup load. But those days are gone. Fall is a melancholy time, all right.

Spectacular abuses occur wherever geese congregate, Shooting Sportsman notes quietly, something that the more cultivated Ducks Unlimited would hesitate to admit. Waterfowl populations are plummeting and waterfowl hunters are out of control. "Supervised" hunts are hardly distinguished from unsupervised ones. A biologist with the Department of the Interior who observed a hunt at Sand Lake in South Dakota said, *Hunters repeatedly shot over the line at incoming flights where there was no possible chance of retrieving. Time and time again I was shocked at the behavior of hunters. I heard them laugh at the plight of dazed cripples that stumbled about. I saw them striking the heads of retrieved cripples against fence posts.* In the South, wood ducks return to their roosts after sunset when shooting hours are closed. Hunters find this an excellent time to shoot them. Dennis Anderson, an outdoors writer, said, *Roost shooters just fire at the birds as fast as they can, trying to drop as many as they can. Then they grab what birds they can find. The birds they can't find in the dark, they leave behind.*

Carnage and waste are the rules in bird hunting, even during legal seasons and open hours. Thousands of wounded ducks and geese are not retrieved, left to rot in the marshes and fields . . . *When I asked Wanda where hers had fallen, she wasn't sure.* Cripples, and there are many cripples made in this pastime, are still able to run and hide, eluding the hunter even if he's willing to spend time searching for them, which he usually isn't . . . *It's one thing to run down a cripple in a picked bean field or a pasture, and quite another to watch a wing-tipped bird drop into a huge block of switch grass.* Oh nasty, nasty switch grass. A downed bird becomes invisible on the ground and is practically unfindable without a good dog, and few "waterfowlers" have them these days. They're hard to train—usually a professional has to do it—and most hunters can't be bothered. Birds are easy to tumble . . . *Canada geese—blues and snows—can all take a good amount of shot. Brant are easily called and decoyed and come down easily. Ruffed grouse are hard to hit but easy to kill. Sharptails are harder to kill but easier to hit* . . . It's just a nuisance to recover them. But it's fun, fun, fun swatting them down . . . *There's distinct pleasure in watching a flock work to a good friend's gun.*

Teal, the smallest of common ducks, are really easy to kill. Hunters in the South used to *practice* on teal in September, prior to the "serious" waterfowl season. But the birds were so diminutive and the limit so low (four a day) that many hunters felt it hardly worth going out and getting bit by mosquitoes to kill them. Enough did, however, brave the bugs and manage to "harvest" 165,000 of the little migrating birds in Louisiana in 1987 alone. *Shooting is usually best on opening day. By the second day you can sometimes detect a decline in local teal numbers. Areas may deteriorate to virtually no action by the third day* . . . The area *deteriorates.* When a flock is wiped out, the skies are empty. *No action.*

Teal declined more sharply than any duck species except mallard last year; this baffles hunters. Hunters and their procurers—wildlife agencies—will *never* admit that hunting is responsible for the decimation of a species. John Turner, head of the federal Fish and Wildlife Service, delivers the familiar and litanic line. Hunting is not the problem. *Pollution* is the problem. *Pesticides, urbanization, deforestation, hazardous waste,* and *wetlands destruction* are the problem. And drought! There's been a big drought! Antis should devote their energies to solving these problems if they care about wildlife, and leave the hunters alone. While the Fish and Wildlife Service is busily conducting experiments in cause and effect, like releasing mallard ducklings on a wetland sprayed with the insecticide ethyl parathion (they died—it was known they would, but you can never have enough studies that show guns aren't a duck's only problem), hunters are killing some 200 million birds and animals each year. But these deaths are incidental to the problem, according to Turner. A factor, perhaps, but a *minor* one. Ducks Unlimited says the problem isn't hunting, it's *low recruitment* on the part of the birds. To the hunter, *birth* in the animal kingdom is *recruitment.* They wouldn't want to use an emotional, sentimental word like *birth.* The black duck, a very "popular" duck in the Northeast, so "popular," in fact, that game agencies felt that hunters couldn't be asked to refrain from shooting it, is scarce and getting scarcer. Nevertheless, it's still being hunted. *A number of studies are currently under way in an attempt to discover why black ducks are disappearing, Sports Afield* reports. Black ducks are disappearing because they've been shot out, their elimination being a dreadful example of game management, and managers who are loath to "displease" hunters. The skies—*flyways*—of America have been divided into four administrative regions, and the states, advised by a federal government coordinator, have to agree on policies.

There's always a lot of squabbling that goes on in flyway meetings—lots of complaints about short-stopping, for example. Short-stopping is the deliberate holding of birds in a state, often by feeding them in wildlife refuges, so that their southern migration is slowed or stopped. Hunters in the North get to kill more than hunters in the South. This isn't fair. Hunters demand equity in opportunities to kill.

Wildlife managers hate closing the season on anything. Closing the season on a species would indicate a certain amount of *mis*management and misjudgment at the very least—a certain reliance on overly optimistic winter counts, a certain overappeasement of hunters who would be "upset" if they couldn't kill their favorite thing. And worse, closing a season would be considered victory for the antis. Bird-hunting "rules" are very complicated, but they all encourage killing. There are shortened seasons and split seasons and special seasons for "underutilized" birds. (Teal were very recently considered "underutilized.") The limit on coots is fifteen a day—shooting them, it's easy! They don't fly high—giving the hunter something to do while he waits in the blind. Some species are "protected," but bear in mind that hunters begin blasting away one half hour before sunrise and that most hunters can't identify a bird in the air even in broad daylight. Some of them can't identify birds in hand either, and even if they can (#%*! *I got me a canvasback, that duck's frigging protected . . .*), they are likely to bury unpopular or "trash" ducks so that they can continue to hunt the ones they "love."

Game "professionals," in thrall to hunters' "needs," will not stop managing bird populations until they've doled out the final duck (*I didn't get my limit but I bagged the last one, by golly . . .*). The Fish and Wildlife Service services legal hunters as busily as any madam, but it is powerless in tempering the lusts of the illegal ones. Illegal kill is a monumental problem in the not-so-wonderful world of waterfowl. Excesses have always pervaded the "sport," and bird shooters have historically been the slobs and profligates of hunting. *Doing away with hunting would do away with a vital cultural and historical aspect of American life,* John Turner claims. So, do away with it. Do away with those who have already done away with so much. Do away with them before the birds they have pursued so relentlessly and for so long drop into extinction, sink, in the poet Wallace Stevens's words, "downward to darkness on extended wings."

"Quality" hunting is as rare as the Florida panther. What you've got is a bunch of guys driving over the plains, up the mountains, and through the woods with their stupid tag that cost them a couple of bucks and immense coolers full of beer and body parts. There's a price tag on the right to destroy living creatures for play, but it's not much. *A big-game hunting license is the greatest deal going since the Homestead Act,* Ted Kerasote writes in *Sports Afield. In many states residents can hunt big game for more than a month for about $20.* It's cheaper than taking the little woman out to lunch. It's cheap all right, and it's because killing animals is considered *recreation* and is underwritten by state and federal funds. In Florida, state moneys are routinely spent on "youth hunts," in which kids are guided to shoot deer from stands in wildlife-management areas. The organizers of these events say that these staged hunts *help youth to understand man's role in the ecosystem.* (Drop a doe and take your place in the ecological community, son . . .)

Hunters claim (they don't actually believe it but they've learned to say it) that they're doing nonhunters a favor, for if they didn't *use* wild animals, wild animals would be useless. They believe that they're just *helping Mother Nature control populations (you wouldn't want those deer to die of starvation, would you?).* They claim that their tiny fees provide *all* Americans with wild lands and animals. (People who don't hunt get to enjoy animals all year round while hunters get to enjoy them only during hunting season . . .) Ducks Unlimited feels that it, in particular, is a selfless provider and environmental champion. Although members spend most of their money lobbying for hunters and raising ducks in pens to release later over shooting fields, they do save some wetlands, mostly by persuading farmers not to fill them in. *See that little pothole there the ducks like? Well, I'm gonna plant more soybeans there if you don't pay me not to . . .* Hunters claim many nonsensical things, but the most nonsensical of all is that they *pay their own way.* They do not pay their own way. They *do* pay into a perverse wildlife-management system that manipulates "stocks" and "herds" and "flocks" for hunters' killing pleasure, but these fees in no way cover the cost of highly questionable ecological practices. For some spare change . . . *the greatest deal going . . .* hunters can hunt on public lands—national parks, state forests—preserves for hunters!—which the nonhunting and antihunting public pay for. (Access to private lands is becoming increasingly difficult for them, as experience has taught people that hunters are obnoxious.) Hunters kill on millions of acres of land all over America that are maintained with general taxpayer revenue, but the most shocking, really twisted subsidization takes place on national wildlife refuges. Nowhere is the arrogance and the insidiousness of this small, aggressive minority more clearly demonstrated. Nowhere is the murder of animals, the manipulation of language, and the distortion of public intent more flagrant. The public perceives national wildlife refuges as safe havens, as sanctuaries for animals. And why wouldn't they? The word *refuge* of course *means* shelter from danger and distress. But the dweeby nonhunting public—they tend to be so literal. The word has been reinterpreted by management over time and now hunters are invited into more than half of the country's more than 440 wildlife "sanctuaries" each year to bang them up and kill more than half a million animals. This is called *wildlife-oriented recreation.* Hunters think of this as being no less than their due, claiming that refuge lands were purchased with duck stamps (. . . *our duck stamps paid for it . . . our duck stamps paid for it . . .*). Hunters equate those stupid stamps with the mystic, multiplying power of the Lord's loaves and fishes, but of 90 million acres in the Wildlife Refuge System, only 3 million were bought with hunting-stamp revenue. Most wildlife "restoration" programs in the states are translated into clearing land to increase deer habitats (so that too many deer will require hunting . . . you wouldn't want them to die of starvation, would you?) and trapping animals for restocking and study (so hunters can shoot more of them). Fish and game agencies hustle hunting—instead of conserving wildlife, they're killing it. It's time for them to get in the business of protecting and preserving wildlife and creating balanced ecological systems instead of pimping for hunters who want their deer/duck/pheasant/turkey—animals stocked to be shot.

30   Hunters' self-serving arguments and lies are becoming more preposterous as nonhunters awake from their long, albeit troubled, sleep. Sport hunting is immoral; it should be made illegal. Hunters are persecutors of nature who should be prosecuted. They wield a disruptive power out of all proportion to their numbers, and pandering to their interests—the special interests of a group that just wants to kill things—is mad. It's preposterous that every year less than 7 percent of the population turns the skies into shooting galleries and the woods and fields into abattoirs. It's time to stop actively supporting and passively allowing hunting, and time to stigmatize it. It's time to stop being conned and cowed by hunters, time to stop pampering and coddling them, time to get them off the government's duck-and-deer dole, time to stop thinking of wild animals as "resources" and "game," and start thinking of them as sentient beings that deserve our wonder and respect, time to stop allowing hunting to be creditable by calling it "sport" and "recreation." Hunters make wildlife *dead, dead, dead.* It's time to wake up to this indisputable fact. As for the hunters, it's long past check-out time.

Questions for Discussion

1. In this essay, which information is knowledge by participation? Is this information necessary?
2. This essay is adversarial persuasion. How might the author revise this essay to make it more conciliatory? What specific changes do you think would be necessary? Would a more conciliatory essay be more persuasive?

3. This essay has visible sections, but no headings for its sections. Why do you think the author decided to omit headings? How would headings influence your reading of this essay? Would you be more or less likely to read the essay?
4. Notice the author's use of italics to indicate direct quotations. Why doesn't the author use quotation marks? What do you think of this use of italics? What are the advantages and disadvantages of this technique?
5. This essay was written for *Esquire,* a men's magazine. How might the author revise this essay for a women's magazine such as *Redbook* or *Vanity Fair*? What specific changes would be necessary? How might the author revise this essay for a hunter's magazine such as *Field & Stream* or *Fins and Feathers*?

Opportunities for Writing

1. In a letter to the editor of *Field & Stream,* offer your opinion of hunting. Do you think hunting is a "killing game"? Is it a "legitimate" sporting activity? Is it ethical? Consider how you will establish your credibility, support your claim, and motivate your audience.
2. Write a comprehensive evaluation of the literature of a local anti-hunting group. Which of their fliers and brochures do you consider persuasive? Which are ineffective? Consider issues such as accuracy, credibility, logical validity, emotional impact, and readability. Offer recommendations for revision. Address your evaluation to the leadership of this group.
3. In a letter addressed to the governor of your state, propose specific changes to state hunting laws. Before writing your proposal, interview both hunting and anti-hunting groups for their observations on the existing laws.
4. Write a letter to a friend who has invited you to join him or her on a hunting expedition. Explain why you are willing or unwilling to go.

Amy Fisher and the Ethics of "Headline" Docudramas

Rod Carveth

Rod Carveth teaches in the Department of Media, Arts, and Philosophy at Worcester State College. He is the co-editor of Media Economics: Theory and Practice *(1993). In this essay, Carveth focuses on the docudrama and argues that producers need to be ethical, accurate, and responsible when they convert sensational news into made-for-TV movies. "Amy Fisher and the Ethics of 'Headline' Docudramas" appeared in the* Journal of Popular Film and Television *and follows the MLA style of documentation.*

On 19 May 1992, 17-year-old Amy Fisher met Peter Guagenti, a 21-year-old college dropout from Brooklyn, to get a .25-caliber handgun. Guagenti then drove Fisher to the home of Mary Jo Buttafuoco, the wife of the man with whom Fisher was allegedly having an affair. There Fisher shot Mrs. Buttafuoco in the head; then, thinking she had killed her quarry, Fisher was driven back to her Long Island home by Guagenti. To Fisher's dismay, she had not killed Mary Jo Buttafuoco, although she had permanently maimed her victim. After emergency surgery, Mrs. Buttafuoco identified her attacker, and Fisher was arrested.

What followed was a media circus of unprecedented proportions, resulting ultimately in three made-for-TV docudramas centering on the tragedy. Volumes have been written about the Amy Fisher case. The docudramas, and the ethical concerns raised by their production, are the focus of this article.

The Evolution of the Docudrama

One of the most popular forms of television programming over the last 20 years has been the "docudrama," a movie that is a hybrid of the documentary and the dramatic film. While there is some disagreement as to what exactly determines a docudrama, this form presents viewers with a purposeful viewpoint or value-laden interpretation of reality and contains some degree of historical accuracy and factual authenticity (Brode 14–17; Hoffer and Nelson 149–63). The television docudrama also draws heavily from such motion picture stylistics as narrative conventions and specific production techniques.

Docudramas are a category of the genre of the made-for-TV movie (Edgerton 114–27; Gomery). More than any other TV programming genre, made-for-TV movies owe their existence to consideration of television economics: Television executives created made-for-TV movies when the rental fees for airing theatrical releases became too expensive. Made at a fraction of the cost of a theatrical movie ($3–5 million versus $25–40 million) and less costly than a series commitment, these TV movies proved popular and profitable.

Docudramas generally fall into two categories. The first is the historical docudrama, a fictionalized retelling of a period of history, such as *Patton: The Final Days*. These telefilms benefit from the perspective of time passage: Much has been written and much is known about the events that have happened.

The second category of docudrama I call the "headline" docudrama. These telefilms are based on events that have occurred much closer to their airing, usually within five years. As Louis Chunovic observes, these docudramas usually follow one of two basic plots (30–33). The first plot revolves around tales of adversity, where the principals display courage and persistence and achieve some form of triumph. A typical docudrama in this category would be *The Ryan White Story*, which portrays a boy's struggle with AIDS.

The second basic plot centers on tales of crime, often involving either greed or lust (or both). Most often, the crimes are murders or sexually related assaults. In the end, justice prevails, and the criminals are held responsible for their crimes. Examples of this type of docudrama are *Good Night, Sweet Wife: A Murder in Boston* (about the Charles Stuart murder case) and *Murder in New Hampshire* (about the Pamela Smart murder case). One of the primary selling points of these docudramas is that they are "based on fact" or "based on real-life events."

Headline docudramas are attractive to producers because the audience has been "presold"—potential viewers are familiar with the story from previous media coverage. Consequently, the more media coverage a story receives, the more interested producers become in obtaining rights to that story. Oftentimes, the amount of media coverage a story receives becomes the determining factor as to why a movie will get made. In this way, the explosion of media coverage set off after Amy Fisher shot Mary Jo Buttafuoco meant the central question was not whether the story would be made into a docudrama but when.

A Media Circus

There are a number of reasons why the Amy Fisher case captured the public's fascination. In 1987, the movie *Fatal Attraction* generated both popular acclaim and critical scrutiny as the story of a woman fatally obsessed with the man with whom she had an affair. So powerful was this story that the term "fatal attraction" became synonymous with any story of obsessive love. It was within this framework that the media first reported the Amy Fisher case—she had a "fatal attraction" for her alleged lover, Joey Buttafuoco.

The case unfolded during the summer months, traditionally a slower period for news, except for wars and natural disasters (in this case, Hurricane Andrew). Because it followed two other highly publicized sex-oriented trials—William Kennedy Smith and Mike Tyson—the story got more play in the press, especially in the tabloids, than it might have otherwise received.

The notion of a young woman's fatal attraction to an older man (with a big assist from the local tabloid *New York Post*) helped propel the story into the national headlines. The story may have had a short shelf life if not for further revelations, however. For one thing, Amy Fisher had a double life. In addition to being a high school student, she was also a call girl. One of her clients, Peter De Rosa, arranged to videotape one of their encounters, then sold the tape to the tabloid news show *A Current Affair*. The revelation that Fisher sold her body changed the frame of the story from "fatal attraction" to "Long Island Lolita," with Fisher as a murderous contemporary version of the Vladimir Nabokov character.

More headlines were generated when Fisher was arraigned on 2 June 1992. Assistant District Attorney Fred Klein argued that her bail should be set at $2 million because of the risk that Amy would flee if released. According to Klein:

> One might describe this defendant as a 17-year-old girl who lives at home with her parents and goes to high school. That would be about as accurate, Your Honor, as describing John Gotti as a businessman from New York. This is not your typical 17-year-old high school student. I emphasize that to the court. She is completely beyond the control of her parents, of the school and of this court. (Kasindorf 36)

The judge at Fisher's arraignment agreed with the prosecution's request for high bail. Fisher's attorney Eric Naiburg appealed unsuccessfully four times to have the bail reduced, spurring headlines at each rejection. Finally, Naiburg was able to obtain a deal with KLM Productions whereby KLM put up $60,000 toward Fisher's bail in return for giving the company the right to negotiate a TV deal (Russell 21). That arrangement drew not only a protest from the prosecution, but provided an interesting new twist to the story for the media.

KLM then negotiated with broadcast tabloid *Inside Edition* to air an exclusive interview with Fisher. During the interview, Fisher charged that she and Joey Buttafuoco had sex many times (including on his boat ironically named *Double

Trouble), he wanted her to wear sexy underwear, he called her on her beeper using the code 007, and he forced her into prostitution. For his part, Buttafuoco claimed to New York radio "shock jock" Howard Stern that he never cheated on his wife. Even Mary Jo's mother got into the act, detailing the torment that Joey was going through to *New York Post* columnist Cindy Adams (Hackett 26–29).

In September, Naiburg and Klein worked out a plea bargain deal whereby Fisher would plead guilty to a charge of reckless assault. On 23 September, Fisher entered her guilty plea in court. That night, Fisher admitted to new "boyfriend" Paul Makely that she deserved something, like a Ferrari, for all she went through. She also asked Makely to marry her so she could have conjugal visits while in prison. Unfortunately for Amy, Makely had videotaped their conversation and sold the tape to the tabloid show *Hard Copy*. When the episode of *Hard Copy* aired, Fisher twice attempted suicide and eventually asked to return to prison so that she could have some peace. More headlines followed.

15   While awaiting sentencing scheduled for 1 December, Fisher completed her exams to obtain her high school diploma and announced plans to pursue a college degree in English literature while in prison. In the meantime, the Buttafuocos filed a multimillion dollar suit against Fisher and sold the rights to their story to Columbia TriStar. *New York Post* reporter Amy Pagnozzi, who had covered the Fisher case extensively, signed on with Capital Cities/ABC to be "technical advisor" to another Amy Fisher project. What resulted were three movies on the Amy Fisher case, all to be aired on each of the three major networks.[1]

NBC aired the first of the docudramas, *Amy Fisher: My Story,* on 28 December 1992. NBC's version was from Fisher's perspective, as the *TV Guide* promotion claimed:

SEE HER STORY FIRST—TONIGHT
You've heard the shocking reports from the news media—tonight, see Amy's side of the story!

CBS and ABC both aired their versions on Sunday, 3 January 1993. The CBS version, *Casualties of Love: The "Long Island Lolita" Story,* was the project on which the Buttafuocos cooperated. The ABC version, *Beyond Control: The Amy Fisher Story,* was based largely on stories written by Amy Pagnozzi of the *New York Post*. The *TV Guide* promotions illustrate the contrast between the two tales. For *Casualties of Love:*

Based on the victims' true story.
Joey Buttafuoco was an auto body repairman.
Amy Fisher was a customer. First she wrecked her car.
Then she wrecked his life.

For *Beyond Control:*

The one you can't miss.
ABC Sunday Night Movie.
"The judge said when Miss Fisher attacked Mary Jo Buttafuoco, her acts were like a wild animal that stalks its prey, motivated by lust and passion."
—*The New York Times*
Drew Barrymore is Amy Fisher.
The Amy Fisher Story.

The three movies drew solid ratings. NBC had a 19.1 rating[2] and 30 share of the audience, barely losing the time period to ABC's football game (which was football legend Joe Montana's first game in two years). In the head-to-head competition, ABC won over CBS: ABC drew a 19.5 rating and 30 share, whereas CBS drew a 14.3 rating and 22 share. All three movies cracked the top 12 of programs for their weeks.

The movies also drew mainly negative reviews (cf. Corliss 47; Hiltbrand 9–10). Most reviews decried the poor acting, trite dialogue, or overall "trashy" nature of the subject matter. None addressed the more troubling aspects of the three docudramas, the questionable ethics employed in retelling this tale to the public.

Ethical Dilemmas of Docudramas

Three major ethical dilemmas exist in terms of docudramas: the effects on the principals of the story, the lack of ideological context, and the techniques used to blur fact and fiction.

Effects on Principals

Unlike many of the earlier docudramas, the quest for converting headlines into movies has produced increasing competition for stories, resulting in behavior that crosses ethical boundaries. For example, the judge during the Pamela Smart murder trial commented that he hoped Clint Eastwood would play him in the TV movie. More recently, it was revealed that one of the witnesses in the Menendez murder case was a producer who held the rights to the story.[3]

The controversy over Amy Fisher selling the rights to her story to raise bail was recently stirred again when KLM Productions (who put up the money for Fisher) assisted the bail for JoAnne Ripic, a woman in New York accused of helping her son murder her husband. Critics worry that this practice rewards perpetrators of crimes, especially those with "juicy" stories to tell. In addition, the production of the subsequent docudrama may compromise the legal positions of the principals, especially during the appeals process.

Producers need to keep in mind that stories that make for good docudramas involve real people with real needs (i.e., fair trials, personal privacy, etc.). When that concept is forgotten, a major ethical line has been crossed.

Lack of Ideological Context

The second ethical concern is more subtle. Most docudramas ignore the social and political forces surrounding an event to concentrate on the personal stories of the characters in the story (Rapping; Schulze 35–60). For example, in *Good Night, Sweet Wife: A Murder in Boston,* the movie barely notes the racial overtones involved in the case. When Stuart called 911 after shooting his wife, he said that a black man had shot them.[4] In the following weeks, most African-American males in Roxbury were rounded up by the Boston police and questioned, sometimes with tactics bordering on being unconstitutional. The incident fueled the simmering racial tensions and fears in Boston. One suspect was arrested, even though police had already begun to suspect Stuart as the murderer. By choosing to concentrate on the character of Charles Stuart, the producers missed an opportunity to explore the issue of race in society.

In terms of Amy Fisher, larger issues of parental abuse, male-female relationships, class, and ethnicity were all ignored in the three docudramas. This is somewhat surprising, considering that Fisher allegedly said to Mary Jo Buttafuoco (and which was repeated in some version in all three movies), "Don't you think a 40-year-old man on top of a 16-year-old girl is disgusting?" Why a teenage girl would try to use sex for power, and why a 40-year-old man would try to exploit a teenage girl were questions that the movies failed to explore. Whether Fisher was being vilified for her sexuality as much as her alleged crime is an important contextual issue that is virtually ignored.

What docudramas largely do is present a restoration of the social order. This is done through the following plot device: An individual (or individuals) creates social chaos. Another individual (or individuals) representing the "system" then works to bring order back to the world. Even when the "system" appears flawed, order is restored in the end. Docudramas are presented as "personal" stories rather than "social" ones. As such, they often fail to critique society's failings, locating wrongs not in the social structure but on a personal and melodramatic level.

Presenting "Reality"

25 The major ethical concern, however, is how well the depiction of "reality" in the docudrama fairly represents the actual event. Due to the narrative constraints of telling a good story, dialogue is often invented, characters are composites of several people, and even certain occurrences are made up. The act of adapting an event to standard narrative formulas changes reality in the process.

Producers do not go out of their way to announce that the docudrama has a point of view. The reality that is portrayed often depends on the perspective of the person or persons who sold the rights of the story to the producer. Depending on which version of the Amy Fisher story was seen, viewers saw that Amy (1) never slept with Joey Buttafuoco (CBS), (2) definitely slept with Joey Buttafuoco (NBC), or (3) most likely slept with Joey Buttafuoco (ABC). These three depictions correspond with the various points of view the movies presented (i.e., Joey's, Amy's, and reporter Amy Pagnozzi's, respectively).

When docudramas are based on books by authors not directly involved in the case, the point of view is presumably neutral and "objective." The docudrama of Jean Harris, who was convicted of the murder of Dr. Herbert Tarnower, the famed "Scarsdale Diet Doctor," was based on Shana Alexander's book *Very Much a Lady*. However, even the "third party" can shade sympathies to one side or the other, as Shana Alexander did with Jean Harris, or Joe McGuiness did with Jeffrey MacDonald in *Fatal Vision*. The subsequent docudramas generally incorporate the authors' leanings.

Producers of docudramas enjoy wide legal latitude regarding the accuracy of docudramas. One good example is the "false light" doctrine. False light means that a person's privacy can be invaded through the coincidental use of names, fictionalization, or the misuse of names and pictures. Damage awards in false light privacy cases are based, as in libel cases, upon false statements of fact.

Examples of false light cases include the Hill family, which was held hostage by three escaped convicts in the 1950s. The family objected to the fictionalization of the episode in both the play and movie versions of *Desperate Hours,* and especially a promotional story preview in *Life* magazine. They sued, arguing that the portrayal of their experience was wildly inaccurate. Although the Hills won in the lower courts, the Supreme Court overturned the judgment (*Time, Inc. v. Hill* 1967). In this case, the Supreme Court ruled that, as in libel cases involving public figures, actual malice must be proved in false light cases. The text has been modified somewhat since (cf. *Gertz v. Welch* 1970) so that private persons seeking actual damages need only prove negligence. In order to collect punitive damages, however, plaintiffs would have to prove actual malice, a very tough standard.[5]

The courts have been very liberal in providing other defenses to false light cases. Beyond privilege (the wide latitude the courts grant through free speech), a producer substantially reduces his/her tort liability potential by obtaining consent through the acquisition of rights to a story. Docudramas may be based on books of events or cases, the rights to which have been secured by the author. Producers may feel protected in such an arrangement. After all, if a principal has been defamed, it could be argued that it was the author's fault and not the producer's.

In addition to privilege and consent, the use of disclaimers, such as "a motion picture based on a true story," go far to prevent litigation potential. Some disclaimers are rather vague. For example, the disclaimer for the docudrama *Guilty Until Proven Innocent* stated: "Martin Sheen stars in a motion picture based on a true story." Other disclaimers are a bit more specific. The disclaimer for *The Preppie Murder Case* read: "The following dramatization is based on police reports, personal interviews, various news reports, and court records. *Some dramatic license has been taken in the creation of certain scenes*" (emphasis mine).[6]

Complicating the process even more is the fact that securing the rights to docudrama stories can often be very difficult and frustrating. Competing companies owning the rights to the same story will rush their product to the screen, sometimes sacrificing accuracy. It is important to be first with airing a property. In January 1987, CBS aired a two-part, four-hour docudrama called *At Mother's Request,* the story about Manhattan socialite Frances Schreuder, who coerced her 17-year-old son to murder her father, one of the richest men in Utah. The production averaged a 35 share of the audience. Two months later, NBC aired its three-part, six-hour version of the story, *Nutcracker: Money, Madness, Murder.* This second version averaged only a 21 share of the audience (Noglows 29–34).

One way of avoiding coming in second in the docudrama "sweepstakes" is to lock up the book rights early. However, such a practice can help up the ante for rights fees. That means that small producers are at a disadvantage and may not pursue a project priced out of their league. As a result, many producers have gone for "smaller" projects with less well-known events and principals with compelling stories (usually of adversity).

In addition, producers are moving more quickly to secure rights. Previously, many producers waited until a book came out, which often was a preliminary test of whether the story generated public interest. Many producers found two problems with this prerequisite, however. First, successful book authors wanted exorbitant fees for the options to their stories. Second, many producers felt hemmed in by the authors' stories, leaving them little room to maneuver in telling their narrative. Consequently, producers first began optioning stories from authors before they finished (or, in the case of the Mayflower Madam, before even writing) their books. Soon, they circumvented authors and moved directly to going after the principals of the stories or the reporters who covered the stories (the very people whose efforts often promoted an event onto the public agenda).

The problem here is that the audience is unaware of who is the source or author of the docudrama. Psychology shows that, over time, individuals forget the source of a message they remember. When a movie airs with a message saying that it is "based on fact," it is highly possible that, over time, viewers will believe that the recreated story is indeed fact rather than fiction.

The believability of docudramas lies in what David Sholle terms the "reality effect" (56–72). Although Sholle applies the concept of the reality effect to broadcast tabloid news shows, such as *A Current Affair,* the same principle can apply to docudramas: The truth content of docudramas depends less on accuracy than credibility, "from what is true to what can be believed to be true" (66). Kenneth Kaufman, executive producer of the *In the Line of Fire* series for NBC and producer of *Ambush in Waco,* defends docudramas:

> We're making a dramatized movie, not a documentary, not a historical analysis, not a tract—a movie. Omission, compression—those are all the things that we have to use in order to tell a story. There are composite characters whose essence is *truth.* (Quoted in Shaw 22–25)

Ironically, one of the devices used to make events appear as if they happened is to include actual or recreated newspaper headlines or news broadcasts within the docudrama. In that way, the appearance in the media validates the events for the viewer. In the case of Amy Fisher, the majority of media coverage emanated from the print and broadcast tabloids, which are generally considered to be less credible than "legitimate" news media such as the *New York Times* or network news. All the Fisher movies included some mention of the tabloids within them. For viewers who saw the Amy Fisher cased played out on the tabloids and then saw the scenes recreated for the docudrama, a sense of validity about the docudrama is created. At the very extreme, viewers may believe these stories without question, thus having a distorted view of the event and the characters.

The line between news and entertainment is becoming increasingly blurred. So-called "reality" programs, such as *America's Most Wanted, Unsolved Mysteries,* and *Rescue 911,* have become increasingly popular, and ratings for broadcast tabloid news programs rival local and network news shows. These programs regularly weave fictionalized dramatic segments, with actors playing criminals, rescuers, and victims, into actual news footage and interviews with real-life participants. It is not always clear where the dramatizations end and the "reality" begins. No disclaimers run on the shows to alert the viewer as to what is fact and what is fiction. The shows blur the line between reality and fiction in the name of narrative—the telling of a story.

Even so-called "legitimate" news organizations have begun to cross the line in terms of what is acceptable news practice. ABC received considerable criticism for its use of a re-enactment in reporting the Felix Bloch spy case on *World News Tonight*. NBC was similarly chastised for actually rigging the explosion of a GM truck on the news magazine *Dateline*. If the major networks continue to employ re-enactments to tell their news stories, the distinction between fact and fiction will continue to diminish.

Alfred Schneider, former vice president of policy and standards at Capital Cities/ABC, authored the following guidelines for "invention" in docudramas: (1) creating composite characters out of two or more actual persons is permissible, but the construction of fictitious characters is not; (2) the chronology of events should be accurate, and the passage of time made clear through the use of dialogue, dissolves, et cetera; (3) characters' personal characteristics should be consistent with those of the actual principals of the story; and (4) created dialogue, when used, should also be consistent with those of the actual principals (75–81). Interestingly, Schneider also notes that "although a conversation between actual persons on a specific matter may not be capable of documentation, depictions of such a conversation may be acceptable if they accurately characterize the individuals portrayed and their specific attitudes at the time in which the scene is depicted" (68). Again, even a network vice president is willing to accept a standard of reasonableness rather than accuracy for recreating reality.

Little research on the impact of docudramas on the audience has been conducted. What few studies do exist suggest that viewers who are least familiar with an event or issue "learn" the most from these docudramas (Surlin 309–20; Whaley, Kaminski, Gorden, and Heisey 285–89). The problem is that what viewers learn may be a misrepresentation of reality.

CONCLUSION

As far as Amy Fisher is concerned, the three docudramas were not the end of the accounts of her case. In January 1993, an off-Broadway theatrical musical of the Fisher case went into production and quickly became a cult hit. An Amy Fisher-Joey Buttafuoco comic book made its debut, and fans snapped up the entire first run of 60,000 copies. Two books appeared, *Lethal Lolita*, written by *People* magazine reporter Maria Eftimiades, and *Amy Fisher: My Story*, by Amy Fisher herself (with writer Sheila Weller). The case continued to be a popular talk show topic, including shows with Amy's high school classmates on *Geraldo* and an appearance by the Buttafuocos on *Donahue* in March 1993. Perhaps the most bizarre twist occurred when an aspiring producer tried to have Amy and Mary Jo appear together on television. The "summit" between these two principals, however, never came off (Marin 37).

On 31 March 1993, the three network TV movies about Amy Fisher were released to video stores. Turner Home Video distributed the NBC version, complete with a WNBC jailhouse interview with Fisher. Suppliers hoped for sales to match the TV ratings, but the high price ($89.95) and the reluctance of video retail outlets to carry the video as a rental (e.g., Blockbuster) limited their impact (Miller 67).

In May 1993, Joey Buttafuoco was indicted on 19 charges of statutory rape because Fisher was a minor when she allegedly first had sex with him. In part, Buttafuoco was victimized by his own high profile in the media. His participation on the Howard Stern and Donahue programs did little to generate sympathy for him. On the contrary, public reaction became increasingly negative. Many people began to question why Buttafuoco had never been charged with a crime. In October 1993, Buttafuoco pled guilty to a charge of statutory rape and subsequently received a six-month prison sentence. Rumors swirled that a sequel to the Amy Fisher movies would be made.

Following the ratings success of the Amy Fisher movies, the networks rushed to get other stories from the headlines onto the small screen, such as *In the Line of Fire: Ambush in Waco*. It took only 10 days from the time of the bombing of the World Trade Towers for producers to secure a TV deal from New York's Rescue One team. Bryan Norcross, the Miami weatherman who broadcasted for 23 straight hours during Hurricane Andrew, sold his rights to NBC five days after the storm ended. In what must be a record, however, it took only one day for former Branch Davidian cultists and wounded federal agents to sell their rights concerning the Waco conflict to a TV-movie producer. Docudramas of all three disasters aired during the May 1993 sweeps on NBC. In fact, the movie on the Waco conflict was in production when the compound burned down. In other words, the story had not even reached its conclusion when the movie was being produced (the movie concludes with the FBI's raid on the compound). Judd Parkin, ABC senior vice-president, has observed that "We've reached the point where TV movies and news shows are competing for the very same stories" (quoted in Waters 58).

A recent example of this competition for stories involves the scandal surrounding pop music star Michael Jackson. Jackson has been accused of molesting a 13 year-old boy. From the time the allegation was first made in August 1993, movie producers and tabloid news representatives have pursued virtually anyone with any knowledge of the incident. Jackson's former maid and bodyguards have been paid thousands of dollars to appear on *A Current Affair* and *Hard Copy*. At the same time, the boy and his family have been approached with offers for the TV movie rights to their story. This media spending spree has created an environment of "checkbook storytelling." What should be noted is that, as of this writing, Michael Jackson has not even been questioned about the alleged molestation, let alone charged with a crime. Yet those involved in the quest for getting the story on the air have conveniently ignored this fact.

Perhaps the next scandal-inspired trilogy will be the Katie Beers case. Katie was abducted and chained by the neck for 16 days in January 1993 before being freed by her captor. In the first two weeks after her release, stories about Katie appeared on *Donahue, The Montel Williams Show, The Maury Povich Show*, and *Inside Edition*. So fierce is the competition for the rights to Katie's story that the court that placed her in foster care is overseeing any subsequent negotiations. Estimates are that the rights to the Beers story may go as high as $500,000 (Lacayo 59; Rudolph and Lieberman 43).

In addition to the saga of Katie Beers, by the end of 1993, docudramas will have been completed on the slaying of Florida abortion doctor David Gunn by an anti-abortionist; the rescue of seven skiers who survived a blizzard in Colorado; and Heidi Fleiss, the "Hollywood Madam." Early 1994 may feature one or more docudramas on the Menendez case or the Bobbitts. Producers have so far demonstrated no more restraint in pursuing those in the headlines or for rushing those stories to the small screen than they did with the Amy Fisher case.

The continuing ratings success of headline docudramas and the concomitant popularity of tabloid news programs ensure that crime and scandal will remain a significant staple of the television viewing environment. As documented in this essay, there is certainly no shortage of sensational stories or of aggressive producers willing to pay large sums for the rights to those stories. What appears to be in short supply is a willingness to tell these tales in a responsible fashion, to protect the principals involved, and to recreate the event as faithfully as possible.

Alfred Schneider recently observed about the ethics of docudrama that the time has come for producers to adhere to "requirements of accuracy, fairness, balance and choice" (81). Unfortunately, it appears that the major goal for most producers in developing a headline docudrama is to get it on the air first. In such a competitive environment, ensuring "accuracy, fairness, balance and choice" is generally irrelevant.

Notes

1. *Village Voice* writer Stacey D'Erasmo observed tongue-in-cheek that a Fox-TV version of the Fisher case was planned, but that *Beverly Hills 90210* star Shannen Doherty, who has generated her own share of tabloid headlines for her erratic off-screen behavior, was already committed to the series and not available (47–48).
2. A ratings point represents 931,000 households.
3. The Menendez murder case, the outcome of which was pending at the time of this writing, involves two brothers who allegedly murdered their parents. Their defense is that they had been long-term victims of parental abuse.
4. In an ironic twist, the "reality" program *Rescue 911* was filming in Boston when Stuart's call came in. The recording of the call and footage shot at the emergency room became the basis of a subsequent episode of the series.
5. Plaintiffs have also tried to sue citing emotional distress. However, to be successful, a plaintiff would have to demonstrate the defendant's action (1) was extreme and outrageous conduct beyond all possible bounds of decency, (2) was intended to inflict emotional distress, (3) resulted in serious emotional distress, and (4) caused a degree of distress equivalent to that which a reasonable person would have suffered (Grunfeld). See *Pawelek v. Paramount Studios* (1983) and *Hustler Magazine v. Falwell* (1988).
6. Curiously, in the opening of *Casualties of Love* (made by securing the Buttafuocos' rights), Joey Buttafuoco is shown doing cocaine in his car. When asked about that on *Donahue,* he said the producers used "creative license" with that scene. It should be noted, however, that Buttafuoco has admitted going through a drug rehabilitation program for cocaine use. In addition, guests on the local New York TV show *9 Broadcast Plaza* charged that Buttafuoco dealt cocaine and was known as "Joey Coco Pops."

Works Cited

Brode, Douglas. "Video Verité: Defining the Docudrama." *Television Quarterly* 20 (1984): 7–26.

Chunovic, Louis. "Looking for Trouble." *American Film* Feb. 1991: 30–33.
Corliss, Richard. "Trashomon." *Time* 11 Jan. 1993: 47.
D'Erasmo, Stacey. "The Three Faces of Amy." *Village Voice* 12 Jan. 1993: 47–48.
Edgerton, Gary. "High Concept, Small Screen: Reperceiving the Industrial and Stylistic Origins of the American Made-for-TV Movie." *Journal of Popular Film and Television* 19.3 (Fall 1991): 114–27.
Gomery, Douglas. "Brian's Song: Television, Hollywood, and the Evolution of the Movie Made for Television." *American History/American Television: Interpreting the Video Past.* Ed. John E. O'Connor. New York: Ungar, 1983. 208–31
Grunfeld, J. "Docudramas: The Legality of Producing Fact-Based Dramas—What Every Producer's Attorney Should Know." *Comm/Ent* 14.4: 483–544.
Hacket, Larry. "Looking for Lolita." *TV Guide* 2 Jan. 1993: 26–29.
Hiltbrand, David. "Picks and Pans." *People* 18 Jan. 1993: 9–10.
Hoffer, Thomas W., and Richard Alan Nelson. "Evolution of the Docudrama on American Television Networks: A Content Analysis, 1966–1978." *The Southern Speech Communication Journal* 45 (Winter 1980): 149–63.
Kasindorf, Jeanie. "Running Wild: The Amy Fisher Story." *New York* 10 Aug. 1992: 28–39.
Lacayo, Richard. "A Little Girl Buried Alive." *Time* 25 Jan. 1993: 59.
Marin, Rick. "Will There Be a TV Summit Between Amy and Mary Jo?" *TV Guide* 3 Apr. 1993: 37.
Miller, Trudi. "Go Fish(er): Retailers Get Their Pick." *Billboard* 20 Mar. 1993: 65, 67.
Noglows, Paul. "How They Got That Story." *Channels* Nov. 1987: 29–34.
Rapping, Elayne. *The Looking Glass World of Nonfiction TV.* Boston: South End Press, 1987.
Rudolph, Reane, and David Lieberman. "Long Island's Latest Scandal Inspires Frenzy." *TV Guide* 6 Feb. 1993: 43.
Russell, George. "'Long Island Lolita' Makes Tabloid Pulse Quicken." *Variety* 3 Aug. 1992: 17, 21.
Schneider, Alfred. "Preserving the Integrity of the Docudrama." *Television Quarterly* 26.2 (1993): 75–81.
Schulze, Laurie. "Getting Physical: Text/Context/Reading and the Made-for-Television Movie." *Cinema Journal* 25 (Winter 1986): 35–60.
Shaw, David. "From Headline to Prime Time." *TV Guide* 22 May 1993: 22–25.
Sholle, David. "Buy Our News: Tabloid Television and Commodification." *Journal of Communication Inquiry* 17.1 (1993): 56–72.
Surlin, Stuart. "Roots' Research: A Summary of Findings." *Journal of Broadcasting* 22.3 (Summer 1978): 309–20.
Waters, Harry F. "Racing the News Crews." *Newsweek* 24 May 1993: 58.
Whaley, A. Bennett, Edmund P. Kaminski, William I. Gorden, and D. Ray Heisey. "Docudrama From Different Temporal Perspectives: Reactions to NBC's 'Kent State.'" *Journal of Broadcasting* 27.3 (Summer 1983): 285–89.

Questions for Discussion

1. In discussing this issue, the author cites twelve different examples of "headline" docudramas. What do you think of this technique of using examples to clarify a point? If you've never seen the docudramas cited, is this technique effective? Explain why you believe it is or isn't.
2. What is the author's claim? How does he support this claim? Which pieces of evidence do you consider especially persuasive? Why?
3. This essay's subordinate aim is referential: the author explains the meaning of "headline docudramas" and analyzes the causes and effects

of this television programming. How might the author integrate a subordinate expressive aim?
4. How would this essay differ if it were written using only knowledge by participation? Which passages would be omitted? Would the essay be more or less effective? Why?
5. How does the author motivate his readers to approve his claim? Does he appeal to their self-interest or their sense of altruism? Cite specific passages to support your answer.

Opportunities for Writing

1. Assess the ethics of a "headline" docudrama you've seen. In your evaluation, compare and contrast the film version of the incident to earlier newspaper and televised news coverage. Consider such issues as the impact on the principals, the presence or absence of ideological context, and the accuracy of the representation. Address your essay to the producers of the film.
2. Voice your opinion of headline docudramas. Do you think such programming is appropriate? desirable? necessary? Would you like to see more or less of this programming? Why? Compose your essay as a guest editorial for the television page of your local newspaper.
3. In a letter to the editor of *TV Guide,* praise or criticize the magazine's coverage of headline docudramas. Review a minimum of twelve issues of the weekly magazine to develop a valid and reliable picture of its coverage. In its stories on headline docudramas, does *TV Guide* identify the film's perspective, specify which principals were paid for their cooperation, or assess the accuracy of this version of the incident?

Hollywood: The Dark Side

SYLVESTER MONROE

Sylvester Monroe writes for Time *and is based in Los Angeles. A native of Chicago, Monroe was a writer for* Newsweek, *specializing in politics and minority affairs. In 1988, working with a team of* Newsweek *correspondents, he published* Brothers, Black and Poor—A True Story of Courage and Survival, *reporting on the lives of black men from his old South Side neighborhood, including himself. He has also written articles for* The Chicago Tribune *and* The Los Angeles Times. *In this essay, Monroe considers a solution to this question: How can blacks become more of a collective force to promote and save quality programming that features blacks? "Hollywood: The Dark Side" appeared in* Essence *in March 1994. The evidence in this essay comes from Monroe's own knowledge of this subject as well as from others' analyses and comments.*

Joan Mosley is a loving but tough single mother raising three children, among them a 5-year-old foster child, in South Central Los Angeles. When she discovers that her teenage son is planning to buy a beeper, every Black mother in America can appreciate her concern. "The day you get a beeper is the day *after* you become a doctor," she admonishes. And when she overhears him exclaim, "That bitch is fine!" she comes down so hard on him that every woman in America is on her side. "Am I a bitch? Is your sister a bitch?" she asks rhetorically, driving her point home.

Joan Mosley, the protagonist of the half-hour show from 20th Century Fox Television called *South Central,* is the mirror image of millions of African-American mothers who can be found in almost any city in America. Where she cannot be found is on major network television. Executives at CBS had "reservations" and passed on it; ABC and NBC weren't interested, either. So what has been described as a "refreshing and realistic" portrayal of a significant slice of African-American life remains at 20th Century Fox Television in the mini network's winter lineup.

Why was it so difficult to get the show on the air? Rose Catherine Pinkney, the former director of programming for 20th Century Fox Television, now with Uptown Entertainment, helped develop *South Central* and was assigned to cover its progress; she says the answer is that *South Central* is a different type of Black comedy. "It's a realistic but positive depiction of life in the nineties," explains Pinkney. "If you're expecting 'ha, ha, ha' every two minutes, you're not going to enjoy this show. But if you want honest laughs from an honest family when it's right, then you'll like it."

South Central is like too many intelligent Black projects that often never make it to prime-time TV or that vanish forever after a few airings. Their chief flaw is that they don't fit neatly into the Black-sitcom formula—that electronic never-never land where stereotypical characters verbally bludgeon one another with insulting one-liners.

As long as we're funny, as long as the public is allowed to laugh at us, then everyone seems to be comfortable dealing with us," says Leisa M. Henry, director of marketing and public relations for new-writer recruitment at Warner Brothers Television. "It's okay to be ethnic. It's okay to wear dreadlocks if you are making people laugh. But as soon as we cross the line and become serious, when we have to be contended with as adults facing serious real-life issues, then we're no longer marketable."

CLOWNS, CUTUPS, AND BUFFOONS

After all these years, Hollywood still doesn't get it. On the big screen, films like *Boyz 'N the Hood, Juice* and *Menace II Society* have been applauded by both critics *and* Black moviegoers for their more honest portrayals. The frustration is their sameness. Studio executives seem to think that hard-core inner-city life is the only slice of Black life there is.

Flick on the small screen, and you're likely to be bombarded with stereotypes of a different stripe: Black men and women depicted mainly as clowns, cutups and loud-mouthed buffoons. "We are more or less told who we are, rather than asked," testified veteran actress and Hollywood activist Marla Gibbs at a hearing held last June by the U.S. Commission on Civil Rights. "We sing, we dance, we tell jokes—that's all we are allowed to do. We entertain."

Among Tinseltown's most vocal critics is one of its biggest stars, Bill Cosby. Temporarily shedding his own comic Jell-O—pudding persona, the most successful African-American in television history took the occasion of his induction into the Academy of Television Arts and Sciences Hall of Fame to urge the industry to cut it out. "Stop this horrible massacre of images that are being put on the screen now," he chided his network peers. "I'm begging you, because it isn't us."

Saundra Sharp, an outspoken African-American actress, writer and independent filmmaker, blames the poor quality of Black TV fare on the nature of the business. "Every once in a while something positive sneaks through like *Frank's Place*," she says. "But I don't hold much hope for Hollywood. The mentality is too low and the greed, too high."

10 But Sharp complains that too many Blacks in the industry have succumbed to the very same dollar-driven shallow way of thinking. Sharp, a former member of the Writers Guild of America, West, Inc., cofounded the activist Black Anti-Defamation Coalition to protest the negative images of Blacks on-screen in the early eighties. She says that if the coalition were still active, they would probably be going after their own people.

"Back then we were going to White producers complaining about how we were being represented as pimps and whores," she says. "But as more and more Blacks got into positions as producers and writers, they began to create the same images."

IT'S ABOUT POWER AND CONTROL

In all fairness, Black executives are still too few and too low on the organizational chart to wield much clout. "There is not one Black person who can 'green light' a television project, who can say, 'Yes, let's make that film or put that show on the air,'" observes veteran actor and producer Tim Reid, who starred in *WKRP in Cincinnati* and *Simon & Simon* before coexecutive-producing the highly acclaimed but short-lived *Frank's Place*. "It's very difficult for a Black person to be taken seriously at the level we are talking about. It's about power and control, and those who have it do not want to relinquish it."

Simply casting more Black actors and actresses in the countless major and minor character roles that routinely go to Whites would go far in getting beyond the same old tired clichés. But with only about eight or ten established Black casting directors for TV and film—that's out of hundreds—Black names, other than those of a star like Denzel Washington, are unlikely to be mentioned. "You can't rely on political correctness," explains Reuben Cannon, veteran Black casting director and producer. "When there's not a person of color in the room when casting is taking place, you can end up with a film that is set in America, yet doesn't have a Black face in it."

Television's biases are so blatant that media scholars and the few outspoken activists within the industry are becoming increasingly vocal in calling for change. George Gerbner, a professor at the University of Pennsylvania's Annenberg School for Communication, directed a ten-year study of the industry commissioned by the Screen Actors Guild and the American Federation of

Television and Radio Artists. The study, released last year, found that White males under 40 work more and earn more than any other group in television. Women, non-Whites and the elderly—in other words, most of America—are greatly underrepresented. That helps explain the enormous diversity of White male characters—from villains to superheroes and just about everything imaginable in between—while everyone else is mainly a type.

15 "Television seems to be frozen in a time warp of obsolete and damaging representations that deprive millions of people of the chance to see themselves growing up with the same opportunities, values and potential as everyone else," Gerbner said.

Another study, commissioned by the Writers Guild of America, West, Inc., found that both the television and the film industries have been shamefully lax in employing women and non-White writers. In 1991 White males still accounted for more than 70 percent of employed television writers and more than 80 percent of the working writers on feature films. In contrast, non-Whites comprise a mere 4 percent of the guild's 7,648 members. That's 3.9 percent of television writers and 2.6 percent of film writers. The result, says the report, is a "numbness and sameness in the storytelling."

The Lowest Common Denominator

Hollywood's long-standing race problems can be explained in large part by an old-fashioned blend of racism and ignorance plus a healthy dose of the industry's legendary arrogance. When it comes to writing for Black characters, for example, most Blacks in the industry would agree that while some White writers can write for Blacks, Black writers are critical to doing it consistently. Most White executives see it differently. "This industry still feels that Whites can write for Black characters simply because they have the power to do it," says Warner Brothers' Leisa M. Henry.

Particularly infuriating to many Blacks in the business is watching White writer-producers become specialists in producing Black shows, while Black writers and producers are routinely locked out of the process. The White husband-wife team of Andy and Susan Borowitz, for example, are the creators of a long list of Black shows, including *The Fresh Prince of Bel-Air*. But industry insiders say it wasn't until Black writer Winifred Hervey became the show's executive producer in June 1991 that it stopped being what one critic described as "a Black caricature of a White caricature" and began noticeably improving.

The industry's flaws are magnified by television's tendency to reduce everyone and everything to its lowest common denominator. "One of the things television does is take reality and pour it into convenient packages of an hour or half hour," says Bridget Potter, senior vice-president of original programming for HBO, "and the process of stereotyping happens."

20 Television executives concede that their industry is the last place to look for displays of multiculturalism. "What the studios have been doing for years is playing to middle-class White Americans," says David Gerber, who was the longtime chairman of the MGM/UA Television Group until the studio phased out its TV operations. "As a result, you won't see Black family shows outside the sitcom genre,

and you won't see Jewish family shows. I'm not sure you have any typical kind of family on television other than a White middle-class one, because the view is that they won't work in a mass audience." He shrugs, "After all, there are only about 30 million African-Americans. But there are 200 million White Americans."

That leaves many African-Americans in the industry in a bind. "If you're working on a show with White executive producers, they have their perceptions of what Black people are like," says P. Karen Raper; Raper and her writing partner, Eunetta Boone, are the only Blacks on a nine-writer staff for the NBC sitcom *Getting By.* "They just don't get it, and in their life they don't have to get it," adds Boone. "It's our job to help them get it." But the burden of speaking up for an entire race can take its toll on even the best Black writers, particularly those working on Black shows. Boone and Raper, who were story editors on *Roc* and *The Fresh Prince of Bel-Air* before writing for *Getting By,* say that at times it's easier *not* to write on Black shows.

"It's easier to sit by and let a White character look stupid," says Raper. "But I am at the point where I am tired of having to defend my race against people who know nothing about our culture. So you are in a position of constantly having to give history lessons to people who act as if you've only existed since 1954. They know nothing about you, and they don't care to know anything about you."

Few people better understand the industry's resistance to quality Black programming than Frank Dawson and his partners in 2002 Communications. For nearly two years the company has had a promising Black dramatic series called *Fox Hills* languishing in "development hell." It's about a thirtysomething African-American couple, both lawyers, in an upper-middle-class Los Angeles neighborhood. The series follows their return from Chicago to Los Angeles, where the husband works for a Fortune 500 company and the wife runs a community law practice in South Central L.A.

Although there hasn't been a dramatic series about an African-American family on network TV since the early 1980's, *South Central* remains tough to sell. "At the studio, they're saying the writing is strong, but they're still not sure whether mainstream audiences want to see these characters on a weekly basis," says Dawson, who spent almost ten years at CBS and Universal Studios before hitting the glass ceiling. "What we're battling are long-standing perceptions not rooted in any truth at all."

25 It doesn't have to be this bad. African-American viewers, today Hollywood's largest and most loyal audience, could make a difference. According to a 1989–90 Nielsen survey, we watch an average of 72 hours of television each week. That's 24 hours, or 49 percent more than non-Blacks watch. We're also frequent moviegoers—by various estimates accounting for between 10 and 25 percent of theater audiences. That puts us in a good position to demand—through petitions, letter writing and telephone campaigns—Black love stories, family dramas and westerns and to see ourselves portrayed as something other than fly girls and clowns from the 'hood. The tragedy is that we rarely exercise our collective power to improve the quality of what we watch.

"Black television audiences are not selective, and they are not vocal," complains Debra Lynn Langford, vice-president of television at Quincy Jones/David Salzman Entertainment. "When we like a show, we don't write in, we don't call in."

Nor do Blacks have a group like the influential Viewers for Quality Television, which saved the popular *Cagney & Lacey* from cancellation nearly half a dozen times when network executives tried to ax the show because of low ratings.

Angry viewers did launch a letter-writing campaign against CBS's decision to drop *Frank's Place*. Unfortunately, it came *after* the show had already been canceled. Black protest did make a difference in deep-sixing an offensive CBS half-hour pilot for a proposed series based on the film *Driving Miss Daisy*. Similarly, if Black viewers want to see *South Central's* Joan Mosley handling the challenges of raising three kids alone in South Central L.A. or any number of other distinctly American issues from an authentic African-American perspective, it will be up to us to start writing letters and making calls to Fox and the other networks and their advertisers.

"It's about teaching people *how* to watch television," says Rose Catherine Pinkney. For many of us, that could turn out to be worth much more than the price of the ticket.

Questions for Discussion

1. This essay was written for the African American readership of *Essence* magazine. If the author were addressing a multiracial audience, would he have to revise this essay? If so, identify specific changes you would recommend. If not, explain why you think revisions would be unnecessary.
2. Would you characterize this essay as adversarial or conciliatory persuasion? Explain your answer.
3. Does the author anticipate and answer possible objections to his claim? If you think he does, cite the pertinent passages. If you think he doesn't, identify the likely objections and compose appropriate answers.
4. How does the author establish his credibility to discuss this subject? Does he display his knowledge and integrity? identify with the audience? practice self-deprecation?
5. How does the writer try to motivate the audience? Does he emphasize the size, severity, or urgency of the issue?

Opportunities for Writing

1. Write a letter to a television executive urging continuation of a show you like or cancellation of a show you dislike.
2. Write a review of a new television show for your school newspaper. Watch at least two episodes of the show before writing your review. In making your recommendation, specifically consider the limited time that college students have for television viewing.
3. Evaluate the characterization of African Americans on a specific television show. Are African Americans depicted strictly as "clowns, cutups, and loud-mouthed buffoons"? Compose your evaluation for the membership of a local civil rights organization.
4. Write a letter to the producer of your favorite television show regarding the frequency with which African Americans appear on the show. Is this

show doing a satisfactory job of incorporating African Americans in both major and minor roles? If so, encourage continuation of this policy. If not, propose a series of corrective actions.

History Is Not a Museum
ROBERT R. ARCHIBALD

Robert R. Archibald is the president of the Missouri Historical Society and served as the 1992–1993 vice president of the American Association for State and Local History. He tackles the question of how museum professionals and historians can judge an artifact's historical significance. In this essay, he argues that no simple measure exists; instead, "to understand and interpret a historical artifact, we attempt to rediscover past thoughts of those people who made, used, and valued the object." "History Is Not a Museum" was published in the May/June 1994 issue of History News, *a magazine of the American Association for State and Local History.*

People make artifacts because they serve useful or aesthetic purposes that humans value. Artifacts acquire meaning over time, as their makers, and the descendants of their makers, use them, appreciate them, and affix significance to them. In seeking to understand and interpret a historical artifact, we attempt to rediscover past thoughts of those people who made, used, and valued the object. Subsequently, we make judgments about those past thoughts and the actions that they impelled.

We are not passive participants in this process of rediscovering and evaluating past human thought and action. Because we cannot circumvent our own time and experience, we can only understand past human thought and action within the framework of our own experiences—what we know of the experiences of others and our own place in time. Artifacts do not tell stories. They are symbols for the thoughts and actions of humans that we actively seek to understand. Active participation in an effort to understand is the process we call *history*.

The symbolism and, therefore, meanings of artifacts vary. Different perspectives arise depending on the observer's place in time, life experiences, age, race, gender, economic status, culture, and all other possible human attributes that establish a unique human identity.

The Missouri Historical Society opened an exhibition entitled "Saint Louis in the Gilded Age" in October of 1993. In this era, after the Civil War but before the end of the century, native St. Louisans derided anyone who seemed alien to them: African-Americans, German, Irish, and immigrants from eastern and southern Europe. The exhibition contains two common 19th-century household objects: cast iron banks formed as grotesque caricatures of an Irish and an African-American man. St. Louisans who owned such items in the Gilded Age found them amusing because they reinforced deeply held beliefs based on stereotypes. Today, we find these banks uncomfortable and even painful to confront, because they represent racial issues that continue to confound us and haunt our society. Unlike many of our 19th-century predecessors, we do not find any humor in them and they are not commonplace in our homes.

5   The exhibit also includes an 1882 banner of the Mystic Order of the Veiled Prophet of the Enchanted Realm, an elite, all-male, all-white fraternal organization founded in St. Louis in 1878 by prominent and mostly wealthy businessmen. The Veiled Prophet organization wielded tremendous economic power on behalf of a few, and it publicly celebrated the achievements of its own members. The organization would now be viewed as a curious relic illustrative of the chauvinism of the city's 19th-century social elite, but for the fact that it continues to function—albeit in a somewhat less militant and exclusive form. Nevertheless, the banner provokes a broad range of emotions and reactions from viewers. While the organization is irrelevant for many, and is simply foolishness to others, some view it as racist, sexist, anti-semitic, and an all-too-much-alive reminder of a frightening past. Others take it quite seriously as an important contemporary organization and aspire to be invited to membership.

The historical significance of artifacts is absolutely dependent upon the meanings society agrees to assign to them. To be precise, we assign primary importance and significance to the meanings and only secondary importance to the artifacts. In so doing, our decisions are implicitly based on the correct assumption that all human thoughts and actions are not of equal importance in understanding and explaining subsequent human actions.

Fantasize with me for a moment. Imagine that we discovered and recorded, either on a 3" × 5" card or as a computer entry, every thought and a description of every resultant action of every human who has ever lived. Once we have warehoused every card in the universe's largest warehouse or stored every bit of data in a gargantuan computer, I say to you, "Our work is finished. We have finally created an absolutely complete and therefore unarguably accurate history of the human species." "Ridiculous," you respond, "because despite your obvious energy and mammoth achievement, you have only managed to create an enormous pile of chaotic data that explains nothing." "Tell me," you continue, "which of these nearly infinite numbers of human thoughts and actions are most critical to an understanding of who we are and how we got here?" Then we engage in the process that we call history by discussing the relative significance of all we have collected and establishing our identities and defining what options exist for the future. In doing so, we give truth to Loren Eisley's beautiful observation in *The Star Thrower* that, "Without knowledge of the past, the way into the thickets of the future is desperate and unclear."

This exercise is, of course, an impossibility on many levels. But, if we could collect every artifact we would confront the same dilemma: Which are most significant? Neither the thoughts, actions, or artifacts will make sense until, using agreed-upon criteria, we rank them in order of priority. Unless we agree upon criteria for the evaluation of past human thoughts and actions, and implicitly for the artifacts that represent them, the meanings of the past will be elusive, fractured, and too-often quaint but not useful. The question of what is historically significant is not strange nor novel. But it is a question that contemporary Americans sorely need to discuss, if not conclusively answer. Ultimately, it holds the answer of who we are and who we want to be.

Our national debate and discord over the appropriate ways in which to mark the Columbian Quincentennary in 1992 are revealing. In October 1992, the Missouri Historical Society organized a symposium on the Columbian legacy featuring presentations by a panel of four experts followed by a public discussion which I moderated. Panelists included a historian, an anthropologist, a professor of Native American studies, and an exchange student from Ghana. The symposium began with predictable descriptions of the aftermath of 1492 by the historian and anthropologist including the progression of European conquest, the opposing world views of European and Indian people, and the nature of contact and exchange between the two, including intermarriage, the spread of European contagious diseases, and the transplantation of American and European foodstuffs.

The professor of Native American studies, herself a Native American, then described an Indian perspective on European conquest. The Indian population, she explained, was decimated by the direct violence of conquest and the importation of European contagious diseases that raged like wildfires across the North American and South American continents. Violent conquests, aided by superior firepower, were followed by cultural clash in which Europeans imposed their values on the now-enslaved native people, resulting in death, cultural destruction, and physical depredation of incredible magnitude. Yet, she noted, Native American people and culture persisted despite the onslaught. Nevertheless, she concluded, Native Americans looking back over 500 years of European contact can in no way conclude that the experience has benefited their people.

The African exchange student analyzed the European conquest from his point of view. The European conquest, he observed, provided an unprecedented stimulus to the enslavement of Africans to work in the fields and in the mines of Mexico and Peru as a captive labor force. Consequently, millions of Africans came to the Americas in chains where their captive status was justified by European ethnocentric claims of their own racial superiority.

After these presentations the audience addressed questions to the panelists. One series of exchanges remains most vivid. "Young man," one woman addressed the student from Ghana, "do you mean to tell me that you think America was a mistake?" "It depends," he answered her. "Upon what does it depend?" she queried. "It depends," he replied, "upon what happens next."

This symposium began with a discussion of 500-year-old events and of a man, Christopher Columbus, who died in May of 1506. It ended with a lively discussion between the audience and panelists about "what ought to happen next?" What is to be remembered and how is it to be remembered? Who should we be? The past, of course, is not dead and, in fact, as others have observed, it is not even sleeping. History, as it was revealed that Sunday afternoon, is a dynamic process in which the participants are changed. History is a discussion about the present and the future, about change as well as continuity.

The question of what constitutes historical significance is, and always has been, inextricably tied to present concerns. History is not the warehouse of facts or artifacts discussed earlier, but rather the process of deciding which facts are most important. We make the selections by constantly referring to our own lives, while under the influence of the times in which we live. As historians and museum professionals, we must assign historical significance based on a consensus of what is important and of enduring concern to the communities that we serve. History has never been objective science, a subject of immutable facts confined to the past. Rather it uses the past to focus on persistent issues in the present and shape our hopes for our future.

15 A year ago I was asked to give a banquet address on the Lewis and Clark expedition. I decided to talk about changing perceptions of the expedition based on descriptions of it in history textbooks of the 19th and 20th centuries.

In 1836 William Grimshaw wrote a *History of the United States,* which included two pages on the Lewis and Clark expedition. In his description, bears were dangerous, wild enemies to be killed. Indian people were described as savages whose behavior was either "martial or ludicrous, or voluptuous and indecent." Grimshaw saw no inherent value in wilderness, only agricultural and commercial potential. The principal achievement of the expedition was that information was gathered on the future commercial and agricultural potential of the territory encompassed within the Louisiana Purchase.

Grimshaw's attitudes towards wilderness, animals and the native people were the dominant attitudes of his time. He wrote during a period of national optimism grounded in the economic growth that accompanied America's first industrial revolution, when possibilities for economic expansion sustained by an infinite supply of natural resources seemed unlimited. Most Americans had neither sympathy nor time for romantic notions about unspoiled nature and native peoples. Both were seen as impediments to progress that would ultimately require exploitation and elimination.

William Grimshaw's perspective prevailed in the American imagination with only slight alteration through the end of the 19th century. Henry Adams published his *History of the United States during the Second Administration of Thomas Jefferson* in 1890. Lewis and Clark, he wrote "were forced to pass the winter in extreme discomfort, among thievish and flea-bitten Indians, until March 26, 1807, when they could retrace their steps." "Creditable as these expeditions were to American energy and enterprise," he concluded, "they added little to the stock of science or wealth. Many years must elapse before the vast region west of the Mississippi could be brought within the reach of civilization." Other histories written at the end of the century reflected similar views.

By the end of World War I, the frontier had receded into memory. The complexity of America's world power status, combined with an increasingly urban landscape and the defeat and confinement of Native Americans to reservations, fostered a climate for non-Native Americans to adopt a romantic and nostalgic view of the frontier, wilderness, and native people, while still maintaining the superiority of "civilization." *The Lure of the Frontier,* authored by Ralph Henry Gabriel, reflected these changing attitudes when it was published in 1929. This volume elevated Lewis and Clark to heroic status and included reproductions of romanticized art by C. M. Russell, E. S. Paxson and others. Sacajawea was imbued with the status of heroine; nature was beautiful and beneficent.

20   In our own time, Lewis and Clark are portrayed as pioneering naturalists and proto-environmentalists. Our perspectives of the expedition are, like the others, shaped by the concerns of our own time and our concerns about the future. Today we realize that natural resources are finite. With wilderness scarce and frontiers eliminated, we have discovered beauty and value in unspoiled nature and seek to preserve what remains. No longer confident in the superiority of the values of our own civilization, we find appeal in the different values that defined the relationships between Native American people and each other and with the planet.

History is a discussion about the present and the future focused on issues of enduring concern. We cannot engage in the discussion if we are distant and unconcerned with the issues that confront our communities, nation, and world. Our work requires that we first study our own time so that the conversations we facilitate about the past are useful, pertinent, and encourage discourse about what ought to happen next. This same axiom must be used to assign significance and establish priorities for all we do, including the collection and preservation of artifacts.

To be explicit, what concerns our communities, concerns us. Issues such as the role of education, economic well-being, livable environment, violence on streets and television, epidemics of drugs and AIDS, neighborhoods, family responsibilities, government and politics, and an understanding of justice and fairness are our concerns. These concerns and others require historical perspective as a prerequisite for understanding varied perspectives and for participating in a reasoned discussion of alternatives.

Alastair MacIntyre commented in *A Short History of Ethics* that "History is neither a prison nor a museum, nor is it a set of materials for self-congratulation." History can be a museum only insofar as we use artifacts as evocative symbols of past human thought and activity. The significance of artifacts and, hence, their ability to stimulate useful and meaningful discussion will be directly proportional to our success in using them to symbolize important and persistent human issues that have endured through time.

Sam Wah, the last Chinese laundryman in St. Louis, is now dead. His laundry has been demolished to make way for a parking garage. A short time ago, a friend of Sam's sent me a cardboard box containing the few things that remained after the settlement of his estate and the shipment of some personal items to his relatives in China. I removed from the carton a small box in which stood a statue of the Buddha, with Catholic rosaries draped through its hands and votive candles in front. It seemed a strange juxtaposition of Buddhist and Christian symbols, indicative perhaps, of Mr. Wah's struggle in the United States and posing for me the perennial and quintessential question of what it is to be American. This artifact, if you will, underscored the need for us to facilitate discussion of the nature of American pluralism, rather than remain a nation of entrenched insiders and marginalized outsiders. Ultimately, it reinforced my conviction that history is not a museum.

Questions for Discussion

1. Which passages of this essay reveal knowledge by participation? How critical is this information to the success of the essay? Which passages reveal knowledge by observation? Would the essay be equally effective without this information?
2. What is the subordinate aim of this essay? Is it expressive or referential? Cite specific passages to support your answer.
3. What do you think of the opening paragraph? Do you think the essay would be more or less effective if it started with the fourth paragraph? Explain your answer.
4. Notice the simplicity of the writing style: little or no technical terminology, relatively short sentences and paragraphs, and a majority of sentences starting immediately with the subject. Does this simple style reinforce the author's credibility? Does it support the claim? Does it motivate the audience? Is this style appropriate?
5. In the second section of the essay, the author records a brief, imaginary dialogue with you. What is the author's purpose in doing so? What is your opinion of this technique? Is it effective? Why do you think it is or isn't?

Opportunities for Writing

1. Review a special exhibit at a local history museum. Does it appropriately display and interpret the historical period or incident? Write your review for your school newspaper.
2. Write a letter to the director of a local history museum regarding the display of a racist or sexist artifact. Do you consider the display of this artifact instructive and necessary?
3. Write a proposal to a local historical society, asking it to support a special exhibition on life in your community during the 1940s, 1950s, or 1960s. In your proposal, identify appropriate subject specialists and potential sources of artifacts. Devise a schedule and budget. Emphasize both the importance and feasibility of this exhibition.

EPILOGUE

In this class you've developed your repertoire of critical reading strategies as well as your ability to compose expressive, referential, and persuasive aim writing. You've explored a variety of subjects and experienced different ways of knowing. Before you finally close the cover on this book, we would like to offer you one more opportunity for critical reading and writing.

Write a letter to us—Gwendolyn Gong and Sam Dragga, c/o English Editor, HarperCollins College Publishers, 10 East 53rd Street, New York, NY 10022–5299—with your evaluation of this book. Tell us which of the readings you liked and which you disliked. Which essays would you like us to keep in a revised edition of this book? Which would you like us to omit? Why? Keep in mind the persuasive aim of your letter: Establish your credibility by showing us what you've learned about critical reading and writing. Prove your evaluation is logical by a fair and judicious review of the essays. Motivate us to approve your recommendations by emphasizing how your advice will make *A Reader's Repertoire* a more useful and usable resource for college students like you.

CREDITS

INTRODUCTION
"The Pie" by Gary Soto from *A Summer Life.* Copyright © 1990 University Press of New England. Reprinted by permission.

PART ONE
"Little Deaths" by T.H. Watkins. Reprinted by permission.

"Meditations on a Stolen Purse" from *Telling* by Marion Winik, pages 109–112. Copyright © 1994 by Marion Winik. Reprinted by permission of Villard Books, a division of Random House, Inc.

"And Then I Went to School" by Joseph Suina from *Linguistic and Cultural Influences on Learning Mathematics* by Rodney Cocking and Jose Mestre, eds. Copyright © 1988 by Lawrence Erlbaum Associates, Inc. Reprinted by permission.

"How It Feels to Be Colored Me" by Zora Neale Hurston. (Originally published in *The World Tomorrow,* May 11, 1928). Reprinted by permission of Lucy Ann Hurston.

"Sylvia Plath: A Memoir" from *The Savage God: The Study of Suicide* by Al Alvarez. Copyright © 1971 by Al Alvarez. Reprinted by permission of George Weidenfeld & Nicolson Limited.

12 lines from "Night Shift" from *The Colossus and Other Poems* by Sylvia Plath. Copyright © 1962 by Sylvia Plath. Reprinted by permission of Alfred A. Knopf, Inc. and Faber & Faber Ltd.

7 lines from "Lady Lazarus" from *Ariel* by Sylvia Plath. Copyright © 1963 by Ted Hughes. Copyright Renewed. Reprinted by permission of HarperCollins Publishers, Inc. and Faber & Faber Ltd.

3 lines from "Daddy" from *Ariel* by Sylvia Plath. Copyright © 1963 by Ted Hughes. Copyright Renewed. Reprinted by permission of HarperCollins Publishers, Inc. and Faber & Faber Ltd.

3 lines from "Kindness" from *Ariel* by Sylvia Plath. Copyright © 1963 by Ted Hughes. Copyright Renewed. Reprinted by permission of HarperCollins Publishers, Inc. and Faber & Faber Ltd.

"Hating Fred" by Harriet Lerner. Copyright © 1994 by Harriet Lerner, Ph.D. Originally published in the *Networker,* March/April 1994, pages 47–49. Reprinted with permission.

"Lessons from a Friend" by Frank DeFord from *Newsweek,* February 22, 1993, pages 60–61. Copyright © 1993 by Newsweek, Inc. All rights reserved. Reprinted by permission.

"Only Daughter" by Sandra Cisneros. First published in *Glamour Magazine,* November 1990. Copyright © 1990 by Sandra Cisneros. Reprinted by permission of Susan Bergholz Literary Services.

"Of Accidental Judgments and Casual Slaughters" by Kai Erikson from *The Nation,* August 3/10, 1985. Copyright © 1985 The Nation Company, L.P. Reprinted with permission from *The Nation* magazine.

"Columbus and His Four Fateful Voyages" by David Gelman from *Special Issue Newsweek,* Fall/Winter 1991, pages 39 and 44–46. Copyright © 1991 by Newsweek, Inc. All rights reserved. Reprinted by permission.

"The Case Of Harry Houdini" from *The Star of Wonder* by Daniel Mark Epstein. Copyright © 1986 by Daniel Mark Epstein. Reprinted by permission. Published by The Overlook Press, Woodstock, N.Y. 12498.

"Fat Like Me" by Leslie Lampert from *Ladies' Home Journal,* May 1993, pages 154–155 and 214–215. Copyright © 1993 Meredith Corporation. All rights reserved. Reprinted from *Ladies' Home Journal* magazine by permission.

"My Grandmother's Pennies" by Cynthia Ozick. First published in *McCall's Magazine,* December 1978. Copyright © 1978 by Cynthia Ozick. Reprinted by permission of the author and her agents, Raines & Raines.

"Ghosts" by Bruce Edward Hall from *New York Magazine,* October 4, 1993, pages 86 and 88–92. Reprinted by permission of the author.

"Living In—and On—the Margins," by Donald McQuade from *College Composition and Communication,* Vol. 43, No. 1, February 1992, pages 11–22. Copyright © 1992 by the National Council of Teachers of English. Reprinted with permission.

"On Being a Cripple" from *Plaintext* by Nancy Mairs. Copyright © 1986 by The University of Arizona Press. Reprinted by permission.

"More Than Just a Shrine: Paying Homage to the Ghosts of Ellis Island" by Mary Gordon from *The New York Times,* November 3, 1985. Copyright © 1985 by The New York Times Company. Reprinted by permission.

"The House Where Martin Wept: Marks, Mississippi" from *Crossings: A White Man's Journey into Black America* by Walt Harrington. Copyright © 1993 by Walt Harrington. Reprinted by permission of HarperCollins Publishers, Inc.

"Grandmother's Country" by N. Scott Momaday from *The Way to Rainy Mountain.* Copyright © 1969 by the University of New Mexico Press. Reprinted by permission.

"A New Monument to Remembering—With a Mission" by Michael Kernan from *Smithsonian,* Volume 24, Number 1, April 1993, pages 51–54, 56, 58–60 and 62. Reprinted by permission of the author.

PART TWO

"Cultural Etiquette: A Guide for the Well-Intentioned" by Amoja Three Rivers from *Market Wimmin* (Gen. Delivery, Auto W. V. 24917, $7 P.Pd). Reprinted by permission of the author.

"Falling for Apples" from *Second Person Rural* by Noel Perrin. Copyright © 1980 by Noel Perrin. Reprinted by permission of David R. Godine, Publisher, Boston.

"Shopping with Children" from *Night Lights* by Phyllis Theroux. Copyright © 1987 by Phyllis Theroux. Reprinted by permission of The Aaron M. Priest Literary Agency, Inc.

"How to Write a Letter" from *We Are Still Married, Stories and Letters* by Garrison Keillor. Copyright © 1982, 1983, 1985, 1986, 1987, 1988, 1989 by Garrison Keillor. Reprinted by permission of International Paper Company, the author and Penguin Books Canada Limited.

"A Practitioner's Guide to Research Methods" by Patricia Goubil-Gambrell from *Technical Communication,* Fourth Quarter November 1992, Volume 39, Number 4, pages 582–591. Copyright © 1992 by the Society for Technical Communication. Reprinted by permission.

"Type A Behavior, Competitive Achievement-Striving, and Cheating Among College Students" by Perry, Kane, Bernesser and Spicker from *Psychological Reports,* 1990, 66, pages 459–465. Copyright © 1990 Psychological Reports. Reprinted with permission of *Psychological Reports* and the authors.

Table 1, "Mean Scores on Word-forming Task" from "Type A Behavior, Competitive Achievement-Striving, and Cheating Among College Students" by Perry, Kane, Bernesser and Spicker from *Psychological Reports,* 1990, 66, page 462. Copyright © 1990 Psychological Reports. Reprinted with permission of *Psychological Reports* and the authors.

"Athenian Democracy" by Josiah Ober and Catherine Vanderpool from *Prologue: Quarterly Of The National Archives,* Vol. 25, No. 2, Summer 1993, pages 127–135. Copyright © 1993 by Josiah Ober and Catherine Vanderpool. Reprinted by permission of the authors.

"The Big New Mix" by Renee Loth from *The Boston Globe Magazine,* October 12, 1991. Reprinted courtesy of The Boston Globe.

"The Underdog Concept in Sport" by Jimmy A. Frazier and Eldon E. Snyder from *Sociology of Sport Journal,* 1991, Volume 8, Number 4, pages 380–388. Copyright © 1991 by Human Kinetics Publishers, Inc. Reprinted by permission of Human Kinetics Publishers, Inc. and the authors.

Figure 1, "Questionnaire used to determine preference for underdog vs.favorite" from "The Underdog Concept in Sport" by Jimmy A. Frazier and Eldon E. Snyder from *Sociology of Sport Journal,* 1991, Volume 8, Number 4, page 383. Copyright © 1991 by Human Kinetics Publishers, Inc. Reprinted by permission of Human Kinetics Publishers, Inc. and the authors.

Table 1, "Student Responses to Underdog Questionnaire" from "The Underdog Concept in Sport" by Jimmy A. Frazier and Eldon E. Snyder from *Sociology of Sport Journal,* 1991, Volume 8, Number 4, page 384. Copyright © 1991 by Human Kinetics Publishers, Inc. Reprinted by permission of Human Kinetics Publishers, Inc. and the authors.

"Communication Stereotypes: Is Interracial Communication Possible?" by Rebecca Leonard and Don C. Locke from *The Journal of Black Studies,* Vol. 23, No. 3, March 1993, pages 332–343. Copyright © 1993 by Sage Publications, Inc. Reprinted by permission Sage Publications, Inc.

Table 1, "List of Terms" from "Communication Stereotypes: Is Interracial Communication Possible?" by Rebecca Leonard and Don C. Locke from *The Journal of Black Studies,* Vol. 23, No. 3, March 1993, page 335. Copyright © 1993 by Sage Publications, Inc. Reprinted by permission Sage Publications, Inc.

Table 2, "Twelve Most Frequently Assigned Traits (Rank Ordered)" from "Communication Stereotypes: Is Interracial Communication Possible?" by Rebecca Leonard and Don C. Locke from *The Journal of Black Studies,* Vol. 23, No. 3, March 1993, page 336. Copyright © 1993 by Sage Publications, Inc. Reprinted by permission Sage Publications, Inc.

Table 3, "Twelve Least Frequently Assigned Traits (Rank Ordered)" from "Communication Stereotypes: Is Interracial Communication Possible?" by Rebecca Leonard and Don C. Locke from *The Journal of Black Studies,* Vol. 23, No. 3, March 1993, page 338. Copyright © 1993 by Sage Publications, Inc. Reprinted by permission Sage Publications, Inc.

"Using Color Effectively: Designing to Human Specifications" by Gerald M. Murch from *Technical Communication,* Fourth Quarter 1985, Volume 32, Number 4, pages 14–20. Copyright © 1985 by the Society for Technical Communication. Reprinted by permission.

Figure 1, "The color spectrum of human vision" from "Using Color Effectively: Designing to Human Specifications" by Gerald M. Murch from *Technical Communication,* Fourth Quarter 1985, Volume 32, Number 4, page 15. Copyright © 1985 by the Society for Technical Communication. Reprinted by permission.

Figure 2, "Processing of color input into opponent channels" from "Using Color Effectively: Designing to Human Specifications" by Gerald M. Murch from *Technical Communication,* Fourth Quarter 1985, Volume 32, Number 4, page 16. Copyright © 1985 by the Society for Technical Communication. Reprinted by permission.

Figure 3, "Perceived intensity as a function of physical intensity" from "Using Color Effectively: Designing to Human Specifications" by Gerald M. Murch from *Technical Communication,* Fourth Quarter 1985, Volume 32, Number 4, page 17. Copyright © 1985 by the Society for Technical Communication. Reprinted by permission.

Figure 4, "Perceived saturation at different wavelengths" from "Using Color Effectively: Designing to Human Specifications" by Gerald M. Murch from *Technical Communication,*

Fourth Quarter 1985, Volume 32, Number 4, page 17. Copyright © 1985 by the Society for Technical Communication. Reprinted by permission.

Table 1, "Best Color Combinations (N = 16)" from "Using Color Effectively: Designing to Human Specifications" by Gerald M. Murch from *Technical Communication,* Fourth Quarter 1985, Volume 32, Number 4, page 19. Copyright © 1985 by the Society for Technical Communication. Reprinted by permission.

Table 2, "Worst Color Combinations (N = 16)" from "Using Color Effectively: Designing to Human Specifications" by Gerald M. Murch from *Technical Communication,* Fourth Quarter 1985, Volume 32, Number 4, page 19. Copyright © 1985 by the Society for Technical Communication. Reprinted by permission.

"Friends, Good Friends—and Such Good Friends" by Judith Viorst. Copyright © 1977 by Judith Viorst. Originally appeared in *Redbook.* Reprinted by permission of Lescher & Lescher, Ltd.

"An Architect Who Takes Stairways One Step at a Time" by Richard Wolkomir from *Smithsonian,* Volume 24, Number 3, June 1993, pages 55–58, 60 and 62–63. Reprinted by permission of the author.

"The Mind of the Puzzler" by Robert J. Sternberg and Janet E. Davidson from *Psychology Today,* 16, June 1982. Copyright © 1982 Sussex Publishers, Inc. Reprinted with permission from *Psychology Today* magazine.

"Luis Jimenez's Outdoor Sculptures Slow Traffic Down" by Chiori Santiago from *Smithsonian,* Volume 23, Number 12, March 1993, pages 87–90, 92 and 94–95. Reprinted by permission of the author.

Photograph, National Museum of American Art, Washington, DC/Art Resource, New York.

"The Bambi Syndrome" by Matt Cartmill from *Natural History,* June 1993, pages 6, 8 and 10–12. (Adapted from *A View to a Death in the Morning: Hunting and Nature Through History* by Matt Cartmill, Cambridge, Mass.: Harvard University Press, 1993). Copyright © 1993 by the American Museum of Natural History. Reprinted with permission from *Natural History.*

"Peach Preserves and 'A New Texas': A Rhetorical Analysis of the Inaugural Addresses of 'Ma' Ferguson and Ann Richards" by Linda Hatchel from *English in Texas,* Volume 23, Number 4, Summer 1992, pages 11–14. Copyright © 1992 by the Texas Council of Teachers of English. Reprinted by permission.

"Alma's Bedside Ghost: Or the Importance of Cultural Similarity" by Marina Oppenheimer from *Hispanic Journal of Behavioral Sciences,* Vol. 14, No. 4, November 1992, pages 496–501. Copyright © 1992 by Sage Publications, Inc. Reprinted by permission of Sage Publications, Inc.

"The Man Who Cries Wolf" by Fred H. Harrington from *Natural History,* Vol. 96, No. 2, February 1987, pages 22–26. Copyright © 1987 by the American Museum of Natural History. Reprinted with permission from *Natural History.*

"The Indian Image" from *Way Out West* by Jane Stern and Michael Stern, pages 276, 278–279, 281–283 and 285–287. Copyright © 1993 by Jane & Michael Stern. Reprinted by permission of HarperCollins Publishers, Inc.

"Gender Bias and the 1992 Summer Olympic Games: An Analysis of Television Coverage" by Catriona T. Higgs and Karen H. Weiller from *The Journal of Sport & Social Issues,* Vol. 18, No. 3, August 1994, pages 234–246. Copyright © 1994 by Sage Publications, Inc. Reprinted by permission Sage Publications, Inc.

Table 1, "Same-Sport Time Results" from "Gender Bias and the 1992 Summer Olympic Games: An Analysis of Television Coverage" by Catriona T. Higgs and Karen H. Weiller from *The Journal of Sport & Social Issues,* Vol. 18, No. 3, August 1994, page 237. Copyright © 1994 by Sage Publications, Inc. Reprinted by permission Sage Publications, Inc.

"Amphibian Alarm: Just Where Have All the Frogs Gone?" by Beth Livermore from *Smithsonian,* October 1992, Volume 23, Number 7, pages 113–120. Reprinted by permission of the author.

PART THREE

"The Outlaw Princesses" from *The Thing Happens* by Terence Rafferty. This piece originally appeared in *The New Yorker.* Copyright © 1991 by Terence Rafferty. Used by permission of Grove/Atlantic, Inc.

"It Is Time to Stop Playing Indians" by Arlene B. Hirschfelder from *The Los Angeles Times,* November 25, 1987. Reprinted by permission of the author.

"Farewell to Fitness" by Mike Royko. Reprinted by permission of Tribune Media Services.

"Inside the Home" by Jill Frawley from *Mother Jones Magazine,* 1991. Reprinted by permission of the Foundation for National Progress.

"I, Too, Am a Good Parent" by Dorsett Bennett from *Newsweek,* July 4, 1994, page 18. Copyright © 1994 by Newsweek, Inc. All rights reserved. Reprinted by permission.

"The 'Bleaching Syndrome': Implications of Light Skin for Hispanic American Assimilation" by Ronald E. Hall from *Hispanic Journal of Behavioral Sciences,* Vol. 16, No. 3, August 1994, pages 307–314. Copyright © 1994 by Sage Publications, Inc. Reprinted by permission Sage Publications, Inc.

Adapted excerpt, "The Data Game" from *Tainted Truth* by Cynthia Crossen. Copyright © 1994 by Cynthia Crossen. Reprinted by permission of Simon & Schuster, Inc. and The Washington Monthly Company, 1611 Connecticut Ave., N.W., Washington, D.C. 20009 (202) 462-0128.

"The Motherhood Myth" by Betty Rollin. Originally in *Look,* Sept. 22, 1970, pages 15–17. Copyright © 1970 by Betty Rollin. Reprinted by permission of the William Morris Agency, Inc. on behalf of the Author.

"Murder, Inc." by Robert Sherrill. First published in *Grand Street,* Spring 1986. Reprinted by permission of the author.

"Letter from Birmingham Jail" from *Why Can't We Wait* by Martin Luther King, Jr. Copyright © 1963 by Martin Luther King, Jr., copyright renewed 1991 by Coretta Scott King. Reprinted by arrangement with The Heirs to the Estate of Martin Luther King, Jr., c/o Joan Daves Agency as agent for the proprietor.

"Warning: Sports Stars May Be Hazardous to Your Health" by Jason DeParle from *The Washington Monthly,* September 1989. Copyright © 1989 by *The Washington Monthly* Company, 1611 Connecticut Avenue, N.W., Washington, D.C. 20009. (202) 462-0128. Reprinted with permission from The Washington Monthly.

"Sexism in English: A 1990s Update" by Alleen Pace Nilsen. (A revised version of "Sexism in English: A Feminist View" from *Female Studies VI: Closer to the Ground Women's Classes, Criticism, Programs*–1972, eds., Nancy Hoffman, Cynthia Secor and Adrian Tinsley, New York: The Feminist Press, 1972). Reprinted by permission of the author.

"The Language of Discretion" by Amy Tan. Copyright © 1990 by Amy Tan. Reprinted by permission of the author and the Sandra Dijkstra Literary Agency.

"From a Native Daughter" by Haunani-Kay Trask from *The American Indian and the Problem of History,* edited by Calvin Martin. Reprinted by permission of the author.

"Give Children the Vote" by Vita Wallace from *The Nation,* October 14, 1991, pages 439–442. Copyright © 1991 The Nation Company, L. P. Reprinted with permission from *The Nation* magazine.

"Why Mow: The Case Against Lawns" from *Second Nature* by Michael Pollan. Copyright © 1991 by Michael Pollan. Used by permission of Grove/Atlantic, Inc.

"Sensationalism Versus News of the Moral Life: Making the Distinction" by Karen L. Slattery from *Journal of Mass Media Ethics,* Vol. 9, No. 1, pages 5–15. Copyright © 1994 by Lawrence Erlbaum Associates, Inc. Reprinted by permission of Lawrence Erlbaum Associates, Inc. and the author.

"The Killing Game" by Joy Williams. First published in *Esquire.* Copyright © 1990 by Joy Williams. Reprinted by permission of International Creative Management, Inc.

"Amy Fisher and the Ethics of 'Headline' Docudramas" by Rod Carveth from *Journal of Popular Film & Television,* Vol. 21, No. 3, Fall 1993, pages 121–127. Copyright © 1993 by the Helen Dwight Reid Educational Foundation. Published by Heldref Publications, 1319 Eighteenth St., N.W., Washington, D. C. 20036–1802. Reprinted with permission of the Helen Dwight Reid Educational Foundation.

"Hollywood: The Dark Side" by Sylvester Monroe from *Essence,* March 1994, pages 83–84 and 127–128. Reprinted by permission of the author.

"History Is Not a Museum" by Robert R. Archibald from *History News,* May/June 1994, Volume 49, Number 3, pages 10–13. Copyright © 1994 by the American Association for State and Local History. Reprinted by permission. *History News* is a bimonthly magazine of the American Association for State and Local History, Nashville, Tennessee.

Author and Title Index

Alma's Bedside Ghost: Or the Importance of Cultural Similarity, 295
Alvarez, Al, 47
Amphibian Alarm: Just Where Have All the Frogs Gone? 325
Amy Fisher and the Ethics of "Headline" Docudramas, 484
And Then I Went to School, 39
Archibald, Robert R., 502
Architect Who Takes Stairways One Step at a Time, An, 260
Athenian Democracy, 208

Bambi Syndrome, The, 282
Bennett, Dorsett, 348
Bernesser, Kevin J., 201
Big New Mix, The, 219
"Bleaching Syndrome," The: Implications of Light Skin for Hispanic American Assimilation, 352

Cartmill, Matt, 282
Carveth, Rod, 484
Case of Harry Houdini, The, 96
Cisneros, Sandra, 64
Columbus and His Four Fateful Voyages, 83
Communication Stereotypes: Is Interracial Communication Possible? 234
Crossen, Cynthia, 359
Cultural Etiquette: A Guide for the Well-Intentioned, 173

Data Game, The, 359
Davidson, Janet E., 267

DeFord, Frank, 61
DeParle, Jason, 409

Epstein, Daniel Mark, 96
Erikson, Kai, 74

Falling for Apples, 177
Farewell to Fitness, 343
Fat Like Me, 107
Fenimore Cooper's Literary Offenses, 386
Ford, Jay, 67
Frawley, Jill, 345
Frazier, Jimmy A., 225
Friends, Good Friends—and Such Good Friends, 256
From a Native Daughter, 443

Gelman, David, 83
Gender Bias and the 1992 Summer Olympic Games: An Analysis of Television Coverage, 314
Ghosts, 118
Give Children the Vote, 450
Gordon, Mary, 146
Goubil-Gambrell, Patricia, 186
Grandmother's Country, 153

Hall, Bruce Edward, 118
Hall, Ronald E., 352
Harrington, Fred H., 300
Harrington, Walt, 150
Hatchel, Linda, 290
Hating Fred, 59
Higgs, Catriona T., 314
Hirschfelder, Arlene B., 340
History Is Not a Museum, 502

516 Author and Title Index

Hollywood: The Dark Side, 496
House Where Martin Wept, The: Marks, Mississippi, 150
How It Feels to Be Colored Me, 44
How to Write a Letter, 183
Hurston, Zora Neale, 44

I, Too, Am a Good Parent, 348
Indian Image, The, 306
Inside the Home, 345
It Is Time to Stop Playing Indians, 340

Kane, Kevin M., 201
Keillor, Garrison, 183
Kernan, Michael, 158
Killing Game, The, 473
King, Martin Luther, Jr., 395

Lampert, Leslie, 107
Language of Discretion, The, 436
Leonard, Rebecca, 234
Lerner, Harriet, 59
Lessons from a Friend, 61
Letter from Birmingham Jail, 395
Little Deaths, 31
Livermore, Beth, 325
Living In—and On—the Margins, 126
Locke, Don C., 234
Loth, Renee, 219
Luis Jimenez's Outdoor Sculptures Slow Traffic Down, 275

McQuade, Donald, 126
Mairs, Nancy, 137
Man Who Cries Wolf, The, 300
Meditations on a Stolen Purse, 36
Mind of the Puzzler, The, 267
Momaday, N. Scott, 153
Monroe, Sylvester, 496
More Than Just a Shrine: Paying Homage to the Ghosts of Ellis Island, 146
Motherhood Myth, The, 366
Murch, Gerald M., 242
Murder, Inc., 375
My Grandmother's Pennies, 113

New Monument to Remembering—With a Mission, A, 158
Nilsen, Alleen Pace, 426

Ober, Josiah, 208
Of Accidental Judgments and Casual Slaughters, 74
On Being a Cripple, 137
Only Daughter, 64
Oppenheimer, Marina, 295
Outlaw Princesses, The, 337
Ozick, Cynthia, 113

Peach Preserves and "A New Texas": A Rhetorical Analysis of the Inaugural Addresses of "Ma" Ferguson and Ann Richards, 290
Perrin, Noel, 177
Perry, Anthony R., 201
Pie, The, 15
Pollan, Michael, 454
Practitioner's Guide to Research Methods, A, 186

Rafferty, Terence, 337
Rollin, Betty, 366
Royko, Mike, 343

Santiago, Chiori, 275
Sensationalism Versus News of the Moral Life: Making the Distinction, 463
Sexism in English: A 1990s Update, 426
Sherrill, Robert, 375
Shopping with Children, 180
Slattery, Karen L., 463
Snyder, Eldon E., 225
Soto, Gary, 15
Spicker, Paul T., 201
Stern, Jane, 306
Stern, Michael, 306
Sternberg, Robert J., 267
Suina, Joseph, 39
Sylvia Plath: A Memoir, 47

Tan, Amy, 436
Theroux, Phyllis, 180
Thoreau, 90
Three Rivers, Amoja, 173
Trask, Haunani-Kay, 443
Twain, Mark (Samuel Langhorne Clemens), 386
20/20 Hindsight, 67

Type A Behavior, Competitive Achievement-Striving, and Cheating Among College Students, 201

Underdog Concept in Sports, The, 225
Using Color Effectively: Designing to Human Specifications, 242

Vanderpool, Catherine, 208
Viorst, Judith, 256

Wallace, Vita, 450
Warning: Sports Stars May Be Hazardous to Your Health, 409
Watkins, T. H., 31
Weiller, Karen H., 314
Why Mow: The Case Against Lawns, 454
Williams, Joy, 473
Winik, Marion, 36
Wolkomir, Richard, 260
Woolf, Virginia, 90